sevensisters@gmail.co.uk

caldifion sorvin

New Voices in Higher Education Research and Scholarship

Filipa M. Ribeiro
University of Porto, Portugal

Yurgos Politis
University College Dublin, Ireland

Bojana Culum
University of Rijeka, Croatia

Carry

A volume in the Advances in Higher Education and Professional Development (AHEPD) Book Series

Information Science REFERENCE

An Imprint of IGI Global

Managing Director:	Lindsay Johnston
Managing Editor:	Austin DeMarco
Director of Intellectual Property & Contracts:	Jan Travers
Acquisitions Editor:	Kayla Wolfe
Production Editor:	Christina Henning
Typesetter:	Michael Brehm
Cover Design:	Jason Mull

Published in the United States of America by
Information Science Reference (an imprint of IGI Global)
701 E. Chocolate Avenue
Hershey PA, USA 17033
Tel: 717-533-8845
Fax: 717-533-8661
E-mail: cust@igi-global.com
Web site: http://www.igi-global.com

Library of Congress Cataloging-in-Publication Data

CIP Data
New voices in higher education research and scholarship / Felipa M. Ribeiro, Yurgos Politis, and Bojana Culum, editors.
    pages cm
 Includes bibliographical references and index.
 Summary: "This book explores the role of higher education in today's society, discussing the rapidly changing nature of higher education around the globe, especially the relationship between higher education and social development"-- Provided by publisher.
 ISBN 978-1-4666-7244-4 (hardcover : alk. paper) -- ISBN 978-1-4666-7245-1 (ebook) -- ISBN 978-1-4666-7247-5 (print & perpetual access : alk. paper) 1. Education, Higher--Research--Methodology. 2. Qualitative research. I. Ribeiro, Felipa M.
 LB2326.3.N48 2014
 378.00721--dc23
                                    2014037377

British Cataloguing in Publication Data
A Cataloguing in Publication record for this book is available from the British Library.

For electronic access to this publication, please contact: eresources@igi-global.com.

Advances in Higher Education and Professional Development (AHEPD) Book Series

Jared Keengwe
University of North Dakota, USA

ISSN: 2327-6983
EISSN: 2327-6991

MISSION

As world economies continue to shift and change in response to global financial situations, job markets have begun to demand a more highly-skilled workforce. In many industries a college degree is the minimum requirement and further educational development is expected to advance. With these current trends in mind, the **Advances in Higher Education & Professional Development (AHEPD) Book Series** provides an outlet for researchers and academics to publish their research in these areas and to distribute these works to practitioners and other researchers.

AHEPD encompasses all research dealing with higher education pedagogy, development, and curriculum design, as well as all areas of professional development, regardless of focus.

COVERAGE

- Adult Education
- Assessment in Higher Education
- Career Training
- Coaching and Mentoring
- Continuing Professional Development
- Governance in Higher Education
- Higher Education Policy
- Pedagogy of Teaching Higher Education
- Vocational Education

IGI Global is currently accepting manuscripts for publication within this series. To submit a proposal for a volume in this series, please contact our Acquisition Editors at Acquisitions@igi-global.com or visit: http://www.igi-global.com/publish/.

Titles in this Series

For a list of additional titles in this series, please visit: www.igi-global.com

Innovative Teaching Strategies and New Learning Paradigms in Computer Programming
Ricardo Queirós (Polytechnic Institute of Porto, Portugal)
Information Science Reference • copyright 2015 • 313pp • H/C (ISBN: 9781466673045) • US $195.00 (our price)

Professional Development Schools and Transformative Partnerships
Drew Polly (UNC Charlotte, USA) Tina Heafner (UNC Charlotte, USA) Marvin Chapman (UNC Charlotte, USA)
and Melba Spooner (UNC Charlotte, USA)
Information Science Reference • copyright 2015 • 363pp • H/C (ISBN: 9781466663671) • US $195.00 (our price)

Models for Improving and Optimizing Online and Blended Learning in Higher Education
Jared Keengwe (University of North Dakota, USA) and Joachim Jack Agamba (Idaho State University, USA)
Information Science Reference • copyright 2015 • 320pp • H/C (ISBN: 9781466662803) • US $175.00 (our price)

Advancing Higher Education with Mobile Learning Technologies Cases, Trends, and Inquiry-Based Methods
Jared Keengwe (University of North Dakota, USA) and Marian B. Maxfield (Ashland University, USA)
Information Science Reference • copyright 2015 • 364pp • H/C (ISBN: 9781466662841) • US $195.00 (our price)

Handbook of Research on Higher Education in the MENA Region Policy and Practice
Neeta Baporikar (Ministry of Higher Education, Oman)
Information Science Reference • copyright 2014 • 527pp • H/C (ISBN: 9781466661981) • US $315.00 (our price)

Advancing Knowledge in Higher Education Universities in Turbulent Times
Tanya Fitzgerald (La Trobe University, Australia)
Information Science Reference • copyright 2014 • 337pp • H/C (ISBN: 9781466662025) • US $195.00 (our price)

Cases on Teacher Identity, Diversity, and Cognition in Higher Education
Paul Breen (Greenwich School of Management, UK)
Information Science Reference • copyright 2014 • 437pp • H/C (ISBN: 9781466659902) • US $195.00 (our price)

Handbook of Research on Trends in European Higher Education Convergence
Alina Mihaela Dima (Bucharest Academy of Economic Studies, Romania)
Information Science Reference • copyright 2014 • 516pp • H/C (ISBN: 9781466659988) • US $315.00 (our price)

Overcoming Challenges in Software Engineering Education Delivering Non-Technical Knowledge and Skills
Liguo Yu (Indiana University South Bend, USA)
Engineering Science Reference • copyright 2014 • 556pp • H/C (ISBN: 9781466658004) • US $235.00 (our price)

www.igi-global.com

701 E. Chocolate Ave., Hershey, PA 17033
Order online at www.igi-global.com or call 717-533-8845 x100
To place a standing order for titles released in this series, contact: cust@igi-global.com
Mon-Fri 8:00 am - 5:00 pm (est) or fax 24 hours a day 717-533-8661

Dedication

Non nubis solum...Not for Ourselves Alone.

Editorial Advisory Board

Table of Contents

Detailed Table of Contents

Chapter 1

The European Union's Lisbon Strategy (2000-2010) set a bold vision of a "Europe of Knowledge" where universities are seen as central actors. A modernisation agenda of universities has been promoted in recent years, focusing on the contribution of the sector to reaching regional and national economic goals. This chapter takes stock of ongoing national reforms across 17 European Union countries. Data pertaining to two key elements—societal relevance (in the form of university-industry relations) and scientific excellence—is analysed. The author discusses the findings in the light of conceptualisations surrounding the relevance-excellence nexus in higher education, as well as current policy dynamics and scholarly debates across the region. The chapter concludes by recommending future research directions.

Chapter 2

This chapter investigates whether and how institutional autonomy enhances strategic management of academic human resources. National regulatory frameworks, available resources, university policies, and practices at the working floor are compared in four European flagship universities. Disciplinary affiliation is taken into consideration through the selection of history and chemistry. The cases reflect different trajectories where substantial changes have been implemented in governance systems when it comes to centralization of decision making, to standardization of procedures, to re-configuration of actors and their room to maneuver. While professorial self-governance in personnel matters remains significant, new boundary conditions constrain substantially choice options in accordance with national, institutional, and disciplinary features. Uncertainty, identity, and flexibility emerge as major dimensions in human resources management, pointing to tensions but also to opportunities for strategic change.

Chapter 3

This chapter examines how knowledge networks of academics shape epistemic authority in higher education institutions. The issue is addressed with the approach of funds of knowledge (Bensimon, 2009) and social network theory. Social networks (of collaboration, influence, friendship, etc.) have been mainly approached with an emphasis on their actual structure and the relationship between position in that network and other features. However, little is known about how those networks of ties affect how knowledge is embodied, encoded, and enacted within higher education institutions at the interpersonal level. Rather than examining the specific qualities of any researcher's fund of knowledge, the authors focus on showing how the approach of funds of knowledge can be operationalised by social network analysis to investigate epistemic authority and epistemic change in research agendas. Knowledge networks are described as epistemic conduits, and the challenges of research in this topic are also discussed.

Higher education is a versatile field where researchers from many different professions take part within a common interest. Usually higher education is seen as an interdisciplinary field, but is it rather a disciplinary field where different researchers discuss higher education development within an interdisciplinary context? What makes the field interdisciplinary? This chapter studies if and how interdisciplinarity is established and played out in international comparative higher education projects. A good way to study if and how interdisciplinarity is established in HE projects is to study their methodological approaches because researchers from different backgrounds who are trained in a range of methodological approaches work together to complete a specific project aim. The methodological approach in one single case is studied to look into how interdisciplinarity can develop within a higher education international research project.

Chapter 5

With this chapter, the authors describe (1) the international, Portuguese, and institutional challenges relating to the quality of doctoral research supervision and (2) systematize the research-based frameworks that exist in the international literature worldwide in what concerns this topic. This is followed by a brief presentation of the research methodology adopted to shed light on the process taken to design an integrative and fluid framework that the authors propose on the quality of doctoral research supervision. Additionally, links are established regarding the international literature and tendencies approached on the theoretical section of this chapter. Finally, the authors reflect on the concerns surrounding the pertinence of the framework that arose from the research to evaluate and monitor the doctoral supervisory process.

Chapter 6

This chapter shows how PhD mobility across organizations constitutes a source of normative isomorphism that has led towards the "collegialization" of some Spanish Technology Centres (TCs). In particular, the study of nine TCs located in four Spanish regions has been essential to identify the normative mechanisms embedded in doctoral training and scientific careers that have promoted the convergence among R&D organizations. Thus, TCs collaborating intensively with higher education institutions through hybrid researchers have adopted academic models of knowledge production. Interestingly, they have also introduced doctoral training programs to reinforce their legitimacy in the eyes of their collaborators and investors. As a result of these changes, TCs move towards a more proactive position in the processes of knowledge transfer to gain an advantageous position in an innovation system.

In this chapter, the authors examine the forces influencing higher education in a digitally globalized, plurilingual, and intercultural world, and how they have already begun to change some traditional notions of what higher education is for, and how it should be adapted to fit new emergent social needs, which are currently under debate in the educational field (Mehaffy, 2012). They go on to propose a connectivist vision for the future of globalized higher education and provide three case studies that illustrate ways of achieving that vision. Each case study has a different orientation: resource orientation, process orientation, transformation orientation. All three of them have the same objective: innovation and adaptation to the new globalized paradigms that have placed higher education in an increasingly complex context.

This chapter presents a comprehensive view of the main activities and findings of a research project entitled TRACER-Portuguese Public Higher Education Use of Communication Technologies, which focused on how the information about the use of Communication Technologies in Higher Education Institutions can be collected, systematized, processed, and deployed to stakeholders. The project was carried out between 2011 and 2014 and its main results are a consolidated proposal of an analysis model to address the use of Communication Technologies in Higher Education institutions, as well as the U-TRACER® tool. This Web-based tool provides support to the process of collecting, processing, and deployment of data related with the use of Communication Technologies in a specific Higher Education or in a group of institutions, based on institutional or geographical criteria.

Daariimaa Marav, National University of Mongolia, Mongolia
Michelle Espinoza, Universidad Arturo Prat, Chile

This chapter is set in the context of two developing countries, Mongolia and Chile, where digital technology is seen as a powerful icon of the knowledge economy. The predominant and common discourses surrounding the uses of digital technologies in education in these developing countries usually assume rather celebratory stances of the roles digital technologies may perform in education in the digital age. Thus, the research reported here explores the realities, opportunities, and challenges that academic staff face when using digital technologies through the perspectives offered by the field of digital literacy studies. The findings illustrate the close and complex relationships between sociocultural contexts, beliefs, values, and digital literacy practices. The study suggests that more attention needs to be paid to the wider contexts affecting the digital practices around teaching and learning rather than to technologies per se.

Emma Murphy, Dublin City University (DCU), Ireland
Yurgos Politis, University College Dublin (UCD), Ireland
Maria Slowey, Dublin City University (DCU), Ireland

This chapter explores current patterns of participation and progression by mature students in undergraduate (Bachelors) programmes in an Irish university. The study was conducted by HERC (Higher Education Research Centre) in collaboration with an Institutional Analysis and Research Office with input from an expert Advisory Group. Based on the suggestions and experiences of students and staff, and informed by good practice examples from literature, a series of recommendations are proposed, aimed at enhancing experiences and successful outcomes of mature students in the future.

Delia Bîrle, University of Oradea, Romania
Daniela Crişan, Tilburg University, The Netherlands
Elena Bonchiş, University of Oradea, Romania
Laura Bochiş, University of Oradea, Romania
Carmen Popa, University of Oradea, Romania

The chapter explores whether the educational policies introduced by the Romanian Government during the last twenty years are examples of good practice for other European countries facing the issue of Roma integration. The authors raise the question of whether the voices of Roma intellectual élites, who represent the "products" of those educational policies, are strong enough to drive the Roma minority towards common and sustained efforts for their social integration. What are the cross products of these educational policies? Additionally, they consider the case of Roma students within the University of Oradea in Romania and examine their attitudes towards academic learning, motivational factors, academic self-efficacy, faced difficulties, and potential ways to achieve higher rates of student retention. For a more in-depth analysis of the role and impact of those policies and the possible challenges/difficulties encountered, the authors interviewed several decision makers, such as academic staff, NGO representatives, and current/former Roma students. The chapter concludes with suggested solutions for detected difficulties.

Chapter 12

To attract a growing number of international students, Higher Education (HE) institutions are striving to differentiate themselves from their competitors. The Eynesbury Institute of Business and Technology (EIBT) is part of a growing number of private providers partnering with universities to establish "pathway" programs. EIBT offers a Diploma of Business leading to either The University of Adelaide or the University of South Australia's degree programs in business-related fields. This chapter investigates EIBT students' own perceptions of "ethics" in a major assessment task embedded in a course titled "Business and Society". The findings, taken from students' reflective papers, reveal their understanding(s) of ethical behaviour and are particularly relevant to contemporary debates surrounding how to improve educational attainment and ethical standards given the emerging importance of partner providers amidst rising numbers of international students seeking HE in Australia and abroad.

The authors are part of a team delivering accredited programmes in teaching at tertiary level, and have collaborated to examine the impact of their work and that of the team over more than ten years in this area: whether accredited professional development programmes for academics have improved teaching— and students' learning—in higher education. A review of the literature is presented, along with new research undertaken in their home institution. The authors' findings from both the literature and their most recent research indicates a range of benefits for higher education in providing and supporting accredited programmes for educators. However, they have also identified methodological issues in measuring these benefits and impact overall. The chapter discusses this work and connects it with the broader themes of this book. The authors emphasise the importance of effective teaching in the midst of the many complex changes influencing higher education at this time.

Chapter 14

Carmen Popa, University of Oradea, Romania
Simona Laurian, University of Oradea, Romania
Laura Bochis, University of Oradea, Romania
Carlton J. Fitzgerald, New England College, USA
Delia Birle, University of Oradea, Romania
Elena Bonchis, University of Oradea, Romania

The goal of this study was to assist instructors and leadership of a hybrid weekend pre-service teacher education program at the University of Oradea to improve their effectiveness with students. Specifically, this study sought to gather and analyze data from three program constituents: students, instructors, and program leadership. The preschool and primary weekend education program at the University of Oradea was developed to be suitable for students who for various reasons cannot attend the traditional day classes. In 2011, the weekend program was changed into a hybrid program in an effort to more directly meet the needs of the student population. In order to more effectively meet the needs of the students, it became obvious that the pedagogy and structure of the program needed refinement. The data gathered in this study allowed the research team to develop recommendations for program, pedagogical, and textbook improvements.

Chapter 15

Sanja Tatalović Vorkapić, University of Rijeka, Croatia
Lidija Vujičić, University of Rijeka, Croatia
Željko Boneta, University of Rijeka, Croatia

The evaluation of the new graduate study program Early and Preschool Care and Education (EPCE) was conducted recently in Croatia. Preschool teachers and graduate students were asked about their motivation for enrolling, the level of competencies developed during their study, and the predictive power of three significantly connected motives in relation to those competencies. Statistical analysis revealed highly positive perception of relevant competences gained. This finding confirmed the hypothesis that continuing professional development through formal higher education contributes significantly to improved preschool teachers' performance while coping with changing and growing job demands. Moreover, subjects demonstrated highly intrinsic motivation for enrolling. Extrinsic motives were indicative of a more negative, while intrinsic motivation led to more positive, perception of learning outcomes and gained competencies. Overall, the evaluation was highly positive and the findings confirmed the importance of satisfying the professional needs of preschool teachers.

Foreword

The core of papers published in this book arose through the opportunity for Early Career Researchers (ECRs) to network and collaborate at an ECR colloquium held in Ireland in 2013 and through the Early Career Higher Education Research (ECHER) network, established in 2011. Networks such as this are valuable in providing a forum for ECRs to exchange information, interact, and engage. This level of peer support is essential, as many ECRs have reported a sense of being isolated in their work; therefore, building networks is critical in enabling ECRs to develop strong ties with peers and develop extended support networks above and beyond those offered by supervisors or associated principal investigators. These networks also allow ECRs to build their scholarly profile and begin a process of developing an academic identity. The quality and breadth of the chapters in this book demonstrates the values of early career researchers in developing networks and building up a body of integrated knowledge in their chosen field; it is hoped that many of the authors in this book will continue to forge working relationships that they have developed as a consequence of this project through the continued formulation of future research grants and publications.

Most of the chapters in the book come from a consortium of authors early in their research careers. The fact that they are in the initial stages of their research careers does not negate the breadth and quality of papers that explore a wide range of issues related to research into higher education. Early Career Researchers (ECRs) are those who are currently undertaking, or have completed, doctoral studies in the last five years and are an important part of research structures within higher education systems. Developing and supporting early career researchers is essential for the future development of disciplinary knowledge. In particular, in the field of research into higher education, ECRs are crucially important to the development of understanding of, and identifying solutions to, the challenges facing higher education systems both nationally and globally. They are also a key component of, and contributor to, the development of higher education systems. In addition, they provide the foundation for the future workforce in all aspects of higher education including teaching, research, policy, and governance in both the public and private sectors.

Although the importance of ECRs to the higher education sector is without question, their voice has not always been heard, and in many cases, their expertise and experience is underutilised. There is also evidence that ECRs are dissatisfied with aspects of their careers, especially in terms of opportunities to take on leadership roles and in accessing forums to highlight and disseminate their work (Åkerlind, 2005; Petersen, 2011). It is important that ECRs are provided with opportunities to publish and present their research findings; projects, such as this book, are imperative in not only allowing ECRs to present their work but also to provide them with an opportunity to publish independently and display their knowledge to a wide audience on their area of study.

In addition, the involvement of ECRs from a variety of disciplines in bringing together the chapters in this book adds scope and innovation in exploring the challenges that face higher education. Bringing together ECRs from different disciplines provides a fresh perspective on higher education research that may not be evident in previously published research. The quality of research in the future is based on the development of skilled researchers who can work together in multidisciplinary teams in advancing knowledge in the field of higher education.

The papers presented in this volume demonstrate how the research undertaken by ECRs can develop new perspectives on higher education research as well as progressing an understanding of areas previously unexplored. In this book, the authors have tackled a diverse range of contemporary challenges facing higher education, including the impact on higher education of information and communications technology, managerial control, academic autonomy, professional development of teachers and academics, the experiences of minority groups in society accessing higher education, non-traditional aged students, internationalisation in higher education, comparative research in higher education, methodology, and doctoral supervision. As well as contributing debate and research on the traditional functions of universities (teaching and research), the authors provide a welcome exploration of new innovations in higher education, not least in the areas of knowledge transfer and the relationships between higher education and industry. The increasing collaborative nature of research into higher education and the enthusiasm of early career researchers in this regard are evident in that the book presents papers by authors from Australia, Chile, Croatia, France, Ireland, Mongolia, Norway, Portugal, Romania, Spain, and the USA. This international interaction and collaboration is to be welcomed as not only does it facilitate understanding of higher education within a global context, but it also allows for cross-national sharing of ideas and methodological innovations. In addition, early career researchers who authored the chapters in this book are using innovative and multiple methods to investigate areas of interest in higher education research. In this book you will find methods, such as case studies, documentary analysis, reflective students' papers, social network analysis, techno-biographies, testimonials, secondary data analysis, and action research, among others, used. All of which push out the boundaries in enhancing our understanding of higher education systems and the actors that work within these systems.

The challenges for ECRs in higher education both in entering the system and progressing careers are well documented; this book demonstrates the value that ECRs can bring to the field and how the future of research into higher education is in safe hands. This is not least down to the editors of the book, all early career researchers themselves, who have shown exemplary leadership skills in bringing together this fine volume of work that will be of interest to all those who work in or research the field of higher education.

Jonathan Drennan
University of Southampton, UK

Jonathan Drennan *is Professor of Healthcare Research at the Faculty of Health Sciences, University of Southampton. He holds a PhD and Master's degree in Education from University College Dublin, a postgraduate diploma in Statistics from Trinity College Dublin, and a bachelor's degree in Nursing from the University of Ulster. He has published a number of papers on higher education in leading international journals, including Studies in Higher Education, Nurse Education Today, Advances in Health Sciences Education, and Assessment and Evaluation in Higher Education. He has also published chapters on engaging university students and the research function of the academic profession in Europe. His specialization is on the impact and outcomes of the Master's degree for health professionals. He has extensive experience in large-scale research projects, having* *worked as principal investigator and co-applicant on a number of nationally and internationally funded studies. He was the principal investigator in a European Science Foundation/Irish Research Council for the Social Sciences-funded programme of research entitled The Academic Profession in Europe: Responses to Societal Change (EUROAC). He also chaired the survey design group, which developed and tested the Irish National Student Survey – a measure of student engagement that is being used throughout the higher education sector in Ireland.*

REFERENCES

Åkerlind, G. (2005). Postdoctoral researchers: Roles functions and career prospects. *Higher Education Research & Development, 24*(1), 21–40. doi:10.1080/0729436052000318550

Petersen, E. B. (2011). Staying or going? Australian early career researchers' narratives of academic work, exit options and coping strategies. *Australian Universities Review, 53*(2), 35–42.

Preface

It has been our belief, for a long time, that *we are what we study*. But how does what we study affect us? Can research on higher education really matter? And how does it matter? The way this book came to exist and the contributions of each author testify the importance of engagement with our own research in our lives. Some reported the way higher education turned out to be a crucial and formative field in a disconcerting and changing society. Others chose to stand up for higher education as a transformative tool of society, underlining both its political and innovative value. All of them, and us as editors, educators, or scholars of education, have shown that higher education *does* matter – it can change the world, at least by changing our *personal* worlds every day.

But if there is a place for higher education research in the 21st century, what kind of place is it, and where are we to find it? This was the underlying concern of a colloquium, Higher Education and Society: Implications and Effects, organized by the editors of this book and funded by the European Science Foundation in April 2013, University College Dublin. Some of the contributors to this book were speakers at the event. Later, that event turned out to be the kick off for this publication, as both innitiatives meant to provide a voice to early career researchers in dialogue with more experienced scholars. The purpose was to create a debate on the implications and effects of higher education on society. And we are happy to present valuable voices from such different locations as Australia, Chile, Croatia, France, Ireland, Mongolia, Norway, Portugal, Romania, Spain, and the USA.

This book not only presents new voices of higher education research; it also aims at mapping contemporary challenges in the field. Thus, the 15 chapters focus on different aspects of higher education: (1) the changing pattern of decision-making in HE, (2) labour market issues, (3) knowledge acquisition and creation in HE, (4) life-long learning, (5) globalisation and internationalisation issues in HE, (6) challenging university teachers' competencies levels, (7) modernising the university, (8) university programme reviews, (9) access to HE by under-represented groups, and (10) multi-disciplinary research in HE. The variety of themes clearly shows that from each of them arises a different discourse. The themes vary from the role and *praxis* of higher education to the several dimensions that stress the dynamic and changeable nature of higher education and of the research carried on it.

In the first chapter, titled "Citius, Altius, Fortius: Mobilising the University for the 'Europe of Knowledge,'" author Rómulo Pinheiro discusses contemporary trends in European higher education policy regarding the debate of university-industry relations and the debate on research excellence. The author does so under the label of the "logic of instrumentality," based on the work by Johan P. Olsen and others. Drawing on data from ongoing national reforms across 17 European Union countries, the analysis discusses the impact of a number of key strategic measures undertaken by policymakers to tackle the excellence-relevance problematic, such as the proliferation of "centres of excellence," the discourse on world rankings, the convergence trends, and the strategic use of research collaboration in order to attain more competitive advantage. Based on these axes, the author suggests that there is a willingness by policymakers across Europe to set in motion a series of mechanisms geared towards supporting both *embedded excellence* (national and supranational efforts towards capitalising on the presence of scientific institutions as regeneration agents and economic catalysts) and *contextual relevance* (mainly related with the dominant emphasis on the role of applied [mode-2] knowledge and innovation in the economic regeneration/growth of localities and regions).

Using case studies, in the second chapter, titled "Strategic Management of Academic Human Resources: A Comparative Analysis of Flagship Universities in Norway, Finland, Switzerland, and Austria," the author, Tatiana Fumasoli, discusses how change has been taking place in personnel policies of four European Flagship universities (University of Oslo, University of Helsinki, University of Basel, University of Vienna), bearing in mind relevant differences between national higher education systems. The author's work has shown that regulatory frameworks (enhancing institutional autonomy), structural conditions (financial resources and students), and actors' identities (academic profession, disciplinary fields, leadership, administration) shape the trajectories of universities and disciplines. In addition, the author discusses three analytical dimensions that emerged from presented comparative analysis that characterize how universities adapt to changing environmental conditions and leadership strategies: uncertainty, identity, and flexibility. Central in this chapter is to understand how universities adapt to pressures for change and develop their strategic management of human resources: how do policy reforms, university strategies, and academic traditions play the role of drivers of change?

The third chapter, titled "Funds of Knowledge and Epistemic Authority in Higher Education," authored by one of the book's editors, Filipa M. Ribeiro and by Miranda Lubbers, focuses on showing how the approach of funds of knowledge can be operationalised by Social Network Analysis (SNA) to investigate epistemic authority and epistemic change in knowledge creation processes in HE. Grounded on authors like Bourdieu, specifically his emphasis on situations of emergent knowledge, the author proposes to extend Bourdieu's concerns to higher education studies, addressing the following questions, What topics seem to occupy hallowed ground? What topics are those to which we consistently turn a blind eye? and What does this say about the era in which we live? The author, then, discusses and describes how the conceptual framework of the theory of funds of knowledge and the methodological frameworks of SNA fits to address those questions and discusses the challenges of researching the relationship between knowledge networks (namely at the interpersonal level) and epistemic authority in HEIs.

In the fourth chapter, titled *"A Need for New Methodological Approaches in Comparative Higher Education Research Projects?," the author,* Kristin Lofthus Hope, aims to contribute to the academic discussion on how international comparative and collaborative projects in higher education research conceptualize the use of methods, and how they practically deal with it. The author analyses the character of international comparative and collaborative research, which is multi-counrty (international collaborative) and often multidisciplinary and multi-method research. Thus, the question raised is if and how interdisciplinarity is established in international comparative higher education projects. The approach chosen was to ethnographically study one international comparative project regarding its choices and use of methods. The author concludes that in international comparative higher education research reflexivity is a highly important feature that needs to be enhanced.

The fifth chapter, titled "Quality of Doctoral Research Supervision: Contributions of an Integrative and Fluid Framework to Evaluate and Monitor the Process," authored by Ana Vitoria Baptista, gives an outline of how quality assurance has evolved in Portugal by introducing different models of external evaluations, including programme accreditation and institutional audits as well as examples of the use of national qualification frameworks and learning outcomes. Internal evaluations are described with examples of common practices—using the case of one Portuguese comprehensive university—such as the monitoring of doctoral candidates' progress. The chapter also contains considerations about the specificity of doctoral education in Portugal and the use of key performance indicators. The conclusion underlines the importance of three basic aspects in the attempt to design an evaluation and monitoring process for the quality of doctoral research supervision: 1) the existence of quality indicators depicted directly from student's and supervisor's reports in order to enhance the critical aspect of the evaluation mechanisms, 2) evaluation and quality should be raised from the institutional culture where they are embedded, 3) the existence of a supportive context to evaluation take place.

In the sixth chapter, titled "Technology Centres: An Extended Internal Labour Market for PhD Holders in Spain," the author, Susana Pablo-Hernando, provides an innovative study on the impact of PhD education and workforce on university-industry collaboration and institutional change of TCs. Based on a qualitative study, the author shows convincingly how Spanish TCs that collaborate a lot with HEI have adopted academic models of knowledge production, something that was absent in the research so far. Thus, the study contributes to closing this gap. Especially interesting is that the author shows how important and prestigious academic norms and knowledge production are even in hybrid spaces like TCs, where more applied projects and R&D activities are the principal task. This result bears important implications for PhD education in Spain, specifically for PhDs in hybrid spaces, as the chapter describes in the discussion section.

In the seventh chapter, titled "Higher Education and Globalization," authors Neus Lorenzo and Ray Gallon provide several case studies in order to illustrate the connectivist stance that the future of higher education should take, in their opinion. Issues like digital democracy, pedagogy of virtuality, and deliberative practices that shape globalization processes are discussed, taking into account the changing context of today's universities. The authors claim that tertiary education—and their chapter clearly justifies the use of the term "tertiary"—must "deeply integrate into the digitally connected universe, while preserving academic freedom and rigor." How? By focusing on three main innovation orientations: resources (e-learning, massive platforms for MOOCs), processes (in-service professional training), and transformational research oriented to a collective good. In line with researchers like Thomas Pfeffer, Lorenzo and Gallon stress that the solution to tackle the vast array of technical innovations and of challenges associated with the distribution of digital media is to engage with well-known collaborative schemas to overcome the "certifying knowledge acquisition" paradigm and promote a shift to "benchmarking learning processes."

The eighth chapter, titled "Tracing the Use of Communication Technologies in Higher Education," authored by Fernando Ramos and a team of his colleagues, presents a comprehensive view of the main activities and findings of a research project titled TRACER-Portuguese Public Higher Education Use of Communication Technologies, which focused on how information about the use of Communication Technologies in Higher Education Institutions can be collected, systematized, processed, and deployed to stakeholders. The project was carried out between 2011 and 2014, and its main results are a consolidated proposal of an analysis model to address the use of Communication Technologies in Higher Education institutions, as well as the U-TRACER® tool. This Web-based tool provides support to the process of collecting, processing, and deploying data related with the use of Communication Technologies in a specific Higher Education or in a group of institutions, based on institutional or geographical criteria.

In the ninth chapter, titled "University Teachers' Use of Digital Technologies: The Realities from Mongolia and Chile," authors Daariimaa Marav and Michelle Espinoza explore the realities, opportunities, and challenges that academic staff face when using digital technologies through the perspectives offered by the field of digital literacy studies. The findings illustrate the close and complex relationships between sociocultural contexts, beliefs, values, and digital literacy practices. The study suggests that more attention needs to be paid to the wider contexts affecting the digital practices around teaching and learning rather than to technologies *per se*. The chapter aims to compare how wider sociopolitical factors are represented in techno-biographies of university teachers from these developing countries and to discuss opportunities and challenges that they encounter in using digital technologies in their everyday lives.

In the tenth chapter, titled "Contributing to an Evidence Base for the Enhancement of the Experiences and Outcomes of Mature Students at an Irish University," authors Emma Murphy, Yurgos Politis (one of the editors), and Maria Slowey explore current patterns of participation and progression by mature students in programmes across an Irish University (IUX), as the proportion of full-time mature entrants to Irish higher education institutions has actually declined in recent years. This chapter reports on a small scale, qualitative exercise. Nevertheless, the consultation with this particular group of mature students delivered an interesting list of conclusions. The students found activity-based learning sessions valuable and suggested the time allocated to them at induction should be expanded; their decision-making processes are quite different from those of school leavers because they do not enter higher education as a cohort; they felt that some of their needs and preferences with regards to the social and, in certain respects, educational activities were not met. Based on the suggestions and experiences of students and staff, and informed by good practice examples from literature, a series of recommendations aimed at enhancing the experiences and successful outcomes of IUX mature students in the future are proposed.

The authors of the eleventh chapter, titled "Roma Social Inclusion through Higher Education Policies in Romania," Delia Bîrle and her colleagues, discuss whether the educational policies that were introduced by the Romanian Government during the last 15 – 20 years are suitable examples of good practices for other European countries that are facing the issue of Roma integration. Their study included Roma students within the University of Oradea in Romania by examining their attitudes towards academic learning, motivational factors, academic self-efficacy, faced difficulties, and potential solutions to achieve higher rates of student-retention during the years of academic training. In attempting to carry out a more in-depth analysis of the role and impact of educational policies that targeted Roma integration in Romania, as well as the possible challenges and difficulties encountered, the authors present data from interviews conducted with several decision makers, representatives of the academic staff, representatives of NGOs, and current and former Roma students.

Using (international) students' reflective papers and managing the large quantity of narrative data received from those papers, the authors of the twelfth chapter, titled "International Student Perceptions of Ethics in a Business Pathway Program," Donna M. Velliaris, Craig R. Willis, and Janine M. Pierce, examine the EIBT (Eynesbury Institute of Business and Technology, Australia) international students' own perceptions of "ethics." The findings reveal students' understanding(s) of their own ethical sensitivity and, hence, behaviour and are particularly relevant to contemporary debates surrounding how to improve educational attainment and ethical standards, given the emerging importance of partner providers amidst rising numbers of international students seeking HE in Australia and abroad. While it is not explored in great detail in this chapter, "culture" is implicit in this discussion because of the way in which international students are required to negotiate meaning through interactions within the sociocultural environment, which in this case is the Australian HE context. Their findings reveal how the vast majority of students referred to their current studies as having opened their eyes to issues surrounding ethical behaviour(s) and/or academic integrity.

In the thirteenth chapter, titled "Does Accredited Professional Development for Academics Improve Teaching and Learning in Higher Education?," the author, Claire McAvinia, and her colleagues focus on evaluation and impact of accredited courses within the academic professional development centers. Since the early 1990s, academic professional development has emerged as a formal activity in most third-level institutions in the UK, Ireland, Australasia, and the US. This trend led to the inception of centres for academic development. Given the range of staff attending, the longevity of the programmes, and the many challenges now facing higher education, the authors sought to re-examine their own provision and to evaluate the impact of accredited courses over some years. The authors are part of a team delivering accredited programmes in teaching at tertiary level, and have collaborated to examine the impact of their work and that of the team over more than ten years in this area. Findings from both the literature and most recent research within their own institution indicate a range of benefits for higher education in providing and supporting accredited programmes for educators. However, they have also identified methodological issues in measuring these benefits and the overall impact.

In the fourteenth chapter, titled "Case Study of a Hybrid Undergraduate Elementary Certification Program," the author, Carmen Popa, and her colleagues present and discuss the only hybrid program developed for preschool and primary certification at the University of Oradea in Romania. The preschool and primary weekend education program at the University of Oradea was developed to work with students who for various reasons cannot attend the traditional day classes. The target groups for this study were the student body of the weekend program and its instructors. Most students work during the day and many have family commitments beyond those of traditional students. One-third of them are already working as teachers and are attending university to earn their bachelor's degree. All instructors in the program are full-time professors at the university. In 2011, the weekend program was changed into a hybrid program in an effort to meet more directly the needs of the student population. The program prepares students to become certified preschool and primary teachers. During the past three years, it has become apparent to the instructors and leadership that the students have different needs than those of the traditional day students. In order to more effectively meet their needs, it became obvious that the pedagogy and structure of the program needed refinement. The data gathered in this study allowed the research team to develop recommendations for program, pedagogical, and textbook improvements.

The authors of the last, fifteenth, chapter, titled "Contemporary Challenges and Preschool Teachers' Education in Croatia: The Evaluation of the New Study Program Early/Preschool Care and Education at Faculty of Teacher Education in Rijeka," Sanja Tatalović Vorkapić, Lidija Vujičić, and Željko Boneta, present results of the evaluation of the graduate study program Early and Preschool Care and Education (EPCE) at the University of Rijeka, which is the first of that kind in Croatia. The salient point of the evaluation was to analyze its usefulness according to preschool teachers' actual job demands in Croatia. Forty-four preschool teachers and graduate students were asked to identify the level of their motivation for enrolling in this particular study program as well as the level of (generic and specific) competencies developed during their graduate study. Their analysis revealed highly positive perception of relevant competences gained during this particular graduate study program as well as highly intrinsic motivation among students for enrolling in this graduate study program. Overall, the findings confirmed the importance of satisfying the professional needs of preschool teachers.

Filipa M. Ribeiro
University of Porto, Portugal

Yurgos Politis
University College Dublin (UCD), Ireland

Bojana Culum
University of Rijeka, Croatia

Acknowledgment

The successful completion of this project was possible due to the tireless effort and true teamwork between all actors involved. We therefore feel the need to thank the Editorial Advisory Board for their help in reviewing the proposals received from the Call for Chapters. Moreover, we would like to thank the reviewers for their valuable contribution with the assessment of the first chapter drafts and the subsequent review of the accepted manuscripts. The authors deserve to be praised for their dedication and commitment in producing a high quality chapter by following the reviewers' and editors' recommendations and suggestions. Special thanks go to Prof. Jonathan Drennan for all his help during the Dublin colloquium, which led to this publication, and for writing the Foreword for this book.

Lastly, we would like to acknowledge the financial contribution offered by the European Science Foundation (ESF), to purchase a number of books from the publisher, with special thanks going to Sarah Moore and Anne Guehl.

Filipa M. Ribeiro
University of Porto, Portugal

Yurgos Politis
University College Dublin (UCD), Ireland

Bojana Culum
University of Rijeka, Croatia

Chapter 1
Citius, Altius, Fortius:
Mobilising the University for the "Europe of Knowledge"

Rómulo Pinheiro
University of Agder, Norway

ABSTRACT

The European Union's Lisbon Strategy (2000-2010) set a bold vision of a "Europe of Knowledge" where universities are seen as central actors. A modernisation agenda of universities has been promoted in recent years, focusing on the contribution of the sector to reaching regional and national economic goals. This chapter takes stock of ongoing national reforms across 17 European Union countries. Data pertaining to two key elements—societal relevance (in the form of university-industry relations) and scientific excellence—is analysed. The author discusses the findings in the light of conceptualisations surrounding the relevance-excellence nexus in higher education, as well as current policy dynamics and scholarly debates across the region. The chapter concludes by recommending future research directions.

INTRODUCTION

Recent reform efforts in European higher education (HE) have been characterised by a strong emphasis on the fulfilment of policy (economic) agendas. As a consequence of a wider process of 'regional integration' (Amaral et al., 2010), a wide variety of endeavors – intergovernmental, supranational, and national - have been undertaken. These do not only aim at enhancing the compatibility (convergence) of HE systems across Europe (Kehm et al., 2009), but, most notably, are seen as significant steps as to propel the region to play a major role in a highly competitive, global,

knowledge-based economy. Significant scholarly attention has been paid to the impact, at the national level, of convergence efforts across Europe (Musselin, 2009; Hsieh & Huisman, 2012; Corbett, 2014), as well as on the repercussions brought by the so-called 'modernization agenda' in European HE (Maassen, 2009; Enders, de Boer, & Westerheijden, 2011), most notably in the realms of governance and funding. These efforts have partly been driven by the strategic goals set forward in Lisbon in 2000 (Gornitzka, 2007).

This chapter contributes to ongoing scholarly efforts towards mapping out the degree of change in European HE. It does so by illuminating policy

DOI: 10.4018/978-1-4666-7244-4.ch001

efforts and strategic initiatives, both at the supranational and national levels, geared towards making universities cornerstones of the 'Europe of Knowledge'. Given the nature of this inquiry, a special attention is given to the prominent role of influential supranational actors, like the European Commission, in help shaping a region-wide reform agenda for the sector. From an empirical standpoint, two policy areas are analyzed in detail: (a) efforts to increase the interaction between universities and industry, in the context of external calls for enhanced responsiveness and societal relevance; and, (b) strategic initiatives aimed at promoting research excellence and foster the global competitiveness of European universities.[1]

The chapter is organized as follows. The next section provides the background for the study, with a particular emphasis on the prominent role played by supranational discourses and strategic initiatives. This is followed by a novel conceptualization regarding the relevance-excellence nexus, and by the empirical section. Towards its final stages, the chapter discusses the findings in the light of the conceptual framework adopted as well as the literature, and concludes by suggesting new avenues for future research inquiries.

HIGHER EDUCATION AND THE 'EUROPE OF KNOWLEDGE'

In Europe, policy makers' interest on the socio-economic role of HE systems and their core actors (universities) precedes the current era. The sector has been part and parcel of the main components characterizing the 'European Agenda' for more than half a century (Corbett, 2005; Gornitzka et al., 2007, p. 195), both in areas pertaining to teaching (e.g. student mobility) as well as research (e.g. framework programs). Notwithstanding, it is undeniable that, in the last decade alone, increasing inter-governmental efforts geared towards the creation of an *European Area for Higher Education* (EHEA) and for *Research* (ERA) have paved

the way for a bold set of reforms at the national level. Historically speaking, the European summit of heads of States (held in Lisbon in 2000) represents a turning point. Facing increasing pressures resulting from sluggish economic growth, high unemployment, and a decline in global competitiveness, policy makers articulated a bold vision for the region's future.

The Union must become [by 2010] the most competitive and dynamic knowledge-based economy in the world capable of sustainable economic growth with more and better jobs and greater social cohesion. (European Council, 2000)

In 2004 a new European Commission, led by former Portuguese Prime Minister José Manuel Barroso, reinvigorated the importance of substantive reforms across Europe, in light of the Lisbon strategy. The setting of the new Commission coincided with the mid-term review of the progress, by individual member-states, of the Lisbon objectives. For the first time a sense of real crisis surrounded the discussions in the corridors of Brussels (Kok, 2004). In a joint effort, the European- Council and the Commission highlighted that, "the success of the Lisbon strategy hinges on urgent reforms" (European Council 2004, p. 2). Amongst other things, it was expressed that synergies between EHEA and ERA should be forged, thus bringing the (inter-governmental and voluntary) Bologna process and the (supranational) Lisbon strategy a step closer to one another (Keeling, 2006; Capano & Piattoni, 2011). In 2003, and for the first time, the Commission explicitly referred to the vital role of universities in the context of the 'Europe of Knowledge'.

Given their central role, the creation of a Europe of knowledge is for the universities a source of opportunity, but also of major challenges. Indeed universities go about their business in an increasingly globalised environment which is constantly changing and is characterised by increasing com-

petition to attract and retain outstanding talent, and by the emergence of new requirements for which they have to cater. Yet European universities generally have less to offer and lower financial resources than their equivalents in the other developed countries, particularly the USA. Are they in a position to compete with the best universities in the world and provide a sustainable level of excellence? (European Commission, 2003a, p. 3)

Two years later, in 2005, a policy document entitled 'Common Actions for Growth and Employment' highlighted that:

The [European] Commission intends to support universities and providers of tertiary education in their efforts to contribute more fully to achieving the Lisbon goals, for example by mobilising all sources of EU funding for their modernisation, and by strengthening cooperation under the Education and Training 2010 programme to complement the Bologna process. The Commission will also examine the establishment of a European Institute of Technology in order to attract the very best minds and ideas from around the world. (European Commission 2005, p. 10)

It was during this period that European Ministers of Education, meeting in Bergen to discuss the Bologna process expressed their commitment towards upholding the principle of 'public responsibility' for HE. They also took the opportunity to stress that, given that "higher education is situated at the crossroads of research, education and innovation, it is also the key to Europe's competitiveness." (Bergen 2005, p. 5) Later, in 2006, the Commission advanced a set of specific recommendations to nation states aimed at a new modernisation agenda for Europe's universities.[2] The Commission identified a set of malaises or 'institutional bottlenecks' to be dealt with, e.g. uniformity and egalitarianism, fragmentation, over-regulation, under-funding, etc. (European Commission, 2006b). The proposals touched upon aspects like student and staff mobility, funding, autonomy and accountability, efficiency, etc. (European Commission, 2006a). Given the limited scope of this chapter, *three* reform areas, as highlighted by the Commission, disserve a special notice:

1. The recognition of the importance of structured partnerships with the business community;
2. Rewarding excellence at the highest level amongst students and researchers;
3. Promoting the global visibility (and competitiveness) of the European Higher Education and Research Areas (European Commission, 2006a, pp. 5-10).

CONCEPTUAL BACKDROP: THE RELEVANCE-EXCELLENCE NEXUS

Scholars have traditionally conceived of strategic efforts towards increasing the relevance and excellence of universities (in Europe and beyond) as somewhat mutually exclusive. Within binary HE systems, the characterisation (and policy discourses) around *teaching (more vocationally-oriented)* HE institutions versus "classic" *research* universities are but one indication of this problematic (cf. Kyvik, 2009). The latter are expected to contribute to global scientific excellence (independently of its direct value for society) whereas the former are seen as having a critical function in transmitting skills and competencies to future (knowledge) workers, as well as providing useful knowledge in the context of application (Kyvik & Lepori, 2010). Similarly, in the realm of knowledge production, discussions around basic (*mode-1*) vs. applied (*mode-2*) research point to a similar direction (Gibbons et al., 1994). Basic or "blue-sky" research efforts, it is stated, should first and foremost be geared towards scientific excellence, albeit the fact that the knowledge generated may (in the long run) be of usefulness to society (Bush, 1945).

In contrast, more applied research initiatives are thought to contribute, first-hand, towards societal relevance by help addressing current problems facing humankind (Nowotny et al., 2002).

Perry and May (2006) propose a novel way of conceiving the interplay between *relevance* and *excellence* in the context of modern HE systems and institutions, and against the backdrop of a globalised knowledge-based economy/society (Rooney et al., 2008). Their conceptual starting point is that both the interdependence and contextualisation of excellence and relevance are rather complex processes to which little scholarly attention has been given. Regarding *interdependence*, it is argued that a dichotomous relation between these two aspects is unhelpful, since "excellence can be relevant, and relevance can be excellent, regardless of funding sources or disciplinary areas." (Perry & May, 2006, p. 76) As a way forward, the authors suggest a typology (see Figure 1) where these two dimensions ('excellence/relevance continuum') are mapped out against degrees of contextualisation (global vs. local); hence, resulting into four distinct, yet not

necessarily mutually exclusive policy discourses regarding the role of universities/knowledge in contemporary societies.

Disembedded excellence pertains to a situation where processes of knowledge production are decoupled from the (local) context in which they are produced, thus being *global* in nature. "Expertise is presumed to be highly mobile, with flows of research personnel and students following and this enhancing existing quality, as judged by league tables or rankings." (Perry & May, 2006, p, 76) In such a situation, hegemonic policy discourses are intrinsically linked to scientific *self-governance* (Nybom, 2007), *selectivity* (Palfreyman & Tapper, 2008), and the concentration of scarce resources, both people and funds, around specialised structures like *centres of excellence* (Aksnes et al., 2012).

Competitive relevance conceives of the application of knowledge assets into specific local (socio-economic) circumstances and strategic priorities, "as a precondition for global success" (Perry & May, 2006, p. 76) Despite of its applied nature, research outcomes are not seen as

Figure 1. The Contextualisation of excellence and relevance (Source: Perry & May, 2006, p. 77)

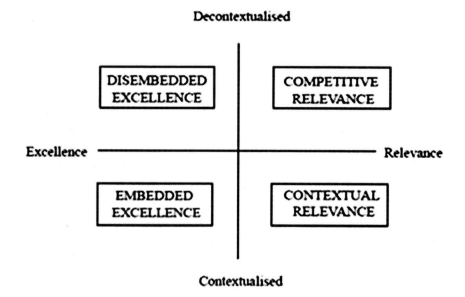

benefiting a particular community or collective (e.g. regional actors). Rather, the idea is that the knowledge being produced/transferred, first and foremost contributes to strengthening the competitive advantage of individual firms or industries (see Porter, 1998). Cutting edge life-science fields such as bio- and nano- technology as well as genomics are compelling examples in this regard (cf. Powell & Owen-Smith, 2002). Concurrently, the prevalent policy discourses tend to put a premium on IP rights, university-industry links, academic spins-offs, etc.; "without seeing context as either a contributing factor or intended beneficiary." (Perry & May, 2006, p. 77)

Turning now to knowledge production that pays attention to contextual (local) dimensions, *embedded excellence* refers to a situation where emphasis is given to the indirect benefits to particular "places and spaces" (Perry & May, 2006, p. 77), i.e. there is an explicit acknowledgment that context does play a role in fostering excellence. The basic idea here is to take advantage of the exploitation of knowledge-laden products and institutions (e.g. universities) for territorial – locality, region, nation as a whole – benefit (cf. Pinheiro et al., 2012). In these circumstances, policy frameworks tend to focus on the framework conditions conducive to attracting "world-class" facilities and expertise (cf. Douglas et al., 2011); "...based on assumptions over the benefits that will indirectly accrue, without any necessary consideration of mechanisms necessary for their realisation." (Perry & May, 2006, p. 78)

Finally, *contextual relevance* is related to both the shaping and creation of research excellence and expertise as well as the exploitation of certain knowledge assets at the local level. In this respect and "within broader processes of knowledge transfer" (Perry & May, 2006, p. 78), critical (policy-related) dimensions such as skills, training and wider participation agendas come to the fore, not necessarily following a linear-dissemination

model; from production to transmission to application (Godin, 2006). Policy frameworks will tend to focus on efforts (partnerships) geared towards connecting the existing research base, either public or private, with industry (Etzkowitz & Leydesdorff, 2000), in addition to equity-related aspects such as social inclusion or economic opportunity.

Whilst this [contextual relevance] discourse appears to be the polar opposite of disembedded excellence, quality is still deemed to be important, but it is judged according to a wider set of scientific, social, economic and political criteria. What is at stake is the values that are seen to inform decision making issues of how benefits from STI [science, technology and innovation] will be realised in practice. In this respect, it is here that we find the greatest challenge to the status quo in terms of issue of justification, legitimation and application. (Perry & May, 2006, p. 78)

EMPIRICAL SECTION

Below we provide new evidence of policy dynamics in the realms of national reforms (broadly speaking), university-industry relations, and strategic efforts aimed at promoting research excellence within European HE systems and institutions.

National Reforms

Reform efforts in European HE are not a novel undertaking, but they have been intensified both, in scale and scope, in the last two decades or so (Gornitzka et al., 2005; Vukasovik et al., 2012). Writing in the early 1990s, on the changing relationship between the State and HE in (Western) Europe and the ability of HE institutions to adapt to external demands, Neave and van Vught (1991, p. 21) pinpointed that:

What has become evident, especially over the past decade, is the apparent inability of higher education to meet the pace of changes as defined from outside the institution, and, more specifically, to respond with a speed which the policy agenda, set by governments, requires.

With respect to the objectives of national policy, i.e. the rationale for governmental intervention in HE, earlier inquiries have suggested that, from the 1960s onwards, governments across (Western) Europe, "have aimed at using their universities to promote regional, economic and occupational policy, and to serve the national interests." (Neave & Rhoades, 1987, cited by Kivinen and Rinne, 1991, p. 58) In the context of an increasingly volatile, highly competitive, and globalised knowledge-based economy, European universities are seen by many – at the national and supra-national levels - as bastions of innovation and competitiveness (Aghion et al., 2008; European Commission, 2003a). Amongst policy circles, a chief assumption "explaining" the lack of competitiveness of Europe lies on the poor degree of engagement between universities and industry, in the context of technological-innovation (Figel, 2006; European Commission, 2006c). Obviously, this does not necessitate that European universities have *not* traditionally engaged with external partners like industry (Geuna & Muscio, 2009; for a recent review of the literature see Perkmann et al., 2013). This is surely the case of the late 19th century English civic universities, which emerged in the vicinity of manufacturing cities like Liverpool, Manchester and Birmingham and, in contrast to their medieval counterparts (primarily located in rural areas), became actively engaged in explorations in the realms of science and technology (Powell & Dayson, 2013, p. 144). What is more, studies (from Northern Europe) suggest that interaction patterns between academics and industrial partners differ amongst technological fields and disciplinary specializations (Meyer-Krahmer & Schmoch, 1998; Pinheiro et al., 2012).

University-Industry Relations

The empirical data on ongoing government-led efforts aimed at fostering the interaction between Europe's universities and industrial sectors, reveal *three* important trends, namely: (a) adjustments in the legal framework; (b) structural measures and financial initiatives; and (c) the development of distinct institutional profiles. The results are briefly presented below.

Adjustments in the Legal Framework

The relationship between academia and industry is, gradually, becoming an important component of the national HE frameworks of many European countries. Across Finland, Sweden, Greece, Italy, and Ireland the interaction between industry and academia is being leveraged by the inclusion of industry representatives in the governing bodies of HE institutions. Governments are also making legal adjustments as to enable universities to enter into direct contractual arrangements with business organizations. For example, the German (federal) government has amended the 'Employee Inventions Act' catering for the direct participation of individual academics in the process of commercialization, through patents. In the Netherlands, the Dutch *hogescholen* (university colleges) are now legally entitled to appoint 'lectors' (a kind of assistant professor) with the explicit task of engaging with industry. Similarly, Hungarian universities have, since 2005, the legal right of founding their own businesses and/or for profit foundations, without the obligation to pay taxes or other governmental duties.

Structural Measures and Financial Incentives

Across Europe, recent reform efforts have stressed the importance of adequate strategic measures aimed at promoting the commercialization of research findings, the creation of new businesses, the utilization of technologies benefiting the economy/ labour market, and the publication of scientific results for the use of all citizens. Across Northern Europe (Sweden and Denmark), governments have funded the creation of Holding Companies, Technological-Bridging Foundations, and Growth Houses (greenhouses for new ideas), all run under the auspices of universities. In Central Europe, the Austrian and Belgium governments have put in place new incentive schemes geared towards attracting industry funds into academia, in the context of applied research. In the Netherlands, a "Smart Mix" financially rewards universities on the basis of their performance in winning competitive research-council contracts and/or contracts with industry. The Dutch Ministry of Economic Affairs has designed a programmatic package targeting "key areas" considered to be of strategic importance to the country, like food and flowers. In a similar fashion, the Ministry of Education has devised an 'Innovation Platform' (chaired by the Prime Minister) acting as an advisory body for HE policy, and responsible for making proposals in reducing the "time-to-market" of (basic) academic research-findings.

In Eastern Europe, the Hungarian government has fostered the creation of Regional Knowledge Centres with the aim of exploring co-research and development opportunities between universities and local industry. Elsewhere (e.g. Czech Republic), special efforts are underway in order to leverage a tighter co-operation between the various stakeholders composing the national R&D infrastructure; universities, academies of science, and industry.

In Britain, the authorities have rationalised existing schemes and boosted the size of the 'Higher Education Innovation Fund' (HEIF) as to further promote knowledge-transfers across the sector. A special focus has been given to building research-capacity and broadening knowledge transfers activities across non research-intensive universities, via the creation of Centres for Knowledge Exchanges, as well as the establishment of *Business Incubators* at British universities.

Finally, in Southern Europe, the Spanish government has, for some time, relied on the Offices for Transference of Research Results as vital structures for promoting and facilitating cooperation in the area of R&D between university-based researchers and businesses. More recently, Portugal's government has pledged substantial financial support to universities interested in registering, via patents, their intellectual property (IP) rights.

Distinctive Institutional Profiles

Finland and Ireland are seen as important success stories in this respect. In Finland, in spite of the fact that the entire sector is expected to contribute to the 'National Development Plan', the more vocational oriented polytechnics have been chosen as the preferable arenas to accommodate the immediate needs of local industry. Whereas polytechnics are to be integrated closer and closer into the national HE system, in line with their specific institutional profiles and missions, universities, on the other hand, are being stimulated to play a larger role in the national/regional innovation systems. Recent amendments of the 'Universities Act' have legally defined "cooperation with the surrounding society" as a core component of universities' formal mission. Finnish universities are now expected to boost their regional impact by developing cooperative endeavours and division of labour with polytechnics and other regional R&D players. The 'regional effect' is expected to increase as a result of the further development of *University Centres or Consortiums* throughout the country. As for the Republic of Ireland, international observers have commented that: "One of the strengths of Ireland's tertiary education system is the extent to which a diversity of mission has been maintained between the university and the institute sectors, as well as within the sectors." (OECD, 2004, p. 20) This conclusion is reinforced by studies shedding light on the role of Irish HE in the 1990s economic boom.

[...] a distinctive feature of higher education in Ireland is the relative concentration of graduates in mathematics and science-related fields at 'college' (ISCED 5A) and even more so at 'polytechnic' (ISCED 5B) level as a result of the creation of Regional Technical colleges that not only improved access to third level education, but, even more importantly, provided a different form of third level education, moving away from purely academic university education to a more technical and modern skills-based system. Consequently, Ireland has a leading position in the output of scientific and engineering graduates, which is also reflected in the disproportionate representation of science graduates in the youth Labour Force. (Ferreira & Vanhoudt, 2004, p. 222)

It is worth mentioning that the strategy of investing in *Technological Education Institutes* is being emulated elsewhere. For example, in Greece where these types of institutions are co-operating with established universities (domestic and overseas) in the provision of postgraduate studies and applied-research. With respect to the traditional research-based universities and their contributions towards national innovation and economic development, these are being stimulated to complement the role of their more vocationally-oriented counterparts in countries such as Belgium, the Czech Republic, Germany, Hungary, and Sweden.

We will now turn our attention to the other modernisation aspect investigated in this paper, the research capacity/global excellence of Europe's universities.

Research Excellence

Across policy circles it is increasingly argued that, the 'Europe of Knowledge' requires adequate investments in R&D infrastructures as to leverage innovative capacity and economic growth across the entire region (European Commission, 2003b), as well as help mitigating 'brain drain' patterns (Barroso, 2006). The sense of "crisis" permeating (supranational) policy debates on European HE (see Figel, 2006, p. 3) is, to a great extent, driven by the relative modest standing of Europe's universities in the global, research-based university rankings (Aghion et al., 2008, pp. 23-27).[3] The national data on reform trends across Europe reveal that efforts are well underway as to strengthen the capacity of institutions, mostly but not exclusively public universities, to compete globally in the knowledge-production frontier. Across the region, the policy measures being used include:

- The concentration of funding in larger units – super universities, centres/clusters of excellence, knowledge centres (Denmark, Finland, Germany, the UK) - and around strategic research areas seen as critical to the global competitiveness of the national economy (the Netherlands);
- Network-type of arrangements aimed at inter-institutional collaboration amongst universities as well as between the university and the non-university sub-sector (Austria, Greece, Belgium), including the participation of overseas partners (Portugal);
- Support for future concepts leading to top-class research (Germany, Finland) and high quality inter-disciplinary research endeavours (The Republic of Ireland, Greece, the UK);
- Structural measures aimed at strengthening the overall capacity of the domestic research system, through mergers/amal-

gamations (Nordic region), and/or the support for the so called 'disadvantaged' fields, e.g. via the creation of a new Arts and Humanities Research Council (the UK).

In addition, recent policy efforts have focused on the general improvement of the conditions leading to the *recruitment*, *training*, and *promotion* (retention) of research talent at universities. Such measures include: allowing institutions greater flexibility in hiring and promoting academic staff (Belgium, France, Italy and Hungary); new financial arrangements (scholarships/grants) targeting young researchers (Denmark, Portugal and the Netherlands); the creation of postgraduate schools (Germany, Finland); enhancements in staff- (professional) training and the overall status of the academic profession (Poland and Austria); recruitment of foreign staff or repatriation of national researchers living overseas (Austria, Belgium, Finland, Germany and the UK); promoting science in broader society and raising the aspirations of the youth (the UK and Hungary); enhancement of gender equity in academia (Germany and Finland); development of special programmes dedicated to the promotion of individual talent/merit amongst young researchers (Denmark, Germany, the Netherlands and the UK); and, the flexible hiring and financial rewarding of the so-called academic 'superstars' (Denmark).

DISCUSSION

It is now time to revisit the conceptual model or typology (Beth & Perry, 2006) presented earlier, in the light of the empirical findings across the selected 17 countries. The first impression one gets is that policy makers – national and supranational levels – have been undertaking a number of key strategic measures as a means of tackling the excellence-relevance problematic in a number of fronts.

The concentration of public funding in/around larger research groups and world-class research units (centres of excellence) is an indication of the importance being attributed to *disembedded excellence*. The current discourse – amongst policy circles and institutional leaders alike – around 'world rankings' (Hazelkorn, 2009; Altbach & Salmi, 2011) is a prevalent feature of this phenomenon, with even marginalised or peripheral institutions mimicking such hegemonic discourses (Pinheiro, 2012b). The European Commission has played an increasingly prominent role in this respect (Deem et al., 2008), by pointing to the US's top research universities - Harvard, Stanford, MIT, etc. - as the blueprint or *organizational archetype* (Greenwood & Hinings, 1993) to follow, i.e. designed for success in an increasingly competitive market place (see Marginson & Rhoades, 2002).[4]

Rankings are a manifestation of what has become known as the worldwide 'battle for excellence', and are perceived and used to determine the status of individual institutions, assess the quality and performance of the higher education system and gauge global competitiveness. (Hazelkorn, 2011, p. 6)

A number of studies have revealed that global models such as the idea of the 'globally-oriented research-intensive university' or 'centres of research excellence' are slowly, but steadily, becoming embedded in the national institutional context in which HE institutions operate (Beerkens, 2009; Mohrman, 2008; Aksnes et al., 2012). As is the case with other parallel processes, like the implementation of the Bologna standards (cf. Witte, 2008), convergence trends are leading to diversification rather than harmonization or *isomorphism* (DiMaggio & Powell, 1983) per se, given the importance attributed to localisation (*adaptation*) processes (see Beerkens, 2010; Pinheiro & Stensaker, 2013).

Moving towards the relevance side of the model, the data suggest that policy makers across

Europe have, for some time, been preoccupied with issues pertaining to *competitive relevance*. The focus attributed to collaborations and partnerships between research-intensive universities and global firms and other knowledge producers/ users (also across the public sector) is indicative of this trend. In countries like Finland (Lester & Sotarauta, 2007), 'triple-helix' arrangements (Etzkowitz & Leydesdorff, 2000) aimed at fostering cross-sectorial collaborations and support the rise of a vibrant *national innovation system* (Nelson, 1993) have become the norm, and have been followed by many across Europe (Meyer et al., 2013). A parallel discourse has emerged nonetheless, namely; that of the rise of the highly responsive institution, in the form of the 'entrepreneurial university' (Clark, 1998; Etzkowitz et al., 2008). Recent studies suggest that the latter model is becoming increasingly pronounced within European HE, providing a global template against which (localised) organizational transformation is to take place (cf. Pinheiro & Stensaker, 2013).

As far as contextualised dimensions go, the data presented above show willingness by policy makers across Europe to set in motion a series of mechanisms geared towards supporting both *embedded excellence* and *contextual relevance*. When it comes to the former, there is evidence of strategic efforts by (national and regional) governmental agencies across Europe towards capitalising on the presence of scientific institutions as regeneration agents and economic catalysts within particular geographies (cf. Gunasekara, 2006), not least regarding their critical role in attracting talent (often from overseas) and scarce financial resources into the locality. Scholars like Richard Florida (2006) have shed light on the importance of HE institutions in the "new global competition for talent", by, *inter alia*, illuminating their critical function in the context of 'talent-magnet regions' (see also Douglas et al., 2011). Recent studies, from Northern Europe, point to the importance of *place* in the development of unique ('world-class') scientific

competencies around particular niches such as community-medicine, artic research, indigenous populations, etc. (Pinheiro, 2012a, 2012b).

Finally, as far as *contextual relevance* is concerned, the empirical data underlines the importance attributed to strategic mechanisms associated with the role of applied (*mode-2*) knowledge and innovation in the economic regeneration/growth of localities and regions (Harloe & Perry, 2004). The appearance of structural arrangements like centres of applied research/innovation, business incubators, and science parks throughout Europe's regions are an example of such ongoing dynamics. The rationale behind such policy measures is to foster sustainable *regional innovation systems* (Cooke et al., 2004) involving a wide variety of R&D actors across public and private sectors. Once again, the Nordic countries are seen as a benchmark in this respect, with HE institutions (of all kinds) expected to play an active role in the manipulation and transfer of knowledge within a given geographic context (Lester & Sotarauta, 2007; Benneworth et al., 2009), thus positively enhancing local *absorptive capacity* (Vang & Asheim, 2006). The expected result is stronger and more competitive local firms and regions (OECD, 2005; Asheim et al., 2007), which are thought to fuel economic growth locally and nationally, thereby contributing to reaching the Lisbon (now 'Europe 2020') objectives.

CONCLUSION

European universities are facing increasing pressure to demonstrate their (economic) relevance to society, whilst competing for scientific status at a global level. These dynamics are not new per se, but they have intensified as a result of national and supra-national efforts towards modernising European HE systems and institutions. Traditional conceptions of relevance and excellence as mutually exclusive are, slowly but steadily, giving way to more re-fined approaches towards assessing the role played by HE institutions (and the knowledge assets they generate) in society/economy. The empirical analysis undertaken here suggests that policy makers across Europe are tackling the issue of modernisation in a number of fronts, with relevance and excellence being two such strategic imperatives, albeit not exclusively.

Going forward, studies – both of a qualitative and quantitative nature - could, for example, investigate how specific institutions and/or academic groups throughout Europe are dealing with having to balance these two critical dimensions – excellence and relevance. In addition, future inquiries could also cast critical light on the interplay between excellence and relevance in the realms of government policy, institutional strategies, as well as specific academic structures and activities; and, in turn, the effects that the institutionalisation of such measures are having on the daily life of HE institutions on the one hand, and the nature of the academic profession on the other. Finally, researchers interested in exploring change dynamics within European HE should, in addition to resort to mixed methodologies, consider adopting a longitudinal research design as a means of capturing dynamics at different points in time as to gain a more accurate (and holistic) understanding of the ways in which developments across specific countries and regions are moving towards either convergence or divergence. And, as a means of tacking stock of the short and long-term effects – for both HE systems and institutions alike – that such processes entail, including the successful realisation of policy ambitions like common European Areas for HE and Research, the idea of a 'Europe of Knowledge', and the global competitive standing of the European continent as a whole.

ACKNOWLEDGMENT

Thank you to an anonymous reviewer for insightful comments and suggestions on an earlier version of the paper. Any remaining errors are the author's.

REFERENCES

Aghion, P., Dewatripont, M., Hoxby, C., Mas-Colelle, M., & Sapir, A. (2008). *Higher aspirations: An agenda for reforming European universities*. Brussels: Bruegel.

Aksnes, D., Benner, M., Brorstad Borlaug, S., Hansen, H., Kallerud, E., Kristiansen, E., et al. (2012). Centres of excellence in the Nordic countries: A comparative study of research excellence policy and excellence centre schemes in Denmark, Finland, Norway and Sweden. *Working Paper 4/2012*.

Altbach, P. G., & Salmi, J. (2011). *The road to academic excellence: The making of world-class research universities*. Washington, DC: World Bank Publications. doi:10.1596/978-0-8213-8805-1

Amaral, A., Neave, G., Musselin, C., & Maassen, P. (2010). *European integration and the governance of higher education and research*. Dordrecht, The Netherlands: Springer.

Asheim, B., Coenen, L., Moodysson, J., & Vang, J. (2007). Constructing knowledge-based regional advantage: Implications for regional innovation policy. *International Journal of Entrepreneurship and Innovation Management*, 7(2), 140–155. doi:10.1504/IJEIM.2007.012879

Barroso, J. M. (2006). *More Europe where it matters: Speech delivered to the European Parliament, Strasbourg, March 15*. Brussels: European Commission.

Beerkens, E. (2009). Centres of excellence and relevance: The contextualisation of global models. *Science, Technology & Society, 14*(1), 153–175. doi:10.1177/097172180801400106

Beerkens, E. (2010). Global models for the national research university: Adoption and adaptation in Indonesia and Malaysia. *Globalisation, Societies and Education, 8*(3), 369–381. doi:10.1080/14767724.2010.505099

Benneworth, P., Coenen, L., Moodysson, J., & Asheim, B. (2009). Exploring the multiple roles of Lund University in strengthening Scania's regional innovation system: Towards institutional learning? *European Planning Studies, 17*(11), 1645–1664. doi:10.1080/09654310903230582

Bergen. (2005). *The European higher education area: Achieving the goals*. Paper presented at the Conference of European Ministers Responsible for Higher Education. Bergen, Norway.

Bush, V. (1945). *Science: The Endless Frontier*. Washington, DC: US Government Printing Office.

Capano, G., & Piattoni, S. (2011). From Bologna to Lisbon: The political uses of the Lisbon 'script' in European higher education policy. *Journal of European Public Policy, 18*(4), 584–606. doi:10.1080/13501763.2011.560490

Clark, B. R. (1998). *Creating entrepreneurial universities: Organizational pathways of transformation*. New York: Pergamon.

Cooke, P., Braczyk, H.-J., & Heidenreich, M. (2004). *Regional innovation systems: The role of governance in a globalized world*. London: Routledge.

Corbett, A. (2005). *Universities and the Europe of knowledge: Ideas, institutions and policy entrepreneurship in European Union higher education policy, 1955-2005*. Basingstoke, UK: Palgrave Macmillan. doi:10.1057/9780230286467

Corbett, A. (2014). The globalisation challenge for European higher education: Convergence and diversity, centres and peripheries. *European Journal of Higher Education*. doi:10.1080/21568235.2014.903575

Deem, R., Mok, K., & Lucas, L. (2008). Transforming higher education in whose image? Exploring the concept of the 'world-class' university in Europe and Asia. *Higher Education Policy, 21*(1), 83–97. doi:10.1057/palgrave.hep.8300179

DiMaggio, P., & Powell, W. (1983). The iron cage revisited: Institutional isomorphism and collective rationality in organizational fields. *American Sociological Review, 48*(2), 147–160. doi:10.2307/2095101

Douglass, J. A., Edelstein, R., & Hoareau, C. (2011). A global talent magnet: How a San Francisco/Bay Area higher education hub could advance California's comparative advantage. In *Attracting international talent and further build US economic competitiveness*. Berkeley, CA: CSHE Publications.

Enders, J., De Boer, H., & Westerheijden, D. (Eds.). (2009). *Reform of higher education in europe*. Rotterdam, The Netherlands: Sense.

Etzkowitz, H., & Leydesdorff, L. (2000). The dynamics of innovation: From national systems and "mode 2" to a triple helix of university-industry-government relations. *Research Policy, 29*(2), 109–123. doi:10.1016/S0048-7333(99)00055-4

Etzkowitz, H., Ranga, M., Benner, M., Guaranys, L., Maculan, A. M., & Kneller, R. (2008). Pathways to the entrepreneurial university: Towards a global convergence. *Science & Public Policy*, *35*(9), 681–695. doi:10.3152/030234208X389701

European Commision. (2006a). *The new Lisbon strategy: An estimation of the economic impact of reaching five Lisbon targets*. Brussels: European Commission.

European Commission. (2003a). *The role of the universities in the Europe of knowledge*. Brussels: European Commission.

European Commission. (2003b). *Investing in research: An action plan for Europe*. Brussels: European Commission.

European Commission. (2005). *Common actions for growth and employment: The community Lisbon programme*. Brussels: European Commission.

European Commission. (2006b). *Delivering on the modernisation agenda for universities: Education, research and innovation*. Brussels: European Commission.

European Commission. (2006c). *Cluster "modernisation of higher education": Summary report of the peer learning activity on university-business partnerships (UBPs)*. Brussels: Directorate-General for Education and Culture.

European Council. (2000). *Diverse systems shared goals: The contribution to the Lisbon strategy*. Brussels: Council of the European Union.

European Council. (2004). *The success of the Lisbon strategy hinges on urgent reforms*. Brussels: Council of the European Union.

Ferreira, M., & Vanhoudt, P. (2004). Catching the Celtic tiger by its tail. *European Journal of Education*, *39*(2), 209–236. doi:10.1111/j.1465-3435.2004.00176.x

Figel, J. (2006). *International competitiveness in higher education: A European perspective*. Paper presented at the Association of Heads of University Administration Annual Conference. Oxford, UK.

Florida, R. (2006). The flight of the creative class: The new global competition for talent. *Liberal Education*, *92*(3), 22–29.

Geuna, A., & Muscio, A. (2009). The governance of university knowledge transfer: A critical review of the literature. *Minerva*, *47*(1), 93–114. doi:10.1007/s11024-009-9118-2

Gibbons, M., Nowotny, H., Schwartzman, S., Scott, P., & Trow, M. (1994). *The new production of knowledge: The dynamics of science and research in contemporary societies*. London: Sage.

Godin, B. (2006). The linear model of innovation: The historical construction of an analytical framework. *Science, Technology & Human Values*, *31*(6), 639–667. doi:10.1177/0162243906291865

Gornitzka, Å. (2007). The Lisbon process: A supranational policy perspective. In P. Maassen & J. P. Olsen (Eds.), *University dynamics and European integration* (pp. 155–178). Dordrecht, The Netherlands: Springer. doi:10.1007/978-1-4020-5971-1_8

Gornitzka, Å., Kogan, M., & Amaral, A. (2005). *Reform and change in higher education: Analysing policy implementation*. Dordrecht, The Netherlands: Springer. doi:10.1007/1-4020-3411-3

Gornitzka, Å., Maassen, P., Olsen, J. P., & Stensaker, B. (2007). Europe of knowledge: Search for a new pact. In P. Maassen & J. P. Olsen (Eds.), *University dynamics and European integration* (pp. 181–214). Dordrecht, The Netherlands: Springer. doi:10.1007/978-1-4020-5971-1_9

Greenwood, R., & Hinings, C. (1993). Understanding strategic change: The contribution of archetypes. *Academy of Management Journal, 36*(5), 1052–1081. doi:10.2307/256645

Gunasekara, C. (2006). The generative and developmental roles of universities in regional innovation systems. *Science & Public Policy, 33*(2), 137–150. doi:10.3152/147154306781779118

Harloe, M., & Perry, B. (2004). Universities, localities and regional development: The emergence of the 'mode 2' university? *International Journal of Urban and Regional Research, 28*(1), 212–223. doi:10.1111/j.0309-1317.2004.00512.x

Hazelkorn, H. (2009). Rankings and the battle for world-class excellence: Institutional strategies and policy choice. *Higher Education Management and Policy, 21*(1), 1–22. doi:10.1787/hemp-v21-art4-en

Hazelkorn, H. (2011). *Globalization and the reputation race in rankings and the reshaping of higher education: The battle for world class excellence.* London: Palgrave MacMillan. doi:10.1057/9780230306394

Hsieh, J., & Huisman, J. (2012). Cross-national policy change in higher education and the Bologna process: a prelude to global convergence? In *Proceedings of the Policy Formation in Post-Secondary Education: Issues and Prospects in Turbulent Times.* Academic Press.

Keeling, R. (2006). The Bologna process and the Lisbon research agenda: The European Commission's expanding role in higher education discourse. *European Journal of Education, 41*(2), 203–223. doi:10.1111/j.1465-3435.2006.00256.x

Kehm, B. M., Huisman, J., & Stensaker, B. (2009). *The European higher education area.* Rotterdam, The Netherlands: Sense Publishers.

Kivinen, O., & Rinne, R. (1991). How to steer student flows and higher education: The headache facing the Finnish Ministry of Education. In G. Neave & F. Van Vught (Eds.), *Prometheus bound: The changing relationship between government and higher education in Western Europe* (pp. 51–64). Pergamon Press.

Kok, W. (2004). *Facing the challenge: The Lisbon strategy for growth and employment.* Luxembourg: European Communities.

Kyvik, S. (2009). *The dynamics of change in higher education: Expansion and contraction in an organisational field.* Dordrecht, The Netherlands: Springer.

Kyvik, S., & Lepori, B. (2010). *Research in the non-university higher education sector in Europe.* Dordrecht, The Netherlands: Springer.

Lester, R., & Sotarauta, M. (Eds.). (2007). *Innovation, universities and the competitiveness of regions.* Helsinki: Tekes.

Maassen, P. (2009). The modernisation of European higher education: National policy dynamics. In A. Amaral, I. Bleiklie, & C. Musselin (Eds.), *From governance to identity* (pp. 95–112). Dordrecht, The Netherlands: Springer. doi:10.1007/978-1-4020-8994-7_8

Marginson, S., & Rhoades, G. (2002). Beyond national states, markets, and systems of higher education: A glonacal agency heuristic. *Higher Education, 43*(3), 281–309. doi:10.1023/A:1014699605875

Meyer, M., Grant, K., & Kuusisto, J. (2013). The second coming of the triple helix and the emergence of hybrid innovation environments. In R. Capello, A. Olechnicka, & G. Gorzelak (Eds.), Universities, cities and regions: Loci for knowledge and innovation creation (pp. 193-209). Milton Park, UK: Routledge.

Meyer-Krahmer, F., & Schmoch, U. (1998). Science-based technologies: University–industry interactions in four fields. *Research Policy*, *27*(8), 835–851. doi:10.1016/S0048-7333(98)00094-8

Mohrman, K. (2008). The emerging global model with chinese characteristics. *Higher Education Policy*, *21*(1), 29–48. doi:10.1057/palgrave.hep.8300174

Musselin, C. (2009). The side effects of the bologna process on national institutional settings: The case of France. In A. Amaral, G. Neave, C. Musselin, & P. Maassen (Eds.), *European integration and the governance of higher education and research* (pp. 181–205). Dordrecht, The Netherlands: Springer. doi:10.1007/978-1-4020-9505-4_8

Neave, G., & van Vught, F. (Eds.). (1991). *Prometheus bound: The changing relationship between government and higher education in Western Europe*. Oxford, UK: Pergamon.

Nelson, R. R. (1993). *National innovation systems: A comparative analysis*. Oxford, UK: Oxford University Press.

Nowotny, H., Scott, P., & Gibbons, M. (2002). *Rethinking science: Knowledge and the public in an age of uncertainty*. Cambridge, MA: Polity Press.

Nybom, T. (2007). A rule-governed community of scholars: The Humboldt vision in the history of the European university. In P. Maassen & J. P. Olsen (Eds.), *University dynamics and European integration* (pp. 55–80). Dordrecht, The Netherlands: Springer. doi:10.1007/978-1-4020-5971-1_3

OECD. (2004). *Review of national policies for education: Review of higher education in Ireland*. Paris: Organisation for Economic Cooperation and Development.

OECD. (2005). *Building competitive regions: Strategies and governance*. Paris: Organisation for Economic Co-operation and Development.

Palfreyman, D., & Tapper, T. (2008). *Structuring mass higher education: The role of elite institutions*. New York: Routledge.

Perkmann, M., Tartari, V., McKelvey, M., Autio, E., Broström, A., & D'Este, P. et al. (2013). Academic engagement and commercialisation: A review of the literature on university–industry relations. *Research Policy*, *42*(2), 423–442. doi:10.1016/j.respol.2012.09.007

Perry, B., & May, T. (2006). Excellence, relevance and the university: The "missing middle" in socio-economic engagement. *Journal of Higher Education in Africa*, *4*(3), 69–92.

Pinheiro, R. (2012a). Knowledge and the 'Europe of the regions': The case of the high north. In M. Kwiek & P. Maassen (Eds.), *National higher education reforms in a European context: Comparative reflections on Poland and Norway* (pp. 179–208). Frankfurt, Germany: Peter Lang Publishing Group.

Pinheiro, R. (2012b). University ambiguity and institutionalization: A tale of three regions. In R. Pinheiro, P. Benneworth, & G. A. Jones (Eds.), *Universities and regional development: A critical assessment of tensions and contradictions* (pp. 35–55). Milton Park, UK: Routledge.

Pinheiro, R., Benneworth, P., & Jones, G. A. (Eds.). (2012). *Universities and regional development: A critical assessment of tensions and contradictions*. Milton Park, UK: Routledge.

Pinheiro, R., Normann, R., & Johnsen, H. C. (2012). *Knowledge structures and patterns of external engagement*. Paper presented at the 34th Annual EAIR (European Higher Education Society) Forum. Stavanger, Norway.

Pinheiro, R., & Stensaker, B. (2013). Designing the entrepreneurial university: The interpretation of a global idea. *Public Organization Review*, *13*(2), 1–20. doi:10.1007/s11115-013-0241-z

Porter, M. E. (1998). *Competitive advantage: Creating and sustaining superior performance.* New York: Free Press.

Powell, J., & Dayson, K. (2013). Engagement and the idea of the civic university. In P. Benneworth (Ed.), *University engagement with socially excluded communities* (pp. 143–162). Dordrecht, The Netherlands: Springer. doi:10.1007/978-94-007-4875-0_8

Powell, W. W., & Owen-Smith, J. (2002). The new world of knowledge production in the life sciences. In S. B. Brint (Ed.), *The future of the city of intellect: the changing American university* (pp. 107–131). Stanford, CA: Stanford University Press.

Rooney, D., Hearn, G., & Ninan, A. (2008). *Handbook on the knowledge economy.* Cheltenham, UK: Edward Elgar.

Vang, J., & Asheim, B. (2006). Regions, absorptive capacity and strategic coupling with high-tech TNCs lessons from India and China. *Science, Technology & Society, 11*(1), 39–66. doi:10.1177/097172180501100103

Vukasovic, M., Maassen, P., Nerland, M., Pinheiro, R., Stensaker, B., & Vabø, A. (2012). *Effects of higher education reforms: Change dynamics.* Rotterdam, The Netherlands: Sense Publishers. doi:10.1007/978-94-6209-016-3

Wangenge-Ouma, G., & Langa, P. (2010). Universities and the mobilization of claims of excellence for competitive advantage. *Higher Education, 59*(6), 749–764. doi:10.1007/s10734-009-9278-x

Witte, J. (2008). Aspired convergence, cherished diversity: Dealing with the contradictions of Bologna. *Tertiary Education and Management, 14*(2), 81–93. doi:10.1080/13583880802051840

KEY TERMS AND DEFINITIONS

Europe of Knowledge: National and supranational attempts – policy efforts - aimed at articulating a common platform for teaching and research across the European Union and its associated members, with direct consequences when it comes to the modernisation of the European higher education landscape.

Knowledge-Based Economy: The strategic importance attributed to knowledge based assets in the context of the economic competitiveness of regions, nations and localities.

Relevance-Excellence Nexus: The importance attributed to scientific excellence and/or societal relevance in the context of local and global dimensions and policy discourses.

Scientific Excellence: The importance attributed to world class research and rankings in the context of an increasingly globalised and competitive higher education landscape.

Societal Relevance: The extent to which the core activities of higher education institutions across Europe contribute to addressing the region's main socio-economic goals (growth and innovation agendas) and pending dilemmas.

University-Industry Links: The strategic importance – by policy makers, institutional leaders and academic communities alike – given to partnerships with the private sector in the context of knowledge transfers and the commercialization of knowledge.

ENDNOTES

[1]   The data is based on the desktop analysis of policy documents (period 2005-2012) across 17 European Union countries, across five sub-regions: Nordic (Sweden, Finland and Denmark); Central Europe (Austria,

Belgium, France, the Netherlands and Germany); Eastern Europe (Poland, Hungary and Czech Republic); Southern Europe (Greece, Portugal, Italy and Spain); and the UK and Ireland.

[2] Under EU law, the Commission has no legal mandate over HE affairs, with these being the sole responsibility of individual member states, but the Commission has enlarged its influence by shaping the dominant 'reform discourse' (Keeling, 2006).

[3] The 2013 Shanghai ranking of world universities (ARWU), shows that of the top-50 contenders only 11 universities were based in Europe. Consult full list at: http://www.shanghairanking.com/ARWU2013.html

[4] In 2013, 17 out of the top-20 research-universities were US based (http://www.shanghairanking.com/ARWU2013.html)

Chapter 2
Strategic Management of Academic Human Resources:
A Comparative Analysis of Flagship Universities in Norway, Finland, Switzerland, and Austria

Tatiana Fumasoli
University of Oslo, Norway

ABSTRACT

This chapter investigates whether and how institutional autonomy enhances strategic management of academic human resources. National regulatory frameworks, available resources, university policies, and practices at the working floor are compared in four European flagship universities. Disciplinary affiliation is taken into consideration through the selection of history and chemistry. The cases reflect different trajectories where substantial changes have been implemented in governance systems when it comes to centralization of decision making, to standardization of procedures, to re-configuration of actors and their room to maneuver. While professorial self-governance in personnel matters remains significant, new boundary conditions constrain substantially choice options in accordance with national, institutional, and disciplinary features. Uncertainty, identity, and flexibility emerge as major dimensions in human resources management, pointing to tensions but also to opportunities for strategic change.

INTRODUCTION

The specific nature of universities as organizations has been stressed in scholarly debate: following Cohen and March work on academia (1974), university distinctive characteristics would allow organizational change only to a limited extent (Whitley 2008, Musselin 2006). Hence, educa-

tion and research cannot be coordinated and controlled because of their inherent unclearness and ambiguity (Cohen & March 1974, p. 3). On the one hand, core operations of teaching and research are unclear processes which cannot be copied, prescribed or reproduced. On the other hand, they are ambiguous, as precise goals cannot be defined or scheduled. Multiple uncertainties

DOI: 10.4018/978-1-4666-7244-4.ch002

influence knowledge production and dissemination (Musselin, 2006; Gläser, 2007) and hamper the possibility to build a strategy based on distinctive organizational capabilities (Whitley, 2008; Bonaccorsi & Daraio, 2007).

Besides, the scientific community has its own distinctive rules characterizing its uniqueness and the conditions of its existence (Merton, 1973). In the professional bureaucracy described by Mintzberg (1979, p. 348) the academic oligarchy coordinates university functioning by establishing standards of quality and by determining entry requirements for new members, based on distinctive skills and training. More specifically in university personnel policies professors apply their own (collegial) system in order to recruit and promote their peers. This is based on scientific and disciplinary criteria that traditionally shape the overall assessment of candidates. More recently, the increasing role of the university board, of the rectorate and of the central administration as well as the formalization and standardization of procedures of recruitment, have put under pressure these practices historically carried out by professors (Fumasoli, 2011, 2013; Fumasoli & Goastellec, 2014).

At the same time, in the last decades public authorities have granted, at different degrees and paces, institutional autonomy to higher education institutions (Brunsson & Sahlin-Andersson 2000; Paradeise et al., 2009; Huisman, 2009; Kehm & Lanzendorf, 2006) with the explicit intent to increase their strategic behavior (Verhoest et al., 2004). Nowadays goals are set for the whole organization; financially, block grants are provided according to contracts of performance. In a governance perspective, university leadership seems to profit from increasing power, while external systems of evaluation have been introduced to standardize education and research (for research see Whitley & Gläser, 2007).

It is then relevant to understand how universities are coping with their human resources[1], to what extent increasing institutional autonomy

has transformed the traditional practices held by the academic profession, where criteria for recruitment and career advancement were based on academic merits and university politics. In sum, it is significant to observe whether and how strategic management of human resources has been developed. The objective of this chapter is to investigate how and to what extent personnel policies have been modified by the recent reforms in European higher education systems. Personnel policies have been addressed as a key organizational area to control and coordinate academic staff, which represents the most important asset for universities. By shedding light on the (shifting) authority between academics, academic leaders and external stakeholders in the management of human resources and the dynamics underlining such changes, it is possible to understand change and stability in higher education. To do so regulatory frameworks, university policies and practices at the work-floor level are analyzed through a multi-level case study, which takes into account national systems, institutional settings, as well as departments, conceived as organizational structures embodying disciplinary fields.

The sample comprises four European Flagship universities: University of Oslo (Norway), University of Helsinki (Finland), University of Basel (Switzerland) and University of Vienna (Austria). Two disciplines have been observed: chemistry (Oslo and Helsinki), history (Basel and Vienna). A Flagship university is defined as a comprehensive, research intensive university, located in a major urban area. In general it is among the oldest and largest higher education institutions of its country. This focus on 'flagships' has implications for the nature of organizational change under scrutiny here, since this category of universities can be expected to be given more leeway than others because of their scientific leading role at the national level (Fumasoli et al., 2014).

The following research questions are addressed:

1. What are the main factors that over the last 10 years have affected the organised university settings and institutional characteristics when it comes to human resources management?
2. How is the increased institutional autonomy in personnel policies interpreted and practised inside European Flagship universities?
3. How do intra-institutional governance relationships play out?
    ◦   To what extent are university internal and external actors involved in key decisions on human resources?
    ◦   How do they differ according to national higher education systems, universities and disciplines?

DRIVERS OF CHANGE: POLICY REFORMS, UNIVERSITY STRATEGIES AND ACADEMIC TRADITIONS

We propose an institutional approach to university autonomy (Olsen, 2009; March & Olsen, 1989, 1995). An institutional approach conceives of institutions as playing a partly autonomous role as well as acting independently, that is beyond environmental determination and strategic choice. In the broader perspective on political and social order university legitimacy is shaped by connections and interdependencies with other actors and institutions (Gornitzka et al., 2007; Olsen, 2009). Moreover universities as institutionalized organizations are infused with values beyond the technical requirements of their task (Selznick, 1957), in this sense their resilience to external influence has to be analyzed against their distinctive structures, routines and identities (Fumasoli & Stensaker, 2013).

Against this backdrop, three main drivers of institutional change are conceptualized here as political ambitions, that is reforms of higher education in the national system; organizational strategies, which represent leadership intentionality and rational definition of goals; and academic traditions, or the different cultures and identities in which universities are traditionally embedded.

Political ambitions reflect the rationale of policy reforms in higher education. This resonates with the assumption that granting increasing institutional autonomy will enhance university effectiveness, efficiency and economy. Free to manage itself, the university will develop a strategic profile, which allows it to compete with other universities. When it comes to human resources, reforms have attempted to centralize, standardize and formalize personnel policies. This means that a shift in the authority from professorial oligarchy to university leadership has been promoted. This should be visible in recruitment processes, which determine entry to academia and have been traditionally controlled by professors. Not only university leadership has been strengthened both at levels of rectorate, of the deans and of the heads of department. Also the university administration has acquired increasingly importance in the implementation of procedures. The re-design of regulatory frameworks is expected to push universities to redefine and implement human resources management in order to support their organizational strategy. For instance, Flagship universities aim to attract the best international researchers in order to compete in the ranking race.

Organizational strategies have emerged as instruments in the hands of academic leadership to shape a specific profile of the university. Here the assumption is that the more a university positions itself strategically, the more it can compete in selected arenas. With respect to personnel policies, it is expected that strategies link organizational objectives to incentive systems to recruit and promote high performing academic staff. This way academics are supposed to concur in enhancing the ambitions of their institution. When it comes to control systems, universities try to cope with a highly diversified academic workforce, which act autonomously according to its professional and disciplinary identities. Flagship universities are expected to put in place incentives for excellent academics – such as performance-related salaries, research funding allocation, additional personnel, increasing academic freedom, minor teaching load. Symbolic and material rewards are also expected to play a role in differentiating high from low performers.

Academic traditions entail academic cultures, identities, practices and routines that make universities resilient organizations (Maassen & Olsen, 2007). In this respect, norms and values of both the academic profession and the disciplinary affiliation, are expected to hinder (but also enable) desired change by reform and managerial intentionality. The structure of academic careers has been in the hands of academics: they decide the different stages, the criteria for evaluation, the degrees and expertise necessary to advance. Even though national regulatory framework contribute to shape academic careers, these practices represent a crucial prerogative of academics, for instance in the case of the Habilitation in countries of German tradition (Fumasoli & Goastellec, 2014). It is then reasonable to expect that academic traditions are difficult to change and that they intertwine with reforms and strategies giving rise to diverse and unexpected outcomes were formal and informal rules, norms and values come into play.

Finally, structural conditions are taken into account in our comparative analysis: financial situation as well as student numbers constitute boundary conditions to actors' behavior, since universities can thrive only when material resources are available. It is expected that university main public funding – the block grant – is based on student enrolment, thus affecting substantially financial conditions of universities and departments. At the same time, intensive competition for the acquisition of external research funding may limit research activities within departments.

Along this line, depending on national, institutional and disciplinary characteristics, different types and degrees of change are expected. Central in this paper is to understand how universities adapt to pressures for change and develop their strategic management of human resources.

PERSONNEL POLICIES IN ACADEMIA

Human resources are fundamental for universities, which need highly qualified individuals to produce and transmit scientific knowledge. Hence, personnel policies represent a major dimension when examining how and to what extent university leadership (members of rectorate, deans, heads of department) are able to manage academic staff. Indeed this has been traditionally controlled by the academic profession, which prescribes skills and training to enter academia. Even existing national regulations, which usually define broad criteria, are negotiated between public authorities, the academic profession and universities, through their associations, e.g. national rectors' conferences and academies. Thus, the shifting authority over recruitment and career advancement comes into play while observing universities as organizations, for managerial control on human resources is instrumental to organizational change (Mintzberg, 1979, 379).

Personnel policies are analyzed according to three components: recruiting, reward and control systems (Aldrich & Ruef, 2006, p. 106). Academic recruitment is a process divided in different stages: defining the need for a position, preparing the call, assessing and selecting candidates and negotiating working conditions with the selected applicant (Musselin, 2005). Academic recruitment, therefore, constitutes an organizational practice within universities: patterns of action are interdependent (e.g. one has to receive applications in order to assess and select a proper candidate). These patterns are collectively recognized by university members who contribute to their enactment (e.g. the heads of department, the professors, the external experts) and share the understanding of the practice's underlying rationale (Feldman & Pentland, 2004).

Reward systems are put in place to attract the best teachers and researchers and to help retain them, while the creation of control structures and routines protects internal structure and coherence of the organization. Indeed, reforms strengthening university leadership and increasing institutional autonomy has been designed to mitigate the perceived internal fragmentation of academia, where several fields, disciplines and sub-disciplines coexist in separated compartments. Procedures related to reward and control systems are performance evaluation, job compensation, and control over workflow. Incentives are usually a mix of material (e.g. salary, infrastructure such as laboratories, technical and academic assistants), symbolic (e.g. reputation), identity-related (sense of personal belonging) components (Aldrich & Ruef, 2006, p. 106). Control of the core activities can be carried out formally, based on conformity with existing procedures and written rules; through peer culture, by informal socialization of staff; and professionally, by means of internalized norms and formal education at entry. Within academia professional control has been historically prominent, however, strengthened administrative and managerial logics may shift the balance towards formal and peer culture oversight.

METHODOLOGY: COMPARATIVE CASE STUDY

In order to investigate change in personnel policies according to regulatory frameworks, organizational strategies, as well as in practices at the work floor, a comparative analysis with four cases has been conducted. The cases are constituted by four flagship universities: University of Oslo (Norway), University of Helsinki (Finland), University of Basel (Switzerland), and University of Vienna (Austria). Four departments

were analyzed: chemistry at Oslo and Helsinki, history at Basel and Economic and Social History at Vienna. This selection supports the attempt to balance similarity and variety. Our four cases have several commonalities: they are located in four smaller Western European countries whose higher education systems are similar as of size, funding schemes, recent reforms and binary structure.

This analysis is based on data from the project European Flagship Universities: balancing academic excellence and socio-economic relevance (FLAGSHIP 212422), funded by the Research council of Norway and coordinated by ARENA, Centre for European Studies, University of Oslo (Fumasoli et al., 2014; Friedrich, 2013). Additionally it draws on data gathered in the framework of EuroAC - The Academic Profession in Europe: Reponses to Societal Challenges, a project of the European Science Foundation and coordinated by INCHER, University of Kassel and on related research (Fumasoli & Goastellec, forthcoming 2015) as well as previous research of the author (Fumasoli, 2011).

Our data sources are threefold: documents, interviews and statistical data. The documents analyzed are university laws, university statutes and personnel policy regulations, strategic plans. Thirty-eight interviews have been conducted with academic leaders, administrators and academics. All respondents were located within the selected departments, academics where usually senior tenured professors with considerable research activities as of national and international funding. Statistical data has been retrieved from national statistical databases (Norwegian DBH, Statistics Finland, Swiss Federal Office for Statistics, Statistik Austria) and university websites have been accessed. The triangulation of data sources and data analysis has been paramount to derive accurate information on structural conditions, policy reforms, university strategies and academic practices.

Reflecting our analytical framework, the research design has focused on the different actors' positions in personnel policies and decision-making as well as on recruitment, reward and control systems. Interviews (Table 1) have been instrumental to observe how the relevant actors make sense of their roles, of their room to manoeuver, and to shed light on their narrative on ongoing practices.

Table 2 shows the differences among the cases when it comes to size (students, total staff, number of professors) and to annual budget. With respect to departments, there is a significant difference in student numbers between Oslo and Helsinki.

Human resources management is analyzed in the four cases according to the national higher education system and the recent reforms, to the university and department governance and strategy. Recruitment of academics, career structures and actors' configurations are highlighted.

CASE 1: UNIVERSITY OF OSLO, NORWAY

The Norwegian higher education system has eight public universities with about 102,700 enrolled students (2013). It has undergone major changes with the Quality Reform in 2003, which has granted institutional autonomy to universities in relation with their governance structures. In 2005 a law on public and private universities has been approved, providing a common framework to higher education institutions when it comes to accreditation, funding and quality. The funding formula is structured around basic state funding (60%), students (credits, degrees, international students – 25%) and research (partly result-based -15%). Norwegian universities remain part of the public sector (i.e. they do not have legal

Table 1. Interviews

University	Country	Department	N	Date	Leaders	Academics	Administrators
University of Oslo	Norway	Chemistry	6	2013	2	3	1
University of Helsinki	Finland	Chemistry	5	2014	1	2	2
University of Basel	Switzerland	History	11	2010-2011	1	9	1
University of Vienna	Austria	Social and Economic History	7	2013	1	5	1

Table 2. Four cases[2]

Cases		University			Department	
		Students (2013)	Staff *Professors	Budget EUR million	Students	Staff *Professors
University of Helsinki	Chemistry	23,800	8,600 (2010) *500 (ca.)	645	800 (ca.)	250 *16
University of Oslo	Chemistry	27,000	6,600 *793	831	148	156 *26
University of Basel	History	13,000	3,300 *272	563 (2012)	158 (own count - 2014)	135 *9 (own count-2014)
University of Vienna	Economic and Social History	92,000 (head-count)	9,500 (head-count) *423	522	164	57 *12

independence) and their staff – both permanent and temporary – is employed according to public service conditions as in all other Norwegian public sector organizations. Academic staff is basically organized in four positions: PhD student, postdoc, associate professor and professor, whereas associate professor and professor are tenured positions. The structure of salaries is regulated through fixed layers, so that professors' salaries can in principle differ quite substantially, from a yearly minimum of Euro 70,000 to a maximum of Euro 125,000.

University of Oslo is the oldest university in Norway, founded in 1814 by the Danish king. It is structured in 8 faculties and 55 sub-units (mainly departments). It enrolls almost 27,000 students and has 6,066 staff (2013). Its budget is EUR 831 million, of which 136,5 million comes from external sources (2012). "Strategy 2020" is the central planning document, from which plans at faculty and department level derive. It defines six main objectives that connect to personnel policies: increasing quality, internationalization, interfaculty cooperation, management, improving working conditions and interaction in research. More specifically, it states that the balance between salaries and operating expenses has to be improved, career planning needs to be better organized. In 2013 the department of Chemistry has 155,5 staff (full time equivalent FTE), of which 26 professors. It enrolls 62 students and employs 86 PhD students. Following the quality reform in 2003, the department has been reorganized: research groups have been merged, priorities have been defined. Increasingly incentives have been offered to the best researchers in terms of equipment, administrative and technical support, PhD students and postdoctoral fellows. More flexibility in increasing salaries has also offered the possibility to acknowledge better performance (measured primarily in research project coordination and publications), so that the differences among professors' remunerations can be quite significant. Recruitment procedures are regulated by the Universities and Colleges Act of 2005, thus

they are the same in the whole higher education sector. In principle the university board is the responsible authority, however it can delegate this task downwards to a subordinate body, usually the department. The evaluation of candidates is based on expert assessment in relation to the description of the post and the advertisement. The appointing body can decide in addition whether to hold an interview, a trial lecture, or other tests. Teaching qualifications should be given separate consideration. In special cases an academic appointment can be made without advertisement, if the university board agrees on such a procedure.

At the chemistry department the recruitment process is organized as follows: the retirement of a professor opens the possibility for a new hiring. This is discussed between the relevant research group and the head of department in order to define which profile is needed. The drafting of the call is crucial, since the selection of applicants rigorously reflects the announcement. The head of department has the final word on the call's wording; then, depending on the applications received, he or she decides on the external reviewers, who rank the candidates based on academic merits, i.e. publications. Usually the first three candidates are invited for an interview and a trial lecture. At this point the head of department organizes an interview committee, which includes him- or herself, the head of administration, a relevant professor within the department, and other professors in the faculty. The head of department may check with the references in case of doubt, doing so usually over the phone. It can happen that the ranking is reshuffled after this stage. The departmental board has to approve the final decision and the faculty also formally agrees, mainly by checking that the process complies with rules and regulations in the university (for instance gender equality). At this point the head of department starts the negotiations, which include the definition of the salary layer and the starting package: equipment, research assistants and starting research grant. It is not rare that international applicants drop out of the process, either because it is long (one year on average), because they have other opportunities, or because the negotiations fail, primarily due to the characteristics of the Norwegian system: relatively low salaries in an very expensive country, impossibility to keep one's own previous research group, poorly perceived starting package (research funding, facilities, PhD students and postdocs).

There are basically two leverages in the hands of the head of department to reward highly performing researchers: salary increase within the limit of what is set by the law and granting administrative, technical and research support for applying for funding, for conducting research and for running laboratories as well as for buying or renting technical equipment. Although the role of the head of department has become more central, there are still significant constraints. First, the financial situation of the department limits hiring and purchase of new equipment; second, the role unions play in salary negotiations. Even if the head of department makes up a list of those to be considered for pay increase, it is the faculty that discusses with unions in broader negotiations including all staff. Hence, the starting salary negotiated at the recruitment is crucial, as it defines an initial position that can only be modified and improved incrementally.

The intrinsic uncertainty in personnel policies is perceived in different ways. For some it is about controlling the recruitment process: conflicting logics are observed as the academic logic – looking for the best candidate according to scientific merits and international competition – is challenged by the necessity of assessing also personal and social skills, by local traditions of inbreeding, by cultural issues (different perceptions of status in other higher education systems) and different institutional settings (e.g. department vs. chair organization). For others the reward system should, if not penalize low performers, at least better acknowledge high performers with more support in administrative, technical and research conditions. Finally, the control system should be improved at university level, in order to keep track of all activities professors are carrying out, e.g. number of (co-) supervisions of doctoral students.

Greater flexibility emerges as a solution for coping with uncertainty: some recommend testing a professor in the first years (for instance by implementing a tenure track system), many would like to provide longer temporary contracts for researchers (according to Norwegian law the maximum is 4 years), others feel necessary to adapt scientific profiles and tasks of researchers according to rapid science dynamics instead of rigidly conforming to job descriptions.

CASE 2: UNIVERSITY OF HELSINKI, FINLAND

Finland has a large network of 14 universities, of which two are private foundations, and 25 polytechnics. In 2010, there were around 111,800 students (FTE) in universities and 104,200 students (FTE) in polytechnics. The university Act in 2009 granted universities autonomous legal status. Against this backdrop universities can choose whether they want to be independent legal entities under public law or foundations subject to private law. Mergers have also taken place: Aalto University was created from the merger of the Helsinki School of Economics, Helsinki University of Technology and the University of Art and Design Helsinki. The University of Eastern Finland was established by the University of Joensuu and the University of Kuopio, while Turku School of Economics was merged with the University of Turku. Finally, the Finnish Academy of Fine Arts, Sibelius Academy and Theatre Academy Helsinki merged in the beginning of 2013 into the University of the Arts Helsinki.

University of Helsinki was founded in 1640 as a Swedish university and primarily trained clergy, civil servants, physicians and officers. Subsequently it became an Imperial Academy and University when Finland was a Grand Duchy of Russia, until 1919 when it became a Finnish university. It enrolls around 23,800 students (FTE 2013) and employs more than 8,600 staff (2010), of which almost 4,400 are academics and about 500 are professors. It has a total budget of Euro 645 million, of which 60% is state funded (2011). With its 11 faculties University of Helsinki defines itself as a "multidisciplinary" top European university. Like at University of Oslo, the board is the supreme body, however faculties are autonomous on academic matters. The rectorate is endowed with some financial resources, which can be allocated autonomously. Employment relations were based on civil servant status until 2011, since 2012 the university employs its staff. After the autonomy reforms, state-university relationships have been organized around control mechanisms such as by legislation (university statutes for instance), budgeting and information. The instability of public funding is perceived as a significant difficulty for the university.

At the department of Chemistry the recruitment procedure is organized upon retirement, which means that the position must appear in the strategic plan. In order to cope with financial constraints joint professorships among faculties can be organized, so that different funds may be allocated for a full position. The head of department coordinates the whole process of hiring. After the faculty has agreed on the call, he or she selects and oversees a group of five internal professors who make a first round of selection and decide which candidates will be assessed by the scientific committee. References are also to be inquired about candidates. The main criteria for selection are ability to attract funds, as well as research plan clarity and sustainability in the long run. All in all the selection is moving towards a mix of 60% concerning research merits, 40% relating to social skills and ability to work with colleagues and with students. Teaching merits, assessed in a trial lecture, are evaluated by the faculty according to formal standards defined by the Faculty of Science. Research merits are assessed

by the external evaluators, it is thus considered strategic in the recruitment process whom the head of department invites in the committee. As of internationalization of staff, competition with other universities and other national higher education systems takes place at salary and starting package level. The latter not only includes technical and research staff but also financial support for housing. Tensions emerge with respect to national duties, e.g. in the use of the Finnish language in teaching and services. At the same time, doubts are expressed on the argument that an international applicant with the same merits should be favored against a Finnish candidate. When it comes to salary negotiations, it appears that the head of department has increasing leeway on deciding the employment conditions. Before the 2005 reforms criteria for salary determination were more rigid but clearer. Today salaries offered by University of Helsinki are not considered truly competitive, even though they are better than before. Finland has introduced grants for visiting professors through the Funding Program for Visiting Top Researchers in Science and Technology (FiDiPro) financed by the Academy of Finland and Tekes (Finnish Agency for Innovation). These grants offer higher salaries for those international academics who want to carry out research in highly reputed fields like the Finnish Institute for Verification of the Chemical Weapons Convention (VERIFIN). External funding is the most important criteria for assessing performance of academic staff. The status of principal investigator (PI) appears to become more relevant than the status of professor. As professor and PI may not always overlap, favoring PI signals that symbolic rewards are being shifted to those researchers able to fund and coordinate big research projects.

Within the boundaries provided by existing regulations salaries can be re-negotiated with the head of department according to performance, as such pay differences among professors are considered legitimate. When it comes to the allocation of resources to the different professors and their (joint) laboratories, intensive bargaining takes place. This happens in the strategic planning process when objectives and priorities are discussed within departments, while the strategic plan frames specific boundary conditions as of allocation of resources.

CASE 3: UNIVERSITY OF BASEL, SWITZERLAND

Swiss higher education has been restructured into a binary system in 1995. The university sector enrolls more than 138'000 students in 10 cantonal universities and 2 federal institutes of technology (2013). Since 2012 a new federal law has provided a common legal framework for both universities and universities of applied sciences. This said, the ten cantonal universities have each their own specific cantonal public funding authorities and legal frameworks. Hence each university is funded by its canton(s), by the federal government (based on the number of students and research activities) and by competitive funding (mainly Swiss National Foundation, Innovation Promotion Agency, EU framework programs).

University of Basel is the oldest university in Switzerland and was funded through papal bull in 1460. It is located under the jurisdiction of the Canton of Basel-City. Since 2006 the Canton of Basel-Country has joined the tutelage authority. The university has 7 faculties (including medicine), enrolls around 13,000 students and employs 3,300 staff, of which two thirds are academics, and 272 professors (2012). The global budget is Euro 563 million (2012), of which 30% comes from external funding. In 1995 a new legal framework granted institutional autonomy in the explicit attempt of creating a unitary organization out of the scattered institutes and faculties. Today the university board decides on personnel policies and regulates the employment conditions of all staff. It rules on the opening for professorships on the basis of faculties' requests and is the highest

authority when it comes to hiring and dismissing a full professor, as well as withdrawing such title. The rectorate, upon request of the faculties, decides on assistant professors and lecturers. With the relevant faculty it prepares the decision on a full professorship to submit to the university board.

The procedure for hiring a full professor is decided by the university board reflecting the objectives stated in the strategic plan, which is also coordinated and finally adopted by the university board. The financial situation is, in this case too, a boundary condition for the opening of a professorial position. While initiating a procedure has to be approved by the institutional leadership, it is the faculty of humanities, in agreement with the rector, that decides the recruitment committee for hiring at the department of History. Equally, the faculty drafts the call that has to be finally approved by the rectorate. Such calls are open-rank and international. The publication in international channels is organized by the human resources section in the central administration. The recruitment committee has to fulfil several formal criteria: maximum 12 internal members, who reflect diversity of competences and of different groups of employees, who represent women, finally the committee chair has to belong to a different discipline. Additionally representatives of the equality office, of the rectorate and at least one external expert are also members of the commission. Candidates have to show quality of their research according to publications and funding, prove teaching merits partly based on experience, partly on formal training and in a trial lecture; they have to possess social skills and leadership qualities, which are assessed through the interview and the references. The final list has to be drafted based on the assessment of at least two external evaluators for research merits. Salary and employment conditions are negotiated by the rector and the administrative director of the university in agreement with the dean. Recruitment procedures have been standardized and substantially centralized in the hands of the institutional leadership and, when it comes to the scientific content, to the faculty. The most significant stage is the definition of the recruitment commission: those who act more actively and convincingly appear to be able to steer the process to a certain extent. On the opposite women seem to remain in a weaker position: there are so few qualified female academics, that always the same are involved and might be overwhelmed by committee work. Research output is considered the most important criteria together with international networking.

However, the members of the committee might profit of large leeway in the initial selection stage, as external evaluators are systematically involved when the final list is being produced.

Professors appear to be more powerful when it comes to hiring research assistants and members of the intermediate corps whether funded internally or externally. In this framework professors are more in control of the process, which, even though formally competitive, for instance as of number of applicants, is based on selection of researchers with similar profiles and shared networks. Unlike the two previous cases, the department of history is organized around the chair model (Neave & Rhoades, 1987). Full professors hold distinctive chairs to which the non-professorial academic staff is attached. This frames not only the workflow, but also opportunities for career advancement, which is perceived to be highly dependent on the will of chair holders.

However the recent introduction of non-structural professorships allows for more independent junior professorships, able to establish autonomous research activities away from the department's dynamics. This said, the sustainability in the long-term of such positions may be questioned. All in all, while the procedures of selection and promotion have been partially shifted in the hands of faculty, rectorate and university board, the internal life of the department seems to remain organized among chair holders, who decide on research, teaching activities and career trajectories.

CASE 4: UNIVERSITY OF VIENNA, AUSTRIA[3]

Austria has become a binary system some years before Switzerland, as universities of applied sciences were introduced in 1990. Since then a small private sector has developed and teacher training schools have been upgraded to tertiary education. In 2012 almost 221,000 students were enrolled in the 23 public universities, which total 78% of overall enrolments in Austrian tertiary education. After the 1993 and the 2002 reforms universities are now autonomous entities under public law, the institutional leadership has been strengthened and academics are employed by the university. Unlike Norway, Finland and Switzerland, Austrian universities are not publicly funded on the number of students. This might be explained by the open admission policy and the traditional free education which has boosted enrolments nationally and internationally (as a measure to counteract this development, since 2008 students overstaying the normal duration of their program have to pay Euro 700 per year).

University of Vienna was founded in 1365 by Duke Rudolph IV, in 1849, following students demand for freedom of teaching and learning, the Austrian basic law, article 17, states that "science and its teaching are free" (art. 17). Nowadays the university enrolls more than 92,000 students, has 15 faculties and 423 full professors (2012). Even though it increased substantially in recent years, the number of professor remains quite low, given the number of students and of employees: almost 9,500, of which more than 6,300 are academics (2012). Equally the senate is composed by only 18 members representing professors, intermediate corps, administrators and students. Personnel planning is not only part of the university strategic plan, but also integrates the performance agreement with Austrian public authorities. The overall budget in 2012 was Euro 522 million. Since 2007 third party funding has increased about 65%, contributing to global budget growth of 15%. The university personnel policies focus on tenure track and flexible management of PhD students, postdocs, lecturers and senior lecturers. Recruitment processes have been considerably centralized and standardized to reduce fragmentation of regulations and practices. Internationalization plays also an important role and a growing number of professors come from abroad.

The department of social and economic history is part of the faculty of historical and cultural studies. It has 5 chairs (full professorships), 7 extraordinary professors and 52 academic staff. The opening of a position takes place according to the development plan of the university and its financial conditions. The senate decides on the appointment commission upon advice of the faculty. The commission is formed by 5 professors, 3 teaching staff and 1 student, it must reflect a broad representation of the relevant discipline and 40% of its members have to be women. The rector approves the shortlist, hence the invitation list, while the head of department is involved in the interview phase. Compliance with internationalization policy and gender equality further shapes the selection of the members of the appointment commission. More significantly, internal appointments, which used to be the norm, have become increasingly rare. The chairman of the commission is very influential and has to come from a different department than the one concerned by hiring. Tenure track positions are decided by the relevant dean and the rectorate, without the department being involved. Salary negotiations are now possible and University of Vienna has been able, in some circumstances, to offer salaries as high as those at some Swiss universities, considered a benchmark for excellence. However pension schemes remain an issue especially with professors coming from German academia. There is presently a shared understanding to compare against excellent German speaking universities such as Lüdwig-Maximilians- Universität München (LMU), Technische Universität München (TUM), University of Zurich and the Federal Institute of

Technology Zurich (ETHZ). This said, international star researchers usually apply at university of Vienna either to leverage and re-negotiate with their own (German) university or to start an intermediate stage of their career before achieving elsewhere their desired position. The support of the dean is paramount at the negotiating stage of recruitment, in fact the dean signals to the rector his or her readiness to offer a good starting package to the new entrant. Accordingly, the rector might strategically negotiate so that the applicant will have to refuse the position. The short list is considered a source of high uncertainty: usually the first or even the second candidate withdraw, while there is a risk that the third candidate is not good enough. On the other side some appointment commissions are considered too ambitious, since they would like to recruit only top candidates. In this sense it can happen that nobody is hired and a new call has to be prepared. The head of department has no formal power, but plays a role of coordinator and moderator, while his or her access to the dean and the rector is perceived by academics as a tactical advantage. At hiring the fight between "traditionalists" and "innovators" is visible, because recruitment is mainly about re-staffing positions remained vacant after retirement. Against this backdrop change can be introduced only incrementally with partial modifications of job description (e.g. increasing focus on global studies is now slowly reorienting the department of Social and Economic History), following pressures by the faculty and the rectorate.

The department of Social and Economic History is entitled to a specific amount of points for its own personnel. Professors count 4 points, assistant professors 3, postdocs 2, PhD students 1. The dean is in principle free to redistribute these points among departments, for instance if two postdocs leave, one professor could in principle be hired. However in order to avoid conflicts, the structure and the type of staff *de facto* remains the same over the years. Moreover the chair system makes the negotiations for the number of assistants very harsh, as professors want to maintain their groups as large as possible, not only for functional reasons but also for signaling their power and status. In general, in order to carry out change in the strategic profile of a department, a long and complex process has to be put in place. First, a round of negotiations and discussions takes place within the department among academics, then the agreed upon changes are proposed to the dean, who in turn will negotiate with the rectorate. If the rectorate is persuaded, the objective agreement between rectorate and subunits has to be modified, finally the university development plan will be changed. Professors can be hired on call and with a fixed time contract of five years. This selection process is under control of dean and rector, who may decide or not to appoint reviewers.

Table 3 summarizes the drivers of organizational change in the university according to policy reforms, organizational strategies, institutional settings and structural conditions.

Table 4 shows how the four universities have adapted to external pressures for change coming from reforms. First, the role of academic leadership has become stronger also in practice: rectors, deans and heads of departments are substantially involved in decision-making related to human resources. This takes different forms according to legal frameworks and internal governance. Personnel policies are increasingly linked to the university strategy: this can be connected to internationalization, to the need of establishing multi- and interdisciplinarity and collaborative research. Limited financial resources play a significant role when it comes to the number of

Table 3. Drivers of change in human resources management

	Policy Reforms	University Strategy	Academic Traditions	Structural Conditions
University of Oslo Department of Chemistry	-Quality reform 2003; Law on public and private universities, 2005 -University remains part of public sector	-Aims to balance salary expenses, improve career planning -Collaborative research and external funding are a priority Internationalization	-Professors hired according to scientific merits (scientific publications) -Formal criteria for assessing academic merits, informal criteria for evaluating social competences	-Block grant is significantly based on student numbers -Low numbers of students at chemistry -Department structure
University of Helsinki Department of Chemistry	-2005 increasing salary flexibility; University act 2009; University becomes employer 2012 -Several mergers redesign the national landscape	-Aims to become a multi-disciplinary top European university -Priority is given to attracting funding and managing research projects Internationalization	-Acceptance of increasing competition for funding and publishing -Questioning internationalization	-Instability of public funding -High numbers of students -Department structure
University of Basel Department of History	-1995 University Act -2006 second canton becomes main public funder - 2011 Federal Act coordinating higher education	-Rectorate and faculty coordination of recruitment -Redefining profile -Internationalization	-Professorial control of recruitment -Powerful chair holders	-Block grant based on student numbers and research output -Chair structure
University of Vienna Department of Socioeconomic History	-1993, 2002 University reforms	-Larger freedom for negotiating salaries internationalization - Benchmarking Swiss and German universities	-Professorial control of recruitment -Powerful chair holders	-Block grant is disconnected from student numbers -Chair structure

Table 4. Emerging strategic management of academic human resources

	Recruitment	Control and Reward System	Discipline-Based Evolution
University of Oslo Department of Chemistry	Process is shifting to take into consideration competences beyond scientific publications. Increasing leeway of head of department, emerging role of head of administration and of (internal) interview committee.	Head of department has increasing leeway in starting package negotiations and salary promotions, in agreement with dean. Tenure track does not exist.	Chemistry has few students and went through difficult financial conditions after a new accounting system was put in place at the university.
University of Helsinki Department of Chemistry	Head of department plays a key role.	Salaries can be negotiated up to a certain point. Harsh bargaining for allocation of laboratory use, PhD students and postdocs. Tenure track introduced in 2010.	Difficult financial conditions require cooperation in laboratory use, in funding of new professorships.
University of Basel Department of History	Process has been standardized. Formally academic recruitment is coordinated by dean and rectorate. Several (mostly internal) actors play a role in the different stages.	It appears to be in the hands of the chair holders. Tenure track exists but is hardly used.	The department has adapted to the new requirements: international staff, external funding, establishment of a doctoral school.
University of Vienna Department of Social and Economic History	Process has been standardized. Internal careers are not possible anymore. Formally academic recruitment is coordinated by dean and rectorate.	It appears to be in the hands of the chair holders, while dean and rector coordinate assistant professorships. Tenure track exists but not is used systematically	The department has become more interdisciplinary through global studies. This shapes significantly academic hiring.

possible hirings, but also to the profile required for new professors. Interestingly, our data show that academics adapt to the new conditions in distinctive ways: while in Oslo the re-discussion of criteria for performance is on-going, Helsinki shows more pragmatism (e.g. concerning funding attraction), Basel complies with requirements for change by reorganizing recruitment of PhD students (establishment of an international doctoral school) and Vienna re-orients its study programs and research agenda.

Differences between national higher education systems are relevant: the Nordic countries have a centralized organization of state. Hence higher education can be steered more centrally (e.g. mergers) and policy relevance of university missions is considered important, for instance when it comes to balancing differences among regions and among higher education institutions. Austria and Switzerland are federal countries: Austria has a national law regulating personnel policies, Switzerland has a rather de-centralized system

where cantons are the main funding authority and cantonal legal frameworks can vary significantly. When it comes to decision-making, in Norway and Finland the room to maneuver is delegated down to the heads of department, while in Switzerland and Austria the rectorate and the dean (eventually supported by the university board) have become increasingly central actors in recruitment.

Although such processes are complex systems of check and balances, the academic leadership at faculty and institutional level has been significantly strengthened. Even if the specific scientific strengths of a candidate are still assessed by academics, the commissions are now appointed according to several criteria such as number of women, external evaluators, and characteristics of the chairperson. Differences can be connected to the different traditions of the academic structure: in Norway and Finland universities are organized around the department model, Switzerland and Austria reflect the chair model, where professors exercise their (individual) power when it comes to department staffing.

DISCUSSION: UNCERTAINTY, IDENTITY AND FLEXIBILITY

This section discusses three analytical dimensions emerged from this comparative analysis, which characterize how universities adapt to changing environmental conditions and leadership strategies: uncertainty, identity and flexibility.

Uncertainty relates primarily to the long-term appointment of a professor, who has to perform well in terms of publications, research funding, but also in relation with teaching and student supervision. There are different mechanisms at play: first, standardization of procedures in order to ensure quality and salary negotiations. Second, internationalization and the (increasing) demise of internal careers provide criteria to comply with in order to select the "best candidate" from a large group. Thirdly, uncertainty is dealt with through formal arrangements systematically considered: thus the university strategic plan constrains the leeway for recruitment, not only as of numbers of recruitments, but also as of profiles candidates. These plans are negotiated within the university, and define actors' influence by intense negotiations and deliberations in multiple formal arenas. Financial conditions are also prominent: while at University of Oslo this refers to departmental finances, in Basel and Vienna it is connected to the broader university/faculty financial situations. In Helsinki this uncertainty is caused by public funding from the state, which has recently varied year by year. The sustainability of research in chemistry remains crucial in the selection of new professors, as laboratories, equipment, technical and research staff represent a major investment. Structural differences between natural sciences and humanities become visible, as history needs "only" a few resources, i.e. individual researchers and access to archives.

Uncertainty is distinctively dealt with by integrating different logics of action which mirror actors' distinctive *identities*. In all cases the academic logic is supplemented by a bureaucratic-administrative logic where formal criteria have to be fulfilled (e.g. composition of commission, introduction of trial lecture) and by a market logic where competition is fostered, and social, managerial and leadership skills are required. Different identities and subsequent ambitions are at play: academics who aim to pursue their own research, thus tending to hire similar colleagues; academic leaders, who try to comply coherently with defined priorities, strategic profiles and financial constraints, administrators and managers, who increasingly take care of internal processes (participating in hiring, overseeing advertisement of call, supporting leadership).

Flexibility has emerged as a dimension balancing uncertainty. Salaries and starting packages have become more and more an arena for negotiations between university and new professors. Different types of professorships have been introduced: based on tenure track, on external funding, fixed-term professorships, hiring through direct call, excellence grants for international professors. These alternative professorships have several functions: they establish a trial period before tenure is granted, they attract excellent researchers by means of higher salaries, they support junior academics in establishing their own career path, they facilitate faster recruitments. However such positions appear to remain vulnerable as long as they are not tightly coupled to the structures, processes and identities of the department where they are located.

CONCLUSION AND FUTURE RESEARCH DIRECTIONS

Policy reforms have all granted institutional autonomy to universities in human resources management, however this has happened according to history, structural conditions and understandings of the role of universities in distinctive national higher education systems. While the universities of Helsinki, Basel and Vienna are now autonomous employers, academic staff at University of Oslo continues to be part of the public sector, which is highly regulated in the Norwegian social-democratic system. As all four universities now have more freedom to organize their structures and processes, on the one hand the Nordic universities have delegated recruitment of professors to departments, i.e. to the discipline as a subunit in the faculty. On the other hand Basel and Vienna have centralized the hiring authority on the dean and on the rectorate levels. Formally the university board (comprising external stakeholders) is the body in charge of approving a professorship, however this power is delegated to faculties at University of Oslo, while it is more significant – at least as a veto-power body – in Basel and Vienna, where the rectorate plays a substantial role in the whole process.

Increasing leeway to negotiate starting salaries and packages is exercised in order to be more competitive in international markets, particularly in comparison with Germany and Switzerland, perceived as benchmark higher education systems. The expectations from applicants vary largely according to the culture of their higher education system: thus researchers from Germany and Switzerland demand higher salaries and several research assistants. This appears to be the case both in Chemistry and History.

Tenure track has been introduced in Helsinki, Basel and Vienna but remains used unsystematically. At the same time in more rigid systems such as University of Oslo, a trial period is advocated in order to cope with the uncertainty of hiring on permanent positions. Besides tenure track for junior researchers, fixed-term professorial positions have been introduced in Helsinki, Basel and Vienna. While little can be done with poorly performing professors (fewer salary increases, additional teaching, for chemistry: reallocation

of the use of and investment on laboratories and equipment), recruitment constitutes a crucial stage in one's career, since it provides the applicant with the largest latitude to shape salary conditions and future research activities which will affect his or her career for the years to come.

Hence it comes to no surprise that recruitment is a central arena where different identities and logics, carried by different actors, come to play. Policy makers are only indirectly involved, unless they sit in university boards approving new professorships (e.g. Basel). Otherwise it is reasonable to say that by granting institutional autonomy, the state expects the university to manage its (human) resources sustainably in order to achieve the broad objectives delineated in the performance agreement. At the same time procedures of recruitment are standardized, formalized, and to some degree, centralized. The necessity for several actors to coordinate among each others can be considered another constraining condition for academics. The systems of checks and balances have become more and more complex in the attempt to accommodate emerging needs (e.g. cooperation to apply for big research projects) but also to take into account all relevant stakeholders (e.g. students). Looking closely at practices it is apparent that the professoriate, while still monopolizing the scientific expertise required for hiring academics, has to comply with a growing number of rules, of layers of decision-making, with an increasing role of the administration and with multiple criteria for assessing non-academic qualifications (social skills, leadership).

This chapter has discussed how change has been taking place in personnel policies of four European Flagship universities. It has shown that regulatory frameworks (enhancing institutional autonomy), structural conditions (financial resources and student enrolments) and actors' identities (academic profession, disciplinary fields, leadership, administration) shape the trajectories of universities and departments.

Even though institutional autonomy has been part of the scholarly debate for two decades, research is needed when it comes to how human resources are managed within universities and the implications for the dynamics of change in higher education. To do this, empirical work has to be conducted at the work floor level in order to understand how changing personnel policies feed back into institutional change at the university and at the national higher education system level. While identities and cultures may be at the fore of such research, structural conditions, formal regulatory frameworks and organizational strategies should not be underestimated as they frame path dependent trajectories according to country, university and discipline (Fumasoli et al., 2014).

Finally, when it comes to the interpretation and practices of autonomy in personnel policies, a discourse on excellence and competitiveness emerges clearly. The necessity of attracting excellent researchers is perceived as hampered by structural conditions in Norway, Finland and Austria (salary span and finances) as well as by the scientific reputation of both university and department. Since 2000 the EU has played a growing role by spreading global scripts as of excellence and relevance, as of how universities shall contribute to socio-economic development, as well as the necessity to increase competitiveness in the global arena. The creation of the European Research Council represent a signal of the will to enhance scientific excellence and link directly European funding to excellent individual researchers (Chou & Gornitzka, 2014). It is then relevant to investigate how European universities receive and implement these ideas on excellence when it comes to human resources management, as well as to explore the dynamics of European integration when it comes to teaching and learning as well as research (Maassen & Olsen, 2007). European flagship universities can be assumed to be at the forefront of such evolution and to play a significant role in the diffusion of such scripts within their national higher education systems.

REFERENCES

Aldrich, H., & Ruef, M. (2006). *Organizations evolving*. London: Sage.

Bonaccorsi, A., & Daraio, C. (Eds.). (2007). *Universities and strategic knowledge creation: Specialization and performance in Europe*. Cheltenham, UK: Edwar Elgar. doi:10.4337/9781847206848

Brunsson, N., & Sahlin-Andersson, K. (2000). Constructing organizations: The example of public sector reform. *Organization Studies*, *21*(4), 721–746. doi:10.1177/0170840600214003

Cohen, M. D., & March, J. G. (1974). *Leadership and ambiguity: The American college president*. Hightstown, NJ: McGraw-Hill Book Company.

Feldman, M. S., & Pentland, B. T. (2003). Reconceptualizing organizational routines as a source of flexibility and change. *Administrative Science Quarterly*, *48*(1), 94–118. doi:10.2307/3556620

Friedrich, P. (2013). University autonomy and professorial recruitment: A case study at the department of economic and social history. (Master Thesis). Oslo, Norway: Faculty of Educational Sciences, University of Oslo. Retrieved from http://www.sv.uio.no/arena/english/research/projects/flagship/publications/friedrich-ma-university-autonomy.html

Fumasoli, T. (2011). *Strategy as evolutionary path: Five higher education institutions on the move*. Lugano: USI. Retrieved from http://doc.rero.ch/record/23135?ln=it

Fumasoli, T. (2013). *The role of organizational routines in academic recruitment: Strategic devices or institutional constraints?*. Paper presented at the EAIR 35th Annual Forum: The Impact of Higher Education. Rotterdam.

Fumasoli, T., & Goastellec, G. (2014). Global models, disciplinary and local patterns in academic recruitment processes. In T. Fumasoli, G. Goastellec, & B. Kehm (Eds.), *Academic careers in Europe - Trends, challenges, perspectives.* Dordrecht, The Netherlands: Springer.

Fumasoli, T., & Goastellec, G. (forthcoming 2015). Recruitment of academics in Switzerland: e pluribus unum? In U. Teichler & W. K. Cummings K. (Eds.), Forming, Recruiting and Managing the Academic Profession – A Varied Scene. Dordrecht: Springer.

Fumasoli, T., Gornitzka, Å., & Maassen, P. (2014). *University autonomy and organizational change dynamics* (ARENA Working Paper 08/2014). Retrieved from http://www.sv.uio.no/arena/english/research/publications/arena-publications/workingpapers/working-papers2014/wp8-14.xml

Fumasoli, T., & Lepori, B. (2011). Patterns of strategies in Swiss higher education institutions. *Higher Education, 61*(2), 157–178. doi:10.1007/s10734-010-9330-x

Fumasoli, T., & Stensaker, B. (2013). Organizational studies in higher education: A reflection on historical themes and prospective trends. *Higher Education Policy, 26*(4), 479–496. doi:10.1057/hep.2013.25

Gläser, J. (2007). The social orders of research evaluation systems. In R. Whitley & J. Glaser (Eds.), *The changing governance of the sciences: The advent of research evaluation systems* (pp. 245–266). Dordrecht, The Netherlands: Springer. doi:10.1007/978-1-4020-6746-4_12

Gornitzka, Å., Maassen, P., Olsen, J. P., & Stensaker, B. (2007). Europe of knowledge: Search for a new pact. In P. Maassen & J. P. Olsen (Eds.), *University dynamics and European integration* (pp. 181–214). Dordrecht, The Netherlands: Springer. doi:10.1007/978-1-4020-5971-1_9

Huisman, J. (Ed.). (2009). *International perspectives on the governance of higher education: Alternative frameworks for coordination.* New York: Routledge Press.

Kehm, B., & Lanzendorf, U. (Eds.), *(n.d.).* *Reforming university governance.* Bonn, Germany: Lemmens.

March, J. G., & Olsen, J. P. (1989). *Rediscovering institutions: The organizational basis of politics.* New York: Collier Macmillan.

March, J. G., & Olsen, J. P. (1995). *Democratic governance.* New York: The Free Press.

Merton, R. K. (1973). *The sociology of science: Theoretical and empirical investigations.* Chicago: The University of Chicago Press.

Mintzberg, H. (1979). *The structuring of organizations.* London: Prentice-Hall.

Musselin, C. (2005). *Le marché des universitaires.* Paris: Science Po Les Presses.

Musselin, C. (2006). Are universities specific organizations? In G. Krücken, A. Kosmützky, & M. Torka (Eds.), *Towards a multiversity? Universities between global trends and national traditions* (pp. 63–84). Bielefeld, UK: Transcript.

Neave, G. (2009). Institutional autonomyu 2010-2020: A tale of Elan – Two steps back to make one very large leap forward. In B. Kehm, J. Huisman, & B. Stensaker (Eds.), *The European higher education area: Perspectives on a moving target* (pp. 3–22). Rotterdam, The Netherlands: Sense Publishers.

Neave, G., & Rhoades, G. (1987). The academic estate in Western Europe. In B. Clark (Ed.), *The academic profession: National, disciplinary, and institutional settings* (pp. 211–270). Los Angeles, CA: University of California Press.

Olsen, J. P. (2009). Change and continuity: An institutional approach to institutions of democratic government. *European Political Science Review*, *1*(1), 3–32. doi:10.1017/S1755773909000022

Paradeise, C., Reale, E., Bleiklie, I., & Ferlie, E. (2009). *University governance*. Springer. doi:10.1007/978-1-4020-9515-3

Verhoest, K., Peters, B. G., Bouckaert, G., & Verschuere, B. (2004). The study of organisational autonomy: A conceptual review. *Public Administration and Development*, *24*(2), 101–118. doi:10.1002/pad.316

Whitley, R. (2008). Universities as strategic actors: Limitations and variations. In L. Engwall & D. Weaire (Eds.), *The university in the market* (pp. 22–37). London: Portland Press.

Whitley, R., & Glaser, J. (2007). *The changing governance of the sciences: The advent of research evaluation systems*. Dordrecht: Springer.

ADDITIONAL READING

Abbott, A. (2001). *Chaos of disciplines*. Chicago: University of Chicago Press.

Carvalho, T. (2012). Shaping the 'new' academic profession: Tensions and contradictions in the professionalisation of academics. In G. Neave & A. Amaral (Eds.), *Higher education in Portugal 1974-2009: A nation, a generation* (pp. 329–352). Dordrecht, The Netherlands: Springer.

Cavalli, A., & Teichler, U. (2010). The academic profession: A common core, a diversified group or an outdated idea. *European Review (Chichester, England)*, *18*(1), S1–S5. doi:10.1017/S1062798709990287

Clark, B. R. (1983). *The Higher education system: Academic organization in cross-national perspective*. Oakland, CA: University of California Press.

Enders, J. (2004). Higher education, internationalisation, and the nation-state. *Higher Education*, *47*(3), 361–382. doi:10.1023/B:HIGH.0000016461.98676.30

Enders, J., & de Weert, E. (2004). Science, training and career: Changing modes of knowledge production and labour markets. *Higher Education Policy*, *17*(2), 135–152. doi:10.1057/palgrave.hep.8300047

Fumasoli, T., Goastellec, G., & Kehm, B. (Eds.). (2014). Academic careers in Europe – Trends, challenges, perspectives. Dordrecht, The Netherlands: Springer.

Gordon, G., & Whitchurch, C. (2007). Managing human resources in higher education: The implications of a diversifying workforce. *Higher Education Management and Policy*, *19*(2), 135–155. doi:10.1787/hemp-v19-art14-en

Gornitzka, Å., & Larsen, I. M. (2004). Towards professionalisation? *Higher Education*, *47*(4), 455–471. doi:10.1023/B:HIGH.0000020870.06667.f1

Huisman, J., de Weert, E., & Bartelse, J. (2002). Academic careers from a European perspective: The declining desirability of the faculty position. *The Journal of Higher Education*, *73*(1), 141–160. doi:10.1353/jhe.2002.0007

Kaulish, M., & Enders, J. (2005). Careers in overlapping institutional context: The case of academe. *Career Development International*, *10*(2), 130–144. doi:10.1108/13620430510588329

Kogan, M., Moses, I., & El-Khawas, E. (1994). *Staffing higher education, meeting new challenges*. London: Jessica Kingsley Publishers.

Lamont, M. (2009). *How professors think*. Cambridge, MA: Harvard University Press.

Oppenheimer, M. (1973). The proletarianization of the professional. *Sociological Review*, *20*(S1), 213–227. doi:10.1111/j.1467-954X.1972.tb03218.x

Selznick, P. (1957). *Leadership in administration: A sociological interpretation.* New York: Harper and Row.

van den Brink, M., Fruytier, B., & Thunnissen, M. (2012). Talent management in academia: Performance systems and HRM policies. *Human Resource Management Journal, 23*(2), 180–195. doi:10.1111/j.1748-8583.2012.00196.x

Waring, M. (2013). All in this together? HRM and the individualization of the academic worker. *Higher Education Policy, 26*(3), 397–419. doi:10.1057/hep.2013.7

KEY TERMS AND DEFINITIONS

Academic Leadership: All those in charge to steer, coordinate, promote core activities in the university and its sub-units. Hence it is located at different levels: rectorate, faculty, department.

Administration: The administrative function takes care of the implementation of authorized procedures and the application of systems to achieve agreed results. It is located centrally or at faculty or department levels.

Institutionalism: An institutional approach assumes that organizational change is not only deterministic (caused by external forces) or intentional (through actors' design). It also conceives of institutions - structures, routines, identities - as elements of order and predictability, with their own distinctive dynamics. Hence, when observing organizational change, one has to consider organizations' resilience and robustness.

Strategic Management: It designs activities and controls their administration according to defined objectives. It aims to achieve intended outcomes through the allocations of responsibilities and resources, and through the monitoring of their efficiency and effectiveness.

University Governance: The structures and processes framing roles of and relationships among actors. It aims to provide organizational coherence.

ENDNOTES

[1] The terms "human resources management" and "personnel policies" relate to academic staff only and are used interchangeably in this chapter.

[2] Data is retrieved by National statistical offices, reports from the Flagship projects and relates to years 2012/2013. While numbers are standardized as much as possible, the objective of table 2 is to provide indications on structural characteristics of universities and departments for general comparison.

[3] The analysis provided in this section draws in part on the data gathered in the framework of a master thesis (Friedrich 2013) supervised by the author.

Chapter 3
Funds of Knowledge and Epistemic Authority in Higher Education

Filipa M. Ribeiro
University of Porto, Portugal

Miranda Lubbers
Autonomous University of Barcelona, Spain

ABSTRACT

This chapter examines how knowledge networks of academics shape epistemic authority in higher education institutions. The issue is addressed with the approach of funds of knowledge (Bensimon, 2009) and social network theory. Social networks (of collaboration, influence, friendship, etc.) have been mainly approached with an emphasis on their actual structure and the relationship between position in that network and other features. However, little is known about how those networks of ties affect how knowledge is embodied, encoded, and enacted within higher education institutions at the interpersonal level. Rather than examining the specific qualities of any researcher's fund of knowledge, the authors focus on showing how the approach of funds of knowledge can be operationalised by social network analysis to investigate epistemic authority and epistemic change in research agendas. Knowledge networks are described as epistemic conduits, and the challenges of research in this topic are also discussed.

INTRODUCTION

The university was and continues to be a compelling force in providing necessary training, among other things, to its community. Apart from the academic expertise espoused by its members to the rest, its function of being a knowledge- based centre to the community at large contributes to creating a learning region wherein the benefits of the university extends beyond its students—for instance, by providing jobs and markets through the attraction of possible companies and other institutions to its vicinity, with such institutions having the chance to further upgrade its members' training as can be offered by the university. This, in turn, contributes to the overall socio economic

DOI: 10.4018/978-1-4666-7244-4.ch003

development of the region as clearly exemplified by this multiplier effect (Publications editor and Full Professor at the Faculty of Education, University of Malaysia).

Yes, I agree that universities are elements of cleavage because there is a huge lack of participation in the construction of a holistic and connected knowledge. What I understand is that the construction of knowledge is done in ways that are compartmentalized, disciplinary, rather than multidisciplinary, which may lead to cleavage, competition and dissection (PhD student at the University of Porto).

Universities privilege certain ways of knowing: academic and competition-driven ways basically. Unfortunately it is not until very late in one's university training (PhD level, more or less) that one can get to develop more personally driven ways of knowing, e.g. through research training. Universities are (usually) old institutions that carry a slow-moving, slow-shifting culture with them, so it is a great struggle for them to keep up conceptually on an institutional basis, even if individual professors are able to. In other words, they are much more likely to stick to, or reproduce, time-honored ways of approaching subject X or Y. Individuals may be identifying new ways on a personal basis, but it takes a long time before these might get institutionalized. There are many ways of knowing in the world. Universities really only cater to the dominant ones (Higher education researcher, publications editor and assistant professor at the Center for International Education, University of Massachusetts-Amherst).

What do these excerpts[1] have in common? Each one of them seems to offer a different way of thinking, of making sense of the role of universities as places where knowledge is created and disseminated and where the nature of knowledge

is at stake. Yet despite of the differences there is something common to the three excerpts. All of them entail rationalities based on networks, diversity and processes (cognitive and institutional) of creating knowledge.

This chapter analyses the issue of epistemic authority regarding the creation of knowledge from the point of view of social network theory and analysis. In this chapter, it will be contended that: 1) the approach of funds of knowledge is an appropriate device to explore the processes of creation and adoption of knowledge by researchers in higher education institutions; 2) social networks are at the same time the site in which these funds arise, grow and change and a component of those dynamic funds.

The claim of this chapter is that emergent processes of knowledge creation – in terms of epistemic states - are highly shaped by the social and knowledge networks in which academics and researchers are engaged. The primary focus of this work will be on knowledge creation. Thus, instead of focusing on the vehicles of distribution of knowledge and scientific outputs (Goldman, 1999) the emphasis will be on the role of knowledge networks – seen as epistemic conduits. Social networks (of collaboration, influence, friendship, etc.) have been mainly approached by focusing on their actual structure and the relationship between position in that network and other features. More recently, there has been an increasing interest on the effect of that network structure, but not on the content of those relations. It is based on the latter that we will look at epistemic authority and at the funds of knowledge of academics using a social network approach.

Knowledge – and social science about it – has to be understood in its cultural, political and economic contexts, but does not reduce to any of those. Why? A possible answer is that we are experiencing a transition period within the academic world, in which scholars put aside both manichean categories of difference and 'heady theories of creative métissage' in favour of 'detailed, individual, vital engagements with specific cases' (Schaffer et al., 2009). In this transition period, knowledge is still created through processes of hybridity, resistance or even reappropriation, but also, and increasingly, by creating new connections, new meanings and novel forms of relation. Gone are the notions of hierarchical expertise, decisive facts, static information, and grand narratives. Additionally, knowledge has taken on network properties (Weinberger, 2012).

By studying the creation and dissemination of knowledge, via the analysis of social and personal networks, we are aware that we are stepping in mined terrain. The weight of both cultural heritage and personal preconceptions cannot be easily dismissed when we think about what is knowledge. By approaching the creation of knowledge at universities through social network analysis our main intention is to retrieve the dialogical view of networks' representation potential, to reaffirm its symbolical and social role and to connect its dynamics to different forms of knowing and of creating knowledge.

Hountondji (1973) made a crucial observation that philosophy is a text-based form of knowledge. So is social theory and in regard to knowledge studies, it turns out to be insufficient given the new cognitive, technological and relational forms of creating knowledge. Especially in the so-called *Europe of Knowledge* and in the *network society*, the hard problem will continue to be to cope with the dawning, intensifying realization of how interlocked we and our collective knowledge are. This chapter also concerns with reading social theory about knowledge in the ways it is being created at universities, and that necessarily concerns the way knowledge communicates beyond its immediate contexts. Ultimately, it tackles the way knowledge encounters ways of being created and established. And this involves a long struggle for understanding how we know what we know and how we translate that into clusters, such as disciplines.

Moreover, if we are concerned with knowledge creation, diversity and knowledge networks at higher education, attention to researchers and university professors is imperative. In this chapter, creation of knowledge is framed by the personal networks in which researchers are embedded. Therefore, on one hand, we will look at the social networks as the epistemic conduits that shape the creation of knowledge in order to explore the concept of epistemic authority at universities. On the other, we will focus on how those networks form and interact with researchers' funds of knowledge. Therefore, combining the funds of knowledge approach with social network analysis is a way of returning to the kinds of relationships addressed by social theories of ordinary people as a means for re-examining how social theorizing is necessarily influenced by the personal and institutional contexts in which it is carried out.

Social Network Analysis (SNA) suggests that it is our relations with others that shape what we share. Combining this view with the approach of the funds of knowledge puts forward how those relations set the personal and professional horizons, the character of contemporary forms of belonging and the complex relations that knowledge creation and adoption entail. As a matter of fact, although researchers have identified many discrete structures in organizational social networks, including dyads, triads, cliques, social circles and other specific and natural structures of communities, the extent to which individuals encode, perceive and give meaning to these structures as entities in themselves remains unknown. The network content of the relations that matter for knowledge creation at universities is still underresearched. Our proposal is to address this issue through the understanding of the funds of knowledge of researchers. The crucial issue for understanding academic social networks also regards its dynamics, its construction and maintenance. Therefore, the novelty of the new approaches on networks and their possible contribution to the study of knowledge processes is that the framework does not realize them as determined and decisive, but as changeable. Thus, also in this regard, the approach of funds of knowledge is suitable as it is built on changing phenomena; it is an approach that has to keep up with continuous change of the object it studies. We will further explore this topic ahead in this chapter. From the point of view of interaccionism, we build upon the simmelian notion that interaction is a principle of analysis *per se*.

The epistemological foundation of this chapter is between critical theory and social constructivism. In constructivism, both knowing and learning are processes of individual knowledge construction and re-construction (Brix & Lauridsen, 2012; Brix, in press). It is therefore the individuals who learn and create knowledge and not organizations: instead, it is the individuals who together make the development in the organization on the behalf on the organization so it can prosper (Argyris, 1999). This perspective is important both for knowledge creation and for innovation studies (e.g.: Crossan & Apaydin, 2010) and for higher education studies as it addresses a process of becoming more knowledgeable, when individuals strive together to reduce the high uncertainty they experience while knowledge moves and changes along time.

In the next section, we will provide a brief overview on the research on knowledge creation at universities and social networks and how it dialogues with the legacy of sociology of education so far. On the third section we clarify the main concepts and theories in order to, at the end, show how the funds of knowledge approach (inspired by Bensimon, 2011) can be operationalised with SNA to explore the relational properties of knowledge creation. We will illustrate the conceptual and theoretical framework with empirical analysis on the influence of specific relational properties on researchers' knowledge creation at the personal level. We finalise by suggesting some future lines of research.

BACKGROUND

On Sociology of Education

In the last two decades western universities have been coping with higher education reforms that are mainly based on the views of the New Public Management frame (Bleiklie & Mathisen, 2011; Braun et al., 2010; Griffin, 2009; Hood, 2011; Kretek et al., 2012; Lohmann, 2002) and the recent research on HE has largely privileged this topic. In fact, the research on knowledge creation has been attached to policy perspectives or to the black box of the "knowledge society" (Välimaa & Hoffman, 2008). In this "imaginary space" of the knowledge society, knowledge is based on intellectual assumptions where everything is included but always in a very general and intangible way. We end up on talking about a concept of knowledge that has no existence in itself, as it is always regarded in relation to the several discourses[2] that dominate it. As a matter of fact, knowledge started to be used by the erudite/academic discourses. Today it is blended with the technocrat language and practices and, thus, its sense is so extended that it cannot mean anything else but the meaning attributed by the one who uses it.

Although knowledge has gained a ubiquitous role in our increasingly political societies (Marginson, 2011), much of this is partly our own devising and partly imposed on us, rapidly changing the flows of knowledge and the map of global relations. Maybe Marginson is right when he says that no global knowledge society is a complete coverage as there are always spaces for new communities of practice. And maybe he is right too when he says that global convergence has ensured that in HE *the global game is dominant* (Marginson, 2011, p. 15).

The dominant circuit is codified academic knowledge in the sciences. This is where value is assigned to knowledge in the form of university-mandated status. Other knowledge has no value. But there is creativity too. There is no justice here – and immense loss. Work in the range of languages, work that challenges accepted disciplinary categories and ways of thought, work from lesser status institutions, or outside the universities altogether (most of the great intellectual breakthroughs have been from outside universities) are consigned to the dustbin (Marginson, 2011, p. 16).

Moreover, Santos (2004) stresses that academic knowledge, i.e, the scientific knowledge produced in universities or in other institutions with university ethos, was, throughout the twentieth century, predominantly disciplinary whose autonomy imposed a somehow decontextualized production process in relation to the requirements of everyday life within societies. According to the logic of this process, researchers in general are the ones who determine which scientific problems are to be solved, set their relevance and establish the research methodologies. It is a homogeneous knowledge and organizationally tiered to the extent that agents involved in their production share the same objectives of knowledge production, according to well-defined organizational hierarchies (Kuhn, 1996). The distinction between scientific knowledge and other knowledges has been absolute.

The topic of knowledge creation has also been related to higher education studies undertaken during the past decades that nourished discussions on cultures and practices of knowledge, with the inclusion of new societal actors and with debates on 'post-normal' or 'post-human' science, both on policy and research arenas (Bourdieu, 2004; Braun et al., 2010; Dybicz, 2011; Felt et al., 2013; Giere, 1993). In a way or another, these studies have discussed knowledge within a discursive war[3] that shifts in turn from a view of scientific knowledge as a superior form of understanding or as a denial of any special status for scientific forms of understanding.

Whether we think of knowledge creation in higher education from a "beyond policy" perspective or heading towards new methodologies of change, those will always be movements in progress, with a constant need in recognising its flaws and gaps. Thus, we must not forget the traditional system's glaring inadequacies or that the political class is still, on the whole, clinging tight to it. In this sense, it is useful to look at the legacy of important education sociologists who have contributed to the critical education of the past and present centuries. It is of interest to frame Bourdieu's work in this perspective as one of the main authors who developed the reproduction model, especially due to two factors: 1) the quality and quantity of his work in sociology of education and in other fields of sociology; 2) his creative heterodoxy, which allowed his ideas to remain active in the realm of sociology of education. One of his ideas was that educational institutions create transferable *habitus* to other social fields. That transference is done through a symbolic violence that legitimates its arbitrary power. As a consequence, any educational culture is a product of a cultural selection of students. Bourdieu insisted on the idea that the agent is not the subject in an attempt to move away from more existentialist approaches. However, we have to bear in mind that Bourdieu, as the rest of the authors of the reproduction model, worked during the 60s under a big pressure of the structuralism. Bourdieu labeled himself as a constructivist structuralist. And, indeed, his work remained within the heterodox structuralism and not outside that movement.

Other authors of the reproduction perspective, such as Jenks (1972) or Bowles and Gintis (2000) highlighted that the reproduction models neglects the cognitive aspects of teaching and pointed the limitations of those models towards a more critical and humanist education in its efforts towards a more diverse education. If the reproduction theories were useful to show the political nature of education and the lack of neutrality in research and teaching practices, there are some limitations to be mentioned. The structuralist perspective assumes reality as a product of the social structures and denies individual's capacity to critically act and transform their surroundings. This implies a segregated vision of society and of education and, as such, the personal will of academics is absorbed by the structures in which they are embedded. One limitation with this perspective is that it leaves all types of solutions to the system, which is not feasible. A second limitation is that it excludes legitimacy to any proposal aiming at transforming society and/ or education. As a consequence both authoritarian and non-authoritarian educational alternatives fall into the same bag.

With Freire (1969), Habermas (1987), Giddens et al. (1994) new words came into the vocabulary of education, such as dialogue[4], transformation, and reflexivity. Then, the model of resistance proposed by Michael Apple (1986) calls for the analysis of processes of resistance in what the author named as *antihegemonic work*. Apple focused on the curriculum, drawing attention to the need of opening new ways to its sociologic analysis. This analysis should focus on the social context of the internal and power relations within schools. This chapter fits this same line of thought but with an extended focus on knowledge creation and research, rather than only on curriculum. The theoretical framework proposed is drawn upon the theory of funds of knowledge and the rest of this chapter shows how that can start to be done.

ON KNOWLEDGE CREATION IN HIGHER EDUCATION

A progressive new paradigm for purposive social change has started to emerge both in policy terms and in the ways we started considering knowledge[5]. One that we can freely call as 'beyond policy', which has many positive aspects but its starting point comprises a number of related critiques – some quite new, some very old – of traditional legislative or quasi-legislative decision-making. One relatively new strand focuses on the problems such decision-making has with the complexity and pace of change in the modern world (Colander & Kupers, 2014).

A second strand argues that the relational nature of knowledge means that change cannot be done to people but must be continually negotiated with them, leaving as much room as possible for local discretion at the interface between different disciplines and knowledges[6]. The key criterion in this trend sees success as 'social productivity'; the degree to which interventions encourage and enable people better to be able to contribute to meeting their own needs. Therefore, even if individuals still communicate inside the same institutions and following similar patterns, they also seek for new activities and identities. They do so neither by ways that are not predetermined instrumentally nor by their own roles. In any case, Beck (1994) does not examine the risk society as a problem or a deadlock, as the risk society also sets a process of world learning in which societies are more and more dialogical (Flecha et al., 2001). Reflecting the way we tend to think about higher education, innovation shows us a better way of making change that lasts.

Bensimon (2007) upholds that if, as scholars of higher education, we wish to produce knowledge to improve student success, we cannot ignore that researchers and teachers play a significant role. Thus, if we intend to do scholarship that makes a difference in the lives of students and in the identity of researchers as such, we have to expand research in order to take into account the various ways researchers build their bodies of knowledge, both positively and negatively. If we continue to focus only on what students accomplish or not and with what quality or on the organizational/institutional settings of universities our understanding of the value of higher education risks to be flawed and incomplete. So, while we have plenty of theories about students and about the academic profession, we do not know much about the relational nature of what knowledge, experiences or types of relations constitute researcher's knowledge and expertise.

A related stream of studies on knowledge creation at universities is well revised by Basov and Oleksandra (2011), who elucidate some of the new trends and transformation mechanisms that knowledge creation is undergoing. Some of them are new and others have been changing for centuries (Bleiklie & Byrkjeflot, 2002). The first trend identified by Basov and Oleksandra (2011) utters that the social mechanisms play a primary role in knowledge creation, which is clearly evidenced by the transformations in scientific practices. Although Kuhn (1996) had already mentioned the relevance of scientific communities as basic structures to create scientific knowledge ('metascientific conditions', according to Kuhn), only after the 1970's, with the rise of sociology of science, the social nature of the scientific process became more clarified and studied.

The second trend identified by Basov and Oleksandra (2011) is the intersection of fields of knowledge combined with narrowing specialization in response to a social demand for deeper knowledge and to the need to create innovative ideas that require different areas of specialized knowledge[7]. This trend is a combination of both interdisciplinary collaboration research and cooperation of different types of knowledge (scientific and common, rational and emotional, technical and spiritual) (Basov & Oleksandra, 2011). The authors summarize these two trends: "In the search for new competences, experience and ideas to synthesize innovations, knowledge creation gradually ceases to be the privilege of a narrow circle of scientists; the number of knowledge workers and creative class representatives grows; and the process of democratization of knowledge creation becomes evident" (Basov & Oleksandra, 2011, p. vii). Yet, some questions remain: to what extent do this cooperation of different types of knowledge is really happening at universities? How is it happening?

Literature on social networks and knowledge creation focuses particularly on how actors' embeddedness within larger structures of co-authorship networks and collaborations in patents and projects is related to individual knowledge outcomes. Little is known about what properties of these networks affect knowledge creation and even less is known about how those networks of ties affect how knowledge is embodied, encoded and enacted[8] within higher education institutions, at the interpersonal level.

In March 2011, a Royal Society report (2011), 'Knowledge, Networks and Nations', stated that over a third of all articles published in international journals are internationally collaborative compared to around a quarter only 15 years ago. Although communication technologies have been a major facilitator, the Royal Society felt that the primary driver of most collaboration is individual scientists aiming to cooperate with the *best* of their peers, though we do not know what "best" means in these cases. Phelps et al. (2012) have called these drivers as knowledge networks (nodes that serve as repositories of knowledge and agents that search for, adopt, transmit, and create knowledge). Those authors were the first to make a review of empirical research on knowledge networks, creating a typology that comprises knowledge networks research in three dimensions: knowledge outcomes (knowledge creation, knowledge transfer and learning and knowledge adoption); knowledge network properties (properties of network structure, relations, nodes, and knowledge flows) and levels of analysis (interpersonal, intra-organizational, and inter-organizational). This large body of literature shows that characteristics of social relationships and the networks influence the efficacy and efficiency by which individuals and collectives create knowledge by affecting their ability to access, transfer, absorb, and apply knowledge. For instance, Rawlings and McFarland (2011) addressed a similar problem on how influence flows in universities by analyzing how different types of affiliations impact on changes in grant productivity. Using the already available amount of affiliation network data, the authors tried to identify the patterns of how individual and dyadic characteristics channel influence among researchers.

Moolenar and Sleegers (2010) also tried to find out more exactly to what extent the characteristics of teacher's social networks affect schools' innovative climate, when the latter is mediated by trust. Their approach was through social capital theory[9] and their attempt was to confirm previous empirical evidences showing that the interplay between social ties, innovative climate and teacher trust was limited. Their survey included 775 educators of 53 schools, in a total of 51 school leaders and 724 teachers. The authors used a whole network approach[10], i.e, they focused on specific network characteristics, such as density (measure of network connectedness), reciprocity and centralization (prominence of an individual), of the social network of the school team as a whole. Findings suggested that the density of the network related to work discussions was significantly associated with school's innovative climate and trust. Krackhardt (1992) argues that strong ties can be depicted by the dimensions of interaction; affection and time. This author also debates about how individual's behavior in processes of information sharing may generate trust.

Hung (2006) showed evidence that some of these characteristics (network density, diversity of relationships, and amount of research funding) have a positive correlation with knowledge creation outputs, while network size has a negative relationship with knowledge creation outputs. Hung's research and a large body of extant research pertaining to social network theory[11] builds on the various benefits of social capital that arise from different social network structures. In order to do so, he draws on the structure hole theory (Burt,

2004), which, by definition, is based on the fundamental sociological principle that there is greater homogeneity of behavior, opinion, information, and ideas within groups of people than between groups of people.

Furthermore, some studies have assessed how direct relationships impact new knowledge creation[12]. McFadyen and Cannella (2004) highlighted the importance of the number and strength of relationships in the context of biomedical research. They analysed patterns of "committed interaction"(Blau, 1964)[13], which is a critical component in knowledge creation[14] (Nonaka & Nishiguchi, 1995). Finally, they examined both the positive and negative aspects of social capital while searching for evidence of diminishing returns to knowledge creation. McFadyen and Cannella (2004) argue that knowledge creation is more dependent on the combination and sharing of tacit knowledge, as information exchange is frequently emergent."This kind of exchange requires very direct interaction, as the parties grapple with research puzzles. In effect, new knowledge emerges through the direct interactions of research partners" (McFadyen & Cannella, 2004, p.735). Based on publication data they have addressed the number and strength of relations among researchers, but have not deepen what exactly is exchanged and how.

In sum, sociology of education and of knowledge have underlined that knowledge is not imposed; it is a network of intense conflicts, negotiations, attempts at rebuilding hegemonies by incorporating less 'powerful' knowledges (Apple, 2000; Young, 2008; Muller, 2009). The network theory has provided a large and growing body of empirical research showing that social relationships and the networks they constitute are influential in explaining the processes of knowledge creation, transfer, and adoption. It has also been shown that the formation and dissolution of the types of collaborative relationships that knowledge networks research examine reflect choices made by individuals or collectives. These choices are often made for systematic, instrumental purposes that may be correlated with desired knowledge outcomes which introduce the possibility of an endogeneity bias[15] (Phelps et al., 2012). Kilduff and Krackhardt (2008) engage three levels of analysis on the actual, perceived and underlying structures of collaboration networks, such as the tendency for people to cluster themselves together on the basis of similarity on dimensions that are considered important. Their work was quite important as they attempted to, as they said, "bring the individual back in" when conducting structural analysis. Thus, this work is placed amidst those that try "to understand the benefits of simultaneously considering individuals and social structures" (Kilduff and Krackhardt, 2008, p.259), bridging in the middle of the durkheimian and weberian views on education and knowledge. If, on one hand, sociology of knowledge and of education, though they are sciences of social relation, have neglected the analysis of the interactions among actors (de Grande, 2014), on the other, sociology and network theory have not paid enough attention to the content of those relations that explain processes of knowledge creation.

So, our proposal intends to move a step further on the understanding of the links between network structure, perceptions, and actions in a dynamic field of interaction such as the knowledge creation at universities. The works of Bernstein (2000) from the beginning of the 1990s have pushed him away from the times when his ideas were complementary of those sustained by Bourdieu due to his profound critics to the reproduction model and the inclusion of "the pedagogical discourse". To Bernstein, what matters is the process of knowledge transmission and not what is transmitted. The proposal of the Funds of Knowledge conciliates both approaches – reproduction and transformation- and adds a lens to analyse how and why the transmission is done and the transmitted is chosen to be included in the process.

CONCEPTUAL AND THEORETICAL FRAMEWORKS

Why Social Network Analysis?

The history of scientific knowledge is full of examples showing that the most powerful views of scientific truth reveal elements of deep webs of relations among scientists. In the past, the delicate nature of the criteria that characterize the scientific value of any theory or discovery has been unveiled by scientific controversies. But the results of those controversies show that the rules of the scientific procedures that we adopt, the beliefs and values that we support are mutually determined. When we speak about scientific inquiry, we recognize both its tradition as its organized authority. The weight of any type of knowledge is then in the relation between its container and its institutions, but also and mostly about the relationships among individuals. Therefore approaches to knowledge in higher education benefit from a networks sensitivity that foregrounds the interpersonal processes through which knowledge becomes entangled with the social. In an early stage, the emphasis was on the cultural values and on the professional features of science as a profession (Merton, 1968; Webber, 2002). Later, Kuhn tried to explain the processes that validate scientific achievements, focusing on the role of controversies and conflicts in scientific paradigms (Kuhn, 1996). The role of interactions between interests and beliefs in scientific community was addressed by the Bath school and by authors such as Collins (1985). Knorr-Cetina (1992), with her laboratory studies, tackled the social and cultural aspects that contextualize the scientific work. Latour (1987) and Callon came out with the Actor-Network theory (ANT), in which a network of actors refers to people, objects or organizations.

The seminal work of Crane (1972) and of other authors (e.g. Garfield, 1979) resulted in a different concept of network with a stronger emphasis on structural aspects, such as bibliometrics. The subsequent development of the network theory and of social network analysis (SNA) proposed other methods to further bibliometrics and the study of co-authorship or citations. SNA, as it is seen now, maps and measures relationships and flows among people, groups or organizations. Identifying, measuring and testing hypotheses about the structural forms and substantive contents of relations among actors have been the distinctive structural-relational feature of SNA in comparison to other more individualistic and variable-centered approaches (Knoke & Yang, 2008).

In the particular case of studying knowledge creation, by focusing the relations and interactions among individuals, SNA is particularly appropriate for examining teams and collaboration networks (which fall between the micro-level of individual's context and the meso level of organizational features). SNA is also useful to draw out precise linkages between agents engaged in collaborative activities as it reveals the structure of informal relationships amongst members and how such relations enhance or hinder certain types of activities that are crucial for the flow of resources, information, and assets. In the particular case of this project, SNA provides empirical data to fill in the schemes of the funds of knowledge; as individuals do not think in terms of network structures, when we show them the structure of the patterns of their relationships that allows a deeper inquiry into the meaning and content of their own relationships.

SNA captures quantitative aspects of relational patterns and makes tacit, informal relationships visible, which is especially helpful in exploring interactions that cross functional / structural boundaries and take place outside of formal channels within organisations. For instance, in this research it has been a useful tool to make invisible the alternative networks that often are strategies of professional demarcation and resistance adopted by academics (though we will not address this topic in this chapter). In this way SNA enables the visualization and understanding of the myriad of relationships that can either facilitate or impede knowledge creation and transfer (Cross *et al.*, 2001). At the group level, the graph-theoretic layouts of SNA helps us to see the shapes of informal networks that underpin much of organisational life, and provides quantifiable existence for the existence or otherwise of a core-periphery structure and/or cliques or sub-groups.

In fact, one of the major advantages of SNA over other methodologies is that it allows to systematically analyse the patterns of interactions among people in various types of social contexts and to quantitatively compare the structural features of such informal social networks. By enabling a visual and mathematical analysis of relationships, it helps to overcome the ideographic nature of much qualitative research by providing a way to nomothetic comparison across social groups (for this reason it is also a useful methodology to the supporters of comparative studies as it adds robustness to the analysis). That said, in this chapter we do not assume a position in which SNA is better or worse than any other methodology. Instead, all the advantages or features of SNA make them a good companion and complement to qualitative approaches as they can compensate each other's natural limitations.

At the individual level, SNA is useful to identify key players in a network, such as those occupying gate-keeping/brokerage/boundary-spanning roles, as well as reveal peripheral, underused or excluded members (Cross *et al.*, 2001). As Scott (1992) says, when using SNA to study teams, one is interested, not in how team members are categorised according to their professional affiliation or job title, but rather in the similarities in their patterns of relations with other team members. Finally, SNA – as it was already seen in this research using egonetwork analysis – proved to be a useful tool to disambiguate contradictory evidence on relational mechanisms and network effects on knowledge creation. Regarding our research questions, this dimension of the methodology is enhanced when used in a complementary way with qualitative methods (in-depth interviews) in order to know the meaning, content and relevance of researcher's ties. In this way it is also possible to better analyse the levels of redundancy of universities' networks of collaboration. In terms of analysing the diversity of knowledges, SNA allows us to study how members of each department are effectively distinct social units, each with its own area of specialized research, expertise, and intellectual and emotional context (or funds of knowledge). Therefore, SNA allows to measure diversity in terms of: 1)the number of different sources of distinct expert knowledge; 2) the research resources that each actor has access to by virtue of their relationships; 3) working styles; 4) research topics; and 4) influential people that shaped the epistemic context in which the researcher moves.

In sum, SNA is a suitable tool to deeper understanding the interpersonal mechanisms among researchers will help us to understand when, why and how do properties of knowledge networks influence knowledge creation and diversity in higher education institutions, which is one of the aims of this project.

Personal Networks as Epistemic Conduits

The concept of network has become ubiquitous in diverse literature on higher education. Yet, the term is mostly used as a metaphor both in studies that do not mobilize any network-related theory as in the studies based on the ANT proposed by Latour. In this chapter, though, we will provide a view on the concept of network based on Social Network theory. Latour was right when he insisted on the utility of the concept of network to explain how knowledge is authorized, but he saw a network as an actor-network – less used to describe or explain and emphasizing only on practices and not on the content, structural properties and perception of networks. While ANT moves away from a focus on separate entities and individuals,

the enactment of knowledge in Latour's view is more due to its materiality (and thus more contingent to the production of knowledge, mainly in the form of artifacts) rather than to its relational nature. In ANT, knowledge is only performative in multiple ontologies (1 perspective, many worlds), whereas SNT focus on the multiple perspectives framed within a single ontology (1 world, many perspectives). It is our belief that there is a need to find ways to analyse the empirical networks that are useful to explain the reciprocal influences of local interactions within organizational settings.

The reason why we chose SNT is because it is the one that best meets our understandings of knowledge, of the concept of network and because it describes and explains how some knowledge becomes sedimented, how they circulate, how they gain or lose power and what practices it sustains upon. It is important to clarify that when we refer to creation of knowledge it is not about the so-called modes of knowledge production usually said as Mode 1 or Mode 2 (Gibbons, 1994), nor we understand knowledge as a mere result of a web of connections, as ANT does. In turn, SNT is mostly concerned with understanding and explaining and not so much with justification by itself. The understanding/explaining orientation is much less atomistic and more social than the certainty/justification orientation. This difference allows us to distinguish between different types of knowledge, for instance, between expert from non-expert knowledge and to see how they interact. Thus, understanding is an epistemic value, a form of knowledge and, as Aristotle already sustained, a special cognitive state. Understanding is an acquired state (e.g.: expertise) that makes it possible to know how to do something reliably. The orientation of understanding fits the purpose of this work as it deepens our cognitive grasp or what and how is already known; this orientation involves seeing how the parts of a certain body of knowledge fit together. In social sciences in general it is quite common to equate this epistemic function of representation structures – such as networks – and erase from that representational process its connections with persons and contexts that matter for what those structures represent. Networks are usually conceived as a sole basis ruled by information-processing mechanisms and modular computational systems. However, the multidimensional aspects of networks of relations in epistemic terms and social foundations based on the content of those relations are rendered invisible. We propose that this should be a theoretical and empirical move that research in SNA should do at this stage of its evolution (Table 1). After all, "at the basis of all knowledge, be it knowledge of the self or knowledge of the object-world, there is the work of representation and understanding" (Jovchelovitch, 2007, p.10).

The social connections among these nodes are seen as channels and/or conduits of information and knowledge (Owen- Smith & Powell, 2004). We agree with this definition, but we add that, particularly with regard to knowledge creation processes, networks are epistemic conduits. This definition involves that the value associated with the formation of ties is not only exogenous and ex-ogenously given and known to all agents. Instead, to research the network phenomena it is important an emphasis on *network epistemics*, i.e., the individual, collective and interpersonal epistemic states of networks agents (Moldoveanu & Baum, 2008). By seeing a network as epistemic conduits where processes of translation of epistemic states and of knowledge take place, one can move a step further in the analysis of network ties. These processes of translation are also co-production processes that evoke the ways in which each type of knowledge is converted into another and how it gains emergence[16] and reliability. Understood in

this way, social networks consider meaning, social and personal context, offering the theoretical and methodological lenses through which SNT and sociology tries to answer questions related to the creation and epistemic authority of knowledge, in our case in higher education. At the same time, they offer a route for an engagement with issues that, despite being with us for a long time, are still important today and indeed have acquired renewed prominence in our contemporary universities.

In the last section, we defined knowledge networks as epistemic conduits where processes of translation of knowledge occur. This view sheds light on specific aspects of the processes of creation of knowledge that can go beyond the idea of knowledge as a single and homogeneous form, achieved as individuals and communities. We will focus now on how the knowledge held by specific subgroups and communities compares to dominant ideas about what knowledge is or ought to be. In other words, we will focus on epistemic authority.

Epistemic Authority through SNA

How does internal coherence or epistemic value of knowledge become valuable? Why and how university professors know what they know and translate it to students? In higher education, epistemic authority has been looked as conceptual practices (Trowler, 2010), as epistemic cultures (Knorr-Cetina,1992) or as disciplinary cultures (Biglan, 1973, Becher & Trowler, 2001; Young & Muller, 2013). All these approaches have looked at epistemic authority with a sole basis on agency without seeing interaction as a principle of analysis *per se*. This principle of interaction

Table 1. Epistemic move on social network research

Self	Self-other relations	Object
Personal/interpersonal	Communicative/interactive	Epistemic/cognitive

involves social control, power, motivation, types of relationships, conflicts and attaining status. By dismissing this interaction principle, and focusing only on the individual belief formation, there remains a lack on fully understanding the whole process of knowledge creation. However, in approaching epistemic authority in science or in higher education one may easily follow several paths: a first one aims at offering a complete normative account of epistemic behavior that includes recommendations for the behavior of individuals and also recommendations for the structure of groups. A second one deals with the relationship between social structure and group reliability (Zollman, 2007). Third, and the one we pursue in this chapter, deals with the relationship between social structures of personal knowledge networks and the epistemic choices individuals make regarding the types of knowledge they privilege and why. That is also why we do not limit our analysis to the practice of publishing in journals and books as scientific results have always, in modern times, been disseminated using those means. Instead, we attempt to find a way to dig the choices, decisions and practices that shapes knowledge creation, in order to evaluate their effect on the educational process in universities.

Lamont (2009) studied panelists who are seen as experts in six disciplines and she found that their action is constrained by the mechanics of peer review, by specific pragmatic procedures, by their respective disciplinary evaluative cultures, and by formal criteria provided by funding competition. She focused on the *black box* of peer review showing how science is not anymore a product of necessity or serendipity, but more the result of a collective belief in the deliberation's fairness between one's personal preferences and criteria of competence.

Blumberga (2012) defines epistemic authority based on the perceptions of students and graduates in relation to teacher's epistemic authority as the content of the professor's epistemic authority develops and manifests in actual and remote in-

teraction between the professor and the student. The author considers that the epistemic authority of a university professor consists of three dimensions of meaning: student-perceived authority of the professor, reasons for reliance, reasoning to explain reliance and a fourth dimension of time. And it depends on the professor's knowledge, the trusting the knowledge of the professor, the readiness to change opinion and the readiness to change behavior. Among the reasons for reliance on professor's knowledge there are: expertness, objectivity, understanding, subjectivity and sympathy, personal acquaintance, similar thinking, intuition, association, friendship and opinion. Previous studies (Raviv, 1993) reported higher ratings for the cognitive aspect of epistemic authority (knowledge) and the cognitively emotional aspect (trust in knowledge) of epistemic authority and the lowest ratings were related to cognitive-behavioral aspects (readiness to change behavior). Moreover, the acceptance of authority is influenced by the professional competence and experience. Blumberga (2012) suggests that for students to perceive a professor as an essential source of information and trust it is essential that students acknowledge the following competences of the professor as reasons for reliance: ability to be impartial (objective) and ability to be an expert. Impartiality is, however, perceived as being more important. Thus, we see that, in the educational realm, epistemic authority is closely related to epistemic self-reliance (autonomy), and autonomy has been treated as an ideal by epistemologists and by higher education scholars and managers. Though intellectual autonomy is compatible with epistemic authority, the latter can be reduced to self-reliance (Zagzebski, 2012). And as Arendt (1968) reminded us, we only ask about authority because it seems to be vanished from the modern world. However, in the educational world it did not vanish, it just changed mechanisms and some of these gained new relevance, such as functional inertia, institutional continuity (Freitag[17], 1995) or the personal endeavors relationships. Educational research has shown us that curriculum and teaching always end in an act of personal knowing. We argue that a critical understanding of these personal relations where knowing happens also encompass relations of dominance and subordination where each actor takes a part. As a matter of fact, through personal relationships we find our most profound experiences of security and anxiety, power and impotence, unity and separateness and these aspects really popped up when interviewing higher education researchers and professors about their significant ties. Personal relationships are indeed important, and sometimes overlooked, as they include a class of relatively stable, internal, personal variables that help to account for certain individual differences in how we conceive our social worlds and live our most significant personal relationships (McAdams, 1988).

Research on personal networks is a subfield of egocentric network analysis, which, in turn, is a subset of social network analysis, the study of patterns of relationships between social actors. As de Grande (2014) defines it, a personal network is the set of ties of a person with the people he/she knows plus the ties among these people. The difference between personal network analysis and other types of egocentric networks is that the boundaries of the network members are unrestrained (McCarty & Molina, forthcoming). For the research question underpinning this work, a whole network analysis could be useful to analyse the weight of institutions in the knowledge creation processes, but it would not give the exact notion of the role of researchers as individuals. We believe that the weight of any flux of knowledge lies on the relationship between its containers and the institutions, not so much in terms of reliance (as most of the studies of epistemic authority or on the epistemic of networks did), but more in terms of the decisions, choices, influences that shape the body of knowledge of a researcher – his/her *funds of knowledge*. Moreover, the dynamics of funds of knowledge are very similar to the dynamics of knowledge networks in terms of epistemic inputs.

Epistemic inputs lead to change of epistemic states, thus, these inputs can be seen and deliverances of experiences or information. But we lacked more detailed information on the researcher's funds of knowledge. This is why the concept of funds of knowledge comprises the translation processes where epistemic authority raises and is negotiated through the networks of personal relationships of the researchers, namely with regard to collaboration, influence and the balance between negative/positive relationships.

Funds of Knowledge and Epistemic Authority through Personal Networks

The theoretical framework of funds of knowledge has firstly been used by researchers, mostly in the K–12 sector, to document the wealth of knowledge existing in low-income households, and to help teachers link the school curriculum to students' lives (Rios-Aguilar et al, 2011). The concept has also been attached to shared mental schema or understandings of how students learn or ought to learn (Gallimore & Goldenberg, 2001); cognitive frames (Bensimon & Neumann, 1993); theories-in-use (Argyris & Schon, 1996), "tools of the mind" (Cole, 1985, cited in Gallimore & Goldenberg, 2001, p. 47); "shared ways of perceiving, thinking, and storing possible responses to adaptive challenges and changing conditions" (Gallimore & Goldenberg, 2001, p. 47); and background understanding (Polkinghorne, 2004). The importance of the funds of knowledge framework for pedagogical action is very well documented in the literature. However, there has been no previous attempt to examine (from a quantitative and qualitative perspective) the relationship between funds of knowledge and higher education professors' knowledge creation processes. Then, the concept of funds of knowledge is here being used in a generously capacious sense and with some flexibility of meaning (since it does not focus on the concept of households as in most studies where the theory was applied), but also include both different types of personal relationships of the researchers and extensive social relations whose actors may not know each other personally (such as experts who were highly important to define a field as a discipline or to include a topic in research agendas of a scientific field).

In higher education, Bensimon (2009) drew attention to "a lack of scholarly and practical attention toward understanding how the practitioner—her knowledge, beliefs, experiences, education, sense of self-efficacy, etc.—affects how students experience their education" (p. 444). She highlighted the role that funds of knowledge play in helping faculty to see students and families in terms of possibilities. According to the author, funds of knowledge reflect how researchers and professors define problems, situations, and make sense of phenomena; they are the know-how (and know-why) that individuals call on to accomplish their work. This is included in our concept of epistemic authority. The author was involved in some projects in which the main purpose was for professors to acquire new funds of knowledge to enhance students' access and equity to universities. We draw upon Bensimon's definition of funds of knowledge, but our focus is not student-related, at least not directly. We were looking for a conceptual device that could reflect the relationship between how collective academic knowledge is established – epistemic authority – and sustained upon individual epistemic practices (such as adoption of certain theories and methodologies, collaboration networks, influence, etc.).

The reader might reasonably expect that the question thus posed – how are funds of knowledge conveyed and sustained? – might lead to a consideration, either of social and individual memory as a dimension of power within academia, or of unconscious elements in individual memory, or both. On SNA, and more specifically on personal network analysis, these issues are straightly touched upon both in theoretical and methodological aspects, but they will not be here addressed in an explicit and systematic way.

Our proposal moves forward the research on funds of knowledge by applying a survey instrument that attempts to measure the various components embedded in the concept of funds of knowledge (i.e., social interactions and its content, educational experiences, work styles, forms of engagement in relationships, properties of their networks, motivations for research, main sources of information, work environment, career, gender, and their use of social media networks).

Sample

The theoretical and conceptual discussion presented in this chapter is grounded on a mixed-method methodological approach aiming at analyzing the knowledge networks of academics and examining the content of the researchers' network of relations. The first instrument is a network survey with multiple name generators – implemented with the software EgoNet (http://sourceforge.net/projects/egonet/)–that aims at describing the knowledge network topology and its properties as well as the work flows of the researchers (motivations for research, main sources of information, working style, work environment, career, gender, and their use of social media networks). The multiple name generators were used to delineate the personal knowledge networks of the respondents The second instrument is an in-depth qualitative interview that aims at: 1) providing the perception and validation of the researcher's network of social and personal relations to create new knowledge; 2) revealing the content and relevance of each network tie in regard to knowledge creation and teaching. The data collection took place in between May and August 2013. The analysis is based on the personal networks of a sample of 32 academic staff members of 4 institutions of the research system in Catalonia, Spain. From the sample of 32 respondents, it was possible to analyse 580 ego-alter and alter-alter relationships. The departments were selected according to the level of knowledge production (Martinez et al., 2007), and the level of interdisciplinarity of the research fields and variety of academic positions (see Tables 2 and 3 for the distribution of respondents in terms of academic positions and discipline).

Challenges

Studying the funds of knowledge of academics through personal networks analysis concerns, for instance, memory as such and social memory in particular. Concerning memory as such, findings suggest that academic's current funds of knowledge largely depends upon their relations of the past. Academics experience their current expertise and research in a context which is causally connected with past relations, and hence with reference to events that were more important for their knowledge creation than the present is. And they will experience their job and knowledge differently – from individual to individual but also from discipline to discipline – in accordance with the different past relations to which they were able to connect and maintain in the present. So, one challenge that continues to be posed in the study of knowledge networks is the one of extracting our past from our present: not simply because present factors tend to influence, or distort, the heritage from the past, but also because past factors tend to influence our experiences in the present. This is something clearly captured by the concept of funds of knowledge.

Concerning social memory in particular, we note that the relations of the past (e.g. PhD supervisor, the disappointment towards certain methodologies, etc.) commonly legitimate a present social order in relation to the knowledge included on research agendas and on curriculum. To the extent that the elicitation of the different types of relationships made by each researcher diverge, for instance according to each discipline, researchers of a same discipline can share neither experiences nor assumptions (e.g.: interviewees E4, E5 and E7). The effect is seen perhaps most obviously within the networks across generations, for instance between a supervisor and his PhD student (E29 and E11) or between an older and a younger researcher from the same department (E1 and E2 or E5 and E6) as knowledge creation is, in those cases, impeded by very similar sets of relations, memories and researchers. Some of the cases analysed indicated that similarity with alters' attributes lowered the possibilities of knowledge creation. For E4, for instance, his/her network is primarily composed of alters from the same

Table 2. Distribution of respondents' academic positions

Position	N° of respondents
Full Professor	2
Emeritus Professor	3
ICREA Professor	3
Associate Professor	11
Senior Researcher	7
Rámon Y Cajal researcher (tenure track)	1
Lecturer (non-tenured)	2
PhD Student	2
Politician / Invited Professor	1
Total	32

Table 3. Distribution of respondents/alters per discipline

Disciplines	Nº of Respondents/Ego	Nº of Alters
Sociology	4	55
Philosophy	3	54
Geography	3	54
History	3	52
Artificial Intelligence	2	46
Physics	3	42
Chemistry	2	38
Communication Sciences	3	35
Arts (music, literature, digital art)		35
Maths	3	35
Chemistry	1	19
Educational Sciences	2	18
Psychology	1	17
Geology	1	14
Biology	1	11
Computer Sciences	-	10
Economy	-	9
Engineering	-	7
Environmental Sciences	-	4
Medicine & Nutrition	-	4
Archaeology	-	4
Anthropology	-	4
Nanotechnology	-	4
Politics	-	3
Linguistics	-	3
Philology	-	2
Business	-	1
Total	**32**	**580**

discipline, with the same personal interests, the same professional trajectories, the same values about research, but, "(...) it's from the people who don't belong to my core department that I get the most interesting inquiries to my discipline", the respondent says.

In those dyads, similar sets of relations, frequently in the shape of implicit background references and research agendas, will encounter each other; so that, although physically and institutionally present, the different generations may remain mentally and physically insulated. In these cases, what happens is twofold: 1) whether the personal networks function as a strange attractor18, i.e., a regular pattern of knowledge creation falls apart and another emerges (e.g.: E26) allowing the transition and translation between forms and types of knowledge; or 2) the relationships of the past serve to legitimate a present knowledge order and is sustained through elective affinities[19]. These processes are conveyed and sustained by (more or less performative) personal relationships. For instance, it is quite common that a researcher engages with researchers who do not belong to their department or university and starts collaborating with researchers he enjoyed being with, that he/she met at a conference or during a scholarship in another university, etc., with whom they developed elective affinities. Those novel forms of relations do not replace the institutional networks, but amplify the range of the researcher as they constitute a meaningful space in which to cultivate the academic self beyond the alienating tendencies of the so-called market oriented modern knowledge production. Those shifts in the research paradigms implied a change in the criteria that researchers (e.g.: E7) uses to select his/her topics of research. For instance, and in contrast to most researchers, E7 does not mention personal values as a major reason to explain his/her ties, but rather it is the clear criteria regarding research topics. These criteria were also an important aspect for researchers whose networks were smaller but with fewer connections among their ties (e.g.: E9). In the case of E9, strong ties are the ones that sustain his/her personal research agenda in opposition to the official research agenda that he/she keeps with his/her collaborators in the department. Other example, such as E9, shows that Faculty networks are often associated to a prescriptive stance on the research agendas selected by the researchers and on their decisions regarding networking with other researchers. Some professors, such as E9, clearly engaged in alternative research agendas arose by means of personal values and scientific preferences that often do not have any correspondence with the institutions or departments as these focuses primarily on institutionalized themes and quarrels, labor conditions and other quantifiable matters.

The findings suggest that the knowledge networks alternative to the research work done within the respondent's department occur simultaneously and not necessarily in opposition to the regular collaboration and co-authorship networks of academics. By not restraining the approach to a dualistic one, it is possible to better understand the contradictions, peculiarities and differences that emanate from the multidimensionality of the knowledge networks of academics. These knowledge networks entail processes that are in continuous negotiation, configuring discourses and practices of subversion and transformation of the dominant research agendas.

Thus, findings suggest that if, on one hand, the emphasis on personal values is important to explain the strength, content and relevance of a tie for knowledge creation, the absence of relation between network size and number of components and structural holes[20] and the importance for knowledge creation may be due to different sort of conflictual nuances in the ties and to the selection criteria of research topics.

Although those relationships are not the most visible ones – in terms of scientific outputs and scores – they are definitely gaining an emergence. In the essay *A critique of lazy reason*, Santos (2004) writes about the modes of productions of the non-inexistent. These are a form of inscribed knowledge (Freeman, 2006) in which devices of creativity and effectiveness are at play in different levels. The reach of these networks is not just a function of their distributed, interconnected and global nature but of the fact that the character and nature of ego networks means that it is able to create and develop spaces and opportunities for emergent forms of knowledge and scientific research, and for groups and individuals to develop and enhance different knowledge culture through scientific collaboration (Newman, 2006; Zuccala, 2006), but that the personal networks potential is not fully accomplished due to institutional constraints (Ribeiro, forthcoming).

Epistemic Authority and Funds of Knowledge: What the Content of Ties Tell

One of the aims of this chapter was to explore the network mechanisms that operatiozalize and relate to researchers' funds of knowledge. Another aim was to show the need of understanding what lies behind a tie in a knowledge network, i.e., its content. Research suggests that decreased connectivity results in slower, but more reliable learning and that network density and clustering coefficient is a stronger predictor of successful learning than any other property (Zollman, 2007). In other words, in some contexts groups of learners are more reliable when the connectivity of the group is low. This occurs because bad experimental results are communicated too widely in highly connected societies, which leads the individuals in those groups to abandon superior theories/paradigms/research methods prematurely. Moreover, the features of a network that make it fast and those that make it accurate are very different. For instance, reliability often has to trade off with speed of dissemination of information. Zollmam (2007) looked at agent based models for the mechanisms of social conformity. He found that from the individual perspective, one would regard social influence as epistemically productive whereas from the group perspective it is better that individuals do not engage in conformist behavior. So, given that scientists are subject to conformity effects, it is better if they are more connected but unequal connectivity should be avoided. That said, it is worth mentioning that Zollman's work is mainly based on the traditional ways ideas are accepted: cultural acceptance, imitation, cooperation and learning.

Based on our data set, we have found that the network mechanism more closely related to knowledge creation and to interdisciplinarity is the strength of ties (Ribeiro & Lubbers, 2013; Ribeiro, forthcoming). As a matter of fact, stronger ties are perceived to be more important for knowledge creation (both in single component

or multiple component networks) and both with dissimilar or similar ties. Surprisingly, similarity, in terms of discipline and academic position, does not affect knowledge creation (Ribeiro & Lubbers, 2013). Findings also suggest that it is not enough to have expertise in one's team. Influential ties (more than collaboration ties) are the knowledge intermediaries defining what counts to be included in research agendas and inducing epistemic change. They perform critical operations and discussions in the knowledge creation, it promotion, constructing legitimacy and adding value through the qualification of that knowledge. Usually they are the responsible for the processes of institutionalization of disciplines. Knowledge of existing expertise can, thus, be a key component in network formation and in network epistemics.

The qualitative analysis of the collected knowledge networks revealed three main phases where the dynamics of the funds of knowledge of the researchers change by epistemic inputs brought about by their personal knowledge networks. Let's look at one example: E10 is a researcher in Medieval Philosophy, whose main topics have been theory of science, interreligious dialogue and cultural traditions. However, his background was on Political Philosophy.

1. **Revision:** A new knowledge is added but not the entire old one is retained. It is a result of conflicting information (in a good sense). Revision is the epistemic state of how one determines which belief or knowledge is to be retained and which is not. For instance, E10 graduated in Political Philosophy. But, during his master, he came across the works of a medieval Catalan philosopher and scientist. He got so interested by the level of interdisciplinarity and pioneering of the medieval thinker that he radically changed the course of his research in a time when Philosophy before Descartes was not well recognized in the academia. However, as his/her background was from German

philosophy his/her turn for a field with a theological tradition was soother. So, his/her turn in his/her research and the input during his master allowed him/her to expand what he had learnt from German Philosophy. If we also look at his main sources of information, we see that he/she does not give reliability or importance to scientific journals and even less to indexed journals.

2. **Contradiction:** As E10 moved from Germany to Spain he/she met several cultural particularities with regard to the type of research, despite the fact that he/she was hired to an advanced research centre where he/she started as a junior researcher. A negative tie with whom E10 had several conflicts due to the fact that he/she was required to "be very submissive" towards that collaborator and "there were forbidden research topics" caused not only a revision of his/her research agenda of E10, but also a retraction. Contradiction happens when knowledges are retracted but no new knowledge is added. For instance, the so-called academic contradiction, controversies or dilemmas are included in this epistemic state.

3. **Expansion:** this stage is a simple way of modeling the epistemic change that follows learning something and, thus, the main causes for this process are observation and information provided by others. This expansion is mainly due to three factors. One relates to the fact that E10 managed to be in a multidisciplinary team, which, he/she believes is the only way to "expand our knowledge". The second were the most important ties for his/her knowledge creation: PhD supervisor, who taught him/her "a lot" of what he/she knows, taught him/her scientific procedures and had "magnificent human qualities". In terms of expansion of his/her knowledge this tie taught E10 how to understand medieval texts with systematic and historical perspectives and to make links

between that knowledge and current times. In epistemic terms, that tie was important to improve E10's ability to formulate problems and raise scientific inquiries. A curious fact is that this strong tie is no longer someone with whom E10 collaborates and, from his/her network of collaborations, he/ she only mentioned two more who he/she considers truly important for his knowledge. This tie was deemed important because of his expertise in academic writing and for sharing knowledge in scientific events; in terms of non-academic knowledge it was this tie's emotional intelligence and capacity to catalyse knowledge that most drew E10's attention. One last tie that was mentioned as important for the respondent's knowledge in terms of epistemic expansion was the isolated node (see Figure 1), which is a type of negative tie (whenever there is conflict, tension, disagreement), with a positive effect in terms of knowledge creation. The third factor that significantly contributes for the epistemic state of expansion is the periods or fellowships in other universities. For instance, E10 included in his/her research agenda topics such as the interreligious dialogue due to the periods he/she spent in other universities where he/she gained a new perspective on the social relevance of linking, through research, the Jewish, Arabic and Latin philosophies. These factors corroborate and explain the quantitative results that suggest that only 32% of the ties form the collaboration network are deemed important for knowledge creation (Ribeiro and Lubbers, 2013) and that the influence network ties are more important for changing and establishing the epistemic states of the funds of knowledge of researchers.

This example, in terms of network measures, shows that network size does not really matter in order to know if a network is more or less global

Figure 1. Personal network of E10. The node's size represents degree centrality, which concerns the prominence of a node within the network

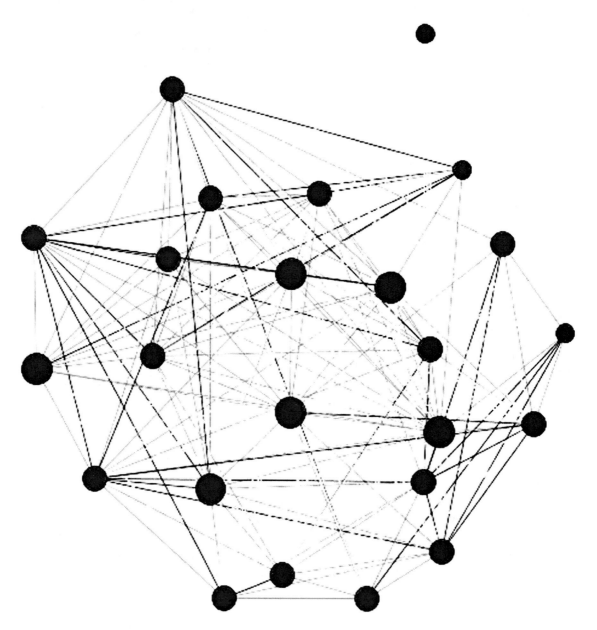

and local or more or less creative and diverse. It also shows that degree distribution only tells half of the story and that is why a qualitative analysis of the content of each tie is important in order to know its meaning and validation in terms of knowledge creation. Centrality[21] and strength of ties are more related to more diverse networks than personal attributes of the researchers such as working styles and creativity and its weight is higher in networks with more ties affiliated to faculty departments than in researchers affiliated to research institutes (author, forthcoming).

CONCLUSION

It is widely demonstrated that network analysis is able to reveal organizational structure via a wide variety of linkages. This chapter conceptually explores how social and personal networks of relationships among researchers influence their funds of knowledge and how those relational funds determine epistemic authority at universities. We focused on how current and emergent processes of knowledge creation – in terms of epistemic states - are highly shaped by the social and knowledge networks in which academics and researchers are engaged.

We proposed to combine the concept of funds of knowledge (Bensimon, 2009) with social network analysis as a way of returning to the kinds of relationships addressed by social theories of ordinary people and as a means for re-examining how social theorizing is necessarily influenced by the social and institutional contexts in which it is carried out. SNA suggests that it is our relations with others that shape what we share. When combined this approach with the concept of Funds of Knowledge, SNA puts forward how those relations set the personal and professional horizons, the character of contemporary forms of belonging and the complex relations that knowledge creation and adoption entail. A previous analysis of our data (Ribeiro & Lubbers, forthcoming) set showed that the collaborative nature of academic knowledge creation is intrinsic to the way that values and meanings are bound up with constitutive of relationships. Even to anyone who has been interested in Durkheim's theory of knowledge, this casts a comforting light and a necessary way to conciliate an empirical filled theoretical framework to academic knowledge creation. So, in this chapter, we argue that the logic of relations, if seen beyond the mere structural aspect, provides a rationale that allows us to bring back the origins of individual thought and how that impacts on *how institutions think* and how new researchers

and new knowledge are socialized, gain or lose presence in higher education institutions.

FUTURE RESEARCH DIRECTIONS

Higher education and the research in the field are widely dominated by topics related to policy reforms, strategies and institutional settings. These are indeed major drivers of change and challenge for higher education. One of the purposes of this chapter is to *draw the individual back in* and highlight individual's funds of knowledge – shaped by the networks they engage in – as another and complementary driver of change and challenge if education is to be education and not just a managerial commodity. After all, what we mean by progress is also what we mean by meaning. And meaning is not anymore the product of an output of intellectual endeavors confronted with reality. It is rather the result of negotiations among individuals. The analysis of the daily relational practices in which we are engaged as researchers and as professors is a privileged way to capture that meaning.

The aim of this chapter was not just to prove how funds of knowledge and knowledge networks are a suitable approach to understand epistemic authority and knowledge creation at universities. Rather, it also aims to reveal how many of our most pressing questions about higher education and universities simply are not fully answered elsewhere. Much of what we take for progress and current challenges in higher education delivers answers that miss the point, distort issues, ignore complications, and may be generated by badly formulated questions or misplaced focus in the first place. How do we want both the policy and political discourses and decision on higher education to change if research on the topic does not praise anymore the main parts of education: professors, students what and how they teach and learn? Higher education is deluged with discourses on new modes to manage and assess higher education and research as knowledge was reduced to be an asset. Higher education research is overwhelmed with ways to track down institutional reforms and management modes. And that is highly useful, but we cannot neglect the core of education and of science: individuals and knowledge. We know that when it comes to figure out why and how researchers research what they research and professors teach what they teach some questions just will not go away. Higher education research can do a lot more in order to come up with its share of answers—and for setting scientists on their way in searching for theirs.

Knowledge networks are privileged modes of engagement of researchers with a wide sort of practices: research collaboration, teaching and curriculum development, institutional demography (student recruitment, mobility, events, etc.), curricular change, transnational engagements (e.g.: collaboration and partnerships with foreign institutions, dual, double and joint Degrees, research partnerships, strategic alliances, etc), academic culture and leadership. This chapter clearly fits in the mechanisms, models and logics of individual initiatives and views on knowledge creations both at universities and research centers. We focused on knowledge networks such as collaboration and influence networks and considered them as epistemic practices through which epistemic states change and evolve. We identified three main mechanisms by which that change occurs: revision, expansion and contraction. However, our findings are based on data from few cases from only four research institutions, even though the variety of their missions expands the scope. To test whether our findings can be generalized and find more possible nuances in the above mentioned mechanisms, this study should be extended to larger scale samples on the one hand and to cross-case comparisons –specially between countries - on the other, to better understand the network determinants of knowledge creation.

Future lines of research should also investigate more deeply the follow-up mote of this research: the link between these emergent modes of knowledge creation with the development and teaching of curricula. For instance, to see how the criteria to select the syllabus in the disciplines vary according to the different weight of the epistemic mechanisms we observed in the knowledge networks? Another line of research would be to explore the potential of egonetwork analysis as a tool of coaching to researchers and university professors. This could, even, provide concrete information to departments in order to better plan and assess the knowledge they create and produce in terms of, for instance, interdisciplinarity. As a matter of fact, when respondents narrate the rise and development of the most relevant ties for their knowledge creation, they seem to go through moments of self-awareness, leading to surprising insights about their own trajectories. These insights could be transformed into useful information both at individual and at the group level. This also opens up a spot into the research on social network analysis in terms of cognitive and epistemic dynamics of social networks.

The grand forward push of human knowledge and education requires each of us to begin by trying to think independently, to recognize that the knowledge we create is more than information it is also what we depict from who we relate with, to see that we are relational beings who must closely interrogate both ourselves and our relations when they have an impact on the knowledge we pass to others—to live, as Socrates might have recommended, an examined education as part of an examined life.

ACKNOWLEDGMENT

First and foremost, I offer my sincerest gratitude to my supervisors, Dr. Miranda Lubbers and Dr. António Magalhães, who have been supporting me throughout my thesis with their patience and knowledge whilst allowing me the room to work my own ideas. Second, I also give my deepest thanks to the reviewer of this chapter for the thoughtful and generous reading of the text, for the usefulness and pertinence of the comments and, especially, for the honesty, elegance, and scientific generosity of those comments. It is blissful to testify such kind stimulus in our path. *Last but not the least*, I thank and cheer my fellow editors of this book, Dr. Bojana Culum and Dr. Yurgos Politis, for the great pleasure of working with them and for having sourced me a high quality work environment that lead to this book.

REFERENCES

Apple, M. (2000). *Official knowledge - Democratic education in a conservative age*. London: Routledge.

Apple, M., & Beane, J. A. (Eds.). (1995). *Democratic schools*. Alexandria, VA: Association for Supervision & Curriculum.

Arendt, H. (1968). *Between past and future*. New York: Penguin.

Argyris, C. (1999). *On organizational learning*. Blackwell Publishing.

Argyris, C., & Schon, D. A. (1996). *Organizational LEARNING II: Theory, method, and practice*. New York: Addison-Wesley.

Basov, N., & Oleksandra, N. (2011). *Understanding knowledge creation - Intellectuals in academia, the public sphere and the arts*. Amsterdam: Editions Rodopi.

Becher, T., & Trowler, P. (2001). *Academic tribes and territories: Intellectual enquiry and the cultures of discipline* (2nd ed.). London: Open University Press.

Beck, U., Giddens, A., & Lash, S. (1994). *Reflexive modernization: Politics, tradition and aesthetics in the modern social order*. Stanford, CA: Stanford University Press.

Bensimon, E. (2007). The underestimated significance of practitioner knowledge in the scholarship on student success. *The Review of Higher Education*, *30*(4), 441–469. doi:10.1353/rhe.2007.0032

Bensimon, E., & Neumann, A. (1993). *Redesigning collegiate leadership*. Baltimore, MD: Johns Hopkins Press.

Bereiter, C. (2002). *Education and mind in the knowledge age*. Mahwah, NJ: Lawrence Erlbaum Associates.

Bernstein, B. (2000). *Pedagogy, symbolic control and identity: Theory, research, critique* (rev. ed.). Lanham, MD: Rowman & Littlefield publishers.

Biglan, A. (1973). The characteristics of subject matter in different academic areas. *The Journal of Applied Psychology*, *57*(3), 195–203. doi:10.1037/h0034701

Blackwell, J., & Gamble, P. (2001). *Knowledge management – A state of the art guide*. London: Kogan Page Publishers.

Blau, P. M. (1964). *Exchange and power in social life*. New York: Wiley.

Bleiklie, I., & Byrkjeflot, H. (2002). Changing knowledge regimes: Universities in a new research environment. *Higher Education*, *44*(3/4), 519–532. doi:10.1023/A:1019898407492

Bleiklie, I., & Mathisen, G. (2011). Organizing knowledge institutions – Standardizing diversity. Paper presented at the 24th Annual Conference of the Consortium of Higher Education Researchers. Reykjavic, Iceland.

Blumberga, S. (2012). Dimensions of epistemic authority of university professors. *Social and Natural Sciences Journal, 5*(0), 1–5. doi:10.12955/snsj.v5i0.299

Bourdieu, P. (2004). *Science of science and reflexivity*. Chicago: University of Chicago Press.

Bowles, S., & Gintis, H. (2000). Schooling in capitalist America revisited. *Sociology of Education, 75*(1), 1–18. doi:10.2307/3090251

Braun, K., Moore, A., Herrmann, S. L., & Könninger, S. (2010). Science governance and the politics of proper talk: Governmental bioethics as a new technology of reflexive government. *Economy and Society, 39*(4), 510–533. doi:10.1080/03085147.2010.510682

Brix, J., & Lauridsen, K. M. (2012). Learning styles and organisational development in practice: An exploratory study of how learning styles and individual learning strategies can facilitate organisational development. *International Journal of Innovation and Learning, 12*(2), 181–196. doi:10.1504/IJIL.2012.048353

Brix, J., & Lauridsen, O. (forthcoming). Improving learning competencies in the context of radical innovation: A team perspective. *International Journal of Innovation and Learning.*

Burt, R. L. (2004). Structural holes and good ideas. *American Journal of Sociology, 110*(2), 349–399. doi:10.1086/421787

Colander, D., & Kupers, R. (2014). *Complexity and the art of public policy: Solving society's problems from the bottom up*. Princeton, NJ: Princeton University Press.

Collins, H. (1985). *Changing order: Replication and induction in scientific practice*. Chicago: Chicago University Press.

Crane, D. (1972). *Invisible colleges: Diffusion of knowledge in scientific communities*. Chicago: Chicago University Press.

Cross, R., Borgatti, S. P., & Parker, A. (2001). Beyond answers: Dimensions of the advice network. *Social Networks, 23*(3), 215–235. doi:10.1016/S0378-8733(01)00041-7

Crossan, M. M., & Apaydin, M. (2010). A multidimensional framework of organizational innovation: A systematic review of the literature. *Journal of Management Studies, 47*(6), 1154–1191. doi:10.1111/j.1467-6486.2009.00880.x

De Grande, P. (2013). Aportes de Norbert Elias, Erving Goffman y Pierre Bourdieu al estudio de las redes personales. *Andamios, 10*(22), 237–258.

Dybicz, P. (2011). Anything goes? Science and social constructions in competing discourses. *Journal of Sociology and Social Welfare, 38*(3), 101–122.

Engeström, Y. (1987). *Learning by expanding: An activity-theoretical approach to developmental research*. Helsinki: Orienta-Konsultit Oy.

Felt, U., Igelsbo, J., Schikowitz, A., & Völker, T. (2013). Growing into what? The (un)disciplined socialisation of early stage researchers in transdisciplinary research. *Higher Education, 65*(4), 511–524. doi:10.1007/s10734-012-9560-1

Flecha, R., Gómez, J., & Puigvert, L. (2001). *Teoría sociologica contemporánea*. Barcelona: Paidós.

Freire, P. (2000). *Pedagogy of freedom: Ethics, democracy, and civic courage*. Lanham, MD: Rowman & Littlefield Publishers.

Freitag, M. (1995). *Le naufrage de l'université et autres essais d'epistémologie politique*. Paris: Ladécouverte.

Gallimore, R., & Goldenberg, C. (2001). Analyzing cultural models and settings to connect minority achievement and school improvement research. *Educational Psychologist, 36*(1), 45–56. doi:10.1207/S15326985EP3601_5

Garfield, E. (1979). Mapping the structure of science. In E. Garfield (Ed.), *Citation indexing: Its theory and application in science, technology, and humanities* (pp. 98–147). New York: John Wiley & Sons, Inc.

Gibbons, M., Limoges, C., Nowotny, H., Schwartzman, S., & Scott, P. (1994). *The new production of knowledge: The dynamics of science and research in contemporary societies*. London: Sage.

Giere, R. N. (1993). Science and technology studies: Prospects for an enlightened postmodern synthesis. *Science, Technology & Human Values, 18*(1), 102–112. doi:10.1177/016224399301800106

Goldman, A. (1999). *Knowledge in a social world*. Oxford, UK: Clarendon Press. doi:10.1093/0198238207.001.0001

Gonzalez, N., Moll, L. C., & Amanti, C. (Eds.). (2005). *Funds of knowledge: Theorizing practices in households, communities, and classrooms*. Mahwah, NJ: Lawrence Erlbaum.

Griffin, G. (2009). *Governance of science in a complex world: Issues for the social sciences and humanities*. Paper presented at the International Conference 'Governance of Science in the 21st Century: Mechanisms and Perspectives'. Moscow, Russia. Retrieved from http://www.issras.ru/conference_2009/index.php

Habermas, J., & McCarthy, T. (1985). *The theory of communicative action: Reason and the rationalization of society* (Vol. 1). Boston: Beacon Press.

Hood, C. (2011). Public management research on the road from consilience to experimentation. *Public Management Review, 13*(2), 321–326. doi:10.1080/14719037.2010.539098

Hountondji, P. J. (1973). *Libertés: Contribution à la révolution dahoméen*. Cotonou: Editions Renaissance.

Hung, W. (2006). *Researching the researcher: A social network analysis of the multidisciplinary knowledge creation process*. (Unpublished master dissertation). University of Waterloo.

Jovchelovitch, S. (2007). *Knowledge in context, representations, communities and culture*. London: Routledge.

Kehm, B. M., & Teichler, U. (2007). Research on internationalisation in higher education. *Journal of Studies in International Education, 11*(3-4), 260–273. doi:10.1177/1028315307303534

Kilduff, M., & Krackhardt, D. (2008). *Interpersonal networks in organizations*. Cambridge, UK: Cambridge University Press. doi:10.1017/CBO9780511753749

King, R. (2011). Power and networks in worldwide knowledge coordination: The case of global science. *Higher Education Policy, 24*(3), 359–376. doi:10.1057/hep.2011.9

Knoke, D., & Yang, S. (2008). *Social network analysis* (2nd ed.). Thousand Oaks, CA: Sage.

Knorr-Cetina, K. (1992). The couch, the cathedral and the laboratory: On the relationship between experiment and laboratory in science. In A. Pickering (Ed.), *Science as practice and culture*. Chicago: Chicago University Press.

Knowledge, N. N. G. c. (2011). *RS policy document 03/11*. London: Royal Society.

Krackhardt, D. (1990). Assessing the political landscape: Structure, cognition, and power in organizations. *Administrative Science Quarterly, 35*(2), 342–369. doi:10.2307/2393394

Kretek, P., Dragšić, Ž., & Kehm, B. (2012). Transformation of university governance: On the role of university board members. *Higher Education, 65*(1), 39–58. doi:10.1007/s10734-012-9580-x

Kuhn, T. S. (1996). *The structure of scientific revolutions*. Chicago: University of Chicago Press. doi:10.7208/chicago/9780226458106.001.0001

Lamont, M. (2009). *How professors think – Inside the curious world of academic judgement*. Harvard University Press.

Latour, B. (1987). *Science in action: How to follow scientists and engineers through society*. Cambridge, MA: Harvard University Press.

Mackenzie, D. (2006). *An engine, not a camera: How financial models shape markets*. Cambridge, MA: MIT Press. doi:10.7551/mitpress/9780262134606.001.0001

Marginson, S. (2011). The new world order in higher education. In M. Rostan & M. Vaira (Eds.), *Questioning excellence in higher education: Policies, experiences and challenges in national and comparative perspective* (pp. 3–20). Rotterdam, The Netherlands: Sense Publishers. doi:10.1007/978-94-6091-642-7_1

McAdams, D. P. (1988). Personal needs and personal relationships. In S. W. Duck (Ed.), *Handbook of personal relationships* (pp. 467–484). New York: John Wiley & Son, lda.

McFadyen, M. A., & Cannella, A. (2004). Social capital and knowledge creation: Diminishing returns of the number and strength of exchange relationships. *Academy of Management Journal, 47*(5), 735–746. doi:10.2307/20159615

McFarland, D. A., Diehl, D., & Rawlings, C. (2011). Methodological transnationalism and the sociology of education. In M. Hallinan (Ed.), *Frontiers in sociology of education* (pp. 87–110). Springer. doi:10.1007/978-94-007-1576-9_5

Merton, R. (1968). *Social theory and social structure*. London: Free Press.

Moldoveanu, M., & Baum, J. (2008). *The epistemic structure and dynamics of social networks*. Science Research Network Paper No 88795. Available at SSRN: http://ssrn.com/abstract=1115311

Moolenaar, N. M., & Sleegers, P. J. C. (2010). Social networks, trust and innovation - The role of relationships in supporting an innovative climate in Dutch schools. In A. J. Daly (Ed.), *Social network theory and educational change* (pp. 235–160). Cambridge, MA: Harvard Education Press.

Muller, J. (2009). Forms of knowledge and curriculum coherence. *Journal of Education and Work, 22*(3), 205–226. doi:10.1080/13639080902957905

Nahapiet, J., & Ghoshal, S. (1998). Social capital, intellectual capital, and the organizational advantage. *Academy of Management Review, 23*, 242–266.

Newman, M. E. J. (2006). Modularity and community structure in networks. *Proceedings of the National Academy of Sciences of the United States of America, 103*(23), 8577–8582. doi:10.1073/pnas.0601602103 PMID:16723398

Nonaka, I., & Nishiguchi, T. (1995). *The knowledge-creating company*. New York: Oxford University Press.

Owen-Smith, J., & Powell, W. W. (2004). Knowledge networks as channels and conduits: The effects of spillovers in the Boston biotechnology community. *Organization Science, 15*(1), 5–21. doi:10.1287/orsc.1030.0054

Phelps, C., Heidl, R., & Wadhwa, A. (2012). Knowledge, networks, and knowledge networks. *Journal of Management, 38*(4), 1115–1166. doi:10.1177/0149206311432640

Polkinghorne, D. E. (2004). *Practice and the human sciences: The case for a judgment based practice of care*. Albany, NY: State University of New York Press.

Raviv, A., Bar-Tal, D., Raviv, A., & Abin, R. (1993). Measuring epistemic authority: Studies of politicians and professors. *European Journal of Personality, 7*(2), 119–138. doi:10.1002/per.2410070204

Ribeiro, F. M. (forthcoming). Interdisciplinarity in ferment: The role of knowledge networks and department affiliation. *Technological Forecasting and Social Change*.

Ribeiro, F. M., & Lubbers, M. (2013). *Social networks and knowledge creation in higher education: The role of similarity and tie strength*. Paper presented at the 10th Conference of Applications of Social Network Analysis. Zurich, Switzerland.

Rios-Aguilar, C., Kiyama, J. M., Gravitt, M., & Moll, L. C. (2011). Funds of knowledge for the poor and forms of capital for the rich? A capital approach to examining funds of knowledge. *Theory and Research in Education, 9*(2), 163–184. doi:10.1177/1477878511409776

Robinson, K. (1999). *All our futures: Creativity, culture and education.* London: National Advisory Committee on Creative and Cultural Education.

Santos, B. S. (2004). *A universidade do século XXI: Para uma reforma democrática eda universidade* (pp. xix–lxii). São Paulo: Cortez Editora.

Santos, B. S., Nunes, J. A., & Meneses, M. P. (2007). Opening up the canon of knowledge and recognition of difference. In B. S. Santos (Ed.), *Another knowledge is possible*. London: Verso.

Schaffer, S., Roberts, L., Raj, K., & Delbourgo, J. (2009). *The brokered world: Go-betweens and global intelligence, 1770-1820*. Sagamore Beach, MA: Science History Publications/Watson Publishers.

Scott, J. (1992). *Social network analysis.* London: Sage.

Sosa, M. (2007). *Faculty & research: Where do creative interactions come from? The role of tie content and social networks*. ISEAD.

Sturdy, S., & Freeman, R. (2014). *Knowledge in policy: Embodied, inscribed, enacted*. Policy Press.

Trowler, V. (2010). *Student engagement literature review*. Lancaster, UK: Lancaster University.

Välimaa, J., & Hoffman, D. (2008). Knowledge society discourse and higher education. *Higher Education, 56*(3), 265–285. doi:10.1007/s10734-008-9123-7

Weinberger, D. (2012). *Too big to know: Rethinking knowledge now that the facts aren't the facts, experts are everywhere, and the smartest person in the room is the room*. London: Basic Books.

Whittle, A., & Spicer, A. (2008). Is actor network theory critique? *Organization Studies, 21*(4), 611–629. doi:10.1177/0170840607082223

Young, M. (2008). From constructivism to realism in the sociology of the curriculum. *Review of Research in Education, 32*(1), 1–28. doi:10.3102/0091732X07308969

Zagzebski, L. T. (2012). *Epistemic authority – A theory of trust, authority and autonomy in belief*. Oxford, UK: Oxford University Press. doi:10.1093/acprof:oso/9780199936472.001.0001

Zollman, K. (2007). *Network epistemology*. (Unpublished doctoral dissertation). University of California, Irvine, CA.

Zuccala, A. (2006). Modeling the invisible college. *Journal of the American Society for Information Science and Technology, 57*(2), 152–168. doi:10.1002/asi.20256

ADDITIONAL READING

Douglas, M. (1986). *How institutions think*. New York: Syracuse University Press.

KEY TERMS AND DEFINITIONS

Epistemic Authority: The relationship between social structures of personal knowledge networks and the epistemic choices individuals make regarding the types of knowledge they privilege and why. Epistemic authority, in this chapter, relies upon the deliverance of experiences provided by the funds of knowledge of researchers and is manifest in epistemic states that occur inside network ties.

Funds of Knowledge: A conceptual device that reflects how researchers and professors define problems, situations, and make sense of phenomena; they are the know-how (and know-why) that individuals call on to accomplish their work. In simple terms, it reflects how knowledge in inscribed, encoded and embodied along the research trajectory of the researcher. Thus, it reflects the relationship between how collective academic knowledge is established – epistemic authority – and sustained upon individual epistemic practices (such as adoption of certain theories and methodologies, collaboration networks, influence, etc.).

Knowledge: A fluid mix of framed experience, values, contextual information, expert insight, and grounded intuition that provides an environment and framework for evaluating and incorporating new experiences and information. It originates and is applied in the mind of the knowers. In organizations it often becomes embedded not only in documents or repositories, but also in organizational routines, practices and norms (Gamble and Blackwell,2001).

Knowledge Networks: A set of actors who are repositories of knowledge and who create, transfer and adopt knowledge (Phelps et al., 2012). The social connections among these nodes are seen as channels and/or conduits of information and knowledge (Owen- Smith & Powell, 2004). In this work, we suggest that networks are epistemic conduits, whose value associated with the formation of ties is not only exogenous and exogenously given and known to all agents. To research the network phenomena it is important an emphasis on network epistemics, i.e., the individual, collective and interpersonal epistemic states of networks actors. So, a knowledge network can be seen as an epistemic conduit where processes of translation of epistemic states and of knowledge take place.

Perception of Expertise: Researchers form ties with others because they perceive them to have expertise; for example many years of teaching experience or training and knowledge of their disciplines.

Social Network Analysis: A multidisciplinary method that maps, measures and represents structural relationships accurately, and explains both why they occur and what the consequences are. In the educational field, the use of SNA meant a shift in perspective as research moved gradually from a rather singular focus on the institution as a unit of change to a more sophisticated conception of nested organizational and individual relationships.

ENDNOTES

[1] These are excerpts of interviews undertaken by the author to the editors of scientific journals in the fields of Higher Education and to PhD students at the University of Porto aiming at understanding if there was a cleavage effect of HEIs on the knowledge created there.

[2] These discourses are analysed by Välimaa and Hoffman (2008).

[3] See, in this regard, for example, Välimaa, J., & Hoffman, D. (2008). "Knowledge society discourse and higher education". *Higher Education*, 56(3), 265-285.

4   Often there has been a restrictive interpretation of

5   Notice this definition by Gamble and Blackwell (2001), "knowledge is a fluid mix of framed experience, values, contextual information, expert insight, and grounded intuition that provides an environment and framework for evaluating and incorporating new experiences and information. It originates and is applied in the mind of the knowers. In organizations it often becomes embedded not only in documents or repositories, but also in organizational routines, practices and norms."

6   The term 'knowledges' rather than 'knowledge' is justified since, as Mackenzie (2006) argues, "knowledge is an engine not a camera", one can only speak in, first, different forms of knowledge and, second in knowledges because these relate to people's understandings of time and temporal processes. These processes, in turn, are not just a matter of application and/ or directionality of critical knowledge, but also a matter of accuracy and power of our models and of ourselves. Moreover, regarding the knowledge-creation metaphor, one may link works like Bereiter's knowledge building (2002), Engeström's expansive learning (1987) and Nonaka & Takeuchi's organizational knowledge creation (Nonaka & Nishiguchi, 1995). Finally, knowledge gets unfolded, read, created and applied by those of us not so sure about reality or about which accounts of it we should trust and act upon.

7   According to Sir Ken Robinson (1999), HE reforms for the future are being drawn with means, tools and minds from the past: cultural age of Enlightenment, industrial revolution, deductive reasoning, "academic ability". Robinson argues that "academic ability" has played a major role in excluding individuals, mainly because it has debarred

and still excludes ways of knowing and of creativity. This "academic ability" is carried out as universities still privilege the orthodoxy by means of the relations among actors. Power is obviously what is at stake in this setting.

8   Freeman and Sturdy (2014) suggest a useful differentiation between the phases of knowledge. These phases are embodied, encoded and enacted. Embodied knowledge is the knowledge held by human actors, mobilized and enacted by them as they go about their work. This includes facts, theories and everything that structures our experience, thoughts, actions and interaction. This kind of knowledge often serves as a marker of social position and status; if acknowledged or accredited by others, it is a source of authority. Encoded knowledge is the one that is embodied or inscribed not in actors, but in artifacts (e.g.: texts, maps, databases, etc). It also encompasses both factual knowledge and know-how. This type of knowledge gives a degree of fixity to knowledge that can help to respond to the variations that arise from the fallibility of human memory or the vagaries of usage. Encoded knowledge serves in effect as a fixed point of reference, around which human action can be coordinated. And since encoded knowledge is also mobile, it additionally serves as a means of coordinating action at a distance. Finally, enacted knowledge refers to what knowledge does or what we do with it. Knowledge informs action but doesn't determine action. As Freeman puts it, it is only when we put it into action that knowledge acquires meaning. In the absence of action, knowledge -whether embodied or encoded- remains latent: thoughts unspoken, skills unexercised, texts unread and instruments unused signify nothing. As Freeman (2006) explains, 'networks and communities have complementary qualities. Networks

have reach but little reciprocity; they are good at sharing knowledge, but less good at producing (or applying) it. Communities are inevitably limited in their scope of reach, but collaboration and reciprocity are tightened, meaning that new knowledge is quickly propagated' (2014, p.376).

[9] Broadly, social capital is defined as the sum of the actual and potential resources embedded or derived from network relationships of an individual or social unit (Bourdieu, 1985; Coleman, 1988; Portes, 1998; Putnam, 2000; Lin, 1999).

[10] In the whole network approach, the focus is on a set of nodes that serve as the population of the study. Then a small number of ties are systematically measured for each pair of nodes in the population. On the other hand, ego-networks represent an individual's overall pattern of relationships. The focus lies on the embeddedness of single actors in their social environment.

[11] Also called as network sociology.

[12] Direct relationships are critical to knowledge creation as direct ties stimulate the exchange of resources embedded within the relationships (Nahapiet & Ghoshal, 1998).

[13] This work by Blau (1964) is of great interest since he conceptualized social relations in terms of trades and exchanges processes, of reciprocity and imbalance (osmose, if we want to use a biological term).

[14] The authors used the Institute of Scientific Information's "impact factor" to assess knowledge creation represented by a given scientist's publications in a given year.

[15] Phelps et al. observe these bias whenever there are similarities between prior and potential adopters (such as demographic characteristics) which can cause them to form relationships with each other (through a process of homophily or assortative matching) and have similar preferences for adopting the same knowledge artifact, thereby creating a spurious relationship between direct ties and adoption.

[16] In refrence to the work on sociology of absences: Santos, B.S., J.A. Nunes and M.P. Meneses (2007) 'Opening Up the Canon of Knowledge and Recognition of Difference', pp. xix–lxii in B.S. Santos (ed.) *Another Knowledge is Possible*. London: Verso.

[17] Freitag (1995) argues that the research mission of universities has become only institutional research and that lead to the wreckship of universities if these are regarded as tecaching and knowledge institutions. The current model of research in most universities, he claims, induces a fundamental change on the nature of universities. These are no longer social and educational institutions, but only organizations of production and control.

[18] Term depicted from the mathematical principle.

[19] Term depicted from the homonimous novel by Goethe and, then, reused by Weber (1946). It refers to the freedom of the actors with respect to their choices of ultimate values. Affinities are manifold: they may refer to intersectoons of meanings, they may exclude elements of the perceived reality form one another, or there maybe no intersection of those elements resulting in isolated meanings. Weber uses it only three times in "The protestant ethic and the spirit of capitalism", but it appears also in several of his other writings, mainly concerning sociology of religion. Weber does not define it, but based on the weberian use of the notion, we can say that elective affinity is a process through which two cultural forms with certain analogies, intimate kinships or meaning affinities enter in a relationship of reciprocal attraction and influence, mutual selection, active convergence and mutual reinforcement. See, for example, Weber, M. (2004). *L'éthique protestante et l'esprit du capitalisme*. Paris: Gallimard, p. 173.

[20] Structural holes are important to avoid redundancies within networks. This means that networks with more structural holes might be more useful to knowledge creation. Literature says that strong ties with individuals who are more structurally apart are more interesting in terms of access to new knowledge. In an egonetwork, structural holes are the individuals who have many ties in common with the ego, but these ties do not know each other.

[21] The prevailing theory is that large institutions need to standardize and mechanize their processes and practices—creating order and structure—therefore unlocking economies of scale. In regard to universities, the level of fragility or resilience of organizations depends in large amount on the distribution of power among researchers. It is known that peripheral positions mean limited ties and access to new resources, whereas more central positions have better and more opportunities to access other researchers who are willing to exchange information. However, some studies (Brass et al., 2004; Burt, 1992) show that the costs of maintaining a large network are high and not always correspond to more exchange of information. In fact, more central actors usually have heavier networks shaped by existing operational structure and organizational constraints (Brass et al., 2004).

Chapter 4
A Need for New Methodological Communication in Comparative Higher Education Research Projects?

Kristin Lofthus Hope
University of Bergen, Norway

ABSTRACT

Higher education is a versatile field where researchers from many different professions take part within a common interest. Usually higher education is seen as an interdisciplinary field, but is it rather a disciplinary field where different researchers discuss higher education development within an interdisciplinary context? What makes the field interdisciplinary? This chapter studies if and how interdisciplinarity is established and played out in international comparative higher education projects. A good way to study if and how interdisciplinarity is established in HE projects is to study their methodological approaches because researchers from different backgrounds who are trained in a range of methodological approaches work together to complete a specific project aim. The methodological approach in one single case is studied to look into how interdisciplinarity can develop within a higher education international research project.

INTRODUCTION

Higher education (HE) research is an applied field where professionals from different subjects collaborate to enhance the knowledge about higher education systems (Teichler, 2009, Altbach, 2014). There has been considerable transformation within the HE system in general, where at the same time new ways of doing research in international cross national projects and collaborating among academics has emerged (Musselin, 2007). International higher education cooperation projects are often composed of researchers from a variety of social sciences, some from the humanities and perhaps researchers from other scientific disciplines as well. Within the area of higher education research there has been a trend of doing research within larger international comparative projects,

DOI: 10.4018/978-1-4666-7244-4.ch004

which is a fruitful and rewarding change and has been a rather steady development the last 20 years (Teichler, 2014; Kosmützky & Krücken, 2014). In addition, international comparative research is a very good data source, often explorative and could provide unexpected outcomes (Teichler, 1996). Nevertheless, several constraints and methodological problems have become visible as well (Bleiklie, 2014, Reale, 2014). How this influences collaboration between different researchers and research communities is a stimulating question, together with the various implications this has for development within HE.

Within the social sciences there is a tendency to opt for more research collaboration and internationalization of research projects. One implication of this development is the methodological challenges this brings, but at the same time the methodological innovations this can generate. This is also a highly relevant question for higher education research projects. Researchers from different disciplines contribute their perspectives to the field thus creating the interdisciplinarity within. Interdisciplinary research is carried out in a variety of areas conducted at institutes and centres (Klein, 1990, p.47). Weingart (2000, p.26) observed that interdisciplinarity has been "proclaimed, demanded, hailed, and written into funding programs". Interdisciplinarity, transdisciplinarity, and multidisciplinary are buzzwords as well (Klein, 2010). A higher education project is not an interdisciplinary project just because researchers from different subjects work together. This chapter will study if and how interdisciplinarity is established in international comparative higher education projects. A good way to study if and how interdisciplinarity is established in HE projects is to study their methodological approaches because researchers from different background who are trained in a range of methodological approaches work together to complete a specific project aim. Is there a middle ground or a method developed for a particular project within international higher education collaboration projects? Or would the

different researchers refer back to their specific discipline and the methodological norms within their discipline? The methodological approach within the Transforming Universities in Europe (TRUE) project will be discussed as an example of the tendency within HE collaborative projects to mix methods and how interdisciplinarity was dealt with.

Higher education is a versatile field where researchers from many different professions take part with a common interest in the field. Could the field be regarded as an interdisciplinary field, or is it rather a disciplinary field where different researchers discuss higher education development within an interdisciplinary context? The methodological approach in the TRUE project will be discussed as a single case study where an extended field report will be the starting point to study if and how interdisciplinarity can develop within a higher education international cooperation research project. This question will be followed up in the analysis part. Bleiklie (2014) advocates for some of the advantages with comparative research. Increasing the number of units under study will most likely lead to a better starting point for generalization within comparative research. Working in an international comparative project could give a better understanding of the study topic because the participants have to discuss and negotiate their positions. Bleiklie (2014) underscores that one of the greatest challenges is to know what is being compared, but by using more systematic comparative strategies the HE field would benefit. The notions of discipline and interdisciplinarity in regards to higher education research will further be discussed.

INTERDISCIPLINARITY IN HIGHER EDUCATION RESEARCH?

First, it is necessary to define discipline. "The term discipline signifies the tools, methods, procedures, examples, concepts, and theories that account coherently for a set of objects or subjects" (Klein, 1990, p.104). No discipline exists in a vacuum concealed from others, but there are variations in the degree of cooperation between subjects. In a way it is necessary for a discipline to do boundary work to distinguish themselves from other disciplines. One way to do boundary work is self-referential communication where, for example, evaluation of relevance and quality of research is limited to members of the specific discipline (Weingart, 2010, p.8). The higher education field could be seen as a speciality and as a research field below the level of a discipline, but with some of the same characteristics as a discipline with its own journals, conferences, research programs, senior experts etc.[1]

How can one be interdisciplinary when we are trained within a discipline? Klein (1990, p.64) mentions four usual ways to be interdisciplinary in practice: a) to borrow something from another discipline, b) solving problems with help from other disciplines, c) increased consistency of subjects or methods, and d) emergence of an interdiscipline. As there is a need for disciplines at the same time as cross collaboration is essential, it will be important to discuss the role of disciplinary behaviour and structure in interdisciplinary work. To work in an interdisciplinary style would be to integrate different approaches, to collaborate, which could be complex, could provoke critique, but could also contribute to problem solving (Klein, 2010). If the aim is to develop interdisciplinary knowledge or change, what kind of project would this produce? Interdisciplinary knowledge or change is more complex due to the fact that it could be perceived as unfamiliar and exotic thinking, contrary to conventional disciplinary thinking. To develop interdisciplinary knowledge from a collaborative project would demand an extra effort from the participants and perhaps the project aim would be different than for other collaborative projects. To work with an interdisciplinary approach or method in mind can represent an innovation in knowledge production where it may make knowledge more

relevant for the public. Many higher education international collaborative projects would be interdisciplinary due to the fact that researchers from different disciplines work together, but the knowledge produced within the project could be more discipline oriented or not. How is it to work within a collaborative project?

Participating in international comparative research could be perceived as more complex than doing single-country studies due to many factors. Firstly, it is a challenge to be part of the academic profession where conditions and expectations change; secondly, one is expected to collaborate in large international projects (Teichler & Höhle, 2013). One implication of collaborative projects is that the project teams are located in different places, and often it takes more time to coordinate and communicate project details (Hoffmann et al., 2014). To publish results from a joint project could potentially be difficult within the limited project time and also because we come from different disciplines. In addition, one is dependent on committed project members to deliver results and publish from the projects. Collaborative projects are often described both as exhausting but also stimulating (Livingstone, 2003). In order to explore the specificities of international collaborative research projects, we must first ask what is a project method and how can we describe the culture of applying a method within a comparative project?

Methodological Boundary Work?

When conducting cross-national research there is always an uncertainty about the generalizability from one case to the next, and the differences between countries and specific national contexts is something that must be discussed. Often the comparative methodological approach is not very much debated within the project, and as a consequence often projects teams "reinvent the wheel" or repeat the mistakes of others (Livingstone, 2003, p.478). When you report from the project the account of the methodological approach could simply be to justify the steps taken and refer to the tradition within the discipline.

To write about methodology is often to engage with norms about how to do research the "right way": The question asked by the research community would be. Have we done the research in accordance with the rules applied to our field? It is an important question because our credibility as researchers would be judged by our methodology and how we have accomplished the task. Therefore, almost every written piece that accounts for research needs to include a paragraph about how the research has been done in accordance with the norms. Often this account is quite straightforward and rather short, where the story about the project process is portrayed as linear where everything went according to plan. Law (2004, p.41) points to the hinterland of research and argues that there is a need for a new language to talk about methods that would help us to recognize and deal with fluidity, leakages and entanglements in a research project. Perhaps these are the more hidden significances of how we work with method. As discussed in the last section, to participate in international project collaboration could be a rather versatile affair. An aim of this chapter is to uncover some of the more hidden aspects of how we as researchers in HE projects work with data and method. Another important point made by Law (2004) is that method is a product of realities rather than a reflection of them, where only parts of reality will be visible.

Research method is good for doing research, but when things are not as expected, perhaps momentarily undefined or irregular, standard methods are not designed to cope with the unexpected (Law, 2004). The problem is not standard research methods in general, but rather the normativity that is attached to them. Law (2004, p.5) claims that research methods are framed in an understanding that the world is *"a set of fairly specific, determinate, and more or less identifiable processes."* This approach opts for a research method that can take into consideration that the world is more unpredictable and in flux than most of the stories about the research methods social science researchers confess to in their account of the method used in their project.

Our own account of the method applied in a research project can be perceived as an account of "rules and norms for best practice" within our field. Law advocates for a new way to talk about method that can instead help us to recognize and give a way to talk about the barriers and uncertainties that also are a part of the research process but rarely are accounted for (Law, 2004). One of the new notions that Law introduces is method assemblage. Assemblage is to bundle together, or recursive self-assembling, where the elements put together are not fixed in shape. These assemblages are not given beforehand, but rather constructed in part as they are put together. These bundles are not fixed, are not good or bad bundles, they can shift, be tacit, unclear and impure according to Law (2004, p.42).

To research is to do a form of puzzle solving, where realities are produced. When doing research one discovers multiplicity, where different realities overlap and interfere with each other. The relationships between them are messy and complex. *"Judgments about method, instead, need to be made in ways that are specific and local"* (Law, 2004, p.103). When puzzling and doing method assemblages one will craft and enact boundaries between them. Each category will depend on the others, but perhaps the boundaries between them could be more flexible. With the help of the method the researcher reinvents, interprets, bundles and re-bundles what she has observed into a new entity that hopefully expands the understanding of the object under study.

For me, the TRUE project will function as a single case study (Yin, 2003; Stake, 2004) and the field report will contribute to a discussion of how interdisciplinarity was conducted within TRUE. The methodological approach and process in the TRUE project will be discussed and reviewed. It is necessary to underline that this story is my interpretation of how the TRUE project developed, and there can likewise be other valid stories of how the project developed. There are 30 probable other stories which corresponds approximately to the number of TRUE researchers. The aim is to give a fuller picture of how the different steps took place and give some clues of the specific development of this project. To create a story of the TRUE project I decided to create a linear description, meaning that the story starts in 2009 when the project started. However, the story is not linear and we have worked on many different angels throughout the project. So the linearity of the story is created to simplify and be able to bundle the different pieces together, to hopefully be more understandable for the readers.

My own participation in the project will also be part of the data source in addition to minutes from joint meetings, e-mail communications, articles, papers and internal project documents. Qualitative research is by definition subjective, but it is crucial to obtain reliability which can be obtained by consistency of judgments, labelling and/or interpretation where one opens up the "black box" of how the research has been done with the help of more specific accounts of the methodological hinterland. In the following analysis of the TRUE project the aim is to study the methodological approach of the project and discuss the interdisciplinary cooperation within.

THE METHODOLOGICAL APPROACH WITHIN TRUE

TRUE was a HE collaborative research project and addressed the topics of governance and steering in a EuroHESC[2] call for proposals. In total, nine different projects were connected to the TRUE project with researchers from eight different countries participating. The aim of the overall research project was to clarify how steering and governance affect essential organizational characteristics of higher education institutions (HEIs) and in turn how this

affects the differentiation of the European higher education landscape. The countries participating in TRUE were England, France, Germany, Italy, the Netherlands, Norway, Portugal and Switzerland. The overall methodological approach was planned to involve national case studies, case studies of individual HEIs including three different institutions in each country (24 institutions in total), surveys of all the HEIs in the involved countries, an in-depth comparative analysis of national policies and instruments (both interviews and document analysis) and a collection of a set of data for a basic characterization of HEIs.

The project had a rather ambitious and wide approach to the object of study which had been developed by the nine project leaders who are senior experts within the higher education field. These nine experts come from different disciplines but dominantly political science, political administration, and sociology. If one reads the project description, the field of interest is the development of higher education system at the European level by studying changes in governance and organisation within specific countries and institutions.[3] The inspiration to do this project - or rather the nine different projects that constitute TRUE - could be read as coming from a mutual interest in higher education institutional development, where each project has their distinctive interpretation of the field and relevant concepts. The overall concepts and notions could be read as coming from political administration, organization studies, political science and sociology.

The project was led by three of the responsible principal investigators from three of the projects, and they met regularly to discuss the progress of the project. In addition the whole project group met six times (Bergen 2009, Rome 2010, Lugano 2010, Porto 2011, Rome 2012, Ranco 2013) during the project period from the kick-off meeting in 2009 until 2013. In addition, project members have met during conferences and contributed to the academic discussion through conference participation, articles and book chapters. The plan as discussed in the project application outline was to initially do the national case studies synthesis (8 case studies), followed by a synthesis report on national case studies, institutional case studies (24 case studies), a synthesis report on institutional case studies, a questionnaire report and analysis. However, the actual data collection in the TRUE project differs from the project application, and has been done in a somewhat different order than planned. The aim is not to criticize those changes, but rather underscore that this is a rather normal development for projects. To obtain a research project one has to promise to do excellent research with a clear cut research design. The day to day research realities are much messier where things not always go according to plan.

The first data collection was planned to be an institutional case study based on a template with eight different topics to be covered. The topics were funding, organizational external relationships, autonomy and institutional governance, academic careers and management of academic work, national policy processes, European level policy, governing instruments, and higher education landscape. These topics were the main themes for the study and these first data collecting attempts were a starting point for the first articles published in a special issue of Higher Education (2013, 65:1).

One of the first data colleting operations was to answer a questionnaire from the team based in the Netherlands about formal autonomy of public universities in the eight countries. Each TRUE country team consisting of higher education researchers completed the questionnaire during the autumn of 2010. The questionnaire was adapted from the taxonomy developed by Verhoest et al. (2004), but the dimensions and indicators were modified to fit the higher education field (Enders et al., 2013). They understand the autonomy concept as relative, multi-dimensional and situational. The written questionnaire contained questions that were all directly related to the indicators. Based on the answers the Netherlands project team

made categories that indicated a scale ranging from 'no university autonomy' to 'full university autonomy'. These scales were used to calculate sub-index scores for each of the seven dimensions that the formal autonomy was measured against. This study can be used together with the data from the survey to discuss developments within higher education systems. Autonomy is a concept from the public administration field employed in the specific higher education area. Therefore this is predominantly a discipline specific study; although the autonomy concept could be understood also as a concept that travels and develops (Bleiklie, 2014). The concepts developed and used within TRUE have been discussed at joint meetings, but with an under communicated relationship to the public administration field.

During the first half year of the project there was an important project leader meeting in Schiphol where the project plan was revised (summer of 2010). After a discussion about the feasibility of the empirical part due to length of the questionnaires and the number of instruments for data gathering that ideally should be used, it was concluded that the project had to be tighter. One important step was to streamline the methods used in the project by doing a survey before a qualitative data collection, in addition to better coordination of the project. For example, it was important that only one interview protocol and one questionnaire per university level were to be used. As a first step to develop the survey, 24 institutional cases were selected (three in each of the eight countries). Next, one institution in every country was selected for qualitative in-depth investigation. During the preparation of the study each project prepared institutional overviews with information about the 26 (five in total from Switzerland) institutions.

Starting to develop the survey during the autumn of 2010 was not a straightforward process. The different project teams had questions related to their own project. Many suggestions were made, and these were presented and discussed at the Lugano project meeting in October 2010. The first attempts were quite chaotic as the surveys were partially overlapping, consisting of questions which were unique to the specific organizational level, questions which applied to more than one organizational level and questions which were addressed to all 5 organizational levels. To master this confusing situation a senior project manager took responsibility to develop the questionnaires further. For example, one area was to cut down on questions and manage overlaps, streamline how the questions were asked, and formulate instructional texts for each section. It was a process that continued over some months to edit the questionnaires and pre-test them. This was a rather labour intensive process, where many took part to develop and improve the content while the three project leaders monitored the process closely. In total there were five separate on-line surveys where the respondents entered their answers directly on-line. In total, five questionnaires (directed to rector, central administrator, middle management, senate members and board members) were developed in which the selected topics were covered.

Almost every country team translated the questionnaires from English to their own language, but without further customization of the national version than a national-language interface of the same survey. Meaning that only the interface was different, but the survey was the same and all the results were entered into an integrated dataset. During the preparation of the survey it was agreed that the TRUE questionnaires were based on a general understanding of the functions inside universities. This meant that the general criterion to identify respondents was the functions rather than the label of function or organizational unit. However, national teams had to manage differences and set up lists over contact persons and handle the communication with the universities involved in the survey. In total 26 higher education institutions took part in the survey, and all in all, the response rate was rather good. The data was collected at two specified periods between May and July 2011 and in November and December 2011.

The project leaders of the different teams took and had much responsibility for the survey process, but with good help from the project members. The results came quickly, and have been integrated into one SPSS file where all institutional-level surveys were united in a single survey (which can be customized). In addition there is an agreement between the different projects that all projects who have contributed to the survey can exploit the whole dataset for their specific research topics. Furthermore, each project team can exploit its own national-level data.

There has been an attempt to publish one article from the survey in which all of the project members took part. The article discusses if the European universities could be understood as complete organizations and is published in the journal "Public Management Review" (Seeber et al., 2014). Identity, hierarchy and rationality are the three different dimensions that have been studied using the survey material. Our efforts have been evaluated to fit into a journal that addresses the public administration discipline.

Comparative questionnaire surveys are a challenge with regard to many factors, for example the high level of cooperation and labour that is needed for a successful outcome. Positive effects from such studies are that they are highly standardized and can give rich information (Reale, 2014). It is often a hard and frustrating process to get everyone in a large cross national project to agree on common suggestions and develop a general questionnaire. At the early stage of the project I was not aware of how important the survey development process was for the project as a whole. In addition, the theoretical approach developed for the project and the experience the senior researchers introduced to the project were extremely important for the outcome. The choices made for the survey cannot be reversed when the survey is launched, and the early effort that all the project teams contributed has perhaps influenced the latter stages of the project. More about this later; first the next data collection process and method will be discussed.

A qualitative case study with interviews at different institutional levels was planned from the beginning of the project. Most of the interview data collection started after the survey was completed. The data collection was concentrated around doing institutional case studies and a policy level study was supposed to follow. The first step was the institutional case study, and there was a discussion among the project members on the topics to be covered starting in 2011. For the case study a common list of topics for the interview guides were developed step by step. The different project teams contributed their opinions to the discussion, and as with the survey development, some senior researchers took the responsibility to further develop the guidelines.

First and foremost, the case study was a study of traditional research universities with a focus on sciences and humanities or social sciences departments. Likewise, as with the survey, the selected respondents were rectors, boards, central administrators, middle management, and academics in management positions. The estimated necessary number of interviews was about 20 in each country. National teams could decide on how many interviews were needed in their country, but had to weigh it against other data sources. The interviews were taped if possible, and a report or summary of the interview was then written in English. This was agreed upon during the Porto project meeting (autumn of 2011). There was also a brief discussion during the Porto meeting on how to handle the perceived vast amount of data from the planned interviews. The French project advocated for a method that could help the project to be more to the point during the data handling process. This method involves writing a country report from each case study where the interview data have been interpreted and presented in an internal report the project called a monograph. It was also promoted as a first development in the analysing process of the interview data. Each project was also to deliver an excel overview of the interviews. On the excel sheet from each country there was an anonymised overview of the persons interviewed and a very short summary from each thematic subject.

Even though the project had an agenda and clear timeline, it took time to collect the qualitative data and to write up the monographs afterwards which delayed the process. It was the French team that led the development of the monograph where they started to write their account from the institutional case interviews. The first draft was briefly discussed in August 2012, and the project group decided to improve this further and work with this concept. It appeared as a rather easy way of handling the data, and some of the project members had worked with this approach before, mostly coming from qualitative research within sociology and political science. The idea was to present the data in a document in which the interview data together with contextual data were presented and discussed to give an overall impression of the institutions in relations to the topics for the project. At the same time, since TRUE is an international project, some national specificities that are particular for the country were also discussed alongside the specific institutional case data to give a broader understanding. Nevertheless, we did not develop a clear list of topics and this was a drawback since almost every project team developed their own approach when writing the monograph. Each country team had the responsibility to describe the interview data in the monograph, but when we compared the six monographs they were not that coherent. Therefore starting to analyse the data further and using them is somewhat challenging. The team from England decided to pull themselves out of this part of the project and the Swiss national monograph has been delayed.

The institutional case monographs with their 20 to 35 pages are a solid documentation of the case studies, but it is not a readymade analysis product so it takes effort to process and use the data for your own research project. Most of the monographs were distributed during spring of

2013. The "excel sheet" as described previously was also an approach meant to help analyse or systematise the vast amount of data, but it turned out to be difficult to read and work with it because it only gives an overview and not a fuller picture.

In addition interview guides were developed to interview a selection of respondents connected to higher education policy progress. The list of about 10 respondents were representatives from relevant stakeholders such as parliament, minister, civil servant, funding agencies, evaluation agencies, association of universities, and unions. In addition, these interviews were connected with the institutional level interviews and the survey, where there were policy questions for rectors/presidents, central administrators and other influential academic leaders. As for the institutional case study, the number of respondents ought to be weighed against other data sources and settled by national teams for each case in collaboration with the policy study responsible in the project. Written interview reports or monographs were supposed to be written in English by each national team. The data handling was, as in the monograph from the institutional case study, written into a report called the policy study template which describes the higher education sector. The aim was to provide key information based on available data of the politico-administrative systems and policy sectors in the TRUE countries. In addition a theoretically guided template was presented with key information about the structural characteristics of the political systems within the TRUE countries (internal report by Michelsen, 2013). This template was developed to function as a basis for a comparative analysis of higher education policies in the eight TRUE countries, and the theoretical point of departure is the public administration tradition.

Five of the eight TRUE countries have delivered the policy study template (Italy, England, Portugal, Norway, and the Netherlands). The topics that were covered were supranational policies (EU, OECD) where the aim was to trace their influence on national policies, and to get an overview of structural characteristics of national political administrative systems. In addition, the actors, policy processes and their outcomes including access, autonomy, regulation, instruments, funding and evaluation were presented. These policy study templates were delivered between late autumn of 2012 and June of 2013.

Reale (2014) underscores that problems can influence the robustness of comparative work, especially in relation to interpretation of empirical results and the outcome of observations. This is especially apparent in the TRUE project where an ambitious project description and goals for the project have led to a solid database with a huge collection of data, although there is a challenge to exploit everything within a rather limited time frame. Since not all of the data has been delivered, some of the project results will be delayed. For example, the late coming of the policy study has been a hindrance for the policy study projects. The knowledge to be drawn from the project is that the data collection that you start with will perhaps have more strength to it. Starting up a new project is exiting and more effort is put into it at the beginning, and therefore perhaps it is better to concentrate the data collection period at the start of a project. In the TRUE project we collected data through the whole project period. Starting out with a huge survey and thereafter an institutional case study has affected the later policy case study.

Furthermore, Reale (2014) argues that in a quantitative study there has to be an extremely high degree of consensus to finalize and get a commonly accepted questionnaire. I will argue that within a comparative project where both survey and a qualitative method are used it is likewise important to work to get consensus within the work group about the project progress and the timeframe for the project. If both surveys and interview data are to be used it is important that one acknowledge that both methods take time to complete and analyse. There will always be some differences within a project group, both regarding professional opinions and vision for the project, regardless of methodological choices. It is important within a project context that the members can negotiate and discuss the project and the process. Theories, methods and facts that influence the start of the project can be very influential on the project as a whole, as seen in the TRUE project.

Working in international teams can bring other problems such as cooperation issues, misunderstandings, and problems with integrating different views, cognitive systems, different ideas, different languages and meanings (Livingstone, 2003). To really create an interdisciplinary project where the project develops a very coherent outcome takes a long time and the project members need to work tightly to create a common reference frame. The TRUE project had a fairly common understanding of the higher institutional framework that made it easier to work together for a common project goal. However, the project did not develop a new reference frame or a coherent outcome so the interdisciplinarity within the project has room for improvement. Especially the autonomy template, the survey and the policy study template had a reference frame coming from the policy administration discipline. One aim of the project has been to develop a better understanding of the HE field, but at the same time enhance the knowledge within the disciplinary traditions we come from.

It has strengthened the project that we have both qualitative and quantitative data with the possibility to triangulate data to more fully explain our research questions. Using mixed method is a key challenge in HE comparative research (Burke, et al., 2004; Creswell, 2013; Ivankova et al., 2006; Creswell & Plano-Clark, 2011:XIX; Reale, 2014). The mixed method approach was not an integrated part of how the TRUE project thought about method, but the project members have the possibility to use this approach when working with the collected material and this can improve the outcome. If the project had explicitly aimed for a mixed method approach from the start this could have strengthened the project and the outcome.

SOLUTIONS AND RECOMMENDATIONS

To sum up some of the thoughts from analysing our methodological approach in the TRUE project I will present some solutions and recommendations. Comparative projects are complicated and take a lot of time to coordinate. Often they last longer than the foreseen project period, perhaps up to twice the predicted time (Teichler, 2013; Reale, 2014). Another time-consuming activity is gaining access to potential participants and getting them to contribute to surveys or qualitative interviews. Coordination of the various project members and their contribution and planning of the data collection could potentially be a quite complex exercise for the project leaders. To succeed one is dependent on very committed project members and financial backing of the projects. It takes time also to develop a conceptual and contextual understanding of the comparative project, and this could be a challenge when the allocated project time is over but there is still work that one would like to finish. The time constraint could hinder the process of developing a shared understanding of concepts and the method in use.

One recommendation to overcome the problem of a limited time frame for HE comparative projects is to opt for longer project periods, where the project members commit themselves to contribute during all the project phases within the agreed timeframe. A research project will benefit from having a mixed experienced group working together from each country. In spite of this, it is important that different experience levels can be utilised and that the project members learn from each other. Another recommendation is to opt for more involvement from senior researchers to do quality checking of the documents delivered to the project.

A lesson learned from the TRUE project is to navigate better when doing case studies, and perhaps do all the data collection during the first trimester of a project. It has especially been a challenge to work with the qualitative data from the project due to the thematic variation within the monographs. The method and the methodological approach in the project could have been discussed more to develop a better utilisation of the data, together with a better understanding of the concepts and project aims. A lesson is that interdisciplinary projects need to discuss how method can function in the project and perhaps develop a better and more common understanding of the concepts applied.

FUTURE RESEARCH DIRECTIONS

National and cultural specific terms, values and concepts are always difficult to incorporate in a comparative study, or are perhaps over-explained because one is afraid of leaving out important information (Kogan & Bleiklie, 2006; Teichler, 2014). It is also a potential pitfall to collect too much information, or to choose too large or massive data collection phases without really regarding the conceptual framework for the project as a whole because different interests within the project ask for more.

Teichler (2013) underscores that in almost all projects there can be difficulty in reaching compromises on the joint and parallel activities needed. In a collaborative project the people involved can have very different backgrounds, come from different disciplines, and differ when it comes to values, communication and working styles for example. This can lead to delays due to inefficient collaboration. As a consequence most projects have their most intensive data analysis and interpretation of findings after the funding of the project is over. So in a very vital stage of a project, often smaller groups are involved where lesser resources and manpower can affect the

outcome of the projects. Then again, one project often generates follow-on studies or new projects, where researchers move between collaboration projects (Hoffman, 2009).

There is a need to look more closely at how international HE projects conduct their research process. There is a need to further develop methodological communication that can explore the data collecting process. Today much of what is written about the data collection and analysing process is covered in a convenient method language to assure the public that the research has been done in a habitual manner. There is also a need to look into how the projects and results are influenced by our disciplines, in addition to national and cultural differences.

CONCLUSION

The overall subject in this chapter has been if and how interdisciplinarity is established and played out in international comparative higher education projects. The methodological approaches in the TRUE project have been discussed as an example of an interdisciplinary project. The question asked was, is there a middle ground or a method developed for a particular project within international higher education collaboration projects? Or would the different researchers refer back to their specific discipline and the methodological norms within their discipline? How have interdisciplinarity been played out within the TRUE project? What became apparent in the TRUE project was that researchers from different disciplines worked together with a specific interest in the HE field, but took their concepts and notions from their disciplinary field to develop both the understanding about higher education systems as well as to broaden the knowledge within their discipline.

The data collected in comparative research is often large-scale survey data or qualitative case studies (see Teichler et al., 2013; Kehm & Teichler, 2013; Teichler & Höhle, 2013; Paradise et al., 2009). The data collection process is often described as a rather straight forward process where the method is known to the project members and the research questions developed. The written account of the projects where the methodological approach is laid out is not very elaborated in any of the books from the comparative projects referred to above.[4] For example, there is little reporting on unexpected methodological problems, project or collaboration problems. The approaches used in these projects are not reported as being new or innovative, but rather as something that is done in accordance with the norms within the subject, something Law (2004) criticizes.

It is not unusual that complex comparative research projects face substantial problems (Livingstone, 2003). A key issue is therefore to discuss all the stages in the project and make sure that there is an open conversation between the members regarding the way forward. To streamline the research process and be able to agree and get a commitment regarding the conceptual and empirical pathway is important when leading a large comparative project, and encourages the project members to deliver according to the agreed time schedule. However, communicating methodology by starting a conversation where the methodological approach in your international higher education project is the topic that could improve the project outcome. Especially through thorough and continuous discussions of what the project concepts and notions would mean, in addition to discussing what implications this has for our methodological way forward.

Kosmützky and Nokkala (2013) underline that there could be different disciplinary methodological cultures and traditions within a project, but there could also be variations regarding understanding of a method within the same discipline in different national contexts. Such hindering could potentially limit the projects when trying to develop a common project understanding. Perhaps it is even more important to be reflective

regarding the whole research process; when we develop a common research project, during data collection, analysing and writing up the results. Especially in international comparative higher education research, it is even more important to be reflective regarding how we as researchers are influenced by the context we are present in when we analyse and interpret the international data. In addition we need more data on the methodological process within the international comparative projects to be able to develop a better method of communication. The aim must be to improve the robustness of the method and the possibility of using measures for comparison within HE. Further, the target must be to develop better and more advanced communication about our methods to explore our research questions in an even better way.

REFERENCES

Bleiklie, I. (2013). Comparing university organizations across boundaries. *Higher Education, 67*(4), 381–391. doi:10.1007/s10734-013-9683-z

Bleiklie, I., & Kogan, M. (2006). Comparison and theories. In M. Kogan & M. Bauer (Eds.), *Transforming higher education: A comparative study* (2nd ed., pp. 3–22). Dordrecht, The Netherlands: Springer.

Burke-Johnson, R., & Onwuegbuzie, A. J. (2004). Mixed methods research: A research paradigm whose time has come. *Educational Researcher, 33*(14), 14–26. doi:10.3102/0013189X033007014

Creswell, J. W. (2013). *Research design: Qualitative, quantitative, and mixed methods approaches* (2nd ed.). Thousand Oaks, CA: Sage Publications.

Creswell, J. W., & Plano-Clark, V. L. (2011). *Designing and conducting mixed methods research*. Los Angeles, CA: Sage Publications.

Enders, J., de Boer, H., & Weyer, E. (2013). Regulatory autonomy and performance: The reform of higher education re-visited. *Higher Education, 65*(1), 5–23. doi:10.1007/s10734-012-9578-4

Hoffman, D. (2009). Changing academic mobility patterns and international migration—what will academic mobility mean in the 21st century? *Journal of Studies in International Education, 13*(3), 347–364. doi:10.1177/1028315308321374

Hoffman, D. M., Blasi, B., Culum, B., Dragsic, Z., Ewen, A., & Horta, H. et al. (2014). The methodological illumination of a blind spot: Information and communication technology and international research team dynamics in a higher education research program. *Higher Education, 67*(4), 473–495. doi:10.1007/s10734-013-9692-y

Ivankova, N. V., Creswell, J. W., & Stick, S. L. (2006). Using mixed-methods sequential explanatory design: From theory to practice. *Field Methods, 18*(1), 3–20. doi:10.1177/1525822X05282260

Kehm, B. M., & Teichler, U. (2013). *The academic profession in Europe: New tasks and new challenges.* Dordrecht, The Netherlands: Springer. doi:10.1007/978-94-007-4614-5

Klein, J. T. (1990). *Interdisciplinarity: History, theory, and practice.* Detroit: Wayne State University Press.

Klein, J. T. (2010). *Creating interdisciplinary campus cultures: A model for strength and sustainability.* Hoboken, NJ: Jossey-Bass.

Klein, J. T. (2010). A taxonomy of interdisciplinarity. In R. Frodeman, J. T. Klein, & C. Mitcham (Eds.), *The Oxford handbook of interdisciplinarity* (pp. 15–30). New York: Oxford University Press.

Kosmützky, A., & Krücken, G. (2014). Growth or steady state? A bibliometric focus on international comparative higher education research. *Higher Education, 67*(4), 457–472. doi:10.1007/s10734-013-9694-9

Kosmützky, A., & Nokkala, T. (2014). Challenges and trends in comparative higher education: An editorial. *Higher Education, 67*(4), 369–380. doi:10.1007/s10734-013-9693-x

Law, J. (2004). *After method: Mess in social science research.* London: Routledge.

Livingstone, S. (2003). On the challenges of cross-national comparative media research. *European Journal of Communication, 18*(4), 477–500. doi:10.1177/0267323103184003

MacDonald, K., & Ritzer, G. (1988). The sociology of the professions: Dead or alive? *Work and Occupations, 15*(3), 251–272. doi:10.1177/0730888488015003001

Marcus, G. E. (1998). *Ethnography through thick and thin.* Princeton, NJ: Princeton University Press.

Musselin, C. (2007). Are universities specific organisations? In G. Krücken, A. Kosmützky, & M. Torka (Eds.), *Towards a multiversity? Universities between global trends and national traditions* (pp. 63–84). Bielefeld, Germany: Transcript Verlag.

Paradise, C., Reale, E., Bleiklie, I., & Ferlie, E. (Eds.). (2009). *University governance: Western European comparative perspectives.* Dordrecht, The Netherlands: Springer.

Reale, E. (2014). Challenges in higher education research: The use of quantitative tools in comparative analyses. *Higher Education, 67*(4), 409–422. doi:10.1007/s10734-013-9680-2

Seeber, M., Lepori, B., Montauti, M., Enders, J., de Boer, H., & Weyer, E. et al. (2014). European universities as complete organizations? Understanding identity, hierarchy and rationality in public organizations. *Public Management Review* doi:. 10.1080/14719037.2014.943268

Stake, R. E. (2004). *The art of case study research.* Thousand Oaks, CA: SAGE.

Teichler, U. (1996). Comparative higher education: Potentials and limits. *Higher Education, 32*(4), 431–465. doi:10.1007/BF00133257

Teichler, U. (2009). *Higher education and the world of work: Conseptual frameworks, comparative perspectives, empirical findings*. Rotterdam, The Netherlands: Sense Publishers.

Teichler, U. (2014). Opportunities and problems of comparative higher education research: The daily life of research. *Higher Education, 67*(4), 393–408. doi:10.1007/s10734-013-9682-0

Teichler, U., Arimoto, A., & Cummings, W. K. (2013). *The changing academic profession: Major findings of a comparative survey*. Dordrecht, The Netherlands: Springer. doi:10.1007/978-94-007-6155-1

Teichler, U., & Höhle, E. A. (2013). The academic profession in 12 European countries – The approach of the comparative study. In U. Teichler & E. A. Höhle (Eds.), *The work situation of the academic profession in Europe: Findings of a survey in twelve countries* (pp. 1–11). Dordrecht, The Netherlands: Springer. doi:10.1007/978-94-007-5977-0_1

Verhoest, K. B., Guy-Peters, B., Bouckaert, G., & Verschuere, B. (2004). The study of organisational autonomy: A conceptual review. *Public Administration and Development, 24*(2), 101–118. doi:10.1002/pad.316

Weingart, P. (2000). Interdisciplinarity: The paradoxical discourse. In P. Weingart & N. Stehr (Eds.), *Practising interdisciplinarity* (pp. 25–41). Toronto, Canada: University of Toronto Press Incorporated.

Weingart, P. (2010). A short history of knowledge formations. In R. Frodeman, J. T. Klein, & C. Mitcham (Eds.), *The Oxford handbook of interdisciplinarity* (pp. 3–14). New York: Oxford University Press.

Yin, R. K. (2003). *Case study research, design and methods*. Thousand Oaks, CA: SAGE.

KEY TERMS AND DEFINITIONS

Communicating Methodology: To start a conversation where the topic is the methodological approach in your international higher education project.

Higher Education Research Project: A project that studies different developments of the higher education systems or field.

Interdisciplinarity: To combine and borrow methods, language, terms, or other substantial elements from another discipline with the aim to develop a new concept or perspective.

International Cooperation Project: A project where different researchers from various countries cooperate to fulfil a specific project aim and research project.

Methodological Approach: To systematically collect data about the research topic.

Methodological Boundary: To account for how one has done the research in accordance to the discipline norms, traditions and rules.

Mixed Method: Both qualitative and quantitative data has been collected with the possibility to triangulate data to more fully explain the research questions.

ENDNOTES

[1] It is an important difference between the US and Europe when it comes to higher education as a research field. In Europe the students take a PhD within a discipline like sociology, public administration, or political science. Within the US higher education is a sub-discipline of education.

2   EuroHESC ''Higher Education and Social change'' by the European Science Foundation (ESF) (2009–2012).Link:http://www.esf.org/coordinating-research/eurocores/completed-programmes/eurohesc.html (15.08.2014)

3   http://www.esf.org/coordinating-research/eurocores/completed-programmes/euro-hesc/projects.html (15.08.2014)

4   The Changing Academic Profession (CAP) study, "The Academic Profession in Europe: Responses to Societal Challenges" (EUROAC), and The Steering UNiversities (SUN) projects.

Chapter 5
Quality of Doctoral Research Supervision:
Contributions of an Integrative and Fluid Framework to Evaluate and Monitor the Process

Ana Vitoria Baptista
University of Aveiro, Portugal

ABSTRACT

With this chapter, the authors describe (1) the international, Portuguese, and institutional challenges relating to the quality of doctoral research supervision and (2) systematize the research-based frameworks that exist in the international literature worldwide in what concerns this topic. This is followed by a brief presentation of the research methodology adopted to shed light on the process taken to design an integrative and fluid framework that the authors propose on the quality of doctoral research supervision. Additionally, links are established regarding the international literature and tendencies approached on the theoretical section of this chapter. Finally, the authors reflect on the concerns surrounding the pertinence of the framework that arose from the research to evaluate and monitor the doctoral supervisory process.

INTRODUCTION

Much research has explored the characteristics of 'effective' supervision, and much has focused on collecting information about postgraduate research students' positive and negative experiences that can inform guidelines about supervision, and improve supervisory arrangements and practices. (Petersen, 2007, p.476)

The agenda that may be found within international Higher Education (HE) institutions and other organizations reveals a growing concern about the impact of research at postgraduate level, where doctoral studies are gathering a greater significance and value. The international and European context demonstrates the existence of an increasing number and a greater diversity of research students enrolling in postgraduate studies, particularly in Doctoral Programmes,

DOI: 10.4018/978-1-4666-7244-4.ch005

where previous doctoral training was not sufficiently considered before the 'massification' phase, namely in the case of Portugal. In fact, in Portugal, the question of massification regarding doctoral degree was not considered so pertinent until a few years ago due to several factors: (1) the growing rate of unemployment among young graduates led them to pursue the 2nd and the 3rd cycles of Bologna consecutively, even if they were not intrinsically motivated to pursue postgraduate degrees; (2) as a consequence, the ratio of postgraduate students *per* supervisors increased immensely, with the latter not being sufficiently prepared for this situation and the institution not providing alternative solutions; and (3) the Bologna Process in Portugal, because it added compulsory disciplines to the research-based PhD and led to a growing discussion regarding training issues at PhD level, something that was not previously discussed.

Consequently, the enhancement of quality at doctoral level is considered to be a pertinent subject to most countries and HE institutions around the world. As such, it is urgent to engage in further public reflection and discussions, as well as to carry out more research on the conceptions that doctoral students and supervisors have on what constitutes the quality of the supervisory process, particularly considering their own responsibilities and roles (Connel, 1985; Cullen et al., 1994; Grant & Graham, 1999; Grant, 1999, 2001, 2005; Kandlbinder & Peseta, 2006; Manathunga & Goozée, 2007; Park, 2005, 2007, 2008; Pearson & Brew, 2002). This is a topic that deserves a close attention from academia in general, and from researchers concerned with this subject in particular.

But, before approaching the quality of doctoral supervision, it seems essential to contextualize this phenomenon within a broader setting. There are many challenges with which HE institutions are struggling. We may systematize the following factors that, at a greater or a lesser extent, are influencing doctoral supervision and research.

From our perspective, each of the following elements may not be considered isolated; they are inter-related and constitute challenges through which the quality of doctoral supervision ought to be reflected on. These include:

- Pressures from external stakeholders over the HE sector (Hodson & Thomas, 2003; UK Council for Graduate Education, 1996);
- Massification at doctoral level, and simultaneously doctoral students with more diverse experiences and characteristics (Harman, 2003; Henard & Leprince-Ringuet, 2008; Taylor, 2009);
- Changes in the research environment at HE institutions, as well as in the conception of research and academic work, namely due to: evaluation, financing, time to complete and completion rates of research projects, the existence of a higher number of inter and trans-disciplinary research, and cross-fertilization between disciplines (Bissett, 2009; Brew, 2001, 2007; Coaldrake & Stedman, 1999; Enders, 2005);
- The emergence of different kinds of doctorates (Park, 2005, 2007), although these may be legally systematized or not;
- Focus on the evaluation of experiences of doctoral students (both training undertaken and research) (Bennet & Turner, 2012; Hodsdon & Buckley, 2011; Park, 2008);
- Rising in the development of training programmes directed to doctoral supervisors (Brew & Peseta, 2004; Pearson & Kayrooz, 2004; Reid & Marshall, 2009);
- Intensification of worldwide discussions and reflections on supervisory experiences and problems, and on the identification of doctoral students and supervisors' competences (Bills, 2004; Cullen et al., 1994; Felton, 2008; Petersen, 2007; Soothill, 2006).

These factors influence the institutional culture (Hodson & Thomas, 2003) and also its dynamics and policies, emphasizing that there are great demands towards doctoral supervision and research. Park (2007), for instance, calls them "drivers of change" (p.13), essential to be considered when we try to answer the following generic questions: (1) what is the value and purpose of a doctorate in today's world?, and (2) is doctoral education taking into consideration all those aspects and other variables which are naturally emerging and complicating this context?

It is important to understand and conceptualize the quality of doctoral research supervision, since the doctorate is considered not only a landmark in the development of highly skilled professionals to work inside and outside academia, but also a product that will give the economy, society and culture important outputs. This latter idea highlights that the doctorate is of great importance to the development of socially relevant research. Thus, doctoral studies and research are rooted in ideals such as originality, creativity and innovation, extending what can be called 'boundaries of quality' in terms of the supervisory and research processes.

Despite the challenge of developing research in this subject (quality of doctoral research supervision), due to the interconnection between so many variables and contextual factors, the author developed a research project at a Portuguese HE institution (the University of Aveiro) with the major objective of designing a framework on the quality of doctoral research supervision. The research project is broader than the description it is made in the chapter. Consequently, within this chapter, the author aims to answer the following 'practical' questions:

- What kind of design a framework on the quality of doctoral research supervision may have?
- What elements will constitute that framework?

- How will those elements be embedded with each other and with the framework?

To address them, we will contextualize the Portuguese case and synthesize what can be found in the international literature, since it establishes a close link to our proposal of integrative and fluid framework on doctoral supervisory quality. Throughout this chapter, the reader will be invited to make the 'journey' of answering those questions with the author. Therefore, we will be unveiling the definition of these concepts, such as 'integrative', 'fluid' and 'framework'.

It must be stressed that, even though the study was developed at a specific Portuguese HE institution, the conclusions the author will present in this chapter may speak not only to the whole Portuguese HE setting, but also to other international contexts, due to the supra-institutional and supra-national character and concerns of this issue. Therefore, this study may add a valid contribution to a continuous discussion and conceptualization about doctoral supervisory quality. This will be visible when making a link between the literature review and the framework that is proposed by the author.

In this chapter we will not only briefly describe the Portuguese and institutional context on this subject, but will also systematize the research-based frameworks that exist in the international literature. We will then present the methodology followed in our research project and will present our integrative and fluid framework on the quality of doctoral research supervision. At the end of the chapter, we will reflect on the pertinence of the framework that arose from our research to evaluate and monitor the supervisory process.

Some Issues of Concern: Contextualizing the Portuguese Case

There is a high volume of theoretical and empirical studies about pedagogic supervision in Portugal (Alarcão, 1996, 2001; Alarcão & Roldão, 2008; Alarcão & Tavares, 2003; Sá-Chaves, 2007; Vieira,

1993; Vieira et al., 2006). Broadly speaking, the pedagogical supervision has its context in schools and is a process and a relationship established between an experienced teacher and a novice teacher (usually a teacher trainee). However, when focusing on research supervision there is a lack of theoretical and empirical studies about this subject. Nevertheless, the Portuguese academic community is starting to be somewhat more aware of the growing number and diversity of students enrolling in postgraduate studies in general, and Doctoral Programmes in particular. Within some scientific domains (for instance, in Education and Social Sciences), concerns are increasing, due to the higher demand from the same number of supervisors to support a growing number of students entering Doctoral Programmes, who are showing (many of them) a lack or a set of low research competences and skills.

The Portuguese legal background demonstrates a gap in the definition of responsibilities and roles that are expected from the doctoral student and supervisor. Taking into consideration the national legal framework that regulates the award of Master's and Doctoral degrees - the Law n. 216/92, 13th October – one may conclude that it only gives a broad 'definition' of the doctoral degree: "innovative and original contribution to the progress of knowledge, a high cultural level within a certain knowledge domain and the competence to carry out independent scientific work" (chapter III, art 17, n.1). This must be considered a pertinent question to take into account, because there are also no definitions of what the roles and responsibilities from doctoral student and supervisor should be nor at institutional or disciplinary levels. While we can find, for instance, in the UK a national regulation – a Code of Practice (QAA, 2012) - that can be incorporated in HE institutions, according to its specificity, the same cannot be said in that regards in the Portuguese context.

Also, one would expect that the main Portuguese funding agency of doctoral grants – the

Foundation for Science and Technology –would approach this issue in more depth, particularly in the Laws which shed light on the legal background for PhD grant holders and their supervisors. It must be stated that the great majority of doctoral students in Portugal are grant holders. As such, from our perspective the funding agency should be concerned with describing the roles and responsibilities of doctoral students and supervisors, in order to have a basis to evaluate the effect and benefits of having this national grant system. However, the Law n. 202/2012, 27th August and the Law n. 12/2013, 29th January do not define any competences or describe the generic profile of doctoral students and supervisors. For instance, when analyzing the "Responsibilities of scientific supervisor" (chapter I, art. 5-A), "Responsibilities of grant holders" and "Rights of grant holders" (chapter III, art. 9 and 12, respectively), only short references can be found about: the completion of the research plans, the existence of true declarations regarding the research process, and the deadlines for the grant holder and supervisor to send their annual reports to the Foundation.

Simultaneously, though the 'traditional' Doctorate has been somewhat re-structured to follow the Bologna Process' guidelines, by becoming Doctoral Programme with compulsory modules and with a shorter period to develop in-depth research, no discussions at academic or governmental level have been carried out. These changes at organizational level of a Doctorate have consequences on what is expected from doctoral students, supervisors and even institutions. Nevertheless, there is a strange 'silence' but 'loud' concerns in the Portuguese context on the processes of doctoral supervision and research, which are conceived as a very private relationship and context. This hinders the stimulation of open and enriching discussions within academia and other external stakeholders.

Setting the Scene at the University of Aveiro

Following European trends, at the University of Aveiro (where we carried out our research), a Doctoral School was legally created (Order n. 6403/2011), focusing on the 3rd cycle of Bologna. Among other objectives, one that may be considered of relevance is: "Monitoring and evaluating Doctoral Programmes (…) in order to enhance quality patterns, in particular in what concerns supervision and training" (art. 5, point g). Nevertheless, this statement begs the question: how to monitor and/or evaluate a certain process that has not been properly described or characterized in Portugal and still persists being covered in 'silent' conceptions, stereotypes and private practices? Therefore, first of all, it was essential to understand what constitutes the quality of a certain phenomenon – the doctoral supervisory process – by involving the members of the academic community in the discussion. Hence, our premises were:

1. Quality is a process of construction, participation, contribution and negotiation from all members of a HE institution. Thus, it involves critical thinking and awareness, capacity of action, (self-)improvement, development and transformation (Conrad, 1999; Demo, 2003; Harvey & Green, 1993);
2. The community members should thus reflect on their own practices in light of the quality culture, and in the monitoring and evaluation mechanisms (Conrad, 1999; Correia, 2010).

Consequently, we searched in the international literature for research-based frameworks on the quality of doctoral supervision to shape the theoretical background and to compare them with the Portuguese research we carried out. We involved the academic community of the University of Aveiro in open discussions regarding this subject through data collection. These two perspectives are described in this chapter.

THEORETICAL BACKGROUND: SYNTHESIS OF RESEARCH-BASED FRAMEWORKS ON THE QUALITY OF DOCTORAL RESEARCH SUPERVISION

In this section, we aim to give a brief overview of the research-based frameworks on the quality of doctoral supervision that we have found in the international literature. It is essential to mention that we have grouped the frameworks under certain more or less general 'umbrella conceptualizations' (expression from our authorship). We use the concept 'conceptualizations', since we intend to analyze several frameworks/models available in the literature, while giving a theoretical meaning to them, following our research objectives. Naturally, the term 'umbrella' is used as a metaphor; we have tried to integrate the frameworks/models, by discovering similarities between them and thus aggregating them. In the case of the boundaries we establish between the conceptualizations, we take into account the level of analysis the authors demonstrate when reflecting and working on the factors that are involved on the quality of doctoral research supervision.

The need to aggregate several authors' perspectives is due to an absence of meta-analysis on the frameworks/models that are presented, perhaps as a result of the 'newness' of the subject and to the incredible recent volume in articles and books emerging, regarding doctoral supervisory process and education. Thus, this lack of integration and the lack of a meta-analysis of the frameworks/models that arise in several parts of the work led us to try a first theoretical integration (although it is not our purpose to do a meta-analysis). As we have mentioned, we will briefly approach several frameworks/models which also inspired us to review the data collected at the University of Aveiro and the design of our framework – another contribution to Academia and a general discussion.

Holistic Conceptualizations

This subsection takes into account more generic frameworks that focus on several contexts that will influence the doctoral supervisory process. So, the emphasis here is less on the doctoral student and supervisor competences and more on the influences that several contexts have on the supervisory relationship.

Holdaway (1997) assumes that the quality of doctoral research supervision is a multifaceted concept. As such, even though the model he proposes is more or less sequential, since the design comprises of three broad moments - inputs, processes and outputs; within each moment several inter-related factors/criteria are gathered, which should identify the quality of the "overall postgraduate programme" (p.62). In fact, the focus is put on the assessment of several macro and/or micro criteria to enhance the quality of doctoral programme.

McAlpine and Norton (2006) present an "integrative framework" organized in three "nested contexts" (societal, institutional and department that "constraints and enhances supervisor-student experience" [p.6]), which influence doctoral retention and completion (p.6). It is, in fact, the latter aspects that stimulate the authors to design this framework. Therefore, in order to increase doctoral attrition rates, it is important to understand the way different factors of diverse contexts interact with each other. Consequently, it will be possible to properly act and enhance the learning experience of doctoral students as well as the quality of the interaction with their supervisors.

Finally, Cumming's proposal (2010) takes into consideration the perspectives of the previous mentioned frameworks. The model presents an integrated perspective composed by two main inter-related multidimensional aspects: "doctoral practices" and "doctoral arrangements" (p.31) that bring together a holistic and comprehensive view of the doctoral supervisory and research processes.

Knowledge-Centered Conceptualizations

In this case, knowledge is at the center of the process and its 'direction' goes towards the doctoral student; knowledge will lead the doctoral student to be deeply transformed. Zhao's (2003) "knowledge management framework for research supervision", as well as Maxwell and Smyth's proposal (2011) – "model for supervision" – clearly demonstrate this description. Zhao's framework (2003) puts the supervisory process and the doctoral supervisor, allied to knowledge, as the 'means to an end': the transformation of doctoral students into "knowledge workers and managers" (p.187). Maxwell and Smyth (2011) put the emphasis on three 'spheres' constituted by the student, knowledge and the research project. These spheres intersect each other and, at the center, we may find the "transformation zone" where, through "critical consciousness", the "student becomes teacher and develops as a researcher" (p.225).

Supervisory Styles' Conceptualization

Even though, these models take doctoral students' profiles into account, the focus is on the supervisor's role, which may then presuppose a 'reaction' from the student. Within this type of conceptualization, we may count several proposals, which we identify below. We will then briefly compare them.

- **Gurr (2001):** Dynamic Model for Aligning Supervisory Styles with Research Student Development;
- **Gatfield (2005):** Dynamic Conceptual Model;

- **Murphy, Bain & Conrad (2007):** Four Orientations to Supervision;
- **Vilkinas (2008):** Integrated Competing Values Framework;
- **Mainhard et al. (2009):** Model for the supervisor-doctoral student relationship / Model for interpersonal supervisor behavior;
- **Lee (2008, 2010, 2012):** Framework of Approaches to Research Supervision.

Comparing the first model (Gurr, 2001) with the last one (Lee, 2012), we find an evolution in terms of the way the supervisory process and relationship is considered; it moves from a more static to a more dynamic perspective. Nevertheless, all those models' descriptions refer to the possibility of moving across styles. Additionally, all proposals may be used as instruments to promote broader discussions and/or individual and dyadic reflections about (daily) supervisory interactions. Also, all proposals consider styles more focused on the task and more focused on the person, which may help characterizing and enhancing the supervisory practice.

Nevertheless, in terms of the differences, it may be observed that throughout the years the authors became more sophisticated in the way they conceptualize the supervisory styles. From quadrant conceptualizations (for instance from Gatfield, 2005; Gurr, 2001), they evolved to a dimensional conceptualization where supervisory behavior is mapped considering degrees (Mainhard et al., 2009). Finally, Lee's proposal (2008, 2010, 2012) suggests that although the focus is also on the supervisor, the doctoral student has a different 'place' when comparing with the previous proposals. In fact, her framework presents three perspectives from which each style can be analyzed: "supervisor's activity", "supervisor's knowledge and skills" and "possible student reaction" (Lee, 2012, p.5). As the author mentions,

all supervisory approaches should be considered inter-related and complementary to each other.

Micro-Level Conceptualizations

What we call micro-level conceptualizations put a particular focus on the supervisory relationship. Styles and Radloff (2001) present a "self-regulatory, synergistic model of supervision" (p.97). Thus, the importance of self-regulated and reflective attitudes of doctoral students and supervisors is stressed, though emphasizing the symmetry of their roles. Grant (2003) shows a "map for supervision" (p.176) constituted by four integrated layers where the emphasis is put on the doctoral student and on the supervisory relationship. Consequently, she refers to this relational process as an institutionalized relationship, where "productive power relations" exist and where there is a mixture of personal, social, institutional, rational and irrational aspects that belong to both supervisor and student.

Intertwining All Conceptualizations

To sum up, when considering the contributions of all authors previously identified, it may be concluded that the research-based frameworks share common characteristics, which are identified below. Therefore, a framework on the quality of doctoral supervision should:

- Be non-deterministic; On the contrary, it should open spaces for unpredictability and changes along the process;
- Focus special attention to different contexts and to the intersection of diverse factors (contextual, institutional, disciplinary, personal), since they all influence the experience of both doctoral students and supervisors;

- Allow permeability and articulation of contexts, situations and personal subjectivities (following the latter point), so the doctoral supervisory relationship and the research process may benefit from the richness of all those contexts which, simultaneously, make a supervisory relationship unique and different from any other;
- Be fluid and allow unpredictability along the process. In fact, when the focus is on the research process, unpredictability may be one of the factors that characterize the research pathway. At the same time, unpredictability also describes the relationship between the members involved in the supervisory relationship;
- Allow the intersection of personal subjectivities (diversity) and contextualization of actions, following previous points already identified;
- Allow flexibility and negotiation of (supervisory and research) approaches, adaptable to contexts, situations and individuals: it requires critical, self and meta-reflection from all who are involved;
- Consider the evolution in terms of (supervisory, research and personal) approaches: it is a non-static phenomenon, also due to its nature of being a process;
- Allow the transformation of those who are involved: doctoral student and supervisor.

When bringing together the data collected in our research, it was a concern to follow those characteristics regarding the integrative and fluid framework we propose in this chapter, since we truly consider that "(…) this phenomenon [the doctoral supervisory process] is in a perpetual state of motion. Hence, it can never be captured in its entirety or fully explained. Only glimpses of its complexity can be revealed at a given moment in time" (Cumming, 2010, p.35). The use of concepts 'integrative', 'fluid' and 'framework' is now hopefully clearer.

METHODOLOGY

This case study was carried out at the University of Aveiro (Portugal) and took into consideration the voices of doctoral students and supervisors from this institution, from several academic domains and with heterogeneous academic and professional experiences. As the main actors of the doctoral research and supervisory processes, it was crucial to hear their voices; the gathered data was analyzed and conceptualized, so a grounded discussion on what should integrate the quality of the doctoral research supervisory process could be stimulated.

The case study was the chosen method due to several reasons (Yin, 2009):

1. The main research questions were supported in the 'how' and 'why' of a specific phenomenon (the supervisory process);
2. A contemporary phenomenon was chosen to be researched, over which the investigator has little or no control;
3. The boundaries of the phenomenon are not clearly evident, since diverse contexts may be articulated. Moreover, conceptual frontiers are complex to be established, because the phenomenon is particularly characterized as a process;
4. It opens the possibility of using multiple sources of evidence (of qualitative and/or quantitative nature), giving a high importance to participants' voices;
5. It allows an analytic generalization. As such, the conclusions (and the particular output presented in this chapter – the integrative and fluid framework) may be important not only to the HE institution where the research took place, but also to other contexts.

This case study started with a qualitative approach (exploratory interviews and focus groups) and then was followed by a quantitative approach (questionnaires). Below, we will describe the phases of data collection, the participants and instruments so it can be better understood the research process that we carried out, particularly to design an integrative and fluid framework on the quality of doctoral research supervision.

Data Collection: Participants and Instruments

Phase 1: Exploratory Interviews

Since this was the first attempt at tackling the doctoral research supervision in Portugal, it was considered essential to start by interviewing the main Portuguese researchers, whose work and contributions to the theoretical, epistemological and empirical advancement of pedagogical supervision has been internationally recognized, validated and well-known. We have made this theoretical and methodological choice, because we assume that pedagogy and research supervision are epistemologically interconnected (Baptista & Huet, 2012). Therefore, we have chosen the main Portuguese experts who could give the first conceptual approach within this subject.

The participants were four well-known Portuguese senior researchers in pedagogical and research supervision. Even though the sample is not statistically significant, their in-depth contributions through semi-structured interviews were essential to contextualize the subject within national and international boundaries and, simultaneously, to validate certain semantic dimensions we wanted to approach in the focus groups. All four senior researchers were women: a Retired Full Professor, Retired Associate Professor, a Full Professor and an Associate Professor. Although the expertise and the research path of each researcher slightly differ from the others, they have strongly contributed to the advancement of HE pedagogy and pedagogical supervision. Also, all of them assume that 'research supervision is a sort of pedagogical supervision' (Baptista & Huet, 2012).

Phase 2: Focus Groups

Due to the unexplored nature of this research topic in Portugal, it was considered that the research could largely benefit from a 'social' approach to the subject. Thus, the data was collected through focus groups with doctoral supervisors (N=25, divided in 6 mini focus groups) in the first instance, and subsequently doctoral students (N=26 participants, divided in 8 mini focus groups), of all academic domains (among the ones that exist at the University of Aveiro) and with diverse characteristics.

Heterogeneity of each group was considered a factor that needed to be assured. Therefore, 6 focus groups with doctoral supervisors, and 8 with doctoral students were carried out. The discussion in each group had the duration of approximately two hours. The focus groups did not have the same number of participants, due to reasons of the participants' availability. Also, we have always tried to assemble very small groups, since we wanted to provoke an intense and open discussion around several topics on those identified dimensions. This was the first time such subject was openly discussed and systematized.

This strategy of data collection (focus groups) was adopted, because it stimulates interaction, discussion, self- and meta-reflection among the participants. Due to the dynamic nature of the process (Greenbaum, 2000, p.13), the research has benefited from this qualitative research technique, since it enabled and encouraged participants to be actively involved and 'think conceptually' (Greenbaum, 2000). This phase of data collection has allowed gathering in-depth perspectives around several interconnected topics, grouped into 2 main dimensions, which we have previously identified in the literature as important to be explored: the context of doctoral research and supervision, and the quality of the doctoral supervision process (Baptista, et al., 2011; Huet et al., 2012).

Both mentioned dimensions were essential to gather data that helped in the construction of the fluid framework that will be presented and described in the next section, due to a set of categories that have emerged from the content analysis. Additionally, at a more particular level and more related to the second referred dimension, it has emerged as the most important competences, from the participants' perspective, that characterize the quality profiles of each element of the supervisory dyad (Baptista et al., 2011; Huet et al., 2012). In this latter case, this output from the content analysis (which we did with the support of NVivo) was the basis to design the questionnaires.

Phase 3: Questionnaires

The questionnaires were directed to the 3rd cycle community (the PhD community) at the University of Aveiro. The data was collected using a self-administered online questionnaire. We had the participation of 197 doctoral students (corresponding to 22% of this population) and 122 doctoral supervisors (corresponding to 12% of this population). The main objective of the questionnaires was to statistically understand the vision of the doctoral community on the competences that (should) characterize doctoral students and supervisors' quality profiles, that is, to understand if a larger number of people considered the competences that emerged from the focus groups were suitable to integrate the quality profiles of each member of the doctoral dyad. In fact, one of our premises was to involve the academic community in this discussion, because they could identify with this process.

The questionnaires comprised of 3 parts: (1) the first one was related to the general characterization of the participants; (2) the second part contained 40 competences of the students' quality profile; and (3) the third part contained 40 competences of the supervisors' quality profile. These competences emerged from the content analysis from the focus groups. The participants had to attribute their level of agreement regarding each competence. Therefore, it was used a scale ranging from: 1=totally

disagree to 7=totally agree. From the statistical analysis of the questionnaires (using SPSS), an articulated system of competences emerged by using a multivariate analysis, in particular the ALSCAL technique. However, this articulated system of competences will not be presented in this chapter.

RESULTS: RECOMMENDATION OF A FRAMEWORK

Where Does the Framework Come From? A Brief Approach

As previously mentioned in the last point of the theoretical section, we have been inspired by certain characteristics of the international research-based frameworks. But, additionally, the data collection was essential to understand the main components, which are identified and described below, that should be considered to integrate what we have called the integrative and fluid framework – qualities that will be further explained in the next subsection.

Although we have mentioned, in the 'methodology', that we have carried out interviews, focus groups and questionnaires, the findings from the qualitative approach were the most important ones to design the framework. Consequently, in order to give the reader a sense of the semantic path followed by the author to design the integrative and fluid framework, Figure 1 presents the main topics (categories and subcategories) that were identified within three main dimensions around the quality of the doctoral supervisory (and research) process.

The other categories and subcategories, identified in figure 1 that do not directly contribute to the design of the framework, were crucial to the design of the questionnaire and for us to achieve the system of competences in terms of the quality profiles that doctoral students and supervisors should demonstrate and enhance.

Figure 1. Where does the framework come from? Contribution from the qualitative data collection

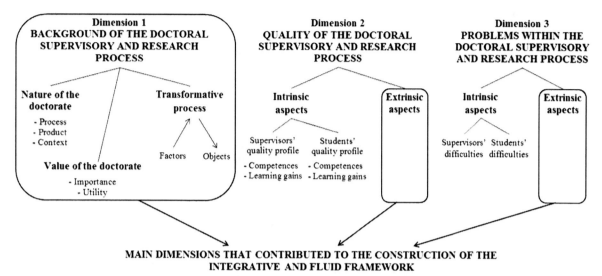

MAIN DIMENSIONS THAT CONTRIBUTED TO THE CONSTRUCTION OF THE INTEGRATIVE AND FLUID FRAMEWORK

(the other parts of dimensions 2 and 3 relate to the 'heart' of the framework that is constituted by the component that is at the centre: the definition of the quality profiles of the supervisory dyad, which is not the focus of this chapter)

Integrative and Fluid Framework on Doctoral Supervisory Quality: Some Initial Remarks and Issues

When proposing and designing our integrative and fluid framework on doctoral supervisory quality, we assumed a holistic and flexible perspective of the concept 'framework'. Nevertheless, the framework should be a systematized, integrative and coherent organization of components, which may be useful in several areas and to achieve diverse goals, namely: (1) to systematize the results of the research carried out; (2) to contribute to the process of (re)constructing knowledge on this worldwide pertinent topic; (3) to design future investigations, considering certain specific components of the framework; and (4) to design several activities/actions with diverse purposes, such as training (for doctoral students and supervisors), formative assessment, institutional evaluation on the quality of the supervisory process and so on.

From our point of view, we agree with Smyth's approach (2004) to this concept:

A conceptual framework is described as a set of broad ideas and principles taken from relevant field of enquiry and used to structure a subsequent presentation (Reichel & Ramey, 1987). When clearly articulated, a conceptual framework has potential usefulness as a tool to scaffold research and, therefore, to assist a researcher to make meaning of subsequent findings. (...) The framework is a research tool intended to assist a researcher to develop awareness and understanding of the situation under scrutiny and to communicate this (p.167-168).

The framework that we present is not only important for research, but also for practice and for academic communities – in Portugal and abroad. This assumption is based on the aspects we have mentioned in the 'introduction' to this chapter and in the 'theoretical background'. Also, we emphasize the importance of a framework to scaffold research and any other sort of activities as well as to understand what may be involved in the quality of doctoral research supervision. In this sense, we strongly believe that a framework may change throughout time, due to modifications of several nature and coming from different contexts and sectors. This is one of the reasons why we have considered that our framework is fluid.

In fact, the fluidity we have mentioned takes into consideration not only time, but also contexts and components. Moreover, it is undeniable that doctoral supervision is characterized as being a process, where research, knowledge and individuals are in the center. As such, the on-going character of this phenomenon, which involves so many variables, is fluid, changeable, and unpredictable; it is not possible to totally define all its frontiers, although it has some regularity – otherwise it would not be an institutionalized process. Therefore, within the framework we propose, there are open spaces between the components that comprise it, so other factors can be included to better capture timely and contextual characteristics. This is the reason why we consider this fluid framework presented below has a supra-institutional and supra-national character.

Components of the Framework

Firstly, it is essential to underline that we observe the phenomenon under study – the quality of doctoral research supervision – as a holistic one. Therefore, following the perspective of authors such as McAlpine and Norton (2006), we also adopt a nested perspective and add a movement nature to the framework: from outside to inside, taking into account a more general and a more specific perspective, respectively.

As we have underlined previously, the holistic nature of this phenomenon leads us to open and give space to other components that, although have not emerged from our research, may be added at a later stage considering the (national, institutional, departmental, research group, disciplinary) context where this framework may be applied. The dashed lines of all macro and micro plans, and components highlights not only the

permeability between the 'spatial plans' but also the fact that the components do not stand alone. The dashed lines demonstrate that the plans and the components:

1. Influence each other;
2. Allow the interaction of contexts and/or components and even the movement between the components from a plan to another;
3. Allow openness to include potential components and/or plans in the future.

Consequently, this is an integrative and holistic framework exactly because one must be aware of the total structure and elements of the framework, regardless of the objectives, so the quality of the supervisory process can be achieved. By analyzing Figure 2, we observe the framework primarily consists of 2 main plans. One is the macro plan – the broader one – which includes diverse challenges, external pressures, (inter) national policies, guidelines and 'tendencies'. This plan gives a background where current HE institutions 'move' themselves and are contextualized. We could establish a link between this plan and the main challenges we have identified in the 'introduction' to this chapter.

The meso plan is the one that corresponds to the HE institution; this is a more specific plan as well as the elements that constitute it. It must be stressed that the location of all components is random, except the central component ('Supervisory Dyad'), which is more specific, when comparing with the other components. This central component is, in fact, the 'heart' of the framework and may lead to another micro plan that will not be discussed within this chapter that is related with an articulated system of competences of the members of doctoral dyad. All components of this meso plan are identified within boxes with the same dimension, which has a purpose. Considering both the theoretical background and the results from our research, it is impossible to understand what are the components that possess a

Figure 2. Integrative and fluid framework on doctoral supervisory quality: A contribution

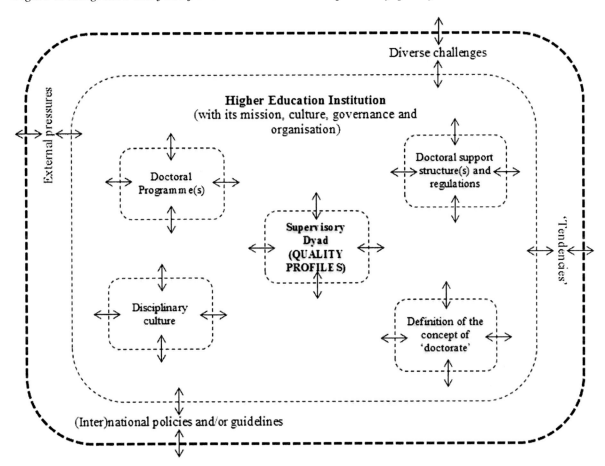

stronger influence and/or relevance on the quality of doctoral research supervision. We assume that national and institutional contexts, the research group context, even the disciplinary context, individual subjectivities and/or other factors may lead to attribute different levels of importance to some components than to others. Consequently, to solve this, by making this framework as supra-national and supra-institutional as possible, we considered the need of having arrows within each box of the components of this meso plan. These arrows signify two main things:

1. The possibility of making the box larger in size (or smaller), according to the level of importance and influence a particular com-

ponent may have on the quality of doctoral research supervision;

2. Movement, allowing different conceptual (re)organization of the components. In this sense each component, which is randomly located within this plan, may move closer to certain components (and/or move apart), may belong to the center or to the 'periphery', considering the 'heart' of the framework. Also, one component that may be in the meso plan may be moved to the macro plan.

All this description emphasizes the nature of the research doctoral supervision:; a process where multiple variables may be considered to be (un) important to its quality. Moreover, it explains why we believe this framework may be operationalized in other contexts and not only in the University of Aveiro where this research took place. Hence, since this was a case study, there is a possibility of analytic generalization (Yin, 2009), as previously underlined.

Some Benefits and Some Cautions Regarding the Integrative and Fluid Framework

We assume, following several international political documents from different parts of the globe (Australian Qualifications Framework Advisory Board, 2007; Council of Graduate Schools of the U.S., 1991; Joint Quality Initiative informal group, 2004; Quality Assurance Agency for Higher Education, 2008), that the PhD degree is both:

1. The enhancement of a set of personal, social, academic and professional competences which will be essential to be successful both in a doctoral research and in a future professional path, which may be inside or outside Academia (thus, we may be talking about a set of high-level transferable competences), and

2. The creation of a final product that is mostly characterized by originality, which may be considered one of the most important aspects that define the nature and/or purpose of the doctorate.

Consequently, the integrative and fluid framework on the quality of doctoral research supervision must be seen as flexible enough to enhance the quality of the relationship without forgetting the 'essence' of the doctorate; what it is and what it is for. Therefore, the components of the framework, specifically their description cannot be seen as a 'list of ingredients'. As previously stated, in the supervisory process, it is essential to be aware of the importance of the context(s), subjectivities, and its unpredictable character (although it has

some regularity). Moreover, it must be regularly reviewed and updated, so the framework can be useful and serve the purposes of the institution and of the individuals.

When considered from an operational perspective, the framework may be used:

*   To create a 'Quality Code', regarding doctoral students and supervisors' quality profile within the Doctoral School at the University of Aveiro;
*   To guide the student to choose his/her supervisor (and vice-versa);
*   To stimulate self, dyadic and group reflections about the supervisory process, both from formal and informal perspectives;
*   To promote discussions on training programmes directed to doctoral supervisors and doctoral students;
*   To design a suitable evaluation and monitoring process on the quality of the doctoral supervisory process. In this case, it will be important to choose the components to be evaluated and monitored, and the variables that may influence that evaluation and/or monitoring objectives.

Recommendations to Design an Evaluation and Monitoring Process on the Quality of Doctoral Research Supervision

In order to achieve the latter objective (identified in the previous subsection) and design a suitable evaluation and monitoring process on the quality of doctoral research supervisory process, it is important to have a specific structure, such as the Doctoral School, to implement it, which is one of its objectives. The centralization of the evaluation and monitor process may benefit the HE institution, since there will be a team focused on this subject and, at the same time, considering the results, may design suitable programmes to help overcome difficulties and enhance successes.

From our perspective, for the design of an institutional evaluation and monitoring process on the quality of doctoral research supervision, it is important to begin with some basic premises:

1. The evaluation and/or monitoring process should not be uncritical nor only support itself with statistical indicators. There should also be qualitative indicators collected regularly, for instance through doctoral students and supervisors' reports;

2. The concepts of evaluation and/or monitoring as well as quality should involve an institutional culture based on meta-critical awareness with the objective of permanent enhancement of the context towards a greater common good and of transformation of the individuals that are part of an institution (Demo, 2003; Harvey & Green, 1993; Houston, 2008; Zhao, 2003). The evaluation and/or monitoring system should assure that formative and summative perspectives of the supervisory process are cyclic, allowing the transformation (namely in terms of competences' enhancement) of those involved in the supervisory process. But these assumptions should be considered at the mission of a HE institution;

3. *Recognising the context in which postgraduate supervision occurs is not the only important factor in effectively managing quality. Creating supportive context for evaluation to improve is also crucial. There must be an atmosphere of trust in which finding weaknesses and addressing them is cause for reward, not blame in which collegial cooperation and mutual support rather than competition are encouraged. It is the institution's responsibility to create such supportive context* (Conrad, 1999, p.20-21).

Consequently, in practice, the evaluation and/or monitoring devices should consider the nature of the doctoral research supervisory process: it is flexible, adaptable and unpredictable. Therefore, this evaluation and monitoring process should have objectives of (1) feedback and feed forward; (2) summative and formative purposes (Henkel, 1998); and (3) self-regulation within the HE institutions and external evaluation. Hence, this process should have several sources of information which should allow the acquisition of a 360° perspective of the supervisory process, so timely activities are designed to solve identified problems and to enhance the identified successes (in the sense of 'empowerment'). Therefore, we consider that a structure as the Doctoral School may (should) have the human and financing resources to carry out a monitoring and evaluation process of this phenomenon.

We consider that, following the previous assumptions, an open and regular reflection and discussion of issues on doctoral supervision that have been covered in 'silences' may be stimulated. These discussions will not only be enriching within the entire academia, but mainly within the supervisory dyad or team. We believe that interesting information on intellectual, social, emotional and intrapersonal factors related to the doctoral supervisory and research processes would become evident and public, as well as expectations, pressures, difficulties and successes felt by each member of the dyad.

FUTURE RESEARCH DIRECTIONS: SOME POSSIBILITIES

The quality of doctoral research supervision is a multidimensional phenomenon. Therefore, considering each component that, for instance, integrates the framework we have proposed and described, future research may be focused on focused investigations regarding each element (and/or others that were not identified) and with diverse objectives.

At a more specific level, many future research pathways are opened to our eyes. We may identify some of them, which, we believe, are central to systematize many studies and research that is being carried out worldwide:

- To gather research-based evidences regarding (1) the types of doctorates (in this case, Portugal must develop conceptual, epistemological and empirical work regarding this issue); (2) the 'space' and the type of involvement and success doctorate holders have in the external market and the professional paths they pursue after finishing doctoral degree; and (3) the impact doctorates (or doctoral holders) have in the economy and society;
- To align the process of doctoral research supervision, the phases of doctoral research and the development of the academic identity of the doctoral student as well as of the doctoral supervisor;
- To design a bi/tri-dimensional model that intersects the components of the framework we have designed (and others that may emerge) with transferable and disciplinary competences that the doctoral student must enhance throughout the doctoral journey and the role of the supervisor.

These are only three examples of future paths. Many others may be opened, since doctoral education and supervision is an ever emerging subject around the world.

CONCLUSION

Increasing demands are coming from different stakeholders over HE institutions, and particularly over the research that is being developed within these organizations, namely at doctoral level. In fact, there are different factors affecting any level of formal education today. Particularly in

what concerns doctoral education, research and supervision, the agenda worldwide is revealing a growing concern with the extension and impact of research produced at this level. Additionally, the international context shows the existence of an increasing number of research students, with diverse backgrounds, enrolling doctoral education. Simultaneously, doctoral supervisors with different sort of experiences may also be found. Actually, worldwide figures demonstrate that there are now more doctoral students and doctorate holders than ever before, having consequences to the labor market and to the knowledge economy.

Simultaneously, an international issue for discussion is the growth of different forms of doctorates and also the growth in the demand for a doctoral education based on quality standards. All of these factors may thus change the nature of research. Therefore, within this background (that could be added and be linked to the 'introduction' of this chapter), the quality of doctoral supervision and education becomes central, as well as the systematization of research on this topic. As previously stated, the design of a framework on the quality of doctoral research supervision where elements of this process can be identified is important, since its operationalization may achieve many goals. One of them we have mentioned in this chapter: the existence of suitable evaluation and monitoring processes regarding this process, in order to enhance its quality, not only by identifying difficulties but also successes.

To conclude, we must stress that the main innovation of the framework that we propose and emerged from our research lies in several interrelated factors:

- Although it shares some characteristics with worldwide frameworks (described in the 'theoretical background' section), the one we suggest is more open to the changes of contexts and time: it may not only be updated regularly, but also the movement allowed between the components and the possibility of integrating other elements give our framework a flexibility which may not be found (so clearly at least) in other frameworks;

- According to its description, the framework may be operationalized according to different HE institutions' intents – just to name a few: to monitor or to evaluate the doctoral supervisory and/or research process, to gather difficulties and successes, to design interventions, to understand the importance of certain component, more in specific, in what regards the doctoral supervisory and research process;

- Consequently, this framework is not only focused on one specific component (namely, doctoral student and supervisors' profiles or contextual factors): it also highlights the importance of other components. In fact, the importance that is given to each component will be assumed and chosen by each HE institution: again, this demonstrates this framework's flexibility to address different goals and concerns.

REFERENCES

Alarcão, I. (Ed.). (1996). Formação reflexiva de professores: Estratégias de supervisão. Porto: Porto Editora, Colecção CIDInE.

Alarcão, I. (2001). Novas tendências nos paradigmas de investigação em educação. In I. Alarcão (Ed.), Escola reflexiva e nova racionalidade (pp. 135-144). São Paulo: Artmed editora.

Alarcão, I., & Roldão, M.C. (2008). *Supervisão: Um contexto de desenvolvimento profissional dos professores*. Mangualde: Edições Pedago.

Alarcão, I., & Tavares, J. (2003). *Supervisão da prática pedagógica: Uma perspectiva de desenvolvimento e aprendizagem*. Coimbra: Edições Almedina.

Australian Qualifications Framework Advisory Board. (2007). Australia qualifications framework: Implementation handbook (4th ed.). Carlton South, Australia: Australian Qualifications Framework (AQF) Advisory Board.

Baptista, A. V., & Huet, I. (2012). Postgraduate research supervision quality: Rethinking the value of doctoral supervision to design an integrative framework. *International Journal of Learning*, *18*(5), 175–194.

Baptista, A. V., Huet, I., & Jenkins, A. (2011). Quality of doctoral supervision: Supervisors' conceptions of learning, supervision and students' profiles. In N. Jackson, L. Frick, C. Nygaard, & N. Courtney (Eds.), *Postgraduate education: Form and function* (pp. 43–58). Faringdon, UK: Libri Publishing.

Bennett, P., & Turner, G. (2012). *Postgraduate taught experience survey 2012 results: Report*. York, UK: Higher Education Academy.

Bills, D. (2004). Supervisors' conceptions of research and the implications for supervisor development. *The International Journal for Academic Development*, *9*(1), 85–97. doi:10.1080/1360144042000296099

Bissett, A. (2009). Academics as entrepreneurs: The changing nature of academic professionalism. In iPED Research Network (Eds.), Academic futures: Inquiries into higher education and pedagogy (pp. 111-123). Newcastle upon Tyne, UK: iPED Research Network.

Brew, A. (2001). Conceptions of research: A phenomenographic study. *Studies in Higher Education*, *26*(3), 271–285. doi:10.1080/03075070120076255

Brew, A. (2007). Evaluating academic development in a time of perplexity. *The International Journal for Academic Development, 12*(2), 69–72. doi:10.1080/13601440701604823

Brew, A., & Peseta, T. (2004). Changing postgraduate supervision practice: A programme to encourage learning through reflection and feedback. *Innovations in Education and Teaching International, 41*(1), 5–22. doi:10.1080/14703290320001726 85

Coaldrake, P., & Stedman, L. (1999). *Academic work in the twenty-first century: Changing roles and policies.* Australian Government, Department of Education Training and Youth Affaires: Higher Education Division.

Connell, R. W. (1985). How to supervise a PhD. *Vestes, 2,* 38–41.

Conrad, L. (1999). Contextualising postgraduate supervision to promote quality. In G. Wisker & N. Sutcliffe (Eds.), *Good practice in postgraduate supervision* (pp. 13–24). Staff and Educational Development Association.

Correia, J. A. (2010). Paradigmas e cognições no campo da administração educacional: Das políticas de avaliação à avaliação como política. *Revista Brasileira de Educação, 15*(45), 456–467. doi:10.1590/S1413-24782010000300005

Council of Graduate Schools of the U.S. (1991). *The role and nature of the doctoral dissertation.* Washington, DC: Report from the Council of Graduate Schools of the U.S.

Cullen, D., Pearson, M., Saha, L., & Spear, R. (1994). *Establishing effective PhD supervision.* Australian Government Publishing Service, Department of Employment, Education and Training.

Cumming, J. (2010). Doctoral enterprise: A holistic conception of evolving practices and arrangements. *Studies in Higher Education, 35*(1), 25–39. doi:10.1080/03075070902825899

Demo, P. (2003). *Educação e Qualidade.* Campinas: Papirus Editora.

Enders, J. (2005). Border crossings: Research training, knowledge dissemination and the transformation of academic work. *Higher Education, 49*(1-2), 119–133. doi:10.1007/s10734-004-2917-3

Felton, S. (2008). *The student experience of supervision: Towards the student-supervisor agreement.* Retrieved January 2009, from http://www.lancs.ac.uk/celt/celtweb/files/SimonFelton.pdf

Gatfield, T. (2005). An investigation into PhD supervisory management styles: Development of a dynamic conceptual model and its managerial implications. *Journal of Higher Education Policy and Management, 27*(3), 311–325. doi:10.1080/13600800500283585

Grant, B. (1999). *Walking on a rackety bridge: Mapping supervision.* Retrieved November 2012, from http://www.herdsa.org.au/wp-content/uploads/conference/1999/pdf/grant.pdf

Grant, B. (2001). Dirty work: "A code for supervision" read against the grain. In A. Barlett & G. Mercer (Eds.), *Postgraduate research supervision: Transforming (r)elations* (pp. 13–24). New York: Peter Lang.

Grant, B. (2003). Mapping the pleasures and risks of supervision. *Discourse (Abingdon), 24*(2), 175–190. doi:10.1080/01596300303042

Grant, B. (2005). Fighting for space in supervision: Fantasies, fairytales, fictions and fallacies. *International Journal of Qualitative Studies in Education, 18*(3), 337–354. doi:10.1080/09518390500082483

Grant, B., & Graham, A. (1999). Naming the game: Reconstructing graduate supervision. *Teaching in Higher Education, 4*(1), 77–89. doi:10.1080/1356251990040105

Greenbaum, T. L. (2000). *Moderating focus groups: A practical guide for group facilitation.* Thousand Oaks, CA: SAGE. doi:10.4135/9781483328522

Gurr, G. M. (2001). Negotiating the "rackety bridge" – A dynamic model for aligning supervisory style with research student development. *Higher Education Research & Development, 20*(1), 81–92. doi:10.1080/07924360120043882

Harman, G. (2003). PhD student satisfaction with course experience and supervision in two Australian research-intensive universities. *Prometheus, 21*(3), 312–333. doi:10.1080/0810902032000113460

Harvey, L., & Green, D. (1993). Defining quality. *Assessment & Evaluation in Higher Education, 18*(1), 26p. doi:10.1080/0260293930180102

Henkel, M. (1998). Evaluation in higher education: Conceptual and epistemological foundations. *European Journal of Education, 33*(3), 285–297.

Hernard, F., & Leprince-Ringuet, S. (2008). *The path to quality teaching in higher education.* Unpublished.

Hodsdon, L., & Buckley, A. (2011). *Postgraduate research experience survey 2011 results: Report.* York, UK: Higher Education Academy.

Hodson, P., & Thomas, H. (2003). Quality assurance in higher education: Fit for the new millennium or simply year 2000 compliant? *Higher Education, 45*(3), 375–387. doi:10.1023/A:1022665818216

Holdaway, E. (1997). Quality issues in postgraduate education. In R. G. Burgess (Ed.), *Beyond the first degree: Graduate education, lifelong learning and careers* (pp. 60–78). Buckingham, UK: SRHE & Open University Press.

Houston, D. (2008). Rethinking quality and improvement in higher education. *Quality Assurance in Education, 16*(1), 61–79. doi:10.1108/09684880810848413

Huet, I., Baptista, A. V., & Figueiredo, C. (2012). Qualidade da investigação doutoral: Enfoque no processo de supervisão na perspectiva de estudantes e supervisores. In A. Noutel, E. Brutten, G. Pires, & I. Huet (Eds.), *Ensino superior: Saberes, experiências, desafios.* João Pessoa: Ideia.

Joint Quality Initiative Informal Group. (2004). *Shared 'Dublin' descriptors for short cycle, first cycle, second cycle and third cycle awards.* Retrieved September 2012, from www.eua.be/.../ pushFile.php?.../dublin_descriptors

Kandlbinder, P., & Peseta, T. (2006). *In supervisors' words... An insider's view of postgraduate supervision.* Sydney, Australia: The Institute for Teaching and Learning.

Lee, A. (2008). How are doctoral students supervised? Concepts of doctoral research supervision. *Studies in Higher Education, 33*(3), 267–281. doi:10.1080/03075070802049202

Lee, A. (2010). New approaches to doctoral supervision: Implications for educational development. *Educational Developments, 11*(2), 18–23.

Lee, A. (2012). *Successful research supervision: Advising students doing research.* London: Routledge.

Mainhard, T., van der Rijst, R., van Tartwijk, J., & Wubbels, T. (2009). A model for supervisor-doctoral student relationship. *Higher Education, 58*(3), 359–373. doi:10.1007/s10734-009-9199-8

Manathunga, C., & Goozée, J. (2007). Challenging the dual assumption of the 'always/already' autonomous student and effective supervisor. *Teaching in Higher Education, 12*(3), 309–322. doi:10.1080/13562510701278658

Maxwell, T. W., & Smyth, R. (2011). Higher degree research supervision: From practice toward theory. *Higher Education Research & Development, 30*(2), 219–231. doi:10.1080/07294360.2010.509762

McAlpine, L., & Norton, J. (2006). Reframing our approach to doctoral programs: An integrative framework for action and research. *Higher Education Research & Development*, 25(1), 3–17. doi:10.1080/07294360500453012

Murphy, N., Bain, J., & Conrad, L. (2007). Orientations to research higher degree supervision. *Higher Education*, 53(2), 209–234. doi:10.1007/s10734-005-5608-9

Park, C. (2005). New variant PhD: The changing nature of the doctorate in the UK. *Journal of Higher Education Policy and Management*, 27(2), 189–207. doi:10.1080/13600800500120068

Park, C. (2007). *Redefining the doctorate*. York, UK: The Higher Education Academy.

Park, C. (2008). *The taught postgraduate student experience: Overview of higher education academy survey*. York, UK: The Higher Education Academy.

Pearson, M., & Brew, A. (2002). Research training and supervision development. *Studies in Higher Education*, 27(2), 135–150. doi:10.1080/03075070220119986c

Pearson, M., & Kayrooz, C. (2004). Enabling critical reflection on research supervisory practice. *The International Journal for Academic Development*, 9(1), 99–116. doi:10.1080/1360144042000296107

Petersen, E. V. (2007). Negotiating academicity: Postgraduate research supervision as category boundary work. *Studies in Higher Education*, 32(4), 475–487. doi:10.1080/03075070701476167

Quality Assurance Agency for Higher Education. (2008). The framework for higher education qualifications in England, Wales and Northern Ireland. Mansfield, UK: QAA's Publications.

Quality Assurance Agency for Higher Education (QAA). (2012). *UK quality code for higher education: Part B: Assuring and enhancing academic quality: Chapter B11: Research degrees*. Retrieved August 2012, from http://www.qaa.ac.uk/publications/informationandguidance/pages/quality-code-B11.aspx

Reid, A., & Marshall, S. (2009). Institutional development fot the enhancement of research and research training. *The International Journal for Academic Development*, 14(2), 145–157. doi:10.1080/13601440902970031

Sá-Chaves, I. (2007). *Formação, conhecimento e supervisão: Contributos nas áreas da formação de professores e de outros profissionais*. Aveiro, Portugal: Universidade de Aveiro.

Smyth, R. (2004). Exploring the usefulness of a conceptual framework as a research tool: A researcher's reflections. *Issues in Educational Research*, 14(2), 167–180.

Soothill, K. (2006). *Experience of supervision: Continuities and change*. Retrieved January 2009, from http://www.lancs.ac.uk/celt/celtweb/files/KeithSoothill.pdf

Styles, I., & Radloff, A. (2001). The synergistic thesis: Student and supervisor perspectives. *Journal of Further and Higher Education*, 25(1), 97-106.

Taylor, S. (2009). The post-Humboldtian doctorate: Implications for supervisory practice. In iPED Research Network (Eds.), Academic futures: Inquiries into higher education and pedagogy (pp. 61-74). Newcastle upon Tyne, UK: iPED Research Network.

UK Council for Graduate Education. (1996). *Quality and standards of postgraduate research degrees*. Retrieved January 2009, from http://www.ukcge.ac.uk/OneStopCMS/Core/CrawlerResourceServer.aspx?resource=6B22F9C5-DC02-4633-9964-579846D4B3A4& mode=link&guid=a57997aa5a9f4450bb141144a86634e6

Vieira, F. (1993). *Supervisão: Uma prática reflexiva de formação de professores*. Rio Tinto: edições ASA.

Vieira, F., Moreira, M.A., Barbosa, I., Paiva, M. & Fernandes, I.S. (2006). *No caleidoscópio da supervisão: Imagens da formação e da pedagogia*. Mangualde: Edições Pedago.

Vilkinas, T. (2008). An exploratory study of the supervision of Ph.D./research students' theses. *Innovative Higher Education*, *32*(5), 297–311. doi:10.1007/s10755-007-9057-5

Yin, R. K. (2009). *Case study research: Design and methods* (4th ed.). Thousand Oaks, CA: Sage Publications.

Zhao, F. (2003). Transforming quality in research supervision: A knowledge-management approach. *Quality in Higher Education*, *9*(2), 187–197. doi:10.1080/13538320308149

KEY TERMS AND DEFINITIONS

Doctoral Research Supervision: A process, where research, knowledge and individuals (student and supervisor) are in the center of this process. We consider this a holistic phenomenon, which should be regarded as a learning process of interactive, dialogic, reflective and transformative nature for both members of the dyad: doctoral student and supervisor. Therefore, it is a process that should be viewed as flexible, adaptable and unpredictable, where a systematic, thoughtful and critical reflection is important to be followed by the supervisory dyad. Doctoral research supervision asks for a mutual commitment established between the student and the supervisor(s), although the research process also occurs in a broader social environment. As Connell (1985) mentions: "Supervision also can be interpreted as a two-way interactional process that requires both the student and the supervisor to consciously engage each other within the spirit of professionalism, respect, collegiality and open-mindedness. Supervision is a complex social encounter which involves two parties with both converging and diverging interests" (p.79).

Evaluation and/or Monitoring Process: This involves an institutional culture based on meta-critical awareness with the objective of permanent enhancement of the context towards a greater common good and of transformation of the individuals that are part of an institution. The evaluation and/or monitoring system should assure that formative and summative perspectives of the supervisory process and cyclic, allowing the transformation (namely in terms of competences' enhancement) of those involved in the supervisory process.

Framework: A systematized, integrative and coherent organization of components about a certain topic. Thus, it may be considered a tool intended to assist an institution, a researcher or a practitioner to develop a better understanding of a specific phenomenon. The framework we present is important both for research and future practice, since the organization it presents may scaffold research and any other sorts of activities as well as to understand what may be involved in a phenomenon – in the case of this chapter: the quality of doctoral research supervision. Thus, we strongly believe that a framework may change throughout time, due to modifications of several nature and coming from different contexts and sectors. This is one of the reasons why we have considered that our framework is fluid. As such, the ongoing character of the phenomenon under study, which involves so many variables that are integrated and establish connections between each other, emphasizes its fluidity, changeability, and unpredictability: it is not possible to totally define all its frontiers, although it has some regularity. Thus, a framework may not be a tool that is finished. Finally, it is an integrative and holistic framework exactly because one must be aware of the total structure and elements, and how the components relate to each other.

PhD Degree: (1) the enhancement of a set of personal, social, academic and professional competences which will be essential to be successful both in a doctoral research and in a future professional path, which may be inside or outside Academia (thus, we may be talking about a set of high-level transferable competences), and (2) the creation of a final product that is mostly characterized by originality, which may be considered one of the most important aspects that define the nature and/or purpose of the doctorate.

Quality: A process of construction, participation, contribution and negotiation from all members of a HE institution: thus, it involves critical thinking and awareness, capacity of action, (self-) improvement, development and transformation.

Chapter 6
Technology Centres:
An Extended Internal Labour Market for PhD Holders in Spain

Susana Pablo-Hernando
IAE de Paris, France

ABSTRACT

This chapter shows how PhD mobility across organizations constitutes a source of normative isomorphism that has led towards the "collegialization" of some Spanish Technology Centres (TCs). In particular, the study of nine TCs located in four Spanish regions has been essential to identify the normative mechanisms embedded in doctoral training and scientific careers that have promoted the convergence among R&D organizations. Thus, TCs collaborating intensively with higher education institutions through hybrid researchers have adopted academic models of knowledge production. Interestingly, they have also introduced doctoral training programs to reinforce their legitimacy in the eyes of their collaborators and investors. As a result of these changes, TCs move towards a more proactive position in the processes of knowledge transfer to gain an advantageous position in an innovation system.

INTRODUCTION

TCs are semi-public R&D organizations whose mission is to transfer scientific knowledge and technology to private sector (especially to Small Medium Enterprises – SMEs - that cannot afford to carry out their own research activities) (Cruz-Castro et al., 2012). It is noteworthy that their intermediate position in innovation systems allows them to bridge the existing gap between academic organizations and industry. In this context, TCs are in charge of acquiring the scientific knowledge generated by universities to solve the real-world problems of their clients.

TCs depend strongly on external resources to achieve their transfer mission. Specifically, they require the scientific knowledge produced in academic organizations and the public funds from multi-level governments (regional, national and European) to face the high diversity of demands coming from a great variety of industrial sectors. The main problem is that these resources are extremely volatile (especially, the scientific knowledge that becomes obsolete in a very brief lapse of time), scarce, and highly demanded by a

DOI: 10.4018/978-1-4666-7244-4.ch006

great variety of R&D organizations. In this context, TCs have implemented several strategies to gain access to these resources that are crucial for their activities. For example, they have diversified their funding schemes increasing their public funds; they have established collaborative relationships and partnerships with local and international universities; and they have recruited skilled employees to obtain scientific knowledge and to increase their opportunities to succeed in calls for funding. This study focuses on the employment of PhD holders in TCs as a strategy to get these resources.

A considerable body of literature has been published about the benefits of PhD mobility across organizations. In particular, several authors state that companies usually recruit PhDs to access scientific knowledge available in academic organizations and they distinguish three reasons for explaining this. First, PhDs have developed research competences during their doctorate that are useful to identify, decode, acquire and apply the scientific knowledge -characterized by being extremely theoretical, abstract and specialized- (Arora & Gambardella, 1997). Secondly, PhDs are used to deal with academic culture (rules and values regulating higher education institutions and their dynamics) because of their long-term socialization in a department (Park, 2005). Thirdly, PhDs have a professional network built during their careers that facilitates the establishment of partnerships with academic community, even at international level (Murray, 2004; Dietz & Bozeman, 2005; Thune, 2009). Interestingly, the majority of these studies have focused on scientific companies located in North American or European countries. However, little attention has been paid to the effects of PhD mobility on intermediate organizations with a technological profile, as the Spanish TCs.

TCs also need to raise public funds from multi-level governments to diversify their funding schemes and to reinforce their scientific capacities (Cruz-Castro et al., 2012). In this sense, some Spanish TCs use public funds to set up

their own R&D agenda and to anticipate future innovation needs of their potential clients. As in other countries, in Spain the national and regional governments have established a high competitive system to distribute equally public funds among R&D organizations according to performance indicators. In particular, scientific productivity (measured by number of publications, scientific communications, patents...) and the percentage of PhDs employed are the main points considered in calls. Thus, TCs are *"forced"* to employ PhDs if they want to succeed in calls for funding.

This research has been structured to pursue three main objectives: First, to describe how PhDs are involved in the acquisition of external resources in TCs, an example of intermediate organization not explored very much in the literature. This is also an excellent opportunity to determine whether a generalist organization with a technological profile use similar strategies to access extramural knowledge than highly specialized companies from scientific sectors.

Secondly, to analyze how the employment of PhDs in TCs impacts on knowledge production models, scientific careers and doctorate programs. In particular, this research aims at exploring whether TCs are introducing academic practices into their organization (process called as *"collegialization of industry"* by Kleinmann & Vallas, 2001) after the number of PhDs has been increased. In this sense, the new institutional theory of organizational change has provided a useful theoretical framework to understand the processes of isomorphism that organizations belonging to the same organizational field experience. Specifically, this theory has allowed describing how the mechanisms related to professionalism influence in the process of organizational change that usually experience organizations that depend strongly on their environment, such as R&D organizations.

Thirdly, to describe the patterns of doctoral education and employment in Spanish non-academic organizations. It is noteworthy that in this country the percentage of PhDs employed in private organizations remains significantly low (less than 20% according to the Survey on Human Resources in Science and Technology, 2009) in spite of the difficulties encountered by PhDs to get a stable position in higher education institutions. In this context, this research provides an opportunity to identify which are the main differences between the academic and the industrial jobs.

The study of nine TCs located in four different Spanish regions allows confirming that the process of collegialization perceived in several TCs has been reinforced by the employment of PhDs from academic origin. In particular, PhDs have pushed TCs to adopt the standards of professionalism of the international scientific community. As a result, TCs are redefining their mission in innovation systems and their objective is to carry out research activities that are not only relevant for their clients, but also excellent for their academic collaborators. Moreover, this chapter provides an interesting discussion about the reforms required to implement new doctoral programs to increase PhD employability in non-academic organizations.

THEORETHICAL FRAMEWORK

The New Institutional Theory of Organizational Change

According to Scott (1992), organizations should be considered as open systems that are exposed to, and conditioned by, their external environment. Specifically, the environment of an organization is composed by a technical dimension – that includes all external resources and information that an organization needs to accomplish their mission – and an institutional dimension – that is formed by values, rules and policies that run a society. Thus, the core idea of the new institutional theory is that the formal organizational structure is not only the result of the technical demands and resource dependencies, but it is also shaped by institutional forces, including rational myths, laws

or knowledge legitimated through the educational system and professions (Meyer & Rowan, 1977). As a result of the strong influence of institutions, organizations usually take decisions more targeted to achieve environmental acceptance and legitimacy than internal efficiency.

DiMaggio & Powell (1983) perceived that the organizations that belong to the same organizational field become less diverse after a period of time, owing to the influence of a common set of environmental conditions. In particular, these authors defined an organizational field as *"those organizations that, in the aggregate, constitute a recognized area of institutional life: key suppliers, resource and product consumers, regulatory agencies, and other organizations that produce similar services or products"* (DiMaggio & Powell, 1983, p. 148). For example, the R&D organizational field is composed by all organizations that produce, apply, diffuse and commercialize the scientific knowledge –as universities, public laboratories, companies-, but also by all the institutions that regulate their life and have an impact on their activities (for example, patent laws). Specifically, these authors identified three mechanisms of institutional isomorphic change for explaining the homogeneity of an organizational field: coercive, mimetic and normative.

All organizations receive pressure, both formal and informal, from government, regulatory agencies, and organizations that control important resources. Thus, coercive forces – usually presented as rules, sanctions or policies – push the organizations to adopt a particular structure, behaviour or technique in their routines which do not conduct necessarily towards more efficiency. By contrast, mimetic isomorphism happens when organizations face high uncertainty coming from their environment. According to Daft (2010), organizations cope with high levels of uncertainty when they need a diverse quantity of resources from their environment which are characterized by being extremely volatile. For example, absorbing the scientific knowledge produced in academic organizations is a source of uncertainty for the majority of the companies from knowledge-driven sectors because this resource becomes obsolete after a short period of time (Lam, 2005).

Finally, normative forces push organizations to achieve standards of professionalism and to adopt techniques that are considered by a professional community to be up to date and effective. In particular, DiMaggio & Powell (1983) found two dimensions of professionalization that are important sources of normative isomorphism: the university degrees and the professional networks. In this sense, Kleinmann & Vallas (2001) supported the idea that the researchers who develop their professional careers in the hybrid space that has emerged between academia and industry constitute an example of professional community that have promoted the collegialization of some companies in the US through normative mechanisms.

To sum up, organizations that act under conditions of dependence, uncertainty, ambiguous goals, and reliance on professional credentials have more probabilities to be under the influence of these mechanisms of isomorphism (Daft, 2010). However, this does not mean that organizations are passive entities that are obliged to conform to the expectations of the fields in which they are members. For example, Olivier (1991) found that organizations have a range of strategies to face institutional pressures that oscillate from conformism to resistance.

The Normative Isomorphism in R&D Organizations: The Collegialization in Non-Academic Organizations

According to Kleinmann and Vallas (2001), in the US a process of convergence is underway in R&D organizations that confirms the tendency towards isomorphism in mature organizational fields. In particular, these authors find that "the codes and practices of industry are infiltrating the academy, even as academic norms are increasingly governing the work practices of selected

knowledge workers in high technology firms and industries" (Kleinmann & Vallas, 2001, p. 451). However, this process of convergence is asymmetric because, although the changes are perceived in both organizations, industry appears to take an advantage in adopting academic culture.

There are at least three factors that can help to explain these dynamics of convergence that are perceived in Anglo-Saxon countries and research-intensive sectors (such as biotechnology or IT companies) (Owen-Smith, 2005; Vallas & Kleinmann, 2008). First, the advance towards a knowledge-based economy implies that companies are more aware of the strategic value of scientific knowledge and technical expertise (Powell & Snellman, 2004). Secondly, the consolidation of a network model of organization has enhanced collaborations and partnerships between university and industry (Lam, 2005). As a result of these fruitful and continuous exchanges, the boundaries between "basic and applied research" and between "public and private sectors" are more diffuse than in the past. Finally, the mobility of researchers across organizations is a source of normative isomorphism that has contributed to the substitution of the administrative principle of vertical control for the occupational principle of horizontal control in companies that depend strongly on knowledge (Kleinmann & Vallas, 2001). Moreover, the mobility is also considered as an efficient mechanism to transfer knowledge in innovation systems (Dasgupta & David, 1994; Stephan, 1996; Arora & Gambardella, 1997; Thune, 2009).

There are several evidences that illustrate the process of convergence in both organizations. In particular, some academic departments have developed a commercial perspective of knowledge that usually coexists with the traditional models of scientific production. For example, several empirical studies have demonstrated that professors use patents as tools for protecting their inventions and coordinating their exchanges with companies (Cassier, 1997; Owen-Smith, 2005). Some authors have revealed that professors specialized in disciplines of social sciences and humanities are also involved in knowledge transfer through consultancy and contract research (Olmos-Peñuela et al., 2014). However, the exchanges with non-academic communities are more important for scientific and technologic fields. In addition, universities have introduced quantitative methods for measuring scientific productivity that increase the control over academic work (Musselin, 2007). In this sense, several authors have signalled two factors for explaining these changes. 1) Universities have diversified their sources of funding in order to avoid the strong dependence on governments and to face the contexts of scarcity (Slaughter & Leslie, 1997). 2) Producing useful knowledge with an economic or social value reinforces the legitimacy of universities at the eyes of public audiences. In a context of more participatory models of citizenship, some professors are appealed to produce a kind of knowledge that should simultaneously be excellent - in scientific terms - and relevant for promoting economic growth and quality of life of citizens (Stokes, 1997; Ziman, 2000).

By contrast, the process of collegialization that some companies are experiencing comes motivated by their continuous dependence on extramural knowledge produced in academia (Lam, 2005). In this context, companies seek to gain greater access to academic departments through strategic partnerships or joint ventures enterprises that allow them to obtain the scientific resources and the support of researchers who own the competences and skills required to apply and commercialize the more basic knowledge. Interestingly, this process has been reinforced by researchers who attempt to maintain their professional identity and to increase their power and prestige within the industrial organizations.

According to Kleinmann and Vallas (2001), there are four manifestations of collegialization that appear in research-intensive industries. First, companies usually compete with universities to attract the most brilliant researchers, offering the traditional benefits of the academic work. Secondly, companies have also appropriated of the norm of publication to reinforce their legitimacy. For example, Hicks (1995) supports that publications help to improve the relationships with other organizations because they constitute a tool to signal the presence of tacit knowledge and to reinforce the technical reputation necessary to engage new collaborators and investors in the technological adventure of the company. The third evidence of isomorphism is the adoption of collegial forms of organizational culture, as collaborations and team work. Fourthly, companies usually design and offer education activities addressed to their employees and users. To conclude, the introduction of these routines contributes to improving the external image of some companies that appear as more legitimate for their workers and other organizations of their environment, because they are not only engaged in profit-making goals.

The Labour Market for PhDs

Traditionally, the main function of the PhD degree has been to reproduce the academic community (Enders, 2002). Thus, the design of doctoral education and the management of academic careers have been private matters regulated by departments, which have worked as internal labour markets (Musselin, 2005; Kehm, 2007). In the majority of the European higher education systems, the training of doctoral students has been assumed mainly by their supervisors who have followed the method of learning-by-doing to transmit the scientific profession to the new generations of researchers. In this context, Shinn (1988) states that doctoral education is a necessary function for academic departments because the technical tasks are usually assigned to doctoral students and, consequently, they contribute to increasing the productivity of their research groups. As a result of these dynamics, doctoral education has been also perceived as a first professional experience in research (Mangematin & Robin, 2003).

However, the emergence of new models of knowledge production and the difficulties to get a tenured position in academic organizations are provoking structural changes in the labour market for PhDs (Cruz-Castro & Sanz-Menéndez, 2005a; Recotillet, 2007; Thune, 2009). In particular, the strategic collaborations between university and industry - that are essential for supporting processes of knowledge transfer - rely on hybrid scientists (as entrepreneurial professors and PhDs who have moved towards private sector) whose main role is to facilitate knowledge circulation across organizations (Arora & Gambardella, 1997; Lam, 2005). It is noteworthy that these trends are promoted by a new political framework that stimulates the approach between both communities and the flow of human resources in both directions. For example, France has successfully implemented an industrial doctoral program (known as "Bourses CIFRE") whose goal is to provide doctoral education with an industrial perspective (Levy, 2005); universities in the United Kingdom have diversified their doctoral training programs to increase PhD employability; and the Spanish government has subsidized the employment of PhDs in private organizations (such as SMEs, TCs, scientific parks...) since 2001 through the "Programa Torres Quevedo" (Cruz-Castro & Sanz-Menendez, 2005b). As a result of these dynamics, the PhD degree has changed its nature and nowadays is considered as *"a passport to different professional journeys"* (Enders, 2005).

The European higher education institutions are facing a common challenge: they need to adapt their doctoral training programs to the new models of knowledge production and to design professional careers that can offer what companies demand. According to Enders and De Weert (2004), there are two main approaches to accomplish this reform. The first approach supports that training for the new qualification needs can be achieved within the traditional PhD programs because they are sufficiently robust to face this change. Whereas the second approach considers that it would be necessary that the traditional model of doctoral education (known as the academic-disciplinary model) should be replaced by a new model with more flexible structures and roles that crosses disciplinary and organizational borders (known as the hybrid model).

This second approach is reinforced by frequent criticisms towards the traditional model of PhD education that come from different sectors of the society. In particular, Nerad (2004) identified in the US six weak points in the academic-disciplinary model, which Kehm (2007) also perceived in the European universities. Specifically, these are the points mentioned: (1) PhDs are educated too narrowly in a high-specialized topic; (2) they usually lack key professional, organizational and managerial skills (such as the ability to work under pressure or to collaborate in a multi-disciplinary team); (3) they have not received a good training to assume teaching duties; (4) the duration of doctoral education is too long (especially, when the funding mechanisms are instable); (5) PhDs are uninformed about the professional opportunities outside academia; and (6) the transitions towards a stable position after completing the PhD are too long and competitive.

Enders (2005) argues that these divergent positions are not irreconcilable and, consequently, universities should recognize the multi-functional role of PhDs by offering a diversity of training approaches. In this sense, Lee et al. (2010) point out that different types of competences from doctoral education are perceived as more suitable for different types of career. For example, the general and transferable skills are regarded as more valuable in employments outside the conventional technical occupations. By contrast, there is enough evidence to support that the composition of the research groups - and their ability to establish academic networks – and the role of the supervisors during the doctorate are important requirements for doctoral students who want to pursue a scientific career in academia after the graduation (Cormina et al., 2011). This chapter provides a perspective of the competences that are advantageous for a career in a non-academic organization, such as a TC.

METHODOLOGY

A multiple-case study design was considered convenient to approach the research question because it enables to analyze an organization in depth and within its real-life context, especially when the boundaries between the organization and the context are diffuse (Yin, 2003). In this sense, this method has been useful to understand the influence of the technical and institutional environment of TCs and, consequently, to study the process of collegialization under the perspective of the new institutional theory of organizational change. Moreover, the continuous comparison and contrast of different types of cases have allowed drawing patterns and obtaining more reliability in the overall results.

Specifically, nine TCs were selected from four Spanish regions for this study: 1 in Madrid, 3 in the Basque Country, 2 in Valencia and 3 in Castile and Leon. It is noteworthy that three main criteria were taken into account to include TCs in the research. 1) TCs had to invest significantly in in-house scientific activities and having a long-term R&D agenda. This condition was essential for studying the four manifestations of the collegialization identified by Kleinmann & Vallas (2001). 2) It was also crucial that the cases had recruited PhDs during the last two years in order to analyze the impact of PhD employment in non-academic organizations. 3) Regional and organizational heterogeneity was aimed to explore the influence of alternative variables (such as organization size, industrial sector, regional innovation policy...) in the advance towards collegialization. As table 1 (see Appendix) reflects, 51 semi-structured interviews were conducted with individuals with five different professional profiles in TC headquarters from October 2009 to February 2010: CEOs (5),

R&D Managers (8), Human Resources Managers (6), PhD Researchers (19) and Researchers (13).

The interview guide was structured in five sections: (1) organization characteristics and functioning, taking into account the relationships with the external environment; (2) R&D activities (funding scheme, organization of R&D department, scientific productivity...); (3) collaborative relationships with academic community; (4) R&D human resources management (with a special focus on scientific careers) and (5) PhD employment in TCs. Each interview lasted approximately 60 minutes and was recorded in its entirety and transcribed verbatim for carrying out a content analysis. Finally, mentioning that data collected through interviews were triangulated with other sources such as observations and document analysis (scientific reports, statistics and website content).

A content analysis of each interview using NVivo 8 was carried out after the fieldwork had been concluded. In particular, the analysis accomplished was divided into four sub-processes. First, each interview was summarized and organized to analyze it from two perspectives: within the interviewee's TC and within the interviewee's professional profile. Second, each interview was coded from a deductive perspective. This means that a coding structure based on the main issues of the interview guide had been previously created which was subsequently developed with emergent codes found during the analysis. Third, data were displayed in a matrix to draw connections and facilitate comparative analysis (Miles & Huberman, 1994). In particular, the matrix ordered data according to two characteristics of TCs: the degree of collegialization – measured through the dimensions identified by Kleinmann and Vallas (2001) – and the percentage of PhDs employed. Finally, an in depth-analysis was conducted in three paradigmatic cases – specifically in TC_3, TC_5 and TC_7 - where PhDs had actively contributed to the introduction of the academic culture within the organization.

Table 1. Interviews conducted in TCs

Region	TC	Profile	Interviews n° / Profile	Interviews n° / TC
Madrid	TC₁	CEO	1	2
		PhD Researchers	1	
The Basque Country	TC₂	CEO	1	9
		R&D Manager	1	
		HR Manager	1	
		PhD Researchers	3	
		Researchers	3	
	TC₃	CEO	1	6
		HR Manager	1	
		PhD Researchers	2	
		Researchers	2	
	TC₄	R&D Manager	1	6
		HR Manager	1	
		PhD Researchers	2	
		Researchers	2	
Valencia	TC₅	CEO	1	8
		R&D Manager	2	
		HR Manager	1	
		PhD Researchers	2	
		Researchers	2	
	TC₆	R&D Manager	1	5
		PhD Researchers	2	
		Researchers	2	
Castile and Leon	TC₇	CEO	1	2
		PhD Researchers	1	
	TC₈	R&D Manager	1	7
		HR Manager	1	
		PhD Researchers	5	
	TC₉	CEO	1	6
		R&D Manager	1	
		HR Manager	1	
		PhD Researchers	1	
		Researchers	2	

RESULTS

The New Models of Knowledge Production

There is a strong consensus among interviewees about the fact that industrial research mobilizes the same cognitive resources and competences than academic research. However, PhDs detected two important differences in the way of conducting scientific activities in both organizations that could be source of adaptation problems at the beginning of their professional career in TCs. The first difference is related to the temporal framework to conduct research projects. In particular, PhDs recognized that it was very stressful for them to get used to work simultaneously in different projects that involve diverse methodologies. Thus, PhDs have had to develop abilities to manage better pressure and to use time more efficiently. Although these difficulties are frequently encountered by the majority of PhDs after completing their doctorate, even when they remain attached to the academic world, they are more intense in the case of PhDs who work in a polyvalent organization because they have to prove a strong flexibility and a great capacity of adaptation. The second difference is related to applicability and the need to solve real-world problems. As some managers explained, the theoretical contributions derived from scientific work are not enough (or even not important) for TCs or clients, the essential is that *"technologies work"*. In this sense, some interviewees felt that moving from basic research to applied research was an interesting challenge and the main appeal for leaving academia.

There are three evidences that reflect how some TCs have introduced an academic model of knowledge production that frequently coexists with the industrial one.

First, some TCs have changed their organizational structure and culture to promote the values of creativity and autonomy among researchers. For example, PhDs recruited by TC_3 or TC_5 work with high levels of autonomy that allow them to define and carry out their own research agenda. In this sense, several R&D Managers have realized that the best ideas frequently come from the initiatives of researchers that work with freedom and flexibility, escaping from the bureaucratic controls that have traditionally characterized private organizations. This change is more evident in TCs that were created by entrepreneurial professors.

Secondly, TCs participate more in research projects funded by multi-level governments (as for example, the projects funded by the European Research Council) than in the past. This means that TCs have included in their research portfolio projects that have more scientific content, that are developed in a long-term period (3 years minimum), that require interacting with academic partners - usually from other countries – and, finally, that are evaluated periodically through scientific indicators by peers. Interestingly, these projects have allowed TCs to achieve three objectives: (1) to diversify funding schemes and reducing the dependence on private funds; (2) to gain better access to scientific knowledge available in academic organizations; and (3) to adopt a more proactive position in innovation systems by anticipating the future innovation needs of their potential clients. Consequently, the development of these projects is considered a profitable strategy to increase legitimacy and to access resources that are essential to accomplish the transfer mission.

According to interviewees, participating in these projects has been possible thanks to the employment of PhDs. In general, calls for funding usually require (or at least privilege) that organizations had employed PhDs with a strong scientific curriculum (measured by number of publications in scientific journals). Moreover, the research profile of PhDs fits well in this kind of projects owing to their strong scientific competences and their socialization in an academic environment during the doctorate. Thus, PhDs are the interlocutor of TCs in these projects.

Thirdly, TCs give out incentives to those employees who publish in scientific journals, as higher education institutions have traditionally done. According to R&D Managers, TCs have appropriated of the publication rule for three reasons. 1) TCs need to have publications in top-journals in order to be eligible to participate in projects funded by governments. 2) Publications help to certify the scientific abilities of the TCs, owing to the fact that only excellent contributions manage to be published by indexed scientific journals. 3) Adopting academic models of scientific productivity increases the legitimacy of TCs at the eyes of investors, collaborators, end-users and clients. In sum, these reasons are similar to those stated by professors.

In spite of the relevance of publications for TCs, writing a paper in a TC is more difficult than in universities or public laboratories, because these organizations are strongly orientated to clients. In particular, several PhDs explained that their daily routines do not allow them to invest much time in working on a paper or to be concentrated on data analysis. Thus, they usually have to dedicate free-time to finish a paper – a duty that not all researchers want to assume because they do not need publications for promoting in a TC or because they precisely decided to move towards a non-academic organization to escape of the academic productivity style. Additionally, the confidential restrictions imposed by some clients make more complicated manipulating empirical data because of the continuous fear to disclose some relevant information to competitors.

To sum up, there are three sources of professionalization related to PhD employment that have influenced in the movement towards excellence envisaged by some TCs: research experience certified by the highest degree delivered by universities, socialization in an academic environment during a long-term period and professional networks. In general, managers corroborated that PhDs have helped to improve the quality of scientific activities, to diversify the kind of projects of the research agenda and to increase the scientific productivity. Moreover, PhDs have enlarged the network of TCs, facilitating the circulation of knowledge across organizations.

The Doctoral Education in TCs

TCs give out economic and professional incentives to those employees who carry out a doctoral research developing projects available within the organization. According to HR Managers, investing in doctoral training for their employees constitutes a profitable strategy to improve the access to public funds and, especially, to scientific knowledge. In addition, a minority of TCs also offers industrial doctoral training as a part of their mission, addressed to their employees and other external candidates. In particular, this training programs offer a doctoral experience fitted to the industrial needs and with strong focus on managerial and organizational skills.

A comparative analysis between academic and industrial doctoral programs – as those proposed by TCs – reveals that there are three main differences related to (1) the content of the thesis and the kind of research conducted, (2) the time dedicated to carry out the doctoral research and (3) the professional opportunities for the new graduates after completing the PhD. Thus, candidates who are trained by a TC focus more on applied research than academic doctoral students and their thesis seek to solve a real-world problem, frequently faced by customers of the TC. As a result of their simultaneous involvement in different projects – boosted by the dynamics and rhythms of the TC -, they only can dedicate a small part of the work day to develop their doctoral research and, consequently, they have to work on it during their free time. After completing the doctorate, the majority of the new PhDs will continue their careers in a private organization owing to the scarcity of PhDs with industrial experience in the Spanish labour market. It is noteworthy that these remarks have been yet mentioned by previous works related to the industrial doctorate.

Interestingly, doctoral employees distinguished three kinds of motivations for justifying their decision of conducting a doctoral research in a TC, an organization that a priori is more orientated to generate economic profit than academic value and with a weak experience in providing education. The analysis of these personal reasons has been crucial to better understand how this alternative system of doctoral education - whose origin was spontaneous and unsystematic for the majority of the cases studied- has emerged.

The first motivation is similar to that signalled by doctoral students from academia: they felt a genuine taste for science and they were interested in learning more about an original topic or a promising technology. The second motivation reveals that some employees invest in a PhD to obtain more professional opportunities and benefits – as mobility or salary augmentation – within the organization. Finally, a minority of employees mentioned that they decided to begin a PhD to facilitate the adaptation of the TC to their external environment. For example, they were aware that governments evaluate the number of publications, the number of PhDs recruited or that of doctoral thesis defended to distribute public funds. Moreover, carrying out a doctoral research, even in a TC, contributes to reinforcing the links with the academic community – a requirement to absorb extramural knowledge.

In spite of the benefits of doctoral education for TCs and employees, there are some barriers that make harder to conduct a doctoral research in a TC than in an academic department. In particular, the majority of R&D Managers recognized that they cannot afford to attach an employee to a single long-term project during the doctorate, the kind of project that allows gaining a deep specialization in a topic to publish scientific papers. As mentioned above, TCs require that their employees can simultaneously work in several projects and be flexible enough to attend unexpected demands. In this

sense, some interviewees explained that they had to give up temporarily their research to solve an urgent problem faced by a client. In addition, the strong market orientation of research activities in TCs makes difficult to use empirical data, owing to the confidential restrictions imposed by clients.

As a result of these difficulties, some TCs offer professional recompenses to engage new employees for a doctorate. According to HR Managers, TCs provide four kinds of incentives to achieve this goal. First, TCs design a personalized time schedule for each employee who is formally conducting a doctoral research to guarantee a better balance between organizational duties and doctoral requirements. Second, TCs provide the resources to carry out the research within the organization (for example, the bibliographic bases) and the empirical data from their projects. Third, TCs give economic grants for affording doctoral expenses, as the universities tax or the acquisition of software licenses or bibliography. Fourth, some TCs promise an improvement of labour conditions after completing the PhD: salary increase, promotion, attribution of more responsibilities in the organization… To sum up, the introduction of this pack of incentives has contributed to reinforcing the process of collegialization in TCs because they have imitated the doctoral training system of universities to retain the best candidates.

TCs have institutionalized their policy for incentivizing doctoral education within the organization after the number of PhDs has increased. In particular, hybrid researchers – as entrepreneurial professors or PhDs who have successfully accomplished their mobility project within the TC– provide the institutional support and the academic culture required to carry out a doctorate. Even if the doctoral research is conducted in a TC, candidates need to be attached to a department and to know the values and rules that regulate academic life, because the thesis is essentially an academic product and the PhD is the highest degree delivered by universities. Consequently, hybrid researchers have developed a dual professional identity during their careers that allow them to transfer the best of both worlds (academia and industry) to doctoral candidates of TCs. For example, they emphasise the importance of disseminating scientific results through publications and scientific communications or to be fluent in English at professional level, owing to the fact that English is the language of scientific community.

The Management of Scientific Careers

There are three reasons that motivate PhDs to move towards a non-academic organization, such a TC. First, TCs constitutes a professional alternative to the academic labour market. In particular, the majority of PhDs interviewed disliked some structural characteristics of the Spanish universities, as the excessive bureaucracy or the endogamic criteria to promote. In this sense, they claimed that the opportunities for getting a stable position in an academic department depend not only on scientific merits, but also (and especially) on professional contacts acquired during the career. Secondly, PhDs who decided to work in a TC were frequently interested in improving their labour conditions. In general, they perceived that private organizations offer more stability and higher salaries than universities, although the social prestigious and the level of autonomy of these positions are lower. It is noteworthy that the labour conditions vary depending on the country, the industrial sector and the field of doctoral specialization. Thus, this result is very specific of this research and not extendable to the case of other PhDs who move towards private sector, even in Spain. Thirdly, several PhDs stated that they wanted to work in more applied research projects. In general, they believed that their positions in TCs were very rewarding because they contributed to the consolidation of the collaborative relationships between academia and industry.

There are two evidences that illustrate how TCs try to imitate academic organizations in the management of scientific careers: the introduction of meritocratic criteria for promoting in TCs and the emergence of an Extended Internal Labour Market (EILM) whose structure and functioning is similar to the academic internal labour markets described by Musselin (2005). In particular, several TCs have created expert positions within their R&D departments (for example, TC_2 use the term "technological leader" to refer to these experts) that they assign to those PhDs who have accumulated more scientific merits along their careers (as publications, communications in conferences, patents...). According to HR Managers, this implicit rule that works in some TCs comes motivated by the notion that authority emanates easier from credentials and scientific merits than from other subjective criteria.

Interestingly, the mobility of PhDs across organizations has enhanced the emergence of a bi-directional EILM (adapting the concept proposed by Lam, 2005). On the one side, TCs constitutes an EILM for some academic departments. In particular, TCs provide financial resources to conduct research activities in universities that help to reduce the strong dependence on public funds. In addition, TCs are more and more perceived by supervisors as a realistic professional choice for the new generations of PhDs. In this sense, supervisors have traditionally succeeded to attract the most brilliant students with the promise of future sponsorship to develop their academic career – this exchange between supervisors and doctoral students has been denominated as implicit contract. However, academic departments (especially those from natural sciences) face severe difficulties to absorb the increasing offer of new graduates and, consequently, to support the careers of their PhDs. In this context, TCs provide a credible alternative to keep the promise of employability that allow recruiting the best students to nourish the productivity of laboratories. On the other side, some academic departments that collaborate intensively with TCs can become EILM for them. For example, TCs use the facilities and equipments of universities to carry out their research activities, influence in the R&D agenda of professors according to their scientific needs and participate in the teaching duties of departments in order to provide a practical perspective of knowledge.

The consolidation of a bi-directional EILM has been possible thanks to the role performed by hybrid researchers in knowledge transfer. Specifically, R&D Managers have realized that their PhDs need to be active members of the academic community if they want to acquire the extramural knowledge. Thus, TCs have redefined the scientific careers within the organization to enhance the relationships of their researchers with the academic community, providing a double set of recompenses and incentives. In this sense, the human resources policy of TCs seeks to extract the advantages of industrial and academic jobs to make the intermediate positions more attractive for PhDs. This change in the management of scientific careers has been facilitated by the reduction of bureaucratic controls in TCs and by the genuine interest of PhDs to continue attached to the academic environments. As a result, the frontiers between TCs and universities are more diffuse than in the past.

DISCUSSION

There is strong evidence to support the idea of the collegialization of TCs, especially of those created by entrepreneurial professors. In particular, data analysis has revealed some manifestations of this underway process that corroborate the results of other studies (Lam, 2005; Vallas & Kleinmann, 2008). Interestingly, TCs have promoted an academic style of knowledge production that has contributed to reinforcing the scientific capacities of their R&D departments and to diversifying their research portfolio. In this sense, the majority of TCs are involved in international research consortia that help them to anticipate the innovation needs of their potential clients. As a result of these

new dynamics, TCs have adapted progressively the management of scientific careers within the organization to recruit researchers from academia. It is interesting to note how some TCs legitimize the introduction of structures and practices that are characteristic of academic labour markets - as the meritocratic system of recruitment and promotion – to make more appealing the professional careers for PhDs in non-academic organizations.

Additionally, an informal and non-structured model of doctoral training has emerged in the majority of the cases studied whose aim is to facilitate the access to external resources (especially, scientific knowledge). Owing to the fact that the academic doctoral programs offered by Spanish universities do not conform to the qualification needs of TCs, these organizations have implemented spontaneously their own doctoral training tailored to their own needs. In particular, TCs offer economic incentives and professional recompenses to those employees who are engaged in the development of a doctoral research whose content is related to the scientific activities conducted in the TC. These incentives attempt to retain the best candidates among the employees for a PhD and to neutralize the typical difficulties of carrying out a doctoral research in a market-orientated organization. As academic departments have traditionally done, TCs promise to their employees that they will support their professional careers within the organization if they carry out a doctoral research from their research projects. On the other side, a minority of TCs also provides a more structured system of industrial doctoral training whose aims are (1) to increase the employability of PhDs and (2) to satisfy the qualification needs of non-academic employers. According to the interviewees of these centres, training PhDs for an industrial career is considered as part of their mission of knowledge transfer to SMEs.

In general, interviewees found that these changes have had a positive impact on the performance of TCs and on the innovation system.

119

In this sense, managers perceived that TCs have successfully moved from a reactive position towards a more proactive one in the management of clients' demands thanks to the development of R&D activities that are simultaneously relevant - for the end-users - and excellent - for the scientific community. To sum up, TCs have assumed some missions that were only provided by higher education institutions -as the doctoral training or the diffusion of scientific results through publications – to reinforce their legitimacy, confirming the thesis of the new institutional theory (Meyer & Rowan, 1977).

According to some interviewees, the mobility of PhDs across organizations has been essential to reinforce the collegialization of TCs, owing to the influence of normative forces embedded in their academic background - as the qualification and experience gained during the doctorate, the long-term exposure to an academic environment and their belonging to professional networks. In this sense, some interviewees agreed that PhDs have provided the academic and institutional basis to guarantee the movement towards excellence in the scientific and training activities of TCs. Moreover, the continuous interaction of PhDs with academic community - in the frame of knowledge transfer processes - feeds back these dynamics.

Contributions and Research Opportunities

The current research confirms that the dynamics of isomorphism in the R&D organizational field - mainly described in Anglo-Saxon countries (Kleinmann & Vallas, 2001; Lam, 2005; Owen-Smith, 2005) - are also perceived in countries with lower resources dedicated to innovation, as in Spain. Moreover, the strategy of increasing legitimacy through the introduction of academic culture is relevant for organizations with a polyvalent and technological profile, and not only for high-specialized and scientific industries (as biotechnological companies). However, these contributions need to be analyzing further in order to better understand the influence of PhD mobility in the process of convergence between academia and industry in Spain. In this sense, two research opportunities have been identified from this study. 1) TCs are an example of intermediate organization that fills the existing gap between universities and companies; although, their hybrid nature constitutes a limitation in the study of isomorphism because, in reality, they are not a company or a university. Thus, it is recommended to test the hypothesis of the asymmetrical convergence stated by Kleinmann and Vallas (2001) in a sample of Spanish companies and universities. 2) Carrying out an ethnographic research is recommended to describe how PhDs keep their professional prestige and power in non-academic organizations with industrial roots.

Implications for the Higher Education Policies

The experience of TCs reveals that in Spain non-academic employers ask for an urgent reform in doctoral programs because of the failure of academic-disciplinary model to satisfy the qualification needs of industry. As in other countries, TCs complain of the lack of managerial skills and the over-specialization of PhDs (Theodosiou & Amir-Aslani, 2013). This problem is aggravated by the lack of an industrial doctoral program in Spain, as those implemented by other countries in Europe (for example, in France or in Denmark).

According to some interviewees, TCs have decided to create an alternative system of doctoral training to face the immobility of Spanish universities that are still attached to the traditional values and, consequently, are unable to answer to the new economic and societal challenges. In this sense, they have perceived that some rare initiatives were developed by some universities to adapt their doctoral studies to the new models of knowledge production without losing the academic nature of this training. Interestingly, some interviewees have considered that the reform of doctoral training should include other stakeholders' insights not only to obtain a better adjustment between offer and demand in the labour market for PhDs, but to increase the legitimacy and acceptance of these changes by employers.

To sum up, the reform of doctoral training has been an important issue in the agenda of policy makers during the last decade worldwide (Nerad & Heggelund, 2008). For example, Bartelese and Huisman (2008) found that doctoral education has been subjected to the intense pressure and scrutiny in the European Union, because of its location between education and research. They signalled that the debates about improving doctoral education in the Bologna Processes sought to shift the functions of doctoral programs to increase their employability outside academia. However, these reforms may bring the risk of transforming the doctoral education in another commodity for increasing technological progress and economic growth, without room for the curiosity-driven investigations. In this sense, it should be necessary to implement a rigorous system of quality to guarantee that the new doctoral training programs that are emerging in non-academic organizations (such as the informal and non-structured model of doctoral training of TCs) continue to produce original scientific research in a specific field of knowledge.

ACKNOWLEDGMENT

The author was awarded an I3P-doctoral fellowship from the Spanish Research Council (CSIC) during the period 2007–2010. The data presented in this study were collected during that period and the fieldwork was funded by a research grant (CSO-2008-03100/SOCI). The author wants to thank all the comments received during the "Higher Education and Society: Implications and Effects" colloquium, organized by European Science Foundation in Dublin, because they have constituted the basis for this work. The reviewers and editors have nicely contributed to the improvement of the chapter.

REFERENCES

Arora, A., & Gambardella, A. (1997). Public policy towards science: Picking stars or spreading the wealth? *Revue d'Economie Industrielle*, 79(79), 63–75. doi:10.3406/rei.1997.1653

Bartelese, J., & Huisman, J. (2008). The Bologna process. In M. Nerad & M. Heggelund (Eds.), Toward a global PhD? Forces and forms in doctoral education worldwide (pp. 101-113). University of Washington Press.

Cassier, M. (1997). Compromis institutionnels et hybridations entre recherche publique et recherché privée. *Revue d'Economie Industrielle*, 79(1), 191–212. doi:10.3406/rei.1997.1661

Coromina, L., Capó, A., Coenders, G., & Guia, J. (2011). PhD students' research group networks: A qualitative approach. *Advances in Methodology & Statistics, 8*(2), 137-155.

Cruz-Castro, L., & Sanz-Menéndez, L. (2005a). Bringing science and technology human resources back in: The Spanish Ramón y Cajal programme. *Science & Public Policy, 32*(1), 39–53. doi:10.3152/147154305781779687

Cruz-Castro, L., & Sanz-Menéndez, L. (2005b). The employment of PhDs in firms: Trajectories, mobility and innovation. *Research Evaluation, 14*(1), 57–69. doi:10.3152/147154405781776292

Cruz-Castro, L., Sanz-Menéndez, L., & Martínez, C. (2012). Research centres in transition: Patterns of convergence and diversity. *The Journal of Technology Transfer, 37*(1), 18–42. doi:10.1007/s10961-010-9168-5

Daft, R. L. (2010). *Organization theory and design.* Mason, OH: South-Western Cengage Learning.

Dasgupta, P., & David, P. A. (1994). Toward a new economics of science. *Research Policy, 23*(5), 487–521. doi:10.1016/0048-7333(94)01002-1

Dietz, J. S., & Bozeman, B. (2005). Academic careers, patents, and productivity: Industry experience as scientific and technical human capital. *Research Policy, 34*(3), 349–367. doi:10.1016/j.respol.2005.01.008

DiMaggio, P. J., & Powell, W. W. (1983). The iron cage revisited: Institutional isomorphism and collective rationality in organizational fields. *American Sociological Review, 48*(2), 147–160. doi:10.2307/2095101

Enders, J. (2002). Serving many masters: The PhD on the labour market, the everlasting need of inequality, and the premature death of Humboldt. *Higher Education, 44*(3/4), 493–517. doi:10.1023/A:1019850524330

Enders, J. (2005). Border crossings: Research training, knowledge dissemination and the transformation of academic work. *Higher Education, 49*(1-2), 119–133. doi:10.1007/s10734-004-2917-3

Enders, J., & De Weert, E. (2004). Science, training and career: Changing modes of knowledge production and labour markets. *Higher Education Policy, 17*(2), 135–152. doi:10.1057/palgrave.hep.8300047

Hicks, D. (1995). Published papers, tacit competencies and corporate management of the public/private character of knowledge. *Industrial and Corporate Change, 4*(2), 401–424. doi:10.1093/icc/4.2.401

Kehm, B. M. (2007). Quo vadis doctoral education? New european approaches in the context of global changes. *European Journal of Education, 42*(3), 307–319. doi:10.1111/j.1465-3435.2007.00308.x

Kleinman, D. L., & Vallas, S. P. (2001). Science, capitalism, and the rise of 'knowledge worker': The changing structure of knowledge production in the United States. *Theory and Society, 30*(4), 451–492. doi:10.1023/A:1011815518959

Lam, A. (2005). Work roles and careers of R&D scientists in network organizations. *Industrial Relations, 44*(2), 242–275. doi:10.1111/j.0019-8676.2005.00383.x

Lee, H. F., Miozzo, M., & Laredo, P. (2010). Career patterns and competences of PhDs in science and engineering in the knowledge economy: The case of graduates from a UK research-based university. *Research Policy, 39*(7), 869–881. doi:10.1016/j.respol.2010.05.001

Levy, R. (2005). Les doctorants CIFRE: Médiateurs entre laboratoires de recherche universitaires et entreprise. *Revue d'Economie Industrielle, 111*(1), 79–96. doi:10.3406/rei.2005.3083

Mangematin, V., & Nesta, L. (1999). What kind of knowledge can a firm absorb? *International Journal of Technology Management, 18*(3), 149–172. doi:10.1504/IJTM.1999.002771

Mangematin, V., & Robin, S. (2003). The double face of PhD students: The example of life sciences. *Science & Public Policy, 30*(6), 405–414. doi:10.3152/147154303781780209

Meyer, J. W., & Rowan, B. (1977). Institutionalized organizations: Formal structure as myth and ceremony. *American Journal of Sociology, 83*(2), 340–363. doi:10.1086/226550

Miles, M. B., & Huberman, A. M. (1994). *Qualitative data analysis: An expanded sourcebook.* London: Sage.

Murray, F. (2004). The role of academic inventors in entrepreneurial firms: Sharing the laboratory life. *Research Policy, 33*(4), 643–659. doi:10.1016/j.respol.2004.01.013

Musselin, C. (2005). European academic labour markets in transition. *Higher Education, 49*(1/2), 135–154. doi:10.1007/s10734-004-2918-2

Musselin, C. (2007). *The transformation of academic work: Facts and analysis.* Center for Studies in Higher Education.

Nerad, M. (2004). The PhD in the US: Criticisms, facts, and remedies. *Higher Education Policy, 17*(2), 183–199. doi:10.1057/palgrave.hep.8300050

Nerad, M., & Heggelund, M. (2008). *Toward a global PhD? Forces and forms in doctoral education worldwide.* University of Washington Press.

Olivier, C. (1991). Strategic responses to institutional process. *Academy of Management Review, 16*(1), 145–179.

Olmos-Peñuela, J., Castro-Martínez, E., & D'Este, P. (2014). Knowledge transfer activities in social sciences and humanities: Explaining the interactions of research groups with non-academic agents. *Research Policy, 43*(4), 696–706. doi:10.1016/j.respol.2013.12.004

Owen-Smith, J. (2005). Trends and transitions in the institutional environment for public and private science. *Higher Education, 49*(1-2), 91–117. doi:10.1007/s10734-004-2916-4

Park, C. (2005). New variant PhD: The changing nature of the doctorate in the UK. *Journal of Higher Education Policy and Management, 27*(2), 189–207. doi:10.1080/13600800500120068

Powell, W. W., & Snellman, K. (2004). The knowledge economy. *Annual Review of Sociology, 30*(1), 199–220. doi:10.1146/annurev.soc.29.010202.100037

Recotillet, I. (2007). PhD Graduates with post-doctoral qualification in the private sector: Does it pay off? *Labour, 21*(3), 473–502. doi:10.1111/j.1467-9914.2007.00385.x

Scott, W. R. (1992). *Organizations: Rational, natural, and open systems.* Englewood Cliffs, NJ: Prentice Hall.

Shinn, T. (1988). Hiérarchies des chercheurs et formes de recherche. *Actes de la Recherche en Sciences Sociales, 74*(1), 2–22. doi:10.3406/arss.1988.2430

Slaughter, S., & Leslie, L. L. (1997). *Academic capitalism: Politics, policies, and the entrepreneurial university.* Baltimore, MD: The John Hopkins University Press.

Stephan, P. E. (1996). The economics of science. *Journal of Economic Literature, 34*(September), 1199–1235.

Stokes, D. E. (1997). *Pasteur's quadrant: Basic science and technological innovation.* Washington, DC: Brookings Institution Press.

Theodosiou, M., & Amir-Aslani, A. (2013). The polyvalent scientist: The added value of management training. *Journal of Commercial Biotechnology, 19*(3), 6–9. doi:10.5912/jcb602

Thune, T. (2009). Doctoral students on the university-industry interface: A review of the literature. *Higher Education, 58*(5), 637–651. doi:10.1007/s10734-009-9214-0

Vallas, S. P., & Kleinman, D. L. (2008). Contradiction, convergence and the knowledge economy: The confluence of academic and commercial biotechnology. *Socio-Economic Review, 6*(2), 283–311. doi:10.1093/ser/mwl035

Yin, R. K. (2003). *Case study research: Design and methods.* Thousand Oaks, CA: Sage.

Ziman, J. (2000). *Real science: what it is, and what it means.* Cambridge, UK: Cambridge University Press. doi:10.1017/CBO9780511541391

ADDITIONAL READING

Auriol, L. (2010). *Careers of doctorate holders: Employment and mobility patterns (No. 2010/4)*. Paris: OECD Publishing. doi:10.1787/5kmh8phxvvf5-en

Beltramo, J. P., Paul, J. J., & Perret, C. (2001). The recruitment of researchers and the organisation of scientific activity in industry. *International Journal of Technology Management*, *22*(7), 811–834. doi:10.1504/IJTM.2001.002993

Enders, J. R. (2004). Research training and careers in transition: A European perspective on the many faces of the Ph. D. *Studies in Continuing Education*, *26*(3), 419–429. doi:10.1080/0158037042000265935

Etzkowitz, H., & Leydesdorff, L. (2000). The dynamics of innovation: From national systems and "mode 2" to a triple helix of university–industry–government relations. *Research Policy*, *29*(2), 109–123. doi:10.1016/S0048-7333(99)00055-4

Fox, M. F., & Stephan, P. E. (2001). Careers of young scientists: Preferences, prospects and realities by gender and field. *Social Studies of Science*, *31*(1), 109–122. doi:10.1177/030631201031001006

Giret, J. F., Perret, C., & Recotillet, I. (2007). Le recrutement des jeunes docteurs dans le secteur privé. *Revue d'Economie Industrielle*, *119*(119), 85–102. doi:10.4000/rei.2123

Greenwood, R., & Hinings, C. R. (1996). Understanding radical organizational change: Bringing together the old and the new institutionalism. *Academy of Management Review*, *21*(4), 1022–1054.

Halse, C., & Mowbray, S. (2011). The impact of the doctorate. *Studies in Higher Education*, *36*(5), 513–525. doi:10.1080/03075079.2011.594590

Harman, K. M. (2004). Producing 'industry-ready' doctorates: Australian Cooperative Research Centre approaches to doctoral education. *Studies in Continuing Education*, *26*(3), 387–404. doi:10.1080/0158037042000265944

Huisman, J., & Naidoo, R. (2006). The professional doctorate: From Anglo-Saxon to European challenges. *Higher Education Management and Policy*, *18*(2), 57–69. doi:10.1787/hemp-v18-art11-en

Kyvik, S., & Olsen, T. B. (2012). The relevance of doctoral training in different labour markets. *Journal of Education and Work*, *25*(2), 205–224. doi:10.1080/13639080.2010.538376

Lam, A. (2010). From 'ivory tower traditionalists' to 'entrepreneurial scientists'? Academic scientists in fuzzy university-industry boundaries. *Social Studies of Science*, *40*(2), 307–340. doi:10.1177/0306312709349963

Mora, J. G. (2001). The academic profession in Spain: Between the civil service and the market. *Higher Education*, *41*(1-2), 131–155. doi:10.1023/A:1026723014731

Mowbray, S., & Halse, C. (2010). The purpose of the PhD: Theorizing the skills acquired by students. *Higher Education Research & Development*, *29*(6), 653–664. doi:10.1080/07294360.2010.487199

Musselin, C. (2013). Redefinition of the relationships between academics and their university. *Higher Education*, *65*(1), 25–37. doi:10.1007/s10734-012-9579-3

Neumann, R., & Tan, K. K. (2011). From PhD to initial employment: The doctorate in a knowledge economy. *Studies in Higher Education*, *36*(5), 601–614. doi:10.1080/03075079.2011.594596

Pablo Hernando, S. (2012). *Dinámicas de cambio en el empleo de los doctores.* (Unpublished doctoral dissertation). Universidad Complutense de Madrid, Madrid, Spain.

Powell, S., & Green, H. (2007). *The doctorate worldwide.* Maidenhead, UK: SRHE and Open University.

Recotillet, I. (2007). PhD graduates with post-doctoral qualification in the private sector: Does it pay off? *Labour, 21*(3), 473–502. doi:10.1111/j.1467-9914.2007.00385.x

Roach, M., & Sauermann, H. (2010). A taste for science? PhD scientists' academic orientation and self-selection into research careers in industry. *Research Policy, 39*(3), 422–434. doi:10.1016/j.respol.2010.01.004

Robin, S., & Cahuzac, E. (2003). Knocking on academia's doors: An inquiry into the early careers of doctors in life sciences. *Labour, 17*(1), 1–23. doi:10.1111/1467-9914.00219

Sauermann, H., & Stephan, P. E. (2010). *Twins or strangers? Differences and similarities between industrial and academic science (No. w16113).* National Bureau of Economic Research. doi:10.3386/w16113

Scott, W. W. R. (2013). *Institutions and organizations: Ideas, interests, and identities.* London: Sage Publications.

Stephan, P. E., & Levin, S. G. (2001). Career stage, benchmarking and collective research. *International Journal of Technology Management, 22*(7), 676–687. doi:10.1504/IJTM.2001.002985

Stephan, P. E., Sumell, A. J., Black, G. C., & Adams, J. D. (2004). Doctoral education and economic development: The flow of new Ph.Ds to industry. *Economic Development Quarterly, 18*(2), 151–167. doi:10.1177/0891242403262019

Stern, S. (2004). Do scientists pay to be scientists? *Management Science, 50*(6), 835–853. doi:10.1287/mnsc.1040.0241

Thune, T. (2010). The training of "triple helix workers"? Doctoral students in university–industry–government collaborations. *Minerva, 48*(4), 463–483. doi:10.1007/s11024-010-9158-7

Wallgren, L., & Dahlgren, L. O. (2005). Doctoral education as social practice for knowledge development: Conditions and demands encountered by industry PhD students. *Industry and Higher Education, 19*(6), 433–443. doi:10.5367/000000005775354446

Wallgren, L., & Dahlgren, L. O. (2007). Industrial doctoral students as brokers between industry and academia: Factors affecting their trajectories, learning at the boundaries and identity development. *Industry and Higher Education, 21*(3), 195–210. doi:10.5367/000000007781236871

Zellner, C. (2003). The economic effects of basic research: Evidence for embodied knowledge transfer via scientists' migration. *Research Policy, 32*(10), 1881–1895. doi:10.1016/S0048-7333(03)00080-5

KEY TERMS AND DEFINITIONS

Collegialization: As a result of the intensification of the collaborations and partnerships between academia and industry, some companies have introduced academic management practices and culture in their organization. For example, these companies promote that their researchers work with high levels of autonomy and creativity, that they publish their results in scientific journals...

Doctoral Education: It is a high-specialized tertiary education addressed to future researchers and whose aim is to provide research training in a specific field during a long-term period. In spite of the fact that the PhD is the highest rank degree awarded by higher education institutions worldwide, the doctorate is perceived as a particular training located between education and scientific research.

Hybrid Researchers: They are researchers who have developed their professional careers in the intermediate space that have emerged between academia and industry. Their main role consists in bringing a considerable volume of relevant scientific knowledge from higher education institutions to a specific company (usually, their employer). Moreover, they have contributed to breaking down the cognitive and institutional barriers existing between both sectors. The entrepreneurial professors, the PhDs students enrolled in industrial doctoral programs or the PhDs who have moved towards the private sector are examples of hybrid researchers.

Normative Isomorphism: Organizations usually receive pressures to achieve standards of professionalism in their activities and to adopt techniques that are considered by a profession to be up to date and effective. Specifically, there are two sources of normative isomorphism related to professions: the credentials and the professional networks. As a result of the influence of these pressures, organizations that belong to the same organization field become similar after a period of time.

Organizational Adaptation: It is a proactive or reactive process begun by organizations to introduce some modifications and changes in their structure or in its components in order to obtain a better adjustment to their external environment. Specifically, organizations respond to some discontinuity or lack of fit that have arisen between them and their external environment.

Scientific Mobility: It can be defined as a cross-border physical, geographical and organizational movement that comprises a stay in another research establishment. It is noteworthy that scientific mobility is a structural characteristic of the professional trajectories of researchers nowadays that is necessary to transfer knowledge and to shape collaborations.

Technology Centres: TCs are non-profit R&D organizations whose mission is to transfer knowledge and technology to private sector (especially to Small Medium Enterprises, SMEs). Their intermediate position in innovation systems allows them to bridge the gap between academic organizations and industry.

Chapter 7
Higher Education and Globalization

Neus Lorenzo
The Transformation Society, France

Ray Gallon
The Transformation Society, France

ABSTRACT

In this chapter, the authors examine the forces influencing higher education in a digitally globalized, plurilingual, and intercultural world, and how they have already begun to change some traditional notions of what higher education is for, and how it should be adapted to fit new emergent social needs, which are currently under debate in the educational field (Mehaffy, 2012). They go on to propose a connectivist vision for the future of globalized higher education and provide three case studies that illustrate ways of achieving that vision. Each case study has a different orientation: resource orientation, process orientation, transformation orientation. All three of them have the same objective: innovation and adaptation to the new globalized paradigms that have placed higher education in an increasingly complex context.

INTRODUCTION

The concept of higher education in a global context is not only evolving, it is becoming ever more complex. All over the world, higher education is expanding the original instructional target to include research, industrial collaboration, or ecological activism, among other functions (Australian Bureau of Statistics, 2002). When we speak of higher education, we can no longer limit ourselves to traditional notions of academically oriented education - a third and final level of formal learning after secondary studies. This

traditional model has often focused on transmitting commonly accepted theoretical knowledge that may (or may not) qualify the learner for a professional field (Harrison & Hopkins, 1967). It is taught at a level that also includes advanced research activity in an environment that facilitates thought and reflection.

The advance of globalized, interconnected exchanges on economic, social, cultural, and academic levels has given rise to new platforms and opportunities for informal and non-formal lifelong learning and economic production (European Commission, 2008). Institutions have responded

DOI: 10.4018/978-1-4666-7244-4.ch007

to demands for transferability of qualifications by attempting to establish a common, global framework for higher education.

The European Bologna Accords of 1999-2010 (European Union, 1999) are a clear example of organizational globalization strategy that tries to converge stages, contents, processes and aims to define a European Higher Education Area (European Higher Education Area, 2010).

In this chapter, we look at the changing context created by physical and digital mobility, and the challenges of interculturalism and plurilingualism that it brings. We'll look at how higher education is dealing with these challenges today, and look ahead to a desired future.

In this context, interculturalism refers to "the conditions, or the 'enabling factors' that characterize a true, meaningful intercultural dialogue," which has been defined by the Council of Europe as "an open and respectful exchange of views between individuals and groups belonging to different cultures that leads to a deeper understanding of the other's global perception" (Council of Europe, 2008, p. 17)." It has been further defined as:

a process that comprises an open and respectful exchange or interaction between individuals, groups and organisations with different cultural backgrounds or world views. Among its aims are: to develop a deeper understanding of diverse perspectives and practices; to increase participation and the freedom and ability to make choices; to foster equality; and to enhance creative processes (European Institute for Comparative Cultural Research website, 2011).

In this chapter, plurilinguism should be understood as:

the intrinsic capacity of all speakers to use and learn, alone or through teaching, more than one language. The ability to use several languages to varying degrees and for distinct purposes is defined in the Common European Framework of

Reference for Languages (p.168) as the ability 'to use languages for the purposes of communication and to take part in intercultural action, where a person, viewed as a social agent, has proficiency, of varying degrees, in several languages and experience of several cultures'. This ability is concretised in a repertoire of languages a speaker can use (Council of Europe, 2003, p. 15; Council of Europe, 2001, p. 168).

It is important to distinguish plurilingualism from multilingualism, which is " the presence of several languages in a given space, independently of those who use them: for example, the fact that two languages are present on a territory does not indicate whether inhabitants know both languages or one only" *(Council of Europe, 2003, p. 16)*.

To conclude, we present three case studies that demonstrate innovative learning environments that are emerging and might provide examples for future higher education projects.

Changing Context: Accessibility and Democratization through Virtuality

In highly developed countries, the generalization of high-bandwidth, always-on Internet connections has meant that computer assisted communication has moved, in 30 years, from a hobby of technically oriented "geeks and nerds" to a fundamental right of all citizens: in 2009, Finland became the first country to pass a law declaring Internet access to be a legal right (Cavaliere, 2011).

Governments are forcing operators to provide high-speed service in rural areas where it is not profitable, as part of their strategies to reinvest poor, deserted areas with new, affluent, and economically productive populations: in 2010, France committed two billion euros toward providing high-bandwidth access throughout the country by 2025 (Jambes, 2011). Although economic improvement is the primary motivation, environmental benefits are also expected (reduction of greenhouse gasses as teleworking increases), and opportunities are created for distance education and professional training. This infrastructure is going to be essential for implementing the actions in the *Erasmus Charter For Higher Education, 2014-2020* (European Commission, 2014), which promotes networks and policy support measures (key action 3), strategic partnerships and knowledge alliances for developing international capacity (key action 2), and creating joint masters degrees and other common training opportunities through student and staff mobility (key action 1). The final aim (European Commission, 2014, pp. 1-2) is:

to contribute to the European Union's modernisation and internationalisation agenda in higher education, which includes 5 priorities:

1. *Increasing attainment levels to provide the graduates and researchers Europe needs.*
2. *Improving the quality and relevance of higher education.*
3. *Strengthening quality through mobility and cross-border cooperation.*
4. *Linking higher education, research and business for excellence and regional development.*
5. *Improving governance and funding.*

Increased access to digital infrastructure acts as a tool for democratization of education and facilitates interchange, collaboration, and social knowledge building - the basic elements of the new concept of higher education, as the process that can bridge the gap between having the knowledge, and being able to use it by networking in real situations (Light et al., 2009).

In developing countries, wireless infrastructure has often become the principal communications channel.

The penetration of mobile phone networks in many low- and middle-income countries surpasses other infrastructure such as paved roads and electric-

ity, and dwarfs fixed Internet deployment," says the World Health Organization in the report "mHealth: New horizons for health through mobile technologies." [p. 5] Increasingly, governmental and non-governmental organizations are using phones in place of physical infrastructure. In developing nations, 79 percent of the population has a mobile phone, according to a 2011 report from the International Telecommunications Union (Steele, 2012).

The ubiquity of telepresence means that students everywhere have potentially equal access, at least theoretically, to the same information (Gallon & Lorenzo, 2013). In the digital context,

"Ubiquity has been referred to as one of the most important characteristics of mobile services." Perceived ubiquity reflects "the benefits derived from continuity, immediacy, portability, and searchability" (Okazaki & Mendez, 2013 p. 98).

One manifestation of this phenomenon is a type of distributed course known as MOOC (Massive Open Online Course), first created in 2008 by Stephen Downes and George Siemens (Downes, 2011). In spite of the emerging debates on the MOOCs' democratic potential (Rhoads et al., 2013), larger connectivity generates several possibilities for international interaction, distance training, and enriched exchanges among students and professionals all over the world. We already have data to study engagement and completion of MOOCs of different types (e.g. Coursera, Udacity, edX) (Hill, 2013).

Open access to research raises the hope that students in poorer countries no longer need to migrate just to be able to complete their studies - and this, in return, implies less "brain drain" caused by emigrating students who do not return to their home countries. At the same time, access to open forums offers students digital mobility. The possibility to exchange knowledge, experiences, and ideas with others around the world, without leaving their home campuses, creates cross-fertilization and prevents isolation. Advanced telerobotics can even provide students with access to expensive equipment found only in major centers, even if they are in isolated rural or underdeveloped locations.

The burgeoning eBook industry has led to the development of "social reading" applications such as Goodreads, where readers share comments or highlights of individual books they are reading, engage in discussions about texts, and evaluate the quality of books, documents, and knowledge sources. Imagine extending these practices in a more structured, pedagogical environment, so that students (across campus or across the globe) can explain difficult texts to each other, share insights, and generate new ideas from the great bullion of interchange and debate!

Virtual digital tools, then, offer:

- Access to the world's knowledge and information
- Opportunities for remote, rural, and isolated areas to develop in new ways
- To equip the young generation with skills related to the new economic and social paradigms that are developing: leadership, participation, digital connectivity, networking, teamwork

The tools are now shaping new forms of higher education instruction, and even institutions. One of the most popular open universities, Khan Academy, was created as a web application in 2006 by Salman Khan (Khan Academy, 2014). It is leaving the institutional model of university as a fixed locale behind, and is becoming a source of new models for structured teaching and learning in formal and non-formal settings. The higher education context is changing forever. The role of technology in higher education may still need further and deeper discussion in order to focus on the best cost-benefit analysis and the fundamentals on which the knowledge-based economy is built. As prescribed in the European Commission's Guide to cost benefit analysis on Investment projects:

Economic growth and welfare depends on productive capital, infrastructure, human capital, knowledge, total factor productivity and the quality of institutions. All of these development ingredients imply - to some extent - taking the hard decision to sink economic resources now, in the hope of future benefits, betting on the distant and uncertain future horizon. (European Commission, 2008 p.13).

The risk comes, for example, from the fact that social returns might not be as expected, or might not be evenly distributed. This could lead to widening the digital gap, or exacerbating regional inequities: "Strategies for investing in education, training, and know-how need to be highly discerning if the desired impact on growth is to be realised. It is vital to understand the national, regional, and institutional context in which human capital investment takes place" (Healy, 2000, p. 36).

Despite the need for further study, we already have useful indicators of the role of information, technology, and learning in economic performance, which allow us to better identify the place of knowledge and technology in modern economies (OECD, 1996; APEC, 2004).

WHERE ARE WE NOW?

With the ubiquity of knowledge on the Internet, as defined above, the professor's role must change. The university campus has traditionally been the gathering place where inquiring minds can exchange and learn from each other, under the tutelage of a professor functioning as gatekeeper. In a global context, where the gathering place is an open, dematerialized campus, many other actors participate in the exchange. Political, economic, and social influences are much more visible in the global university. Paradoxically, the universities have the longest experience of anyone using digital media, and now, these globalized virtual media are changing the role that the university plays in shaping society (Selwyn, 2007).

University: Ivory Tower or Socioeconomic Tool?

The ivory tower question, of course, is an old debate. Today, however, there are increasing pressures that bring it to the fore, and perhaps, tilt the debate in a new direction. No matter how strong the ivory tower argument, universities have always had a role in changing society, simply because they explore new ideas and develop new knowledge in public spaces. Inside the ivory tower itself, there is a tension between the roles of preserving and communicating an institutionalized model of past hierarchical knowledge, and the research function that develops new connective knowledge, based on interaction (Nackerud & Scaletta, 2008) and individualization (Li & Pitts, 2009).

The connectivist model of learning (Siemens, 2006) claims that learning, as a process, is more relevant than knowing, as a product: connective knowledge is seen as the dynamic ecosystem where learning takes place and where scientific content grows (Siemens, 2009). Implicit in this ecosystem are social development and collectivity building. The connectivist model also stresses keeping, as primary learning objective, the holistic learning experience that enables cognitive, constructive, social and situational development (Mayes & de Freitas, 2007). The ivory tower opens to the socioeconomic world in this process; higher education becomes an institutional tool to create trans-sectorial opportunities for cooperation across Educational, Labor, Political or Leisure sectors throughout the world (European Union, 2013).

It is, all the same, difficult to define "knowledge" when what is true this morning might be changed by this afternoon. Notions of rigor go out the window when information can change during the time it takes to verify it. In a world of the ephemeral, concepts such as universal values, founding principles of civilization, even basic

scientific and mathematical theorems are called into question. Rumors circulate freely on the Internet, and are often accepted as fact without any serious verification by any method - journalistic, experimental, or empirical. This implies that lifelong learning skills to unlearn and to relearn (Kaipa, 1999) are perhaps more important than any degree or diploma we are able to earn.

Students develop professional skills, social strategies and many non-academic but essential abilities not just by attending classes, but also by the fact that they interact and relate digitally. It is essential to embed this kind of informal learning in the instructional offer that the university provides. This is the space where young generations are discovering and creating new ways of occupying the digital environment: on-line studying, teleworking, on-line social movements, digital politics, eGovernance, crowd funding and other open source economic models.

Although they are often faster than their professors in exploring digital possibilities (Junco & Cole-Avent, 2008), students take risks that are difficult to detect or that didn't exist before, in the physical world. Developing a digital identity means becoming a *digital resident* (White & LeCornu, 2011). Digital residents live in an emerging virtual space that is being shaped at the same time that it is shaping its inhabitants' abilities. As John Culkin said, "we shape our tools, and thereafter our tools shape us" (Culkin, 1967 p. 70). Studies show that almost 94% of university students publish content to the web without thinking of its impact, and 80% of them admit to having erased material that they published, after having second thoughts (Castaneda & Camacho, 2012). One might think this represents a preoccupation with privacy, but in fact, the same study shows that 80% of the students admit that they are not aware that people other than their friends can see what they publish. At the same time, 23% indicate that they are not concerned with that possibility and that they are more worried about the image their friends might have of them from their online behavior. Moreover, 26% agree that they are totally unconcerned about the impact this can have on their future carriers.

We can infer that this generation is developing a very different perception of privacy, ethics, and identity, and research tends to back up this claim: "Young people do not conceive social media as a 'public' space, reflecting a shift in our understanding of the delineation of what is public and private" (Tene, 2010). In fact, they build their reputation differently than their teachers did, however they might not be fully aware how they are doing that (Moorman & Bowker, 2011). Consciously or unconsciously, students are sharing knowledge all the time on social media. This public information sharing becomes part of their university experience, too, and has long been considered part of essential learning to develop individual higher mental processes (Vygotsky, 1978) and socially structured thinking skills (Sally, 1995).

The tension between controlling knowledge for economic gain and sharing it is a classic debate that puts the university at the center. In todays connected world, the power of knowledge comes from sharing it. The more information we share, the more we become known as an expert, or a "go-to" person. As our digital reputation expands, so does our influence. "Knowledge is power" is an old adage that continues to be true, but its meaning has evolved: the power comes from facilitating the flow of knowledge rather than from hoarding it (Bastian, 1994).

In this context, the question of "intellectual property" as expressed in copyrights, patents, etc. is brought into question everywhere, and most especially in the university, where there is massive access to digital information (Haggard, 2011). Copyright, in particular, has traditionally represented an industrial model for the output of creative and intellectual workers. Much of that output is, in fact, intangible, and copyright has usually been applied to the production and reproduction of physical supports for representing that intangible work. In an era where intellectual and creative output can remain intangible, and become ubiquitous at the same time, it no longer makes sense to continue with this model (Gallon & Lorenzo, 2013b). More than that, in the university, this traditional concept of copyright obstructs the natural processes of innovation that come from framing, reframing, reshaping and reusing ideas (White & Manton, 2011).

In many countries, universities receive funding for research from private companies who expect to control the rights to the results of such research. Just think of the "growing role that market forces and commercial values have assumed in academic life" (Washburn, 2005 p. ix). Internet itself was developed for the U.S. military as a way for universities to exchange research data in a closed network (Veà, 2013). Paradoxically, it was the military's insistence on the network being proof from nuclear attack that resulted in the open, multi-route structure that today fosters access to information, rather than hoarding.

Universities are now collaborating with public institutions and private enterprises in exploring areas of common interest to researchers and industries. Such involvement obviously influences the content of the studies offered by the university. We are already seeing a trend towards more and more university masters programs that lead to professional qualifications rather than to doctoral studies (the Bologna process focuses on this change [European Union, 1999]) In fact, a master's degree is no longer a final step, in a world where knowledge is evolving and changing at lightning speed. New masters are regularly introduced, shaped by the immediate needs of enterprises to serve labor markets. Others disappear as demand for the skills they provided fade out. Degrees and diplomas that have fixed, established criteria, need to be continually updated; their value is continuously put in question. The days of single careers are finished, and most students will have from two to five different professions during their working life (Meister, 2012) Tertiary education in and beyond the university becomes a lifelong learning process without end, especially in a context of changing economic models.

Collaboration skills are essential, not only for individuals, but for organizations. Collaboration between educational institutions and enterprises is not only necessary for economic reasons, it is also essential for transferring knowledge, applying innovative solutions to the productive world, and making long term research sustainable.

Collaborative Problem Solving

The Organization for Economic Cooperation and Development (OECD) has identified the ability to solve problems collectively as a major objective for the next round of PISA evaluations in 2015 (OECD, 2013). The OECD considers that students entering higher education should be proficient in:

- Establishing and maintaining shared understanding
- Taking appropriate action to solve problems
- Establishing and maintaining team organization

If a global economic organization expects 15-year-olds to develop these skills, it's because they believe that adults today are hardly competent without them (PIAAC, 2012). Universities also need to collaborate to find new funding sources. The model where private industry supplements the public purse is one obvious way to go, but it poses problems of conflicting agendas that can influence academic freedom and limit the educational offer in ways that might not be desirable for society as a whole. A worldwide policy concern is to assure regular funding and quality for higher education institutions, generating innovative approaches and opening new business models (Christensen, 2003).

Universities, networking at global level amongst themselves, have designed virtual platforms that enable students to connect not only with teachers, but with experts, professionals, and society in general, as we'll see in one of our case studies. As part of the process of democratized access, eLearning (computer-based learning) has evolved from new forms of delivering learning content to individuals, into a universal offer of systematic courses that can be taken by anybody, on any device, (Wiley & Hilton III, 2009). This evolution makes mLearning (mobile learning) attractive in these times of economic uncertainty and high long-term unemployment. (Yuan & Powell, 2013).

The verdict is still out on some of these, such as Massive Open Online Courses (MOOCs) (de Freitas, 2013), but the experimentation that lies behind these and similar ventures is here to stay, in existing types of MOOC or new ones to come (Lane, 2012). The European Commission has already expressed its full support for exploring the possibilities of MOOCs and has created a space to publish MOOCs for educational communities (European Commission, 2013). The first European MOOCs Stakeholders Summit took place in June, 2013 in Lausanne, and the Second MOOCs Stakeholders Summit was held in February, 2014. A new website was launched along with its communication on "Opening Up Education" and the "OpenEducationEuropa.eu Portal" (European Commission, 2014b).

Professional higher education studies and technical degrees also require alternating sequences of classroom training and apprenticeships. These collaborations can both open institutional reflections on the essential policy needed to succeed, and also solve problems as concrete as the need for equipment and classroom space (UNESCO, 2002). Computers, libraries, and facilities need to serve multiple audiences in different ways. At the Université de Paris Diderot, for example, two professional degrees, undergraduate and graduate, run on a two-week cycle: every two weeks, students alternate between classroom work and practical internships on site at a company. When the master's students are in the field, the undergraduates use the classroom, and vice versa. Thus one room (and its 20 computers) is serving 40 students in two programs (Gallon, 2013). The university's investment in facilities and computers is doubled and the students gain valuable practical experience at the same time. Teacher training can also be organized in similar fashion, as we show in one of our case studies.

WHERE DO WE WANT TO GO?

Exploring new paths in higher education implies opening fields and assessing experiences from their results, processes and costs. The process of developing evaluation frameworks and needs detection tools cannot collapse in theoretical debates, in spite of the importance of theory; it must build models of effective practice (see case studies below). Universities have been the spearhead of open source movements, have developed decentralized decision-making processes, and developed human-based problem-solving methodologies, but they have yet to define transferable epistemological models and sustainable resource management for applying them.

New Models for Knowledge Creation

The university model of learning needs to evolve, given that learning to learn has become the basic skill for compulsory education when developing reading, math, and science literacies (OECD, 2013). Professional key competencies are the target of vocational training in post-obligatory higher education. The university, though, should at least be focused on a combination of research, innovation, and social knowledge creation for enriching both economic systems and social demands (Scardamalia, 2004).

It is first of all important to associate *knowledge creation* with teaching and learning in every physical or virtual field, tied to a problem-solving approach: proactive knowledge, social action, student protagonism (Scardamalia, 2002). Second, *teachers' roles should change*, and even be

supplemented by the intervention of other educational agents from private enterprises, or from socio-cultural associations, with different roles:

- **Professor-Tutor:** For providing individual academic support.
- **Enterprise-Mentor:** For professional coaching and training.
- **Animator-Facilitator:** For personal guidance and accompaniment.

Third, students must also acquire proactive habits of leadership, participation, and knowledge management. This guides students away from mere information consumption, towards heightened awareness, increased engagement, and autonomous research that higher education requires: knowledge building, community building, and social transformation management (Scardamalia & Bereiter, 2003). In our opinion, the university and other institutions of higher education should focus less on providing answers and more on facilitating the skills to formulate good questions, and so leave each student to find their own way of structuring relevant knowledge and integrating it into their own life project. It is necessary to explore interactive teaching and learning, based on action/research and action/reflection models, such as the Nemetics Sequence that promotes "Notice, Engage, Mull, Exchange (NEME)," where "exchange" is a technique for teaching and learning (Josefowicz, 2012).

Fourth, higher education organizations must be in touch with multiple communities, networking with different institutions and creating spaces for different interactive learning activities. By creating collaborative and reflective learning spaces on the Internet, higher education institutions would, at the same time, participate in developing the Internet of the future, and facilitate methodological renewal. To engage students in real research and help them feel authentic cognitive challenges, higher education needs to become experiential. There is sufficient research to show that we anchor theory better in our memories if we learn it through performing actions. Theory is still an important part of the process, but the theory comes in the course of practical exercise, not separated from it.

To use Roger C. Shank's terminology (Schank, 2011), *learning by doing* implies exploring and building new scenarios, while also gaining inferential experience and cognitive reframing. It is this theoretical grounding that allows us to generalize from one task-oriented situation to another, without having to re-learn via a rote process. This sort of *inferential or associative learning* (Carroll, 1965) activates the brain's enquiry processes, encouraging creativity. This required state of mind not only enables theoretical innovation and research, but also focuses on practical application and lateral thinking. The relationship between knowledge and creativity has been deeply studied, since it can help both lifelong critical thinking and performance in many domains of the arts and sciences (Dietrich, 2004).

Moreover, we are becoming aware of the urgent need to focus on *learning to lead*. Higher education should devote a huge amount of effort to creating structured self-organization in class, and on social networks in different domains. Collaboration on line creates Personal Learning Environments (PLEs) that will be essential for intellectual and professional development (Lubensky, 2006). Community building is already seen as a profitable working strategy in leadership, teamwork, networking or any other field of endeavor.

The Challenge of Culture and Language

Leadership in the context of global institutional collaboration brings us to the challenge of knowledge dissemination across cultures and languages. The simple solution, historically, has been to adopt one common "lingua franca" to work in – Latin in medieval ages; French in the 18th century; most commonly English, in modern times. But in a global world, different languages offer different modes of thinking. Anyone who has actually had to negotiate use of a lingua franca in real life knows that speaking English to a French person, and speaking English to a Chinese person, are totally distinct experiences, and it's difficult to be sure that all parties take away the same understandings. Knowing multiple languages opens up a world of new thought - first simply by acquiring the different thought processes of a new language, and second, by contact with speakers of that language, their culture, and their thought patterns. 954,6 million people in the world speak and think in Mandarin (14,1% of the Earth's inhabitants), 406,7 million speak Spanish (5,85%), 358,9 million speak English (5,52%) and 311,4 (4,46%) speak Hindi (Nationalencyklopedin, 2010). Enlarging international training opportunities with on-line scenarios is creating new needs for plurilingualism and for intercultural mediation. Studying in a foreign language requires complementary efforts and skills. Teachers and students, co-workers and team colleagues will have to communicate with foreign collaborators as well as conational colleagues, in production and for peer reviewed publication, to name just two examples.

In a global context, it is in the self-interest of content providers in higher education to use major languages to respond to international accreditation, certification and quality concerns. Minority languages can be threatened by globalization, if they do not find proper adjustments to the global world. The Council of Europe already sounded an alert in 1992 (Council of Europe, 1992) to increasing challenges within the European Charter for Regional or Minority Languages (ECRML), which proposed in Part III, Article 8, paragraph e, to:

i) make available university and other higher education in regional or minority languages; or

ii) to provide facilities for the study of these languages as university and higher education subjects; or

iii) if, by reason of the role of the State in relation to higher education institutions, sub-paragraphs i and ii cannot be applied, to encourage and/or allow the provision of university or other forms of higher education in regional or minority languages or of facilities for the study of these languages as university or higher education subjects;

Seeing language diversity as a common richness, the Council of Europe also declares

...that the right to use a regional or minority language in private and public life is an inalienable right conforming to the principles embodied in the United Nations International Covenant on Civil and Political Rights, and according to the spirit of the Council of Europe Convention for the Protection of Human Rights and Fundamental Freedoms.

The *Common European Framework of Reference for Languages: Learning, Teaching, Assessment* (CEFR), published after twenty years of European research (Council of Europe 2001), provides the guidelines for curricular development of modern language studies in upper secondary and higher education with six levels of foreign language proficiency. It is now translated into more than 39 languages, and it promotes a common European policy to include the study of two modern languages in compulsory education, other than the language of instruction, for every student in Europe.

In the university, where research and international collaboration should take place on a regular basis, using a foreign language won't be enough. We have to understand how geolocalization and machine translation might provide a fertile area for new research, with regard to big-data and information-flow analytics. Tracking and gathering

data about information flow in learning networks should be used, eventually, to provide not only valuable data on how they perform, but also to predict and anticipate the danger of impending course failures, increasing international demand for registrations, or dropouts of specific student profiles (Leskovec, 2011).

A New Institutional Role for the University

If universities still want to have the near-exclusive power to certify graduates with degrees, they will need to evolve the basis of their benchmarks towards a more process-based system. Universities, vocational schools, and colleges are trying to maintain their role as official certifiers amid pressure for both quality improvements and wider access, without raising cost. In many countries, access to higher education is perceived to be a social right, but such wide access is also seen by institutions as a menace to quality standards. Strong endogamy in the selection of university professors, which is still too common in many countries (Horta et al., 2010), must disappear. Self-aggrandizing research, closed assessment and lack of evaluation transparency seem to be a clear path to social failure for university institutions.

We need to focus first on the kinds of interactions we want to promote, and then design tools around it. This process is design thinking (Brown, 2008), and it is built around three main axes:

- **Desirability:** Hearing, detecting and understanding what people need
- **Technological Feasibility:** Can it be built?
- **Economic Viability:** Creating or facilitating success

Instead of thinking of a specific product, object, or output, we should use integrative thinking to develop a problem-solving orientation in higher education (Nonaka, 1994; Grant, 1996; Engestrom, et al., 1999). It is important to create the framework where non-formal learning can exist and be recognized, in addition to formal courses. Higher education institutions should provide professors and students with alternative or complementary learning experiences, involving external actors from professional fields. This implies a revalorization of the adjunct instructor, who must become a major player in higher education, and not simply an inexpensive extra faculty member.

Professors must take a different approach to their own roles, and need to explore different interactive models of teaching and training, to become face-to-face and on-line innovators, as well as guides and facilitators. As the UNESCO *"Rethinking education in a changing world"* report says, "The role of teachers and other learning professionals remains central for the change of mind-set that we seek in our quest for new sustainable models of societal development." (UNESCO, 2013).

Society, in general, has to become aware of the enormous power of collective engagement in higher education, which could find creative solutions for funding university research, for focusing community work to improve vocational training, or for promoting collaborative solutions in higher education. The university, at its best, should become a resource for acquiring and updating new strategies and adapting to change flexibly and responsibly, towards a more sustainable and just world. How some institutions are initiating this type of action is the main focus of the case studies presented in this chapter.

CASE-STUDIES

This chapter draws upon case studies carried out as part of the authors' professional experience, training and research, during 2012-2014. All share organizational issues that include participants from different sectors, blended interaction and training, and institutional leadership. The results can be seen as part of the current search for meth-odological innovation and for updating training systems in higher education. The main common characteristic of all the presented case studies is the transversal and trans-sectorial design, which includes strong vertical interaction – students, teachers, professionals - and broad horizontal permeability. Each case-study presents a creative change in focus involving new student learning activities, innovative exploratory teaching techniques, and enriched institutional development:

1. **Student Learning:** The aim of the teaching process in these cases is that students go beyond simple participation. They are asked to assess, give opinions, and evaluate processes, according to their age or situation, as much as their teachers do.

2. **Exploratory Teaching Techniques:** Teachers are seen here as strategic managers of the curriculum, and the initial promoters of learning projects. Their engagement makes the students' participation and research possible. Their role in leading, adapting and assessing the different student activities is seen as valuable professional development.

3. **Enriched Institutional Development:** All of these cases were initiated by institutions that seek to have a wide-scale impact. Nevertheless, the question of generalizing the pilot project to a larger institutional framework remains to be solved.

Each of the case studies described in this chapter has evolved around a collaborative 'pilot learning project,' involving different on-line participation tools and fostering the use of technology in education, networking, and institutional collaboration. Considered together, they demonstrate how higher education is embarking on a path of highly diversified teaching and training models, where *content ubiquity, distributed leadership* and *digital work* spaces are going to be the common hallmarks.

Case Study 1: Resource-oriented - EduPLEmooc, Personal learning environments (PLE) for teacher professional development

Introduction

EduPLEmooc is an experimental MOOC offered as free, open, on-line, non-formal education, without official certification nor associated final standard levels, in Spain. The research question is to determine if a training modality that doesn't offer any reward other than personal experience can be attractive to higher education students, school teachers, learners from educational fields, professors, or other professionals in higher education.

As is explicitly mentioned in the official Spanish web for this course:

This new form of training is done experimentally without providing final certification. Digital badges (mentioned in the presentation) are only delivered as a form of recognition of the learning process developed in the course activities. The estimated workload is only indicative, and "training hours" will not be certified. It is expected that participation in this course has - as its principal motivation - personal learning, professional development and collaboration with other teachers. (translation by the authors)

The main aim of this initiative seems to be to create, for the first time in the Spanish Ministry of Education, a framework for on-line professional training and community building for Spanish speaking teachers or teachers-to-be. It is a MOOC that developed seven interactive units, which demand very different activities to stimulate ways of learning and teaching through ICT and digital content, mainly through the development and availability of open education research. Students

arc supposed to develop digital skills by using several media tools and digital programs: SlideShare, Google-drive, Google-hangout, YouTube, Pinterest, Twitter, Facebook, Eventbrite, Storify, etc.

Instructions are presented via YouTube videos and text documents, with a profusion of help-links and interactive forums. Students from all over the world can participate at different speeds and following their own calendars, but a collective global MeetUp or Hangout is promoted on a fixed date, mid-course. Continuous performance and weekly delivery is expected from every student, without penalty for lateness. Community building is essential to accomplishing some of the tasks, and teamwork is encouraged by many different activities: weekly chats, open forums, and even a face-to-face meeting encouraged in every locality.

Trans-sectorial collaboration is promoted. Task guidelines propose transferring acquired techniques from the training sessions into primary or secondary classes, and into related professional fields. Gamification is universally present, both explicitly (with three badges that can be won during the course) and implicitly (with strong competition and continuous emerging challenges for teamwork, networking, and peer collaboration), within a meta-analysis level of action-reflection in the Google+ Community, "eduPLEmooc Gamification".

Overview

Within the panorama of on-line training, EduPLEmooc follows a traditional sequence of instructional content, increasing technical difficulty and participation in every unit, but it is able to generate very dynamic interactions among students. They can assume leadership to develop creative initiatives and become highly proactive. Mutual support for solving other people's problems is appreciated.

Content includes extra readings and independent access to information to be chosen by every student, but it is *strategic content curation* that seems to be the backbone of the syllabus, focused on explicit learning about digital tools. A final team project is an obligatory assignment, presented after an action-research challenge.

Peer-to-peer assessment is embedded in the course platform; multiple readings of randomly selected work by at least three other students is required to achieve positive marks in every task.

The main elements and key players in this training course are:

- **Level:** Higher Education, Vocational Education and Training, Adult Learning
- **Provider:** *Ministerio de Educación, Cultura y Deporte* (Spain), designed and coordinated through INTEF-EducaLAB (*INTEF: Instituto Nacional de Tecnologías Educativas y Formación de Profesorado. El correo electrónico: webmaster@mooc. educalab.es*).
- **Language of Instruction:** Spanish.
- **Presentation:** "The course offers a connected learning experience through which we can build or redesign our Personal Learning Environment, reflect on our digital identity and our learning processes and establish personal contact with other professionals and other people interested in education, through various virtual communities".
- **Professors:** David Álvarez, Clara Cobos Jurado, Diego García García (@ eduPLEmooc).
- **Number of Attendees:** 10,310.
- **Dates:** 13 January 2014 - 03 March 2014.
- **Hashtags:** #eduPLEmooc, #eduPLEreto, #eduPLEchat.
- **License:** *Creative Commons Reconocimiento-NoComercial-CompartirIgual 3.0 España.*

- **Official Site:** https://mooc.educalab.es/course/entornos-personales-de-aprendiza-je-ple-para-el-des/
- **Included in the European Commission register of MOOCs, Open Education Europa:** http://openeducationeuropa.eu/en/node/133966

Results of Research

Partial results are available in the personal Course-Portfolio of @NewsNeus (Lorenzo, 2014) and will be completed with references to the on-going publications and further data published by the @eduPLEmooc professors. As of this writing, results are incomplete, but the data we have show that 10,310 people registered for the MOOC, of whom 2,641 did not participate in any activities. There were 10,000 posts to 1,500 blogs created as a direct result of this program. The 3,400 followers of @eduPLEmooc produced 7,423 tweets in a 20-day period. Our action-research included different personal experiences in diverse protagonist roles, several directly recorded interviews and comparative opinion surveys among secondary students (16-18 years old).

Innovation

The specificity of this MOOC is its use of a digital instructional tool to teach about digital resources for education. It also encourages the generation of networks and professional communities, and active participation of students, teachers and other educational agents as the basis of social learning. (Conecta13, 2013)

Training Acceptance

Given the lack of formal recognition after following this course, we focused on collecting the reasons why attendees were participating: they expressed their motivations in weekly chats (#eduPLEchat, in Twitter), and on their personal bogs (#eduPLEmooc). Among the most common ones, were professional development and individual engagement in on line interaction:

- Updating professional skills
- Personal development and personal learning interest
- Interpersonal engagement with colleagues and friends
- Exploratory possibilities for transference to professional fields
- Opportunities for networking and exchanging ideas on common interests
- Innovative spirit and curiosity

It is highly relevant to see how this particular MOOC has been followed by 3401 followers in Twitter (February 22, 2014), while @AulaMentor_sede, the other training initiative that has existed longer on the same site, has only achieved half of this number, with 1520 followers. One explanation could be found in the open approach that this MOOC is using, when facilitating strong interaction among participants every week. @AulaMentor_sede courses tend to offer on-line materials, without such intensive interpersonal relationships.

Professionals' Involvement

The design of this MOOC includes extremely flexible possibilities for open interaction, and demands intense connectivity within networks and communities. Analysing 'Content Strategy in Education,' one of the Google+ Communities opened for this course by @NewsNeus in her role of course attendee as educator and trainer, we find 60 members from different countries, and with different professional backgrounds: for example, an international university professor, primary teacher, plurilingual advisor, upper education headmaster, content industry professional, content curator, professional web managers university students, European policy makers, a former Catalan minister of education, inspectors of education, a content strategist, and a web designer, among others.

Figure 1. Twitter followers for @eduPLEmooc and @AulaMentor_sede, two different training initiatives on-line promoted by Ministerio de Educación, Cultura y Deporte (Spain), and coordinated through INTEF-EducaLAB (24th February 2014)

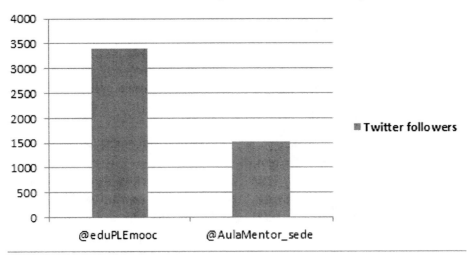

Figure 2. Members of Content Strategy in education, Google+ Community created by @NewsNeus in her role of attendee to the #eduPLEmooc course, as educator and trainer (24th February 2014)

This extremely rich community profile, the result of a MOOC task requirement, is an example of how Personal Learning Environments can enlarge exponentially into other professional domains, and collateral research fields.

Transferability

Our initial data (Regí & Lorenzo, 2014) shows that at the beginning of their teacher's training course, 45% of upper grade secondary students said they would be interested in following a Master's degree or post university studies via eLearning; when their teacher had completed the MOOC, which included the students in using several ICT tools and doing teamwork on line, 59% of upper secondary students said they would ask for an eLearning university course. This 11% increase in on-line acceptance doesn't mean a rejection of more traditional face-to-face classes, 55% of the students declared that combining face-to-face classes and MOOCs would be more efficient for learning at University, while only 4% considered 'just MOOC' the most efficient way:

Impact

The methodological impact on the educational system is difficult to measure from a structural point of view. What we do know, is that this Spanish course was followed by students in South America, Mexico, and France, among others. The evidence of their participation can be seen in the general open face-to-face meeting (#MOOCafe) that was followed worldwide on 20 February 2014, as part of the course.

Current Hypothesis

According to the existing data, the interviews, and the on line evidence, this MOOC course is opening a different model of lifelong training, which offers the opportunity for crossing boundaries: intergenerational participation, mixed professional-vocational-academic interchange of information, and international collaboration in training and networking. Results seem to show a strong engagement and continuity of participation, based both on clear understanding of the roles of ICT tools in education, and on the intense interpersonal relations created through collective

Figure 3. Which technique would be more efficient for learning content in the University? Survey results from 74 Upper secondary students in Virolai School (Barcelona, Spain), whose teacher (Coral Regí) was attending the #eduPLEmooc course, as school headmaster (24th February 2014)

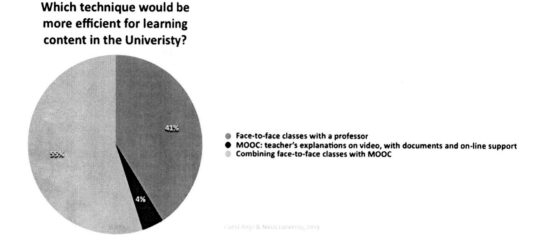

tasks and projects in the MOOC assignments. The mentors' Twitter account (@eduPLEmooc) gained double followers in three months compared to the more traditional advisors' on-line Twitter account in the same training institution. Further research needs to be done to identify the particular tasks, texts or documents in the course syllabus that are responsible for the increased fidelity and

commitment among different profiles of students and attendees. The main question will be whether and how MOOCs can complement the structures and instruments developed in the European Higher Education Area, both for Universities and for Professional development (European Commission, 2013b).

Figure 4. Google Map, tagging #eduPLEmooc open event #MOOCafes, face-to-face meetings planned in unit 6 to facilitate personal exchange among students, professionals and educators participating in the MOOC. From: https://mapsengine.google.com/map/u/1/edit?mid=zgsxo9czXgss.ktQBkDcSm7vg (20th February 2014).

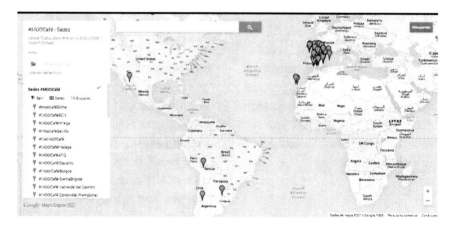

Case-Study 2: Process-Oriented - GEP Project, Grup Experimental per al Plurilingüisme, an Experimental Group for Plurilingualism: Promoting Language Learning at School through Collaborative and Digital In-Service Training

Introduction

GEP Project is an educational experiment to consolidate inclusive policies for foreign language teaching and learning in Catalonia (Spain), to increase plurilingualism by training teachers to transfer leadership and collaborative processes to their own classes. This project combines an alternative method for classroom teaching (using CLIL and other integrated methodologies), training teachers (in-service training and action-reflection) and creating collaborative networks between private enterprises and public institutions. It includes teamwork among different publishers to create text-book materials, training sessions for content teachers in partially face-to-face and partially on-line training, Sheltered Instruction Observation Protocol (SIOP) system classes at schools for primary and secondary levels, and diffusion of the school's production as new teachers' materials for the following year.

The research question is to know how innovative training that includes new private-public collaboration and funding schemes is perceived by teachers. Private-public collaboration is a new initiative in this context, in-service training is not usually compulsory, content teachers are not normally trained in a foreign languages, and training does not usually demand active content creation and reflection from teachers.

Overview

The main elements and key players in this experience are:

- **Level:** Teachers' Training and professional development, to transfer "learning-to-learn" and "collaboration for problem solving" strategies to Primary and Secondary education learners.
- **Provided by:** *Subdirecció General de Llengua i Plurilingüisme del Departament d'Ensenayment* (Spain), designed and coordinated through *Servei de Llengües Estrangeres*.
- **Language of instruction:** Course in English, on a bilingual MOOC, in the Catalan plurilingual education system.
- **Presentation:** The GEP Project offers a teaching-and-learning experience through which schools can redesign their Linguistic Project or build their Language Learning Environments, reflect on their teaching techniques and their networking processes and establish common strategies with publishers, universities and other professionals, through in-service digital training and cross curricular communities".
- Professors provided by British Council Barcelona, Trinity College London, Oxford University Press, Cambridge University Press, Universitat Autònoma de Barcelona (Grup CLIL-SI).
- **Number of attendees:** 52 schools, 145 teachers with 5075 students from Primary and Secondary public schools.
- **Course Dates:** 12 January 2014 - 31 March 2014.
- **Moodle:** http://odissea.xtec.cat/course/view.php?id=10442
- **Licensed:** published with license *Creative Commons Reconocimiento-NoComercial*.
- **Official Site:** http://www.xtec.cat/web/projectes/plurilinguisme/pluri/gep
- Included in the Catalan Educational network, XTEC (Xarxa telemàtica Educativa de Catalunya).

Results of Research

The Department of Education (Catalan ministry of education) promoted official collaboration between educational authorities, local Universities and the main publishers of language teaching and learning textbooks in Europe, to create teaching sequences of Content and Language Integrated Learning (CLIL) in Maths, Natural Science, Literature and Cultural Tradition, Arts and Theatre, Social Science and Vocational Education, for plurilingual students.

Innovation

The project was carried out using a networked structure. Networks were organised in 6 clusters of plurilingual teachers (speaking Catalan, Spanish and English), who attended classes according to curricular content. They had the support of local advisers and of the Catalan Inspectorate of education for implementing the GEP-Project at school. The objective was focused and well accepted: achieving major improvement in student learning, teacher implication, and collective support in the schools for inclusive policies. Training was also provided for headmasters and principals for them to organise, coordinate, and assess activities, in order to focus on creating learning environments at school, and reflective attitudes among teachers - both necessary for language learning and plurilingualism development.

Training Collaboration

This private-public collaboration was necessary to align institutional policies and market tendencies. The European Union is promoting social networking and global collaboration to achieve the Europe 2020 aims for language learning. These aims were also adopted by the GEP project: every child of 15 will have to achieve a mastery level of language literacy in at least two languages (50% with a B2 level) and 75% of the students will have to have study at least a second foreign language. Teach-ers' production was shared in open collaboration and became part of the collective digital teaching resource available in Catalonia.

Professionals' Involvement

Plurilingualism is a strategy for increasing employability and empowering students' lifelong learning, a key element in Catalan educational policy. As Head of the Foreign Language Service (2007-2014), Neus Lorenzo had the opportunity to participate in the design of the GEP project, and the assessment of products, results and impact in the educational system. Data shows that teachers' professional involvement came mainly from collective engagement, personal research and content creation, as well as from seeing their own students engaged and actively learning.

Transferability

Teaching and learning units were used to train teachers in-service and to ask them to implement, assess and perform research about their teaching techniques, transferring strategies to their own primary or secondary school classrooms (students from 10 to 14). Teachers were asked to produce - and share online - educational material, following the same principles as the training they had attended, in a recursive process of sharing. Scaling up is planned from the existing Moodle to train more schools and teachers.

Impact

In the on-line assessment surveys, attending teachers showed a strong acceptance for the training, and self-satisfaction for the products and content creation. Results were presented by the authorities on the educational web, XTEC, and offered as a starting point for other schools. These are now accepted good practice examples for other levels in the same schools, other schools, or different languages.

Current Hypothesis

The private-public collaboration is a new initiative that was well accepted by teachers, who generally rated the trainers very highly. Teachers also said they enjoyed transferring what they learned to their classes, and felt encouraged to consolidate their new habits. Teachers also reported feeling much more implicated in overall educational policy, as they had a role to play in a larger picture.

Case-Study 3: Transformation Oriented - 'ILE-Leadership' (ODCE), An International Collaboration for Action-Research Development in Education Systems

Introduction

Innovative Learning Environments-Leadership (ILE-Leadership, ODCE) is a comparative study done by an international research group and disseminated by OECD Publishing. It follows action-research and reflection-practice approaches, and it has been coordinated at local, national and international levels to analyze leadership impact in educational innovation at micro, meso and macro levels of success. The OECD describes the resulting report as presenting "a wealth of international material and features a new framework for understanding innovative learning environments" (OECD webpage, 2013).

Universities, private educational organizations, and schools with different institutional models participated in the research process, in an informal and non-formal training offer. The research itself provides learning environments for participants, where they can collaborate to detect, compare, and reflect on the role of context and learning climate in learning situations. Neus Lorenzo participated in this research in her role as inspector of education, by observing and evaluating classrooms and schools at local micro level in Catalonia (Spain) (Lorenzo & Martínez, 2013).

This international research was developed using on-line tools for communicating and exchanging data, collaborating and coordinating different visions, creating collaborative documents and debating procedures. A public conference was organized to disseminate the results of the experience in a final collaborative report presented internationally by the OECD. The research question is to determine if collaborating in international research might become a sustainable training modality in higher education, or if it would be seen more as a personal experience that develops educational growth informally. Challenges to acceptance of research as common generalized training in higher education may increase because individual teachers, students, or researchers are not commonly recognized and mentioned in every official report.

Overview

In this research, several schools and learning institutions were selected and studied on five continents, to identify the relevant teaching practices and the most efficient organizational processes that best facilitate innovative learning environments. In Europe, the research was applied in Catalonia (a historical autonomous region in Spain) coordinated by the Jaume Bofill Foundation. International policymakers, secondary and primary school headmasters, university researchers, education supervisors, inspectors of education, school teachers, and students all participated with their own voice. Not all the schools that were visited and analyzed are mentioned in the reports, but all the selected examples have in common the leadership practices that promote school climates for learning success.

The official international OECD report was delivered in Barcelona (Spain), on 4-5 December 2013, at the '*International Conference: Innovative Learning Environments (ODCE & Jaume Bofill*

Foundation),' under the format of teacher training, and credited as non-formal education, with an associated official certification of attendance and recognition of training for participant presenters (supported by the *Generalitat de Catalunya* and the *University of Barcelona* among other institutions). Conferences are usually credited as professional training by universities worldwide, and original research is a required component of higher education.

In Catalonia, the schools observed in this project ranged from state schools with students from difficult economic backgrounds, to private schools in well-to-do neighborhoods, providing several different models of leadership. At the Col·legi Sant Pere Claver (Barcelona), for example, Neus Lorenzo and other researchers could collect evidence of the transformative connection between the headmaster's vision, distributive leadership among the school teachers, and the students' awareness and self-organization in the classroom.

The main settings and key actors in this project were:

- **Level:** This study looks at Education Systems worldwide, from classroom level to national policymakers and international organizations.
- **Coordinated by:** Organization for Economic Cooperation and Development (OECD), in collaboration with national and local institutions, universities and private foundations such as Jaume Bofill (Catalonia, Spain).
- **Presentation of Final International Report:** 4-5 December, 2013 at *International Conference: Innovative Learning Environments (ODCE, Jaume Bofill Foundation)*, in Barcelona (Spain). http://learningleadershipconference.cat/en/informacio-general/

- **Language of research:** All local research was done in the instructional languages of the schools studied. The final report is available in English and French. The international presentation of results took place in English, Catalan and Spanish.
- **Presentation:** The international report explicitly states that a contemporary learning environment should:
  o Innovate the elements and dynamics of its "pedagogical core".
  o Become a "formative organisation" through strong design strategies with corresponding learning leadership, evaluation and feedback.

  o Open up to partnerships to grow social and professional capital, and to sustain renewal and dynamism.

  o Promote 21st century effectiveness through the application of the ILE learning principles (OECD 2013).
- **Catalan researchers:** Màrius Martínez i Muñoz, Joan Badia i Pujol, Anna Jolonch i Anglada, Roser Salavert, Maite Górriz, Joaquim Núñez, Jordi Longás, Carmina Pinya, Antoni Tort, Neus Lorenzo, Imma Buñuel, Eugeni Garcia, Begoña Gros, and Josep Menéndez.
- **Research Dates:** March 2011- December 2013.
- **License:** Copyright, all rights reserved.
- **Official site:** On-going project 2011-2014, Website at http://www.oecd.org/edu/ceri/innovativelearningenvironments.htm
- **Included in the Organization for Economic Cooperation and Development (OECD) register of international documents, and available on line:** http://www.keepeek.com/Digital-Asset-Management/oecd/education/innovative-learning-environments_9789264203488-en#page4

Results of Research

Partial results are available on the national partners' webs worldwide, but here we refer to the research we have participated in:

- **Macro Level research:** (OECD, 2013).
- **Meso Level research:** (Istance *et al.*, 2013).
- **Micro Level research:** (Martínez *et al.*, 2013).

This multilevel research shows similar recursivity at school level analysis, where organizational leadership (macro) is seen in alignment with teachers' pedagogical leadership (meso) and students' leaning autonomy (micro). Even in the classroom observation process, the three levels are identically reproduced, at fractal scales, when assessing a school's planning and the classroom's organization, teachers' performance and professional implication, and students' learning engagement.

Innovation

According to the OECD's final report, this research offers pointers to how effective distributed leadership can be achieved, including the role of technology, teamwork, and networking, in order to change organizational cultures. This research project proved to be an invaluable resource for training and personal development for all those who participated directly, those who were involved in schooling and leadership observation, and those who attended the international conference where the final report was presented: teachers, headmasters, university professors, higher education students, inspectors of education, researchers, educational advisers and other school management professionals (OECD, 2013).

Training Acceptance

This vertically structured project offers different levels of higher education and lifelong learning. It provides an opportunity for informal experiential training to the teachers and headmasters in the schools that were observed and assessed; implicit structural training for the research groups worldwide; explicit non-formal professional training for those who attended the international conference in Barcelona, where the final report was presented; informal higher education and professional development for the readers of the different local and national reports, in different languages. From a personal point of view, Neus Lorenzo participated in a professional lifelong learning and networking experience, together with colleagues from different backgrounds and educational fields, in an enriched and reflective personal growth process.

Professionals' Involvement

Participation in transversal international projects like this one offers valuable possibilities for academic improvement and professional development. Trans-national teamwork demands online interaction, and requires stable connectivity within participant networks and communities. The systematized publishing of the results at micro, meso and macro levels in separate documents, also calls for the involvement of new publishing technologies and content management systems. Not receiving publication credit for work done might be an obstacle to finding participants, or might affect credibility and external perception in a negative way, so it is important to make sure that every participant feels fulfilled with acceptable rewards and adequate recognition.

Transferability

The research itself is an attempt to transfer macro level policies through reflective practice and action-research methodologies into the micro level performance of school education, in primary and secondary school classrooms. It also tries to reach professionals all over the world through a final report and several local publications that point out the urgent need to create synergies to improve education systems: families, students, teachers, headmasters, advisers, supervisors, and the whole education community should share the vision of the school project, the processes to achieve it, and the responsibility for assessing and readdressing the results.

The knowledge gained from this research can be transferred to other fields in a targeted fashion, but it is even more desirable to promote the generalization of the leadership practices that were identified and understood as good pedagogical and organizational management. Not only can schools and professionals benefit from this research, but also families, associations and social communities. As (OECD, 2013 p. 39) says, there are many examples where parents are also learners:

In some cases, however, they also welcome the parents as learners – whether in order to enable them to better support their children's learning, or to build a collective sense of community around the learning environment, and often both

Impact

The direct impact of this research was felt during the research visits to the schools, and at the round tables or research meetings where all the education professionals could exchange, share, and interact to build social knowledge and community bonds.

Another level of impact is explicitly promoted in the mentioned published documents. They include orientations for improving educational synergies and for applying innovative flexibility to curriculum, school organization or communication strategies that mediate between teachers, parents, and students. "Several of the cases in our study have moved towards bringing together learners of different ages, in part to avoid disruption that can occur especially in the primary-to-secondary transition." (OECD, 2013, p. 42)

Current Hypothesis

Taking into account the acceptance mentioned on the published reports that the attendees at the final conference made, and the feedback form the schools and professionals that participated in the Catalan project, "collaborating in this international research was an excellent experience and should be repeated for other similar educational research topics". The institutional initiative, on the other hand, is hardly sustainable without systematic planning that guaranties control of costs, quality, and generalized access to this training experience. It needs to go from a handcrafted study to a reproducible and transferable system to be able to adapt to different contexts.

CONCLUSION

Social Information processing is an activity through which collective human actions organize knowledge. (Daniel Durant)

The three practical examples presented in our case-study section show three projects that focus on different directions for innovation:

- **Resource Oriented:** eLearning and virtual platforms for massive open online courses.
- **Process Oriented:** In-service sequences for training and professional growth
- **Transformation Oriented:** Research and collaboration for collective development.

All three are examples of the kinds of activities that universities should explore.

Tertiary education in general and the university in particular, need to deeply integrate into the digitally connected universe, while preserving academic freedom and rigor. This implies adopting a connectivist paradigm, which can be understood as social constructivism in the digital era. Under this paradigm, the professor's role emerges from that of preparing a *coherent narration* that he or she can offer on a particular discipline, to that of a storyteller, where s/he is able, not only to structure a meaningful scientific discourse, but also help learners find their own voice and participation space in the social and professional environment (Siemens, 2009b).

The university's role metamorphoses from that of certifying knowledge acquisition to one of benchmarking learning processes. Problem-based learning, project-based approaches, inquiring minds, or any other of the many well-known collaborative schemas (Boud & Felleti, 1999), need to replace the inefficient "cramming" for exams that leaves students with poor thinking strategies, in order to pass tests that require memorizing seldom-used material.

The university needs a collaborative role in society, interacting with institutions of business and government. Social action and practical application of knowledge in the labor market are explicit ways of fostering knowledge dissemination. Alternative communication strategies, which today are largely moving towards gamification, should explore other engagement scenarios. The line between personal hobbies and professional lives will become increasingly blurred. When they converge toward common objectives, they can also form hybrid communities that should be effective learning spaces, if managed in a structured way. Non-formal scenarios (intergenerational debates, on-line communities, open projects, network research) should also offer enriched opportunities for examining problems and devising solutions. As Neus Lorenzo has stated, " teaching is not transmitting knowledge for students to learn what the teacher knows, it is moving others to inquire and learn what nobody knows yet...and this is essential for collective improvement!" (Lorenzo interview, 2013)

ACKNOWLEDGMENT

We are deeply grateful to the professionals in *Servei de Llengües Estrangeres* of Department of Education, in Catalonia, for their support during the GEP project observation. We also thank the colleagues and participants in the eduPLEmooc Course, for the data they provided. We are grateful to the Jaume Bofill Foundation for their open access to tools and methodology used in their project.

REFERENCES

APEC. (2004). *Indicators of knowledge based economy*. APEC Economic Committee.

Australia Bureau of Statistics (ABS). (2002). *Measuring a knowledge-based economy and society – An Australian framework* (Discussion Paper cat. No. 1375.0). Author.

Boud, D., & Felleti, G. (Eds.). (1999). *The challenge of problem-based learning* (2nd ed.). London: Kogan Page. First published 1991, reprinted 1999. Retrieved February 15, 2014, from http://books.google.es/books?id=zvyBq6k6tWUC&pg=PA137&redir_esc=y#v=onepage&q&f=false

Brown, T. (2008). Design thinking: Thinking like a designer can transform the way you develop products, services, processes—and even strategy. *Harvard Business Review, 2008*(June). Retrieved from http://www.lacountyarts.org/UserFiles/File/CivicArt/Harvard%20Business%20Review-on-Design-Thinking.pdf

Carroll, J. B. (1965). The contributions of psychological theory and educational research to the teaching of foreign languages. *The Modern Language Journal, 49*(5), 273-281. Retrieved February 15, 2014, from http://www.jstor.org/stable/322133

Castaneda, L., & Camacho, M. (2012). Desvelando nuestra identidad digital. *El Profesional de la Información, 21*(4), 354-360. Retrieved February 15, 2014, from http://eprints.rclis.org/17350/1/2012EPI.pdf

Cavaliere, P. (2011). Catch me if you can: The OSCE report and the hunt for the elusive "human right to the internet". *Media Laws.* Retrieved February 15, 2014, from http://www.medialaws.eu/catch-me-if-you-can-the-osce-report-and-the-hunt-for-the-elusive-%E2%80%9Chuman-right-to-the-internet%E2%80%9D/

Christensen, C. M. (2003). *The innovator's solution: Creating and sustaining successful growth.* Boston: Harvard Business Press.

Conecta13. (2013). '#eduPLEmooc, un MOOC para el desarrollo profesional docente'. *EducaLab, spin-off de a Universidad de Granada.* Retrieved February 15, 2014, from http://conecta13.com/2013/12/eduplemooc-conecta13/

Council of Europe. (1992). *The European charter for regional or minority languages (ECRML).* Retrieved February 15, 2014, from http://conventions.coe.int/Treaty/en/Treaties/Html/148.htm

Council of Europe. (2001). *Common European framework of reference for languages: Learning, teaching, assessment (CEFR).* Strasbourg, France: Language Policy Unit. Retrieved February 15, 2014, from http://www.coe.int/t/dg4/linguistic/Source/Framework_en.pdfOfficial

Council of Europe. (2003). *Guide for the development of language education policies in Europe: From linguistic diversity to plurilingual education.* Strasbourg, France: Language Policy Unit. Retrieved July 26, 2014, from http://www.coe.int/t/dg4/Linguistic/Source/FullGuide_En.pdf

Council of Europe. (2008). *White paper on cultural dialogue: Living together as equals in dignity.* Retrieved July 26, 2014, from http://www.coe.int/t/dg4/intercultural/source/white%20paper_final_revised_en.pdf

Culkin, J. M. (1967). A Shoolman's Guide to Marshall McLuhan. *Saturday Review.* Retrieved February 15, 2014, from http://www.unz.org/Pub/SaturdayRev-1967mar18-00051

de Freitas, S. (2013). *MOOCs: The final frontier for higher education?* Coventry, UK: Coventry University. Retrieved February 15, 2014, from http://benhur.teluq.uquebec.ca/ted/Ressources/mooc.pdf

Dietrich, A. (2000). The cognitive neuroscience of creativity. *Psychonomic Bulletin & Review, 11*(6), 1011-1026. Retrieved February 15, 2014 from http://download.springer.com/static/pdf/163/art%253A10.3758%252FBF03196731.pdf?auth66=1392965651_1c41ea592320ab0865bef5c8dc28bef1&ext=.pdf

Downes, S. (2011). *The MOOC guide.* Retrieved July 26, 2014, from https://sites.google.com/site/themoocguide/3-cck08---the-distributed-course

Engeström, Y., Reigjo, M., & Raija-Leena, P. (Eds.). (1999). *Perspectives on activity theory.* New York: Cambridge University Press. Retrieved July 26, 2014, from http://ebooks.cambridge.org/ebook.jsf?bid=CBO9780511812774

European Commission. (2008). *Guide to cost-benefit analysis of investment projects*. Brussels: Directorate General Regional Policy. Retrieved February 15, 2014 from http://ec.europa.eu/regional_policy/sources/docgener/guides/cost/guide2008_en.pdf

European Commission. (2013a). Startup Europe - Using MOOCs to foster web talent in Europe. *Open Education Europa: The Gateway to European Innovative Learning*. Retrieved February 15, 2014, from http://openeducationeuropa.eu/en/groups/startup-europe-using-MOOCs-foster-web-talent-europe

European Commission. (2013b). Communication from the Commission to the European Parliament, the Council, the European Economic and social Committee and the Committee of the Regions. *Opening up Education: Innovative Teaching and Learning for all Through new Technologies and Open Educational Resources*. Retrieved February 15, 2014, from http://new.eur-lex.europa.eu/legal-content/EN/TXT/?qid=1389115469384&uri=CELEX:52013DC0654

European Commission. (2014a). Annotated guidelines. *Erasmus Charter for Higher Education, 2014-2020*. Retrieved February 15, 2014, from http://eacea.ec.europa.eu/funding/2014/documents/annotated_guidelines_en.pdf

European Commission. (2014b). EMOOCs 2014, the second MOOC European stakeholders summit, will be held on February 10-12, 2014 in Lausanne. *Open Education Europa: The Gateway to European Innovative Learning*. Retrieved February 15, 2014, from http://openeducationeuropa.eu/en/news/save-date-second-mooc-european-stakeholders-summit-be-held-february-2014

European Higher Education Area. (2010). Welcome to the EHEA official website! *Bologna Process - European Higher Education Area*. Retrieved February 15, 2014, from http://www.ehea.info

European Institute for Comparative Cultural Research. (2008). *Sharing diversity: National approaches to intercultural dialogue in Europe*. Bonn, Germany: European Institute for Comparative Cultural Research. Retrieved July 26, 2014, from http://www.interculturaldialogue.eu/web/intercultural-dialogue.php

European Union. (1999). Joint declaration of the European Ministers of Education. *The Bologna Declaration of 19 June 1999*. Retrieved February 15, 2014, from http://www.ehea.info/Uploads/Declarations/BOLOGNA_DECLARATION1.pdf

European Union. (2013). Erasmus+ programme: Call for proposals 2013. *Official Journal of the European Union, C 362*, 62-65. Retrieved February 15, 2014, from http://new.eur-lex.europa.eu/legal-content/EN/TXT/PDF/?uri=OJ:JOC_2013_362_R_NS0004&from=EN

Gallon, R. (2013). Communication, culture, and technology: Learning strategies for the unteachable. In R. D. Lansiquot (Ed.), *Cases on interdisciplinary research trends in science, technology, engineering, and mathematics - Studies on urban classrooms*. Hershey, PA: IGI Global. doi:10.4018/978-1-4666-2214-2.ch005

Gallon, R., & Lorenzo, N. (2013a). Transcending space: Ubiquitous knowledge. *Crossing Boundaries: Implications for the Content Industries*. Retrieved from http://adobe.ly/15NgqPx

Gallon, R., & Lorenzo, N. (2013b). *Crossing boundaries: Implications for the content industries*. Adobe Technical Communications White Paper. Retrieved February 15, 2014, from http://www.adobe.com/cfusion/entitlement/index.cfm?event=custom&sku=FS0003677&e=tcs_whitepaper

Grant, R. M. (1996). Toward a knowledge-based theory of the firm. *Strategic Management Journal, 17*(S2), 109–122. doi:10.1002/smj.4250171110

Haggard, S. (2011). *The coming MOOC copyright problem and its impact on students and universities.* Retrieved February 15, 2014, from http://moocnewsandreviews.com/category/commentary/

Harrison, R., & Hopkins, R. L. (1967). The design of cross-cultural training: An alternative to the university model. *The Journal of Applied Behavioral Science, 3*(4), 431–460. doi:10.1177/002188636700300401

Healy, T. (2000). *The appraisal of investments in educational facilities.* Paris: OECD Programme on Educational Building. Retrieved July 26, 2014, from http://files.eric.ed.gov/fulltext/ED439593.pdf

Hill, P. (2013). Emerging student patterns in MOOCs: A (revised) graphical view. *E-Literate.* Retrieved from http://mfeldstein.com/emerging-student-patterns-in-moocs-a-revised-graphical-view/

Horta, H. V. F., & Grediaga, R. (2010). Navel gazing: Academic inbreeding and scientific productivity. *Management Science, 56*(3), 414–429. doi:10.1287/mnsc.1090.1109

Istance, D., Stoll, L., Jolonch, A., Martínez, M., & Badia, J. (2013). Liderar per aprendre: Del diàleg entre la recerca i la pràctica. *Informes Breus 46 EDUCACIÓ.* Retrieved February 20, 2014, from http://www.fbofill.cat/intra/fbofill/documents/publicacions/580.pdf

Jambes, J. P. (2011). Développement numérique des espaces ruraux: Peut-on transformer un problème en ressource Territoriale? *Networks and Communication Studies, 25*(3-4), 165-178. Retrieved February 15, 2014, from http://www.netcom-journal.com/volumes/articlesV253/Netcom165-178.pdf

Josefowicz, M. (2012). *Connecting to complexity & change: Connecting urban design to people.* The International Nemetics Institute. Retrieved February 15, 2014, from http://cochange.wordpress.com/2012/12/18/connecting-urban-design-to-people/

Junco, R., & Cole-Avent, G. A. (2008). An introduction to technologies commonly used by college students. *New Directions for Student Services, 124*(124), 3–17. doi:10.1002/ss.292

Kaipa, P. (1999). What is unlearning? *The Mithya Institute for Learning.* Retrieved February 15, 2014, from http://mithya.prasadkaipa.com/learning/whatunlearn.html

Khan Academy. (2014). What's Khan Academy all about? *Khan Academy.* Retrieved February 15, 2014, from https://www.khanacademy.org/#mission-statement

Lane, L. M. (2012). Three kinds of MOOCs, Lisa's (online) teaching blog. Retrieved from http://lisahistory.net/wordpress/2012/08/three-kinds-of-moocs/

Leskovec, J. (2011). Tracking, modeling and predicting the flow of information through networks. in *KDD 2011 tutorial, social media analytics.* Stanford University. Retrieved February 15, 2014, from http://snap.stanford.edu/proj/socmedia-kdd/

Li, L., & Pitts, J. (2009). Does it really matter? Using virtual office hours to enhance student-faculty interaction. *Journal of Systems Education, 20*(2), 175–185.

Light, G., Cox, R., & Calkins, S. C. (2009). *Learning and teaching in higher education: The reflective professional.* London: Sage Publications.

Lorenzo, N. (2013). Daily adventure with Neus Lorenzo. In *Daily Edventures: Anthony Salcito's 366-day Look at Global Heroes in Education.* Retrieved February 15, 2014 from http://dailyedventures.com/index.php/2013/10/23/neuslorenzo/

Lorenzo, N. (2014). Curso MOOC- Personal learning environment: eduPLEmooc, del ministerio de educación, ciencia y deportes. In *NewsNeus blog de formación docente*. Retrieved February 15, 2014, from http://newsneus.wordpress.com/curso-mooc-pel/

Lorenzo, N., & Martínez, M. (2013). Col·legi sant pere claver (Barcelona). In *Lideratge per a l'aprenentatge: Estudis de cas a Catalunya*. Barcelona: Jaume Bofill Foundation.

Lubensky, R. (2006). The present and future of personal learning environments (PLE). In *Deliberations: Reflecting on learning and deliberating about democracy*. Retrieved February 15, 2014, from http://www.deliberations.com.au/2006/12/present-and-future-of-personal-learning.html

Martínez i Muñoz, M., Badia i Pujol, J., & Jolonch i Anglada, A. (Eds.). (2013). *Lideratge per a l'aprenentatge: Estudis de cas a Catalunya*. Barcelona: Jaume Bofill Fundation. Retrieved February 20, 2014, from http://www.fbofill.cat/intra/fbofill/documents/publicacions/580.pdf

Mayes, T., & de Freitas, S. (2007). Learning and Elearning: The role of theory. In H. Beetham & R. Sharpe (Eds.), *Rethinking pedagogy in the digital age*. London: Routledge.

Mehaffy, G. L. (2012). Challenge and change. *EDUCAUSE Review*. Retrieved June 3, 2014, from http://net.educause.edu/ir/library/pdf/ERM1252.pdf

Meister, J. (2012). Job hopping is the 'new normal' for millennials: Three ways to prevent a human resource nightmare. *Forbes Magazine*. Retrieved June 3, 2014, from http://www.forbes.com/sites/jeannemeister/2012/08/14/job-hopping-is-the-new-normal-for-millennials-three-ways-to-prevent-a-human-resource-nightmare/

Moorman, J., & Bowker, A. (2011). The university Facebook experience: The role of social networking on the quality of interpersonal relationship. *The American Association of Behavioral and Social Sciences Journal (AABSS), 15*, 1-23. Retrieved February 15, 2014, from http://aabss.org/Journal2011/04MoormanFinal.pdf

Nackerud, S., & Scaletta, K. (2008). Blogging in the academy. *New Directions for Student Services, 124*(124), 71–87. doi:10.1002/ss.296

Nationalencyklopedin. (Ed.). (2010). *Världens 100 största språk 2010, the world's 100 largest languages in 2010*. Retrieved February 15, 2014, from http://www.ne.se/spr%C3%A5k/v%C3%A4rldens-100-st%C3%B6rsta-spr%C3%A5k-2010

Nonaka, I. (1994). A dynamic theory of organizational knowledge creation. *Organization Science, 5*(1), 14–37. doi:10.1287/orsc.5.1.14

OECD. (1996). *The knowledge-based economy: General distribution*. Paris: OECD. Retrieved February 15, 2014, from http://www.oecd.org/science/sci-tech/1913021.pdf

OECD. (2013). *Innovative learning environments*. Paris: OCDE. Retrieved February 20, 2014, from http://www.oecd-ilibrary.org/deliver/fulltext?contentType=%2fns%2fOECDBook%2c%2fns%2fBook&itemId=%2fcontent%2fbook%2f9789264203488-en&mimeType=freepreview&containerItemId=%2fcontent%2fserial%2f20769679&accessItemIds=&redirecturl=http%3a%2f%2fwww.keepeek.com%2fDigital-Asset-Management%2foecd%2feducation%2finnovative-learning-environments_9789264203488-en&isPreview=true

OECD. (2013b). *PISA 2015: Draft collaborative problem solving framework, March 2013*. Retrieved February 15, 2014, from http://www.oecd.org/pisa/pisaproducts/Draft%20PISA%202015%20Collaborative%20Problem%20Solving%20Framework%20.pdf

Okazaki, S., & Mendez, F. (2013). Perceived ubiquity in mobile services. *Journal of Interactive Marketing, 27*(2), 98–111. doi:10.1016/j.intmar.2012.10.001

PIAAC. (2012). *Program for the international assessment of adult competencies.* Retrieved February 15, 2014, from http://nces.ed.gov/surveys/piaac

Regí, C., & Lorenzo, N. (2014). *Nuevas estrategias para la gestión de contenidos en educación: Análisis de la situación.* Retrieved February 15, 2014, from http://newsneus.wordpress.com/curso-mooc-pel/

Rhoads, R. A., Berdan, J., & Toven-Lindsey, B. (2013). The open courseware movement in higher education: Unmasking power and raising questions about the movement's democratic potential. *Educational Theory, 63*(1), 87–110. doi:10.1111/edth.12011

Sally, D. (1995). Conversation and cooperation in social dilemmas: A meta-analysis of experiments from 1958 to 1992. *Rationality and Society, 7*(1), 58–92. doi:10.1177/1043463195007001004

Scardamalia, M. (2002). Collective cognitive responsibility for the advancement of knowledge. In B. Smith (Ed.), *Liberal education in a knowledge society.* Chicago: Open Court. Retrieved February 15, 2014, from http://ikit.org/fulltext/2002CollectiveCog.pdf

Scardamalia, M. (2004). *Ask the experts: What's the next revolution in education going to be?* [Video series]. Toronto: Ontario Institute for Studies in Education, University of Toronto. Retrieved February 15, 2014, from https://tspace.library.utoronto.ca/handle/1807/2994

Scardamalia, M., & Bereiter, C. (2003). Knowledge building. In J.W. Guthrie (Ed.), *Encyclopedia of education* (2nd ed.). New York: Macmillan Reference. Retrieved February 15, 2014, from http://ikit.org/ulltext/2003_knowledge_building.pdf

Schank, R. C. (2011). *Teaching minds: How cognitive science can save our schools.* New York: Teachers College Press.

Selwyn, N. (2007). The use of computer technology in university teaching and learning: A critical perspective. *Journal of Computer Assisted Learning, 23*(2), 83–94. doi:10.1111/j.1365-2729.2006.00204.x

Siemens, G. (2004). Connectivism: A learning theory for the digital age. *Elearnspace Everything Elearning.* Retrieved February 15, 2014, from http://www.elearnspace.org/Articles/connectivism.htm

Siemens, G. (2006). Knowing knowledge. *Elearnspace Everything Elearning.* Retrieved February 15, 2014, from http://www.elearnspace.org/KnowingKnowledge_LowRes.pdf

Siemens, G. (2009). *Connectivism and connective knowledge.* Retrieved February 15, 2014, from http://ltc.umanitoba.ca/connectivism/?p=189

Siemens, G. (2009b). *Connectivism and the role of the teacher.* Retrieved February 15, 2014, from http://www.connectivism.ca/?p=220

Steele, C. (2012). How the mobile phone is evolving in developing countries. *PC Magazine.* Retrieved February 15, 2014, from http://www.pcmag.com/slideshow/story/297822/how-the-mobile-phone-is-evolving-in-developing-countries

Tene, O. (2010). Privacy: The new generations. *International Data Privacy Law, 1*(1), 15-27. Retrieved July 26, 2014, from http://idpl.oxford-journals.org/content/1/1/15.full#xref-fn-78-1

UNESCO. (2002). *Final report: Forum on the impact of open courseware for higher education in developing countries.* Paris: UNESCO. Retrieved February 15, 2014, from http://unesdoc.unesco.org/images/0012/001285/128515e.pdf

UNESCO. (2013). *Rethinking education in a changing world: Meeting of the senior experts' group.* Paris: UNESCO. Retrieved February 15, 2014, from http://unesdoc.unesco.org/images/0022/002247/224743e.pdf

Veà, A. (2013). *Cómo creamos internet: Grup editorial 62.* Barcelona: S.L.U. Edicions Península.

Vygotsky, L. (1978). *Mind and society: The development of higher mental processes.* Cambridge, MA: Harvard University Press.

Washburn, J. (2005). *University Inc.: The corporate corruption of higher education.* New York: Basic Books.

White, D. S., & Le-Cornu, A. (2011). Visitors and residents: A new typology for online engagement. *First Monday, 16*(9). doi:10.5210/fm.v16i9.3171

White, D. S., & Manton, M. (2011). *Open educational resources: The value of reuse in higher education.* Oxford, UK: University of Oxford. Retrieved February 15, 2014, from http://www.jisc.ac.uk/media/documents/programmes/elearning/oer/OERTheValueOfReuseInHigherEducation.pdf

Wiley, D., & Hilton, J. III. (2009). Openness, dynamic specialization, and the disaggregated future of higher education. *International Review of Research in Open and Distance Learning, 10*(5), 1–16. Retrieved from http://www.irrodl.org/index.php/irrodl/article/view/768/1414

Yuan, L., & Powell, S. (2013). MOOCs and open education: Implications for higher education – A white paper. Bolton, UK: The University of Bolton. Retrieved from http://publications.cetis.ac.uk/2013/667http://publications.cetis.ac.uk/wp-content/uploads/2013/03/MOOCs-and-Open-Education.pdf

KEY TERMS AND DEFINITIONS

Connectivism: A representation of the learning process in the digital age, through work experience, learning, and knowledge building, that integrates informal relationships, networked community building, technology, and information metaphors.

E-Learning: The use of electronic media, educational technology, and information and communication technologies (ICT) as digital educational tools, that can provide self-paced, asynchronous or synchronous learning, including multimedia learning, computer-based training (CBT), computer-assisted instruction or computer-aided learning (CAL), internet-based training (IBT), online education in virtual learning environments (VLE), or social media platforms.

Globalization: The process of international integration arising from the interchange of world views, products, ideas, and other aspects of culture, and which present challenges such as public-private boundaries, transparency, governance, economic and social equity, and educational transformation.

Interculturalism: A process that comprises an open and respectful exchange or interaction between individuals, groups and organizations with different cultural backgrounds or world views, to develop a deeper understanding of diverse perspectives and practices, increase participation and the freedom and ability to make choices, foster equality, and enhance creative processes

M-Learning: The exploitation of ubiquitous handheld hardware, wireless networking and mobile telephony to facilitate, support, enhance, and extend the reach of teaching and learning, that can take place in any location, at any time.

Plurilingualism: The intrinsic capacity of all speakers to use, learn, and function in more than one language and culture, as opposed to monolinguals, who can only manage in one language, and regardless of whether the society offers multilingual opportunities or not.

Telepresence: The effect of a set of technologies which allow a person to feel as if they were present, to give the appearance of being present, communicate, and participate socially, at a place other than their true location.

Training: The acquisition of knowledge, skills, and competencies through a guided learning process in formal, informal, and non-formal fields, with specific goals of improving one's capability, capacity, productivity and performance.

Transformation: The dynamic process whereby cultures, education, economics, and other defining aspects of world civilisations are changing and adapting to external or internal forces, such as globalization, advances in digital information technologies and communication, infrastructure and transport improvements, and military expansion.

Ubiquity: The impression of being everywhere at once - in digital terms, the result of mobility, continuity, immediacy, portability, and searchability.

Chapter 8
Tracing the Use of Communication Technologies in Higher Education

Fernando Ramos
University of Aveiro, Portugal

Pedro Almeida
University of Aveiro, Portugal

Marta Pinto
University of Aveiro, Portugal

João Batista
University of Aveiro, Portugal

Dalila Coelho
University of Aveiro, Portugal

Nídia Morais
University of Aveiro, Portugal

Rui Raposo
University of Aveiro, Portugal

Francislê Souza
University of Aveiro, Portugal

Lúcia Pombo
University of Aveiro, Portugal

Ana Balula
University of Aveiro, Portugal

Luís Pedro
University of Aveiro, Portugal

Margarida Lucas
University of Aveiro, Portugal

António Moreira
University of Aveiro, Portugal

ABSTRACT

This chapter presents a comprehensive view of the main activities and findings of a research project entitled TRACER-Portuguese Public Higher Education Use of Communication Technologies, which focused on how the information about the use of Communication Technologies in Higher Education Institutions can be collected, systematized, processed, and deployed to stakeholders. The project was carried out between 2011 and 2014 and its main results are a consolidated proposal of an analysis model to address the use of Communication Technologies in Higher Education institutions, as well as the U-TRACER® tool. This Web-based tool provides support to the process of collecting, processing, and deployment of data related with the use of Communication Technologies in a specific Higher Education or in a group of institutions, based on institutional or geographical criteria.

DOI: 10.4018/978-1-4666-7244-4.ch008

INTRODUCTION

Since the revolution fostered by the dissemination of the Internet, Communication Technologies (CTs) have been playing a major role in Higher Education (HE) as a trigger to new and challenging approaches to teaching and learning. Besides, the strategic options of Higher Education Institutions (HEIs) have also been strongly influenced by the power that CTs – such as email, blogs, wikis, social networks, videoconferencing systems, Virtual Learning Environments/Learning Management Systems, 3D virtual worlds – provide as a way to address new and diverse target audiences, opening possibilities for the broadening of the activity of HEIs in new markets through lifelong learning and internationalization approaches.

The reinforcement of the role CTs have in a new generation of Education policies in the European Union has been widely envisaged in several strategic decisions, namely regarding the effort to establish a European Higher Education Area. The Europe 2020/Horizon 2020 research framework clearly addresses the need for new approaches to helping people of all ages anticipate and manage change through investment in skills and training, paving the way to modernizing labour markets and raising employment levels leading to smart and inclusive growth.

The international research community has also widely addressed the need for deepening the understanding on how CTs may positively influence how students learn, discussing the role of topics such as CTs mediated collaborative learning practices, CTs based/online distance education or, more recently, massive open online courses (MOOCs). The success of several MOOC initiatives are pointing out the importance students are giving to the way HEIs use CTs in deploying new teaching and learning models that provide advanced levels of flexibility and openness in time, space, context, contents and curricula (Anderson, 2013; Gillani & Eynon, 2014; Nkuyubwatsi, 2014).

This move towards the relevance of the use of CTs in HE requires research on analysis models and methods aiming at characterizing the use of CTs in HEIs and on tools that may help deploying systematized information to stakeholders. These include regulatory and institutional policy makers, teachers, students, families, i.e., everyone having responsibility on options about the use of CTs in HEIs or willing to acknowledge the information about how HEIs use CTs as a basis for deciding which HEI to apply for.

In this chapter, some information as to these topics is put forward, by presenting and discussing the main findings and results of a research project entitled TRACER-Portuguese Public Higher Education Use of Communication Technologies (http://cms.ua.pt/TRACER), through which it was aimed to study how information concerning HEIs' use of CTs can be systematized, retrieved, processed and deployed to stakeholders. Despite the existence, in specialized literature, of several reports about research on this topic (Conole & Alevizou, 2010, Coutinho & Junior, 2008; Dahlstrom et al., 2011; EHEA, 2012; Franklin & Harmelen, 2007; O'Neill & Colley, 2006; Pempek et al., 2009; Puente, 2007; Santos et al., 2011; Selwyn, 2007; UNESCO, 2009; Vercruysse & Proteasa, 2012), the lack of a comprehensive and systematic approach to the analysis of the use of CT in HEIs was identified. Consequently this project also aimed at contributing to improve awareness and transparency in the Portuguese HE system by deploying a web-based data retrieval tool enabling open and easy access to the details about how Portuguese HEIs' use CTs.

This project, funded by FCT (Fundação para a Ciência e a Tecnologia – the Portuguese research funding agency, ref. PTDC/CPECED/113368/2009COMPETE:FCOMP-01-0124-FEDER-014394), started in 2011 and was conducted by a team of researchers from the University of Aveiro – Portugal, with hybrid educational and technological scientific backgrounds.

The project included five main phases (Figure 1). During phase 1, an online survey was prepared and conducted with the universe of Portuguese public HEIs aiming at retrieving the institutional perspective about the adoption and use of CTs. Phase 2 was devoted to the design and implementation of the online U-TRACER® tool. In phase 3, the teaching staff of the Portuguese public HEIs was invited to collaborate in a survey aiming at retrieving data about the use of CTs in teaching and learning activities. Phase 4 was dedicated to the identification and retrieval of relevant data as to best practices on the use of CTs in the HEIs. During phase 5 all data retrieved during the project was integrated in the U-TRACER® tool, and further deployed to relevant stakeholders.

The main results of the project are a consolidated proposal of an analysis model to address the use of CTs in HEIs, the analysis resulting from the data collection processes carried out during the project execution and a web-based tool, the U-TRACER® tool, which provides support to the online collection, processing and deployment of

data related with the use of CTs in a specific HEI or in a group of HEIs, based on institutional or geographical criteria.

Besides this introduction the current chapter also includes the following sections: literature review; research methods and main outcomes; the U-TRACER® tool; and conclusions.

Literature Review

Communication Technologies are being used in HEIs worldwide (Conole & Alevizou, 2010), producing changes in the design of teaching and learning practices, giving rise to learning paradigms such as e-learning, b-learning, m-learning and cloud learning. Some evidence of this change is the use of Personal Learning Environments (PLE) in HE (Downes, 2005; Santos et al., 2011), the emergence of MOOCs or Open Courseware (Liyoshi & Kumar, 2008) or the online availability of educational videos, both in closed and in open access contexts (Katz, 2008).

Figure 1. Main phases of the TRACER project

① Survey PPHEI 1: institutional perspective of CT use

② TRACER: Tool conception and prototyping

③ Survey PPHEI 2: CT use by teachers

④ CT use in PPHEI: dissemination of good practices

⑤ PPHEI: TRACER tool delivery

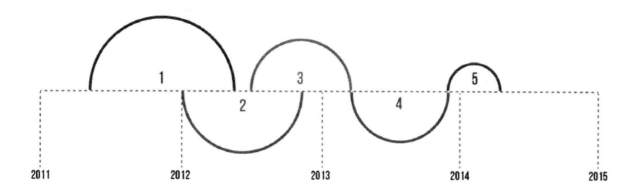

In the last decades, HEIs worldwide have been making a strong investment to offer CTs infrastructures for more independent and distance learning students, blending CTs into many aspects of teaching and learning (Selwyn, 2007; Bielschowsky et al., 2009; Schlosser & Simonson, 2009).

Research related to the use of CTs in HE embraces two main perspectives regarding the impact in teaching practices. The first perspective emphasizes that CTs use is not potentiating innovation or disruptiveness of more traditional forms of education, arguing that teachers need training to integrate CTs in teaching practices in a more innovative way (Blin & Munro, 2008). The second perspective argues the existence of disruptiveness which is becoming ever more powerful, promoting changes in the roles and in the way teachers and students work and interact (Garrison & Anderson, 2003; Bielaczyc & Blake, 2006; Siemens & Tittenberger, 2009).

From the literature review already published, particularly in the context of the TRACER Project (Pinto et al., 2012) and from the literature regarding the use of CT in HEIs in Portugal (e.g. Batista & Ramos, 2011; Batista et al., 2011; Morais et al., 2011; Gomes et al., 2011), it may be concluded that the ubiquity of Web 2.0 tools leads to the strengthening of its use in environments of teaching and learning practices, although its use doesn't always enhance innovation.

Several international studies related to the use of CT (e.g. Johnson et al., 2011; JISC, 2012) refer changes in the teacher's and student's roles, leading to the adoption of new approaches compared to traditional learning scenarios in HE. However, the literature review that includes only Portuguese studies during the last five years (Pombo et al., 2013) could not lead to the conclusion that these changes also occur in the national context. In general, it is considered that CTs are primarily being used for "delivery" with the underlying perspectives of teaching by transmission, targeting mainly at the student's knowledge development. From this point of view, students are not

being properly prepared to face the challenges of information society or new labor markets (JISC, 2012). However, some cases may be identified where these practices are changing.

In the Portuguese HE context, a national study shows the use of CTs mostly focuses on the use of Learning Management Systems/Virtual Learning Environments (LMS/VLE), content sharing and Web 2.0 tools, with research evidence showing little use of 3D virtual environments and social networks (Batista, 2011; Morais, 2012). In general, LMS/VLE are used to provide class and additional materials to students; to propose activities to be undertaken inside or outside the classroom; and to disclose other elements, such as process and outcome evaluation, for which interpersonal CTs (email, skype, etc.) are also largely used (Duarte & Gomes, 2011; Morais et al., 2011; Silva, 2012). In fact, LMS/VLE, more specially the Moodle platform, are widely used in Portuguese HE to support teacher training process, in face-to-face sessions, to promote learning communities or even to foster research projects (Duarte & Gomes, 2011).

Another type of widely used technologies in HE are interpersonal CTs, such as e-mail, in particular for the interaction between teachers and students and among themselves. It is often used as an alternative to face-to-face activities (O'Neill & Colley, 2006), namely to answer the students' questions or to disseminate information (Morais et al., 2011). Interpersonal CTs, and especially e-mail, remain as one of the most effective forms of communication in learning contexts (Dahlstrom et al., 2011).

With regard to the use of Web 2.0 in HE learning contexts, numerous works have been published (Franklin & Harmelen, 2007; Coutinho & Junior, 2008; Conole & Alevizou, 2010). Some of the advantages often referred for the use of these CTs are that they are freeware and user-friendly, and allow for collaboration and interaction (Aresta, 2009; Marques & Carvalho, 2009). However, some constraints associated with the use of these technologies are also identified, such as the lack of institutional control, the lack of knowledge about these technologies and the lack of training for its use (Aresta, 2009; Marques & Carvalho, 2009).

Some documents published as to Web 2.0 deal with the use of specific tools such as blogs, wikis, websites for sharing photos and videos, social bookmarking tools, content aggregators and social networks, among others. For example, the construction of blogs and wikis, characterized by the production and sharing of new, or repurposed, content (Coutinho & Junior, 2007; Ros-Rodríguez et al., 2011) seems to stimulate the involvement and the responsibility of students in more participatory activities (Puente, 2007).

Podcasts also have been explored in educational contexts in HE (Edirisingha et al., 2007; Carvalho, 2008), as a way to motivate students to learn and to complement the more traditionally designed content materials created and disseminated by teachers. Such type of resources also allows greater autonomy and mobility of students in their learning processes, in particular because they can hear the learning contents and exercises anywhere and anytime (Edirisingha, et al., 2007; Carvalho, 2008). Several studies also report experiments conducted on the use of collaborative tools. These tools require the participation of teachers and students in the development of learning activities. Examples are Google Drive, mindmaps and social bookmarking tools (Lomas, 2005; Grodecka et al., 2009). Despite the potential and the user-friendliness of these tools, as well as the students' recognition of its value, its adoption is still not very common in educational contexts in HE in Portugal (Coutinho & Junior, 2008a; Morais et al., 2011).

The widespread use of social networks, like Facebook, has also given rise to its exploitation in learning contexts, particularly in HE. The motivations for its use include ease in establishing interpersonal contacts, providing and sharing content, such as news, events, and visual materials related to the subjects under study (Pempek et al., 2009; Patrício & Gonçalves, 2010; Miranda et al.,

2011). Although they are widely used in personal contexts, research shows lower use rates in learning contexts (Batista et al., 2011).

From the above-mentioned, an evolution of teaching and learning practice enhanced by the integration of CT in HE is expected, as recommended by the Digital Agenda for Europe (DAE, http://ec.europa.eu/digital-agenda). The aims of this initiative are to help European citizens to get the most out of digital technologies, and thus support the effective development of digital literacy in favor of science, society, employability, economy, and innovation in Europe.

The development of digital literacy is becoming an urgent priority across HE, as referred in the Horizon 2011 Report (Johnson et al., 2011), as the frequency of digitally-mediated contexts increases across all professional fields. According to the European Commission, while the labour market crisis in Europe leads to high levels of youth unemployment, there is a CT jobs' gap, which means that companies cannot find enough employees with proper digital competencies, which as a huge impact in the European economy.

To have insights and knowledge regarding HEI and their use of CTs is an asset little disputed, although there is difficulty in accessing comparable data between countries and institutions regarding this field of knowledge. In the scenario of comparable data about HE worldwide, we find instruments such as university rankings and transparency tools (Costes et al., 2010; Hazelkorn, 2013; Marope et al., 2013), which are being gradually grasped as assets in the involvement of stakeholders, for benchmarking practices, communicating the diversity of institutional profiles, analyzing strengths through comparable data and adequate indicators (ENQA, 2011; EHEA, 2012; EUROASHE, 2012; Vercruysse & Proteasa, 2012).

The worldwide phenomenon of the uses and outcomes of HE rankings and transparency tools have generated debates with opposite perspectives: recognizing their usefulness; criticizing its main approaches that privilege research outcomes over teaching and learning (Hazelkorn, 2013; IIIEP, 2009). Marope et al. (2013) stress that regarding the perspective of students "[t]here is a growing need for simple-to-use but sophisticated tools to filter out the noise and shortlist options that merit further research" (p.58). Furthermore, the authors alert that, regarding the perspective of HE decision makers, there are limitations in global rankings in particular because of data interpretation, i.e., "global rankings will never be able to provide a complete picture regardless of how sophisticated data collection mechanisms may become. Indeed, in almost all cases, such rankings were intended for use as a guide to decision-making rather than an alternative" (p.63).

Although varying in their methodologies and underlying measures, these instruments facilitate the collection of comparable data about HEIs (Marope et al., 2013), mostly based on indicators concerning the institutions' performance as to research, citations and publications, grounded on bibliometric databases such as Scopus and Thomson Reuters. Disproportionately, data about teaching and learning is approached only by two rankings, offering distinct data (van Vught & Ziegele, 2011). Additionally, the use of information visualization features to present data has also a disproportionate adoption, with the majority presenting as league tables and a minority of 3 ranking platforms using information visualization features. Nevertheless, none of the instruments allows the collection of data as to the use of CTs in institutions for management or pedagogical purposes.

This is where the U-TRACER® tool emerges as an information visualization tool that accomplishes the purpose of supporting data collection focused on the use of CTs, and translates that data into comparable information which can be visualized, filtered and customized according to interests of the user, in open access to HE stakeholders.

Research Methods and Main Outcomes

A first challenge of this project was the definition of an analysis model of the research object – the use of CTs in HEIs from the institutional and the teaching perspectives – that could be used as theoretical reference regarding the most relevant domains, dimensions and indicators to be addressed (OECD/JRC, 2008; UNESCO, 2009; Quivy & Campenhoudt, 2005). Consequently and bearing in mind the literature review, a complex theoretical framework was designed, grounded on the institutional and the teaching points of view (Figure 2).

For each of these perspectives several conceptual domains were defined, as well as the respective dimensions and indicators, which underpinned the design and implementation of two questionnaires, validated by an external consultant, two external experts, as well as by a pilot-study held with sixteen teachers of four different public HEIs. These questionnaires supported two online surveys – the first was implemented during the academic year 2011/2012 (Figure 1, Phase 1) to gather data regarding the institutional perspective of CT use; the second during the academic year 2012/2013 (Figure 1, Phase 3), aiming to gather data concerning the teachers' perspective of CT use.

In the first survey, focused on the institutional perspective, there were two main target respondents in each HEI: the person responsible for the CT domain at the rectory level (e.g. rector, pro-rector, president, vice-president) and the person responsible for CT services at the technical level (e.g. director, chief officer, manager). Therefore, the questionnaire used to gather data related with the institutional perspective was composed by two interdependent parts with the following sections: profile, policies towards CT use, CT resources and functionalities, infrastructures to support CT use, current institutional challenges relating to future CT use (1st part – rectory/presidency level) and training provision for CT use and CT use (2nd

Figure 2. Main conceptual domains and dimensions of the TRACER reference model

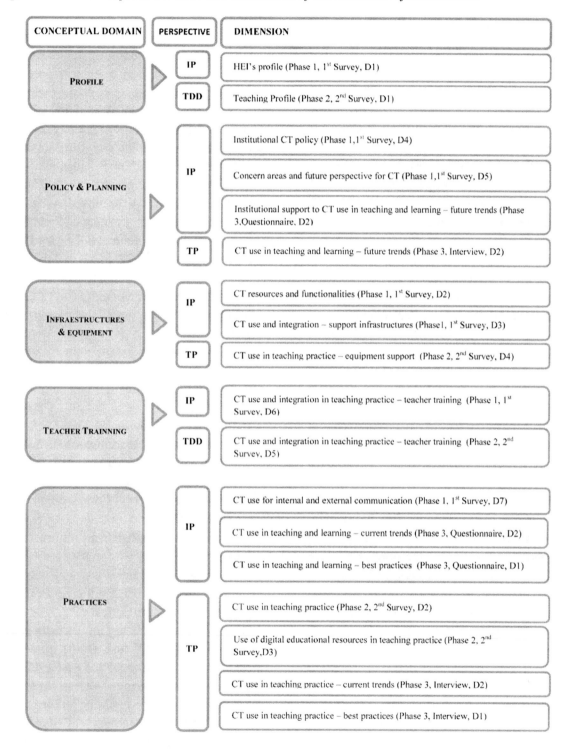

part – technical level). In order to identify the respective leaders at the rectory/presidency and technical level, a database with several contacts was built, supported on the public information available at each HEI's website. Relying on that information, a first contact was made to present the project and the study, and each HEI was asked to confirm the respective interlocutor for each of these levels, in order to submit the formal invitation for their participation in the survey. Considering the distinct organization of each HEI in what concerns CT policies, services and staff, and the need of enrolling different departments in the institution in order to obtain the data required, this invitation was send to the main responsible for the CT domain at the rectory/presidency level, that coordinated the answering process within the institution and delivered the final submission.

From a total of thirty-five existing Portuguese public HEIs, including universities and polytechnics, all invited to participate in the study, seventeen accessed the online survey and nine have fully completed and submitted the information required. Data was provided by decision-makers at the rectory level in universities and at presidency level in polytechnics, as well as by the person responsible for institution's CT services, whenever existent, thus involving nearly twenty stakeholders (around 2 per institution). Results globally show that the HEIs that have fully answered the questionnaire are aware of the need to have an overall online presence, through an institutional website (n=9) and in social networks (n=8), also the most common options selected for presenting departments, research centers and courses online. A less preferred choice for the online presence and for institutional communication is 3D virtual environments (n=1).

Results reveal that HEIs are making an effort to bring together policies and practices, although formal political strategies were only reported by three HEIs. More specifically, results point out to an overall concern with teachers' training and professional development, i.e., with embedding

CTs in teaching practice and with the use of technology devices and resources by teaching and non-teaching staff. The existence of specific guidelines about distance education was reported also by three HEIs. Despite their differences, respondent HEIs seem to agree on the main concerns regarding institutional adoption of CTs, which are mostly connected to funding (n=8), to the creation and expansion of infrastructures to support students and staff (n=6) and to equipment and infrastructure management (n=5). The less common concerns seem to be related to emerging technologies, namely, the creation or deployment of Open Educational Resources (OER) (n=0), the institutional use of Web 2.0 (n=1) and the introduction and diffusion of educational resources supported by mobile technologies (n=1).

From the 821 courses of all cycles offered by the respondent HEIs, 5.9% were delivered entirely online and 4.2% in a blended environment, most of them at 1st and 2nd cycle level, thus representing nearly 10% of the training offer and pointing out to a slow movement to online education. Regarding the provision of online learning LMS/VLE to support teaching and learning, results indicate that the open source platform Moodle is the most commonly adopted (n=9), sometimes coexisting with other similar platforms. From the analysis of the access of teachers and students to these online platforms, results show there were more accesses in the case of institutions with courses available in online settings. Digital repositories of scientific content exist in eight HEI, in all cases based on the open source platform DSpace.

The majority of HEIs has infrastructures and services to support CT use (n=8), providing support to every department and sector, both in technical and online teaching and learning issues. Seven institutions provide training for supporting CT integration and use in the teachers' educational practice, delivered in face-to-face (n=4) or blended scenarios (n=4), through workshops (n=6), focusing on the use of institutional platforms (LMS/VLE and digital repositories) (n=6).

The second survey (Figure 1, Phase 3) focused on the teachers' perspective regarding CT use in their teaching practice, and it was subdivided into five domains: profile, pedagogical use of CTs, CT resources used, equipment and support for CT use, and training for CT use in teaching and learning. From an overall 578 teachers that accessed the questionnaire, 185 answers were considered valid, representing nineteen public HEIs. Despite intense dissemination of the survey through a variety of channels, in a first moment through official invitation sent to the leaders at the rectory/presidency level contacted in the first survey and then through social media and relevant channels of research in education and ICT, the overall response rate was low and did not include answers from every public HEI. Therefore, data obtained are considered necessarily limited, although regarded as an important asset for future studies.

Considering the subsystem, 60% of the respondent teachers belong to universities and 40% to the polytechnic subsystem. Around 75% of the teachers reported to have ten or more years of teaching experience in HE. Moreover, the scientific areas taught by the respondents are Education (13,5%), Health and Social Welfare (13,0%) and Business Management (10,8%). Most of the respondents are teaching in 1st (88.1%) and 2nd cycle courses (63.8%), in face-to-face settings.

Global results show that interpersonal CTs (62.2% in 1st cycle; 42.7%, in 2nd cycle) and LMS/VLE (35.7% in 1st cycle; 23.8% in 2nd cycle) are the most used in teaching and learning activities, usually on a daily basis. This is consistent with results gathered as to CT use per specific activity type – dissemination, discussion, discovery and assessment –, although some differences exist within activity types and subtypes. LMS/VLE are mainly used for delivering class materials (89.7% – dissemination), whereas interpersonal CTs are the most common option for answering students' doubts (80.5% – discussion). Discovery activities bring together more different types of CTs, with an important role played by collabora-

tion CTs in searching and selecting information (39.5% – discovery). In general, assessment activities seem to represent the lower CT integration level, except for the use of LMS/VLEs for receiving students' assignments (69.2%). Between 70%-90% of teachers rate the CT use positively, notably regarding the possibility of communicating with students in (extra-)class time (95.7%) and of making educational resources available to them (93.5%). Oppositely, the volume of tasks demanded for integrating CT in the educational process is perceived by teachers (44.3%) as the most negative aspect. Nevertheless, quality and innovation purposes are put forward as the main reasons for using CT, i.e., to motivate students for learning (77.8%) and to innovate in teaching practice (74.6%).

Images or visual materials are the most commonly used digital educational resources in all course modalities (95%-98%) and study cycles (60%-90%). Interactive games are the least used type, with 75.1% (course modality) and 77.3% (study cycles) of declared non-users. Around 30% of teachers (n=54) attended training related to CT use in education during the academic year 2012/2013, in most of cases, one workshop (48.1%) or one theoretical course (22.2%). Such training has been delivered mostly in face-to-face environment (79.6%); nevertheless, there is growing evidence of training in online modalities (42.6% blended; 37.0% fully online). Common themes are the use of institutional platforms (63.0%), use of Web 2.0 tools for educational purposes (40.7%) and teaching and learning strategies support by CT (38.9%).

The two questionnaires concerning institutional and teaching perspectives are integrated in U-TRACER® as data gathering tools; nonetheless, U-TRACER® also enables the visualization of the inserted data from an individual and aggregated viewpoint, as described in the next section.

The U-TRACER® Tool

This section provides an overview of the U-TRACER® tool, a web-based tool that enables the online collection, processing and deployment of data about the use of CTs in HEIs. It includes a general description of the main functionalities provided by U-TRACER®, and some examples of the individual and aggregated statistical information users may access.

Main Features

The U-TRACER® online tool is composed by two areas: the front-office, which offers end-users access to distinct information about the project and diverse visualization features of the collected data, and the back-office, which supports all the platform's management functionalities (users, HEIs, data collection, surveys).

The U-TRACER® web portal (front-office) includes common information and explanation areas. It consists of a typical open web platform, which serves the purpose of disseminating the data collected in the back-office, through information visualization (interaction and graphical) features (Figure 3). This particular area of the platform has the following main sections (Figure 3, main menu):

- **Registration and Login:** allows common users to register and login, accessing the list of HEIs, which he/she chooses to receive notifications with up-to-date data;
- **About Area:** information about the TRACER project;
- **News:** access to the news published;
- **Methodology:** description of the methodology used in the project, namely for the data collection and analysis;
- **How to Use:** information on how to use the U-TRACER® tool to filter information and generate graphs according to criteria defined by the user;

- **Publications:** list of publications authored by the TRACER project;
- **U-TRACER®:** information visualization features of the tool that allows information customization, interaction with information filters that generate the corresponding visual displays of data.

The core area of the portal is devoted to displaying the results of the surveys through a set of graphical representations that may be customized through an extensive list of filters and indicators. Specifically, it allows a common end-user to retrieve data by interacting with filters based on specific parameters, which include (Figure 3, left menu):

- **Perspective:** 'Institutional Perspective' confines the use of CT to data fields related to the institutional adoption of CTs to support educational practice; 'Teachers Perspective' includes data related to the use of CTs by teachers;
- **Context:** 'Region' aggregates data of HEIs from a specific region organized by NUTS II geographical criteria; 'Higher Education Institution' aggregates data for each HEI;
- **Academic Year:** 'Academic year' confines data per academic year; 'Comparison between academic years' allows the selection of two or more years to frame data;
- **Theme:** distinction between 'Uses of Communication Technologies' and 'Best practices in the use of Communication Technologies' with each topic being structured in sub-themes with data subsets;
- **Graphical Display of Data:** allowing data to be represented by stacked bar graph or pie-donut graph.

Additionally, the U-TRACER® tool section includes other features which include:

Figure 3. The visualization area of the U-TRACER® public web portal

- **Glossary:** a list of common used terms and their definitions;
- **Download:** the ability to download the dataset that generated a graphic, and the graphic in .pdf or .xls formats;
- **Share:** sharing features, allowing the promotion of graphics in the most common social networks (Facebook, Twitter, LinkedIn, Google+).

In Figure 3, a particular example of a data graphical display is presented, which can also be downloaded and/or shared in social networks.

Three examples illustrate the institutional and aggregated statistical information by region that users may request:

- The total number of courses offered by an institution, according to the teaching and learning modality adopted (face-to-face, blended or fully online) (Figure 3, main graph area);

- The number of courses offered in a whole region, according the teaching and learning methodologies and per study cycle;
- The frequency with which an institution offers teacher training on how to use CTs.

The back-office provides support to administrators and respondents of both surveys (HE institutional leaders and teachers). In this area, the following information and editing features are available (Figure 4):

- Institutional profile information (available to the institutional leader);
- The ability to fill in the surveys (available to the institutional leader and teachers) (Figure 4, main area);
- The history of completed surveys (available to the institutional leader);
- Information: help and contacts sections (available to the institutional leaders and teachers).

Figure 4. A view of the U-TRACER® back-office

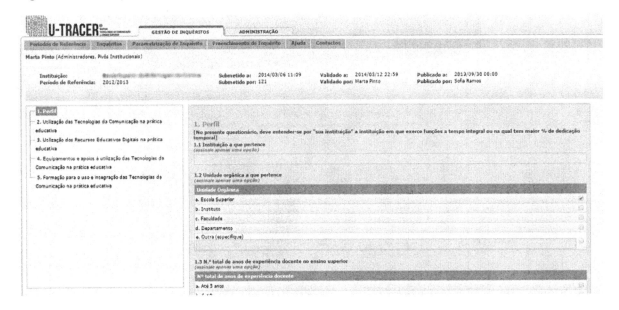

Evaluation of the U-TRACER® Tool

Ten institutional decision makers, belonging to eight of the nine of the HEIs that provided data in survey 1 were interviewed concerning the usefulness of the U-TRACER® tool. Globally, results show that the majority considers the tool useful to provide:

- Information to support activities: using the tool to access information about the institution's competitors, to collect systematized information about their own institution, and to deploy information about the institution;
- Information for research and development: scholars and teachers can use the tool for research and development purposes.

There were no disadvantages identified for the tool, and the advantages focused on the possibility of positioning the institution in the HE market, and allowing for some comparative analysis with other institutions of similar size. The comparison is seen as an advantage because it allows the observation of trends of CT use, and therefore contributes to evaluate and better position the institution in the HE market. The fact that the information visualization can be customized in the tool, enabling the user to search for specific information, was also considered as an asset.

The concerns expressed regarded the confidentiality of the HEIs identification, suggesting it should be maintained, as well as the sustainability of the U-TRACER®, since it requires resources and at the moment the tool is supported by a funded project ending in 2014.

Usability tests to the prototype of the U-TRACER® tool were also performed, addressing the efficiency and user satisfaction dimensions as to with the general use of the tool.

These tests followed ISO 9241-11 (International Organization for Standardization, 1998) – human-computer interaction related – and were developed with the close monitoring of the performance that resulted from the application of a task list to a group of seven participants.

These tasks encompassed the efficiency of the information architecture and interface of the tool, namely concerning the:

- General browsing of the tool through the exploration of specific information in several areas;
- Retrieval of specific information through the selection of particular criteria and display options.

The results of these usability tests revealed that some of the visual metaphors, initially used in the interface, were not completely understood by the users, namely in tasks related with the application of information filters/criteria. The display options were also often mentioned, namely regarding the information labels and format.

After performing every task, the participants answered a questionnaire about their overall satisfaction in using the back-office and front-office of the U-TRACER® tool, noting their opinions in a Likert scale from 1 (not satisfied) to 5 (highly satisfied). The results concerning the use of the back-office revealed an overall moderate to high satisfaction (between levels 3 and 4). In terms of the use of the front-office, the results point out a greater diversity of opinions, ranging from levels 2 to 4.

In the overall results regarding satisfaction of use, two users indicated to be somewhat satisfied, three users quite satisfied and one highly satisfied. Regarding the satisfaction of interacting with the data filters (context, school years and themes) users mostly revealed to be satisfied (three) and one highly satisfied. Regarding the interaction with the graphs, five of the participants indicated their satisfaction to be between 1 and 3, which indicates a low satisfaction, understood as a consequence of the comments made during the interaction with the graphs, as described earlier. Finally, the satisfaction in what the graphical representation types are concerned reveals more satisfaction from the participants, since five of them indicated to be quite satisfied.

The results of the usability tests were integrated as improvements to the tool, and covered changes to the graph labels, the introduction of

contextualized help buttons near the filters, as well as the introduction of the word 'or' between the drop-down menus for the filters 'region' and 'higher education institution' to help clarify the user about the option of selecting one or another filter. Besides, a new tab called 'How to use' replacing the existing button was included and improvements were made to the result of interaction tasks performed with the filters, by adding an immediate alteration of the chart area when the user changes the filter. Finally, concerning the graphs, suggestions pointed out that the words in the labels should be complete; the color labels for the bar and pie-ring graphs should be standardized; the tooltips of the graphs should include the description of the measurement unit; the color label of the map should not indicate the region, and the title of the selected region should be closer to the image of the map.

CONCLUSION

The TRACER project pursued a comprehensive research approach to the analysis, gathering and deployment of relevant data about the CT use by HE. The scope of the project was defined as the Portuguese Public Higher Education system, which includes universities and polytechnic schools, but the theoretical and methodological framework adopted may be reused and adapted to other contexts.

Results from the analysis of the data collected show that the use of CT in the Portuguese Public Higher Education system follows other international patterns, still reflecting a somewhat conservative attitude of the HEIs. Nevertheless, the results also show that there is a great interest from the teaching staff to explore innovative uses of CTs to foster students' motivation and learning outcomes by increasing the interaction among students and teachers and promoting their relevance in the learning processes.

In the literature review, information about the CT use in HEIs is vast and scattered in a huge number of publications and data is deployed in a myriad of formats. There is a serious need for an expedite systematization of that information to understand the effective use of CTs, which is being made by institutions to support education. Although this need exists, some HEIs were reluctant to participate in the project, i.e. to provide data, which may be due to a limited institutional awareness of the transformative impact CT may have in HE.

The online visualization U-TRACER® tool proved to be a valid approach for gathering data and delivering information about the use of CTs in HEIs. However, further research will help to enlarge its application, namely by the introduction of other relevant perspectives such as the students' perspective.

It is expected that the results of this project will contribute to raise awareness and transparency on the institutional and teaching practices concerning CT use. Besides, by providing examples of good practices, results may also have a great impact on Portuguese HEIs by fostering the discussion about how CTs may help them to achieve their strategic goals and to promote better teaching and learning conditions for teachers and students.

A huge challenge is now the sustainability of the U-TRACER® tool, since its maintenance and further development requires resources that recommend the convergence with other existing systems intended to offer information transparency to the European HE system and institutions, such as the U-Multirank platform.

ACKNOWLEDGMENT

This work is financed through a FEDER Grant under the "Programa Operacional Factores de Competitividade – COMPETE" and National Funds by FCT – Fundação para a Ciência e a Tecnologia (Project reference PTDC/CPE-CED/113368/2009 COMPETE:FCOMP-01-0124-FEDER-014394).

REFERENCES

Anderson, T. (2013). *Promise and/or peril: MOOCs and open and distance learning.* Retrieved from http://www.col.org/SiteCollection-Documents/MOOCsPromisePeril_Anderson.pdf

Aresta, M. (2009). *As ferramentas web 2.0 e as comunidades de aprendizagem: Estudo de casos sobre as comunidades de aprendizagem no mestrado em multimédia em educação.* (Master thesis). Universidade de Aveiro, Aveiro, Portugal.

Batista, J. (2011). *O Uso das tecnologias da comunicação no ensino superior.* (PhD thesis). Universidade de Aveiro, Aveiro, Portugal.

Batista, J., Morais, N. S., & Ramos, F. (2011). Frequency and user satisfaction on using communication technologies to support learning: the case of Portuguese higher education. In A. Moreira, M.J. Loureiro, A. Balula, F. Nogueira, L. Pombo, L. Pedro, & P. Almeida (Eds.), *International council for educational media (ICEM) and the international symposium on computers in education (SIIE) joint conference (ICEM&SIIE'2011)* (pp. 372-380). Aveiro, Portugal: Universidade de Aveiro.

Batista, J., & Ramos, F. (2011). The institutional perspective on the use of communication technologies in Portuguese public higher education: A research proposal. In *Proceedings of 5th International Technology, Education and Development Conference.* Valencia, Spain: Academic Press.

Bielaczyc, K., & Blake, P. (2006). Shifting epistemologies: Examining student understanding of new models of knowledge and learning. In *Proceedings of the 7th International Conference on Learning Sciences (ICLS '06)* (pp. 50-56). International Society of the Learning Sciences.

Bielschowsky, C., Laaser, W., Mason, R., Sangra, A., & Hasan, A. (2009). *Reforming distance learning higher education in Portugal.* Lisbon: Ministry of Science, Technology and Higher Education.

Blin, F., & Munro, M. (2008). Why hasn't technology disrupted academics' teaching practices? Understanding resistance to change through the lens of activity theory. *Computers & Education*, *50*(2), 475–490. doi:10.1016/j.compedu.2007.09.017

Carvalho, A. A. (2008). Os podcasts no ensino universitário: Implicações dos tipos e da duração na aceitação dos alunos. In A. A. Carvalho (Ed.), Actas do encontro sobre web 2.0 (pp. 179–190). Braga: Universidade do Minho. Retrieved from https://repositorium.sdum.uminho.pt/bitstream/1822/8566/1/Marques%26CarvalhoSIIE_08.pdf

Conole, G., & Alevizou, P. (2010). A literature review of the use of web 2.0 tools in higher education. Milton Keynes, UK: The Open University. Retrieved from http://www.heacademy.ac.uk/assets/EvidenceNet/Conole_Alevizou_2010.pdf

Costes, N., Hopbach, A., Kekäläinen, H., van IJperen, R., & Walsh, P. (2010). *Quality assurance and transparency tools - Workshop report*. Helsinki: European Association for Quality Assurance in Higher Education.

Coutinho, C., & Junior, J. (2007). Blog e wiki: Os futuros professores e as ferramentas da web 2.0. In M. Marcelino & M. Silva (Eds.), *Actas do SIIE'2007 – Simpósio internacional de informática educativa* (pp. 199–204). Porto: Escola Superior de Educação do Instituto Politécnico do Porto.

Coutinho, C., & Júnior, J. (2008). Web 2.0 in Portuguese academic community: An exploratory survey. In Proceedings of the 19th International Conference of the Society for Information Technology & Teacher Education (SITE 2008). Las Vegas, NV: SITE.

Coutinho, C., & Junior, J. (2008a). Using social bookmarking to enhance cooperation/collaboration in a teacher education program. In *Proceedings of World Conference on Educational Multimedia, Hypermedia and Telecommunications*. Chesapeake, VA: AACE.

Dahlstrom, E., Boor, T., Grunwald, P., & Vockley, M. (2011). The ECAR national study of undergraduate students and information technology, 2011 (research report). Boulder, CO: EDUCAUSE Centre for Applied Research. Retrieved from http://www.educause.edu/ecar

Downes, S. (2005). E-learning 2.0. *eLearn Magazine*, *2005*(10). Retrieved from http://elearnmag.acm.org/featured.cfm?aid=1104968

Duarte, J., & Gomes, M. J. (2011). Práticas com a Moodle em Portugal. In P. Dias & A. J. Osório (Eds.), *Atas da VII conferência internacional de TIC na educação, challenges 2011* (pp. 871–882). Braga: Centro de Competência da Universidade do Minho.

Edirisingha, P., Salmon, G., & Fothergill, J. (2007). *Profcasting – A pilot study and guidelines for integrating podcasts in a blended learning environment*. Retrieved from http://hdl.handle.net/2381/404

EHEA. (2012). *Transparency tools*. Flanders: Flemish Ministry for Education and Training. Retrieved from http://www.ehea.info/article-details.aspx?ArticleId=145

ENQA. (2011). ENQA position paper on transparency tools. Helsinki: European Association for Quality Assurance in Higher Education (ENQA).

EURASHE. (2012). EURASHE policy paper on quality assurance and transparency tools. Brussels: European Association of Institutions in Higher Education (EURASHE).

Franklin, T., & Harmelen, M. (2007). Web 2.0 for content for learning and teaching in higher education. Bristol: JISC - The Joint Information Systems Committee. Retrieved from http://www.jisc.ac.uk/media/documents/programmes/digitalrepositories/web2-content-learning-and-teaching.pdf

Garrison, D. R., & Anderson, T. (2003). *E-learning in the 21st century: A framework for research and practice*. London: Routledge. doi:10.4324/9780203166093

Gillani, N., & Eynon, R. (2014). Communication patterns in massively open online courses. *The Internet and Higher Education, 23*, 18–26. doi:10.1016/j.iheduc.2014.05.004

Gomes, M. J., Coutinho, C., Guimarães, F., Casa-Nova, M. J., & Caires, S. (2011). Distance learning and e-learning in Portugal: A study of the perceptions, concepts and teaching practices at the Institute of Education, University of Minho. In *Proceedings of EDULEARN11 Conference*. Retrieved from http://repositorium.sdum.uminho.pt/bitstream/1822/12852/1/edulearn11-1.pdf

Grodecka, K., Wild, F., & Kieslinger, B. (Eds.). (2009). How to use social software in higher education: iCamp project. In *How to use social software in higher education: A handbook for the iCamp project*. Retrieved from http://www.icamp.eu/wp-content/uploads/2009/01/icamp-handbook-web.pdf

Hazelkorn, E. (2013). How rankings are reshaping higher education. In V. Climent, F. Michavila, & M. Ripolles (Eds.), *Los rankings universitarios: Mitos y realidades* (pp. 1–8). Tecnos.

IHEP. (2009). *Impact of college rankings on institutional decision making: Four country case studies*. Washington, DC: Institute for Higher Education Policy. Retrieved from http://www.ihep.org/assets/files/publications/g-l/impactof-collegerankings.pdf

International Organization for Standardization. (1998). *ISO 9241-11: Ergonomic requirements for office work with visual display terminals (VDTs) - Part 11: Guidance on usability*. Geneva: International Organization for Standardization.

JISC. (2012). *Researchers of tomorrow: The research behaviour of generation y doctoral students*. London: JISC/British Library. Retrieved from http://www.jisc.ac.uk/publications/reports/2012/researchers-of-tomorrow.aspx

Johnson, L., Smith, R., Willis, H., Levine, A., & Haywood, K. (2011). *The 2011 horizon report*. Austin, TX: The New Media Consortium.

Katz, R. (Ed.). (2008). *The tower and the cloud: Higher education in the age of cloud computing*. EDUCAUSE.

Liyoshi, T., & Kumar, M. (2008). *Opening up education: The collective advancement of education through open technology, open content, and open knowledge*. Boston: The MIT Press.

Lomas, C. (2005). *7 things you should know about social bookmarking*. EDUCAUSE Learning Initiative. Retrieved from http://www.educause.edu/library/resources/7-things-you-should-know-about-social-bookmarking

Marope, P., Wells, P., & Hazelkorn, E. (2013). *Rankings and accountability in higher education: Uses and misuses*. Paris: UNESCO.

Marques, C., & Carvalho, A. A. (2009). Contextualização e evolução do e-learning: Dos ambientes de apoio à aprendizagem às ferramentas da web 2.0. In *Challenges'09 - VI Conferência Internacional de TIC na Educação* (pp. 985-1001). Braga: Universidade do Minho. Retrieved from http://repositorium.sdum.uminho.pt/handle/1822/10028

Miranda, L., Morais, C., Alves, P., & Dias, P. (2011). Redes sociais na aprendizagem. In D. Barros, C. Neves, F. Seabra, J. Moreira, & S. Henriques (Eds.), Educação e tecnologia: Reflexão, inovação e práticas (pp. 211-230). Lisboa: Universidade Aberta.

Morais, N. (2012). *O género e o uso das tecnologias da comunicação no ensino superior público Português*. (PhD thesis). Universidade de Aveiro, Aveiro, Portugal.

Morais, N., Batista, J., & Ramos, F. (2011). Caracterização das actividades de aprendizagem promovidas através das tecnologia da comunicação no ensino superior público Português. *Indagatio Didactica, 3*(3), 6–18.

Nkuyubwatsi, B. (2014). Cultural translation in massive open online courses (MOOCs). *eLearning Papers, 37*, 23-32. Retrieved from http://www.openeducationeuropa.eu/en/paper/experiences-and-best-practices-and-around-moocs

O'Neill, R., & Colley, A. (2006). Gender and status effects in student e-mails to staff. *Journal of Computer Assisted Learning, 22*(5), 360–367. doi:10.1111/j.1365-2729.2006.00186.x

OECD/JRC. (2008). *Handbook on constructing composite indicators – Methodology and user guide*. Paris: OECD. Retrieved from http://www.oecd.org/dataoecd/37/42/42495745.pdf

Patrício, M., & Gonçalves, V. (2010). Utilização educativa do Facebook no ensino superior. In *Proceedings of the l Conference Learning and Teaching in Higher Education* (pp. 1-15). Évora: Universidade de Évora, Gabinete para a Promoção do Sucesso Académico.

Pempek, T., Yermolayeva, Y., & Calvert, S. (2009). College students' social networking experiences on Facebook. *Journal of Applied Developmental Psychology, 30*(3), 227–238. doi:10.1016/j.appdev.2008.12.010

Pinto, M., Souza, F., Nogueira, F., Balula, A., Pedro, L., Pombo, L., et al. (2012). Tracing the use of communication technology in higher education: A literature review. In L. Chova, A. Martínez, & C. Torres (Eds.), *Proceedings of the 6th International Technology, Education and Development Conference* (pp. 850-859). Valencia: INTED2012.

Pombo, L., Morais, N., Batista, J., Pinto, M., Coelho, M., & Moreira, A. (2013). Five years of communication technologies use in higher education in Portugal: An overview. In M. Marcelino, M. Gomes, & A. Mendes (Eds.), *XV International Symposium on Computers in Education* (pp. 99-103). Instituto Politécnico de Viseu.

Puente, X. (2007). New method using wikis and forums to evaluate individual contributions in cooperative work while promoting experiential learning: results from preliminary experience. In *Proceedings of the WikiSym 2007 - International Symposium on Wikis - Wikis at Work in the World: Open, Organic, Participatory Media for the 21st Century* (pp. 87-92). Montréal, Canada: WikiSym 07. doi:10.1145/1296951.1296961

Quivy, R., & Campenhoudt, L. (2005). *Manual de investigação em ciências sociais* (4th ed.). Lisboa: Gradiva.

Ros-Rodríguez, J., Encinas, T., Picazo, R., Labadía, A., Artalejo, A., Gutiérrez-Martín, Y., & Gilabert, J.A. (2011). Use of wikis as collaborative tools in a b-learning course of Pharmacology. In L. Chova, I. Torres, & A. Martínez (Eds.), *Proceedings of INTED2011 - International Conference on Technology, Education and Development* (pp. 586-590). Valencia: INTED2011.

Santos, C., Pedro, L., Ramos, F., & Moreira, A. (2011). Sapo campus: What users really think about an institutionally supported PLE. In *Proceedings of PLE Conference 2011*. Southampton, UK: Academic Press.

Schlosser, L. A., & Simonson, M. (2009). *Distance education: Definitions and glossary of terms* (3rd ed.). Charlotte, NC: Information Age Publisher.

Selwyn, N. (2007). The use of computer technology in university teaching and learning: A critical perspective. *Journal of Computer Assisted Learning, 23*(2), 83-94. DOI:10.1111/j.1365-2729.2006.00204.x

Siemens, G., & Tittenberger, P. (2009). Handbook of emerging technologies for learning. Winnipeg, Canada: Learning Technologies Centre, University of Manitoba. Retrieved from http://umanitoba.ca/learning_technologies/cetl/HETL.pdf

Silva, F. (2012). *A utilização de recursos educativos digitais no ensino superior a distância: A perceção do estudante e o modo como utiliza os recursos digitais para fins educativos.* (Master thesis). Universidade Aberta, Lisbon, Portugal.

UNESCO. (2009). *Guide to measuring information and communication technologies (ICT) in education.* Quebéc, Canada: UNESCO Institute for Statistics. Retrieved from http://unesdoc.unesco.org/images/0018/001865/186547e.pdf

van Vught, F., & Ziegele, F. (2011). *Design and testing the feasibility of a multidimensional global university ranking.* Brussels: Consortium for Higher Education and Research Performance Assessment.

Vercruysse, N., & Proteasa, V. (2012). Transparency tools across the European higher education area. Helsinki: European Association for Quality Assurance in Higher Education (ENQA).

KEY TERMS AND DEFINITIONS

Analysis Model: A definition of the relevant indicators that are used for research purposes to characterize a specific phenomenon.

Communication Technologies: Digital tools that provide support for sharing information and/or interpersonal communication (email, blogs, wikis, social networks, videoconferencing systems, Virtual Learning Environments/Learning Management Systems, 3D virtual worlds).

Digital Literacy: The ability to find, evaluate, utilize, share and create content using information and communication technologies.

Higher Education Institutions: In Portugal Higher Education Institutions include Universities and Polytechnic Institutes. Universities offer 1st, 2nd and 3rd cycle programs. Polytechnic Institutes offer 1st and 2nd cycle programs.

Higher Education Rankings: Listings of Higher Education Institutions organized according to a specific assessment criteria. Examples: Times Higher Education, U-Multirank.

Information Visualization: Graphical representation of information aiming at helping a human user understand the meaning of specific information.

Learning Management Systems/Virtual Learning Environments (LMS/VLE): Computer programs that offer an integrated environment to support learning and teaching activities, including sharing of documents, interpersonal communication, online assessment and activity monitoring.

Social Network: Dedicated website or other computer application which enables users to communicate by posting information, such as texts, comments, messages, images, videos, etc.

Chapter 9
University Teachers' Use of Digital Technologies:
The Realities from Mongolia and Chile

Daariimaa Marav
National University of Mongolia, Mongolia

Michelle Espinoza
Universidad Arturo Prat, Chile

ABSTRACT

This chapter is set in the context of two developing countries, Mongolia and Chile, where digital technology is seen as a powerful icon of the knowledge economy. The predominant and common discourses surrounding the uses of digital technologies in education in these developing countries usually assume rather celebratory stances of the roles digital technologies may perform in education in the digital age. Thus, the research reported here explores the realities, opportunities, and challenges that academic staff face when using digital technologies through the perspectives offered by the field of digital literacy studies. The findings illustrate the close and complex relationships between sociocultural contexts, beliefs, values, and digital literacy practices. The study suggests that more attention needs to be paid to the wider contexts affecting the digital practices around teaching and learning rather than to technologies per se.

INTRODUCTION

The last decades have witnessed a massification of higher education in both Chile and Mongolia due to the value embedded in higher education and the prestige it represents to people in both countries (Marav & Espinoza, 2014). According to statistics on higher education in Mongolia by its Ministry of Education and Science (2014), in the 2012-2013 academic year there were 99 higher education institutions, consisting of 15 public, 79 private and 5 branches of foreign institutions. There are 3 types of higher education institutions in Mongolia: university, institute and college. Since 1990, after socialism collapsed, a rapid expansion of the higher education system of Mongolia was triggered by the liberalisation of the economy and the legalisation of private higher education in the 1991 Education Law of Mongolia (World Bank, 2010). The number of students in higher

DOI: 10.4018/978-1-4666-7244-4.ch009

education institutions doubled between 2000 and 2013, 84,985 to 175,591 (Ministry of Education and Science, 2014), supported by the expansion of private universities and colleges that began in the 1990s.

Meanwhile, Chile has also experienced an increase in the number of students who pursue tertiary studies mainly due to private institutions which cater for 65 per cent of higher education students. After the 1981 educational reform, the Chilean higher education system was transformed from a system of eight state-financed universities to a system which includes four types of higher education institutions: universities, traditional and private; professional institutes; technical training centres and the institutions in charge of training the armed forces and police (Espinoza & Gonzalez, 2013).

Chile's economic success, mainly through the exploitation of its mining resources, has been placed as an example for Mongolia to follow, framed by the mining boom they are currently experiencing. Also, even though Chile is located to the global opposite of Mongolia, collaboration between both countries has been constant in the last decade and co-operation has strengthened. In the context of higher education in these two countries, even though, historically, the higher education system in Chile outperforms that of Mongolia over the past hundred years, the current tendencies and directions for higher education are going on the same track in both countries (Marav & Espinoza, 2014). For example, they each have adopted a neoliberal agenda for the development and improvement of their higher education systems to position their countries within the knowledge economy and technology integration has become of paramount importance for both countries to increase their economic and educational competitiveness. Although national policies to integrate digital technologies in education in both countries have been enacted since the late 20th century, there has not been a policy which specifically promotes

the inclusion of digital technologies in higher education in either country.

As digital technologies and social media have become integral parts of people's everyday life, currently, there is a global trend for integrating them in education effectively. However, much of the digital and new media research takes place in predominantly Anglo-American contexts (Prinsloo & Rowsell, 2012) and not much is known about what shapes university teachers' use of digital technologies. Thus, the study reported in this chapter aims to examine the 'messy realities' of digital technology use of university teachers from two developing countries, Chile and Mongolia. In addition, as there is a need for systematic studies to explore technology use in teaching and learning in higher education (Lai, 2011), the chapter aims to compare how wider sociopolitical factors are represented in techno-biographies of university teachers from these developing countries and to discuss opportunities and challenges that they encounter in using digital technologies in their everyday lives. To achieve these aims, first, we will discuss the existing literature in relation to teachers' use of digital technologies in higher education. Then, we will critically review the social and political factors shaping university teachers' use of digital technologies.

TEACHERS' USE OF DIGITAL TECHNOLOGIES IN HIGHER EDUCATION

Digital technologies have been infiltrating every sphere of our societies, including higher education. For example, using PowerPoint to support their lectures and using the internet as a resource for their teaching and learning are typical examples of teachers' technology use in higher education. In fact, digital technologies have become an icon of higher education provision not only in developed but also in developing countries in the 21st century (Selwyn, 2007). Some studies of university students' internet use in Australia and the UK (Kennedy et al., 2008; Oliver & Goerke, 2007; Selwyn, 2008a) indicate that most of the students use mobile phones, computers and the internet in their everyday lives to do their assignments, learning, searching for information, communication and leisure. Therefore, it can be assumed that university teachers, as well-educated individuals and also as educators of those changing learners most of whom find themselves in the digital environment, use digital technologies in their everyday lives for personal and academic purposes. However, depending on their different backgrounds and different levels of resources in using technologies in both personal and professional contexts, it is impossible to generalise about their technology use. There is a need for detailed studies about their digital technology use to enhance teaching and learning in higher education, or even more so, taking the focus out of the teaching and learning and more on why things are done the way they are (taking into account the wider social, political, cultural, historical background of these people) (Facer & Selwyn, 2013). Above all, there is a lack of research on university teachers' digital literacy practices. As Goodfellow (2011) comments, "higher-education research and practice has been slow to engage with the cultural impact of the new communications order on its literacy practices" (p. 135). Lea and Jones (2010) also state that there is a lack of fine-grained research on literacies and technologies in higher education. These observations stressed the need for the present study.

Digital technology use in higher education is "a multi-faceted concept which encompasses a variety of activities and practices, via a range of hardware platforms and means of connectivity, requiring a number of different competencies and resulting in a number of outcomes" (Selwyn, 2010, p. 39). Clearly, to understand how and why technology may or may not be used by teachers in higher education we need to examine not only teachers' personal contexts but also broader social, political

and economic contexts (Lai, 2011; Selwyn, 2007). However, it is hard to understand how technologies are used in teaching and learning in higher education and their effects on higher education as "there are simply too many new developments in digital tools and researchers cannot catch up with all of these" (Lai, 2011, p. 1267). Lai (2011), thus, calls for systematic and longitudinal studies to provide a better understanding of technology use in teaching and learning in higher education.

Digital technologies, particularly the internet, have been found to be useful in teaching effectively and supporting a pedagogy as they motivate learners; become a resource in teaching and learning; help to facilitate learner-centred teaching; and can bring the potential learning benefits through collaboration amongst teachers and students and flexible learning (Bennett et al., 2012; Tess, 2013; Tibebu et al., 2010). Importantly, the internet can be used as a platform for collaborative learning in educational settings (Lankshear & Knobel, 2011). Learning is situated in social practices on the internet; because of the internet, the borders between everyday informal learning and formal learning in educational contexts are becoming indistinct. Digital literacies, then, enable teachers not only to teach in engaging ways to students but also to access knowledge and develop themselves.

According to Schneckenberg (2009), the lack of technology use by the majority of teachers in higher education is due to the fact that they pay more attention to their research outcome and career advancement instead of to their teaching practices. Simply, it is time-consuming for teachers to learn how to use new technologies in their teaching. In addition, teachers' pedagogical beliefs, their beliefs about the role, value and use of technologies, teaching experiences, their context and the affordances of different technologies play main role in using technologies in their teaching (Steel & Levy, 2009). Obviously, teachers' personal beliefs about teaching, learning and technologies and their willingness to engage in technology-enhanced teaching practices affect their technology use. It seems that teacher training programmes can promote the potential application of educational technologies by role-modelling pre-service teachers and ongoing professional development for teachers also can assist them to enhance their teaching and learning through technology use as Rawlins and Kehrwald (2010) suggest. In fact, learning new literacies can be a life-long journey for teachers due to the changing landscape of higher education and rapid development of technology.

SOCIAL AND POLITICAL FACTORS SHAPING UNIVERSITY TEACHERS' USE OF DIGITAL TECHNOLOGIES

Grand claims about the revolutionary capabilities of digital technologies in higher education pervade the media and academia (Snyder et al., 2007). The recent discussions around massive open online courses (MOOCs), for instance, highlight how higher education institutions, academic staff and the ordinary people conceptualise the incorporation of digital technologies in learning and professional environments as detached from disputes and sociopolitical conflicts (Department for Business Innovation and Skills, 2013; Flynn, 2013). On the one hand, they point to the possibilities of enhancing educational attainment for large numbers of students. However, the reality points to the high number of drop-outs in MOOC courses and a persistent traditional view of learning as merely knowledge transmission (Yang et al., 2013).

From a sociological perspective, Selwyn (2013) urges researchers to consider that "any account of digital technology use in education needs to be framed in explicit terms of societal conflict over the distribution of power" (p. 2). Such perspective brings up to attention the complex, multifaceted and dynamic relationships at play when digital technology use is incorporated in (higher) education contexts. Moreover, Selwyn

(2013) points to the need of questioning the assumptions and values underlying the discourses of digital technology use in education. His analysis shows how conflicting and contradictory agendas are represented as conciliatory in the realm of digital technology use. Selwyn (2013) argues:

At best, then, current forms of 'educational technology' appear to be doing little to challenge or disrupt the prevailing individualization, commodification and privatization of contemporary education. Conversely, there is far less that actively promotes 'positive' concerns of social justice, inequality and the notion of education as a collective public good. If education technology is to be a genuinely positive project then there is clearly much rethinking and recalibration to be done (p. 15).

If we consider specifically the contexts of digital technology incorporation from developing countries, such as Chile and Mongolia, the sociopolitical challenges are embedded in the struggles over what higher education should be for and its underlying values. Discussing the roles digital technologies may play at the restructuring of education, Kellner (2002) argues that incorporation of digital technologies in learning and teaching is not only a matter of having or not having access to such devices. Rather, the author suggests that a more nuanced view that focuses on access, quality and power struggles over the beneficiaries of such incorporation might be more useful if we aim to maintain higher education as the locus of knowledge production, dissemination and universalisation. Such an argument is based on:

With the proper resources, policies, pedagogies and practices, we can work to reduce the (unfortunately growing) gap between have and have nots, although technology alone will not suffice to democratize and adequately reconstruct education. That is, technology itself does not necessarily improve teaching and learning, and will certainly not of itself overcome acute socio-economic division. Indeed, without proper resources, pedagogy and educational practices, technology might be an obstacle or burden to genuine learning and will probably increase rather than overcome existing divisions of power, cultural capital, and wealth (Kellner, 2002, p. 156).

One of the questions which needs, thus, to be addressed is how university teachers, who are responsible for educating future teachers and professionals, conceptualise digital technology use in their own realities. Moreover, it seems necessary to understand how sociopolitical factors, such as lack of infrastructure, deterioration of teaching work conditions, attempts of privatising higher education, shape university teachers' encounters with digital technologies.

Johnson (2013) investigates how academic staff from research-intensive universities conceptualise the incorporation of digital technologies in their institutions. The author bases his research on the premise that "we possess little knowledge of faculty perceptions of new instructional technologies, which is crucial to understanding whether implementation could contribute to the erosion of professional control" (Johnson, 2013, p. 137). The results point out that academic staff usually integrate digital technologies into their teaching due to marketing strategies and not academic-based arguments, and the incorporation of digital technologies contributes to constraining academic staff's autonomy in relation to higher education institutions.

Similarly, Snyder et al. (2007) carried out 15 case studies in Australian higher education institutions to investigate how digital technologies were incorporated in terms of educational, technological and organisational relationships. One of their study findings highlighted how "the discourse of student-driven learning articulated to market-driven models of students as consumers, an approach which tended to be more concerned with administrative scope and efficiencies than

with critical pedagogical outcomes" (Snyder et al., 2007, p. 200). This finding points to the need of discussion around the struggles between the corporatisation of universities and its role as knowledge producer and disseminator for the common good.

As briefly discussed here, the literature points to the complexities inherent to digital technology use in higher education contexts. University teachers' beliefs, values and appreciation of digital technology are enmeshed with wider sociopolitical factors of the contemporary capitalist society. How such factors shape university teachers' everyday encounters with digital technologies in developing countries may thus highlight the tensions emerging and the arena of struggles onto which different agendas and values are conceptualised when integrating digital technologies in the higher education context.

METHODOLOGY

As previously mentioned, our research has been framed against the lack of research on teachers' digital engagement in higher education. In the context of higher education, Lea and Jones (2010) highlight the importance of applying sociocultural perspectives of literacy within the field of Literacy Studies to studying new literacy practices in higher education. Thus, our study is informed by the perspectives offered by the field of digital literacy studies, which views technology use as a social practice and as shaped by diverse contexts. Our intention in this research was to explore university teachers' use of digital technologies including their personal and professional contexts of digital engagement.

We used technological biographies or techno-biographies as our data collection tool. According to Barton and Lee (2013), "…a techno-biography, in short, is a life story in relation to technologies. The notion itself is apparently inspired by the traditional narrative approach to interviews, where an interviewee tells a story about certain significant events in life" (p. 71). Furthermore, they state that "every single technology user is unique" and "people develop their own set of practices in response to what they think technologies can do for them in their lives" (Barton & Lee, 2013, p. 71). In this sense, the researchers requested the teachers from four universities, two universities in Chile and two in Mongolia, to write their techno-biographies as narratives to gain an in-depth understanding of their past and present experiences and practices with digital technologies in the context of their life stories. The participants were given prompts as to what to include in their techno-biographic narratives in our research. They were asked to include their educational and professional background; personal experiences in relation to digital technology use (internet, laptops, cell phones, tablets, applications, software, games, and so on); a detailed account of their technology use in relation to their teaching, learning and researching; their reflections on their personal and professional use of digital technologies in teaching, learning and researching; and the opportunities and challenges they face in relation to digital technology use in higher education in their countries.

In total, seven teachers volunteered to be involved in the research. Pseudonyms were used to protect the identity of the participants in this research because of the ethical concerns. The participants included: two English teachers and a teacher in science and technology at two different universities in Mongolia; three academic staff from the Faculty of Humanities in a university in northern Chile and an academic at the Faculty of Educational Sciences at a university in the south of Chile. The participants were requested to send their techno-biographies to the researchers via email. The techno-biographies helped the researchers to explore the participants' digital literacy backgrounds, the opportunities and challenges they had had and were having with their use of digital technologies in their personal and professional contexts and their beliefs about the role, value and use of technologies.

The researchers used open coding which "expresses data and phenomena in the form of concepts" (Flick, 2002, p. 177). Our data indicate the teachers' engagement in digital literacies and illuminate the interplay between teachers' background, digital literacies and professional contexts, including the opportunities and challenges of using digital technologies in higher education. Furthermore, our data from different universities in two developing countries show that teachers in higher education have some similarities in their digital literacy practices despite the differences in their focus of their teaching and broader socio-cultural contexts.

FINDINGS

Mongolia

Two female English teachers, Nomin and Badam, in the same university and a male teacher, Bold, in science and technology at a different university in Mongolia volunteered to participate in this study by writing their techno-biographies. They were in their late twenties and had been working as lecturers for five to six years at the time of data collection. Their techno-biographies reflected both the educational context in Mongolia but also aspects of their personal lives. Clearly, context is important for accessing and developing literacies, particularly when the literacies are new for people. At a macro-level, their access to digital technologies was influenced by social and economic factors such as the changes in post-socialist Mongolia and the context where they lived – urban and rural – which is the main factor that determines access to digital technologies in Mongolia. Rural areas in Mongolia depend on infrastructure development to cater for remoteness, people's socio-economic status, (i.e., their education and income level) and their limited access to computers and digital literacies. Because of social differences between rural and urban areas, people living in urban areas are more advantaged in using digital technologies (Marav, 2013). At a micro-level, their family background and their own agency around technology use also contributed to developing their digital literacies and to practising them for personal benefits.

When the internet service was introduced in Mongolia in 1996 the participants were ten to eleven years old. They did not take the technologies up at that time. Nomin had lived in a rural area of Mongolia until her family migrated to Ulaanbaatar, the capital city, when she was 12 in 1998. The only technology, she was familiar with at that time, was black and white TV with only one channel available for limited hours, 6 pm to 11 pm, in the rural area where she lived. She had learnt some basics of a computer in her final years at a secondary school; however, she had to learn how to use a computer for real to type up her assignments after she became a university student. She started using the internet frequently after she became a lecturer to prepare her teaching materials in 2010. By contrast, Bold, who lived in the city, had the opportunity to become familiar with computers at her mother's workplace when he was 12. He mentioned that a computer had been his hobby since then. He said:

I gain almost 90 per cent of my information on the internet, which is a necessary tool for my teaching, learning, researching and working. Usually, I manage my data using software which integrates my laptop, home PC, office PC and cell phone. (Bold)

Evidently, his life revolved around digital technologies. Another participant, Badam, who grew up in the city, was introduced to the computer when she was in grade 8. She had to study informatics at secondary school. However, there were not enough computers available at her school: 5-6 children in her class had to share one. Therefore, she did not learn much about using computers at that time: "no more than pressing a few buttons" (Badam). Later, after she became a university student she took a private course in using computers. In fact, not only in this study but also in Marav's (2013) study about Mongolian university students' everyday digital literacy practices, the connection between the academic dimensions of schooling and digital technologies was weak in the context of Mongolia. As in most Mongolian educational settings, the participants were taught to use computers but, as Warschauer (2003) puts it, it was "computer literacy in isolation from broader skills of composition, research, or analysis" (p. 112).

The three teachers were all engaged in the following digital literacies in their everyday lives:

- Google/Wikipedia searches;
- Downloading from Google/Wikipedia
- Gaining information online;
- Checking and sending email;
- Reading local and international news online;
- Searching for information for their teaching materials online;
- Presentation using PowerPoint;
- Texting/Yahoo messenger;
- YouTube;
- Using projector for teaching;
- Preparing lecture notes/tests/handouts in Word;
- Printing/photocopying lecture notes/tests/handouts;
- Using Facebook.

There were other digital literacy activities in which two English teachers, Nomin and Badam, were engaged:

- Using online dictionaries;

- Uploading data about students' attendance and results into university internal online system;
- Using smartboard/CD player/TV for teaching.

Only Bold was engaged in:

- Writing PhD thesis/book in Word;
- Preprint a book using Adobe InDesign;
- Analysis of data using SPSS/Excel;
- Presentation using Prezi/Adobe Flash Professional;
- Making calendar plan using MS-Office Project;
- Preparing e-lesson files using Articulate Engage/Articulate Quizmaker;
- Scanning from books;
- Sharing data with students via Facebook;
- Creating a blog for students with lecture notes/assignments;
- Uploading lecture notes using file sharing websites;
- Paying bills online;
- Checking bank account online;
- Online communication via Skype.

Nomin was the only participant who used Twitter and received students' assignments via email. These teachers' engagement in digital literacies in their everyday lives indicate that there is an interplay between technologies, practices, institutional contexts and their areas of teaching. For example, though two English teachers did not use digital technologies as much as another teacher in science and technology, they mostly used the internet as resource for their classes because of the availability of the materials in English. They also had to learn how to use smartboards which were recently installed in most of the classrooms in their university. One of them said:

After smart boards were installed in the classrooms, teachers were given general information about the boards and how to use them. In reality, this was not enough for teachers. Therefore, now teachers use those boards like a computer, not like a 'smart technology'. (Badam)

Obviously, the teachers lack expertise in using new technologies, such as smartboard, as no comprehensive training is offered to teachers. In addition, Nomin also said that sometimes technical failures, such as broken computer and having no internet connection, had disrupted her teaching. Despite some challenges and differences in their digital literacy practices because of their areas of teaching and institutional contexts, their agency around digital literacies has shaped their literacy practices with digital technologies. They were all using digital technologies in their personal and professional contexts to learn, to access up-to-date information in their areas of teaching and study, to communicate, to entertain themselves and to prepare for their classes/lectures. Overall, they wanted to benefit from their technology use personally and professionally as one of the participants mentioned: "Digital technologies are making my life easier and less costly" (Bold).

It is noteworthy here that the issue of plagiarism has been brought up by the three teachers as the biggest challenge related to technology use in higher education in Mongolia as also indicated in Marav's (2013) study. They were concerned about their students' misuse of the internet. For example, Nomin commented: "Most of the students plagiarise their essays and assignments on the internet". Not only plagiarism but also some students' cheating during exams has become a problem for teachers as Bold said: "All students use smart phones which makes it easy to scan books and lecture notes and send them to other students using the internet during exams". In Mongolian university context, students thus need to be educated about the consequences of plagiarism and their critical use of the internet should be promoted.

Chile

Four teachers from Chile participated in this investigation. Three of them, Annie, Francisco and Camila, belonged to the Faculty of Humanities in a northern university in Chile. Alicia worked in the Faculty of Educational Sciences in a university in the centre-south of the country. They were all in their thirties and had been working as lecturers for eight to fourteen years. All of them had English majors but were specialised in different areas (creative writing, CALL [Computer Assisted Language Learning], translation, language teaching methodology, and linguistics). Their techno-biographies provided some information about the 'state of the actual' (Selwyn, 2008b) in relation to technology use in the context of higher education in Chile, as well as their own everyday digital literacy practices. Data show that personal access to technology is not an issue for the Chilean academics but the heavy workload, the constraints of academic life and the lack of proper infrastructure to use with the students in the classroom prevent them to make better use of the technologies available.

The participants accessed digital technologies for the first time at different stages of their lives and they had integrated technologies into their lives in different ways. Francisco and Annie mentioned that their first access to digital technologies was before the age of ten when they had started using arcade consoles or Atari. In the case of these two participants, video games played an important part in their relationship with technology. The games helped them to develop certain abilities not only for gaming but also for working around technological devices.

Annie regarded her first encounters with technology as a lesson for life because it had allowed her to incorporate technology in her work as a translator in a smooth way. Nevertheless, this 'easiness' to use technology in her work as a translator does not imply that she incorporated digital technologies in the same way in her work as an academic:

I must confess, though, that I have not been updating my digital-technological knowledge to make the best use of it in teaching. This is mainly because I consider myself more of a traditional person, someone who gives great value to a white board and a marker than technology in classes. I think I can do more things with just a marker.

This indicates that teachers' beliefs and values play important roles in integrating technologies in their teaching. She also acknowledged that in her classroom she used PowerPoints sometimes and she also used emails to communicate with students, and the university platform for registering the students' grades, and for posting messages to students.

First internet connection in Chile took place in January, 1992 (Piquer, 2012). It is not surprising then that for three of the participants, the first encounter with computers and the internet took place when they were studying at university. Francisco recalled that he had learned to use it by himself, via trial and error, observing, sneaking out of the classroom to be in the lab to enter chat rooms, browse some new websites or explore MS Office. During his first years as a teacher, he was able to use the internet as an 'open library resource'. Because of the resources available on the internet, he had been able to explore different language practice activities such as collaborative writing or voice recording. He mentioned:

I've had the chance of testing interactive web tools in which learners can upload pictures and record voice comments, others that allow them to create cartoons and comics, and some where they can embed videos and write their own collaborative wikis. The language learner is not only a passive receptor anymore because these tools provide chances to exploit learner's creativity.

Francisco praised the potentials of technology use for students to build up on their own knowledge; to use these digital technologies in creative ways and be actively engaged in these activities. Besides his personal interest on technology and his eagerness for his students to see technologies the way he sees them, we believe that the nature of the subjects he taught (creative writing and CALL) were fertile soil for him to promote students' engagement with digital technologies. However, we did not have enough data to infer whether he was successful in his attempts or not.

Generally, all four teachers were engaged in the following digital literacy practices:

- Searching for information for their teaching materials online;
- Checking and sending email;
- YouTube;
- Using projector for teaching;
- Gaining information online.

Francisco and Alicia were also engaged in social networking and other hardware, like tablets. Only Francisco was engaged in:

- Using activities posted on TEFL (Teaching English as a Foreign Language) chatrooms and taking advice from colleagues in other countries by e-mail;
- Exploring various resources to practice grammar, listening or vocabulary in EFL (English as a Foreign Language) teaching, directly with the students in the labs;
- Using websites like elllo.org; ompersonal.com.ar; or a4esl.org in his teaching;
- Using smart boards.

Only Alicia was engaged with Prezi. Because of their role as directors of the Translation and the EFL teaching program, Annie and Camila used the university platform for accountability purposes. As a translator, Annie also used online

dictionaries, data bases, corpus of terms and translation software.

For Camila, digital technologies did not play such an important role in her personal life or in her teaching practice. She said that she was not a very technological person. She also acknowledged using her mobile phone but only for making calls or sending messages. She enjoyed watching videos, musicals, concerts on the internet in her leisure time. She had a Facebook account but she was not very active. She did not like playing video games at all. In her teaching, she said, she started to incorporate digital technologies ten years ago, mainly by making use of the internet to get some of the resources to use in the classroom. She attached greater values to her printed books, which she still had been using most of all.

Using social media was the main reason for Alicia's engagement with technology in her personal life. As she was living away from her hometown she needed to keep in touch with her loved ones. In her teaching, the use of technology was limited:

This is due to the fact that not all the technologies, devices or software are available to everyone (students) or not all of them are working properly. Also, if I am not completely familiar with or if I don't manage [a technological] resource very well, I tend not to use it.

According to her, one of the main challenges for technology use in higher education in Chile was the lack of permanent training to use the technological resources available, as in most cases, it was all done in just one session. She also claimed that there is not proper maintenance of the equipment and that many of the necessary conditions for good functioning of digital technologies are not met (i.e. internet connection to support a large number of people connected at the same time).

There is evidently a visual representation culture of technology use in the Chilean classrooms (Reedy, 2008). For all the Chilean participants, except for Francisco, there is a default tendency to use technology for visual representations in their teaching. All of the participants mentioned that they needed to keep their technology knowledge updated because the new generations of university students had the advantage of being 'digital natives'. There are many challenges to be addressed. As Francisco argued:

I have to confess that I have been "dazzled", if one can put it like that, at the possibility of using these new tools with my students. But I can be critical about it. As a "digital immigrant" who has become fluent in this "language", I cannot say that technology is the one thing that the learning process needs. No teacher can disregard the value of oral practice, human contact, direct observation and non-verbal language, or a 100% reliable synchronous communication.

Hence, although Francisco was the most enthusiastic of our Chilean participants for integrating technology in the classroom, he reflected on the importance of human contact. He believed that technology had been a wonderful tool to be used with the new generations of university students, mainly because this was the world they live in, but he also agreed that technology had not been the most important token that can be passed on to our students. He, as other academics who participated in this study, believed in the need to prepare students to critically use what digital technologies have to offer.

DISCUSSION

The incorporation of digital technologies into the university classrooms and their use have been framed by a series of negotiations which have not been struggle free between the different actors intervening. The push for 'effective' integration of technologies has overlooked the fact that teachers can be regarded as "pragmatic strategic technology users" (Selwyn, 2011, p. 104), as they incorporate digital technologies when they 'fit' their job and resist its integration when they do not see the real benefit of them. Although in the case of our participants, access to digital technologies in the universities they work at (understood as a computer lab, data projector or internet connection) was not of special concern, the concrete and practical application of technology in the classroom was full of hassle. Having to carry their own equipment from room to room when using technology or even moving from the classroom to the computer lab with their students was another factor that inhibited these teachers' use of technology. In that sense, academic staff actually embedded ICT within existing practices rather than using digital technologies in innovative ways.

Unlike the study by Schneckenberg (2009), our participants did not avoid using digital technologies in their teaching practices because of career advancement or research outcome. In the case of these Chilean and Mongolian academics, it is not that they did not have time to 'learn' how to use technologies. Instead, three of the main reasons for not incorporating digital technologies in their everyday classroom practices were the lack of explicit skills training, reliability of the technology and their heavy workloads. The universities our participants worked at were not research oriented but teaching oriented. For many of them, dealing with the job of a university teacher, the day-to-day struggles they go through, the constant negotiations, the competitions for scarce resources, the increasing culture of assessment and accountability of universities nowadays, at best leave technology as a resource to be used for getting work done as a substitute for "work well done" (Apple & Jungck, 1990, p. 235).

Our data do not support the claims that ICT is transforming the teaching and learning processes in higher education. It is clear that the social, political, historical and cultural backgrounds of our participants and the place they work at were of crucial importance for shaping their digital literacy practices. Their interest in technology varied according to many factors such as their personal drive to use digital technologies. As we have found in our data, most of our participants 'enjoyed' using technologies in their everyday lives, for rather personal purposes. Those ones who had the same eagerness to use technology in their classrooms as they did in their personal lives were the exception to the rule. It turns out that they were also the only males in our data set. In addition, depending on their fields of teaching and research, teachers had different levels of knowledge of digital technologies and software. For example, English teachers in Mongolia did not engage in as many technological activities as the teacher in a university of science and technology did.

Also, most of the participants claimed to be either autodidact or had learned how to use computer and the internet while they were studying at university. They were also concerned with their performances in front of students. They said that students were clearly outperforming their teachers when it comes to technology use and that was something that either promoted the teachers' own interest in 'learning' how to use new digital technologies or inhibited their uses of technology in the classroom.

Another issue that has arisen from our data is what Reedy (2008) refers to as a "PowerPoint mindset", especially in the case of the Chilean academics. Even though our participants used the internet for researching materials for their classes and personal leisure, they also were prompt to think of PowerPoint as synonymous with ICT. However, teachers considered preparing PowerPoint presentations as "giving students everything" and leaving little room for them to think, reason, and write. As a result, some of our participants continued preferring to be more 'traditional' when it comes to technology in their classrooms and even PowerPoint is relegated to a second place.

Overall, it can be argued that even though higher education institutions in Chile and Mongolia have been early adopters of digital technologies,

the institutional policy decisions which have led to the implementation of computer labs, internet access (cable and Wi-Fi), etc. have failed in their effort to promote 'innovative' engagement of academics with digital technologies. There may be some partial explanations as to why some university teachers seem to adapt better to changes and innovations, such as the lack of explicit skills training in how to make the most of the new technologies. However, expecting teachers to embrace digital technologies for the mere reason that they are available is not as simple as that. Engaging with technology does imply investing hours of class preparation, not to mention the prior development of the skills needed to effectively do so.

CONCLUSION

Despite the limited number of participants, the research findings provide evidence that teachers in higher education have different levels of technology use for their teaching, researching, and leisure in their everyday lives depending on their academic fields, digital literacies, and beliefs and mindsets not only about digital technologies but also about teaching and learning. Obviously, this complexity and diversity needs to be acknowledged and accommodated. From their first encounters with digital technologies, it seems that the participants' mindsets about technology have been influenced by both local and global contexts. Importantly, the study highlights the tight-knit relationships between sociocultural contexts, beliefs, values and digital literacy practices. The participants' digital literacy practices provided them with opportunities for enriching and supporting their teaching and learning experiences and involved both traditional and new literacies. Most teachers in this study tended to use digital technologies to support their teaching practices, in other words, as accessories to their pedagogies. Generally, though, most teachers were enthusiastic about technology use in their everyday lives, however some of them were not eager to integrate digital technologies in their classrooms as teachers. There was a sense of resistance. This is like resisting technological imperialism which is imposed on students and teachers, coming from the top of the hierarchy, from policy-makers to the lowest level, where theory fails to meet praxis: the classroom.

The study contributes to the research on university teachers' digital literacy practices by illuminating what opportunities are provided and what challenges are faced with when the university teachers engage with digital technologies in their everyday lives, including both personal and professional contexts. Although the research provides evidence that higher education institutions where these teachers work at are implicated in their digital literacy practices, mostly, teachers' own agency around technology use has shaped their digital literacy practices. The results of this study can have important implications for the educational policies in Mongolia and Chile as the study illuminates that teacher education programmes cannot overlook the important role of the academic staff in educating the professionals for the near future. Critical digital literacies need to be promoted among teachers since using digital technologies as a mere presentation tool may promote the focus of a teacher as being a presenter of information and inhibit their thinking, reasoning and writing that should take place in a classroom, especially at university level. Future studies can employ more than one data sources, e.g. interviews, observations, classroom visits, to gain different perceptions and perspectives and to achieve greater validity of the data.

ACKNOWLEDGMENT

We would like to thank Lucas Moreira Dos Anjos-Santos, a Brazilian PhD candidate at Monash University, Australia, for his encouragement to conduct this research and his contribution in the early stages of this investigation.

REFERENCES

Apple, M. W., & Jungck, S. (1990). You don't have to be a teacher to teach this unit: Teaching, technology, and gender in the classroom. *American Educational Research Journal*, 27(2), 227–251. doi:10.3102/00028312027002227

Barton, D., & Lee, C. (2013). *Language online: Investigating digital texts and practices*. London: Routledge.

Bennett, S., Bishop, A., Dalgarno, B., Waycott, J., & Kennedy, G. (2012). Implementing web 2.0 technologies in higher education: A collective case study. *Computers & Education*, 59(2), 524–534. doi:10.1016/j.compedu.2011.12.022

Department for Business Innovation and Skills. (2013). *The maturing of the MOOC: Literature review of massive open online courses and other forms of online distance learning*. London, UK: Department for Business, Innovation and Skills. Retrieved May 1, 2014, from https://www.gov.uk/government/uploads/system/uploads/attachment_data/file/240193/13-1173-maturing-of-the-mooc.pdf

Espinoza, Ó., & González, L. E. (2013). Accreditation in higher education in Chile: Results and consequences. *Quality Assurance in Education*, 21(1), 20–38. doi:10.1108/09684881311293043

Facer, K., & Selwyn, N. (2013). Towards a sociology of education and technology. In R. Brooks, M. McCormack, & K. Bhopal (Eds.), *Contemporary debates in the sociology of education* (pp. 218–236). London: Palgrave Macmillan. doi:10.1057/9781137269881.0016

Flick, U. (2002). *An introduction to qualitative research* (2nd ed.). London: Sage.

Flynn, J. T. (2013). MOOCs: Disruptive innovation and the future of higher education. *Christian Education Journal.*, 10(1), 149–162.

Goodfellow, R. (2011). Literacy, literacies and the digital in higher education. *Teaching in Higher Education, 16*(1), 131–144. doi:10.1080/135625 17.2011.544125

Johnson, D. R. (2013). Technological change and professional control in the professoriate. *Science, Technology & Human Values, 38*(1), 126–149. doi:10.1177/0162243911430236

Kellner, D. (2002). Technological revolution, multiple literacies and the restructuring of education. In I. Snyder (Ed.), *Silicon literacies: Communication innovation and education in the electronic age* (pp. 154–169). London: Routledge.

Kennedy, G., Dalgarno, B., Bennett, S., Judd, T., Gray, K., & Chang, R. (2008). *Immigrants and natives: Investigating differences between staff and students' use of technology.* Paper presented at the Hello! Where are You in the Landscape of Educational Technology? Melbourne, Australia. Retrieved March 3, 2011, from http://www.ascilite.org.au/conferences/melbourne08/procs/index.htm

Lai, K. W. (2011). Digital technology and the culture of teaching and learning in higher education. *Australasian Journal of Educational Technology, 27*(8), 1263–1275.

Lankshear, C., & Knobel, M. (2011). *New literacies: Everyday practices and social learning* (3rd ed.). Maidenhead, UK: Open University Press.

Lea, M. R., & Jones, S. (2011). Digital literacies in higher education: Exploring textual and technological practice. *Studies in Higher Education, 36*(4), 377–393. doi:10.1080/03075071003664021

Marav, D. (2013). *We can do anything in the cyberworld except conceive: Mongolian university students' everyday digital literacy practices.* (Unpublished doctoral dissertation). Monash University, Monash, Australia.

Marav, D., & Espinoza, M. (2014). Equity and access in higher education: A comparative perspective from Chile and Mongolia. In Z. Zhang, P. W. K. Chan, & C. Boyle (Eds.), *Equality in education: Fairness and inclusion* (pp. 169–182). Rotterdam, The Netherlands: Sense Publishers. doi:10.1007/978-94-6209-692-9_13

Ministry of Education and Science. (2014). *Statistics on the higher education sector.* Retrieved June 30, 2014, from http://www.meds.gov.mn

Oliver, B., & Goerke, V. (2007). Australian undergraduates' use and ownership of emerging technologies: Implications and opportunities for creating engaging learning experiences for the net generation. *Australasian Journal of Educational Technology, 23*(2), 171–186.

Piquer, J. M. (2012). *Internet en Chile: 20 años después.* Retrieved February 19, 2014, from http://www.fayerwayer.com/2012/01/internet-en-chile-20-anos-despues/

Prinsloo, M., & Rowsell, J. (2012). Digital literacies as placed resources in the globalised periphery. *Language and Education, 26*(4), 271–277. doi:10.1080/09500782.2012.691511

Rawlins, P., & Kehrwald, B. (2010). Education technology in teacher education: Overcoming challenges, realizing opportunities. In R. Luppicini & A. Haghi (Eds.), *Cases on digital technologies in higher education: Issues and challenges* (pp. 50–63). Hershey, PA: IGI Global. doi:10.4018/978-1-61520-869-2.ch004

Reedy, G. B. (2008). PowerPoint, interactive whiteboards, and the visual culture of technology in schools. *Technology, Pedagogy and Education, 17*(2), 143–162. doi:10.1080/14759390802098623

Schneckenberg, D. (2009). Understanding the real barriers to technology-enhanced innovation in higher education. *Educational Research, 51*(4), 411–424. doi:10.1080/00131880903354741

Selwyn, N. (2007). The use of computer technology in university teaching and learning: A critical perspective. *Journal of Computer Assisted Learning, 23*(2), 83–94. doi:10.1111/j.1365-2729.2006.00204.x

Selwyn, N. (2008a). An investigation of differences in undergraduates' academic use of the internet. *Active Learning in Higher Education, 9*(1), 11–22. doi:10.1177/1469787407086744

Selwyn, N. (2008b). From state of the art to state of the actual? Introduction to a special issue. *Technology, Pedagogy and Education, 17*(2), 83–87. doi:10.1080/14759390802098573

Selwyn, N. (2010). Degrees of digital division: Reconsidering digital inequalities and contemporary higher education. *Redefining the Digital Divide in Higher Education, 7*(1), 33-41. Retrieved October 15, 2012, from http://rusc.uoc.edu/ojs/index.php/rusc/article/view/v7n1_selwyn/v7n1_selwyn

Selwyn, N. (2011). *Schools and schooling in the digital age: A critical analysis*. Hoboken, NJ: Taylor & Francis.

Selwyn, N. (2013). *Discourses of digital 'disruption' in education: A critical analysis*. Paper presented at the Fifth International Roundtable on Discourse Analysis, Hong Kong.

Snyder, I., Marginson, S., & Lewis, T. (2007). An alignment of the planets: Mapping the intersections between pedagogy, technology and management in Australian universities. *Journal of Higher Education Policy and Management, 29*(2), 187–202. doi:10.1080/13600800701351769

Steel, C., & Levy, M. (2009). *Creativity and constraint: Understanding teacher beliefs and the use of LMS technologies*. Paper presented at the Same Places, Different Spaces, Auckland, New Zealand. Retrieved December 14, 2013, from http://www.ascilite.org.au/conferences/auckland09/procs/steel.pdf

Tess, P. A. (2013). The role of social media in higher education classes (real and virtual) – A literature review. *Computers in Human Behavior, 29*(5), 60–68. doi:10.1016/j.chb.2012.12.032

Tibebu, D., Bandyopadhyay, T., & Negash, S. (2010). ICT integration efforts in higher education in developing economies: The case of Addis Ababa University, Ethiopia. In R. Luppicini & A. Haghi (Eds.), *Cases on digital technologies in higher education: Issues and challenges* (pp. 279–303). Hershey, PA: IGI Global. doi:10.4018/978-1-61520-869-2.ch019

Warschauer, M. (2003). *Technology and social inclusion: Rethinking the digital divide*. Cambridge, MA: The MIT Press.

World Bank. (2010). *Tertiary education in Mongolia: Meeting the challenges of the global economy* (Report No. 52925 – MN). Human Development Sector Unit, Mongolia Country Management Office, East Asia and Pacific Region.

Yang, D., Sinha, T., Adamson, D., & Rose, C. P. (2013). *Turn on, tune in, drop out: Anticipating student dropouts in massive open online courses*. Retrieved April 30, 2014, from http://lytics.stanford.edu/datadriveneducation/papers/yangetal.pdf

KEY TERMS AND DEFINITIONS

Access: In this study, access has been understood as the availability of resources to be used by the participants to fully engage with digital technologies.

Chile: A country located at the very south of Latin America, bordering Peru, Bolivia and Argentina.

Context: The social, cultural, political, historical and economic setting which has framed the study.

Digital Literacy Studies: The research field which views technology use as a social practice and as shaped by diverse contexts.

Digital Technologies: The use of digital resources such as personal computers, laptops, mobile phones, tablets, Wi-Fi, internet, programming tools and software applications, etc., to effectively find, analyse, create, communicate and use information in a digital context.

Higher Education: It refers to post-secondary education which leads to the attainment of a degree at a university or other similar educational establishments.

Mongolia: A country located in east-central Asia bordered by Russia and China.

Techno-Biography: Teacher's life story related to technologies and a detailed account of their digital technology use in relation to their teaching, learning and researching.

Chapter 10

Contributing to an Evidence Base for the Enhancement of the Experiences and Outcomes of Mature Students at an Irish University

Emma Murphy
Dublin City University (DCU), Ireland

Yurgos Politis
University College Dublin (UCD), Ireland

Maria Slowey
Dublin City University (DCU), Ireland

ABSTRACT

This chapter explores current patterns of participation and progression by mature students in undergraduate (Bachelors) programmes in an Irish university. The study was conducted by HERC (Higher Education Research Centre) in collaboration with an Institutional Analysis and Research Office with input from an expert Advisory Group. Based on the suggestions and experiences of students and staff, and informed by good practice examples from literature, a series of recommendations are proposed, aimed at enhancing experiences and successful outcomes of mature students in the future.

INTRODUCTION

Ireland has a binary higher education system comprising seven universities and thirteen institutes of technology (IoTs)-all publicly funded.

The full-time undergraduate student population is 70,090 in the Universities and 62,376 in the IoTs. Universities have a majority of female students (53%) while the IoTs enrole a majority of male students (56%) (HEA, 2013). In addition, there are

DOI: 10.4018/978-1-4666-7244-4.ch010

colleges of education and a number of specialist colleges and a small number of private higher education institutions. Universities in Ireland are relatively small by international standards, ranging from approximately 24,000 students in the largest to approximately 9,500 students in the smallest. In 2014, the Irish university involved in the study described in this chapter had around 12,000 registered students. There has been a substantial growth in the higher education sector in Ireland which is exemplified by the fact that in 1965 there were approximately 19,000 full-time students in the sector and by 2013 this has risen to approximately 165,000 (HEA website/ Statistics 2013).

Despite a strategic priority to increase the number of mature students[1]** in higher education in Ireland (HEA, 2008), the number of students over the age of 23 participating in higher education remains relatively low (HEA, 2012, 2013). With a view to improving participation rates and enhancing outcomes for mature students, an exploratory study was conducted with students at one Irish university (referred to from here as IUX – abbreviation of Irish University X). In IUX, mature students enter programmes across the university through a variety of routes. While they are widely recognized as constituting a valuable part of the student community, little was known about their profile, their patterns of participation across the university, and, importantly, what factors appear to shape successful outcomes. This study is an exploration of current patterns of mature students' participation and experiences in programmes across IUX. Based on the suggestions and experiences of student participants, and informed by relevant literature, a series of recommendations aimed at enhancing the experiences and successful outcomes of mature students have been developed. Before presenting the results of the consultation with mature students at IUX we provide a brief overview of literature related to the experiences of mature students and their profiles, and where available, with particular reference to an Irish context.

Diversity of Motivations and Experiences of Mature Students

There is a danger that mature students are presented as a homogenous group (McGivney, 2004). While all students are distinct individuals, because they do not 'progress' directly from school as a cohort, the even wider range of motivations and life circumstances of mature students must be taken into account in seeking to meet their educational, personal, social and occupational needs. A twelve country comparative analysis identified seven groups of adult learners in higher education (Slowey & Schuetze, 2012).

1. Second chance learners;
2. Equity groups;
3. Deferrers;
4. Recurrent learners;
5. Returners;
6. Refreshers;
7. Learners in later life.

These sub-groups may be diverse, but at the same time they are interconnected and it is therefore unsurprising that mature students' motivation to study in higher education is equally diverse. Their decision to enter higher education may relate to personal, financial or family responsibilities (Davies, 2001) that usually require bigger life changes than for younger, 'traditional' age students (Waller, 2006).

Some studies suggest general life circumstances activate the decision-making process (Britton & Baxter, 1999; McGuire et al, 2003) while other studies suggest that entering higher education is a long-standing goal or ambition of mature students (Fleming & Murphy, 1997; Bowl, 2001; Osbourne et al., 2004). A significant life-changing event such as redundancy or divorce can also prove a motivator (Gallacher et al., 2002; Lawton, 2005; MacFadgen, 2007; McCune et al., 2010) or that obtaining a qualification may be part of a long educational journey (Foster, 2009); whereas many studies refer to dissatisfaction with employment or career prospects (Mathers & Parry, 2010). Honneth (2007) found that mature students in Ireland perceived society as 'highly credentialised', where gaining a third level qualification is seen as the norm in terms of securing meaningful employment and recognition from society.

In another Irish study, Fleming and Finnegan (2011) reinforce this point, suggesting that gaining higher education qualifications may fulfil the need people have for respect and social recognition. Also on the topic of recognition, Tett (2000) records how mature working class students entering higher education perceived their participation in terms of 'breaking the mould' or being 'role models' in their communities. Wainwright and Marandet (2010), for example, indicate that mature students' entry to higher education is driven by a desire to be a role model for their children (especially for female students). The authors report that: 'As their powerfully articulated motivations suggest, higher education and being at university are perceived as tools for social mobility, enabling a transformative experience for both parent and child and impacting on the learner as well as their family' (ibid, p.456). Moreover, Britton and Baxter (1999) have identified that female mature entrants' dissatisfaction with their current life role can act as a powerful catalyst for re-entry, due to a sense of unfulfilled potential and expressing the feeling of 'wanting to do something for myself' (Fleming & Finnegan, 2011; see also Blair et al, 2010).

A qualitative study from another Irish university found that mature students are generally very positive about their experiences in HE (Keane, 2009). It is however important for them to feel involved, to become integrated into their institution both academically and socially; the influential study by Tinto (1993) suggests that this will enhance student retention. On the social front, Thomas (2002) reports that mature student retention and progression in higher education is significantly dependent on the degree to which they feel they have access to support via good friend-ships and social networks; that they experience a sense of connectedness to their institution and its members, especially relationships with their non-mature peers (c.f. Tinto, 1993; Thomas, 2002).

In fact, Tinto suggests that the frequency and quality of students' interactions with other students and staff constitutes an independent predictor of student persistence (2002). This can be explained by the fact that mature students tend to grow apart from their former friends as a result of their higher education participation. In order to avoid feelings of isolation and disconnectedness, it is even more important for them, compared to their non-mature peers that they need to develop social networks in their new environment (Keane, 2009).

However, the reality is that many students 'juggle' study and coursework with employment, family responsibilities, civil engagement and the like. This means less time and energy to engage in social activities on campus and with extra-curricular activities. Moreover, on the academic front, their academic experience can be shaped by difficulties in their relationships with younger students (Bowl, 2003; Merrill, 2001; Inglis & Murphy, 1999; Edwards, 1993). Some research suggest that the two groups seem to take a different approach to learning; while mature students' approach is to try to understand the teaching material, their younger peers may engage in a relatively superficial way (Richardson, 1995). Low levels of participation in tutorials from the younger students can be a source of conflict with the mature students (Merrill, 2001; Edwards, 1993). It is also documented that mature students feel frustrated with what they perceive as the immature behaviour and less serious attitude towards academic work of their younger counterparts; and they also feel isolated from them as a result of being older and having more life experience (Bow, 2003; Merrill, 2001; West, 1996; Edwards, 1993).

An added benefit to students and staff alike of larger number of mature students can be diversity and inclusion. Professional development for staff may be beneficial assisting in understanding diversity and individuals' differential needs (Keane, 2009; Trant, 2006; Kelly, 2005; Macdonald & Stratta, 2001; Brown & Atkins, 1986). The integrated approach to diversity training, which entails an infusion of principles of diversity and inclusion throughout the academic programme, is preferable to 'add-on' approaches (Zeichner et al., 1998). Significant steps forward have been achieved in this regard in Irish HEIs both in policy and practice. There is an increased focus on academic staff development and on developing a broader range of innovative and student-centred teaching and learning strategies (c.f. Trant 2006; O'Neill et al., 2005; Slowey et al., 2014).

Socio-Demographic Profile of Mature Students in Irish Higher Education

As mentioned above, Irish higher education has grown substantially over the past couple of decades. Concerns about the declining numbers of traditional-age participation in higher education along with equity concerns (HEA, 1995) brought mature students to the limelight. The White Paper on Adult Education (2000) highlighted the low level of participation of mature students in higher education, noting that Ireland had the 'lowest mature-aged participation rates in the industrialised world' at the time (p.138); an observation which was repeated in an OECD Review of higher education in Ireland (2004). Although the situation has improved since then (Table, 1), the current participation rate remains short of entry rates in some other western industrialised countries. For example, graduation rates for mature students

(defined in Ireland as students over 23 years of age on entry, and 25 years or older in many other countries) account for a quarter of university graduates in Iceland, Israel, New Zealand, Sweden and Switzerland (OECD, 2011).

As Table 1 shows, despite targets set by the HEA to increase the proportion of mature students to 20% by 2013 the proportion of full-time mature entrants to Irish higher education institutions actually declined in 2011-13 (HEA 2013). Those figures compare favourably to some other European countries (for example, Germany and Austria) but unfavourably to others (Slowey & Schuetze 2012). In the UK, for example, where percentage of full-time undergraduate mature entrants to English, Welsh and Northern Irish HEIs was 21.2%, 20.3% and 19.3% respectively in 2012/13 (HESA website, Table 2a_1213). The reality though was different because after a period of modest growth up to 2004, part-time undergraduate numbers started to decline thereafter, with a substantial (18 per cent) drop between the academic years 2008/09 and 2009/10, and an overall reduction in the proportion of undergraduates defined as part-time over the period 2000 to 2009 (Slowey, 2012). While some of this variation may reflect a statistical blip (due to changes in definitions) the relatively high level of fees charged for part-time study and the lack of incentives for HEIs to deliver part-time programmes are undoubtedly factors.

In terms of age breakdown, it is evident that the majority of full-time mature new entrants are at the younger end of the age spectrum: that is, in the 23-25 year age group (HEA, 2012). In contrast, students aged 49 upwards represent less

Table 1. Percentage of full-time mature undergraduate students in Ireland (1999 – 2013)

YEAR	1999*	2002*	2008	2009	2010	2011	2012	2013°
% of new Mature students	6.9	8.3	10.8	13.6	15.6	14.5	14.0	13.0

Sources: HEA (2012) [* HEA (2006); °HEA (2013)]

than 0.5% of mature new entrants. Also, for most age brackets a higher proportion of mature full-time new entrants enter the IoTs than universities.

The gender breakdown for universities and IoTs is presented in Figure 1. Across higher education as a whole a majority (57%) of full-time mature new entrants are male. Full-time mature students are predominantly male in the IoTs, whereas in the universities there is a gender balance.

In terms of socio-economic background there is some evidence to suggest that many are indeed 'second chance' learners. In the universities for example, the largest socio-economic group (SEG) for mature respondents is skilled manual at 18.8% of respondents. This compares to 10.2% for the same group in the 'traditional' younger student population. However, the Employer and Manager (16.8%) and Higher Professional (10.8%) group figures suggest a return to education cross-skilling/retraining. A smaller proportion of mature new

entrants are classified as Employer and Manager (15.6%), Higher Professional (8.1%), Lower Professional (9%) and Farmers (7.4%) than their non-mature peers, which traditionally are highly represented groups in higher education. In the IoTs the largest socio-economic group for mature respondents is skilled manual group at 25.2% of mature respondents (HEA, 2012).

The percentage of full-time mature undergraduates studying at universities and IoTs in the period 2008-12 is presented in Figure 2. The figures have remained static for the university entrants whereas, up to 2011 the proportion of mature entrants in the IoT sector had been growing. According to the HEA (2012), 14% of full-time undergraduate entrant students in 2012 were mature students. This figure is comparable to those for the UK, where the percentage of full-time mature undergraduate students to English, Welsh and Northern Irish HEIs is 7.8%, 14.3% and 12.4%

Figure 1. Percentage of male mature students by sector (HEA, 2012)

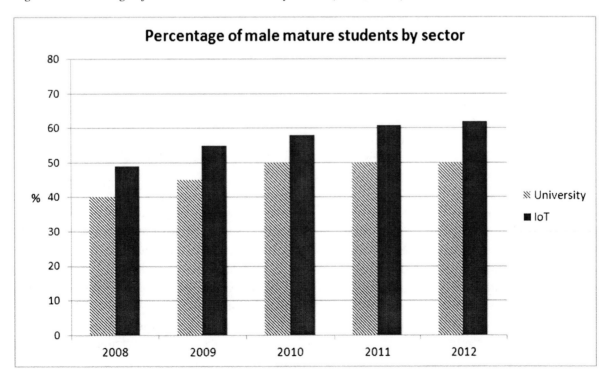

Figure 2. Percentage of full-time mature students by sector (HEA, 2012)

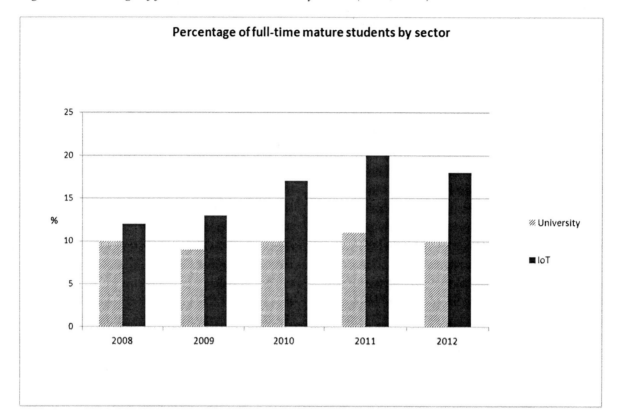

respectively in 2012/13 (HESA website, Table 2b_1213). The fact that the majority of mature students are part-timers can be attributed to the desire of enhancing their employment and career prospects, academic achievement and economic/financial reasons (Connor et al., 2001). Although respondents recognised that being employed and studying would bring added stress, they thought it would be worthwhile in the end.

There is some evidence pointing to the importance of qualification 'ladders' for adult learners. In Irish universities, for example, 93% of all new entrants studying at Level 6 in the national framework of qualifications (advanced certificate/higher certificate) are defined as mature (full- and part-time). The majority of these students are enrolled in Healthcare Certificate programmes. In 2012, 81% of Level 7 (ordinary bachelor degree)

new entrants were mature but just 9% of Level 8 (honours bachelor degree/higher diploma) new entrants. In the IoTs, the proportion of mature new entrants studying at level 6 is 28%, level 7 is 20% and level 8 is 18% (HEA, 2012).

With regards to progression rates, 15% of mature students in both universities and IoTs did not progress to their second year of study. This compares unfavourably to the situation in the UK where non-progression rates for mature students in English, Welsh, Scottish and Northern Irish HEIs is 10.3%, 10.8%, 12.1% and 7.3% respectively in 2011/12 (HESA website, Table 3a_1213). Figure 3 shows breakdown of non-progression by level of course study and sector. According to the HEA (2010) mature non progression in universities was 12% for level 8 courses, compared to 9% for the traditional students. On the other hand, at levels

Figure 3. 'Non-progression' rates by level of course and sector (HEA, 2010)

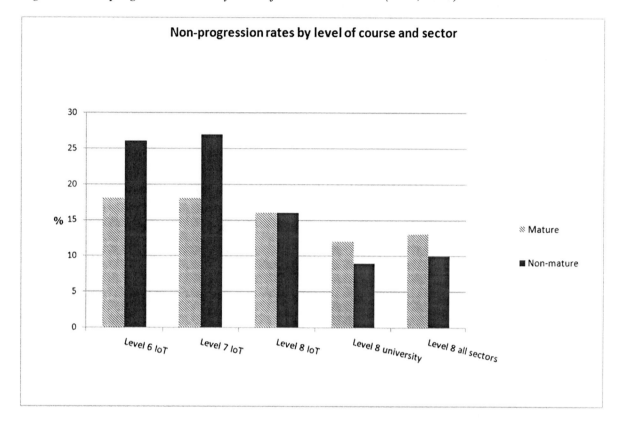

6 and 7, mature students were more likely to progress than younger counterparts.

Research on adult learners reveals many reasons for 'non-progression'. Success is influenced by a range of factors including motivation for study, student support within and beyond the institution, pre-entry preparation, curriculum congruence, issues related to student identity, self-confidence and the risks taken in becoming a mature student (Harvey et al., 2006). For example, the Swedish system highlighting the importance of flexible higher education is responding to adult educational needs through systems which allow for the facility to 'drop-in' and 'drop-out' in line with changing career, domestic, civic and personal requirements (Bron & Thunborg, 2012). It is interesting though to point out that most studies show, mature students tend to outperform their younger peers (van Rooyen et al., 2006; El Ansari, 2003).

MATURE STUDENTS AT IUX: A CONSULTATION

With a view to finding out more about the actual experiences of mature students in IUX, a group of full-time undergraduate mature students were invited to take part in a consultation facilitated by members of an Advisory Group and project researchers.

These participants were recruited via an active Mature Students Society, an InterFaith Centre (which provides support for the latter) directly by email. The group was not designed to be representative of all mature students. Given the limited time and resource available for the project, the objective was to gain insights which might inform IUX policy and practice, as well as identifying areas for further investigation.

This session took the form of a roundtable discussion with breakout panel discussions. Nine IUX mature undergraduate students participated in the consultation, which initially provided them with a brief overview of the study aims and objectives before breaking into two groups for a roundtable discussion.

Participants ranged in age between 39 and 60- hence older than the average age of mature students in the university- and comprised four women and five men. All were full-time undergraduate students. They divided almost equally between first and second year students and were mainly taking programmes in the social sciences. Both discussion panels were audio recorded for analysis purposes. The questions addressed can be grouped under the following three broad headings:

Access to IUX

This section explored the access paths taken by participants, from when they first considered studying through to acceptance of a place at IUX and their experience of initial reception and orientation. Specific questions included:

- What were the factors determining your choice of a course and university?
- What were the barriers to access your undergraduate course at IUX?
- Can you describe your experiences of orientation for mature students at IUX?

Mature Student Identity

As adult learners, participants were asked about the groups or communities with which they most identified on campus. (For example, other mature students, students on their programme, university staff.)

Proposal to Enhance Experiences

Participants were asked to identify the single proposal which they felt would best enhance the experience of mature students at IUX

The participants were assured that their anonymity would be protected. In order to ensure that they could not be identified, every measure was taken to remove names of individuals and higher education institutions, as well as specific courses. A draft of the text was returned to participants for approval and, in the following quotations universities and IoT Institutions are referred to as University 1, 2 etc.

FEEDBACK FROM IUX MATURE STUDENTS

All participants actively engaged in discussion throughout the consultation and all contributed answers to the questions presented above. The feedback that they provided is detailed below and grouped according to emerging themes.

Factors Determining Mature Students' Choice of a Course and University

There were many reasons offered as to why the participants chose to study in higher education as adults. For example they may not have been encouraged to do so at a younger age:

I left school in 1978 and it just wasn't the done thing to go to college, you just didn't go. I worked all my life. I gave up work when the kids were younger and I did some voluntary work, community work I would have got involved in adult literacy... They started to pay me to do it and it snowballed from there...finances threw me back into the workplace full-time... I always had a desire to do a degree...when it came to the stage where I had the time and the money to do it, the only thing

I was interested in and the only thing that I put on the CAO [national Central Applications Office] was the... degree here in IUX ...I don't intend to work when I finish which is very unusual I get a lot of stick for that ...but I am here for knowledge just for knowledge (Participant 2)

Others went a step further and suggested that it was a personal interest and self-motivation that was the main driver:

I always wanted to do a degree... It was constant it was niggling and of course I got married I had children. I worked in insurance for about 15 years...when they were small I stayed at home I was always doing courses...I set up my own business...it was very successful, but at the same time I had in the back of my mind that I had to do more... I did computer courses, HR courses, cookery courses, all kinds of courses ...and I saw an advertisement in the paper one day... access courses [offered by University 2]...I applied for University 3 as well... University 3 offered me a place... I took up that place... I studied History and Politics for the year on the access course... and that was the motivating factor for Contemporary Culture and Society...it is very broad...and I love it...I actually made the right choice..."(Participant 3)

I did the --- access programme [offered by University 2]...during the year we were shown all the options...my first instinct was to go to University 1 because I live [close by]...I saw this course...I spent 1980 in the army here I was over in Lebanon a few times...all that area of conflict and policy interests me and it has always stuck with me... so that's why I chose the International Relations (Participant 6)

I've been a plumber for years...until 2008...I started doing various short courses...I did counselling...I came up to the open day here...I was talking to people doing the CCS...I liked that ...I

had tunnel vision ...I didn't look anywhere else... it just worked out for me...(Participant 5)

I don't know what I'm going to do afterwards but I am going to do something, I'm thinking of further study ...I have to try and forget about my age and just go with what I want to do and I intend to do that when I get this degree next year please God (Participant 3)

Some participants felt the need for a change of careers:

Having grown up in an institution, a boy's home I would be very social minded ...I always had a leaning towards social issue...If I'm going to go somewhere else I'd like it to be in that direction... complete change of [career] direction a lot [of the motivation] has to do with my wife, I think she knows me better than I know me ...she knew it was a direction I should go into (Participant 7)

I started off in my job as a chef... I needed to change careers...I went on an access course in University 3...I wanted to get into teaching young adults about healthy eating...I heard about IUX when I was in University 3...IUX was the only place that had a specific course for teaching and training...this was my first choice...another factor was that it was closer to me...this is the ideal place for me (Participant 8)

The economic crisis, not surprisingly, featured high on motivating factors-due to diminishing income and/or unemployment:

Very much timing the whole process started two and a half years ago...the future looked pretty bleak in this country...I was working as a taxi driver and the income had just plummeted... [a friend] put me in touch with access programme [offered by University 2] and that's how it started really...she pointed me in the right direction" (Participant 6)

199

I worked construction all my life until I came to Ireland when the Celtic tiger was kicking off... I think it was 2009 I ended up I was driving cranes and the job I was on finished and there was just no other work... I tried a building course with FAS... [Then did a welding course]... Then I went to FETAC level 5 in [X College]...I did an economics course there I said to myself I can get employment in economics...applied for all the universities...I got into University 2... [BESS Programme]...although I had done psychology and the social sciences it wasn't something I was going to continue...as soon as I found out I was accepted here and when I heard what the course entailed and once I was accepted here it was a no brainer... This was the course for me (Participant 1)

I was out of work for about 3 years...It was my wife who suggested I go back...having left school at about 15 or 16 I was a bit dubious ...I applied for the Access Programme [offered by University 2]...but got refused for that...the following year she said just apply directly...my first choice was University 2...didn't get that...second choice was CCS here in IUX and after an interview here I got accepted... and enjoy it now that I'm here (Participant 7)

Some interviewees stated that they were inspired when their children enrolled in a higher education degree programme:

When I was trawling through the CAO for my children because I did that job and marked out all the things that they may be interested in doing ...so that was my job I knew every course in every university in the whole of Ireland! (Participant 2)

I raised my children, did a few part time posts and I did an access course 5 years before I plucked up the courage to attempt to go to university. All my life it didn't even come into my head to do a

degree but I think having kids and seeing how well that people can do that would have inspired me. (Participant 4)

It seems though, that some of the participants had self-doubt or low self-esteem when applying for their courses:

...at the interview I didn't think that I had a chance and I am delighted to be here I love what I am studying (Participant 3)

...So I applied and surprise surprise I got the course and it feels right (Participant 4)

Self-doubt and low self-esteem can be considered as impediments to the participation of mature students to higher education. We will discuss other barriers in more depth in the following section.

Barriers to Access

Issues with the Undergraduate Courses at IUX

Participants outlined the barriers that they had encountered in accessing their undergraduate degree. Issues related to finance arose for a number of participants:

I would have found finance a barrier because I had 2 daughters here [at IUX] at the time ... I have to be honest it was a barrier ...now it didn't stop me but it made things very difficult but I had to be sure that I wanted to do it, to put myself under the pressure that I did financially (Participant 2)

the expense...I had to be in a position for me to go to college once they [children] were settled then I came third or fourth on the list ...and one of the advantages of coming to IUX is that I just live around the corner ...and to be honest if I had to travel...I would have gone into town I wouldn't have gone out to University 3, I wouldn't have gone to University 1 because they would have been barriers (Participant 4)

When most of us were at school, going to university was never seen as an option, first of all the cost of it ruled it out and my [secondary school] I'd say less than 3 or 4 per cent went to college and they were seen as the swots they were always going to do well...it was never an option whereas it is nowadays there seems to be easier access to 3rd level than when we were in school... (Participant 6)

Participants also described how family life and caring for children can be a barrier to enrolling in full-time education:

And if you have children pulling out of you as well that is an obstacle to getting on with your own studies. So you have to detach yourself. Now I have adult children but they are living at home and their attitude to their mother not always being available ...they have gotten used to mother not being available as mother always was...but mothers have to detach themselves. (Participant 3)

Five years before when I got my place in IUX my children were much younger and they were at junior cert and leaving cert level so there was no way I was going to put myself in front of them ...and the one year access course that I did ... [laugh] when I was studying in my bedroom my son was about 11 at the time and he would put notes under the door "when are you coming out?" so the guilt of that! I felt awful! And I couldn't put myself before them (Participant 4)

Academic preparedness was highlighted as a potential barrier to succeeding at third level (higher education) as a mature student.

Part of your economics [course] you've got to do a recap on your maths...IUX ran a week's course... without me doing that I would have been in serious trouble coming back...I spoke to one of the tutors...I was keeping up but I felt like I was swimming against the tide so we [mature students] got an extra hour tutoring a week... It was up to yourself whether you went or not... because whatever you were doing he would say what was the problem...I didn't even know what differentiation was...there was only three or four of us [mature] students going to it but a couple of the other students did take advantage of it ...I'm going to the maths learning centre now myself... (Participant 1)

The academic writing; I struggled a lot with that...I'm slowly coming around to seeing how it is done...I know they run a course in the library. I didn't find it very useful...more about referencing (Participant 5)

The writing is bad but you know the reading is ten times worse so a speed reading course would be good (Participant 8)

Some participants had completed an access course before coming to IUX and they described this experience as invaluable.

Anyone coming to third level having been out of school for 10 or 20 years they would sink. I think that it is essential to do a pre-university course because if I had not done ...that [access] course...I think I would have just gone home and cried. (Participant 4)

I did the level 5 FETAC in college Y and without that there is no way I would have survived here (Participant 1)

You are at a great advantage if you have done an access course (Participant 8)

Mature Students' Experiences of Orientation at IUX

Participants described IUX in positive terms as a smaller and more comfortable institution to navigate, compared to some other Irish HEIs:

I was out in the University 3 campus [for access course] it was a scary place, this place is a doddle in comparison ...it is such a small campus...University 3 is a village. It was daunting I struck it out because I wanted the [qualification] it got me here (Participant 3)

Participants had a generally positive experience of the orientation process at IUX, especially with regards to help from staff members related to support on computing or academic issues:

Orientation that all the mature students (do) before they start in 1ˢᵗ year (is) excellent. It is very informative...they have mature students in the college who talk to you and tell you what the college is like ...they offer a computer to tell us about Moodle which is essential to your degree and in general the staff are extremely helpful and nice...I had no barriers personally but if I had one I'd feel confident going to one of the staff members and asking for help. (Participant 3)

[The maths learning centre at IUX is] a great support...I didn't need to do [maths]...I went to that and it really built my confidence because I realised I am really good at this...it was an even better way of meeting mature students than the big orientation ...and I still meet a lot of the people that were on that maths course ...so an add advantage to the mature student orientation, which is fantastic ...something where you would have a chance to work together in small groups... like a day in small groups ...I just found going to

that maths class, it was smaller, it was focused rather than the big thing [orientation meeting] (Participant 2)

Isolation is an issue that seems to affect certain mature students:

A lot of us felt we had too much time off and left us sort of isolated... (Participant 8)

I joined the mature student society...they seemed to be more active last year...there is a lunch every Wednesday...it is difficult to organize...you know people have kids, husbands. Difficult to organize for matures to meet up...it is hard getting organization for matures because they have so much going on in their lives (Participant 9)

Some mature students feel out of place either due to the fact that they co-exist in classes with non-mature students or due to the fact that even the mature student cohort is not a homogenous group.

I still haven't found my feet...I am basically just coming into the lectures and meeting for group work and stuff ...and going to the library...but as far as social life in here is basically non-existent for me ...I was thinking of the first talk in the Helix in with all the 18 and 19 year old...it just felt very weird (Participant 8)

There is a bit of a difference between 23 and 40 [years of age] (Participant 9)

This last point also appears prominently in the next section of the chapter.

Mature Students' Identity

Participants spoke at length about the relationship with their younger student peers. Some, as stated above, felt that there was a big gap between them (mature students) and the younger students, but that given time, the situation improves:

There definitely is that gap, the difference between us and them and the orientation week allowed for us to settle because we had the place to ourselves, we didn't have the kids running around the place so it gave us that week to get a feel for the place and to acclimatize. (Participant 4)

I'm starting to be able to talk to the younger students in the course...but there is only a certain few that will talk to (us) (Participant 6)

It does take time...by the second year they will be more chatty and receptive (Participant 9)

Yeah, it is starting to mellow a little between mature (students) and the rest of the students but at the start of the year it was completely separate... the barriers are starting to break down. We start to see that we are all in the same boat together the only difference is age really (Participant 6)

A minority felt marginalised or almost invisible to the younger cohort, however some felt comfortable with their mature peers:

This is not a closed campus you know you see people walking through with their dogs, you could be staff, you could be a lecturer...I am older than most of the lecturers...it doesn't bother me...I could be anything...it is when they walk right into you or stand in front of doors after a lecture...maybe I am impatient (Participant 9)

You are pushed a bit to the side...but we tend to have a clique as well...if you get to make up your own group you sit with the group you are more comfortable with... (Participant 5)

Some respondents suggested that younger students may want to develop a relationship with mature students, while others stated that the reason this is not feasible is the way the programmes are set-up:

I just find they are so clever ...and they have respect for you because of your age ...they are always asking me to go out socializing...but I'm not going to go out socializing with 19 year olds (Participant 1)

In my degree there are only 4 mature students ... there is a big divide between us and the school leavers...there is very little interaction... I would prefer if I was put in with my fellow students [for group projects] rather than placed here there and everywhere with language and international students from other degree programmes...I'm second year and we have no relationship...with the younger students ...there is such a huge gap... (Participant 3)

Others felt a clear divide between them and lecturers but that there was no clear need to identify with any other group:

There is a divide there really [between students and lecturers] I could not identify with them I am a student...I identify with myself...I love what I study I am happy really I don't need to identify with anyone (Participant 3)

For me I'm still the school girl and they are the teacher...I know that there has to be a barrier and I would like to relax into it...I suppose it is from years of negative schooling negative teacher...I'm still only 16 in my head (Participant 4)

I can get through this whole course without identifying with anyone. There is a barrier with the tutors...but I prefer it that way (Participant 1)

A minority though did want to fit in:

I do think it is important to identify with someone... (Participant 4)

One participant was under the impression that the course modules would actually be targeted at mature students:

When I interviewed for this course I was under the mistaken impression that this course was actually for mature students ...I go in there ...I was expecting much older age range... (Participant 9)

It is interesting that many participants identified a sub-group of mature students, the "younger matures", which is the student cohort between the ages of 23 and 29 (maybe even in their early 30s). They felt that this group may be experiencing more issues with identity:

the younger mature students have a hard time ... (some have) nothing in common with the 18 year olds 19 year olds and (others are) totally isolated ... (Participant 3)

The 23 year olds have a much bigger problem than us [in terms of identification] and none of them is here today... (Participant 2)

I think there should be an interim group...23 is very young to be one of us and yet very old to be 18 (Participant 2)

They are not accepted by the 18 or 19 year olds and in fairness they don't want to be (Participant 3)

The over 23s are really isolated and there is a gap... (Participant 3)

Participants believe that the integration of younger and mature students falls to the student cohort themselves. It is not something which can be 'forced':

No, it is just a building process (Participant 7)

It is part of the younger groups learning experience to start to speak to us...it is part of life to be able to start talking to adults (Participant 8)

You have to realize they have just come from school the only adults have been teachers so it is a learning process for them as well (Participant 6)

I think the best icebreakers were talking to them about the academic work and reading... (Participant 9)

An observation some respondents made is that younger students seem to need help on academic issues from their mature counterparts:

The younger ones are actually starting to gravitate towards the matures [for group work] because they know they'll do well (Participant 3)

And they come to you ...when they need questions answered that they don't have to go to their tutors they come to the mature students and ask them (Participant 4)

Don't go in and try and be one of the young guys...hang back...after 2 or 3 weeks... If I don't understand what he's saying I will ask...they are desperate at the back for me to ask...they won't because they are embarrassed. It takes a lot to get me embarrassed...and after a couple of weeks they say I wanted to ask that question as well... (Participant 1)

This could be due to different levels of expectation and commitment to their studies:

I think that the mature students have higher expectations...the younger students are happy to scrape by whereas we set the bar higher...we want a good result and they are happy to pass (Participant 4)

Academic Issues: Team Work and Technology

However, some respondents suggested that they can be intimidated by the academic ability of their younger classmates.

I find I am surprised at how smart some of my [younger] classmates are, how focused they can be which is the complete opposite to what I expected you know ...we were doing a project recently and I had put several hours into it and the young student basically started from scratch and had it done in 50 minutes and it was one of the best things I'd ever read it was very impressive you know (Participant 6)

Participants were also impressed with their younger colleagues' grasp of technology:

Well the technology I wouldn't be great with ...I actually asked to get the group to meet up but every time ...it just never happened so it all just happened through e-mails ...or Google docs or whatever (Participant 5)

I find that the younger ones would be doing stuff in class on their phone ...they all have Internet on their phone...I don't think I'd be able for a smartphone (Participant 8)

Participants were asked whether lecturers break the class up to proactively integrate younger and mature students. Some were negative:

Not really (Participant 5)

In other cases, group work was encouraged. Frequently, mature students would need to take the lead; other times the work was divided:

As the time went on...the younger ones in the group...they were afraid to talk, it took a while for them to talk...they were leaving us to come with the ideas...they needed a little nudge and encouragement...but once they started they came up with some great ideas and becoming more creative in the group work and the task (Participant 8)

Personally I wouldn't find any issue between the young and the [mature students] (Participant 6)

They would have issues though with the different approach of the non-mature students to learning when it comes to group work:

I just handed in a [group] assignment and I never met anyone in the group they just did it all online (Participant 5)

I find some of them haven't read their email... Facebook they will reply instantly (Participant 9)

Some participants had a real fear of failing their course exams which had a significant impact on their confidence:

Just pure fear I failed one of my exam for the semester...when I failed that it really knocked me back...I had an idea that I had already failed it was really difficult for me to do the exam...I was surprised that I actually got a mark...I was afraid when I saw it in print I wondered is it really for me (Participant 8)

I think it just knocks your confidence a bit...if I feel I haven't done something to my own standards I beat myself up about it but then after getting over that initial giving out to yourself but I would kind of try and concentrate on that and bring it back up to where it should be ...but I find it can bring down other things then ...it can kind of know you on other things... (Participant 7)

Proposals to Enhance the Experience of Mature Students

Some participants suggested that it would be helpful if there could be some practical workshops and skills training as part of the orientation process:

I'd like to suggest for the orientation...I would have done a lot of workshops at the beginning ...and I would like to see a couple of those for matures ...maybe the essay writing one or the reading one for the mature students to put us into the smaller groups...I'd like to see a few of them for the orientation (Participant 2)

Some general skills [training]...as part of the orientation...and it is not only for the skill it is for the meeting people ...I know someone from everywhere [every faculty] because of that maths course (Participant 2)

Study groups I would like to see more study groups...not just for the mature students but I think the matures would use it a lot (Participant 4)

Others didn't focus their suggestions just on the orientation week, but rather felt there was a need for help on academic issues throughout the year:

More tutorials (Participant 1)

Some sort of class on the technology end of things... maybe a one hour class just for mature students... to update their skills...I had a lot of problems with Microsoft...Moodle... (Participant 6)

[Technology] is Second nature to most of them [younger students] you see (Participant 5)

Open centre – where you can get help with certain things...access to machines (Participant 9)

Another suggestion was the need for a space on campus specifically for mature students. Al-

though there is mature student lunch once a week this did not suit everyone due to timetable clashes and general availability:

I would like to have like an interfaith centre that is designated for mature students ...just a room... that you can go to...I think it would be invaluable for me as a mature student...literally a space with couches...just a drop in centre, not a study place (Participant 2)

Even a room in the interfaith just for mature students...I'd often have a two hour break...I go up and sit in the car in the car park ...if I had a room to go to (Participant 3)

A room where we can sit down... (Participant 1)

One thing that struck me is that are not many benches and places to sit around the campus (Participant 4)

Respondents suggested that promoting shared interests and group work between mature and younger students could improve social interactions between the groups.

I think that separation is always going to be... they have never interacted with adults in a different situation. I just hope that as second and third year goes on there will be more interaction (Participant 6)

I think that the group work helps [with social interaction] (Participant 5)

Common interests are important [for social interaction] (Participant 6)

However, some participants proposed that there should be mechanisms in place to deal with the imbalance of effort in group work between those groups:

I have a problem with group work...the imbalance that is there..."Some penalty for not turning up (Participant 3)

There should be some sort of a checking system... the tutor has some sort of checking system (Participant 4)

There was also a recommendation for the offer of more continuous feedback provided to mature students:

Feedback on all courses is continuously offered to mature students ...if you don't do well...go to the lecture and find out why... (Participant 9)

CONCLUDING OBSERVATIONS

This chapter reports on a small scale, qualitative research study. Nevertheless the consultation with this particular group of mature students delivered an interesting list of recommendations which could form the basis of a more comprehensive investigation.

The students, for example, found activity based learning sessions valuable and suggested the time allocated to them at induction should be expanded and continued further in the semester. This would boost their academic skills and also improve social interaction. This kind of student-centred, activity based learning is also promoted in best practice literature and guidelines (Machellan & Soden, 2004; Kember, 2009) and should be organised to continue beyond orientation. Academic reading and writing and technology skills were highlighted as important skill areas for mature students. They also believe that every effort should be made by the university to publish its timetables earlier. Allowing early access to timetables would make it easier for mature students to embark on their studies as they have to plan for family and financial commitments. This would have benefits for other students.

Mature students do not embark on higher education as a cohort, the nature of their enquiries and decision making processes are quite different from those of school leavers. Those involved with the focus group discussions described the length of time they had taken to decide to apply for an IUX programme. Some also described their lack of knowledge and full understanding of what they were actually embarking upon. While there is much expertise around the university in working with adult students, there is no clear route of enquiry for adults who are seeking more generic advice on the range of IUX options which might be open to them, and appropriate to their interests. Thus they recommend that a position for a mature student liaison/outreach officer is created.

While all facilities in IUX are open to any registered student, the social and, in certain respects educational activities are orientated towards the majority of the student body: in practice, the needs and interests of many, if not most, adult learners are quite different to those of 18-23 year olds. This is reflected in the strong recommendations of participants that there should be a space on campus dedicated to mature students. As the needs and interests of mature students in full-time programmes are likely to overlap with those of other adult learners, for example in evening, part-time, distance and/or e-learning programmes, consideration might therefore be given to a space which might serve this wider community of adult learners.

This study was designed as an exploratory process to expand our knowledge about the diverse interests and needs of mature students in one specific Irish university. To take this exploratory work further it would be valuable that larger, more detailed studies of adult students as well as staff are undertaken across the Irish system. One specific issue that we believe merits further investigation are the interests and perspectives of 'younger' mature students, in the 23-29 – none of which opted to participate in the consultation. This could be due to the fact that this group do not identify with the term "mature" and therefore did not respond to the call for participation. Alternatively, there could be other factors such as time pressures that affect this group. It would be interesting to explore these issues in a more detailed study involving "younger mature" students.

Other priority topics for investigation include:

- The overlap and the differences with other 'non-traditional' student groups such as Access Students and students with disabilities.
- A follow up study of the experiences and outcomes for a range of IUX adult learners: including part-time, distance students and others (undergraduate and postgraduate).
- The potential of intergenerational learning.
- Participation of mature students in the institutional governance; any mechanisms through which they can influence decision-making?
- Institutional strategy regarding mature students; does it exist and how is it implemented?

ACKNOWLEDGMENT

This study was supported by a University Quality Improvement and Development fund. The authors of this chapter are particularly grateful for the assistance of Dr. Ekaterina Kozina for her help in writing the research proposal for this study, Aisling McKenna for her statistical expertise and the members of the advisory board for their valuable contributions, namely Mathew Gunning, Celine Jameson, Susan Jones, Teresa Murray, and Ita Tobin.

REFERENCES

Blair, E., Cline, T., & Wassis, J. (2010). When do adults entering higher education begin to identify themselves as students? The threshold-of-induction model. *Studies in Continuing Education*, *32*(2), 133–146. doi:10.1080/0158037X.2010.488355

Bowl, M. (2001). Experiencing the barriers: Non-traditional students entering higher education. *Research Papers in Education*, *16*(2), 41–160. doi:10.1080/02671520110037410

Bowl, M. (2003). *Non-traditional entrants to higher education: They talk about people like me.* Stoke on Trent, UK: Trentham Books.

Britton, C., & Baxter, A. (1999). Becoming a mature student: Gendered narratives of the self. *Gender and Education*, *11*(2), 179–193. doi:10.1080/09540259920681

Bron, A., & Thunborg, C. (2012). Higher education and lifelong learning in Sweden. In M. Slowey & H. G. Schuetze (Eds.), *Global perspectives on higher education and lifelong learners* (pp. 97–111). London: Routledge.

Brown, G., & Atkins, M. (1986). Academic staff training in British universities: Results of a national survey. *Studies in Higher Education*, *11*(1), 29–42. doi:10.1080/03075078612331378441

Carroll, D., & Patterson, V. (2011). *A profile of undergraduate mature new entrants.* Dublin: HEA.

Connor, H., Dewson, S., Tyers, C., Eccles, J., Regan, J. & Aston, J. (2001). *Social class and higher education: Issues affecting decisions on participation by lower social class groups.* Sheffield, UK: DfES

Davies, P. (2001). *Widening participation in higher education in England: Report to Scottish executive.* Stirling, UK: Centre for Research in Lifelong Learning/Scottish Executive.

Edwards, R. (1993). *Mature women students: Separating or connecting family and education.* London: Taylor and Francis.

El Ansari, W. (2003). Satisfaction trends in undergraduate physiotherapy education. *Physiotherapy, 89*(3), 171–185. doi:10.1016/S0031-9406(05)61033-4

Fleming, T., & Finnegan, F. (2011). *Nontraditional students in Irish higher education: A research report.* Retrieved from http://www.ranlhe.dsw.edu.pl/

Fleming, T., & Murphy, M. (1997). *College knowledge policy, power and the mature student experience at university. NUI Maynooth.* Centre for Adult and Community Education.

Foster, T. (2009). *Research paper no.4: Alternative routes into and pathways through higher education.* London: Department for Business Innovation and Skills (BIS). Accessed online at http://www.bis.gov.uk/assets/biscore/corporate/migratedD/publications/B/BIS-RP-004

Gallacher, J., Field, J., Merrill, B., & Crossan, B. (2002). Learning careers and the social space: Exploring fragile identities adult returners and the new further education. *International Journal of Lifelong Education, 21*(6), 493–509. doi:10.1080/0260137022000016172

Harvey, L., Drew, S., & Smith, M. (2006). *The first year experience: A review of literature for the higher education academy.* York, UK: HEA.

HEA. (2008). *National plan for equity of access to higher education 2008-2013.* Dublin: HEA.

HEA. (2010). *A study of progression in Irish higher education.* Dublin: HEA.

HEA. (2012). *Higher education: Key facts and figures 2011-12.* Dublin: HEA.

HEA. (2013). *Higher education: Key facts and figures 2012-13.* Dublin: HEA Higher Education Statistics Agency (HESA) Website. Accessed at https://www.hesa.ac.uk/pis/urg

Higher Education Authority (HEA). (1995). *Report of the steering committee on the future development of higher education.* Dublin: HEA.

Higher Education Authority (HEA). (2006). *An overview of applications and acceptances to higher education.* Dublin: HEA Website. Accessed at http://www.hea.ie/en/policy/national-access-office

Honneth, A. (2007). *Disrespect: The normative foundations of critical theory.* Cambridge, MA: Polity.

Inglis, T., & Murphy, M. (1999). *No room for adults? The experience of mature students in University College Dublin.* Dublin: Social Science Research Centre & Adult Education Office, University College Dublin.

Keane, E. (2009). Frictional relationships … tension in the camp: Focusing on the relational in under-represented students' experiences in higher education. *Irish Educational Studies, 28*(1), 85–102. doi:10.1080/03323310802597358

Kelly, M. (2005). The effects of increasing numbers of mature students on the pedagogical practices of lecturers in the institutes of technology. *Irish Educational Studies, 24*(2-3), 207–221. doi:10.1080/03323310500435497

Kember, D. (2009). Promoting student-centred forms of learning across an entire university. *Higher Education*, *58*(1), 1–13. doi:10.1007/s10734-008-9177-6

Lawton, M. (2005). *Working class heroes*. Paper presented at University of Wolverhamton, Wolverhamton, UK. Retrieved from http://asp.wlv.ac.uk/Level3.asp?UserType=11&Level3=1659

Leathwood, C., & O'Connell, P. (2003). It's a struggle: The construction of the 'new student' in higher education. *Journal of Education Policy*, *18*(6), 597–615. doi:10.1080/0268093032000145863

Macdonald, C., & Stratta, E. (2001). From access to widening participation: Responses to the changing population in higher education in the UK. *Journal of Further and Higher Education*, *25*(2), 249–258. doi:10.1080/03098770120050909

MacFadgen, S. L. (2007). *Mature students in the persistence puzzle: An exploration of the factors that contribute to adult learners' qualify of life and retention in post-secondary education*. (Unpublished doctoral dissertation). Simon Fraser University, Burnaby, Canada.

Maclellan, E., & Soden, R. (2004). The importance of epistemic cognition in student-centred learning. *Instructional Science*, *32*(3), 253–268. doi:10.1023/B:TRUC.0000024213.03972.ce

Mathers, J., & Parry, J. (2010). Older mature students' experiences of applying to study medicine in England: An interview study. *Medical Education*, *44*(11), 1084–1094. doi:10.1111/j.1365-2923.2010.03731.x PMID:20880007

McCune, V., Hounsell, J., Christie, V., Cree, V., & Tett, L. (2010). Mature and younger students' reasons for making the transition from further education into higher education. *Teaching in Higher Education*, *15*(6), 691–702. doi:10.1080/13562517.2010.507303

McGivney, V. (2004). Understanding persistence in adult learning. *Open Learning*, *19*(1), 33–46. doi:10.1080/0268051042000177836

McGuire, D., Collins, M., & Garavan, T. (2003). Tackling social exclusion at third level: A profile of participants on access courses. *Irish Educational Studies*, *22*(1), 41–68. doi:10.1080/0332331030220107

Merrill, B. (2001). Learning and teaching in universities: Perspectives from adult learners and lecturers. *Teaching in Higher Education*, *6*(1), 5–17. doi:10.1080/13562510020029563

O'Neill, G., Moore, S., & McMullen, B. (Eds.). (2005). *Emerging issues in the practice of university learning and teaching*. Dublin: AISHE.

Organisation for Economic Cooperation and Development (OECD). (2004). *Review of higher education in Ireland*. Paris: OECD.

Organisation for Economic Cooperation and Development (OECD). (2011). *Education at a glance*. Paris: OECD. Accessed online at http://www.oecdlibrary.org/docserver/download/fulltext/9611051ec008.pdf

Osbourne, M., Marks, A., & Turner, E. (2004). Becoming a mature student: How adult applicants weigh the advantages and disadvantages of becoming a mature student. *Higher Education*, *48*(3), 219–315.

Richardson, J. (1995). Mature students in higher education: An investigation of approaches to studying and academic performance. *Studies in Higher Education*, *20*(1), 5–17. doi:10.1080/03075079512331381760

Slowey, M. (2012). Lifelong learning and higher education in Ireland: Turbulent times. In M. Slowey & H. G. Schuetze (Eds.), *Global perspectives on higher education and lifelong learners* (pp. 60–81). London: Routledge.

Slowey, M., Kozina, E., & Tan, E. (2014). *The voices of Irish academics: Perspectives on professional development*. Dublin: All Ireland Society for Higher Education.

Slowey, M., & Schuetze, H. G. (2012). *Global perspectives on higher education and lifelong learners*. London: Routledge.

Tett, L. (2000). I'm working-class and proud of it: Gendered experiences of non-traditional participants in higher education. *Gender and Education, 12*(2), 183–194. doi:10.1080/09540250050009993

Thomas, L. (2002). Student retention in higher education: The role of institutional habitus. *Journal of Education Policy, 17*(4), 423–442. doi:10.1080/02680930210140257

Tinto, V. (1993). *Leaving college: Rethinking the causes and cures of student attrition* (2nd ed.). Chicago: University of Chicago Press.

Tinto, V. (2002). *Taking student retention seriously: Rethinking the first year of college*. Paper presented at the Annual Meeting of the American Association of Collegiate Registrars and Admission Officers, Minneapolis, MN. Retrieved from http://suedweb.syr.edu/Faculty/Vtinto/Files/AACRAOSpeech.pdf

Trant, M. (2006). Creative and innovative teaching in the context of wider access to higher education in Ireland. Paper presented at the 4th Annual International Conference on Teaching and Learning, Galway, Ireland.

van Rooyen, P., Dixon, A., Dixon, G., & Wells, C. (2006). Entry criteria as predictor of performance in an undergraduate nursing degree programme. *Nurse Education Today, 26*(7), 593–600. doi:10.1016/j.nedt.2006.02.002 PMID:16624454

Wainwright, E., & Marandet, E. (2010). Parents in higher education: Impacts of university learning on the self and the family. *Educational Review, 64*(4), 449–465. doi:10.1080/00131911.2010.487643

Waller, R. (2006). I don't' feel like a 'student' I feel like 'me'! The oversimplification of mature learners' experiences. *Research in Post-Compulsory Education, 11*(1), 115–130. doi:10.1080/13596740500508019

Website, H. E. S. A. (n.d.b). *Table T3a - Non-continuation following year of entry: UK domiciled full-time first degree entrants 2011/12*. Accessed at https://www.hesa.ac.uk/pis/urg

Website, H. E. S. A. (n.d.a). *Table T2b - Participation of under-represented groups in higher education: UK domiciled part-time undergraduate entrants 2012/13*. Accessed at https://www.hesa.ac.uk/pis/urg

West, L. (1996). *Adults, motivation and higher education: A biographical analysis*. London: Taylor and Francis.

Zeichner, K., Grant, C., Gay, G., Gillette, M., Valli, L., & Villegas, A. (1998). A research informed vision of good practice in multicultural teacher education: Design principles. *Theory into Practice, 37*(2), 163–171. doi:10.1080/00405849809543800

KEY TERMS AND DEFINITION

Access Programme/Students: The Access Programme helps to create equality of access to higher education for students from groups currently underrepresented.

Industrialized World: An explicit system that categorizes countries based on their development level (developing/industrialized)

Institutes of Technology (IoTs): Ireland's Institutes of Technology are flexible and dynamic university-level Institutes focused on teaching/learning, purpose-driven research, and public service.

Intergenerational Learning: Bringing together students and older people aged 60 years and over in a teaching and learning opportunity that values the equitable role of both participants as tutors and learners

Mature Student: The term is used in Ireland to describe students over the age of 23 (on the 1st of January of the year they enrol), participating in formal education.

National Framework of Qualifications (NFQ): The NFQ provides a way to compare qualifications, and to ensure that they are quality assured and recognised at home and abroad. (http://www.nfq.ie/nfq/en/)

Springboard Initiative: This Initiative in Higher Education offers free courses at certificate, degree and masters level leading to qualifications in areas where there are employment opportunities in the economy.

ENDNOTES

[1] The term mature student is an official category in Ireland for students over the age of 23 when entering post-initial education.

Chapter 11
Roma Social Inclusion through Higher Education Policies in Romania

Delia Bîrle
University of Oradea, Romania

Elena Bonchiş
University of Oradea, Romania

Daniela Crişan
Tilburg University, The Netherlands

Laura Bochiş
University of Oradea, Romania

Carmen Popa
University of Oradea, Romania

ABSTRACT

The chapter explores whether the educational policies introduced by the Romanian Government during the last twenty years are examples of good practice for other European countries facing the issue of Roma integration. The authors raise the question of whether the voices of Roma intellectual élites, who represent the "products" of those educational policies, are strong enough to drive the Roma minority towards common and sustained efforts for their social integration. What are the cross products of these educational policies? Additionally, they consider the case of Roma students within the University of Oradea in Romania and examine their attitudes towards academic learning, motivational factors, academic self-efficacy, faced difficulties, and potential ways to achieve higher rates of student retention. For a more in-depth analysis of the role and impact of those policies and the possible challenges/ difficulties encountered, the authors interviewed several decision makers, such as academic staff, NGO representatives, and current/former Roma students. The chapter concludes with suggested solutions for detected difficulties.

INTRODUCTION

The issue of integrating the Roma population within the European context is a topic that breeds a great deal of debate while politicians and non-governmental institutions often find themselves standing on different or even opposing positions. However, there is one thing they have reached consensus on, that the most certain way of facilitating the social integration of Roma population

DOI: 10.4018/978-1-4666-7244-4.ch011

is through education. This view was supported at the conference called "Strategies for the inclusion of Roma people - from good intentions to actual results", by Mariana Campeanu, the Ministry of Labor, Family, Social Protection, and Elderly (from May 2012-February 2014) who stated that:

Education is the only solution for the social integration of Roma people... As long as they do not benefit from an optimal level of education, this category of people will always be on a lower social level. If Romania and Europe would be focusing on solving the problem of education, their situation could get better" (Brebenel, 2013).

Moreover, the mission of Roma Education Fund Romania (a European NGO) is to "close the gap in educational outcomes between Roma and non-Roma" (Roma Education Fund Romania, 2014).

It has been more than twenty years since Eastern European and Central European countries have started to make the transition towards a market economy. Even though prior to 2007, when Romania entered the European Union, a law existed that granted funded places at universities to Roma students, there weren't any systematic efforts for the education and integration of the Roma population, mainly due to lack of financing. Once Romania entered the EU, the non-for-profit organizations (NGOs) have had the ability to access EU funds for projects aimed at educating Roma people, starting with children, and continuing with youths and adults. O'Higgins (2009) argues that the Roma population has taken the least advantage of the transition towards a market economy - on the contrary, at the macro level they have been excluded both from the labor market and from the social services sector. This chapter aims to bring under discussion the Romanian higher education policies for the Roma students and their role in the formation of a Roma intellectual élite as an important actor in future promotion of the social integration of the Roma minorities.

Problems Related to the Education of Ethnic Minorities Across Central-Eastern European Countries and the USA

Statistics show that the proportion of Roma within certain Eastern and Central European countries is between five to ten percent (European Commission, 2012). There have been multiple unsuccessful attempts of solving the issue of Roma minorities across Europe, which suggests that a new direction is needed, one in which education represents the starting point of any action. Education is an important tool for promoting the social, cultural and economic particularities of the Roma population, including prevention of assimilation, support for Roma's cultural autonomy, and training for occupations that are specific of their tribal groups. Any implementation of an organized system for the education of the members of Roma communities has to consider their (local and regional) socioeconomic and religious status as well as the existence of their specific tribal groups. While most authors agree that Roma people are marginalized (increased unemployment rates, low social status, poor health, households with poor facilities, increased illiteracy among adults and children, feelings of inadequacy in relation to the rest of the population), they pinpoint the importance of synergetic and structural approaches for the advancement of Roma's progress and success. This kind of marginalized phenomena can not be approached nor solved by targeting just one segment of their integration. The progress and success of Roma minorities' education could be achieved by improving their socioeconomic status, with consideration for the national, cultural and religious characteristics that portrait this minority group (Posavec & Hrvatic, 2000).

In Croatia[1] for example, the rate of school non-completion among the Roma population is extremely high, and it is caused by the poverty of the Roma communities (Posavec & Hrvatic, 2000). In addition to socioeconomic factors, pedagogic influences have been identified that explain the low rates of school attendance and the low academic performance: insufficient knowledge of the language, insufficient knowledge at the entry-level, poor personal health and hygiene skills, poor parental involvement, lack of good and encouraging study conditions at home, lack of teachers who speak the Romani language, peer rejection, and their poorly defined national identity. The same issues identified by the Croatian specialists are also encountered amongst the Roma population from Romania. It is believed that specific activities for facilitating the education of Roma individuals are needed at each level of education. More specifically, preventive actions against school non-completion in kindergarten and primary school, interventions in secondary school, and rehabilitation are required (Posavec & Hrvatic, 2000).

In Bulgaria[2], the issue of education of Roma individuals has become a salient point during Bulgaria's transition period from the communist regime to democracy. Problems in this direction occur when trying to change the attitude of the society towards Roma children's bilingualism and cultural differences. It has been shown that it is very important for children in kindergarten and primary school to be taught in their mother language. However, this aspect is poorly addressed in Bulgaria, with regard to Roma children. There are negative attitudes toward providing Roma children with education in the Romani language since the Bulgarian society does not consider that the Romani language is a necessary tool in the cognitive development of the Roma children (Kyuchukov, 2007).

Ball et al. (2002) have analyzed, in a study conducted on 65 students belonging to several ethnic minorities, the decisions these students make regarding their participation in higher education. Two important findings of this study are worth mentioning: the first is that the decision-making process varies across the social classes. The second finding is that, for 25 out of the 65

participants, an important factor in deciding to which institution of higher education to apply is the institution's "ethnic mix".

If nowadays the issue of access to higher education is set in a discourse of ethnic minorities, in the past it was set in a discourse of racial minorities. Moreover, this is not at all a recent issue, and it is encountered all around the globe. In 1947, the USA Commission for Higher Education reported that the percentage of African-American students in higher education was only 3%, whereas their proportion in the general population was 10%. Out of these 3% of African-American students, 85% were enrolled in some segregated institution. In the same year (1947) there were 4000 advanced degrees awarded in the USA, out of which Historically Black College and Universities (HBCUs) awarded only 481. None of the degrees awarded by Black institutions were doctoral degrees. Unsegregated institutions for higher education, however, had awarded, in the same year, 8 doctoral degrees to African-American students, and 3775 to white students (Kephart, 1949).

Harris and Tienda (2010) have examined administrative records from two Texas public universities for the purpose of analyzing the number of applications, admissions, and enrollments in relation to the Affirmative Action policy as well as with the policy of implementation of the top 10% admission rate regime. By means of simulations of the gains and losses in the number of Hispanic and African-American students within each stage of higher education, and comparing those two admission policies, the authors showed that the Affirmative Action policy is the most efficient policy for maintaining ethnic and racial diversity in universities, even within highly segregationist states such as Texas (Harris & Tienda, 2010). Ramey & Suarez (1985) attributed some of the minorities' lower intelligence level to their less than adequate living conditions and to early social difficulties encountered by the minority children. Correlation studies from sociology have generally concluded that the main limiting factor in the educational process of ethnic minorities is their low socioeconomic status (Bond, 1981). Other researchers argue that the obstacles to minorities' education pertain to the differences in language and culture, and the conflicts arising from these differences. Their argument is that minority children are more or less forced to get educated in an environment that is very different from their own, in terms of culture and language (Philips, 1976).

What is the Current Situation of Roma Minority Regarding their Education?

It is common knowledge that education is directly related to income level, hence the explanation for the poverty of the Roma population from this part of Europe is pretty straightforward: they have a significantly lower level of education, compared to the majority populations within this area. To make things worse, Roma employees have lower wages than employees with similar positions but of different ethnicity, regardless of their gender (O'Higgins, 2009). According to the most recent census (2011), there are approximately 620 000 Roma living in Romania at the moment; however, there are many other Roma people who have emigrated to other European countries. Therefore, in the remaining of this chapter we will refer to Roma population as those who actually live in Romania, unless stated otherwise.

An important question is what is the perception of the majority of Roma minority population and how it is formed. Why are Roma people viewed as uneducated and why so many of them are illiterate? What exactly influences their decision to avoid going to school? Zamfir (2013) argues that negative perceptions of the majority population towards the Roma minority still prevails, mostly because its communities are closed, and have a strong traditional culture. From a social standpoint, however, Roma's relations with the majority population are rather symbiotic. Concerning their economic integration, in most cases they

continue to practice their traditional handicraft trade, or take low paid jobs characterized by low social status that is associated with them. The fact that Roma people are socially and economically disadvantaged may be explained both by their low education level and high levels of discrimination against them (O'Higgins, 2009). Roma populations who have a low socioeconomic status and a marginalized traditional life style are being pushed towards the lower levels of the society, where they form homogeneous communities. However, Roma people who manage to grasp the flow of modern life are being easily accepted and integrated within the social boundaries of the population majority (Zamfir, 2012).

In the literature it is argued that the lack of education is, undoubtedly, the major obstacle preventing Roma people from rising (Zamfir, 2012). Most often it is Roma families who take their children out of secondary school, mostly due to poverty. Another explanation for withdrawing 11-12 years old girls from school is their parents' fear of them being tempted to get involved in a romantic relationship outside the realms of the Roma tradition that entails marital arrangements between families to marry their children very young. Roma people's participation in education differs between those who live in compact communities and those who are spread across the country or who declare themselves to be Romanians.

For the last twenty-five years, since the anti-communist revolution, the Romanian society has been trying several methods to educate the Roma population. One of the issues with educating Roma children is that their teachers are not familiar with Roma traditions, Roma linguistic and cultural particularities; meaning, they do not possess the necessary knowledge about Roma people to be able to communicate efficiently with the children's parents and with the children themselves. Tamas (2012) discusses this issue in his paper on Roma children/s attitudes towards education and in particular of those Roma children who live in European or North American countries and whose parents are immigrants. The low frequency of class attendance is a major problem for these children, which is recognized by the teachers. Because Roma people place very little value on education, they don't seem to feel that attending school regularly is important and they do not understand very well the medium- and long-term effects of absenteeism. Unfortunately, often-prolonged absenteeism leads to school dropout for many of these children (Moise, 2013, September 19). At the moment there are no data available on whether school dropout rates are higher for Roma children who go to mass schools where they study together with children from the majority population, or for those who attend schools that are placed in areas where compact Roma communities live, and which are attended only by Roma children.

Romanian Educational Policies Regarding Higher Education for Roma Minorities

Romanian society has attempted many times to keep Roma children in school, either through governmental policies driven by The Ministry of National Education, or through projects carried out by local communities or NGO's. There are some positive results, but major changes regarding the quality of life of Roma ethnics in Romania are happening slowly and over longer periods of time. The most criticized aspect of Romanian policies for Roma minority integration is that these policies were implemented in a sporadic manner, mainly by NGO's, with no sustenance from established public policies, at the national level (Zamfir, 2012).

Although Romanian higher education can be traced back between the 16th and 17th centuries, the first two Romanian modern universities were founded in 1860 and 1864 in Iasi and Bucharest, respectively. Its sinuous track from then on until 1990 is mainly accounted for by socioeconomic factors as well as the historical and geographical context. The December 1989 Revolution that led

to the fall of Communism in Romania, marked the beginning of a restructuring process. Nevertheless, the alignment of Romanian higher education to the European framework is evident: more state and private universities are being founded, the range of academic specialties is increasing, and the number of university students is increasing. According to Mihnea Costoiu, the delegated minister for the higher education, in the year 1995 there were 336,141 students, and in 2012 their number was 464,592 (Pantazi, 2013).

Romanian higher education has three levels: undergraduate (bachelor) studies, master (graduate) studies, and doctoral studies. In the Law of Education from 1995, which has regulated the structure and functioning of national educational system (Title 1 - General Dispositions, Art. 5), it is stated that all Romanian citizens are equally entitled to all forms and levels of education, regardless of financial and social status, gender, race, nationality, and political and religious affiliation. The Law of Education from 2011 adds to the prior stipulations of the right to lifelong learning for all, without any form of discrimination. In Romania, the principles of democratic education are being promoted, and the right to differentiated education based on educational pluralism, is guaranteed. Thus, in Chapter XVIII, Art. 118 it is mentioned that all individuals who belong to national minorities have the right to be educated and trained in their mother tongue language, at all forms and levels of education.

The first legal norm regarding the education of Roma minority had been adopted in Romania in 1992, designating special places in institutions of higher education to Roma people. Accordingly, ten such places were offered to Roma prospective students at the University of Bucharest's department of Social Services, which was intended to create an élite that would attempt at alleviating some of the difficulties faced by this minority (Zamfir, 2012). Consequently, other universities followed the example set by the University of Bucharest in 1995, such as those from Iasi, Cluj-Napoca, and

Timisoara; later on, universities form Oradea, Craiova, and Sibiu followed the lead. Whereas in 1992 only ten places in higher education were offered to Roma young individuals who were interested in following undergraduate studies in Social Services, for the calendar year 2012-2013 the Romanian Government had offered 594 free places in higher education for Roma students. In addition to no tuition fees, Roma students are also offered scholarships and places in the student residences.

Since 1992, the number of places in universities for Roma individuals has been continuously growing, with 49 state universities all over the country providing such places at present. Yet almost a third of these places remain unoccupied every year. The admission criteria are minimal; in fact, Roma people are only required to provide a proof of their ethnicity, a document that can usually be provided by the NGO representing them, whereas regular prospective students may have to take certain admission tests or to have acquired certain grades during high-school or at the national exam. There are split, and often unvoiced, opinions regarding these educational policies. Pantea (2014) argues that because of these policies Roma people are negatively perceived as getting undeserved privileges.

In 1998, the department of Romani Language and Literature was founded at the University of Bucharest. Since then, a number of free places are offered to Roma young individuals at this specialization, every year. Romanian students, who are motivated by the desire to better understand Romani language and culture, and to assist Roma people towards social integration, also follow this specialty. Apparently, Roma students, and especially those who benefit from government-funded places in institutions of higher education, are more likely to come from poor Roma communities and, as Daniela Tutos, the coordinator of Ruhama Foundation's programmes for community development, states, "they receive career guidance mostly from their high-school teachers and not

so much from their parents, since in many cases their parents are illiterate" (personal communication, February 24, 2014). Community traditions and traditional religious institutions within Roma communities might represent an impediment for children's education, since "in their culture girls should marry young and leaving for college might jeopardize their purity". These cultural beliefs might represent an important cause of school dropout because often "married girls are no longer allowed to continue their studies and they are coerced by their families to leave school" [Ioan Lakatos, the president of Bihor Roma's Party and of Ciore Roma NGO; personal communication, February 26, 2014].

Is Free Access to Higher Education for Roma People from Romania a Means Towards Social Inclusion? The Case of Roma Students from the University of Oradea, Romania

A closer look at the profile of Roma individuals with higher education, or Roma scholars, might point out the positive trend regarding the social integration of Roma population through education. Following this line, Zamfir and Zamfir (2012) have shown, on a sample of 192 Roma scholars, that over 45% of Roma individuals with higher education are under 31 years old, and more than 35% are between 31 and 40 years old. In other words, the measures adopted during the last 20 years regarding free schooling at the university level for Roma people have had an enormous impact. Over 50% of the participants in the Zamfir and Zamfir's (2012) study were not married, which is a rather odd thing in their culture, where marriage occurs at a very early age. This finding represents an indicator of educated Roma's desire to dedicate themselves to study while they are very young, and only after should they take the responsibility of starting a family. Moreover, educated Roma people postpone conceiving a child, as opposed to those who drop-out school, who usually get married before the age of 18 and have children while still very young.

In order to better understand the important link between the young Roma scholars and the social integration of Roma minority, we further present some of the findings reported by Zamfir (2012) in the same study mentioned earlier: of the 192 Roma scholars that had participated in the study, 45 had graduated from their studies in Social Services, 20 had graduated in Economics, 18 had graduated in Law, 15 had graduated in Public Administration, and so on. We can therefore ascertain that their studies allow them to work in institutions that can contribute to the improvement of social inclusion of Roma minority or to the improvement of their quality of life. It is known that many children are born in Roma families; however, 129 out of the 192 highly educated Roma individuals included in the study have one, two or three children. In turn, these scholars will be able to ensure better living conditions and a better education for their children, as they face considerably less financial difficulties.

From the total of 620,000 Roma individuals registered in Romania by the 2011 census, 0.56% have a higher education, with women in a higher proportion than men. The percentage of highly educated Roma individuals is, however, considerably small compared to the percentage of illiterate Roma people (over 10% of Roma individuals of age ten or older cannot read). Regarding illiteracy, an important progress has been recorded for the past fifteen years, as the number of illiterate Roma people has dropped by more than 30 percent.

The Case of Roma Students at the University of Oradea, Romania

The vast majority of scientific research on the education of Roma people in Romania focuses mainly on the pre-university level or on policies regarding the education of Roma people in Romania, in general (Butler & Gheorghiu, 2010; Cozma et al., 2010; Georgiadis et al., 2011; McDonald,

2006; Olah, 2009; Roth & Moisa, 2011; Schvey et al., 2005). There are, however, a small number of studies that had investigated the issue of Roma individuals who attend higher education in Romania (Pantea, 2014; Chipea & Bottyan, 2012).

For a clearer understanding of Roma students' attitudes towards higher education, we will be presenting the results of a study conducted at the University of Oradea, a state-university situated in the North-West of Romania. The participants are Roma individuals currently enrolled at one or more of the schools within the University of Oradea. According to the official lists certified at the university level (which are not made public to protect the students' identities), within the last three years, that is between 2011 and 2013, there have been 88 Roma students enrolled on the places held for Roma: 30 (34.1%) students were enrolled in the year 2011-2012, 27 (30.68%) were enrolled in the year 2012-2013, and 31 (35.2%) students were enrolled in the year 2013-2014. Twenty-eight of them (31.8%) are students within the Faculty of Social and Behavioral Sciences (departments of Social Services and Psychology), 23 (26.1%) are Medical students (most of them follow General Practice or Pharmacy), 16 students (18.2%) are studying specializations such as Law, Public Administration, International Relations and European Studies, and the remaining students (23.9%) are enrolled within faculties of Engineering, Economics or Arts.

The study has been approved by the university's board and it aims to identify the attitudes of Roma students towards higher education, their academic self-efficacy, certain difficulties that they have faced, their short-, medium-, and long-term career plans, and also a layout of perceived difficulties that might lead them to cease their studies.

With the help of the university management, in particular the vice-rector for students and students' concerns and social life matters, we contacted (first by phone) the Roma students who were enrolled on government-funded places for the period 2011-2013. Of these 88 students, 40 of them (43.2%)

gave their verbal consent to participate in the study and, thus, to fill out the online questionnaire, 2 (2.27%) persons refused to participate. Out of those forty students who had primarily agreed to participate, unfortunately 21 of them (52.5%) have never returned the questionnaire. Participants' verbal consent (via telephone) was followed by two separate reminders sent via e-mail, first reminder at an interval of 8 days after the first contact (the questionnaire was sent to them in the same day the first contact was made by phone), and the second reminder at an interval of 4 days after the first reminder. However, the 21 students mentioned above have never replied to any of the emails, nor did they return the questionnaire, albeit they were informed about the fact that the study was being conducted under the approval of the university board. Based on our knowledge from past research (e.g., Pantea, 2004) that most Roma students feel uncomfortable with being identified by their professors or fellow students as being of Roma ethnicity, we decided not to summon them in the lab to fill out the questionnaire. We decided to only contact them via telephone and e-mail, to ensure their anonymity as much as possible. The university board provided their contact details. A number of 46 students could not be reached by phone. Although the exact number of students who have dropped out is unknown to us at this point, we know that the dropout rates among Roma students are quite high, thus it is possible that several of the students we were unable to contact are in this situation. In total we have gathered 19 filled out questionnaires.

The low response rate might be surprising. Regarding this issue, Pantea (2014) argues that often the Roma students perceive this affirmative action negatively. When they make the request to be enrolled on government funded places, they need to declare their ethnicity, and not all of them feel comfortable doing so. It might be that the request to participate in the study and possibly the content of the items regarding their academic and familial situation had once more made salient to them their ethnicity, and perhaps this made them feel uncomfortable and possibly ashamed. Even though students were guaranteed the confidentiality of their answers, this seems not to have been reassuring enough for most of them.

The authors for the purpose of the present study created the questionnaire that the students had filled out. The questionnaire consists of five sections, as following: the first section is comprised of socio-demographic questions, such as their age and gender, marital status, familial situation (number of brothers, number of children, if any), their academic specialization, and their parents' education. The second section consists of a measurement of students' attitudes towards education (the semantic differential). The third section consists of items measuring students' academic self-efficiency: the participants were asked to specify, on a 5-point Likert type scale, how confident they are regarding their ability to achieve several educational goals. With the fourth section of the questionnaire we wished to see whether the Roma students have positive academic role models, i.e., other highly educated Roma individuals within their general community, their families or their circle of friends. The last section of the questionnaire represents the qualitative part of our research. In this section we asked students to identify and write the major difficulties that they have encountered during their studies, their short-, medium-, and long-term objectives regarding their academic and professional development, and the major difficulties that they feel they might encounter in the future, which could jeopardize the fulfillment of their previously-mentioned goals and objectives. The findings of our study are presented within the next few paragraphs.

RESEARCH FINDINGS

The socio-demographic characteristics of our sample are as follows: of the total of 19 participants, 14 (73.7%) are female participants and 5 (26.3%)

are male participants, all aged between 19 and 48 years old (with an average age of 28.2 years and a standard deviation of 10.53 years). Most of these students are not married (70.6%). Students who are married (29.4%) have an average age of 44 years old, with a standard deviation of 4.53 years. None of the students who are unmarried have children, and those who are married have between one and four children.

All participants are currently 1st (36.8%), 2nd (26.3%) or 3rd (36.8%) year bachelor students within various academic specializations. Regarding their personal background and the education level of their parents, participants have between zero and five siblings (with 50% having only one sibling and 27.8% having no siblings), and their parents have an average level of education of approximately 11 years, with a standard deviation of approximately 2.5 years.

From the analysis of the socio-demographic characteristics of our participants, we may conclude that Roma young individuals choose to focus on their academic and professional development rather than on following their cultural traditions and start a family at a very early age. Also, they come from families in which the level of education of their parents is, on average, approximately 11

years, which indicates that these parents also value education. Few students also declared that their parents have graduated from high school and some of them had even gained an undergraduate degree.

Next, we were interested in Roma students' attitudes towards education. To measure this, we asked them to rate the word "education" on a 7-point Likert scale in terms of ten pairs of bipolar adjectives that were presented to them in the questionnaire. The averaged ratings for each of the 10 pairs of adjectives are presented in Figure 1. The reader might notice that the average ratings are concentrated on the right half of the scale, i.e., towards the positive end of the continuum. There are several possible explanations for this: either Roma students have, on average, very strong and positive attitudes towards education or their ratings have been affected by social desirability, which we haven't controlled for. Either way, clearly the Roma students have a strong desire to be educated.

The bipolar pair "useless/useful" has the highest ratings on average ($M=6.94$, $SD=0.23$), and the bipolar pair "difficult/easy" has the lowest ratings on average ($M=4.67$, $SD=1.84$). This indicates that Roma students perceive the level of difficulty of their academic training as high enough as to give them a sense of accomplishment and

Figure 1. The averaged responses of students' ratings of the 10 pairs of bipolar adjectives for the word "education" (N=18)

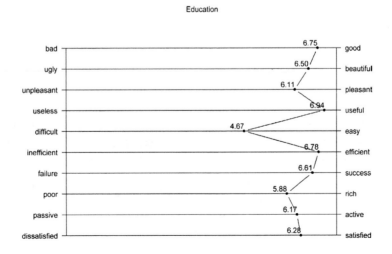

self-worth, but not so high that they would feel incapable to follow. They also evaluate education as being very useful to them. High ratings on average we also find for the pairs "inefficient/efficient" (M=6.78, SD=0.54) and "failure/success" (M=6.61, SD=0.85), which would indicate that Roma students evaluate their education as highly efficient and leading to success.

To sum up the results from the semantic differential, Roma students evaluate their education within the University of Oradea as highly useful, very efficient, fairly difficult, and leading to success.

Regarding Roma students' academic self-efficacy, significantly more students than we would expect by chance said that they were very confident in their ability to pass their exams (61.1%), to graduate from their studies (94.4%), and to gain the necessary skills for practicing their profession (21.1%). Also, significantly more students than we would have expected by chance said that they were confident enough in their ability to assimilate (52.6%) and to understand (47.4%) the information that is presented to them during their lectures and seminars. Five students (26.3%) said that sometimes they are not very confident in their ability to apply in practice the knowledge and abilities that they have gained during their studies. However, this proportion is not significantly higher than the proportions of students who feel very confident about this or who feel confident enough. To summarize this study's results regarding Roma students' academic self-efficacy, we may conclude that significantly more students than we would have expected by chance feel very confident or confident enough in their abilities to perform well academically.

With this study we also wished to see whether Roma students from the University of Oradea know other highly educated Roma individuals and the extent to which these people represent role-models for the students from the University of Oradea. Thus, our results show that when asked whether they know examples of Roma personalities (actors,

singers, etc.) who have higher education, 47.4% indicated that they knew two or more examples, 31.6% indicated that they only knew one example, and 21.1% indicated that they did not know any example. Of those who indicated that they knew at least one example, 26.7% indicated that these individuals very much represent a role model for them, 33.3% - much and a little, and 6.7% indicated that these people do not represent a role model for them at all. These proportions are not significantly different from each other.

When asked whether there are any members in their families who have graduated or who are attending university, 57.9% gave an affirmative answer, and 42.1% gave a negative answer. Of those who indicated that there are highly educated people in their family, 54.5% students indicated that these persons very much represent role models for them, and 9.1% indicated that these persons represents a little or they do not represent at all role models for them. There are no statistically significant differences between these proportions.

When asked whether they have any friends who are highly educated and who are of Roma ethnicity, 52.6% of the students indicated that they have such friends. The variation in answers to the item regarding the extent to which students' Roma highly educated friends represented role models for them is high, thus the differences between proportions are not statistically significant. Apparently, there is a roughly equal proportion of Roma students whose highly educated Roma friends represent role models for them on the one side, and of students whose Roma highly educated friends do not represent role models for them, on the other side.

Perceptions of the Role of the Educational Policies for Roma Students

It is worthwhile to try to understand the motivations and reasoning behind the advancement of such educational policies for Roma young individuals.

We therefore have asked for the opinion of several decision-makers or individuals who are directly involved in this matter and who are very knowledgeable of the issue of Roma students. Hence, Prof. Elena Bonchis, who is a former vice-rector within the University of Oradea and was in charge of students' social matters for almost four years, states the following:

The allocation of funded places within universities for Roma students has been part of the educational policies promoted by the Romanian Government, aimed at reducing school dropout rates among Roma students, at offering them financial and moral support, and at facilitating their subsequent involvement in educational activities and projects within their own communities. [Prof. Elena Bonchis, former vice-rector in charge of students matters within the University of Oradea, Romania; translated from Romanian]

This endeavor happens in a context in which school dropout rates are increasing not only amongst the Roma students' population, but also amongst the general students' population, perhaps due to the poor economy, which leads to financial costs that are hard to manage for many families. In spite of all these efforts to support Roma students, efforts that consist of full funding for the entire duration of their studies, at any specialization of their choice, regardless of their academic results, the dropout rate is still surprisingly high. Students who do not drop might, however, decide to temporarily suspend their studies, for reasons such as the necessity to work in order to provide for their everyday life. Tracking the dropout rates is not as straightforward as it may seems at first glance, mainly because students are given the opportunity to re-enroll after a temporary suspension of their studies.

Regarding Roma's opportunity of having their university studies funded by the Romanian Government, a key leader of the Roma community from Bihor county (whose capital city is Oradea, where the study was conducted), stated:

This initiative is highly regarded. Without these fundings, the proportion of Roma students would be extremely low, due to poverty. Furthermore, students who obtain good results, that is a grade point average above 7.5, can benefit from a special scholarship offered by some NGOs [Ioan Lakatos, the president of Bihor Roma's Party and of Ciore Roma NGO].

When asked about the possible causes of school dropout, Prof. Elena Bonchis argues:

The fact that the Romanian Government covers for the Roma students' tuition fees does not imply that they and their families have sufficient financial resources to support themselves, especially so for families who live outside the city where the university is located. Furthermore, the recession that has installed in our country in the last few years significantly lowers the odds of being employed after graduation. Also, I have noticed in the recent years a growing gap from one generation to another, between students' pre-university academic training, on one hand, and the university curricula and professors' demands, on the other hand. [Translated from Romanian]

Daniela Tutos, the coordinator of the community development programmes within the Ruhama Foundation, believes that creating a Roma intellectual élite might be able to facilitate the education and integration process of poorer Roma communities. Ruhama Foundation is active in Oradea, and its mission is to improve the quality of life for individuals and communities at risk (in Romania, a large proportion of these individuals are Roma). Nevertheless, the Ruhama Foundation together with the University of Oradea has been collaborating on several social programs. When asked about the educational policies for Roma students and about the problem of school dropout, Daniela Tutos states:

The fact that Roma students are given the possibility to study at the higher education level without having to pay for their studies offers them a big advantage, and not because otherwise they would be unable to take an admission exam, but because they come from financially disadvantaged families and they would not afford to bear the costs of their tuition fees. Regarding the causes of dropout, we don't have an exact percentage of students who actually graduate from their studies. From our interviews with Roma students, the main reason for dropout is the lack of money to support the day-by-day life. Then it's the discrimination. We have students who feel discriminated both by their fellow students and by their teachers. [Translated from Romanian].

With regards to discrimination, a University of Oradea alumnus (I. S.), who graduated the faculty of Social Humanistic Sciences, with specialization in Social Work is pleased with the fact that the discrimination against him during high school, which he felt was hurtful and unfair, is not at University level. He states that:

To my surprise, my fellow classmates didn't have any problem with me being a Roma. I was often seen as the "go to" person for information related to our course assignments. Moreover, they even proposed me as the year-leader, but I refused the position, mainly because of my rather negative past experience with being the class leader during my entire high-school period. [I. S., University of Oradea alumnus; translated from Romanian].

I. S. is one of the students whom the system hasn't failed and who was not discouraged by the financial difficulties. As he himself had said when he talked about his desire to finish his studies, he had the proper motivation and desire to do so, in spite of the difficulties. Due to a certain situation that he had encountered in his life, he was a rather prudent person: he had learned not to make long-term plans during high school, but instead to follow through with short-term (1-2 years) objectives. What has followed is the result of successes that he already had, and of battles that he has already won. He put a real effort into accomplishing his mission, that of contributing, with the knowledge he has gained, to the improvement of the quality of life of poor Roma communities.

Not all Roma students' experiences are success stories. In her attempt of finding possible solution for this problem, Daniela Tutos, program-coordinator within the Ruhama Foundation, talks about the difficulties faced by Roma people, as herself and her colleagues have witnessed:

Many of the Roma students need tutoring. They need someone to work with them individually, according to their personal needs. They need these tutoring sessions because they face diverse and novel situations, which they are not able to cope with.

Ioan Lakatos, one of the Roma leaders in Bihor County, talks about the shortcomings of those policies, as they are viewed as extremely important by all those involved:

The Government should focus its attention more on the Roma young people who really want to study and who are finishing their studies, maybe being helped, also, by different NGOs. If it would create an opportunity for them to have jobs in Roma communities or Roma colonies, then Roma social inclusion and education would be quicker and more efficient. We know that Roma people living in the colonies are more open to other Roma people to enter the colony as educators and health mediators, compared to Romanian ones. I am confident that Governmental representatives are aware of it, but there is no political will to finish the process of Roma social inclusion. [Ioan Lakatos, the president of Roma Party and the president of Ciore Roma NGO]

Free access to higher education for Roma people is a solution to the problem of their social inclusion, however we need to ensure a fertile ground for it to be a complete success; it would be better if efforts were made to prevent school dropout among Roma young pupils, an idea consistent with the findings of Posavec and Hrvatic (2000). Likewise, children with academic potential should be identified early on, and guided towards proper schools. Free access to higher education would no longer be perceived as just another form of *unconditional support to Roma people*, but as a real opportunity for personal and professional growth. For hundreds of years Roma people have benefited from unconditional support without acknowledging the full utility and the real necessity of the help they were given, hence this tactic of social integration has pretty much failed so far. As an example, in spite of the "Bread stick and milk" programme, a Governmental normative act running since 2007 through which a bread stick and a cup of fresh milk is offered every day to each child in primary school, the rate of school dropout is still high among Roma children.

Can Roma Élites Facilitate the Integration of Roma Minority in a European Society?

The participation of Roma young individuals in the implementation of European projects that have the purpose of facilitating the integration of the Roma minority, contributes to the expansion of the Roma scholars' perspective from one that is focused on the local community, to one that is focused on the integration in the European society. Pantea (2014) talks about Roma students' sense of needing to "give something back" to society, as the result of the educational policies of funded places in universities for Roma students. According to the study, the leaders of Roma NGOs often send the message to Roma students that they ought to support their community subsequent to their graduation.

We do not believe the motive of giving back to the community is purely extrinsic. Young graduates do empathize with the members of their community who haven't had the chance to participate in higher education. Moreover, students often find at least some moral support within these foundations, thus they certainly have a genuine desire to remain close to those who have offered them support, consistent with the *social exchange theory* (Thibaut & Kelly, 1959). This "need to stay" is more related to students' emotional comfort and to the strong relationships that they had built with people who understand their struggles.

This view is shared by I.S., who believes that:

... an individual who comes from a community with a low social and economic status, and who has an intimate understanding of the vulnerabilities of that community, ought to find ways to contribute with the knowledge and skills that they have gained, regardless of their professional specialization, to the development of their community, to support their community, and to be a role-model for the members of their community. Their role is to help in finding ways of improving the well being of facilitating the prosperity of the community in which they belong. [I.S. University of Oradea alumnus, Social Work diploma; translated from Romanian].

He goes on to talk about the period following the graduation of his studies in social work: "I graduated from university in 2009, after which, in 2010, I was employed by the Ruhama Foundation as a social worker to help with its ongoing social and educational programs" [I.S., University of Oradea alumnus; translated from Romanian].

Young Roma students' intrinsic motivation of giving back to the community might also be explained by the fact that a large proportion of them choose to follow one of the medical specializations or social work. It might be that their role models are social workers responsible with supporting their communities and the medical personnel, which lately have played an important role in educational programs for health implemented within the poorer and/or Roma communities.

The Roma leader, Ioan Lakatos, also speaks about the NGO's expectations toward the Roma students to "give something back" to the community:

Yes, I do believe that there are some expectations that they should go back in the community, to support it, but the Government doesn't create jobs for them. It is suitable that they get a job at the town halls, where the local population lives in poverty, with low resources and without access to education. [Ioan Lakatos, the president of Bihor Roma's Party and of Ciore Roma NGO].

The positive experience during his studies, the feeling of accomplishment, the need to prove that he can do better, and perhaps his desire to find his calling, has made I.S. determined to follow his artistic inclinations and to enroll into the program of a prestigious Romanian school of Theatre where, although he is the only Roma student in his class, he does not feel discriminated or marginalized. The Roma people's propensity for the arts is well known and the Romanian culture is rich in prestigious artists of Roma ethnicity: Johnny Raducanu - international jazz performer, Damian Draghici, whose band is promoting Gypsy's traditional songs and dance all over the world, Anca Parghel, also a jazz singer, Madalin Voicu, music performer and politician, etc.

Roma Students' Suggested Solutions and Recommendations

Recent studies have collected data on the issue of Roma students' attitudes towards government-funded places in higher education by targeting

them directly. For example, Pantea (2014) analyzed 57 in-depth interviews with Roma students at several Romanian universities regarding the affirmative action and their perception of the importance of these policies, but also the tensions that these policies create. The author argues that Roma students who are enrolled on government funded places are faced with two kinds of dilemmas: the first dilemma arises from their perception that they are being put in the situation of having to "give back" or to return the investment in some way, and the other arises from the tacit imperative of having to disclose their ethnicity. Pantea's (2014) study concludes that the policy of funded places is inclusive and debilitating in the same time, since it produces social costs for Roma students who come from a stigmatized social group.

Chipea and Bottyan (2012) have also analyzed the issue of Roma students from the University of Oradea. Data analysis on the number of enrolled Roma students, their age, gender and faculty, together with the data gathered through interviews, indicate that Roma students from the University of Oradea are facing problems related to poverty, which forces them to find a job. A significant number of Roma students talk about how little support they have received from the community and NGOs, and also about the low academic level in their high schools.

The students also mention the issue of discrimination against Roma individuals, with regards to their ethnicity. However, I.S. expressed the view that he had not experienced discrimination during university studies, compared to the discrimination he faced on the streets and in public spaces, where, he said "I feel that I am being watched by the bodyguards from the shops or I am being called: hey, Gypsy guy!". Such discrimination is experienced and perceived in different ways by Roma students, varied from real dramas to life lessons:

The fact that I was surrounded by rich people who used to wear fancy and expensive clothes made me feel very humiliated during classes or during the whole time I was at the university. Because everyone was avoiding me, [...] I was determined to go through with it, to prove them that a Roma student can be as good as any other Romanian student, or even better! [a Law student].

Roma students have medium- and long-term objectives: "I would like to open a care center for elderly people", says a student, "I want to be a doctor", says e medical student, "I am planning on following a master's program", says a Psychology student, and a Law student says:

As an attorney, I would like to work with an NGO in order to be able to encourage as many Roma children as possible to fight to earn their respect and not to give up, and to show everybody that we are all equal, regardless of our ethnicity or religious views. We are different, but equal!

Participants in our study point out that discrimination and poverty are main reasons for encountering difficulties during their studies, thus eliminating or at least reducing the impact of these factors would be important. Regarding the issue of poverty, a feasible solution could be addressed by policies for government-funded places together with access to scholarship and accommodation facilities in the university campuses. Regarding the issue of discrimination, in Romania there is an institution called The National Council for Combating Discrimination that advocates for equality among people and for the abolition of discriminatory practices. There is also a need for continuous actions to inform people about the equality of rights, and about the consequences of violating these principles.

FUTURE RESEARCH DIRECTION

Insofar as defining the problems faced by the young Roma people who want to pursue higher educa-

tion in Romania and other Central and Eastern European countries who are hosting them, there is a need for evidence base. Their problems and difficulties are the product of poverty, discrimination and ancestral traditions and all these make the access and retention of young Roma in academia more difficult. They also lack an understanding of the rules of society, other than the Roma community. Unfortunately, at least some societies, Romania included, are not ready to nurture the young Roma people, the future Roma élite that will be the engine of the Roma social integration through education.

There is also a need to analyze the significant predictors that have the power to explain the academic success and the academic and career self-efficacy of Roma students, in order to indicate to the decision-makers the exact needs of these people and the possible solutions to their problems. The results of such research have to be made known in the geographical and political area of interest, in order to increase decision-makers' awareness.

CONCLUSION

Attempts are being made to achieve social integration of Roma people by enabling them to enter the labor market, but with little success. Despite of the several initiatives funded by NGOs (e.g., the Ruhama Foundation, the Roma Education Fund), the number of Roma participants to these projects is small, as indicated by the high rates of unemployment, namely 51% for individuals between 15-64 years of age and 73% for individuals between 15-24 years of age (The World Bank/ European Commission statistics, 2011). Material and social support are provided for those who did not succeed in attaining a job. This scenario has the shape of an endless loop.

We believe that the education of the Roma people and the creation of a nontrivial Roma élite could be the foundation for socially integrating the Roma minority. This élite will encounter less difficulties in getting employment, they will represent positive role-models for other members of their community, they will be better informed, and will have a positive attitude towards education and its roles. As O'Higgins (2009) mentioned, those who benefit the least from the transition towards European integration are the Roma people; they continue to have low employment rates and low economic status, and the most likely explanation for this is, again, their low level of education. Even though the labor market has been expanding, illiteracy, ethnic discrimination and / or lack of education makes it almost impossible for them to get a job. Needless to say, there is a severe need for action that increases the educational attainment among the Roma population, and to eliminate the discrimination against them especially regarding their chances of being employed and their economic status.

As we have already argued, education is a paramount factor in the social integration of the Roma minority. The policy of free access to higher education for Roma individuals has the role of facilitating their educational process and creating élites that will be able to change the lives of Roma people, but these policies must be complemented by influences at social, educational and political levels, and by actions coming from non-for-profit organizations. Keeping records of the rate of school dropout should lead to the adoption of new measures of prevention, other than those that were attempted in the past, by which Roma people were granted several facilities without informing them about, and making them aware of the role and importance of these facilities for their social integration. It is not enough to merely tell a young mother, who herself has completed no more than the fourth class, that she must send her children to school because in Romania the first ten years of school are mandatory by law. It is important that she understands *why* it is so important to send her children to school, insofar as their own laws, their own court of law called "Stabor", does not

sanction parents for not sending their children to school, and they do not acknowledge other laws other than their own. Provided that social assistance alone is not a viable solution for their social integration issues, we believe that coherent and articulated educational policies can be, and we hope that this will be proven in the years to come.

REFERENCES

Ball, S. J., Reay, D., & David, M. (2002). Ethnic choosing: Minority ethnic students, social class and higher education choice. *Race, Ethnicity and Education*, 5(4), 333–357.

Bond, G. C. (1981). Social economic status and educational achievement: A review article. *Anthropology & Education Quarterly*, 12(4), 227–257. doi:10.1525/aeq.1981.12.4.05x1811q

Brebenel, A. (2013, April 22). Mariana campeanu: "Education is the only solution for integrating Roma people". *Adevarul*. Retrieved from http://adevarul.ro/news/societate/marianacampeanu-singura-solutie-integrarea-romilor-esteeducatia-1_517509d0053c7dd83f3464c4/index.pdf

Butler, M., & Gheorghiu, L. (2010). Exploring the failure to protect the rights of the Roma child in Romania. *Public Administration and Development*, 30(4), 235–246. doi:10.1002/pad.562

Chipea, F., & Bottyan, Z. (2012). Issues regarding the integration of young Roma in higher education: Qualitative analysis at University of Oradea. In T. Kozma & K. Bernath (Eds.), *Higher education in the Romania-Hungary cross-border cooperation area* (pp. 73–85). Oradea, Romania: Partium Press.

Cozma, T., Cucos, C., & Momanu, M. (2010). The education of Roma children in Romania: Description, difficulties, solutions. *Intercultural Education*, 11(3), 281–288. doi:10.1080/14675980020002439

Dobrica, P., & Jderu, G. (2005). *The academic education of Roma children: Socio-cultural determinants.* UNICEF. Retrieved from http://www. unicef.org/romania/ro/Educatie_romi.pdf

European Commission. (2012). *National Roma integration strategies: A first step in the implementation of the EU framework.* Belgium: European Commission. Retrieved from http://ec.europa.eu/ justice/discrimination/files/roma_nat_integration_strat_en.pdf

Flecha, R., & Soler, M. (2013). Turning difficulties into possibilities: Engaging Roma families and students in school through dialogic learning. *Cambridge Journal of Education, 43*(4), 451–465. doi:10.1080/0305764X.2013.819068

Foszto, L., & Anastasoaie, M. V. (2001). Romania: Representations, public policies and political projects. In W. Guy (Ed.), Between past and future: The Roma of Central and Eastern Europe. University of Hertfordshire Press.

Georgiadis, F., Nikolajevic, D., & van Driel, B. (2011). Evaluating a project on Roma education. *Intercultural Education, 22*(1), 105–113. doi:10 .1080/14675986.2011.549649

Harris, A., & Tienda, M. (2010). Minority higher education pipeline: Consequences of changes in college admissions policy in Texas. *The Annals of the American Academy of Political and Social Science, 627*(1), 60–81. doi:10.1177/0002716209348740 PMID:23077374

Kephart, W. M. (1949). Minority group discrimination in higher education. *Journal of Educational Sociology, 23*(1), 52–57. doi:10.2307/2264358

Kyuchukov, H. (2007). Good practices in Roma education in Bulgaria during the years of transition. *Intercultural Education, 18*(1), 29–39. doi:10.1080/14675980601143645

Marin, L. (2012). *Contemporary challenges in accessing high quality education for Roma children.* Retrieved from http://romaeducationfund. ro/download/Policy%20Brief%205%20--%20 Politici%20educationale%20pentru%20romi%20 in%20context%20FSE-POSDRU.pdf

McDonald, C. (2006). Roma in the Romanian educational system: Barriers and leaps of faith. European. *Journal of Intercultural Studies (Melbourne, Vic.), 10*(2), 183–200.

Miskovic, M. (2009). Roma education in Europe: In support of the discourse of race. *Pedagogy, Culture & Society, 17*(2), 201–220. doi:10.1080/14681360902934442

Moise, I. (2013, September 19). UNICEF, the Cilibia school, and the fight against school dropout. *Sanatatea buzoiana.* Retrieved from http://www. sanatateabuzoiana.ro/

O'Higgins, N. (2009). *It's not that I'm racist, it's that they are Roma: Roma discrimination and returns to education in South Eastern Europe.* IZA discussion papers, No 4208. Retrieved from http:// nbn-resolving.de/um:nbn:de:101:1-2009061932

O'Nions, H. (2010). Divide and teach: Educational inequality and the Roma. *International Journal of Human Rights, 14*(3), 464–489. doi:10.1080/13642980802704304

Olah, S. (2009). The school dropout in Bihor County: A qualitative approach. *Revista Universitara de Sociologie, 1*(11), 95–128.

Pantazi, R. (2013, October 1). Mihnea Costoiu, the delegated minister for the higher education: The number of students in public universities has grown by approximately 10% from last year. *HotNews.* Retrieved from http://www.hotnews. ro/stiri-esential-15701687-mihnea-costoiu-ministrul-delegat-pentru-invatamant-superior-numarul-studentilor-universitatile-publice-crescut-aproximativ-10-fata-anul-trecut.htm

Pantea, M.-C. (2014). Affirmative action in Romania's higher education: Roma students' perceived meanings and dilemmas. *British Journal of Sociology of Education.* doi:10.1080/014256 92.2013.869172

Philips, S. U. (1976). Access to power and maintenance of ethnic identity as goals of multicultural education: Are they compatible? *Anthropology & Education Quarterly, 7*(4), 30–32. doi:10.1525/ aeq.1976.7.4.05x1657s

Posavec, K., & Hrvatic, N. (2000). Intercultural education and Roma in Croatia. *Intercultural Education, 11*(1), 93–105. doi:10.1080/14675980050005424

Ramey, C. T., & Suarez, T. M. (1985). Early intervention and the early experience paradigm: Toward a better framework for social policy. *Journal of Children in Contemporary Society, 17*(1), 1–13. doi:10.1300/J274v17n01_01

Roma Education Fund Romania. (2014, August 7). *Mission.* Retrieved from http://romaeducationfund.ro/en/

Roth, M., & Moisa, F. (2011). The right to education of Roma children in Romania. *International Journal of Children's Rights, 19*(3), 501–522. doi:10.1163/157181811X584587

Schvey, A., Flaherty, M., & Higgins, T. (2005). The children left behind: Roma access to education in contemporary Romania. *Fordham International Law Journal, 29*(6), 1155–2006.

Tamas, J. (2001). A hidden minority becomes visible Romani refugee children in the schools. *Childhood Education, 77*(5), 295–302. doi:10.1 080/00094056.2001.10521653

Thibaut, J. W., & Kelley, H. H. (1959). *The social psychology of groups.* New York: Wiley.

Vlase, I., & Voicu, M. (2013). Romanian Roma migration: The interplay between structures and agency. *Ethnic and Racial Studies.* doi:10.1080/ 01419870.2013.809133

Zamfir, E. (2013). Roma people within the global process of change. *Revista de Cercetare si Interventie Sociala, 40,* 149–165.

Zamfir, E., & Burtea, V. (2012). *The present and future perspectives of Roma culture from the perspective of Roma intellectuals, leaders, and other successful individuals.* Bucharest: The Press, Typography, and Distribution PPB Group.

ADDITIONAL READING

Achim, V. (2004). *The Roma in Romanian history.* Budapest: Central European University Press.

Cahn, C., Chirico, D., McDonald, C., Mohacsi, V., Peric, T., & Szekely, A. (1998). Roma in the educational systems of Central and Eastern Europe. *European Roma Rights Centre Report.* Retrieved from http://www.errc.org/article/roma-and-the-right-to-education--roma-in-the-educational-systems-of-central-and-eastern-europe/53

Cretan, M., & Turnock, D. (2008). Romania's Roma population: From marginality to social integration. *Scottish Geographical Journal, 124*(4), 274–299. doi:10.1080/14702540802596608

Csepeli, G., & Simon, D. (2004). Construction of Roma identity in Eastern and Central Europe: Perception and self-identification. *Journal of Ethnic and Migration Studies, 30*(1), 129–150. doi:10.1080/1369183032000170204

Dorius, S. (2013). The rise and fall of worldwide education inequality from 1870 to 2010: Measurement and trends. *Sociology of Education, 86*(2), 158–173. doi:10.1177/0038040712456558

Herakova, L. (2009). Identity, communication, inclusion: The Roma and (new)Europe. *Journal of International and Intercultural Communication*, 2(4), 279–297. doi:10.1080/17513050903177318

Kelso, M. (2013). 'And Roma were victims, too': The Romani genocide and Holocaust education in Romania. *Intercultural Education*, 24(1), 61–78. doi:10.1080/14675986.2013.768060

Kyuchukov, H. (2011). Roma girls: Between traditional values and educational aspirations. *Intercultural Education*, 22(1), 97–104. doi:10.1080/14675986.2011.549648

Stulberg, L., & Chen, A. (2013). The origins of race-conscious affirmative action in undergraduate admissions: A comparative analysis of institutional change in higher education. *Sociology of Education*, 87(1), 36–52. doi:10.1177/0038040713514063 PMID:25309003

Thornton, G. (2014). The outsiders: Power differentials between Roma and non-Roma in Europe. *Perspectives on European Politics and Society*, 15(1), 106–119. doi:10.1080/15705854.2013.873260

Zamfir, C., & Preda, M. (2002). *The Roma in Romania*. Bucharest: Expert.

Zamfir, E., & Zamfir, C. (1993). *Roma between ignorance and concern*. Bucharest: Alternative.

KEY TERMS AND DEFINITIONS

Affirmative Action: civic actions in favor of those who are victims of discrimination.

Discrimination: unfair and prejudiced behavior towards particular people or groups of people, based on their ethnicity, race, religion, sexual orientation, etc.

Minority Group: a sociological demographic category, different from the majority group and defined in relation to it. The differentiation of a minority group from the majority group can be based on a human characteristic, their relative frequency in the population, or lower social power.

NGO: an organization that is not part of the Government or any profiting business. NGOs may be founded by the Government, foundations, natural persons, or private businesses.

Roma People from Romania: also known as "tzigani", they represent a minority population in Romania, approximately 3% of the entire population of Romania. They have settled down in Romania in the 10th century.

School Dropout: the act of withdrawing or abandoning one's studies before completion of the current instruction level.

Social Inclusion: giving civic rights to all members and groups of a society, rights regarding job opportunities, health and social protection, education, living conditions, etc.

ENDNOTES

[1] A unitary democratic parliamentary republic at the crossroads of Central Europe, Southeast Europe, and the Mediterranean, member of the EU from 1st July, 2013.

[2] EU member from 1st January 2007, Bulgaria is a South-Eastern European country, a unitary parliamentary republic with a high degree of political, administrative, and economic centralization.

Chapter 12
International Student Perceptions of Ethics in a Business Pathway Course

Donna M. Velliaris
Eynesbury Institute of Business and Technology, Australia

Craig R. Willis
University of Adelaide, Australia

Janine M. Pierce
University of South Australia, Australia

ABSTRACT

To attract a growing number of international students, Higher Education (HE) institutions are striving to differentiate themselves from their competitors. The Eynesbury Institute of Business and Technology (EIBT) is part of a growing number of private providers partnering with universities to establish "pathway" programs. EIBT offers a Diploma of Business leading to either The University of Adelaide or the University of South Australia's degree programs in business-related fields. This chapter investigates EIBT students' own perceptions of "ethics" in a major assessment task embedded in a course titled "Business and Society". The findings, taken from students' reflective papers, reveal their understanding(s) of ethical behaviour and are particularly relevant to contemporary debates surrounding how to improve educational attainment and ethical standards given the emerging importance of partner providers amidst rising numbers of international students seeking HE in Australia and abroad. 10.4018/978-1-4666-7244-4.ch012

INTRODUCTION

International students play a vital and increasing role in the internationalisation of Higher Education (HE). In order for them to succeed in their academic study and for the host nation to continue to attract greater numbers of overseas students, social, cultural and educational issues must be addressed (Zhang & Mi, 2010). For example, international students need to meet the same challenges their Australian peers face while navigating a new cultural terrain, an education

DOI: 10.4018/978-1-4666-7244-4.ch012

system with different rules and expectations than in their home country, and often in English as an Additional Language (EAL). They may experience difficulty adjusting to Western (a) *pedagogical* practices such as peer-assisted, problem-based, real-world, self-directed, and student-centred approaches (Velliaris & Warner, 2009, p. 1) and (b) *dialogical* practices such as critiquing, debating, persuading, questioning, and refuting (Major, 2005, p. 85). Rigorous academic demands together with adjusting to a new culture has the potential to place those students at "greater risk of academic failure" (Li & Gasser, 2005, p. 562).

BACKGROUND

Eynesbury Institute of Business and Technology (EIBT)

The Eynesbury Institute of Business and Technology (EIBT) is one of a growing number of private providers linking up with partner universities to establish programs that create opportunities to promote Australian HE globally. The main objective of pathway providers is to attract international students early in their education lifecycle and secure their tertiary destination prior to them meeting

entrance requirements (Fiocco, 2006; Velliaris & Willis, 2014). EIBT has established pre-university pathways and offers the same courses that constitute the first-year of a Bachelor of Business, Information Technology, or Engineering at the destination university.

Specifically, EIBT's Diploma of Business leads to nine Bachelor of Business degree programs at *The University of Adelaide* when students achieve an average of 65% across all eight courses (Table 1). Consistently ranked in the top 1% of universities worldwide, the Business School specialises in Accounting, Finance, International Business, Management and/or Marketing, with degree programs accredited by the Association to Advance Collegiate Schools of Business (AACSB) International. This accreditation represents the highest standard of achievement for business schools worldwide and is only achieved by 5% of universities globally (The University of Adelaide, 2014).

EIBT's Diploma of Business leads to 13 Bachelor of Business degree programs at the *University of South Australia* when students achieve a minimum Grade Point Average (GPA) of 4.0 across all eight courses (Table 2). The state's largest and one of the nation's premier business schools, it offers a diverse range of degrees that have been

Table 1. EIBT diploma requirements for The University of Adelaide business degree programs (2013-2014)

EIBT Pathway	Business Degree Programs
6 Core Courses: ■ Accounting for Business ■ Accounting Method 1 (Pre-requisite: Accounting for Business) ■ Foundations of Business Law ■ Management Principles ■ Marketing Principles: Trading & Exchange ■ Quantitative Methods for Business 2 Electives from the following 3 Courses: ■ Business & Society ■ Communication & Information Systems in Business ■ Principles of Economics	1. Bachelor of Commerce 2. Bachelor of Commerce (Accounting) 3. Bachelor of Commerce (Corporate Finance) 4. Bachelor of Commerce (International Business) 5. Bachelor of Commerce (Management) 6. Bachelor of Commerce (Marketing) 7. Bachelor of Economics 8. Bachelor of Finance 9. Bachelor of Finance (International)

Table 2. EIBT diploma requirements for University of South Australia business degree programs (2013-2014)

EIBT Pathway	Business Degree Programs
8 Core Courses: ■ Accounting for Business ■ Business & Society ■ Communication & Information Systems in Business ■ Foundations of Business Law ■ Management Principles ■ Marketing Principles: Trading & Exchange ■ Principles of Economics ■ Quantitative Methods for Business	1. Bachelor of Applied Finance 2. Bachelor of Business (International Business, Finance & Trade) 3. Bachelor of Business (Property) 4. Bachelor of Business Administration 5. Bachelor of Commerce 6. Bachelor of International Relations 7. Bachelor of Management 8. Bachelor of Management (Human Resource Management) 9. Bachelor of Management (Logistics & Supply Chain Management) 10. Bachelor of Management (Marketing) 11. Bachelor of Marketing & Communication 12. Bachelor of Sport & Recreation Management 13. Bachelor of Tourism & Event Management

created in collaboration with industry to equip graduates with a competitive mix of knowledge, skills and experience to embrace a successful career in Commerce, Law, Management and/or Marketing. It is one of eight Australian business schools accredited by the European Quality Improvement System (EQUIS) (University of South Australia, 2014).

EIBT serves as a bridge to degree-level studies and offers an extended period of academic preparation for entrance into HE, with specific focus on the preparation of students who may be deemed "lower-level" in terms of their language proficiency and/or previous academic results (Gillett & Wray, 2006, p. 7). Over the years, EIBT students have represented [in alphabetical order]: Bangladesh; China [mainland, Hong Kong and Macau]; Egypt; Fiji; India; Indonesia; Iran; Kenya; Lebanon; Malaysia; Nepal; Nigeria; Oman; Pakistan; Saudi Arabia; Singapore; South Korea; Sri Lanka; Turkey; Vietnam; and Zimbabwe. With a 98% international student demographic—the remaining 2% are "international" students with Australian Permanent Residency (PR)—EIBT lecturers face several "interconnecting" challenges that include, but are not limited to: *acculturating* international students to Australian HE; *confronting* English language-related teaching and learning barriers; and *improving* students' academic integ-

rity and overall academic performance (Velliaris & Willis, 2014).

This chapter is borne out of issues arising from the link between English-language proficiency and discipline-specific HE preparation. Throughout this chapter, the term "international students" or "students" is specific to individuals enrolled in EIBT on temporary student visas and who are almost exclusively Non-English Speaking Background (NESB). "Acculturation" will refer to Redfield et al.'s (1936, p. 149) seminal definition, "those phenomena which result when groups of individuals having different cultures come into continuous first-hand contact with subsequent changes in the original cultural patterns of either or both groups". In attempting to acculturate its international students, EIBT lecturers consider pedagogical practices that address three primary influences: (a) academic English language proficiency; (b) social, cultural, and educational dispositions; and (c) institutional barriers.

Academic English Language Proficiency

For international students from linguistic backgrounds other than mainstream English, rapid HE disciplinary acculturation is often through EAL. Problems may arise, however, from differences in the linguistically determined discourse of intercultural/interpersonal communication and the cultural distance of such patterns (Campbell & Li, 2008, p. 376). In order to acquire appropriate skills, international students must first recognise that their existing knowledge and abilities—based on learning in their home culture—may not suffice. Difficulties in assessing independent learning notwithstanding, getting them to articulate their learning needs, related to issues of "self-efficacy" (Bandura, 1994), is in itself problematic. That is, they may not be aware of their needs and it is, therefore, through inclusive pedagogical practices that they can come to connect with the academic literacies of their chosen discipline and become acculturated to Australian HE (Russell, 1991; Velliaris & Warner, 2009).

By virtue of their entry into a new societal and organisational culture, international students may face the dilemma of performing below their true capabilities. As Sawir (2005, p. 568) posited, it is inevitable that they will be predisposed to the "kinds of pedagogies that were used before coming to Australia". Angelova and Riazantseva's (1999) work emphasised how international students would benefit from explicit dialogue concerning the expectations of the discourse community. The reality is that when international students are faced with discipline-specific academic texts their ability to process information may become overshadowed by language-related barriers. An enormous array of higher-order vocabulary has most likely been woven into sophisticated works that are "culturally bound" (Corson, 1997, p. 673). The culture of academic literacy is, therefore, frequently a product of institutional forces and experiences not shared by all cultures. Accordingly, they are hardly logical and rational in every setting, because they represent sectional interests' (Corson, 1997, p. 675).

Academic staff may regard the principles inherent in their discipline as apparent and for that reason, expectations about learning and assessment as examples, are not made entirely explicit (McLean & Ransom, 2005). Limited

aptitude to think critically and to write in a non-native language places international students at a disadvantage and may substantially increase their workload (Hayes & Introna, 2005). In particular, international students' English language proficiency may cause some academics to consider them a "homogeneous group of learners" (Chalmers & Volet, 1997, p. 87) and to some extent "remedial" in ability level. In the absence of any guidance and/or positive affirmation, "[international] students often accept and internalise misinformed negative views of themselves as lacking in initiative, linguistically impoverished, and passive or rote learners' (Dawson & Bekkers, 2002, p. 2). Lecturers may encourage international students to "use their own words" and though well-intended, this advice is not likely to produce instantaneous results i.e., academically precise writing. The English language proficiency scores that allow international students to enter into Australian HE are no guarantee that they are capable of applying that level of English to discipline-specific learning (McGowan, 2005a, 2005b).

Social, Cultural and Educational Dispositions

International students transitioning to Western HE—particularly at the undergraduate level—are expected to adjust to discipline-specific language without yet having had exposure to the discipline in question (Velliaris & Warner, 2009). Successful transition into a new educational environment requires adaptation to the teaching and learning culture of the host institution (Hellsten, 2002; Prescott & Hellsten, 2005). However, while international students acquire the latest academic discourse and obtain concepts/skills important for them to become members of the mainstream scholarly community, they inevitably draw on their own cultural resources and rely on previous—natural and more familiar—learning approaches and writing conventions that may not meet the demands of their new scholarly activities. In agreement with

McGowan (2005a, p. 51), when foreign students embark on Western HE, they need to understand that they are entering into a new culture and are becoming members of a "community of scholars". They are about to take their place within a research tradition that involves drawing on evidence from prior research, and one day, potentially having their own work drawn on by others.

While it is not explored in great detail in this chapter, "culture" is implicit in this discussion because of the way in which international students are required to negotiate meaning through interactions within the sociocultural environment, which in this case is the Australian HE context (Bodycott & Walker, 2000, p. 83). In this scenario, the dominant culture is seen in terms of academic expectations and interpretations that are often taken-for-granted. The assumptions embedded in culturally-related "good" or "bad" academic behaviours are developed within a Western context. As such, they may unfairly discriminate against those from non-Western backgrounds. Hence, lack of understanding of the norms of Western academic practices has implications for teaching and learning, and in turn these can impact upon measures to ensure that international students develop effective academic skills.

Hayes and Introna (2005) noted that many international students learn from textbooks and their preference is focused on the "recall" and rote learning of information. In their home country, they may have been taught to "not" challenge the ideas of an expert author (Lund, 2004). That is, in some cultures, students are advised to accept knowledge without exploring and creating new knowledge; merely memorising information by retelling and delivering it in its exact form (Spack, 1998). To them, this is not an act of intentionally falsifying information; these students may not even realise their actions as they already knew the information and did not, therefore, see the need to cite the "original". It is accepted practice to incorporate direct quotations from reading material—but without acknowledgment—as this shows respect, while critical thinking is perceived as a sign of disrespect. Echoing the original work shows that the new author [the student], believes that the work is highly knowledgeable and thus, copying may be a valid strategy. Such a perspective is supported by research into academic misconduct in India. Gitanjali (2004) described academic dishonesty in Indian medical colleges at the undergraduate level as consisting of international students copying from textbooks and more surprisingly, "each other" in examinations. These students may have not previously faced issues surrounding academic integrity until such time as they changed educational institutions.

Anecdotally, there appears to be consensus that international students entering (Australian) HE are under-equipped for tertiary-level studies, and concerns around language together with students' basic academic study skills may be accentuated by their cultural unfamiliarity with Australian pedagogical preferences. HE requires a diverse range of skills: active listening; brain-storming; critical thinking; essay and report writing; effective study habits; independent learning; note-taking; oral presentations; proof reading; referencing; study strategies; and time management as examples (Velliaris & Warner, 2009). International students who lack some or all of these skills are likely to struggle.

Institutional Barriers

Academic acculturation necessitates adjustments on the part of the institution with the goal of creating greater alignment between/among teaching and learning styles, and establishing effective student-teacher partnerships. In promoting effective learning, it is important that international students are made culturally aware, through gradually initiating them into the norms, values, and conventions of the institution (Velliaris & Warner, 2009). Such acculturation better enables and prepares students to understand "otherness" i.e., Australian HE key reference points such as fairness, honesty, respect, responsibility and trust.

Foremost, it is the responsibility of HE educators to clarify their expectations to students of all cultures, which may require differing and numerous attempts and methods. "Firstly, we must make the rules of the game clear to the student and secondly, we must assist them to develop skills and strategies to succeed at this new game" (Leask, 2006, p. 191). For example, it is important for international students to be made aware of accurate citation methods. This can take extra time for lecturers who may feel that they are not English for Specific Purposes (ESP) instructors and should only need to focus on course content rather than the conventions of scholarly writing. However, as McCabe (2005, p. 30) expressed "[j]ust as the African tribal maxim proclaims that *"it takes a village to raise a child"* ...it takes the whole campus community—international students, faculty, and administrators—to effectively educate a student".

Two practices that can increase alignment and bridge the social, cultural and education gaps are "integration" and "scaffolding" (Velliaris & Warner, 2009, pp. 2-3). Integration involves the "process of linking new knowledge to old and modifying and enriching existing knowledge" (Grabinger & Dunlap, 1995, p. 11). By increasing the number of access points international students have to new information, they will be more likely to comprehend and retain new learning. Complementarily, scaffolding can provide exposure to model readings and assignments where evidence of critical thought are explicitly highlighted, thereby reducing ambiguities inherent in the discourse community. Scaffolding can operate at a controlled, guided or independent level, with variation in the degree of exposure to and use of academic English needed to cope with tertiary-level studies (Hawkins, 2008; Turner & Pointon, 2009).

RESEARCH METHODOLOGY

An action research methodology was considered best suited to this study as it involved critical enquiry by a practitioner into their own practice and had the ability to combine "action and reflection, theory and practice" (Reason & Bradbury, 2001, p. 1). Carr and Kemmis' (1986, p. 162) definition of action research stated, "[a] form of enquiry undertaken by participants...to improve rationality and justice of their own social or educational practices, as well as their own understanding of these practices and situations in which these practices are carried out".

This methodology deals with the practices of people—quite often educators within their own setting—with the aim being to improve praxis; either one's own or the effectiveness of an institution (Koshy, 2005, p. 9). Several objectives for achieving this goal include: to *pursue* action in an integrated fashion through a cyclical and participatory process; to *construct* knowledge of specific issues through planning, acting, evaluating, refining and learning from experiences; to *develop* situations under investigation by assessing the quality of teaching and learning, and then enabling new and successful action strategies; and to *aid* in the professional development of educators and their practical theories and competence in action through reflection (Koshy, 2005). Altrichter, Posch, and Somekh (2000, p. 4) stressed that action research directs attention to one of the most essential motives for conducting research; to improve the quality of teaching and learning as well as the conditions under which staff and students work.

Carr and Kemmis (1986) viewed action research as empowering practitioners to take control of the development of their own educational practice(s). Elliott (1991) considered action research to be essential in the development of schools as flexible and dynamic learning environments, and crucial to "genuine" school improvement. Action research is intended, therefore, to support educators to cope with pedagogical challenges and then to relay new insights for the purpose of contributing to the knowledge base of their profession. This involves an iterative process whereby practitioners and researchers collaborate together on a particular cycle of activities encompassing: (a) *problem diagnosis*; (b) *action intervention*; and (c) *reflective learning* (Avison, et al., 1999).

To help readers better understand the complex and rapidly changing nature of Australian HE in an era of increasing globalisation, this chapter examines EIBT international students' own perceptions of "ethics" in response to an undergraduate first-year level assessment task delivered by one author in mid-2013. EIBT's Diploma of Business comprises eight courses, in which "Business and Society" is one; an "elective" course for *The University of Adelaide* (Table 1) and a "core" course for the *University of South Australia* (Table 2). The primary aim of this course is articulated as "...to develop students" understanding of the relationship among society, business, government, and the not-for-profit sector, and to enable students to identify a range of professional capabilities necessary for participation in a sustainable society".

In 2013-02, (Trimester 2, Table 3), 53 Diploma of Business students in two separate classes were required to submit a major assessment task worth 30% in the form of a "personal reflection" (total 2000 words). This assessment task involved three unrelated and reflective responses to questions based on specific activities covered during the trimester. In preparation, students were required to bring together: (1) a designated reading or activity and concepts from the relevant part of the curriculum; and (2) their personal experiences in a first-person account of their considered view.

This was an "exploratory" study (Neuman, 2004, p. 15) that involved becoming familiar with one setting and its particular features, gathering data from one selected course, and creating a preliminary picture of international students' perceptions of ethics to be able to generate teaching and learning improvement, and ideas for future empirically-based projects. Data were collected from students' first reflection in which they were required to respond in narrative form to the question: *What does "ethics" mean to you as a student in your time at university?*

The aim of this research was to utilise the qualitative data—derived from the students themselves—to evaluate how the EIBT teaching and learning environment has improved their understanding of ethics; essentially issues surrounding academic integrity. The objectives of this research were to: *acknowledge* EIBT students' comments/experiences as rich source of description and insight; to *identify* cultural factors that may have impacted on how EIBT international students have become informed of the concept; and to *share* findings with EIBT colleagues.

Table 3. Business and Society course and associated data over the past two years (2012-2014)

EIBT Trimester	No. of Students	No. of Classes	Pass Rate	Fail Rate
2012-01	66	2	53 (80%)	13 (20%)
2012-02	50	2	42 (84%)	8 (16%)
2012-03	62	2	46 (74%)	16 (26%)
2013-01	62	2	43 (69%)	19 (31%)
2013-02	53	2	49 (93%)	4 (7%)
2013-03	34	1	29 (85%)	5 (15%)
2014-01	55	2	35 (64%)	20 (36%)

Prior to the presentation of their reflections, the following section of this chapter explicates the three action research informed phases, namely: (a) *conceptualisation*; (b) *implementation*; and (c) *interpretation*, in relation to the assessment task from which the data was derived (McLean, 1995).

Conceptualisation

EIBT has an agreement to use the partner university's intellectual property and is contractually obliged to deliver courses with equivalent outcomes. Any changes in staffing, text books, and/or assessment procedures as examples, are made known to EIBT through the university's course coordinator. As articulation and credit transfer agreements are in place, courses delivered by EIBT are continually monitored to ensure that the validity of these arrangements is maintained. In other words, all EIBT courses and their contents are university approved and moderated.

Embedding an ethics component in a "business" course provides a potential means of increasing students' ethical sensitivity and hence, behaviour. In brief, a study by McCabe and Trevino (1995) described how business students were found to be: more likely to commit academic misconduct; more tolerant of such conduct; and more socially accepting of poor ethical behaviours than other students. In a related work, scholars stressed that "…in light of recent scandals in corporations, business schools have been searching for ways to send students the message that ethics is important… there is reason to believe that cheating may be more of a problem in business schools than it is elsewhere" (McCabe et al., 2006, p. 294). Glater (2006) described the alarming magnitude of "cheating" among university students and the growing concern on the part of University Deans and society in general, about the escalating pervasiveness of this phenomenon and its detrimental impact on "business and real world" ethics.

"Ethics" education may reduce students' academic misconduct in the "present" and hopefully have a positive effect on their conduct in the business community in the "future". Universities are being called to educate and influence the ethics of future business person/leaders (e.g., Hall & Beradino, 2006; McCabe & Trevino, 1995; McGill, 2008; Swanson, 2004; Trevino et al., 1998). Therefore, "[h]elping students become more socially responsible and ethically sensitive is a substantive part of our [teacher's] responsibility as we prepare a new generation of business practitioners" (Giacalone & Thompson, 2006).

Implementation

This reflective assessment task, and final piece of coursework worth 30%, was introduced to students synchronously (face-to-face) and asynchronously (Eynesbury intranet) several weeks prior to the submission date. The descriptor for this assessment task included the following guidelines:

Assignment 3 should be in the form of three pieces of reflective writing. Each reflection provides an opportunity for students to practice critical reflection and recognise its value in professional life. Each piece should be 2-3 paragraphs in length, but that is a general guide, not a requirement; the total length is 2000 words.

The ability to reflect is an important element of professional business life. It enhances the capacity to evaluate knowledge and to understand and accept personal strengths and weaknesses. A reflection is a record of the writer's thoughts. It is important that students share their "own" ideas. There will be exercises in class to assist you in understanding the concept of reflection and to provide an opportunity to practise this writing style.

Refer to the course texts, for example, Cohen's (2004) chapter on descriptive and prescriptive ethics. Students may also choose any of the other readings from the ethics section of this course, such as Platts (2003) and Provis (2004). If the reflection uses material written by "others" then it must be clear. Reference all sources that are included in your work. Final submissions will be uploaded to Turnitin, which will help to identify the originality of a student's paper.

Interpretation

As with all qualitative research, it was important to properly manage the large quantity of narrative data (approximately 35,000 words). The first draft represented students' "word-for-word" reflections. The second draft aimed to accurately represent the substance and meaning of original excerpts, but was edited for fluency; simplifying the text by removing colloquialisms and errors of grammar and punctuation. In essence, a type of data reduction was undertaken; abstracting, focusing, selecting, and simplifying the reflections to present in this chapter. Eliminating data not relevant—or extracting data that are relevant—is usually the first and arguably the simplest form of reduction (Hughes & McCabe, 2006, p. 58). As a form of analysis, it discards, focuses, organises, sorts and sharpens data (Koshy, 2005, pp. 113-114). Far from diminishing the process of qualitative research, the aim here was to enhance students' commentary and present a free-flow of response as a literal record was not warranted given that this was not a linguistic study.

The researchers decided against the use of computer-based analytic tools in order to remain open to flexible analysis and interpretation. Hence, rather than looking for meaning(s) in discrete words, the researchers concentrated on pools of information and in this way issues of reliability were addressed by making the analysis as contextualised as possible. Significantly, using existing data had advantages over data collected through a contrived process. Not only was it collected relatively quickly, but it would appear to have higher credibility because it was independent of the teacher's research activit(ies) (Altrichter, et al., 2000, p. 82).

The excerpts presented below are based on students' own personal experiences and do not make any generalisable claims. They provide an insight into EIBT international students' "beliefs" and should be conceived as a subjective process realised in a specific historical context. Importantly, the selected excerpts do not disclose any information that may prejudice participants. Students are not identifiable either by name or description. The focus of this study and the contents of each passage were considered non-controversial and no apparent consequences for the participants could arise. Student perceptions were categorised into several common themes for assembling and comparative purposes, however, many comments were relevant across multiple themes and selected excerpts are indicative of the type of student work received.

FINDINGS AND DISCUSSION

First and foremost, students should have made direct reference to the EIBT context. Indeed, the vast majority of students referred to their current studies (at the time of completion) as having opened-their-eyes to issues surrounding ethical behaviour(s) and/or academic integrity.

Acting ethically at EIBT has taught me that I should follow rules and policies and continue to upgrade my skills and knowledge. In order to show the respect of other people's ideas or work, I must not plagiarise, otherwise I have encroached on other people's copyright which is forbidden in a global world.

At EIBT, there is a strong focus to not plagiarise or copy other students' work. This is an important and serious problem for all international students.

When students plagiarise or copy the work of others, they will get a zero or fail the whole course.

Even though I am currently undertaking a diploma program, I am on the pathway to becoming a full-time university student. EIBT has deepened my understanding of what ethics means, not only from our lecturers, but everyone who is working within EIBT.

It is an important issue to focus on at EIBT—do not plagiarise or copy work. From this, I realised that I must not do this kind of mistake. Acting ethically includes contributing to group assignments, following the lecturer's rules, and improving my academic skills.

There is a focus at EIBT to not copy the work of others; following the rules and trying to improve my study skills and knowledge.

University is an academic place and learning in university means trying to become a "professional". Academic integrity is so important and I have grasped this concept a lot in EIBT.

The vast majority of students, but not all, referred to "academic integrity" in their reflection. This was a key expression that needed to be included/addressed in each narrative, and an expectation that was repeatedly emphasised in the lead-up to submission of this work.

Academic integrity is a strong focus at EIBT to not copy work of others, following the rules and trying to improve study skills. That is because it is an important part of study. I think doing my assignment in a timely way; by myself; going to school on time; contributing to group assignments etc. is good study ethics. I am building my knowledge and trying to be professional.

I am studying a Diploma of Business in EIBT and I am going to university next year. Although

I am still a student and not yet in the workforce, I have come to realise what being a professional means since studying this course. In our lecture on "professionalism", I learnt about key values such as academic integrity, being ethical and having social responsibility. Learning these values I realised was quite similar to the core learning values that I need as a student at EIBT. In particular, the value of "respect".

In order to maintain trust among members of the university community, lecturers and students must follow basic ethical principles in regard to academic integrity. Academic dishonesty is against the integrity of EIBT and is a threat to every student and the standards of The University of Adelaide.

Impressively, one student provided a breakdown of issues related to academic integrity in an explicit and thoughtful personal interpretation.

EIBT's focus is on academic integrity. It includes honesty, trust, fairness, respect and responsibility. Those five values are more important than plagiarism. First, "honesty" means that students should have their own ideas, do not steal or present others' ideas, and do not make up results or data. Second, "trust" means students and lecturers share their ideas and information together without those ideas being stolen. Third, "fairness" means students should have fair treatment in their work. Next, "respect" means lecturers and students have to respect each other. They have to listen and pay attention to each other's ideas and attend all learning activities. Finally, "responsibility" means that students have to be honest while they are learning. Those values are not only important in student life, but also important in the workplace. Such ethics is helpful for my future in business.

EIBT uses Turnitin plagiarism prevention software. Students are required to submit their assessment tasks to Turnitin via the online portal (intranet), which checks the originality of their document. Valued for its rapid processing of results and ability to compare submitted work with the submissions of students—past and present—and may act as a deterrent to academic dishonesty. EIBT students initially find this process over-whelming, as their ability to paraphrase in English is put to the test. The following excerpts made direct reference to this software.

At the beginning of this term, my lecturers asked all students to promise that "you will not plagiarise". EIBT has an online system called Turnitin to stop students plagiarising. Plagiarism means stealing, although this is not money or wealth products, it is other people's work that does not belong to you. I noticed that we could not plagiarise doing our assignments, so we have to put ourselves into a self-regulation situation.

In EIBT, there is a system called Turnitin that can check the similarity and plagiarism of homework and every assignment submitted through EIBT's online portal. In the past, lecturers would check homework manually to make sure your work is done by yourself. If you get caught plagiarising by Turnitin, you will be warned by the Academic Advisor and if you repeat the same mistake again, you may be expelled from EIBT.

All My Own Work (AMOW) is an online tool designed to help "new" EIBT students follow the principles and practices of good scholarship. Students are required to complete AMOW during the first four weeks of their first trimester, otherwise their results are withheld.

Eynesbury has a strong focus on AMOW. AMOW is a program designed to help EIBT students to follow the principles and practices of good scholarship. This includes understanding, valuing and using ethical practices when locating and using informa-tion. Students who have completed the program

will know about penalties for cheating and how to avoid this when preparing their homework.

Since I completed AMOW, I understand more about academic integrity and plagiarism. In the past, I never realised that plagiarism was such a crucial problem, but now I agree that taking other's ideas without acknowledgement is just like stealing.

As instructed in the assignment guidelines, stu-dents needed to reflect on their past experience(s) in their home country, and prior to their studies in Australia. These excerpts provide a fascinat-ing account of the degree to which their previous educational encounters were in contrast to their diploma studies.

As an EIBT student, "ethics" means being hon-est and professional in our studies which means to do homework by ourselves and no cheating. I still remember my first assignment which got so much plagiarism. The Academic Advisor talked with every student. I was shocked by that, because it is not a big issue to get some copies from the internet or books when we do essay; it is a com-mon thing in China. It was the first time I was asked to talk about my essay which had a reading of 40+% plagiarism, but I was too scared to col-lect my paper. I did not get my assignment back, but after one week I tried to talk to her and since then, I have tried to avoid the same problems and ensure a much lower percentage.

During my studies in EIBT, all students need to have lessons about plagiarism. In other words, copying assignments or having no referencing is unacceptable. At first I was very confused, because in high school in Vietnam, I was allowed to copy and paste anything off the internet for my home-work. Here, the ethics is completely different. We may still copy other people's work, but we must tell our lecturers where we found the information.

By referencing, I am still paying respect to the original author.

When I was doing my assignments in Hong Kong, I copied information directly from the internet and did not provide any citations. I even did not understand or look for the information. As a university student, now when I am doing my assignments I will understand and look carefully to prevent cheating or plagiarism. This process will help me to reach more different information and expand my knowledge. Also, I feel good because I am respecting authors and important writing rules.

There were a several examples where students shared a dramatic event(s) to highlight their understanding of inappropriate ethical behaviour by a university student.

This topic reminds me of a Chinese university event that happened a few months ago. A student poisoned his room-mate just because of his jealousy. After I heard this news, I was shocked and ashamed. This student disobeyed the ethics of students and the law. This event made many people reflect on ethical issues. Of course, this is unethical and a serious matter at university. Due to study pressures and different habits of students, inevitably problems will arise. Therefore, it is really important for students' education.

Interestingly, many students shared experiences of academic misconduct during their time at EIBT. The two examples below are of students' "own" occurrence of academic misconduct; the first intentional and the second unintentional.

My lecturer found me and said "You did not write this essay". He said, "plagiarism is not acceptable behaviour". Plagiarism is not acting in good faith. It is not a right option to copy other people's work. As you can guess, I got zero marks and I realised my mistake. I apologised to my lecturer

and promised never to plagiarise again. Since then I have never copied any assignment. Self-review is a necessary method to improve my studies and professional life. According to the lecture, I learned that ethics relates to fairness. If I copy an assignment, and if I get marks for this assignment, it is unfair for other students, because they spent more time achieving it, but I did nothing. I received a zero, which means I must take the consequence for my unethical behaviour.

From my experience, I studied Quantitative Methods for Business (QMB) last trimester. I did the assignment by myself at my home and one of the students in the class asked me to do it with him and his friend. I went to the computer room with them, but I just gave them what I did on assignment and they copied it onto their USB. After I gave my assignment to the lecturer, he found that the similarity was really high. I told him that I did the assignment with friends, then he told me a story about honesty and to not do assignments with other people, because the assignment needs to demonstrate what I learned in class and what my knowledge is. Now, I remember it all the time.

One student posed a hypothetical cultural dilemma related to sharing their work with "friends". This situation may or may not have actually occurred.

Hypothetically, a friend wants me to help with an assignment and I decide to give my own assignment for reference voluntarily. After I realise that my assignment was copied word-by-word. Should I blame my friend for this problem? Obviously, I do not want to rattle my friend, but I want to get out of this trouble as soon as possible. Such an ethical issue will make me choose to be loyal to my friend or be truthful to my lecturer? I believe most students will struggle with this problem when the same situation happens to them.

There are concerns in HE that some students may refer to "ghost writing" services through "cheat sites" or "essay mills" (e.g., LazyStudents.com, SchoolSucks.com, Cheathouse.com). Oftentimes, the work submitted by contract cheaters has been produced exclusively for them. This means that sources for their submissions may not be found on the internet and may be not detected using Turnitin. Unfortunately, when cheating goes undetected, it may appear to be condoned. Seeing peers get away with deceptive practices may produce a sense of injustice and undermine morale. Fortunately, in the following case, justice prevailed.

I have found that some students who come from overseas to study in Australia have a hard time to do their assignments by themselves, because they need to do their work in English, which is their second language. Instead of spending more time on their work, they rather choose to pay for their assignment. They pay other students or even some company that helps to do assignment, but eventually they got zero marks for plagiarising and cheating. From this I realised I must also not do this especially when I am working in my career.

Many students referred to the fact that they had heard of "other" students purchasing assignments, but did not provide specific details.

I know that English for the majority of international students is a challenge, because it is not our first language. I heard some students want to get high marks and they chose to copy someone else's work or pay for others to help them to do their homework.

In my study time in China and Australia, I often heard things about cheating and plagiarism. Some students pay for assignments in order to get a good grade. They even pay for the lecturer to change the original marks and get a higher one to pass

the course or even worse. My view is that these things are unethical and wrong.

The majority of students in this course acknowledged that their understanding of ethics had advanced since they first arrived in EIBT. Many students reflected on what action they were taking in the present (i.e., as a continuing EIBT student) and what action they will take in the future (i.e., at the partner university) to avoid potential misconduct.

I now understand that I should follow university rules as this would be no risk to my study situation. As a result, I should write in my own words in every assignment, as it is a part of learning. As a university student this is my obligation. Therefore I could never cheat, forge, plagiarise or help others to engage in such behaviour. This course has definitely strengthened my awareness.

To an EIBT student just like me, we need to do our own assignment and do not copy from others. If I cannot understand what the lecturer said, I need to ask questions and study harder, but cannot just copy work. I will remember these lessons and instructions, so that my time at university will be safe.

Finally, in helping to address concerns about students in business programs being more likely to condone cheating than in other discipline areas, few students mentioned their future as a business professional. The following example was the most succinct.

This course helps us to become ethical students and we will become ethical business professionals in the future. We have learned about scandals, deceit, corruption and deception. I do not want to be involved in bad events in the future, because I will disgrace myself and my family. By my actions and my example, I will promote honesty, responsibility, and respect. I want to feel proud and make a positive contribution to society.

IMPLICATIONS AND RECOMMENDATIONS

Lecturers often have limited opportunity to dedicate time, energy and funds to designing and then conducting elaborate research projects. Fortunately, the authors of this chapter were able to utilise existing data to conduct a preliminary investigation into the perceptions of a sample cohort of its student demographic. This study proved to be invaluable, as an abundance of rich narrative data could be gathered from students' own understanding(s) associated with "ethics". One limitation of this study, however, was that students could hide or even distort their true attitudes and behaviours in an attempt to achieve high marks in this course. Despite this, the authors believe that the student cohort who contributed to this study was representative of EIBT.

While the effectiveness of this course and more specifically this assessment task in curbing academic misconduct in the present and unethical business practices in the future would be impossible to measure with any certainty, it has proven to be a useful starting point. The recommendations for advancing EIBT's teaching and learning practices include, but are not limited to:

- *Articulating* the concept of academic integrity from the Western construct;
- *Asking* students for their input on how to create a community of integrity at the start of each course and establishing them as stakeholders in the teaching and learning community;
- *Continuing* to provide effective, targeted and ongoing language support for students whose first language is not the medium of instruction—English;

- *Delivering* focused training to support the development of key academic language and learning skills such as critical analysis, synthesis, evaluation, reflection, and referencing technique;
- *Disseminating* information about ethical student behaviour via a plethora of different avenues e.g., EIBT brochures, application for admissions forms, student handbooks, covers of examination booklets, and posters on walls in classrooms;
- *Educating* students about "intellectual property", why it matters, how to legitimately access other people's work, and how to protect their own;
- *Ensuring* that staff are interculturally competent, i.e., at least aware of students' social, cultural and educational backgrounds to be able to provide superior support for their academic development;
- *Incorporating* academic integrity strategies into EIBT professional development and faculty training offerings;
- *Making* information pertaining to academic integrity easily accessible on the student online portal, in course information booklets, and within specific assignments;
- *Ongoing* use of Turnitin software with guidelines and resources, and lecturer support in class to further facilitate students' understanding(s) related to the development of their writing;
- *Promoting* a campus environment that demands ethical behaviour by all members of the community by upholding the ethos and values of academic integrity, and encouraging students to adopt these values in their professional practices;
- *Reminding* students of assignment expectations prior to submission dates and being explicit about which resources are permitted/not-permitted; and

- *Revising* policies, procedures and invigilation practices to ensure that students have the support and understanding of all EIBT administrators and faculty.

Further study will be conducted; perhaps to identify the impact of certain ethnic groups, gender, age and/or educational background that may influence internationals students' academic preferences/practices/performance, and thereby better determine more effective pedagogical approaches for supporting them on their pathway to university.

SUMMARY

It is important to ensure that students from diverse backgrounds and experiences are supported in a variety of ways throughout their HE studies, so that they may develop academic proficiency within the context of their program of study. Ethical practices such as those related to academic integrity continue to be a problem for many tertiary institutions. Using a robust data source such as international students' own reflections will facilitate outcomes with several compelling advantages. In terms of EIBT, these include demonstrating an institutional commitment to: (a) learning and engagement; and (b) university partners in a common educative endeavour that is likely to strengthen cooperation.

Improving strategies that encourage international student reflection, autonomy, and performance success, together with appropriately integrated language and learning support, will not only benefit them, but may aid in augmenting the potential of every student. This study is only the beginning as EIBT is committed to gathering and assessing its strengths and weaknesses in effectively acculturating its international students. Understanding their perspective(s), in terms of what "ethics" means for them is one direction

that can be taken towards establishing a more effective student-teacher partnership and making responsibility equitable. Authentic assessment tasks, such as the one highlighted in this chapter, enables students to develop valuable skills that will serve them well in Australian HE, future "business" workplaces, and throughout their lives.

REFERENCES

Altrichter, H., Posch, P., & Somekh, B. (2000). *Teachers investigate their work: An introduction to action research across the professions.* New York: Routledge.

Angelova, M., & Riazantseva, A. (1999). If you don't tell me, how can I know: A case study of four international students learning to write the US way. *Written Communication, 16*(4), 491–525. doi:10.1177/0741088399016004004

Avison, D. E., Lau, F., Myers, M. D., & Nielson, P. A. (1999). Action research. *Communications of the ACM, 42*(1), 94–97. doi:10.1145/291469.291479

Bandura, A. (1994). Self-efficacy. In V. S. Ramachaudran (Ed.), *Encyclopedia of human behaviour* (pp. 71–81). New York: Academic Press.

Bodycott, P., & Walker, A. (2000). Teaching abroad: Lessons learned about inter-cultural understanding for teachers in higher education. *Teaching in Higher Education, 5*(1), 79–94. doi:10.1080/135625100114975

Campbell, J., & Li, M. (2008). Asian students' voices: An empirical study of Asian students' learning experiences at a New Zealand university. *Journal of Studies in International Education, 12*(4), 375–396. doi:10.1177/1028315307299422

Carr, W., & Kemmis, S. (1986). *Becoming critical: Education, knowledge and action research.* London: Falmer Press.

Chalmers, D., & Volet, S. (1997). Common misconceptions about students from South-East Asia studying in Australia. *Higher Education Research & Development*, *16*(1), 87–99. doi:10.1080/0729436970160107

Cohen, S. (2004). *The nature of moral reasoning: The framework and activities of ethical deliberation, argument and decision-making*. Melbourne: Oxford University Press.

Corson, D. (1997). The learning and use of academic English words. *Language Learning*, *47*(4), 671–718. doi:10.1111/0023-8333.00025

Dawson, J., & Bekkers, C. G. (2002). *Supporting international students' transition to university*. Paper presented at the 11th Annual Teaching and Learning Forum: Focusing on the Student, Perth, Australia.

Elliot, J. (1991). *Action research for educational change*. Buckingham, UK: Open University Press.

Fiocco, M. (2006). *An evaluation of a pathway program: The students' view*. Paper presented at the Australian International Education Conference, Perth, Australia. Retrieved from www.idp.com/aiec

Giacalone, R. A., & Thompson, K. R. (2006). Business ethics and social responsibility education: Shifting the worldview. *Academy of Management Learning & Education*, *5*(3), 266–277. doi:10.5465/AMLE.2006.22697016

Gillett, A. J., & Wray, L. (2006). *Assessing the effectiveness of EAP programmes*. London: BALEAP.

Gitanjali, B. (2004). Academic dishonesty in Indian medical colleges. *Journal of Postgraduate Medicine*, *50*(4), 281–284. PMID:15623972

Glater, J. (2006, May 18). Colleges chase as cheats shift to higher tech. *The New York Times*.

Grabinger, R. S., & Dunlap, J. C. (1995). Rich environments for active learning: A definition. *Association for Learning Technology*, *3*(2), 5–34. doi:10.1080/0968776950030202

Hall, A., & Beradino, L. (2006). Teaching professional behaviours: Differences in the perceptions of faculty, students, and employers. *Journal of Business Ethics*, *63*(4), 407–415. doi:10.1007/s10551-005-2411-6

Hawkins, B. (2008). Using sociocultural theory to examine the context(s) of language teaching and learning. *Working Papers in TESOL & Applied Linguistics, 8*(1).

Hayes, N., & Introna, L. D. (2005). Cultural values, plagiarism, and fairness: When plagiarism gets in the way of learning. *Ethics & Behavior*, *15*(3), 213–231. doi:10.1207/s15327019eb1503_2

Hellsten, M. (2002). *Students in transition: Needs and experiences of international students in Australia*. Paper presented at the 16th Australian International Education Conference, Macquarie, Australia.

Hughes, J. M. C., & McCabe, D. L. (2006). Understanding academic misconduct. *Canadian Journal of Higher Education*, *36*(1), 49–63.

Koshy, V. (2005). *Action research of improving practice: A practical guide*. London: Paul Chapman Publishing.

Leask, B. (2006). Plagiarism, cultural diversity and metaphor: Implications for academic staff development. *Assessment & Evaluation in Higher Education*, *31*(2), 183–199. doi:10.1080/02602930500262486

Li, A., & Gasser, M. (2005). Predicting Asian international students' sociocultural adjustment: A test of two mediation models. *International Journal of Intercultural Relations*, *29*(5), 561–576. doi:10.1016/j.ijintrel.2005.06.003

Lund, J. R. (2004). Plagiarism: A cultural perspective. *Journal of Religious & Theological Information, 6*(3/4), 93–101. doi:10.1300/J112v06n03_08

Major, E. M. (2005). Co-national support, cultural therapy, and the adjustment of Asian students to an English-speaking university culture. *International Education Journal, 6*(1), 84–95.

McCabe, D. L. (2005). It takes a village: Academic dishonesty and educational opportunity. *Liberal Education, 91*(3), 26–31.

McCabe, D. L., Butterfield, K. D., & Trevino, L. K. (2006). Academic dishonesty in graduate business programs: Prevalence, causes, and proposed action. *Academy of Management Learning & Education, 5*(3), 294–305. doi:10.5465/AMLE.2006.22697018

McCabe, D. L., & Trevino, L. K. (1995). Cheating among business students: A challenge for business leaders and educators. *Journal of Management Education, 19*(2), 205–218. doi:10.1177/105256299501900205

McGill, S. (2008). Integrating academic integrity education with business law course: Why and how? *Journal of Legal Studies Education, 25*(2), 241–282. doi:10.1111/j.1744-1722.2008.00053.x

McGowan, U. (2005a). Academic integrity: An awareness and development issue for students and staff. *Journal of University Teaching and Learning Practice, 2*(3), 6.

McGowan, U. (2005b). Does educational integrity mean teaching students NOT to 'use their own words'? *International Journal for Educational Integrity, 1*(1).

McLean, J. E. (1995). *Improving education through action research: A guide for administrators and teachers.* Corwin Press.

McLean, P., & Ransom, M. L. (2005). Building intercultural competencies: Implications of academic skills development. In J. Carroll & J. Ryan (Eds.), *Teaching international students: Improving learning for all* (pp. 45–63). New York: Routledge.

Neuman, W. L. (2004). *Basics of social research: Qualitative and quantitative approaches.* Pearson Education Incorporated.

Platts, J. (2003). Developing competence and trust: Maintaining the heart of a profession. *Professional Ethics (Gainesville, Fla.), 11*(1), 3–18. doi:10.5840/profethics20031116

Prescott, A., & Hellsten, M. (2005). Hanging together even with non-native speakers: The international student transition experience. In P. Ninnes & M. Hellsten (Eds.), *Internationalizing higher education: Critical explorations of pedagogy andf policy* (pp. 75–95). Springer Publications. doi:10.1007/1-4020-3784-8_5

Provis, C. (2004). Guanxi, relationships and ethics. *Australian Journal of Professional and Applied Ethics, 6*(1), 47–57.

Reason, P., & Bradbury, H. (Eds.). (2001). *Handbook of action research: Participative inquiry and practice.* London: Sage.

Redfield, R., Linton, R., & Herskovits, M. J. (1936). Memorandum for the study of acculturation. *American Anthropologist, 38*(1), 149–152. doi:10.1525/aa.1936.38.1.02a00330

Russell, D. R. (1991). *Writing in the academic disciplines, 1870-1990: A circular history.* Southern Illinois University Press.

Sawir, E. (2005). Language difficulties of international students in Australia: The effects of prior learning experience. *International Education Journal, 6*(5), 567–580.

Spack, R. (1998). Cultural backgrounds: What should we know about multilingual students? *TESOL Quarterly*, *32*(4), 740–746. doi:10.2307/3588006

Swanson, D. L. (2004). The buck stops here: Why universities must reclaim business ethics education. *Journal of Academic Ethics*, *2*(1), 43–61. doi:10.1023/B:JAET.0000039007.06014.24

Trevino, L. K., Butterfield, K. D., & McCabe, D. L. (1998). The ethical context in organizations: Influences on employee attitudes and behaviors. *Business Ethics Quarterly*, *8*(3), 447–476. doi:10.2307/3857431

Turner, K., & Pointon, M. L. (2009). *Contextualising the learning of assessment practices: Meeting the academic skills of international students*. Paper presented at the ALTC First-year Experience Curriculum Design Symposium, Queensland, Australia.

University of Adelaide. (2014). *Adelaide business school*. Retrieved 25 June 2014, from http://www.business.adelaide.edu.au/

University of South Australia. (2014). *Business school*. Retrieved 25 June 2014, from http://www.unisa.edu.au/Business/

Velliaris, D. M., & Warner, R. (2009). *Embedding 'learning guides' in a flexible delivery mode: Improving academic acculturation for international students at an Australian university*. Paper presented at the 20th ISANA International Education Conference, Canberra, Australia.

Velliaris, D. M., & Willis, C. R. (2014). Getting personal: An autoethnographic study of the professional identit(ies) of lecturers in an Australian pathway institution. In P. Breen (Ed.), Cases on teacher identity, diversity, and cognition in higher education (pp. 87–110). Hershey, PA: IGI Global. doi:10.4018/978-1-4666-5990-2.ch004

Zhang, Y., & Mi, Y. (2010). Another look at the language difficulties of international students. *Journal of Studies in International Education*, *14*(4), 371–388. doi:10.1177/1028315309336031

KEY TERMS AND DEFINITIONS

Academic Integrity: The moral code or ethical policy of academia; adherence to honest and responsible scholarship. This includes, as examples: values such as avoidance of cheating and plagiarism; maintenance of academic standards; and respect and rigor in academic research and publishing.

Acculturation: In its simplest sense, this includes the change(s) that arise following contact between/among individuals from different cultural backgrounds. This may lead to progressive adoption of elements of the other culture (e.g., ideas, words, values and/or behaviours).

Action Research: A form of enquiry undertaken by participants—quite often educators within their own setting—to improve educational practices, as well as their own understanding of those practices and the situations in which they are carried out. The aim of action research is to improve praxis.

All My Own Work (AMOW): An online tool designed to help "new" EIBT students follow the principles and practices of good scholarship. The program has been developed as part of the New South Wales Government's "Respect and Responsibility" strategy and is designed to be delivered flexibly as self-paced online learning modules for students.

Business and Society: A first-year undergraduate business degree course that develops students' understanding of the relationship among society, business, government, and the not-for-profit sector. This course enables students to identify a range of professional capabilities necessary for participation in a sustainable society.

Business Ethics: Ethical and moral principles that arise in business environments. It applies to all aspects of business conduct and is relevant to both the behaviour of individuals and/or organisations.

Eynesbury Institute of Business and Technology (EIBT): One of a growing number of private providers linking up with partner universities to establish programs that create opportunities to promote Australian HE globally. EIBT offers pathways to a Bachelor of Business, Information Technology, or Engineering at one of two South Australian higher education institutions: The University of Adelaide; or the University of South Australia.

International Student: Individuals enrolled in EIBT on temporary student visas and who are almost exclusively from a Non-English Speaking Background (NESB).

Pathway Provider: Educational institutions that offer students alternative forms of entry into university programs. Applicants may include: early school leavers; those who have not achieved the academic and/or English requirements to obtain direct entry; or students looking to return to study after a period of absence.

Turnitin: An internet-based plagiarism detection and prevention program, which checks documents for unoriginal content. The results can be used, for example, in: (a) formative assessment to help students learn how to avoid plagiarism and improve their writing; and/or (b) summative assessment to identify students' similarities to existing sources.

Chapter 13
Does Accredited Professional Development for Academics Improve Teaching and Learning in Higher Education?

Claire McAvinia
Dublin Institute of Technology, Ireland

Orla Hanratty
Dublin Institute of Technology, Ireland

Roisin Donnelly
Dublin Institute of Technology, Ireland

Jen Harvey
Dublin Institute of Technology, Ireland

ABSTRACT

The authors are part of a team delivering accredited programmes in teaching at tertiary level, and have collaborated to examine the impact of their work and that of the team over more than ten years in this area: whether accredited professional development programmes for academics have improved teaching—and students' learning—in higher education. A review of the literature is presented, along with new research undertaken in their home institution. The authors' findings from both the literature and their most recent research indicates a range of benefits for higher education in providing and supporting accredited programmes for educators. However, they have also identified methodological issues in measuring these benefits and impact overall. The chapter discusses this work and connects it with the broader themes of this book. The authors emphasise the importance of effective teaching in the midst of the many complex changes influencing higher education at this time.

INTRODUCTION AND OBJECTIVES

Since the early 1990s, academic professional development has emerged as a formal activity in most third level institutions in the UK, Ireland, Australasia and the US (Gosling, 2009). This trend led to the inception of centres for academic

development, including the Learning, Teaching and Technology Centre (LTTC) at Dublin Institute of Technology (DIT) in Ireland. Since 2000, the LTTC has provided accredited academic development programmes and short courses for academics within and externally to the Institute. DIT spans a number of sites in Dublin city, with some 20,000

DOI: 10.4018/978-1-4666-7244-4.ch013

students from apprentice to doctoral levels. Disciplines are organized into four Colleges: Arts and Tourism, Business, Engineering and the Built Environment, and Sciences and Health. Given the range of staff attending, the longevity of our programmes, and the many challenges now facing higher education, we sought to re-examine our provision and to evaluate the impact of accredited courses over some years.

The value of teaching as a professional area of activity in higher education has only relatively recently been identified and studied (Hanbur et al., 2008; Kandlbinder & Peseta, 2009). The past two decades have seen concerted efforts made to develop teaching as a formal professional activity in higher education in many parts of the world (Fink, 2013; Kandlbinder & Peseta, 2009). A strong trend for professional development programmes has emerged, particularly for new staff, and many universities have developed postgraduate qualifications in higher education (Chalmers & Thompson, 2008). Critical reflection on practice in higher education has emerged as potentially an important means to develop teaching practice (Bamber & Anderson, 2012; O'Connell & Dyment, 2006).

Funded initiatives have also foregrounded teaching enhancement. In Ireland and the UK, funding has been connected directly with the creation and implementation of institutional learning and teaching strategies (for example, the Teaching Quality Enhancement Funds in the UK (2000-2004) and Strategic Innovation Funds in Ireland (2006-2011)). National forums and academies for teaching and learning have emerged (http://www.heacademy.ac.uk; http://www.teachingandlearning.ie/), defining priority themes for academic professional development and the enhancement of students' learning.

Academic development units and services began to challenge the predominance of traditional teaching methods, taking more constructivist approaches in their workshops and courses (Bostock, 1998; Laurillard, 2001; Entwistle, 2009; Jordan,

et al., 2008), gaining funding as well as senior level support for their efforts. Innovation and change in teaching and learning were articulated in a manner that was appropriate to institutions and to their lecturers through the development and launch of accredited programmes (Kandlbinder & Peseta, 2009).

In light of this history, our objectives in this Chapter are twofold. First, we examine in detail emergence of accredited teaching courses at tertiary level, and where these may fit in the evolving landscape of higher education nationally and internationally. Second, we consider the evidence in relation to this kind of professional development, and whether it can be said to have improved teaching and learning. We draw both on the literature, and on a local evaluation of accredited courses at DIT. We will identify the learning points from this work, and the future directions in which research could be taken.

CONTEXT AND LITERATURE REVIEW

A review of the literature related to our research objectives indicated three over-arching themes for discussion:

- The development of teaching as a formal, professional activity in higher education;
- The evolving national and international contexts for this work;
- The potential impact of accredited programmes and measuring this impact.

Each of these will be addressed in this section.

Professionalising Teaching in Higher Education

For approximately 20 years, programmes of continuing professional development have been established in universities and other tertiary institutions in Europe, the US and Australasia. Fink (2013) identifies four levels of growth internationally, ranging from limited or no activity (for example, in Africa and parts of Asia and Europe) to well-embedded systems of continuing professional development by all faculty (Sweden). Ireland is not mentioned in Fink's survey, but could arguably be placed at Level 3 of this framework, in that there is activity in academic development at nearly all higher education institutions, with some obligatory participation in workshops. In the case of the DIT, there is mandatory participation in the Postgraduate Diploma in Third Level Learning and Teaching for newly appointed lecturers since 2006.

In common with the UK, Ireland has seen a trend from the late 1990s onwards towards the gradual provision of formal academic development opportunities and ultimately accredited courses. The Staff and Educational Development Association (SEDA) in the UK launched an initiative to accredit teachers in higher education in 1990, with a pilot at eight institutions. Following the publication of the Dearing Report (NCIHE, 1997), and the recommendation that staff should undertake formal courses in teaching and learning, these programmes began to grow. Some 168 Higher Education Academy accredited courses existed in 2007 (Kandlbinder & Peseta, 2009, p. 20), and the Academy aligns courses and other forms of professional development to its Professional Standards Framework (http://www.heacademy.ac.uk/ukpsf). In Ireland, there is a smaller sector of 21 publicly-funded higher education institutions. Academics have a range of qualifications to choose from, some leading to further study at Masters and doctoral level. In addition, standalone accredited modules have been developed and delivered collaboratively by the Learning Innovation Network (www.lin.ie) and Dublin Region Higher Education Alliance (www.drhea.ie.).

Researchers have asked why such activities have grown in the past number of decades, and suggest a number of reasons: that growing evidence pointed to the limitations of "traditional" modes of teaching, that training was previously piecemeal, that students were only achieving some of the attributes they should at third level, that student retention figures have become a cause for keen concern in many countries, and that new technologies offer a further and very significant challenge (Fink, 2013; Lueddeke, 2003). Governments expect higher education to meet these challenges. Gibbs and Coffey (2004), researching the experiences of staff and students in 20 universities across eight countries found that where teachers participated in academic development programmes, their focus became more student-centred, and lecturers' feelings of self-efficacy and confidence grew. Students in turn adopted strategies for deep learning and reported that their learning experiences were better. Similar findings have been reported more recently by a study in Durham College, Ontario (Rodgers et al., 2014). The purpose of professionalizing activities of various kinds is ultimately to enhance student learning but more importantly, to prevent students from leaving (Lueddeke, 2003). Fink (2013) defines academic development in terms of an individual's immediate goals, longer term aims, and ultimately the wider benefit to education and society. The formal development of teaching is argued to feed into these goals, but challenges remain in finding the most appropriate ways of doing this. Lueddeke (2003) suggests that we need to theorise further on the kinds of professional development academics undertake, given that academics' own preference is often to learn professionally through social networks, keep close to their 'home' disciplines, and that any professional development they undertake is subject to the pressures of time and workload. These are significant challenges indeed, and nowhere more so than in the case of the 'silent majority': those who do not engage with academic professional development. Lueddeke (ibid) found that early and late career academics were most likely to participate, as well as those who had already pursued higher studies in their own careers.

Notwithstanding the challenges of designing appropriate forms of professional development, the value of pedagogic knowledge and learning design has risen dramatically within Irish HEIs over the last few years, with rewards for the development of good practice in these areas now becoming instituted. In the UK, delivery has emphasised institutionally led strategies and provision (accredited or not). Parsons *et al.* (2012) report that for new and aspiring academic staff, the qualification pathway is becoming a more established feature of institutional strategies. The next section will examine these national and international trends in more depth.

Evolving International and National Context

Higher education (HE) in Ireland and internationally is part of a dynamic and shifting landscape, challenged by the global economic recession since 2008, and by technological change. These factors are important of themselves, but also affect our interactions with our stakeholders, how we react, and how we might influence change as it happens. The increasing profile of teaching in higher education since the 1990s, and its gradual steps towards becoming a more formally recognized activity, now take place against the backdrop of radical shifts in how people access knowledge and information, and what they may expect to gain from any professional qualification.

Generally HEIs are not well known for responding quickly, but the unregulated world of MOOCs, open sharing, relentless innovation, co-curricular development, and moves towards greater cross-organisational collaboration, have come to the fore of conversations and agendas for change. In the Irish context, the high magnitude changes that have taken place in the economy and in society since 2007 require academic developers to reflect and re-examine professional programmes in teaching and learning (along with other disciplines) (Donnelly, 2008).

There has been ongoing discussion in the Irish HE system about a proposed reconfiguration of the number of HEIs and their geographical distribution due to what has been called "*laissez-faire* development" (HEA 2012, p.5), leading to duplication of effort and blurred missions in some areas. Ireland's *National Strategy for Higher Education to 2030* (DES, 2011) is framed against a range of new challenges facing higher education; it has argued that:

Irish higher education itself will need to innovate and develop if it is to provide flexible opportunities for larger and more diverse student cohorts. It will need to do this while simultaneously enhancing quality and relevance, and connecting better with the wider needs of society and the economy, while operating in a more competitive globalised environment (2011, p.32).

To address this, the newly formed National Forum for the Enhancement of Teaching and Learning in Higher Education (http://www.teachingandlearning.ie/) has identified four priority enhancement themes: supporting teachers in helping students make effective transitions; setting up a national learning impact award system; benchmarking a professional development framework; and building digital capacity. With this focus on recognition of and reward for teaching, maximizing digital learning opportunities, and the introduction of a professional development framework for academics, the National Forum has the potential to be a powerful driver of change in Irish higher education. Existing accredited provision for academic professional development may well have a renewed emphasis in this context.

The Impact of Professional Development Programmes

In light of the established trend towards accrediting professional development in teaching and learning, and the likelihood that this will grow in importance over the next number of years, it is important to examine evidence in the literature as to whether professional development programmes have had the positive impact desired. Studies have investigated whether this kind of professional development has had the effect of improving teaching and learning, and what might be learned from various approaches to this work. It is important to acknowledge that there is still relatively little research evaluating the impact of programmes, and limited evidence to link participation in teaching development programmes with enhanced student learning (Bamber, 2008; Bamber & Trowler, 2005; Gibbs & Coffey, 2004; Porritt, 2014). In 2006, Pickering concluded that investigating the impact of these programmes on the practices and beliefs held by academics is not simple or even feasible. We will focus in this section on the work that has been undertaken by (amongst others) Prosser *et al.* (2006); Rust (2000, 2006); Kahn *et al.* (2006); Knight *et al.* (2006); Stes *et al.* (2007); Hanbury *et al.* (2008); Trigwell *et al.* (2012) and Bamber (2013a). We consider also the limitations of this research, and the calls for more robust methodologies to be developed.

Hanbury *et al.* (2008) researched with programme completers from 32 UK higher education institutions, as well as programme leaders, heads of department and pro-vice-chancellors, and set out to explore the perceived impact of UK-accredited teaching development programmes upon participants and departments. Findings centred on perceptions of impact, with participants perceiving themselves to be significantly more student-focused in their teaching after attending a programme, with those from newer institutions and health sciences disciplines experiencing the greatest conceptual change and rating the programmes most positively. There were some positive examples of departmental impacts, and the programmes were seen to align more closely with institutional teaching and learning strategies than mission statements.

A review by Kahn *et al.* (2006) for the Higher Education Authority (HEA) in the UK, on the use of reflective practice in postgraduate programmes for academic staff emphasised that such programmes are intended to create meaning around practice. Accomplishing this is an inherently collaborative and social process that can lead to changes in practice, capacity for change and changes in professional identity. The evaluative study by Prosser *et al.* (2006) found that such programmes encouraged the academic staff participating to be more student focused and to help form linkages between departments. The conclusion of the study by Knight *et al.* (2006) on the effectiveness of postgraduate certificates in the field was that there were varying levels of satisfaction for teacher development as an outcome of these programmes.

It may also be challenging to find sufficient time to evaluate, to recognise that professional practice is complex, and to reconcile evaluation processes with the potential to influence management beliefs (Bamber, 2013a). The challenge we face as academic developers is how we can establish shared understandings with those who will assess our value. Bamber (2013a) emphasizes the importance of professional judgment in complex, multi-factoral situations and the recognition of the value of experience, and knowledge of the context, intelligently used. Ultimately it is key for us to remember that academic development (and its programmes), has long, slow-burning effects.

Reviewing the literature which addresses the impact of accredited teaching development programmes points to positive effects, albeit with some tentative conclusions and a growing awareness of the complexity of teachers' own conceptions of teaching and learning in the context of an increasingly busy workload. Carrying these findings forward, we sought to design an appropriate evaluation of our own accredited programmes.

MEASURING IMPACT: A CASE STUDY

Context

The previous review and discussion of the literature has shown that although there has been formal development of teaching as a professional activity in higher education, and this has been articulated through accredited programmes, there are important challenges in tracing the impact of this work. Methodological challenges exist, and researchers are still working to build an evidence base in this area.

In seeking to assess the impact of our own courses, we engaged first with the evaluation literature. Stake (2004) has suggested that evaluation is the discernment of the good in our work. Baume (2008) indicated three purposes for such evaluation - to account, to improve, to understand. He argues that we should look at the setting, the people, the atmosphere, the environment as well as what is happening and why. It is good practice to think about evaluation being collaborative, and indeed how evaluation fits with the key elements of the change lifecycle: preparing, planning, implementing, and sustaining change to practice. Fleming (2012) believes that in order to add value to the evaluation of complex change, evaluation questions need to energise rather than stifle innovation and it is important to keep the thinking about any initiative nuanced, flexible, responsive and rigorous. It is useful to consider the use of 'double loop learning' – what did and did not work and use the findings to facilitate innovative thinking about the initiative as it progresses. These varying models for evaluation point to the complexity of the task, and perhaps explain in some measure the methodological difficulties facing academic developers in the evaluation of the impact of their work. But they also indicated the need for deep, rich descriptions of experience and the potential of qualitative research methods, rather than attempting a positivist study to measure impact (Cohen et al., 2011).

Bamber (2013b) suggests a useful eight step framework for evidencing the value of our academic development work: explore the evaluation literature; elucidate our theory of change; plan the evaluation; choose an evidence mix; adopt a systematic approach; remember the role of judgment and subjectivity; bring in evidence-based cases; and contribute to the literature. We have followed this model to support the design of this evaluative study:

- We consulted the evaluation literature and the existing research available.
- We theorised that 'change' in the context of academic professional development would likely be evidenced by changes in teaching practice towards more student-centred learning, and away from transmission-oriented approaches to teaching.
- We planned and undertook an evaluation project to examine the impact of our three accredited programmes: the *Postgraduate Diploma in Third Level Learning and Teaching* (previously known as the Postgraduate Certificate in Third Level Learning and Teaching), as an accredited course which has been in place since 2000 and completion of which is a requirement since 2006 for members of staff new to teaching at DIT; the *MA in Higher Education* (in place since 2000) and the *MSc in Applied eLearning* (established in 2006).
- Our chosen methods determined the evidence mix: a questionnaire to internal and external alumni of the accredited programmes and short courses; focus groups with members of staff at the Institute who had completed accredited programmes or short courses.

- A systematic approach to the study was adopted and is reported in the *Implementation* section below.

- Our own roles as course co-ordinators and tutors were consciously recognised throughout the process. This was especially important in addressing the ethical issues associated with the research. The authors work with graduates of our programmes as colleagues in DIT and at the external institutes. Many of our DIT colleagues return to our Centre to participate in other courses, or as members of working groups and committees. It was appropriate to use the Institute's procedures for ethical approval of the research, and following submission of our project proposals and data collection instruments, approval was granted. The questionnaire was distributed by a colleague in our administrative office, to remove the authors one degree from the data collection. The focus groups were facilitated by the colleague newest to the team, who had not previously met the programme alumni.

- Evidence-based cases: the longevity of our courses, which were established in the 2000s, indicated a large group of alumni from whom data could be collected. We gathered data from those both internal and external to the Institute, who were engaged in teaching in other higher education institutions in Ireland or in a teaching/training role within their organisations. We asked whether accredited training and professional development for academics had led to changes in their teaching, whether these changes had been positive, and whether the student learning experience had been enhanced.

- We seek here to make a contribution to the literature, deriving from this work. In addition, the research has been presented at two conferences (Harvey et al., 2013; McAvinia

et al., 2014) and reported through formal channels at the local level.

Implementation

227 internal and external alumni of our courses were contacted via email to invite their participation. 78 of them returned questionnaires, representing a response rate of 34%. The questionnaires were administered using an online survey system.

Frequency data was provided in a range of charts by the online system. This system also allowed us to compare the quantitative results across the two surveys. Most of the respondents were working in Institutes of Technology[1], and there was some distribution of responses across the disciplines. A higher proportion of the internal respondents were at an earlier point in their teaching careers, teaching for less than five years. This may reflect the requirement since 2006 for newly appointed DIT teaching staff to take the Diploma course within their first two years of employment. For the external group, length of time teaching was more varied.

Graduates of the Certificate/Diploma and Masters courses, and also the accredited short courses, from 2008-2013 were contacted and invited to attend a focus group. Eight participants attended as two separate groups. Notwithstanding the small sizes of these groups, three of the four Colleges of the Institute were represented, and each participant came from a separate department or school within his/her College. As participation was on a voluntary basis, we could not guarantee attendance from all four Colleges and unfortunately one College was not represented. The focus groups were recorded and fully transcribed, with a thematic analysis of the data undertaken (Bryman & Burgess, 1994).

Limitations of the Research Design

It is important to acknowledge the limitations of the research design adopted, notwithstanding the eight-step approach we have taken informed by the work of Bamber (2013b) in researching academic development. Even with an awareness of the limitations of similar studies (*Literature Review*), we could not necessarily design these out of the evaluation reported here. An interpretivist approach drawing on qualitative methods is appropriate to our stance as researchers, but for ethical reasons participants were self-selecting, and data is self-reported. The data reflect the participants' perceptions of the impact of the accredited programmes on their students' learning, but we do not have data from the students themselves. Even with such data it would be difficult to identify where and how (precisely) student learning had been enhanced, but we make some recommendations to address this point later in the Chapter.

FINDINGS

Questionnaire

This section presents summary findings from the closed questions on the questionnaire, to provide context for the analysis of qualitative data which follows in the subsequent section. The data showed that alumni had a high degree of satisfaction with their chosen courses, they reported benefits for their departments and for their students, and many had continued studying.

93% of the questionnaire respondents said their expectations had been met by their course, with 96% saying their teaching practice had changed. 92% said they had seen changes in their students' learning as a result of their changed practices. 82% of the respondents reported benefits for their departments as a result of their having taken the course, particularly around development of teaching, and also their skills in taking on course redesign and development. Nearly 80% of respondents said they could identify an underlying ethos to the programmes, most identifying the student-centred focus of LTTC courses, which was encouraging

as our team has sought to instil a student-centred approach to our work.

The vast majority of respondents did not have a teaching qualification before undertaking their chosen programme. Overall, five people had completed short courses, 54 had completed the Certificate/Diploma, 23 had completed the MA in Higher Education and 10 had completed the MSc in Applied eLearning. Some people had completed more than one course at the LTTC, and for both internal and external groups there was evidence of progression from the Certificate/Diploma to either the MA or MSc. 25% were continuing their studies at doctoral level, but DIT staff were over-represented in this group: external staff were less likely to be undertaking doctoral level studies.

Analysis of Qualitative Data

This section presents analysis of the qualitative data obtained in the questionnaire and the two Focus Groups. Data were analysed thematically (Bryman & Burgess, 1994). We present first the findings in respect of the identified themes, in order of importance. These findings will be discussed in relation to the research objectives in *Solutions and Recommendations*.

Colleagues in Collaborative Learning

The most important theme to emerge from the focus group discussions, and which emerged repeatedly in response to a range of questions, was the benefit of working as part of a class cohort and interacting with colleagues during an accredited course.

Certainly being able to meet people from such a broad range of disciplines, to be put into that kind of mix, to see how the Engineers think, to see how the Chemistry people think, from [named College] for example, it was very, very stimulating (Participant 3, Focus Group 1)

These interactions were separate to the collegial relationships participants had in their own teams or disciplines, and were characterised as being beneficial precisely because of the differences, and because of the opportunities to meet people from other institutions or subject areas. While it might be argued that such networks could be fostered independently of accredited programmes, participants commented on the value of their courses as a safe space to discuss their teaching. The potential to confer with colleagues on new approaches to teaching, new methods, tools and techniques, was of crucial importance and could not be replaced by reading or accessing the information in other ways.

The fact that you are meeting like-minded people, like-minded people in the same place, and that's really the big thing for me, you know that you're put in with a group of people who are talking about things, and if you get people talking about things, then you get to improve them and start thinking about things in a different way yourself. So that was the key benefit for me. (Participant 1, Focus Group 1)

More formal – and formative – collaborations were undertaken through groupwork, which was identified as a key benefit of participation in an accredited course. However, this was also a significant challenge for some people, and their experiences informed their own use of groupwork in their classrooms. Once they had become accustomed to group work, it became a valuable learning experience. Following completion of the Certificate/Diploma, in particular, there was a sense of belonging to a network or even a group of alumni, and the social dimension of being in that group persisted, providing additional support to participants:

When you talk to people, (..) when you do the Cert or Diploma or whatever, and the next question usually is, who was on it when you did it?

[laughter] Because we all knew each other to a certain extent, and there's a huge benefit and support in that. (Participant 2, Focus Group 1)

Developing Confidence in Teaching

The second theme to emerge consistently throughout the focus group discussions was that of confidence. For many of the participants, there was no difficulty in thinking about introducing changes to their teaching, but initial reluctance or a fear that something could go wrong. There were repeated references to the development of confidence in teaching, confidence in making changes to programmes, and in the introduction of new methods for assessment or feedback:

You could still try new things but it's easier and you have more confidence because of learning about it first and – crucially – having had the chance to discuss it with other people in the class (Participant 2, Focus Group 1)

While other settings could afford the development of confidence in teaching, the accredited courses provided authentic exercises in making significant change (for example, introducing problem-based learning, or redesigning modules) before making these changes in reality. There was a keen awareness that lecturers could not just experiment in class – they had to be mindful of their students' needs too:

it would be very difficult to attempt something like that without having been here [in the course]. You could probably do it but you would probably have casualties along the way, which are people's future, and you can't mess with people's future (Participant 2, Focus Group 1)

Enhancing Students' Learning

Participants reported numerous examples of how their accredited courses had positively impacted on their teaching and their students' learning. For some, these experiences had been transformational in nature:

Well, I mean when I first started I could see that the lecturing thing wasn't really very, a very positive experience for all involved, so by attending the course here and by talking to others outside I was sort of able to transform practice, so it has totally changed (Participant 1, Focus Group 2)

They responded keenly to the question of whether students' learning had improved as a result of their own participation in accredited courses in teaching and learning:

I would have to say absolutely (..) I would have to say there's been a transformation in the way that students have engaged.

Positive learning experiences affected their students' confidence too:

you can see that they're more confident, and when they're going into project work as well they're much more confident and self-assured, and like that's fantastic (Participant 5, Focus Group 2)

We have previously stated some of the limitations of this research inasmuch as participants were drawn from programme alumni, and measuring the impact of accredited programmes from the perspective of students was not practicable in this particular study. However, participants did comment on factors supporting their observations of change in discussing student engagement and retention. For example, Participant 4 (Focus Group 2) describes a change in attendance rate following the introduction of active learning methodologies in his teaching:

And you know that's very easily measurable I guess in the way that they will attend modules because if, you know, if it's not working out the way they

expect, or if it's not exceeding their expectations, they'll drift away quickly, and in some very difficult modules that don't sound at all sexy, the attendance rates have rocketed and students are fully engaged, and producing extraordinary work. (Participant 4, Focus Group 2)

The discussion also focused on sustaining changes in teaching which could lead to greater levels of student engagement. Change in one topic or module led to thinking more about how and where it fitted with the full programme. The challenge then was to continue to innovate, and to try to redesign the curriculum rather than just isolated pockets of activity within it, and this was linked with the expectations of students:

you start to realise that and you start to think well if there was more of this in the programme, they might be more prepared for these modules then when they get to them. So I've been sort of trying to chip away on the curriculum level with others and to try and sort of not just reform my teaching practice but to try and help reform the curriculum (Participant 1, Focus Group 2)

But the focus group participants were also very clear about the challenges they had encountered. Introducing different methods of learning and teaching brought its own difficulties, and again the place of student-centred modules in a broader curriculum could be difficult to reconcile:

student-centred learning isn't necessarily student-friendly. Student-centred learning can be quite hard on students, it's much more, independent thinkers and so on, and if they're just getting little islands of it in the curriculum I don't know (..) if the entire curriculum had a student-centred learning approach it should be more effective (Participant 1, Focus Group 2)

These examples show that graduates of the accredited courses changed their own teaching methods and practices, had seen increased levels of student engagement, and had begun to look at sustaining change in the wider curriculum. The feedback indicating that student motivation is raised, that retention in class has improved, and that the quality of students' work has been significantly enhanced, suggests a range of positive outcomes from their experiences of accredited professional development.

Learning the Language

Engaging with the scholarship of teaching and learning had contributed to the confidence people had in their work, as well as giving them a new area in which to research and publish. They felt they had the language and terminology to engage with teaching and learning issues, and research. Participants described significant personal benefits and a sense of achievement as they had published their work, and spoken at conferences about their pedagogical research. Participant 3 in Focus Group 2 described three separate publications derived from the MA, and an invitation to present at an upcoming conference:

I would never have thought four years ago that I would ever have been doing anything like that or have the confidence to do something like that and I think doing the MA and having to write a conference paper and having to present it you know even just here in front of your peers (..) that really enabled me, and I think the peers that were on the course at the time to be able to do things like that (Participant 3, Focus Group 2)

Having acquired the 'language' of teaching and learning, participants were also better equipped to deal with institutional programme documentation, validation processes and other issues (Participant 2, Focus Group 1). Their studies had enabled them not only to manage course administration, but also to develop and validate new courses and to respond to the changing economic climate which called for programme modernisation (Participants 2 and 3, Focus Group 1).

Positive Impact on Home Department/School

There was frequent discussion in the focus groups of the broader impact their experiences had had back in their Schools and Departments. Different threads could be identified here: participants had been successful in winning institutional project funding (Participants 1 and 2, Focus Group 1; Participants 1, 2 and 3, Focus Group 2). They were able to share their knowledge and experiences with colleagues, and contribute to innovations:

you can see the benefit across, as a School, it's been useful and I know we've shared a lot of information as well within the College not just within the School (..) we've revamped a lot of programmes and modules, in terms of how you assess, and just aligning all our learning outcomes with our assessment and looking at the big picture (Participant 5, Focus Group 2)

In a few cases, the work undertaken with colleagues in a School or Department had led into the establishment of semi-formal groups. These groups were focused on issues in teaching or "educational research" (Participant 5, Focus Group 2). They examined the development of teaching and learning in the discipline, and often coordinated efforts to obtain funding, try new methods or to look at on-going professional development opportunities together. These examples point to the potential longer-term added value of the accredited courses, and additional return for Departments and Schools investing in continuing professional development for their staff.

Practical Issues and Challenges

In both the questionnaire and the focus group strands of this research, we sought to hear from participants in detail about the practical issues and challenges associated with attending an accredited programme. The investment of time in an accredited course (from both individual and home department) is significant, and although positive outcomes had been reported these needed to be balanced against the practical difficulties and challenges encountered. These will be summarised here in the interests of space, but have been reported them in greater detail locally.

Internal and external respondents to the questionnaire were motivated to enrol in programmes because they were interested in the topics, wanted a teaching qualification or wanted to experience new teaching methods from a student's perspective. Practical arrangements around the courses did not seem to influence the decision to enrol, although time pressures once studying were considerable. Obtaining permission to be away from teaching in order to study was difficult, and was referred to by all participants in the Focus Groups. Their studies were often accommodated only in their spare time:

I would have done a lot of the assignments in, at Christmas, Easter, whenever you had a break, and just fly through them, which was, all of your holidays was used to do your assignments, because like you have 20 hours teaching, and that's just teaching, then there's correcting and so on, so it's at the worst stage of your career but it is when you need it most (Participant 5, Focus Group 2)

Participants in both Focus Groups felt that it was essential for new lecturers to have a teaching qualification. Without professional development, it was felt that new lecturers would naturally teach in the way they had been taught themselves:

..very easy to get into a rut where you say, this is how I teach, you give your notes and you walk away again, particularly if you're given a lot of hours at the start and once you get into that sort

of situation you might just say that's the way it is and never move on (Participant 1, Focus Group 1)

In spite of the time challenges, the practical arrangements for the courses were not considered to be obstacles. In terms of the content of the accredited courses, some participants felt that some modules might be too theoretical, and that there might be greater use of new technologies and social media. But they also recalled having enjoyed modules when they had not expected to (Participant 3, Focus Group 1), and argued against changing challenging activities such as micro-teaching and teaching observation. There is also evidence from some of the examples discussed at the focus groups (and in the questionnaires) of a greater engagement with e-learning, including the institutional virtual learning environment, audience response systems, and podcasting/screencasting following completion of an accredited course.

Alternative forms of accreditation were discussed, such as more flexible modular structures for courses or independent completion of a teaching portfolio. However, although there had been positive responses to this in the questionnaires, there was much more caution amongst the focus group participants. It was felt that more flexible forms of accreditation could encourage people to work strategically, rather than participate and engage fully with course materials and activities. Once again, the importance of learning with colleagues and interacting with them emerged from this discussion:

the course isn't really content-driven, it's not really you have to attend these classes and you have to read the notes and you have to... it's I think what you learn is by attending and actually communicating with the other people on the course and I think for a lot of postgraduate courses even within your discipline that would be the same, it's not really what you're reading, it's a sharing of different perspectives and how things work (Participant 5, Focus Group 2)

The Wider Importance of Learning and Teaching in an Institution

We asked participants about whether and how teaching was valued within their home departments and organisations. This issue relates to the broader discourse on the importance of qualifications in teaching at third level, and the status of teaching in higher education (discussed in the opening sections of this Chapter). Aside from their informal working groups, and keeping in contact with fellow alumni, participants were not sure of the broader importance attributed to teaching development. Their work, including their educational research, might not be recognized as readily as disciplinary research. Research metrics did not include educational research and it was not counted (Participant 5, Focus Group 2). However, when other metrics for quality assurance in teaching were being applied, the work then became valued.

Re-designed courses using active learning methods were often regarded as being more resource-intensive than those taught through lectures, making them a hard sell to colleagues. Notwithstanding institutional support for the development of teaching, it could be difficult for individuals to implement the kinds of changes they felt programmes and modules then needed. In one case, a participant felt his department was making a more conscious effort to recognise the work of staff in gaining qualifications in teaching and the innovations they were making to curricula. This may have been related to the requirements of their allied professional body, but nonetheless he felt that "at least it's there, and the moment is there" (Participant 1, Focus Group 2). This perhaps indicates the importance of certain external drivers, including professional bodies' accreditation processes, in supporting academic development in higher education.

The focus group participants appeared to agree that it would take time, and also a 'critical mass' of qualified and/or interested colleagues before recognition of the importance of teaching would be achieved across an organisation. Even then, however, it would be unlikely to help with an individual's chances of promotion.

DISCUSSION

In this Chapter, we have asked whether accredited training and professional development for academics has led to changes in their teaching, whether these changes have been positive, and whether the student learning experience has been enhanced. We adopted an interpretivist stance for this research, using qualitative methods and framing the work in the evaluation model proposed by Bamber (2013b). We sought to address the experiences of more than 200 alumni of our accredited professional development programmes through a systematic approach to the study, and conscious recognition of our own roles in the research process.

Our review of the literature indicated mixed findings from the work of other researchers, but also identified the theoretical and methodological difficulties inherent in gathering evidence in relation to the impact of programmes. We experienced similar challenges in our own work. In particular, the issue of measuring impact from the perspective of students themselves is unresolved, and results in research reliant on the reports of those doing the teaching. This may be mitigated through the evidence mix: the strength of the data from our closed questionnaire questions validates the detailed reported experiences of the participants in our focus groups. However, other approaches to this issue could include the analysis of examination results, student retention and progression rates, and qualitative data-gathering with the students themselves – provided an ethically sound design could be made for this.

The results of our research indicate that academics have changed their teaching as a result of undertaking accredited professional development, and that they feel their students have benefited as a result. Participants saw many positive changes in students' learning, and were able to give numerous examples from their practice. Students were engaged with their courses, retention within courses had been improved, and students' work was of a higher quality. The personal and professional benefits to participants were also clearly evident, with many participants continuing their studies and moving into both educational research and research in their disciplines. These benefits should not be seen only in terms of one individual's continuing professional development, but also in terms of the relationship between teaching and research, with teaching leading into research and into new fields of research for some. Participants were reporting longer term impacts as they may have completed the programme a number of years previously and therefore had time to develop and change their practice. Taken together, these findings indicate the value of accredited development for the enhancement of teaching and learning, even if as researchers we face a range of challenges in measuring this value accurately.

These benefits have emerged notwithstanding the struggles and challenges both academics and students face in undertaking their studies. Institutional strategies prioritise excellence in disciplinary research, and resource constraints may well favour traditional modes of transmission-oriented teaching. While there is greater recognition emerging at national level for academic development, this exists in the context of both government proposals to reconfigure the tertiary sector, and the continuing funding challenges facing higher education.

It is important to acknowledge again the limitations of the research presented here, as a short study conducted on the basis of self-selection by participants. One recommendation emerging from this work is that researchers should expand the methods used to evaluate the impact of accredited programmes over a longer period of time, drawing on the evaluation models discussed earlier

in order to build up a clearer picture of impact (Bamber, 2013a, 2013b; Fleming, 2012). If the impact of accredited programmes on classroom teaching and learning is difficult to measure, estimating the impact of such programmes on the institution and on a national higher education sector is an even greater challenge. However, the indications from our work suggest that accredited programmes have an impact far beyond the immediate loci of participants' teaching and that this is worthy of further exploration. Through the work of the programme alumni, curricular change and constructive alignment (Biggs, 2003) are being addressed in schools and departments. Institutions therefore have the opportunity to make substantial progress towards their strategic objectives of excellence in teaching and learning. Course development and validation processes are engaged with in-depth, rather than being regarded at a superficial level. Research activity is being developed and enhanced. These developments occur organically as the undefined longer-term learning outcomes of accredited programmes such as ours. The high level of satisfaction amongst external participants demonstrates the appeal of the accredited courses to people outside the 'provider' Institute. Their involvement is highly valued by internal participants for the enriched discussion in class. The sector as a whole is enriched through sharing continuing professional development activities. Furthermore, the appeal of these courses to external participants is also something that can be valued in terms of income generation for the Institute going into the future

There were few indications from this study that participants and graduates of our programmes would suggest major change or restructuring of those programmes, and they have helped to discern the good in our work (Stake, 2004). However, we can identify recommendations for the future too. Impact needs to be researched through more methodologically eclectic designs, and across external contexts as well as the immediate contexts of our programmes. It may be appropriate to increase provision in certain areas, notably in short courses which could build towards particular qualifications. This structure, in tandem with the existing provision, would offer some additional flexibility to staff and perhaps accommodate them more easily given the increasing pressures on their time.

FUTURE RESEARCH DIRECTIONS

Our review of literature, and the case study presented in this Chapter have sought to examine the impact of accredited academic professional development programmes in higher education. Evidence has been presented to support the conclusion that such programmes are valuable, and are having a positive impact on teaching and learning. However, this evidence has also demonstrated the complexity and difficulty of developing appropriate research methods to evaluate and measure impact in this area. Future research should address this issue in the first instance, before seeking further evidence from stakeholders and course participants

Stefani (2003) has alluded to the need to become more businesslike in our thinking and approach to evaluation of practice. It is challenging to move in this direction as we know well that HEIs have different purposes to for-profit organisations. They have different ambitions, goals and needs. Whatever metrics we ultimately develop to evaluate the effectiveness of our professional development programmes and initiatives, they will be different to those in business. But they could nonetheless demonstrate cost benefits, for example through student retention and progression. There is a clear sense of the importance of integrating professional development with efforts to improve strategic implementation in our institutions. Our programmes can be evaluated to tabulate their benefits more precisely. In turn, our evaluation should provide better and organisation-specific indicators of what types of development are appropriate, and which should be strengthened, changed or even abandoned.

Other studies have drawn on national surveys of student engagement to compare data with that reported by programme alumni. This could become possible in Ireland with the introduction of a national survey in 2013. Instruments such as the *Approaches to Teaching Inventory* have also been used to triangulate data in at least one study (Lueddeke, 2003). We propose that this area of work should be the focus of future research efforts in the short term.

CONCLUSION

In this Chapter, we asked whether accredited training and professional development for academics has led to real changes in their teaching, whether these changes have been positive, and whether the student learning experience has been enhanced. There is emergent evidence in the literature of the effectiveness of accredited programmes, and this is supported by our findings most recently at DIT.

We asked in turn, if it could be possible through the enhancement of teaching and learning, to create a more responsive higher education sector, and whether staff could better address their roles in context through reflective practice. This question is much more difficult to address, and perhaps it should be redefined at the more granular level of changes to lessons, modules and programmes. If we consider change at this level, then there is evidence pointing to positive changes in methods, teaching and assessment practices, and the engagement of students in their learning. As these changes become embedded and grow, we may come to see a more responsive sector, contributing more readily to society and better able to meet fresh challenges in a more complex world.

REFERENCES

Bamber, V. (2008). Evaluating lecturer development programmes: Received wisdom or self-knowledge? *The International Journal for Academic Development, 13*(2), 107–116. doi:10.1080/13601440802076541

Bamber, V. (2013a). Evidence, chimera and belief. *SEDA Special, 34.*

Bamber, V. (2013b). A desideratum of evidencing value. *SEDA Special, 34.*

Bamber, V., & Anderson, S. (2012). Evaluating learning and teaching: Institutional needs and individual practices. *The International Journal for Academic Development, 17*(1), 5–18. doi:10. 1080/1360144X.2011.586459

Bamber, V., & Anderson, S. (2012). Evaluating learning and teaching: Institutional needs and individual practices. *The International Journal for Academic Development, 17*(1), 5–18. doi:10. 1080/1360144X.2011.586459

Bamber, V., & Trowler, P. (2005). Compulsory higher education teacher training: Joined-up policies, institutional architectures and enhancement cultures. *The International Journal for Academic Development, 10*(2), 79–93. doi:10.1080/13601440500281708

Baume, D. (2008). A toolkit for evaluating educational development ventures. *SEDA, 9*(4).

Biggs, J. (2003). Aligning teaching and assessing to course objectives. *Teaching and Learning in Higher Education: New Trends and Innovations, 2*, 13–17.

Bostock, S. J. (1998). Constructivism in mass higher education: A case study. *British Journal of Educational Technology, 29*(3), 225–240. doi:10.1111/1467-8535.00066

Bryman, A., & Burgess, R. G. (Eds.). (1994). *Analyzing qualitative data.* London: Routledge. doi:10.4324/9780203413081

Chalmers, D., & Thompson, K. (2008). *Snapshot of teaching and learning practice in Australian universities.* Carrick Institute Report on Behalf of Australian Learning and Teaching Council.

Cohen, L., Manion, L., & Morrison, K. (2011). *Research methods in education* (7th ed.). London: Routledge Department for Education and Skills.

Entwistle, N. (2009). *Teaching for understanding at university.* London: Palgrave Macmillan.

Fink, L. D. (2013). The current status of faculty development internationally. *International Journal for the Scholarship of Teaching and Learning, 7*(2). Retrieved from http://w3.georgiasouthern.edu/ijsotl/v7n2.html

Fleming, A. (2012). Developmental evaluation and the "double loop": Adding value to the evaluation of complex change. *SEDA Special, 33.*

Gibbs, G., & Coffey, M. (2004). The impact of training of university teachers on their teaching skills, their approach to teaching, and the approach to learning of their students. *Active Learning in Higher Education, 5*(1), 87–100. doi:10.1177/1469787404040463

Gosling, D. (2009). Educational development in the UK: A complex and contradictory reality. *The International Journal for Academic Development, 14*(1), 5–18. doi:10.1080/13601440802659122

Guardian Professional – Higher Education Network. (2013). *Stick or twist: The postdoctoral dilemma.* Last accessed 15th March 2014 at http://www.theguardian.com/higher-education-network/blog/2013/jun/21/postfoc-dilemma-stick-or-twist

Hanbury, A., Prosser, M., & Rickinson, M. (2008). The differential impact of UK accredited teaching development programmes on academics' approaches to teaching. *Studies in Higher Education, 33*(4), 469–483. doi:10.1080/03075070802211844

Harvey, J., Donnelly, R., & McAvinia, C. (2013). *Engaging lecturers as students: Building sustainable professional development.* Paper presented at the 6th Annual Learning Innovation Conference: Sustainable Models of Student Engagement – Rhetoric or Achievable? Dublin, Ireland.

Higher Education Authority (HEA). (2012). *A proposed reconfiguration of the Irish system of higher education.* Report of the International Expert Panel for the Higher Education Authority of Ireland. Retrieved from http://9thlevel.ie/wp-content/uploads/International_Panel_Report.pdf

Jordan, A., Carlile, O., & Stack, A. (2008). *Approaches to learning: A guide for teachers.* Maidenhead, UK: Open University Press.

Kahn, P., Young, R., Grace, S., Pilkington, R., Rush, L., Tomkinson, B., & Willis, T. (2006). *The role and effectiveness of reflective practices in programmes for new academic staff: A grounded practitioner review of research literature.* York, UK: Higher Education Academy.

Kandlbinder, P., & Peseta, T. (2009). Key concepts in postgraduate certificates in higher education teaching and learning in Australasia and the United Kingdom. *The International Journal for Academic Development, 14*(1), 19–31. doi:10.1080/13601440802659247

Knight, P., Tait, J., & Yorke, M. (2006). The professional learning of teachers in higher education. *Studies in Higher Education, 31*(3), 319–339. doi:10.1080/03075070600680786

Laurillard, D. (2001). *Rethinking university teaching: A conversational framework for the use of educational technology.* London: Routledge.

Lucas, L. (2006). *The research game in academic life.* London: Palgrave.

Lueddeke, G. R. (2003). Professionalising teaching practice in higher education: A study of disciplinary variation and 'teaching scholarship'. *Studies in Higher Education, 28*(2), 213–228. doi:10.1080/0307507032000058082

McAvinia, C., Harvey, J., Donnelly, R., McDonnell, C., & Hanratty, O. (2014). *What has been the impact of accredited professional development for people teaching in higher education?* Paper presented at the UK Higher Education Academy 10th Annual Conference, Birmingham, UK.

National Committee of Inquiry into Higher Education (NCIHE). (1997). *Higher education in the learning society.* Norwich: Crown Copyright.

National Strategy for Higher Education to 2030. (2011). Dublin: Department of Education and Skills.

O'Connell, T., & Dyment, J. (2006). Reflections on using journals in higher education: A focus group discussion with faculty. *Assessment & Evaluation in Higher Education, 31*(6), 671–691. doi:10.1080/02602930600760884

Parsons, D., Hill, I., Holland, J., & Wills, D. (2012). *Impact of teaching development programmes in higher education.* York, UK: Higher Education Academy.

Pickering, A. (2006). Learning about university teaching: Reflections on a research study investigating influences for change. *Teaching in Higher Education, 11*(3), 319–335. doi:10.1080/13562510600680756

Porritt, V. (2014). Evaluating the impact of professional learning. In S. Cowley (Ed.), *Challenging professional learning.* Abingdon, UK: Routledge.

Prosser, M., Rickinson, M., Bence, V., Hanbury, A., & Kulej, M. (2006). *Formative evaluation of accredited programmes.* York, UK: Higher Education Academy.

Rowland, S. (2002). Overcoming fragmentation in professional life: The challenge for academic development. *Higher Education Quarterly, 56*(1), 52–64. doi:10.1111/1468-2273.00202

Stake, R. E. (Ed.). (2004). *Standards-based and responsive evaluation.* Thousand Oaks, CA: Sage Publications.

Stefani, L. (Ed.). (2011). *Evaluating the effectives of academic development: Principles and practice.* Abingdon, UK: Routledge.

Stes, A., Clement, M., & Van Petegem, P. (2007). The effectiveness of a faculty training programme: Long-term and institutional impact. *The International Journal for Academic Development, 12*(2), 99–109. doi:10.1080/13601440701604898

THE. (2014). *World rankings 2014.* Accessed 15th March 2014 from http://www.timeshighereducation.co.uk/world-university-rankings/

Trigwell, K., Caballero-Rodrigues, K., & Han, F. (2012). Assessing the impact of a university teaching development programme. *Assessment & Evaluation in Higher Education, 37*(4), 499–511. doi:10.1080/02602938.2010.547929

ADDITIONAL READING

Bamber, V., & Anderson, S. (2012). Evaluating learning and teaching: Institutional needs and individual practices. *The International Journal for Academic Development, 17*(1), 5–18. doi:10.1080/1360144X.2011.586459

Bamber, V., Walsh, L., Juwah, C., & Ross, D. (2006). New lecturer development programmes: A case study of Scottish higher education institutions. *Teacher Development, 10*(2), 207–231. doi:10.1080/13664530600773069

Donnelly, R. (2006). Exploring lecturers' self-perception of change in teaching practice. *Teaching in Higher Education, 11*(2), 203–217. doi:10.1080/13562510500527735

Fitzmaurice, M. (2013). Constructing professional identity as a new academic: A moral endeavour. *Studies in Higher Education, 38*(4), 613–622. doi:10.1080/03075079.2011.594501

Gibbs, G. (2010). *Dimensions of quality.* York, UK: Higher Education Academy.

Gibbs, G. (2012). *Implications of dimensions of quality in a market environment.* York, UK: Higher Education Academy.

Gosling, D., & Hannan, A. (2007). Responses to a policy initiative: The case of centres for excellence in teaching and learning. *Studies in Higher Education, 32*(5), 633–646. doi:10.1080/03075070701573799

Knight, P. (2002). A systemic approach to professional development: Learning as practice. *Teaching and Teacher Education, 18*(3), 229–241. doi:10.1016/S0742-051X(01)00066-X

Knight, P. (2006). Quality enhancement and educational professional development. *Quality in Higher Education, 12*(1), 29–40. doi:10.1080/13538320600685123

Kreber, C., Brook, P., & Policy, E. (2001). Impact evaluation of educational development programmes. *The International Journal for Academic Development, 6*(2), 96–108. doi:10.1080/13601440110090749

MacCormack, C., & Kelly, P. (2012). How do we know it works? Developing and evaluating a professional development program for part-time teachers. In F. Beaton & A. Gilbert (Eds.), *Developing effective part-time teachers in contemporary universities: New approaches to professional development* (pp. 94–113). London: SEDA Routledge.

Nasr, A., Gillet, M., & Booth, E. (1996). Lecturers' teaching qualifications and their teaching performance. *Research and Development in Higher Education*, *18*, 576–581.

Nicholls, G. (2005). New lecturers' constructions of learning, teaching and research in higher education. *Studies in Higher Education*, *30*(5), 611–625. doi:10.1080/03075070500249328

Prebble, T., Hargraves, H., Leach, L., Naidoo, K., Suddaby, G., & Zepke, N. (2004). Impact of student support services and academic development programmes on student outcomes in undergraduate tertiary study: A synthesis of the research. Ministry of Education, New Zealand

Prince, M. J., Felder, R. M., & Brent, R. (2007). Does faculty research improve undergraduate teaching? An analysis of existing and potential synergies. *The Journal of Engineering Education*, *96*(4), 283–294. doi:10.1002/j.2168-9830.2007.tb00939.x

Rodgers, R., Christie, J., & Wideman, M. (2014). *The effects of a required faculty development program on novice faculty self-efficacy and teaching*. Toronto, Canada: Higher Education Quality Council of Ontario.

Rust, C. (2000). Do initial training courses have an impact on university teaching? The evidence from two evaluative studies of one course. *Innovations in Education and Training International*, *37*(3), 254–262. doi:10.1080/13558000050138498

Rust, C. (2006). The impact of educational development workshops on teachers' practice. *The International Journal for Academic Development*, *3*(1), 72–80. doi:10.1080/1360144980030110

Sharpe, R. (2004) How do professional learn and develop? Implications for staff and educational developers. In D. Baume & P. Kahn (Eds.), Enhancing staff and educational development. Abingdon, UK: RoutledgeFalmer. doi:10.4324/9780203416228_chapter_8

Smith, J. (2005). From flowers to palms: 40 years of policy for online learning. *Association for Learning Technology Journal*, *13*(2), 93–108.

Stefani, L., & Elton, L. (2002). Continuing professional development of academic teachers through self-initiated learning. *Assessment & Evaluation in Higher Education*, *27*(2), 117–129. doi:10.1080/02602930220128706

Stes, A., Clement, M., & Van Petegem, P. (2007). The effectiveness of a faculty training programme: Long-term and institutional impact. *The International Journal for Academic Development*, *12*(2), 99–109. doi:10.1080/13601440701604898

KEY TERMS AND DEFINITIONS

Academic Professional Development: While this may take many forms in higher education institutions, we refer in this Chapter most often to the professional development undertaken by academics to enhance their teaching and their students' learning.

Accredited Programmes: Short courses of a module or more, certificate, diploma or master's level qualifications taken for credit in a higher education institution.

Evaluation: There are various definitions of evaluation in education, in this Chapter we regard evaluation as process-oriented research into practice drawing on multiple sources of data.

Institutes of Technology: Tertiary level institutions in Ireland offering awards from apprentice through to doctoral levels, and traditionally having a closer relationship with applied practice and industry than universities.

National Forum for the Enhancement of Teaching and Learning: Established in Ireland in 2012 in order to enhance the quality of the learning experience for all students at third level, with a focus on recognising and enhancing teaching quality in higher education.

Reflective Practice: There are many definitions of reflective practice, and a lengthy discussion of these is not possible here for reasons of space. In this Chapter we use reflective practice to mean the process by which professional educators observe, analyse and interrogate their teaching in order to identify areas for development and change.

Scholarship of Teaching and Learning: There are various definitions of this area of activity, in this Chapter we define scholarship of teaching and learning as formal research into students' learning, and teaching practices in higher education.

UK Higher Education Academy: Established in the UK in 2004 to enhance teaching and learning development across higher education, initially through a network of subject centres and latterly through funded initiatives and awards.

ENDNOTES

[1]   Institutes of Technology are tertiary level institutions in Ireland offering awards from apprentice through to doctoral levels, and traditionally having a closer relationship with applied practice and industry than universities.

Chapter 14
Case Study of a Hybrid Undergraduate Elementary Certification Program

Carmen Popa
University of Oradea, Romania

Carlton J. Fitzgerald
New England College, USA

Simona Laurian
University of Oradea, Romania

Delia Birle
University of Oradea, Romania

Laura Bochis
University of Oradea, Romania

Elena Bonchis
University of Oradea, Romania

ABSTRACT

The goal of this study was to assist instructors and leadership of a hybrid weekend pre-service teacher education program at the University of Oradea to improve their effectiveness with students. Specifically, this study sought to gather and analyze data from three program constituents: students, instructors, and program leadership. The preschool and primary weekend education program at the University of Oradea was developed to be suitable for students who for various reasons cannot attend the traditional day classes. In 2011, the weekend program was changed into a hybrid program in an effort to more directly meet the needs of the student population. In order to more effectively meet the needs of the students, it became obvious that the pedagogy and structure of the program needed refinement. The data gathered in this study allowed the research team to develop recommendations for program, pedagogical, and textbook improvements.

INTRODUCTION

The University of Oradea, which was charted in 1990, is housed in Oradea, Romania. There are 108 undergraduate programs, 86 master degree programs and 10 doctoral programs offered by the university. The university is organized into 15 faculties at the undergraduate and graduate levels and three independent departments: the Teacher Training Department, the On-line Department, and the Life Long Learning Department. The University has adopted the European Credit Transfer and Accumulation System (ECTS) in

DOI: 10.4018/978-1-4666-7244-4.ch014

order to allow students to participate in classes throughout Europe and transfer their credits to the University of Oradea. This agreement also allows students from other European countries to attend classes in Oradea and transfer those credits to their home universities. Approximately 11781 undergraduate students are enrolled at the university and 2931 students attend graduate levels classes. The Sciences of Education department houses 457 students. The weekend program for primary and pre-school pre-service teachers hosts 184 students.

The mission statement for the university states that its goal is to promote knowledge, research and training through partnerships among teachers, students and the community. According to its mission the University seeks to train and educate undergraduate and graduate students on a large scale and at a high level. The weekend education program was developed to be aligned with and assist the university in accomplishing this mission.

The Pedagogy of the Primary and Pre-School Education program is housed in the Department of Sciences of Education from the Faculty of Social and Humanistic Sciences. There are seventeen full-time instructors in the department. Associate instructors are also hired by the university on a need basis. The certification program is a three year process. Students progress through the program as a cohort with all students taking the same courses together during their program. Each cohort is assigned an advisor who remains with the cohort for their three years at the university. Students participate in 60 courses in three categories: Core Education courses (9 courses), specialty courses (43 courses), and elective courses (8 courses). Students participate in community schools every semester, usually one day per week. Courses are usually divided into two types, theoretical and practical. In the theoretical classes students learn educational and psychological theory. The practical seminars are organized to give students more real life experiences related to the theories studied in the theoretical classes. In their specialty courses students also participate in laboratory (e.g. music,

art, etc.) and practicum courses (methods of teaching), based on the discipline under study. At the completion of the program students are certified as Pre-School and Primary Teachers.

The teacher certification program has a long tradition, starting in 1785 with a vocational high school. In 1989 the state changed the certification process and required all teachers to be college graduates. The first weekend classes for education majors began in 1997 as an independent department. In 2005 the program was transferred to the faculty of Social and Humanistic Sciences in the Department of Sciences of Education. University weekend classes were endorsed by the national government in 2001 based on Government Decision No. 1101, and the law was updated in 2011 by the National Education Law. According to national standards weekend programs can only be instituted if there is an identical program in the day program. The education weekend program at the University of Oradea is the only teacher certification program that uses a hybrid weekend model.

In 2011, during the accreditation process, the weekend program acquired its present hybrid format. The program changed its philosophy from being a traditional weekend program running traditional face-to-face classes to a hybrid program based on a tri-dimensional pedagogical model. Online resources were added to the program and policies and procedures changed to adapt to the new roles of instructors in a more student centered and hybrid process. The program identified the non-traditional nature of its weekend students and developed the present instructional philosophy. Instructors who were not experienced working online had to learn how to use a new platform, new procedures, and new technology. Some instructors quickly adapted to the new systems while others struggled with their new teaching environment. Some instructors use the online portion of the program as a significant part of their teaching while other use the online resources to give out information and class resources for students. The format and content of the class texts changed significantly. Instructors are now required to differentiate their teaching in their texts. The text became a student centered resource to assist the students in their independent learning. The format and activities in the new formatted textbooks are set to assist students in their self-assessments and allow students to learn content in a progressive fashion. Instructors are now asked to include graphics and other visuals to assist students in their learning. In addition, the goals and competencies of the course and the content, activities, formative assessments and summative assessments are connected as an integrated whole in each textbook.

Instructors are also now asked to differentiate their teaching to meet the needs of adult full-time workers. Teachers are also asked to consider the travel issues encountered by their students in the development of the three aspects of their classes (face-to-face, online, and the instructor developed textbook). For example, instructors are asked to integrate the content and experiences of the texts and online experiences with their face-to-face work in order to give students multiple access points to the important course content. As the program has developed during the past three years professionals who work in the program have recognized that the weekend student body is extremely different from a traditional day class program. This recognition allowed the program to identify who its students are: older working adults, with families, diverse educational backgrounds, who live in a large geographic area with transportation issues, and most of whom have been out of school for many years. A group of these students is already teaching but have not graduated from a university, while another group is attempting to make a career change. Once the program recognized who the students are it became obvious that the philosophy of teaching and learning had to change from teacher centered teaching to student centered learning.

The purpose of our chapter is to describe the weekend program's progress as we have attempted to develop a high quality hybrid program for our elementary pre-service teachers. Our goal is to develop teachers who will enter the field prepared both theoretically and practically to engage their students in high quality educational activities. As we reflect on our work and the data we have collected our hope is that other programs will learn from both our failures and successes.

BACKGROUND

Introduction

Most people today would agree that modern technologies have drastically changed our world. Students have different situations and needs and it makes sense that our programs should adjust to meet those needs. The weekend pre-school and primary certification program at the University of Oradea has adapted its weekend program in an attempt to adjust to the needs of our future teachers. Blended learning has become an important area of review for many educators. There are various definitions for blended learning (Staker & Horn, 2012) and the program at the University of Oradea is developing the weekend program to be in line with the following definition: Blended learning is composed of a teaching and learning process in which students spend part of their time in face-to-face practical classes supervised by teachers, in schools supervised by a mentor and a classroom teacher, and at home learning independently. Students and teachers have access to an online platform for a portion of their work and most of the class resources (Staker & Horn, 2012).

The weekend program is a unique program for the University. There are two faculties that employ online programs at the University for students in traditional type of programs. In Romania there are various online teacher education programs (e.g. Cluj, Brasov, Bucharest, Iasi, Timisoara) but the weekend program at the University of Oradea is the only hybrid program developed for preschool and primary certification. Hybrid programs are developing at a rapid rate around the world (Picciano et al., 2013). As these programs develop people are learning how to integrate what they see as best practices from both face-to-face and online learning (Staker & Horn, 2012). To be successful, hybrid programs have to do more than just use technology to start discussion boards. Programs that have been successful work to develop a sense of community with the use of various tools and methods to engage students and their instructors in interacting (Lord & Lomicka, 2008). As the weekend program has developed it has been important to attempt to make it more student centered (Leese, 2009). The goal is to have students become immersed in deep and complex activities (Caine et al, 2009) in which students take more control over their learning (Tucker, 2012). Instructors have to change their focus from disseminators of information to coaches who guide their students in their learning (Tucker, 2012; Whipp, 2009). In this process part of the traditional classroom has been flipped (Berhmann & Sams, 2012) in order to give students more time to interact with each other and with their instructor (Hall, 2007).

At New England College, in Henniker, New Hampshire, USA, we have developed a fully online program for three of our majors, psychology, business, and criminal justice. The college has also developed a hybrid evening program for master of education students who are full-time teachers. Instructors at the college are using flipped classroom concepts in some of their teaching (Berhmann & Sams, 2012). Blended classrooms are becoming popular throughout the nation (Clark, 2011; Lloyd-Smith, 2010; Means et al, 2013). These blended classes take on many forms depending on the preferences of the instructors. The program at the University of Oradea is unique with its ability to include seminar, online, and practicum experiences in every class.

Our search into the relevant literature indicates that the use of blended classes will benefit our students (Clark, 2011; Lloyd-Smith, 2010; Means et al, 2013). We understand that just introducing technology will not give us blended classes (Clark,

2011; Glading, 2004). Therefore, the program has been developed to enhance the teaching and learning process by attempting to adapt the program using basic constructivist activities (Brooks & Brooks, 1999). We believe that our students must be engaged in the development of their own learning and students must interact more with the curriculum, their peers and their instructors (Hall, 2007). Brain research also agrees with the notion that active engagement leads to more student effort and higher achievement levels (Sousa, 2011).

Textbooks for the weekend program are developed by the instructors so that students can independently accomplish the reading assignments and follow-up activities. This version of a flipped class (Berhmann & Sams, 2012) has the students using the text either in hard copy or online to learn the basics of the theories. Then students are asked to apply their knowledge and skills during the practical and in-school portions of the program. This process was developed as an attempt to create an effective blended instructional system for students and instructors (Staker & Horn, 2012) that will enhance their engagement and learning (Clark, 2011; Lloyd-Smith, 2010; Toyama et al, 2013). The weekend program's vision is to create and use pedagogical techniques aimed to differentiate learning (Tomlinson, 2003) and move from teacher-centered to student-centered practices (Sousa, 2011).

Institutional Data

A review of the institutional data was conducted in relation to student numbers, GPAs, student grades by groups (i.e. 9.5 – 10, 8.5 – 9.49, etc.), retention rates, and graduation rates. The graduating class of 2012 began the program with 119 students of which 64 graduated in 2012. This gave that class graduation rate of 53.78%. In their second year there were 88 students for a retention rate from year one to year two of 73.94%. This class began their third year with 79 students for a retention rate between year two and three of 89.77%. The graduation class of 2013 began the program with 61 students of which 45 of those students graduated in 2013. This gave that class a graduation rate of 73.77%. The graduating class of 2014 started the program with 48 students and began their second year with 38 for a retention rate of 79.16%. This class began their third year with 34 students for a retention rate of 89.47%. If all of these students graduate in 2014 their graduation rate will be 70.83%. The graduating class of 2015 began the program with 55 students and in their second retained 49 of those students for a retention rate of 83.63%.

Data in relation to grades for the current program were reviewed for the 2012 – 2013 school year. First year students earned an average grade of 6.32 (using a 10 point scale). Seven students failed due to non attendance to classes, practicums, and exams. When those grades of zero are removed from the data, the average for those students who attended school was 7.09. For this group of students 1.8% earned a grade average of 9.5 to 10; 29; 1% earned an average of 8.5 to 9.4; 20% earned an average of 7 to 8.49; 23.6% earned an average of 5; 25.45% earned failing grades.

Second year students earned an average grade of 7.78 (10 point scale). Two students failed due to non attendance to classes, practicums, and exams. When those grades of zero are removed from the data, the average for those students who attended school was 7.94. For this group of students 6.12% earned a grade average of 9.5 to 10; 36.73% earned an average of 8.5 to 9.4; 43% earned an average of 7 to 8.49; 6.12% earned an average of 5; 8.19% earned failing grades.

Third year students earned an average grade of 8.05 (10 point scale). Five students failed due to non attendance to classes, practicums, and exams. When those grades of zero are removed from the data, the average for those students who attended school was 8.19. For this group of students 20.33% earned a grade average of 9.5 to 10; 30.51% earned an average of 8.5 to 9.4; 34%

earned an average of 7 to 8.49; 5.09% earned an average of 5; 10.17% failed.

PRE-SCHOOL AND PRIMARY WEEKEND PROGRAM

Program Overview

The Pedagogy of Primary and Pre-School Education Weekend Classes program works as a hybrid program with face-to-face practical seminars, laboratories, and practical classes and online theoretical classes. Students attend face-to-face activities on Saturdays and Sundays each semester for three years. Students participate in these classes for between twelve and fourteen hours per week. In all cases the curriculum and expectations for students is the same as the regular day program for the university teacher preparation program.

Schedule

Each semester is fourteen weeks in length. Students attend classes on the weekend (Saturday and Sunday) throughout the term. Professors are required to meet with their students between one or two hours per week face-to-face, depending on the course. Students usually attend classes for six or seven hours per day each weekend. For those students who do not have access to the internet at home the library has internet access available for weekend student use. Students are expected to work on the theoretical portion of their courses online at home. Each instructor schedules assignments and activities with her or his individual class. At the completion of each semester the instructors engage with their students in exams during a two or three week period of time.

Curriculum and Instruction

All students in the program are pre-service teachers working toward certification as pre-school and primary teachers. Students participate in sixty courses during their three year program. The curriculum consists of nine core education courses (15%), forty-three specialty courses (72%), and eight compulsory general study courses (13%). All students also must engage in a capstone action research project at the conclusion of their program. Students present their final results and research paper to a professor committee at the completion of the sixth semester.

The program philosophy to create specific pedagogy for our non-traditional students has led us to create a tri-dimensional approach to instruction: face-to-face engaging activities, online access, and independent learning resources. It is important for our program professors to use instructional strategies that are flexible and that enhance independent learning for our students. Our instructors also have to develop strategies that are effective with older and more experienced adults.

One of the goals of the weekend program is to develop our system so that student learning can occur as independently as possible. Each professor must create a text for the course she or he teaches. This class text is written with the understanding that students will have to use the material individually outside of class time.

Online Elements

The weekend classes use Moodle as the technological platform for the online portion of the program. Students have access to all program resources through this platform including syllabi, announcements, discussion forums, assignments, communications from instructors and administration, and textbooks. Students also have access to the Secretariat in order to access schedules, grades and other important information necessary for students. Students are expected to engage in the theoretical portion of their class work using the online text and other resources. Administration and the three mentors post announcements, schedules and important information that students

nced during the year. Mentors also use the online program to engage with their students in a general forum in which the mentor or any student may pose questions or work to resolve issues that develop during a semester.

Assessment

Students are assessed by all teachers both formatively and summatively. In seminars and theoretical classes 50% of the students' final grade is determined through the use of formative assessments and 50% of the final grade is determined through the use of summative assessments. In laboratory and practical classes 60% of the final grade is determined through the use of formative assessment and 40% of the final grade is determined through the use of the summative assessments. Each instructor develops formative assessments that match the discipline of the course. Every teacher implements a summative exam connected to the organization of the discipline. Instructors may use written, oral performances, final portfolios, writing prompts or real classroom activities as part of their assessment process. At the completion of their program all students develop and implement an action research project that they present either to a panel of professors or at a conference.

Professional Development

Each year instructors must provide evidence of professional development in their discipline. Every five years instructors in the weekend program must participate in training organized by the Department of Online Education. Each instructor in the program must participate in training for teaching in the weekend program. In order to qualify to teach in the program an instructor must pass an online test. In addition, each instructor must successfully develop a weekend course online using the program platform. The Director of Online Learning and the administrator of the program platform review and assess the course developed by the potential instructor. Once both aspects of the exam are successfully completed the Director of Online Learning awards a certificate of completion to the instructor who is then eligible to teach in the weekend program. The program director and coordinators also attend yearly state run training sessions developed by national online experts.

METHODOLOGY

In order to gather appropriate data for analysis this study used a case study approach for its research. According to Bogdan and Biklen (2003) the case study approach gives the researcher the opportunity to study complex social relationships and processes that change over time in order to develop a more complete understanding of the case under study. This approach enables the researcher to develop the story behind the quantitative numbers. We chose this case study approach because it allowed the researchers to gather both quantitative and qualitative data directly from the participants in our program, instructors, students, and administration. Quantitative data used in this study was gathered by surveying students and instructors and by analyzing institutional data: retention rates, graduation rates and student grades. Qualitative data was gathered through interviews of the director of the online department, the administrative assistant for finances and the weekend program budget, weekend program advisors, and the coordinator of the weekend program.

The student survey consisted of 20 items. The survey was divided into four categories: student background and demographic information, reasons for choosing the weekend program, online platform and technology use, and assessment of and recommendations for the program. The instructor survey consisted of eight sections: the use of the e-learning platform, use of text, face-to-face activities, a comparison of typical day classes to weekend classes, media used in the program,

assessment of the program, professional development, and recommendations.

RESEARCH RESULTS

Student Survey

Background and Demographic Information

Of the total students in the program 126 students participated in the student surveys (68.48%). The results indicate that most students have positive attitudes about the program with 96.8% of the students indicating that they recommend the program for other students. The student body is diverse in its demographic make-up with 53.2% of the students living in urban areas and 46.8% living in rural areas.

Weekend program students may be considered to be non-traditional students in other ways. The students are generally older than a typical day program student body. For the weekend program 42.1% of the students are between 18 and 25 years old, 45.3% are between 24 and 39 years of age, and 12.7% are 40 years of age or older. When they enter the program approximately 25% of the students are 23 years old, meaning that although they are in the youngest category, they are older than typical graduating students in the day program. The majority of the weekend program students work (76.3%). Of this group of working students 84.4% of them work full time. From this group 35.7% of the students work as teachers. Of these teachers 23 (51% of the people who work) have been teaching for ten or more years. Forty-four percent of the weekend program students are married and 39.7% of the students have children of their own, with 26 students having two or more children in their homes.

The weekend program students have a variety of program and career needs. Approximately 23% of the weekend program students already hold a degree of some kind and 29% of the students are working to earn two degrees simultaneously. Approximately 50% of the weekend program students enrolled at the university four or more years after graduation from high school.

Transportation is a major issue for many of the weekend program students. Approximately 40% of the students travel to school by automobile, either their own car or through car pooling. The most common mode of transportation is through the use public transportation, bus or train (55%). For students who live in the city in which the college is housed this is not a major issue but for those students who live in other cities or in rural areas transportation schedules cause issues. People often have to travel significant distances to get to a train or bus station and students have to travel based on the schedule of the bus or train (which may or may not coincide with class schedules). The range of distances from the university to the residencies of the students ranged from 3 kilometers to 840 kilometers. The mode and mean distance from the university is 60 kilometers.

Reasons for Choosing Weekend Program

In addition to questions about their backgrounds, the survey asked students to select from a list one or more reasons for choosing the weekend program. The list included: 1. Their older age, 2. Family obligations, 3. Work obligations, 4. Free time, 5. They live outside of the city which houses the university. Students also had the opportunity to add their own reasons (no students did so). The Students indicated that the most important reason for choosing the weekend program was their working obligations (54.8%). The majority of the weekend program students work (76.3%). Of this group of working students 84.4% of them work full time. Approximately 17% of the students chose the weekend program in order to change their careers or job situations. From that group, most of the students chose this program because they work in a school and have decided that teaching would be a good career choice for them. Thirty-two percent of the students chose the program as their university choice upon graduating from high school. Thirty-five point seven percent of the students are already working as teachers and want to or have to complete their degree for their work. The preponderance of these students are forty years of age or older and have been working in the field for a number of years.

The second most important reason chosen was family obligations (34.9%). Forty-four percent of the weekend program students are married and 39.7% of the students have children of their own. Twenty-six students have two or more children in their homes. The majority of these students also work full time.

Their third most important reason for choosing the weekend program was that students live in another city than where the university is (29.4%). Students indicated that transportation is an issue and the weekend program offers them the opportunity to not have to travel every day to the university. Free time was the fourth most important reason for choosing the weekend program (15.9%). The survey did not ask the students to define what fee time meant to them (e.g. leisure, time to work, time for family obligations, etc.). The fifth reason for choosing the program was the older age of the students (10.3%). The students are generally older than a typical day program student body. For the weekend program 42.1% of the students are between 18 and 25 years old, 45.3% are between 24 and 39 years of age, and 12.7% are 40 years of age or older. When they enter the program approximately 25% of the students are 23 years old, meaning that although they are in the youngest category, they are older than typical graduating students in the day program.

Technology Use and Online Platform

All of the students in the weekend program indicated that they are at least somewhat familiar with using a computer to access the internet. Data from the survey indicated that 69% of weekend program students are familiar or very familiar with using a computer. Another 25.4% of the students indicated that they have average familiarity with using a computer. Six students indicated that they were somewhat familiar with using a computer. No students indicated that they were not at all familiar with using a computer.

No students indicated that they were totally unfamiliar with using the online platform for the weekend program. Sixty-five percent of the students indicated that they were familiar or very familiar with using the online platform. Another 29.4% indicated that they were somewhat familiar with the online platform, and 5.6% of the students indicated that they were unfamiliar with the program. As students gain more experience in the program they become more familiar with the program. In the first year 54.7% of students indicated they were familiar or very familiar with the online program; in the second that number was 76.5%; in the third year the number rose to 78.7%.

The survey also asked students to indicate how often they use the online platform for their school work and/or learning. Forty-six point eight percent of the students indicated that they access the online platform on a daily basis. Another 32.5% of students indicated they use the online platform 2 or 3 times per week. Twelve point seven percent of the students indicated they use the platform daily during the exam periods. Five point six percent of students indicated they use the platform at least once per week. Lastly, 2.4% of students use the platform once per month. First year students (64.2%) use the platform at a higher rate than do second and third year students (35% and 33.3%).

Students were asked to prioritize their reasons for using the online platform (scale of 1 – 7). The first priority for students was to access posts uploaded to the platform by their instructors (mean 5.35). Their second priority was to post assignments for their classes (mean 4.95). The third most frequent reason were individual student reasons

that they added to the list (mean 4.83). The fourth most important reason to access the online platform was to communicate with their instructors (mean 3.62). Students chose forum discussions as their fifth most important reason to access the online platform (mean 3.45). The sixth priority for accessing the online platform was to communicate with their mentor (3.04). Students' final choice was to use the online platform to communicate with secretariat (mean 1.42).

The survey also asked students about how much help they needed in using the online platform. One third of the students indicated they needed assistance with using the online platform, while the other two thirds indicated they did not need assistance. The youngest group of students (18 – 23) indicated they needed assistance at the highest rate (43.4%). The students from age 24 to 39 indicated the lowest need for assistance (22.6%). Students were also asked by the survey to indicate their preference for lowering the face-to-face time of the program and substituting that time with online work. This would include doing more of their assignments and discussions in the online format. The majority of the students (65.9%) indicated they did not want to change the face-to face to online ratio as it now exists.

In response to the survey students indicated that almost all of them (96%) have access to the internet at home. Three percent indicated that they have access at their work, and one student indicated the she or he does not have internet access.

Program Leaders Survey

Introduction

The program implemented an open ended survey with five people: program administrator, coordinator of the weekend program, and the three program advisors. All participants responded to the same six questions: What are the strengths of the program? What can be improved in the program? What are the needs of the students in our program? What are the needs of the instructors in the program? How effective are the resources provided by the program (i.e. text, online resources, program library)? Are there any other comments you would like to add?

Results

For question one, strengths of the program, there were three major themes raised by the respondents. All five participants responded that although the program is presented in an alternative format the students receive the same level of training and certification as do students in the traditional day program. Four of the five respondents noted that the weekend program offers easier access to the textbooks and classes for their students. Three participants responded that the flexibility of the program and its use of weekend classes, online resources, and independent learning opportunities allow students to be successful within their family and work situations. Two people stated that the cooperation among online instructors and classroom instructors is effective. In addition, two respondents noted that the instructors are well prepared to teach in the program.

The second questions asked for ways to improve the program. Three participants responded that although the program is working with non-traditional students, a significant number of instructors do not differentiated their instruction and assessment practices to adjust to their students' needs. These respondents believe the weekend program should develop a professional development system to ensure that instructors understand the needs of the program, their students, and the program's pedagogical philosophy and best practices necessary for student success. Two respondents noted that they are not sure that the textbooks they created are accurate in terms of the time students need to accomplish the tasks. They recommended that the program could assist instructors in the process of developing texts and of researching the accuracy of the time require-

ments for the students. Two participants noted that working with smaller classes would improve their effectiveness.

The third questions referred to the student needs in the program. The responses to this question did not develop any major themes. The different responses discussed the general concepts that the students have diverse needs and need flexibility in order to meet those needs. The theme of the responses appeared to be that the program should constantly assess the student needs and respond to each group of students as necessary. For the fourth question, needs of instructors, all five respondents indicated that the salary for their efforts should be more in line with the work required of the instructors, mentors, and administrators in the program.

The fifth question asked about resources in the program for students. Three people noted that the content of texts should be "essentialized" in order to give a more accurate set of activities in terms of the amount of time students need to complete text activities. Two participants suggested that the program should develop more ways to motivate students to access the online platform on a more regular basis.

Participants were asked to give other recommendations. Two people responded to this question. Their suggestion was to improve the consultation time offered by the program. Instructors offer two-hour blocks of time for students to come to the university to get assistance of any kind. Few students take advantage of these opportunities. The suggestion was to have the program look into other ways to format the consultation time (e.g. include online office hours, etc.).

Instructor Survey

Introduction

The program implemented an instructor survey that was organized into eight sections: 1. Online Platform, 2. Textbooks, 3. Face-to-Face Activities, 4. Comparison with Day Program, 5. Use of Media, 6. Assessment, 7. Professional Development, 8. Other Comments. Sixteen full-time instructors (66.67%) responded to the survey. There are two types of classes offered by these instructors, online theoretical classes and face-to-face practical classes.

Results

Section 1 asked instructors three items: How important is the online platform for the weekend program? What aspects of the platform are important for you? How often do you access the online platform? For the first question the instructors' mean was 4.43 (scale of 1 – 5) indicating that instructors believe the platform is important to the program. When asked how often instructors access the program 81% responded that they use the online platform on a weekly basis. Instructors indicated that they use the platform to post information (mean 5.00) for their classes (e.g. syllabus, text book, assessments, schedules, etc.). The second most important reason (4.64) given was to create the buttons for the assessment tasks for students. The third purpose for accessing the online program was for the online discussions (4.40).

Section 2 referred to the program textbooks (12 questions). There were four questions in this section that related to student use of the text. Instructors indicated that the textbooks were effective for students use and needs (means 4.42, 4.57, 4.42, 4.42). The rest of the questions for Section I referred to the required elements of the texts according to program standards. Instructors indicated their texts followed program standards, with mean scores ranging from 4.14 to 4.71.

Section 3 referred to face-to-face activities (eight questions). There were five questions related to the effectiveness of the face-to-face classes in helping students to learn and apply the concepts of each course. Instructors indicated in four of the five questions that the classes were successful for students. The means for those questions ranged from 4.40 to 4.60. The fifth question asked if the

materials used in the classroom were useful for the future careers of these pre-service teachers. The mean score for this question was 3.93 which was the lowest mean for this section. The other three questions for this section asked about the content of the classes as they related to program requirements. Instructors indicated that their content was in line with program requirements with means between 4.4 and 4.73.

Section 4 asked instructors to compare the weekend program to the traditional day program. This section gave instructors ten typical teacher functions, and they were asked to choose which, if any, were more difficult in the weekend program as compared to their work in the day program. A majority of instructors (11 of 16) indicated that presenting the same content is more difficult in the weekend format as compared to the day program format. For question nine (motivating students) nine of the sixteen instructors indicated that it is more difficult to motivate their students in the weekend program. Five instructors indicated that it is more difficult to organize the class time effectively in the weekend program format. For the other seven questions a minimum of 13 of the 16 instructors indicated there is no difference in difficulty in preparing and implementing their classes in the weekend program.

Section 5 asked instructors their ideas about video use in the program. Three of the 16 instructors indicated that they sometimes use videos, while 6 instructors indicate that they use videos often or very often. Seven instructors indicated they either rarely or never use videos. Thirteen instructors indicated that the use of videos is somewhat important, important, or very important. Three people indicated that video use in class is not at all important. When asked if the program created videos how they would like to use them three instructors indicated they would like the videos to use in both the day and weekend program and seven instructors indicated the videos should be developed specifically for the weekend students. One person indicated that the videos should be prepared by someone other than her. Five people gave other written ideas which included: three of them suggested recording lessons in the schools and kindergarten and use them as models and for class discussions for students; two of respondents suggested creating an electronic presentation program with audio (e.g. Powerpoint).

Section 6 asked instructors about their assessment practices. This survey asked three questions about assessment, one in relation to formative and summative assessments, one question asking instructors to indicate the formats their assessments take for their students, and one question about feedback to students. Sixty-nine percent of the instructors indicated that they use formative assessment strategies with their students and 94% of the instructors indicated that they use summative assessments. Nineteen percent of the instructors indicated that they also use other forms of assessments: pre assessments and differentiated or personalized assessments.

Instructors were asked whether or not they use oral, written, and practical assessment techniques. Forty-four percent of the instructors indicated they use oral assessments. Sixty-three percent indicated they use written assessments, and 44% indicated they use practical assessment techniques. Thirteen percent of the instructors also indicated they use other assessment techniques which include: portfolios, structured essays, and individual projects. The third question asked teachers to rate at what levels instructors believe their students understand how they receive the grades they achieve on their assessments. The results for formative assessments indicated that 81.3% of the instructors believe that students have a good or very good understanding of why their grades are what they are. Thirteen percent of the instructors believe that students have little understanding of what their grades mean. For summative assessments 75% of the instructors indicated that students have a good or very good understanding of what their summative assessment scores mean about their learning. Thirteen percent of the instructors indicated that students

do not understand what their grades mean about what they have learned.

Section 7 asked instructors to share their ideas about professional development. Ninety-four percent of the instructors indicated that the professional development provided by the weekend program was useful to the instructors. When asked how often instructors would like to participate in professional development activities provided by the weekend program 50% indicated they would like professional development to occur every other year, 13% indicated they would like to have annual professional development activities, and another 13% indicated they would like professional development to occur every semester. Thirteen percent also indicated they would like professional development to occur every five years.

The final section of the instructor survey asked instructors for recommendations to improve the weekend program: four people suggested to reduce the content volume of the material taught in the textbooks; four people suggested making attendance mandatory for the face to face meetings; three people stated that the curriculum content should be coordinated throughout the program, three people indicated they thought working with smaller groups of students would benefit teachers and students; three instructors indicated that learning should be more adapted to the individual needs of students.

DISCUSSION

The weekend program consists of students who have diverse backgrounds, experiences, and needs. Students range in age from 18 to older than 50, and their experiences in the world of work and life are vastly differently from each other. A significant group of students work full time, many as teachers, a large group of students has families of their own, and a significant number of students live long distances from campus. These peculiarities mean that the weekend community members have a variety needs for the program to address. This diversity suggests the necessity for a program that is also diverse. From an instructor perspective the program goals suggest flexible teachers who understand older and more experienced students, while at the same time understanding young adults. The weekend program has an obligation to maintain high standards for future educators while creatively integrating the curriculum for its students. Data indicates that instructors could take more advantage of the online portion of the program, especially to communicate with and give feedback to students.

The people who work in the weekend program understand that they are working with a diverse population that has varied needs. An analysis of the data from the study indicates that leaders and instructors in the program should regularly assess the program and its students' and instructors' needs in order to build in the necessary flexibility for the success of its students. The hybrid nature of the program implies a pedagogical philosophy that all instructors should understand, buy-into, and participate in appropriate professional development.

The results of the instructors survey indicates that there is a wide range of experiences and needs among instructors. In general it appears that instructors have worked hard to prepare their classes to be in line with the requirements of the program. There are some areas of concern in these results. For example, the low mean from the instructors with regards to whether the materials used in the classroom were useful for the future careers of these pre-service teachers is disconcerting. Another area of concern is the fact that 31% of the instructors surveyed indicated they do not use formative assessments. Twenty-six percent of the instructors indicated they would like professional development to occur yearly or during each semester. That means that 74% of the instructors indicated they want or need professional development less than yearly, with 13% indicating once every five years. When combined with other results from this research from students

and program leaders, it appears that there is a wide range of understanding of and commitment to the philosophy, pedagogical requirements, and goals of the weekend program from its instructors. This area of the program is going to require further review to determine needs and develop appropriate refinements in the program.

From the review of the data in relation to retention and graduation the program appears to maintain higher retention and graduation rates with smaller classes. For the class that started with 119 students the graduation rate was 53.48% and the graduation rates for the smaller classes were 73.77% and 70.83%. As students progress through the program they do better both in terms of retention rates and in terms of grades. The percentage of students who attain low or failing grades during the first year is significantly higher than in the second and third year of the program. The program leaders should look to develop a system to work with first year students in order to help them transition into the university and into the rigors of higher education. Additionally, program leaders will attempt to develop ideas with program instructors to create systems to work with students in alternative ways during their first year. The system in place for class mentors may also be able to adapt to the needs of program students, especially first year students. Strategic online learning strategies could play a significant role in the process of working with program students.

SOLUTIONS AND RECOMMENDATIONS

It is clear from this research that the weekend program should continue to move toward a student-centered teaching and learning structure. Instructors and students indicated that more personalized instruction and materials would be useful. The program would do well to strategically create and implement a professional development program to assist instructors in the creation and use of constructivist teaching and learning strategies. The online component of the weekend program has not been used to its fullest potential. Instructors use the online platform to make curriculum resources, textbooks, schedules, and other information available to students but the interactive potential of more discussions, lessons, meetings, and other kinds of learning activities are underutilized. Students asked for more consistent communication and feedback among instructors and students online. The incorporation of online office hours could assist in this request. Instructors will need training and support to effectively use the technological tools available to them.

In order to develop a more student-centered approach the program might contemplate ways to lower the student to teacher ratio. For example, creating a schedule in which instructors can meet with students in smaller groups with flipped classroom activities for the rest of the class might assist instructors in this matter. The program might incorporate more cooperative grouping techniques to assist with the class size issue. The weekend program has done a great job of developing its ideas in relation to the texts. Students would benefit from further development. The program could consider ways to make the activities more in line with the time required from students to accomplish the requested readings and tasks. It appears that the content of the texts and the content of the practical classes could be more coordinated so that students are getting into complex activities rather than being introduced to a myriad of ideas with little depth. In line with the differentiated instructional philosophy of the program it makes sense to consider creating video lectures and interactive video activities for instructors and students. Finally, we recommend that the discussion aspects of the online platform could be used more effectively. This aspect of the program could allow students and instructors to communicate more regularly and for students to interact more frequently with their peers in connection to important curriculum.

The weekend program is working with a diverse group of students and instructors. There is no question that it needs instructors who are committed to working in such a program because the success of our future teachers cannot be left to chance. The program and its instructors are working hard to identify needs and develop the philosophical and pedagogical structures to make the program highly effective. This will require a full commitment on the part of both the program and its instructors. The program should commit to a systematic and strategic professional development program for its leaders, advisors, and instructors. As part of this professional development system the program should develop procedures to ensure ongoing support and training for all staff. It is imperative that all instructors understand, buy-into, and receive the support necessary to be effective in meeting the requirements and goals of the weekend program. Since teaching in the weekend program is voluntary, people who disagree with the goals and philosophy of the weekend program should not volunteer to work in the program. On the other hand any person who wants to teach in such a program should receive great training and the full support from the program.

The use of hybrid programs such as the weekend program is going to continue to play an important role for students, and the trend appears to indicate that more students will be attracted to and need such programs. We believe that the recommendations made above will assist the program in its continued growth as it works to meet as many needs of their students and instructors as possible.

FUTURE RESEARCH DIRECTIONS

Further research into the connection between online activities and academic achievement would benefit the weekend program and so would research in the area of working with diverse populations in effective ways and exploring the use of texts in a hybrid program, which has potential for such a program as the weekend classes. Instructors agree that individualized learning is important and further research into techniques that work to differentiate instruction and assessment with diverse groups would help instructor growth. Research in relation to the building of a cooperative culture for students and instructors working together in a weekend model would assist all participants in the program. The advisors in the weekend program would benefit from research into the roles of advising in an alternative model such as the weekend program. Finally, research into the development of a highly effective professional development program and support system for instructors in an alternative program such as the weekend program would be beneficial to everyone involved in the program.

The weekend program is developing an exciting model for its instructors and students. This model is probably going to attract more students in the coming years. The program has the potential of changing how universities prepare their future public school teachers.

CONCLUSION

As we move to prepare teachers for the rest of the 21st century and beyond it is clear that to be successful universities must adapt to the changing times and technologies. Teaching in a world in which borders and travel no longer limit access will require adapted or completely different models of teaching and learning. It appears that the model in which professors have more access to information than do the students has to change. In the area of open access the needs of the students is changing and programs should adapt to meet those emerging needs. In this chapter we reviewed one case study of a program that is working hard to adjust to the present and future needs of its students and their future students. The willingness of the people in

this weekend program to venture into alternative strategies for teaching and learning is commendable. Hopefully, their hard work will assist others as they contemplate how to adapt for the future in their programs. Teacher preparation programs have the impossible task of preparing students to be successful teachers who exhibit the habits and abilities of veteran teachers on their first day of teaching. University teacher preparation programs must transcend the curriculum and help students to develop into knowledgeable, dedicated, and caring human beings. The job is impossible but that is what great teachers do, accomplish the impossible with their students.

REFERENCES

Berhmann, J., & Sams, A. (2012). *Flip your classroom: Reach every student in every class every day*. Alexandria, VA: Association for Supervision and Curriculum Development and International society for Technology in Education.

Bogdan, R. C., & Biklen, S. K. (2003). *Qualitative research for education: An introduction to theories and methods* (4th ed.). New York: Pearson.

Brooks, J. G., & Brooks, M. G. (1999). *In search of understanding: The case for constructivist classrooms*. Alexandria, VA: Association for Supervision and Curriculum Development.

Caine, R. N., Caine, G., McClintic, C., & Klimek, K. (2009). *12 brain/mind learning principles in action*. Thousand Oaks, CA: Corwin Press.

Clark, B. (2011). *Moving the technology into the classroom project blended delivery: A literature review*. College Sector Committee for Adult Upgrading. Retrieved from ProQuest

Gladings, N. (2004, March 8). Blended learning in K-12 social studies instruction. *Literature Review*.

Hall, A. (2007). Vygotsky goes online: Learning design from a socio-cultural perspective. *Learning and Socio-Cultural Theory: Exploring Modern Vygotskian Perspectives, 1*(1), article 6. Retrieved from http://ro.uow.edu.au//llrg/vol1/iss1/6

Leese, M. (2009). Out of class - Out of mind? The use of virtual learning environment to encourage student engagement in out of class activities. *British Journal of Educational Technology, 40*(1), 70–77. doi:10.1111/j.1467-8535.2008.00822.x

Lloyd-Smith, L. (2010). Exploring the advantages of blended instruction at community colleges and technical schools. *MERLOT Journal of Online Learning and Teaching, 6*(2), 508-515. Retrieved from http://jolt.merlot.org/vol6no2/lloyd-smith_0610.htm

Lord, G., & Lomicka, L. (2008). Blended learning in teacher education: An investigation of classroom community across media. *Contemporary Issues in Technology & Teacher Education, 8*(2), 158–174.

Means, B., Toyama, Y., Murphy, R., Bakia, M., & Jones, K. (2009). *Evaluation of evidence-based practices in online learning: A meta-analysis and review of online learning studies.* Washington, DC: U.S. Department of Education, Office of Planning, Evaluation, and Policy Development.

Means, B., Toyama, Y., Murphy, R. F., & Baki, M. (2013). The effectiveness of online and blended learning: A meta-analysis of the empirical literature. *Teachers College Record, 115*(3), 1–47. Retrieved from http://www.tcrecord.org/library

Picciano, A., Dziuban, C., & Graham, C. (2013). *Blended learning: Research perspectives* (Vol. 2). London: Routledge.

Sousa, D. (2011). *How the brain learns* (4th ed.). Thousand Oaks, CA: Corwin.

Staker, H., & Horn, M. B. (2012). *Classifying K-12 blended learning.* INNOSIGHT Institute. Retrieved from http://files.eric.ed.gov/fulltext/ED535180.pdf

Tomlinson, C. A., & Imbeau, M. B. (2013). *Leading and managing a differentiated classroom.* Alexandria, VA: Association for Supervision and Curriculum Development.

Tucker, B. (2012). The flipped classroom. *Education Next, 12*(1). Retrieved from http://education-next.org/the-flipped-classroom

Whipp, J., & Lorentz, R. R. (2009). Cognitive and social help giving in online teaching: An exploratory study. *Educational Technology Research and Development, 57*(2), 169–192. doi:10.1007/s11423-008-9104-7

ADDITIONAL READING

Akinsola, M. K., & Awofala, A. A. (2009). Effect of personalization of instruction on students' achievement and self-efficacy in mathematics word problems. *International Journal of Mathematical Education in Science and Technology, 40*(3), 389–404. doi:10.1080/00207390802643169

Allen, I. E., & Seaman, J. (2013). *Changing course: Ten years of tracking online education in the United States.* Babson Survey Research Group and Quahog Research Group, LLC. Retrieved from http://www.gedcouncil.org/publications/changing-course-ten-years-tracking-online-education-united-states

Alliance for Excellent Education. (2012). *Culture shift: Teaching in a learner-centered environment powered by digital learning.* Washington, DC: Alliance for Excellent Education.

Arnold-Garza, S. (2014). The flipped classroom. *College & Research Libraries News*, *75*(1), 10–13.

Aspden, L., & Helm, P. (2004). Making the connection in a blended learning environment. *Educational Media International*, *41*(3), 245–252. doi:10.1080/09523980410001680851

Ausburn, L. J. (2004). Course design elements most valued by adult learners in blended online education environments: An American perspective. *Educational Media International*, *41*(4), 327–337. doi:10.1080/0952398042000314820

Aycock, A., Garnham, C., & Kaleta, R. (2002). Lessons learned from the hybrid course project. *Teaching with Technology Today, 8*(6). Available from http://www.uwsa.edu/ttt/articles/garnham2.htm

Beecher, M., & Sweeny, S. M. (2008). Closing the achievement gap with curriculum enrichment and differentiation: One school's story. *Journal of Advanced Academics*, *19*(3), 502–530.

Benjamin, A. (2005). *Differentiated instruction using technology: A guide for middle and high school teachers*. New York, NY: Eye on Education.

Bergmann, J. (2011). Flipped classroom offers new learning path. *Electronic Education Report*, *18*(23), 1–3.

Bergmann, J. & Sams, A. (2014). Flipped learning: Maximizing face time. *Training+Development*, *68*(2), 28-31.

Berrett, D. (2012). How 'flipping' the classroom can improve the traditional lecture. *The Chronicle of Higher Education*, *58*(25), 16–18.

Boyle, T. (2005). A dynamic, systematic method for developing blended learning. *Education Communication and Information*, *5*(3), 221–232. doi:10.1080/14636310500350422

Boyle, T., Bradley, C., Chalk, P., Jones, R., & Pickard, P. (2003). Using blended learning to improve student success rates in learning to program. *Journal of Educational Media*, *28*(2-3), 165–178. doi:10.1080/1358165032000153160

Brown, B. W., & Liedholm, C. E. (2004). Student preferences in using online learning resources. *Quality in Higher Education*, *11*(1), 56–67.

Bull, G., Ferster, B., & Kjellstrom, W. (2012). Inventing the flipped classroom. *Learning and Leading with Technology*, *40*(1), 10–11.

Choudhury, S., Charman, T., & Blakemore, S. (2008). Development of the teenage brain. *Mind, Brain, and Education*, *2*(3), 142–147. doi:10.1111/j.1751-228X.2008.00045.x

Christiansen, C., Horn, M., & Staker, H. (2013). Is K-12 blended learning disruptive? An introduction of the theory of hybrids. Clayton Christensen Institute. Retrieved from www.christenseninstitute.org

Clark, B. (2011). Moving the technology into the classroom project blended delivery: A literature review. Ontario, Canada: LBS Research and Development Fund, Ministry of Training, Colleges and Universities. Retrieved from ProQuest.

Clark, I., & James, P. (2005). Blended learning: An approach to delivering science courses online. In *Proceedings of UniServe Science Blended Learning Symposium* (pp. 19-24). Available from http://science.uniserve.edu.au/pubs/procs/wshop10/index.html

Collins, A., & Halverson, R. (2009). *Rethinking education in the age of technology: The digital revolution and school in America*. New York: Teachers College Press.

Crouch, M. (2014). The flipped classroom. *Scholastic Parent & Child*, *21*(5), 59–59.

Darling-Hammond, L., & Bransford, J. (Eds.). (2005). *Preparing teachers for a changing world: What teachers should learn and be able to do*. San Francisco, CA: John Wiley and Sons.

Davies, J., & Graff, M. (2005). Performance in e-learning: Online participation and student grades. *British Journal of Educational Technology, 36*(4), 657–663. doi:10.1111/j.1467-8535.2005.00542.x

Du, C. (2011). A comparison of traditional and blended learning in introductory principles of accounting course. *American Journal of Business Education, 4*(9), 1–10.

Elebiary, H., & Mahmoud, S. (2013). Enhancing blended courses to facilitate student achievement of learning outcomes. *Life Science Journal, 10*(2), 401-407. Retrieved from http://www.lifesciencesite.com

Ellis, R. A., Marcus, G., & Taylor, R. (2005). Learning through inquiry: Student difficulties with online course-based material. *Journal of Computer Assisted Learning, 21*(4), 239–252. doi:10.1111/j.1365-2729.2005.00131.x

Esfandiari, M., Barr, C., & Sugano, A. (2006). *Examining the effectiveness of blended instruction on teaching introductory statistics*. Unpublished Manuscript. Available from EbscoHost.

Flynn, A., Concannon, F., & Ni Bheachain, C. (2005). Undergraduate students' perceptions of technology supported learning: The case of an accounting class. *International Journal on E-Learning, 4*(4), 427–444.

Fulton, K. P. (2013, September). Byron's flipped classrooms. *Education Digest, 79*(1), 22–26.

Garrison, D. R., & Anderson, T. (2003). *E-learning in the 21st century: A framework for research and practice*. New York: RoutledgeFalmer. doi:10.4324/9780203166093

Garrison, D. R., & Vaughn, N. (2008). *Blended learning in higher education*. San Francisco, CA: Jossey-Bass.

Global Engineering Deans Council. (2012). *Six articles on online and blended learning*. Milwaukee, WI: Global Engineering Deans Council. Retrieved from http://www.gedcouncil.org/publications/six-articles-online-and-blended-learning

Greener, S. (2008). Self-aware and self-directed: Student conceptions of blended learning. *MERLOT Journal of Online Learning and Teaching, 4*(2), 243-253. Retrieved from http://jolt.merlot.org/vol4no2/greener0608.htm

Hess, K. K., Jones, B. S., Carlock, D., & Walkup, J. R. (2009). *Cognitive rigor: Blending the strengths of Bloom's taxonomy and Webb's depth of knowledge to enhance classroom-level processes*. Online Submission. Retrieved from http://eric.ed.gov/?id=ED517804

Lim, D. H., Morris, M. L., & Kupritz, V. W. (2007). Online vs. blended learning: Differences in instructional outcomes and learner satisfaction. *Journal of Asynchronous Learning Networks, 11*(2), 27–42. Retrieved from http://www.editlib.org/p/104046

Lim, D. H., & Yoon, S. W. (2008). Team learning and collaboration between online and blended learner groups. *Performance Improvement Quarterly, 21*(3), 59–72. doi:10.1002/piq.20031

MacDonald, J. (2008). *Blended learning and online tutoring* (2nd ed.). Hampshire, UK: Gower Publishing.

Mangan, K. (2013). Inside the flipped classroom. *The Chronicle of Higher Education, 60*(5), 18–21.

Mitchell, P., & Forer, P. (2010). Blended learning: The perceptions of first-year geography students. *Journal of Geography in Higher Education, 34*(2), 77–89. doi:10.1080/03098260902982484

Musallam, R. (2011). *Should you flip your classroom?*. Retrieved from Edutopia.

Nielsen, S. M. (2008). Half bricks and half clicks: Is blended onsite and online teaching and learning the best of both worlds? In *Proceedings of the Seventh Annual College of Education Research Conference: Urban and International Education*. Academic Press.

November, A., & Mull, B. (2012, March 26). Flipped learning: A response to five common criticisms. *eSchool News*.

Pane, D.M. (2009). Third space: Blended teaching and learning. *Journal of the Research Center for Educational Technology, 5*(1), Article 8.

Parker, D. R., Robinson, L. E., & Hannafin, R. D. (2007). Blending technology and effective pedagogy in a core course for pre-service teachers. *Journal of Computing in Teacher Education, 24*(2), 49–54.

Pearcy, A. G. (2009). *Finding the perfect blend: A comparative study of online, face-to-face, and blended instruction*. Dissertation Prepared for the Degree of Doctor of Philosophy. Retrieved from ProQuest.

Reach Every Student. (n.d.). Retrieved from http://www.edugains.ca/resourcesDI/Brochures/DIBrochureOct08.pdf

Roehl, A., Reddy, S. L., & Shannon, G. J. (2013). The Flipped classroom: An opportunity to engage millennial students through active learning strategies. *Journal of Family and Consumer Sciences, 105*(2), 44–49. doi:10.14307/JFCS105.2.12

Rowntree, D. (1990). *Teaching through self-instruction: How to develop open learning material*. London: Kogan Page.

Sousa, D., & Tomlinson, C. A. (2011). *Differentiation and the brain: How neuroscience supports the learner-friendly classroom*. Bloomington, IN: Solution Tree Press.

Sousa, D., & Tomlinson, C. A. (2011). *Differentiation and the brain: How neuroscience supports the learner-friendly classroom*. Bloomington, IN: Solution Tree Press.

Sprenger, M. (2010). *Brain-based teaching the digital age*. Alexandria, VA: ASCD.

Springen, K. (2013). Flipped. *School Library Journal, 59*(4), 23.

Staker, H. (2011). The rise of k-12 blended learning. Boston: Innosight Institute. Retrieved from http://www.innosightinstitute.org/blended_learning_models/

Sweeney, J., O'donoghue, T., & Whitehead, C. (2004). Traditional face to face and web-based tutorials: A study of university students' perspectives on the roles of tutorial participants. *Teaching in Higher Education, 9*(3), 311–323. doi:10.1080/1356251042000216633

Tomlinson, C. A. (2004). *Fulfilling the promise of the differentiated classroom*. Alexandria, VA: Association for Supervision and Curriculum Development.

Tomlinson, C. A. (2008). *The differentiated school: Making revolutionary changes in teaching and learning*. Alexandria, VA: Association for Supervision and Curriculum Development.

Tucker, B. (2012). The flipped classroom. *Education Next, 12*(1). Retrieved from http://education-next.org/the-flipped-classroom

Tucker, C. (2012). Blended learning in grades 4-12: Leveraging the power of technology to create student-centered classrooms. Thousand Oaks, CA: Corwin.

U.S. Department of Education. (2013). *Evaluation of evidence-based practices in online learning: A meta-analysis and review of online learning studies*. Washington, DC: Office of Planning, Evaluation, and Policy Development Policy and Program Studies Service. Retrieved from http://www.gedcouncil.org/publications/evaluation-evidence-based-practices-online-learning-meta-analysis-and-review-online-lear

Uzen, & Senturk, A. (2010). Blending makes the difference: Comparison of blended and traditional instruction on students' performance and attitudes in computer literacy. *Contemporary Educational Technology, 1*(3), 196-207. Retrieved from ProQuest.

Vignare, K. (2007). Review of literature blended learning: Using ALN to change the classroom – Will it work? In A. G. Picciano & C. D. Dziuban (Eds.), Blended learning: Research perspectives (pp. 37–63). Needham, MA: Sloan Consortium. Retrieved from http://msuglobal.com

Yapici, I., & Akbayin, H. (2012). High school students' views on blended learning. *Turkish Online Journal of Distance Education, 13*(4), article 8. Retrieved from http://www.academia.edu/2089803/HIGH_SCHOOL_STUDENTS_VIEWS_ON_BLENDED_LEARNING

Yapici, I., & Akbayin, H. (2012). The effect of blended learning model on high school students' biology achievement and on their attitudes towards the internet. *The Turkish Online Journal of Educational Technology, 11*(2), 228–237.

KEY TERMS AND DEFINITIONS

Blended Learning: Blended learning occurs in an environment in which the student work and learn in a classroom part of the time and work outside of the classroom part of the time. For the portion of the work accomplished outside of the classroom students have some control over timing and pace. In a blended environment the use of technology is integrated into the learning process in order to give students more time working with the curriculum, their peers, and the teacher.

Differentiated Instruction: In a classroom that differentiates instruction the teacher attempts to adjust her/his teaching to the needs of the students. The differentiated teacher attempts to teach at different levels using a variety of approaches and thinking level processes to assist all students in learning all of the important material.

Flipped Classroom: The concept of a flipped classroom approach to teaching is to allow students to accomplish the lower level activities outside of the classroom in order to give the students and the teacher more time to work together in higher levels of engagement. For example, a teacher may video her/his lecture and have the students view the lecture as homework. When the students come to class the teacher and students then engage in application and guided practice activities rather than note-taking activities.

Practicum Experiences: Pre-service teachers gain experiences in the field at public schools under the guidance of a university supervisor and a public school teacher. Practicum experiences occur every semester for all students.

Seminar Experiences: In the weekend program students participate in face-to-face seminar classes built each week to give students practical experiences in relation to the theory learned from their text and online activities.

Student-Centered Learning: In a student-centered classroom the focus is on student learning rather than teacher led activities. In this process the teacher sets up the learning activities in ways that engage students in active ways. The teacher role becomes more of a coaching and guiding role as opposed to a dissemination of information role.

Weekend Program: For the purposes of this study, a weekend program is one in which students attend classes on the weekend as opposed to the week days of a traditional program. The weekend program also uses a blended model of learning in which the students are responsible for the text learning in an independent fashion. This includes independent reading and activities, self assessment activities, and online learning. The weekend program utilizes face-to-face practical classes, independent and online theoretical learning, and in-school practicum experiences.

Chapter 15
Contemporary Challenges and Preschool Teachers' Education in Croatia:
The Evaluation of the New Study Program of Early/Preschool Care and Education at Faculty of Teacher Education in Rijeka

Sanja Tatalović Vorkapić
University of Rijeka, Croatia

Lidija Vujičić
University of Rijeka, Croatia

Željko Boneta
University of Rijeka, Croatia

ABSTRACT

The evaluation of the new graduate study program Early and Preschool Care and Education (EPCE) was conducted recently in Croatia. Preschool teachers and graduate students were asked about their motivation for enrolling, the level of competencies developed during their study, and the predictive power of three significantly connected motives in relation to those competencies. Statistical analysis revealed highly positive perception of relevant competences gained. This finding confirmed the hypothesis that continuing professional development through formal higher education contributes significantly to improved preschool teachers' performance while coping with changing and growing job demands. Moreover, subjects demonstrated highly intrinsic motivation for enrolling. Extrinsic motives were indicative of a more negative, while intrinsic motivation led to more positive, perception of learning outcomes and gained competencies. Overall, the evaluation was highly positive and the findings confirmed the importance of satisfying the professional needs of preschool teachers.

DOI: 10.4018/978-1-4666-7244-4.ch015

INTRODUCTION

Recent theories concerning child development and studies in the field of developmental neuroscience (Gopnik et al., 2003) were utilised in preparing students to become quality preschool teachers. The role of preschool teachers has been changed dramatically in recent years (Bowman et al., 2001; IOM & NRC, 2012; Jacobson, 2009a; Tobin et al., 2004). Contrary to 'just looking after the kids' as well as in contrast with working methods employed before, today's preschool teachers actively listen and respond to children's thoughts and feelings, observe their activities and take account of their actions, while trying to find the appropriate procedures to assist children's development (Rinaldi, 2006). One preschool teacher believes that:

Our job does not present only preparation for one joint activity that shall be carried out during the day and over anymore, for what we have been educated at the university. Therefore, I consider it necessary to immediately make changes within college programs for preschool teachers and their duration for to be prolonged, otherwise new generations of kids will know more than their preschool teachers (Vujičić, 2011, p. 80).

New developmental theories suggest that a rather different approach in the education of future preschool teachers is required. In addition to developing their knowledge and skills, professional development courses should reflect the role of preschool teacher as a researcher. This role has been perceived as the one in which preschool teachers take the initiative to create, rather than consume new knowledge and new practices (Hopkins, 2001). Contemporary work in the institution of early and preschool education requires that preschool teachers make decisions, build professionalism by encouraging research and collaborative habits during all phases of preschool educator training (Kipper & Mischke, 2008). This

is important to ensure that teachers are not merely the mean of knowledge transfer.

The theoretical underpinning of this chapter is based on the work of such contemporary researchers as Fullan (1993, 1999, 2007), Elliot (1998), Bruner (2000), Stoll & Fink (2000), Datnow et al. (2002), Senge et al. (2003), Gardner (2005), Vujičić (2011) and Whitebook et al. (2012). They suggest that access to professional development of preschool teachers should be based on joint research and understanding of the complex phenomena that arise directly from educational practice. It is particularly important therefore, to reflect on the organisation of the academic education of future preschool teachers and how this provides for the: a) contemporary and dynamic roles of preschool teachers; b) new paradigm of early and preschool care and education based on changing relationships between adults and children; c) co-construction of curriculum based on the idea of reflexive practitioner educator; and d) the current perception of kindergarten as a learning organisation. All of these preschool teachers' properties were taken into account while new graduate study program of *Early and Preschool care and Education* at the University of Rijeka was developed. Therefore, the main research question that guided the evaluation of this graduate study program refers to program's usefulness for preschool practice and work in Croatia.

Development of Graduate study program: Early and Preschool Care and Education (EPCE)

The Faculty for Teacher Education at University of Rijeka initiated the graduate study program "Early and Preschool education and Care" (EPCE) in the academic year 2010-2011 when the first cohort of students was enrolled. This initiative put forward the University of Rijeka as the first one in Croatia to provide the graduate level of academic education for preschool teachers. The development of this academic degree could provide increased opportunities for the advancement and mobility within the preschool teaching profession, especially for those preschool teachers who aim to engage in researching the practice and enroll on a postgraduate study program.

Today's competent preschool teacher should be knowledgeable about how to successfully embed two important roles, of being a researcher and a practitioner. As a researcher and practitioner, as Roldao (2007) puts it, a preschool teacher must be able to galvanize a large amount of knowledge and situations. It is assumed that the preschool teacher should become a member of a large *"learning community"*, one that will continually adapt and reshape existing practices into a new practice and even *"theorize practice"*. In the context of early and preschool care and education, preschool teachers are primarily presented as initiators of change. In addition, they are portrayed as the promoters of learning who take care of their own personal and professional development, as well as members of a learning organization. As such, preschool teachers are primarily the subjects of a wide spectrum of interests, sensitive to changes in their working, learning and living environment. Not only do they actively engage in various changes in their working environment, but they also often initiate them. Such an expert is capable of easily responding to the challenges of contemporary society characterized by constant change. To summarize, the modern preschool teacher is a rather complex professional characterised by reflective thinking, continuous professional development, autonomy, responsibility, creativity, research and personal judgment (Vujičić et al., 2010).

Recent European documents (Children in Europe, Policy Paper 2007, OECD 2006, UNICEF, 2008, etc.) indicate that early and preschool care and education has gained increased attention in both public and political life. This development involves building an entirely new educational approach - one not based on the role of preschool teacher as merely a supplier of static knowledge, but as one who has major influence on shaping the conditions in which children are educated and who takes responsibility for managing their own learning process.

Creating a modern educational policy is inconceivable without the recognition of professionals in the field of early care and education of children. In the light of these policy papers mentioned above, many European countries have enhanced the design of their educational policy and strengthened their commitment to professionalism in early and preschool care and education. This is particularly important for the quality of professional training of preschool teachers, which requires the creation of policies that stimulate further development of their profession (Key Competences for Lifelong Learning - A European Reference Framework, the European Parliament and The Council of the European Union, 2006). A growing number of research studies seek to answer the question whether preschool teachers should have a four-year degree (Jacobson, 2009b). At the same time other researchers are more concerned with the question of which higher education degree (if any) is an appropriate standard of the quality of preschool teacher preparation (Barnett, 2003; Burchina et al., 2008; Whitebook & Ryan, 2011). However, there is general agreement that the quality of preschool teaching is of great significance, thus the organization of the program for the academic degree should be of a major concern in every country. While any kind of teacher education related to early childhood development or education is better than none, preschool teachers with bachelor's and specifically with graduate degrees appear to be the most effective (Arnott, 1989; Whitebook et al., 1989; Dunn, 1993). Therefore, the launch of the graduate study Early and Preschool Care and Education at the University of Rijeka impinges on fundamental theoretical considerations related to qualitatively different definitions of the role, importance and perspectives of experts who work in preschool institutions.

Graduate Study Program Competencies and Actual Job Demands of Preschool Teachers in Croatia

Any educational action, regardless of the place where it is happening or the population that is designed for, requires a highly competent approach based on the professional and social responsibility for the selected profession. It is a complex activity that requires a high level of intellectual ability followed by appropriate practical actions. Such competencies can be achieved primarily by appreciating the base of contemporary scientific knowledge in the field to which it relates. By constructing the appropriate (academic) educational model based on current curricular approaches, such competencies flow into a successful model of education at graduate level in which both theoretical and practical dimensions are balanced in order to achieve quality educational actions (Lepičnik-Vodopivec & Vujičić, 2010). That's the path of achieving the goal of educating preschool teachers as critical intellectuals and reflective practitioners.

Therefore, following current trends in (higher) education of preschool teachers, the competence-based approach grounded on a complex system of learning outcomes and competencies was used while creating the concept of graduate study of *Early and Preschool Care and Education* (EPCE) at the University of Rijeka. Specifics of working models and curriculum within Croatian cultural context were taken into account while the study program was being created (Tatalović Vorkapić, Vujičić & Čepić, 2014). Learning outcomes in the curriculum are, at the same time, relevant for the basic vocational training, for the labor market, and for further (formal) education of preschool teachers. The structure of the study program was based on the 'Bologna 3+2 model' (3 years of undergraduate and two years of graduate studies). The levels involved were defined by describing the essence of qualifications in terms of generic and specific competencies, and specific learning

outcomes expected to be achieved after successful completion of a study program,. Differentiation between these is to be achieved through knowledge and understanding, judgment, communication and learning skills in the context of the contemporary definition of the selected fieldwork.

While developing the university graduate study program *Early and Preschool Care and Education,* the national context of the labor market and job demands for preschool teachers were taken into account, as well as the international contemporary trends in the field. It is expected that new graduates will have less challenges in their pursuit for a job in Croatia, and get employed more frequently than their colleagues who do not have graduate degree. This might have a positive effect in relation to prospective students' motivation and their engagement in pursuing further (graduate) education.

Motives for Enrolling Graduate Study Program *Early and Preschool Care and Education* (EPCE)

From the individual perspective, it is possible to distinguish two sets of reasons why someone is involved in lifelong education (Aspin et al., 2012). The first is the desire to expand their knowledge (learning as pleasure), which results in self-realization of an individual, as well as his/her more competent participation in a social life. This type of motivation is commonly referred to as intrinsic or internal. The second set of motives involves the desire to improve an individual's own position in the labor market (higher salaries, advancement to a better position), and may relate to job loss or non-usefulness of existing qualifications. It has a pragmatic nature and is referred to as an extrinsic or external motivation. Studies indicate greater success among intrinsically motivated students rather that those who are externally motivated. Of course, one should always have in mind the spectrum of social conditions that largely affect (any) individual's decision.

Table 1. Percentage of participation in lifelong learning programs in European countries in 2011

	Countries							
	Denmark	**Romania**	**Greece**	**Hungary**	**Italy**	**France**	**Croatia**	**EU average**
Percentage	32.3%	1.8%	2.4%	2.7%	5.7%	5.5%	2.3%	8.9%

Participation in continuing education programs is represented in different ways in various European countries, according to the records of Eurostat in 2011 and it can be observed in Table 1. For example, in Demark around one third of people between 25 and 64 years attend some lifelong learning program, which outperforms the EU average (8.9%). Some other EU countries lack behind the Denmark as well as behind the EU average – Italy (5.7%), France (5.5%), Hungary (2.7%), Greece (2.4%) and Romania (1.8%). In Croatia, in 2011 there were 2.3% of adults included in lifelong learning programs.1. It is clear that both intrinsic and extrinsic motivation is important in making a decision to take part in lifelong educational programs. Comparing this finding with other EU countries, the percentage of adults included in lifelong learning programs in Croatia is rather small. Therefore, it is advisable to emphasize the importance of lifelong learning in the Croatian society and make lifelong learning programs more accessible as well as based on the needs assessment.

Houle (1961; according to Jarvis, 2004, p. 73/4), identifies three types of students with regards to motivation: goal-orientated learners; activity-orientated learners; and, those whose main orientation is learning for its own sake. Johnstone and Rivera (1965, p. 46; according to Jarvis, 2004, p. 74) discuss the problem of motivation for research purposes and identify ten possible motives related to lifelong learning: *"prepare for a new job; help with the present job; become better informed; spare-time enjoyment; home-centered tasks; other everyday tasks; meet new people; escape from daily routine; other or*

none – a miscellany of unclassifiable responses". This classification appears to include a new motive - meet new people. This motive suggests that lifelong learning for students has an important social function.

An important aspect of any analysis of preschool teachers' motivation is the fact that at this moment the labour market in Croatia does not have a graduate qualification listed as a requirement for job entry as a preschool teacher. It is therefore reasonable to assume that students will be triggered by intrinsic motives. Additionally, there are gender differences in motivation – men are more likely to have instrumental reasons (such as salary), while women are more likely to have intrinsic reasons (Woodley et al., 1987, Sargant, 1990; according to Jarvis, 2004, p. 73).

SETTING THE STAGE: AIMS OF THE STUDY

The salient point of the evaluation of the *Early and Preschool care and Education (EPCE)* graduate study program at the University of Rijeka was to analyze its usefulness according to preschool teachers' actual job demands in Croatia. The evaluation study was guided by the research question - Does continuing professional development through formal graduate education contribute to the development of preschool teachers' competences that are indicated as relevant for the actual job demands of preschool teachers in Croatia? In other words, the main aim of this study was to analyze if the new graduate study program contributed to the development of relevant knowledge and skills for preschool teachers enabling them to better respond to the growing demands of their job and working surrounding. In order to answer that question, graduate university students of Early and Preschool Care and Education at Faculty of Teacher Education in Rijeka have estimated the degree of development of all the competencies they were expected to acquire throughout the 2-years of graduate study, and how much those competencies served them in their preschool practice. Therefore, students were introduced to the aim of this study and our goals to explore their attitudes toward an enrolled graduate study program, competencies they have gained and the usefulness of those competencies in the real preschool practice and work. Since we earlier described that the graduate study program has been developed in collaboration with preschool teachers in practice, following the major changes in child development and all new factors in satisfying children needs within institutional context, we expected that students would evaluate their gained competencies as high and very high. Furthermore, it was expected that students would have found their continuing professional development through formal education satisfying for actual job demands and contributing to their career advancement.

The second aim of this study was to analyse the relationship between motives that preschool teachers have for enrolling this new graduate study program and perceived competencies gained. In order to find significant relationship between those two sets of variables, this study explores the enrolment motives as significant predictors for perceived competencies gained during the graduate study. According to theoretical models and previous research, it was expected to find that intrinsic motives would be positive significant predictors of perceived competencies gained during the graduate study, while extrinsic motives would be negative predictors. In order to answer that question, the graduate university students of EPCE at Faculty of Teacher Education in Rijeka have estimated the level of each motive for en-

rolling the graduate study program presented in the questionnaire. Subsequently, the prediction strength of each motive was analysed according to previously determined perceived competencies gained.

Besides the two main aims of this study, we also analysed all possible correlates of preschool teachers' attitudes as well as some socio-demographic variables: working experience, employment status or grade average.

RESEARCH METHODOLOGY

Research Study Participants

Forty-four preschool teachers participated in this study, all females with a mean age of 34 years (SD=7.5), ranging from 23 to 51 years of age. The mean of their working experience was 10 years (SD=7.92), ranging from 2 to 32 years of working within preschool care and education. At the time of this study, 41 of them were employed (37 of them as preschool teachers and 4 of them as directors of preschool), and 3 of them were unemployed. According to the Ordinance on the conditions and opportunities for the personal advancement and professional promotion (promotion within the profession and promotion within the workplace) of preschool teachers and associates in Croatian kindergartens (Ministry of Education and Sports, 1997), 37 participants were preschool teachers, 6 of them were preschool teachers-mentors and one of them was preschool teacher-advisor. Half of the students/participants were living in Rijeka at the time, while the others were coming from other parts of Croatia. All of them were enrolled in the second year of the new graduate program *Early Childhood and Preschool Education and Care* (EPCE) at the Faculty of Teacher Education in Rijeka. Participants were asked to estimate their grade average at the time; five of them reported to have grade average between 2.5 and 3.49; thirty-three reported to have grade average between 3.5

and 4.49; and six of them reported to have grade average 4.5 and higher. The sample was suitable because it presented the first cohort of Croatian students enrolled in the new ECPCE graduate study program and almost all of them (except 3 participants) were employed at the same time. Therefore, the evaluation of gained competencies and of their use in order to satisfy job demands within their particular preschool setting was the only applicable method for answering our research question. Collected data from that sample is extremely valuable as an evidence-base that could have a great impact on future development of the study program itself.

Measuring Instrument

To explore the evaluation of specific competencies development among preschool teachers and usage of those competencies for better performance and more successful coping with their job demands as well as for the influence on their career advancement, the thirty-nine-item pool has been used (Table 2). Participants were supposed to estimate their level of agreement with each item on 5-point Likert's scale (*1-I totally disagree; 2-I partially disagree; 3-Maybe; 4-I partially agree; 5-I totally agree*). Even though it was created only for the purposes of this research, its psychometric characteristics have been analysed. The reliability analysis showed very high and respectable reliability level of used instrument according to determined Cronbach alpha $r=.97$. In addition, to analyse the preschool teachers' motives for enrolling this graduate study program a set of ten items was used to explore their main reasons for enrolling to the EPCE program (Table 3). Participants were supposed to estimate the influence level of each reason for enrolling the graduate study program on 5-point Likert's scale (*1-no influence; 2-small influence; 3-moderate influence; 4-big influence; 5-total influence*). Finally, at the end of questionnaire students were asked about age, working

experience, employment status, working position and professional title during the graduate study.

Procedure

At the beginning of the fourth (last) semester of the two-year graduate study the enrolled preschool teachers (N=44) completed the questionnaire. That particular moment was selected for this study because the only engagement students have in their last semester is writing their thesis. Therefore, it was presumed that most of the expected competencies were gained within the prior three semesters. Students were told that the aim of this study was to explore their attitudes toward their study program, competencies they could built based on the study course and the usefulness of those competencies in preschool practice and work. Their participation in the study was completely voluntarily and anonymous and they were promised to be provided with feedback on research results. Administering the questionnaire took about twenty minutes. SPSS 18.0 was used to perform necessary statistical procedures: descriptive analysis, correlation analysis, Mann-Whitney test for testing the difference significance in non-parametric conditions and Multiple regression analysis.

CURRENT CHALLENGES FACING THE STUDY PROGRAM: RESEARCH RESULTS

The Preschool Teachers' Opinions about Competencies Gained During the Graduate Study and their Relevance to Actual Job Demands

The results of the descriptive analyses related to students' perception of competencies gained as well as their relevance for their actual job demands as preschool teachers are presented in Table 2. In general, it could be said that continuing professional development through formal higher edu-

Table 2. Descriptors of each attitude (N=39) toward gained competencies and their relevance to the labour market, their averages per items, and their average sum

Questionnaire items	Mean	SD	R	C
1. Preschool teachers need this graduate study program in theoretical and practical sense.	4.43	0.82	1-5	B
2. It is important and useful that future preschool teachers attend this study program.	4.3	0.9	1-5	B
3. Study program helped me in upgrading general competencies needed for a modern preschool teacher.	4.34	0.74	2-5	B
4. Every preschool teacher should have knowledge and skills acquired in this study program.	4.43	0.79	1-5	B
5. I would recommend this study program to any other preschool teacher.	4.11	1.06	1-5	B
6. If I could return the time, I would enroll this study program again.	4.39	11.2	1-5	B
7. Content of offered mandatory courses is interesting.	3.82	0.69	2-5	C
8. Content of offered elective courses is interesting.	4.07	0.86	2-5	B
9. This study program has completely met my expectations.	3.39	0.99	1-5	D
10. Competencies I have acquired in this study are relevant for my position on labor market.	3.82	0.87	1-5	C
11. Competencies I gained from this study program are relevant for my further education.	4.18	0.69	3-5	B
12. After this study, I have higher level of knowledge and understanding based on abilities of analyzing, synthesizing and evaluating within theory and practice of preschool care and education.	4.32	0.67	2-5	B
13. After this study, I will have higher ability of learning by problem solving in novel situations within interdisciplinary context of my professional working field.	4.14	0.76	2-5	B
14. My ability of constructive problem solving and making decisions within my professional role is higher after attending this study program.	4.11	0.87	2-5	B
15. Thanks to this study, I can better demonstrate the use of foreign language in verbal and written communication on the level of advanced use.	3	1.16	1-5	D
16. I can more efficiently act interdisciplinary in team work with experts in my and other scientific fields due to this study program	3.84	0.99	1-5	C
17. This study helped me to develop ability to work in international context based on comprehension and acceptance of multiculturalism.	3.27	1.06	1-5	D
18. Due to this study, I have higher ability of using new education possibilities (informal and non-formal learning, e-learning).	4.2	0.85	2-5	B
19. I developed new skills of learning as prerequisites of lifelong learning due to this study (informal and non-formal learning, e-learning and other).	4.34	0.74	2-5	B
20. After this study, I will be able to create new ideas based on development of creative dimension of my profession.	3.98	0.76	2-5	C
21. This study enabled me to acquire qualitatively higher levels of interpretation and evaluation of research findings in my profession.	4.16	0.61	3-5	B
22. After this study, I am able to efficiently anticipate developmental actions and manage them.	3.8	0.82	2-5	C
23. Due to this study, I have greater possibility of further development of ability to application of my knowledge by reflecting and evaluating my own practice work.	4.37	0.79	2-5	B
24. During this study, I have developed the ability of independent action within teamwork of interdisciplinary team experts who are active in my field of profession.	3.81	0.82	2-5	C
25. Due to this study, I have better comprehension, acceptance and encouragement of differences in achievement of developmental effects in children of early and preschool age.	4.27	0.79	2-5	B
26. After this study I show more personal dedication and commitment to early educator profession	4.25	0.94	2-5	B

continued on following page

Table 2. Continued

Questionnaire items	Mean	SD	R	C
27. This studying enabled me to show my knowledge about different theoretical aspects and practical applications within studies about "institutional childhood".	4.2	0.93	2-5	B
28. During study, I acquired knowledge and comprehension of contemporary childhood on interdisciplinary level (pedagogy, anthropology, psychology, culture, history, sociology).	4.27	0.82	2-5	B
29. I am able to think about new strategies in construction of integrated curriculum due to this study	4.27	0.73	2-5	B
30. After this study, I can show the higher level of knowledge and comprehension in the field of expert and scientific aspects within chosen study subjects.	4	0.75	2-5	B
31. Thanks to this study, I am able to participate actively in creating the education politics in the field of early and preschool care and education.	3.84	0.86	2-5	C
32. During study, I have learned to analyse, evaluate and improve concepts, theories, politics and practice of contemporary and institutional early and preschool care and education.	4.04	0.81	1-5	B
33. After this study I will be able to independently write a scientific and expert paper.	3.77	0.86	2-5	C
34. All knowledge, skills and abilities acquired during a study I can adequately use in my practice.	4.09	0.83	1-5	B
35. Besides improving preschool teacher in practice, this study program definitely increased the level of preschool teacher profession dignity in order to other professions.	4.34	1.01	1-5	B
36. Courses in this study are corresponding to the real needs of competencies in preschool teachers.	3.59	1.26	1-5	C
37. During this study I experienced significant positive and useful changes on a professional level	4.27	0.76	2-5	B
38. Attending this study led me to significant positive changes on a personal level.	4.34	0.64	3-5	B
39. Please, estimate your overall satisfaction level with this study program.	3.64	0.81	2-5	C
Average answers per items	4.07	0.59	2.05-4.87	
Average sum of answers	158.57	23.01	80-190	

Standard deviations (SD), results' range (R) and category (C) collected in sample of N=44 preschool teachers

Table 3. Participants 'stated reasons for enrolling in the graduate study program (n=44)

Participants' reasons for enrolling in the graduate study program	Mean	SD	Range
1. The possibility of career/employment advancement	2.40	1.28	1 - 5
2. The opportunity to continue my professional development	4.05	1.01	1 - 5
3. Opportunity for personal & professional training through new knowledge	3.50	1.25	1 - 5
4. The possibilities for better finances	4.80	0.46	3 - 5
5. The possibilities of higher salary	3.75	1.14	1 - 5
6. A wish to feel like a student again	2.11	1.54	1 - 5
7. My potentials are not completely utilized in my job	1.86	1.11	1 - 4
8. To satisfy the demands of my working institution	3.43	1.23	1 - 5
9. The possibility of successfully meeting job demands	1.52	1.00	1 - 5
10. Efficient use of free time	4.45	0.63	3 - 5

Standard deviations (SD), results' range (R) collected in sample of N=44 preschool teachers cation definitely contributes to the development of relevant knowledge and skills for preschool teachers in Croatia, thus making them more agile to respond to the growing job demands. The findings of this study present empirical validation of other theoretical studies (Bowman et al., 2001; Jacobson, 2009b; IOM and NRC, 2012; Whitebook et al., 2012) that suggest the same preschool teachers' knowledge and skills that were applied within existing the graduate study program and while developing the questionnaire for the purpose of this evaluation research.

Graduate university students of Early and Preschool care and Education at Faculty of Teacher Education in Rijeka have a rather high average estimation on all items (M=4.07) presented in a Table 2. In other words, they partially agree with all presented items, so it could be concluded that due to this specific study program they have developed all those competencies that form the base of the 2-year graduate study program in terms of expected learning outcomes and competencies. Moreover, the finding implies that gained competencies served them in their preschool practice. Both hypothesis concerning gained competencies due to the study program and their relevance to the actual job demands of preschool teachers are confirmed. To briefly analyze data from Table 2, the means are categorized in four categories according to the specific mean range: A = means from 4.5 to 5; B = means from 4 to 4.49; C = means from 3.5 to 3.99; and D = means from 3 to 3.49. Therefore, the analysis and interpretation of data would be better elaborated within those four categories.

Categories A & B. The statistical analyses showed (Table 2) that there was no average estimation within mean range from 4.5 to 5 (category A). On the other hand, the majority of average estimations are situated within the mean range 4 to 4.49, in category B. Preschool teachers showed a higher level of agreement with 26 items. It could be seen that they agree about the need of such graduate study program in theoretical and practical

sense; that they have built general competencies needed for a modern preschool teacher; that they would recommend this study program to any other preschool teacher; and if they could turn back time, they would enroll in this study program again. Furthermore, they think that it is important and useful for future preschool teachers to attend this study program, that every preschool teacher should have the knowledge and skills acquired in this study program, those competencies they have acquired in this study are relevant for their further education, and that the content of offered elective courses was interesting. Also, they share the opinion that after finishing this study they have higher level of knowledge and understanding based on acquired abilities of analyzing, synthesizing and evaluating within theory and practice of preschool care and education as much as a higher ability of learning through problem solving in new and novel situations within interdisciplinary contexts of their professional working field. They also think that their ability of problem-solving and decision-making within their professional role and ability of using new educational possibilities (informal and non-formal learning, e-learning) are higher after attending this study program. They agreed that due to this study they have developed new skills of learning as prerequisites of lifelong learning (informal and non-formal learning, e-learning and other). Also, they have a greater possibility of further applying their knowledge by reflecting and evaluating their own practice. Finally, they have a better comprehension of differences in achievement of developmental effects in children of early and preschool age. This study enabled them to acquire qualitatively higher levels of interpretation and evaluation of research findings in their profession; to show more personal dedication and commitment to the early educator profession; and to show their knowledge about different theoretical aspects and practical applications within the study of *"institutional childhood"*.

During this study, preschool teachers stated that they acquired knowledge and comprehension of contemporary childhood on interdisciplinary level (pedagogy, anthropology, psychology, culture, history, sociology) and that they have learned to analyze, evaluate and improve concepts, theories, politics and practice of contemporary and institutional early and preschool care and education. Consequently, preschool teachers are now able to think about new strategies in construction of an integrated curriculum; they can show the higher level of knowledge and comprehension of expert and scientific aspects within their chosen study subjects; and they can adequately use all skills and abilities acquired during their study in their practice. They agreed that besides improving their practice, this study program definitely increased their level of professional dignity in relation to other professions and that during this study they have experienced significant positive and useful changes at both, professional and personal level. The highest average estimations were on agreements with first and fourth item (Table 2). Therefore, preschool teachers showed the highest agreement with the attitude that they need this graduate study program in theoretical and practical sense and that every preschool teacher should have knowledge and skills acquired in this particular study program.

Category C. Considering the average estimations within mean range from 3.5 to 3.99 (Table 2), it could be seen that preschool teachers showed a lower level of agreement with 10 items. They thought that the offered mandatory courses were interesting and that competencies they have acquired in this study are relevant for their position in the labor market. They agreed that due to this study they could perform better in interdisciplinary teamwork with experts in theirs and other scientific fields. Also, they are able to create new ideas based on development of creative dimension of their profession. Finally, they perceive to be more able in efficiently anticipating developmental actions and managing them, so that they are more able to write a scientific/expert paper. They lightly agreed that during this study they

have developed the ability of independent action within an interdisciplinary team of experts who are active in their field and the ability to actively participate in creating the education discourse in the field of early and preschool care and education. Finally, they agreed that courses in this graduate study program are corresponding to the real needs of competencies in Croatian preschool teachers' profession.

Category D. Descriptive analysis of category D (mean range between 3 and 3.49) showed that preschool teachers were ambiguous toward three items. Therefore, based on these findings it could be concluded that this study program completely met all expectations of some preschool teachers. In addition, this study has helped some preschool teachers to develop the ability to work in an international context based on comprehension and acceptance of multiculturalism. The lowest average estimation has been determined for item 15 (3-maybe), where some preschool teachers think that they can demonstrate the better use of foreign language in verbal and written communication on the level of advanced use, but some of them do not share that opinion. Those last three items definitely deserve more attention concerning possible intervention within the study program. Their evaluation concerning the developed ability to work in an international context based on comprehension and acceptance of multiculturalism and the ability of demonstrating the use of foreign language in verbal and written communication on the level of advanced use is moderate and the lowest in comparison to other developed competencies. These findings implied that their previous formal education was weak in the use of a foreign language, which unfortunately is beyond the remits of this programme. So, it is very important to think about giving preschool teachers the option to enhance their foreign language use through the lifelong learning program at our faculty, so that the expected competencies concerning advanced use of foreign language could be accomplished at higher level.

Some Correlates of Preschool Teachers' Opinions about their Competencies Gained During Graduate Study Program and their Relevance to the Actual Job Demands

Correlation analysis showed significant correlations between only one demographic variable (employment status) and preschool teachers' attitudes toward gained competencies and their usefulness in preschool practice. Furthermore, within this research problem, *Anova* was performed to test the significance level of possible differences in preschool teachers' attitudes according to their employment status. It could be seen that significant negative correlation between employment status and preschool teachers' attitudes toward gained competencies and their usefulness in preschool practice has been determined (r_{ho}=-.40, p<.01). Consequently, the significant difference has been determined between employed preschool teachers and unemployed in their opinion toward gained competencies. Considering the small number of unemployed preschool teachers (only three), Mann-Whitney test was run which has confirmed previous result of significant difference in opinions (M-Wu=6, z=2.56, p=.01).

Employed preschool teachers showed significantly more positive attitudes toward their gained competencies and their usefulness in preschool practice in comparison to the unemployed preschool teachers. Employed preschool teachers expressed the perception of more developed competencies due to graduate study program and they perceive significantly greater usefulness of those competencies concerning their job demands. This actually indicates that the expression of positive attitudes towards their own learning outcomes and competences between the employed and unemployed teachers was determined by their working status, i.e. by the factor of social-economic safety perceived at the personal level.

The Preschool Teachers' Motives for Enrolling Graduate Study Program

Since this type of graduate study has been the first one in Croatia, and because of the meaningful role of enrolment motives, it was very useful and interesting to explore preschool teachers' motives for enrolling to this graduate study program. Ten possible motives for enrolling are presented in Table 3.

The following motive had the highest rate: "I have enrolled this study program because it provided me with the possibility of personal and professional training through new knowledge". Moreover, the possibility of career advancement (or employment possibilities for unemployed), the possibility of successfully meeting the job demands and the possibility of better finances (higher salaries) were estimated as the motives with high influence for enrolling to this graduate study program. Based on the findings, it could be concluded that when enrolling to the graduate study program, preschool teachers expected to acquire those skills, knowledge and competencies that would serve them in their practice and helped them to meet all contemporary job demands. More intrinsically motivated preschool teachers are those who are more dedicated to their professional development in general and their profession. They have recognized their own shortcomings in certain areas of knowledge and skills that could be acquired through this graduate study program. They enrolled and through this evaluation found it worthwhile regarding their actual job demands. Therefore, those results are very satisfying since they reflect the intrinsic motivation for enrolling the graduate study program, which is very important concerning the learning outcomes and the whole purpose of this graduate program. Motives for enrolling the study because it provided them with possibilities for continuing their professional development at graduate and postgraduate level and it enable them to work on and develop their potentials which have not been completely utilized at their job, showed moderate influence. There was small influence by motives regarding the efficient use of free time; enrolling the study because a friend has enrolled too; the wish to feel like a student again; or to satisfy the demands of their workplace.

The Relationship between Preschool Teachers' Motives for Enrolling Graduate Study Program and their Perceived Gained Competencies during Study

Correlation analysis showed significant correlations between three motives for enrolling graduate study program and preschool teachers' attitudes toward gained competencies and their usefulness in preschool practice. Furthermore, within this research problem, *Anovas* were performed to test the significance level of possible differences in preschool teachers' attitudes according to the relevant motives for enrolling the graduate study. The third, the fourth and the sixth motives showed significant relationship with preschool teachers' attitudes. According to these findings, the preschool teachers with significantly more positive attitudes toward gained competencies and their usefulness in preschool practice gave higher rate of two motives for enrolling this graduate study. The correlation between their positive attitude and the first motive of enrolling this study because of the opportunity to continue their professional development at graduate and postgraduate level, was positive and significant ($r_{ho}=.35$, p<.05). Furthermore, more significant and positive was determined relationship between their positive attitude and the motive of enrolling this study because of the possibility of personal and professional training ($r_{ho}=.45$, p<.01). Even though the significant correlation has been determined between the third motive and preschool teachers' attitudes, its significance level is lower, what consequently led to determined non-significant differences in attitudes between group of lower

and higher third motive for enrolling the graduate study (M-Wu=152.5, z=1.44, p=.15). Analyzing the relationship between the fourth motive and preschool teachers' attitudes it could be seen that the group with higher fourth motive showed significantly more positive attitudes toward gained competencies due to graduate study and their usefulness to preschool practice (M-Wu=47.5, z=2.84, p=.00).

Both of those findings are very important because they imply the importance of type of motivation for enrolling the study which is obviously relevant for the way in which that same study program is perceived, as well as learning outcomes and their relevance for the actual job demands. The following finding also confirmed these implications, since correlation analysis showed significantly negative relationship between *"enrolling the study because of my friend has enrolled too"* and attitudes toward gained competencies and their usefulness in preschool practice ($r_{ho}=-.33$, p<.05). In other words, those preschool teachers who showed lower rate on this motive for enrolling the study also showed significantly more positive attitudes toward gained competencies and their usefulness in preschool practice (M-Wu=119, z=2.31, p=.02). It is clear that the more extrinsic motivation for enrolling the study is, the more negative perception of that same study program learning outcomes and their relevance for job demands would be. Therefore, this study confirmed that the motivation for enrolling graduate study present a significant correlate of preschool teachers' attitudes toward gained competencies and their usefulness in preschool practice – extrinsic motives led to more negative perception of the study program and learning outcomes and intrinsic motives led to more positive perception of study program and its learning outcomes.

To examine the predictive power of three significantly connected motives in relation to perceived competencies gained during the study program, regression analysis was conducted.

Table 4. Multiple regression analysis of three motives for enrolling this graduate study as predictors of average perception of gained competencies during study in preschool teachers

Motives for enrolment	B	Beta	Independent contribution	General contribution	F	p
Opportunity for personal & professional training through new knowledge	0.079	0.163	0.022	0.056	4.31	0.01
The possibilities for better finances (higher salary)	0.470	0.375	**0.111***	**0.176***		
I wanted to feel like a student again	-0.040	-0.097	0.009	0.022		
R				.504**		
R²				.254**		

*p<0.05; **p<0.01

Overall, it was determined that those three motives explained 25.4% of variance in students' perception of their gained competencies during study, as Table 4 shows. The highest predictive power had the fourth motive: its total contribution in prediction is 17.6% and independent contribution in prediction is 11.1%. Therefore, enrolling this study program provides students with a possibility of their personal and professional training. Furthermore, this finding significantly predicts highly positive perception of their gained competencies during study. This result is very important since it implies at the fact that the perception of the enrolled study program is conditioned by the enrolling motives of the students. If those motives are intrinsic, the students will show positive perception of the gained competencies. Therefore, if the motives were strong and intrinsic, this would successfully influence students' capability for learning, which might have the competencies developed on higher level as a result at the end. Even though this causality could not be drawn from these results, this discussion could serve for some future studies. Moreover, even smaller, the third motive: *"I have enrolled this graduate study because it provided me with the opportunity to continue my professional development at graduate and postgraduate level"* also showed its general contribution to prediction (5.6%) and independent contribution (2.2%). In addition, the sixth motive

of *"enrolling the study because of my friend has enrolled too"*, showed the smallest general contribution to prediction of criterion variable (2.2%), the smallest independent contribution (0.9%), and its prediction is negative in relation to criterion variable. It could be concluded that these last two motives are still important even though their predictive powers are rather small in comparison to fourth motive. General remark of this section could be drawn in the light of great importance of measuring students' enrolling motives when their perception of the study program or their gained competencies will be examined.

CONCLUSION

The evaluation of the new graduate study program *Early and Preschool Care and Education* at the Faculty of Teacher Education at the University of Rijeka offers legitimate base to conclude that this study program, as a mean of continuous professional development of preschool teachers in Croatia, contributed significantly to students' own knowledge and skills and their better coping with the growing job demands in the institutions of preschool and early education in the Republic of Croatia. Overall evaluation of participants, who are at the same time students and preschool practitioners, suggests that the acquired competencies from the designed graduate study program are very useful for their practice and relevant for their job, i.e. for actual labor market and job demands of preschool teachers in our country.

Based on the evaluation of this study program, employed preschool teachers found the competences gained very useful in their working environment, as it was expected. Furthermore, their motivation for enrolling the study program is mainly intrinsic, that according to motivational theory implies high dedication to their own professional development and profession quality.

Education for the profession is defined as a dynamic, open and permanent process based on the requirement that the professional development and continuing professional training presents an obligation which arises from professional ethics and responsibility of every person who chooses to be a preschool teacher. This study confirmed expectations toward perceived usefulness of gained competencies and it also serves as a solid base to continue monitoring the quality of graduate study program and its usefulness for challenging growing job demands of preschool teachers in practice.

ACKNOWLEDGMENT

We would like to thank all preschool teachers who have participated in this study. In addition, we would like to thank our dean, Prof. Jasna Krstović, Ph.D., for her support in running this research. Finally, we thank to Maja Homolka, MA, for her help with proofreading.

REFERENCES

Arnett, J. (1989). Caregivers in day-care centers: Does training matter? *Journal of Applied Developmental Psychology, 10*(4), 541–552. doi:10.1016/0193-3973(89)90026-9

Aspin, D. N., Chapman, J., Evans, K., & Bagnall, R. (Eds.). (2012). *Second international handbook of lifelong learning*. Dortrecht, The Netherlands: Springer; doi:10.1007/978-94-007-2360-3

Barnett, S. W. (2003). *Better teachers, better preschools: Student achievement linked to teacher qualifications*. New Brunswick, NJ: National Institute for Early Education Research.

Bruner, J. S. (2000). *Kultura obrazovanja [The culture of education]*. Zagreb: Educa.

Burchinal, M., Hyson, M., & Zaslow, M. (2008). Competencies and credentials for early childhood educators: What do we know and what do we need to know? *NHSA Dialog Brief, 11*(1).

Čepić, R., & Krstović, J. (2008). Cjeloživotno učenje i organizacije koje uče za održivu budućnost: Izazovi i pitanja [Lifelong learning and learning organizations for a sustainable future: Challenges and Issues]. In L. Vujičić & V. Uzelac (Eds.), *Cjeloživotno učenje za održivi razvoj part I [Lifelong learning for sustainable development]* (pp. 139–144). Rijeka: Faculty of Teacher Education, University of Rijeka.

Datnow, A., Hubbard, L., & Mehan, H. (2002). *Extending educational reform: From one school to many*. London: RoutledgeFalmer.

Dunn, L. (1993). Proximal and distal features of day care quality and children's development. *Early Childhood Research Quarterly, 8*(2), 167–192. doi:10.1016/S0885-2006(05)80089-4

Education Statistics at Regional Level. (n.d.). Retrieved on July 15th 2012 from http://epp.eurostat.ec.europa.eu/statistics_explained/index.php/Education_statistics_at_regional_level

Elliott, J. (1998). *The curriculum experiment, meeting the challenge of social change*. Buckingham, UK: Open University Press.

Faculty of Teacher Education, University of Rijeka. (2010). *Early childhood and preschool education – Course program.* Available from http://www.ufri.uniri.hr/data/RipO-eng.pdf

Fullan, M. (2007). *The new meaning of educational change* (4th ed.). New York: Teachers College Columbia University.

Fullan, M. G. (1993). The complexity of the change process. In M. G. Fullan (Ed.), *Change forces: Probing the depth of educational reform* (pp. 19–41). London: Falmer Press.

Fullan, M. G. (1999). *Change forces: The sequel.* Philadelphia, PA: Falmer Press.

Gardner, H. (2005). *Disciplinirani um [Disciplined mind].* Zagreb: Educa.

Gopnik, A., Meltzoff, A. N., & Kuhl, P. K. (2003). *Znanstvenik u kolijevci – što nama rano učenje kazuje o umu [A scientist in the crib - What early learning tells us about the mind].* Zagreb: Educa.

Hopkins, D. (2001). *School improvement for real.* London: Falmer Press. doi:10.4324/9780203165799

Institute of Medicine (IOM) & National Research Council. (NRC). (2012). The early childhood care and education workforce: Challenges and opportunities: A workshop report. Washington, DC: The National Academies Press.

Jarvis, P. (2004). *Adult education and lifelong learning: Theory and practice* (3rd ed.). London: Routledge.

Kipper, H., & Mischke, W. (2008). *Uvod u opću didaktiku [Introduction to general didactics].* Zagreb: Educa.

Lepičnik-Vodopivec, J., & Vujičić, L. (2010). The development of professional competencies: The educator as a reflective practitioner in tertiary education. *Scientia Paedagogica Experimentalis: International Journal of Experimental Research, 47*(1), 111–131.

Ministry of Science, Education and Sports, Republic of Croatia. (1997). *Pravilnik o načinu i uvjetima napredovanja u struci i promicanju u položajna zvanja odgojitelja i stručnih suradnika u dječjim vrtićima [Ordinance on the conditions and opportunities for promotion in profession and promotion in position titles of preschool teachers and associates in Croatian kindergartens].* Zagreb, Croatia: Ministry of Science, Education and Sports.

Niemi, H. (2007). The Bologna process and the teacher education curriculum. In *Proceedings of the European Union Conference: Teacher Professional Development for the Quality and Equity of Lifelong Learning* (pp. 50-65). Lisbon: Ministry of Education.

Noordegraaf, M. (2007). From "pure" to "hybrid" professionalism: Present-day professionalism in ambiguous public domains. *Administration & Society, 39*(6), 761–785. doi:10.1177/0095399707304434

Óhidy, A. (2008). *Lifelong learning interpretations of an education policy in Europe.* Wiesbaden: Verlag für Sozialwissenschaften.

Petrović-Sočo, B., Slunjski, E., & Šagud, M. (2005). A new learning paradigm – A new roles of preschool teachers in the educational process. *Zbornik Učiteljske Akademije u Zagrebu, 7*(2), 329-340.

(2009a). Pre-K issues step to the front. In Jacobson, L. (Ed.), *Covering the pre-K landscape: New investments in our littlest learners* (pp. 1–4). New York: Hechinger Institute.

Rinaldi, C. (2000). Utopia? Considerazioni tra passato e futuro sull' educare nelle istituzioni infantili. In G. Rabitti & P. Rametta (Eds.), Intorno a un percorso di formazione, il quaderno del now (pp. 55-61). Municipality of Reggio Emilia, Italy: Reggio Children.

Rinaldi, C. (2006). *In dialogue with Reggio Emilia: Listening, researching and learning*. New York: Routledge. doi:10.4324/9780203317730

Roldão, M. C. (2007). Research-based teacher education and reflective practice: Teacher professional development for the quality and equity of lifelong learning. In *Proceedings of the Council of the European Union Conference: Teacher Professional Development for the Quality and Equity of Lifelong Learning* (pp. 39-49). Lisbon: Ministry of Education.

Senge, P., Kleiner, A., Roberts, C., Ross, R., Roth, G., & Smith, B. (2003). *Ples promjene – izazovi u razvoju učećih organizacija [The dance of the change – The challenges in development of learning organizations]*. Zagreb: Mozaik knjiga.

(2009b). Should preschool teachers have four-year degrees? In Jacobson, L. (Ed.), *Covering the pre-K landscape: New investments in our littlest learners* (pp. 13–14). New York: Hechinger Institute.

Slunjski, E. (2008). *Dječji vrtić: Zajednica koja uči: mjesto dijaloga, suradnje i zajedničkog učenja [A kindergarten: The learning community: The place for dialog, cooperation and mutual learning]*. Zagreb: Spektar Media.

Slunjski, E. (2011). *Kurikulum ranog odgoja – Istraživanje i konstrukcija [Early childhood education curriculum – Research and construction]*. Zagreb: Školska Knjiga.

Stoll, L., & Fink, D. (2000). *Mijenjajmo naše škole: Kako unaprijediti djelotvornost i kvalitetu škola [We should change our schools: How to improve effectiveness and quality of schools]*. Zagreb: Educa.

Tatalović Vorkapić, S., & Vujičić, L. (2012). Do we need positive psychology in Croatian kindergartens? The implementation possibilities evaluated by preschool teachers. *Early Years: An International Journal of Research and Development, 33*(1), 33–44. doi:10.1080/09575146.2012.662214

Tatalović-Vorkapić, S., Vujičić, L., & Čepić, R. (2014). Preschool teacher identity. In P. Breen (Ed.), *Cases on teacher identity, diversity, and cognition in higher education* (pp. 22–60). Hershey, PA: IGI-Global. doi:10.4018/978-1-4666-5990-2.ch002

Tobin, J., Karusawa, M., & Hsueh, Y. (2004). Komatsudani then and now: Continuity and change in a Japanese preschool. *Contemporary Issues in Early Childhood, 5*(2), 128–144. doi:10.2304/ciec.2004.5.2.2

Vujičić, L. (2008). Research and improvement of one's own practice – Way to development of teachers'/preschool teachers' practical competence. In I. Žogla (Ed.), *Teacher of the 21st century: Quality education for quality teaching* (pp. 184–194). Riga, Latvia: University of Latvia Press.

Vujičić, L. (2011). *Istraživanje kulture odgojno-obrazovne ustanove [The research of the culture of the preschool institution]*. Zagreb: Mali professor d.o.o.

Vujičić, L., Čepić, R., & Pejić Papak, P. (2010). Afirmation of the concept of new professionalism in the education of preschool teachers: Croatian experiences. In Chova G.L. Belenguer, M.D. Cande lT.I. (Eds.), *Proceedings of EDULEARN10 Conference* (pp. 242-250). Valencia, Spain: IATED.

Whitebook, M., Austin, L. J. E., Ryan, S., Kipnis, F., Almaraz, M., & Sakai, L. (2012). *By default or by design? Variations in higher education programs for early care and teachers and their implications for research methodology, policy, and practice*. Berkeley, CA: Center for the Study of Child Care Employment, University of California.

Whitebook, M., Howes, C., & Phillips, D. (1989). *Who cares? Child care teachers and the quality of care in America—Final Report of the National Child Care Staffing Study*. Oakland, CA: Child Care Employee Project.

Whitebook, M., & Ryan, S. (2011). *Degrees in context: Asking the right questions about preparing skilled and effective teachers of young children. NIEER Policy Brief (Issue 22)*. New Brunswick, NJ: National Institute for Early Education Research.

KEY TERMS AND DEFINITIONS

Competencies of Preschool Teachers: A set of defined behaviours that provide a structured guide enabling the identification, evaluation and development of the behaviours in the context of an early and preschool care and education. They present a combination of practical and theoretical knowledge, skills, behaviour and values used to improve performance in early and preschool care and education, and could be general and specific.

Evaluation: A systematic verification of certain program or project, using criteria governed by a set of standards, in this case a verification of a new graduate study program Early and Preschool Care and Education. Defined set of standards used in this study is supposed preschool teachers' competencies in relation to existing job demands. The primary purpose of evaluation, in addition to collect basic data about the program is to enable objective analysis of the program and to determine possible guidelines for future modification.

Extrinsic Motives: Presents one form of motives that are directed to attain an outcome, whether or not that activity is also intrinsically motivated. Extrinsic motivation comes from outside of the individual. Common extrinsic motivations are rewards or the threat of punishment.

Intrinsic Motives: Presents one form of motives that are stem from an interest or enjoyment in the task itself, and exists within the individual rather than relying on external pressures or a desire for reward.

Job Demands: The degree to which working environment contains stimuli that imperatively require attention and response. In other words, job demands are all those things that have to be done in the context of early and preschool care and education. The more adequate competencies preschool teacher have, more successfully (s)he can adequately respond to actual job demands.

Motives: Psychological features that induce an individual to act towards a desired goal. They also, elicit, control and sustain certain goal-directed behaviours. In addition, they are considered as driving forces in, for this case, studying desirable program.

Preschool Education in Croatia: Croatian curricula of early and preschool education is based on two theoretical programs: humanistic-developmentally and socio-constructivist models. The purpose of institutional early and preschool care and education presents a successful satisfaction of the children needs and children self-actualization in the age range from six months until the age of entering the primary school. It is an integrated system of early and pre-school education, which falls under the jurisdiction of the Ministry of Science, Education and Sports.

Preschool Teachers as Students/ Early and Preschool Care and Education: Students at Faculty of Teacher Education in Rijeka, University of Rijeka, Croatia. They are attending new graduate university study program called Early and Preschool Care and Education.

Study Program EPCE: Faculty of Teacher Education in Rijeka, University of Rijeka launched the undergraduate university Early and Preschool Education Study in the academic year 2009/2010, and the graduate study in the academic year 2010/2011. The name of the study is Early and Preschool Care and Education. It is the first-of-a-kind study in the Republic of Croatia. The University of Rijeka is the first university in our country that enabled university education of future preschool teachers (3 years of undergraduate + 2 years of graduate study).

ENDNOTES

[1]   For more statistics visit http://epp.eurotat.ec.europa.eu/.

Conclusion

In the higher education *millieu* it is common to hear that it is a meta-field rather than a field for itself. There is a point of truth that, in general, we often fail to pay enough attention to the underlying structure of a debate or of a discipline; is it, for example, one in which matters of detail stand for much more fundamental differences of values, or one in which relatively small differences in starting points have somehow ballooned into what feels like a much more polarised debate than it needs to be? Most of the ground of debate comprises the arid territory of one side's distorted portrayal of the other side's views. A leading goal of this book is to contribute to overcome this myopia by providing chapters that are themselves reflexive in how each topic or research is presented. Maybe it is time, for higher education researchers, agree to differ, as long as important issues continue to be tackled. Imagine a world where the organised effort of policy, education and research was to make things clearer and, where possible, more consensual diverse. Not only would we waste a lot less time and probably make wiser decisions, but we could focus our arguments on stuff that are genuinely important and on which we really do profoundly disagree.

The success of most social interventions – the interventions that could help foster mass creativity – rely on what has been called 'civic effects' that is the public engagement, mobilisation and behaviour change. Most of the chapters included in this book relate to these three dimensions in the field of higher education, which affect many practical aspects of educational development practitioners. But those civic effects are more likely to emerge from leaders articulating a clear vision, convening new conversations and collaborations, leading by doing than through the slow, cumbersome process of developing and implementing policy. The word 'new' in the title of this book does not only relate to the emphasis it is given to research done by ECRs, but also to the proposal of enlarging the span of actors and of research types in that process of implementing policy and, especially, research. That said, effects and impact of educational research are most effective when they build from what already exists; honoring current efforts and engaging established organizations, rather than creating an entirely new solution from scratch.

The chapters included in this book, but also some of the ones that, for various reasons, could not be included, gave rise to the following topics that we can reflect upon not only with regard to higher education research but to social sciences in general.

THE CHALLENGES

Research on higher education touches global issues and, at the same time, investigates national, local and individual specificities. Nevertheless, this is a field in which there is a clear and visible will to deal with contemporary 'burning' issues. When research on the field does that, often the field hesitates between a more general view of the issues, with a strong theoretical weight, and the inputs of more empirical data. This leads us to a very first challenge, which is one of the *leitmotifs* for this book: how to better articulate more precise data and scenarios with broader visions and theories within the field?

The book also deals with the comprehension of changing phenomena in higher education, understanding its past and preparing for the future of the field. Some implied searchlights from the different chapters of this book give us cues on the debate that is taking place around those issues and for each ongoing sociocultural situation. We work outward from situations rather than impose boundaries. Contemporary higher education can make use of proposed benchmarks and guidelines. As a field, it has a formidable toolkit, numerous and varied instruments to produce rigorous knowledge and enable all stakeholders of the collective life to be helpful to raise their ability to think and, hence, to act.

ENGAGEMENTS

The deficit of sight or of thought in higher education research is not theoretical, but rather a lack of general perspective enabling it to integrate, beyond its diversity, the different visions that the field is likely to propose. It is also the relationship between higher education and collective life, politics, whether national or international, regional, global, and the great changes that are taking place. Researchers in higher education, from this standview, may therefore have points in common with the actors that animate the social, cultural, economic or political scene.

Researchers in higher education are willing to invest in the public space, but provided they can do so as producers of scientific knowledge. They do not want to be the ideologues of the present time, and many of them do not confuse their role with that of an expert or consultant. We recognize the obligation of the higher education field towards society, and therefore the participation of researchers towards a more reflective and active research arena.

A NEW INTELLECTUAL SPACE

Among the changes that require higher education to transform its modes of approach, the most evident ones can be summarized conveniently under two expressions: globalization, on the one hand, and on the other hand, individualism. These are two logics that mark the space inside which research is increasingly called upon to move.

Globalization encourages us to analyze social facts taking into account their global dimensions. But it must also consider a second and more diffuse phenomenon that has changed and will increasingly change the work of social sciences and higher education research: the thrust of individualism, in all its dimensions. This boost has resulted in the search by a sustained interest in the theories of rational choice, but also, and especially more recently, by increasingly taking into account the subjectivity of individuals. It weakens the holistic approaches, and is one of the major, if not one of the sources of the debate of the structuralist approaches from the mid-1970s.

LEVELS AND THEIR ARTICULATION

Since 1977, with the book *The actor and the system*, by Michel Crozier and Ehrard Friedberg, we have been invited to articulate, in our analysis, those two levels. Today, this articulation remains necessary, but there are more levels that ougth to be considered: the global logics of the individual – and its subjectivities reflected in education systems – are much more nuanced and richer than the ones regarding the social actor, and settings such as society, state and nation. In fact, half a century after C. Wright Mills had said that "neither the life of an individual nor the history of a society can be understood without understanding both," researchers have now to deal with global and individual trends and at the same time avoid the temptations of fragmentation (which lead to a relativism) and of the mix or fusion of levels of analysis, which is typical in an abstract universalist style.

THE FRAGMENTATION OF HIGHER EDUCATION RESEARCH

Most often, research on the social sciences has set the goal of describing a phenomenon, a problem, a situation, an event, an interaction, or to bring a new contribution to the knowledge of the causes of a certain phenomenon. The majority of research proposes to improve the comprehension of a phenomenon by highlighting a new variable that will add towards the explanation to that phenomenon. In these cases, knowledge has the advantage of being cumulative, but it is restricted to a very precise question, often not linked with broader contextual concerns. And it is rare that this type of knowledge may have a social purpose or feed public debate. It will contribute to legitimate its author, to the game of "publish or perish," maybe to be discussed among authors of similar work, or to be presented at a congress or conference. However, an effort must be made that higher education research escapes the trap of falling into a hyper specialisation that usually leads to its corollary; an ideological and metaphysical chitchat and a sterile essayism. We try to avoid this temptation in the chapters selected as well as to show general issues in the higher education field without losing the richness of empirical analysis. The chapters presented do not divide so much among different paradigms or theoretical orientations—though we can find some dominant ones, such as the institutional logics—but between families of objects of analysis.

The organization of university systems often does not encourage this struggle against the fragmentation of knowledge. Thus, it is our hope that this book may contribute to place some of the challenges that higher education is currently facing within a larger social debate. More than the scientific integration of topics and researchers in a closed professional arena, this book aims at promoting the intellectual participation of young and senior researchers in a public and social debate that research on education may benefit from. This social responsibility does not have to be imputed only to the system or to institutions; researchers themselves have their own share of responsibility in this matter and it also depends on them how they define their social role.

BEING A HIGHER EDUCATION RESEARCHER

If higher education researchers have any legitimacy to intervene in the public sphere, it is not only because they are, most of the time, teachers disseminating knowledge to their students. This task is crucial, but it is distinct from the specific activity of doing research, which should lead to the production of knowledge. It comes close when the teacher-researcher provides for his/her students research training, especially when this training involves strong practical dimensions, for example on the field. But let us not confuse the production of knowledge with other activities. This production stresses, with its own criteria, scientific activity. On many of the issues that fall within higher education research, everyone has an opinion, a point of view, possibly certainties without any apparent need to have expertise or special knowledge. In addition, a powerful trend is at work, in many societies; promoting an anti-intellectualism that goes head-on with the social sciences, then accused of irrelevance, or worse (in populist terms), participating in the domination of the elites on the masses. Isn't the contribution of higher education beyond its appearances of meta-discipline, due to its representations to provide informed, competent analyses being honest about its own limits?

One of the important characteristics of higher education as a field is that it is relative to the opinion, to the audiences, and to the actors who are always likely to judge its contribution. A specificity of the contributions of higher education researchers at the collective life is that it is distinguished from the mere opinion, while they are in contact with carriers of opinion. Their work is necessarily based on the results of research, even if they import rules of other disciplines. We must distinguish between the respect of strict rules and the validity or relevance of the results obtained by researchers. In the first case, it is within the professional realm that we must tell if a research, a study, an investigation satisfies the cannons of the normative and ethical discipline concerned, if it was carried out with rigour.

It is also necessary that this field is not fragmented into chapels mutually excluding each other; that it is able to ensure the unity of the disciplines considered while recognizing the diversity of theoretical orientations, approaches, methods, objects, and about being able to take their path to innovation and originality.

The validity or relevance of a research project poses even more delicate problems. It is not enough that a study, a survey, a participant observation, etc. is conducted with all the desirable rigour so we can say that it is relevant. The method applied in a research does not only determine its quality or its social usefulness. Those who fetish the method, the selection of techniques, the seriousness of their application are likely to miss the point, which is the intellectual content of his contribution, the interests of its assumptions and its assertions, as indeed of its doubts. The test, here, cannot come from the professional research community, at least not exclusively. If one accepts that the production of knowledge on higher education must have a social utility, based on its scientific contribution, then one must recognize that its relevance lies in what will be done for this contribution in other areas than theirs.

This poses very directly the question of the evaluation. Higher education research has its cost, provided by the public power, by international organizations, by private institutions, and by foundations. In all cases, it is legitimate that researchers are accountable, and it is one of the functions of the assessment to enable it. But there are other functions. Evaluation ought to help organize careers, to ensure the proper functioning of universities and other higher education and research organizations. Higher education professionals rise frequently not so much against the principle of an assessment but against its terms. For instance, they criticise its normative character, which might constitute an encouragement to the conformism

Sometimes, higher education scholars also fear to be judged by powers that may subordinate the research to interests of specific actors - large businesses for example. How to combine the necessary freedom of researchers, the recognition of the fundamental nature of the critical dimensions of research with the idea that it must be at the service of all of the common good, of the companies, and for that, assessment procedures are necessary?

INSTITUTIONS

There is a danger that this input from higher education research functions to only advantage of the field and institution leaders. But research may also, and above all, help transform a crisis, a problem, a blockage in exchange, discussion, negotiation and positive conflicts. It can prevent a higher education institution from being locked in the logic of management and devastating organizational practices. The most critical of the researchers, those who developed supercritical approaches, will argue against the idea of participating in the study of problems of this type, internal to an organisation. They will see in it a support to practices of pacification which ultimately allow the dominant to ensure the reproduction of their domination. This type of argumentation is still well alive in the so called post-modernist times.

Higher education is not necessarily intended to be boxed in the relatively confined space of university life. Moreover, this is not where it was born; rather in social reform movements, or in the establishment of welfare institutions. It is not void for young minds, for doctoral candidates seeking to strive in the labour market to bring their skills, including as researchers, in other worlds than that which they have been trained. However, there is the risk that their skills are deteriorating, that they become mediocre consultants, that they follow directions of institutions or companies in political manipulation or suppression.

LIMITS AND TABOOS

As in all fields, research in higher education needs freedom. Researchers must be able to choose the issues they intend to tackle, make their hypotheses, determine their chosen method, etc. But this principle is facing two types of limits, which come from what might be called social demand, possibly even driven by public or private instances. To access the necessary resources, the researcher must pass through the turbulent quests for funding, scholarships, programs, etc. Research institutions have also increasingly tend to establish codes or charters that can go very far in defining what is acceptable and what is not for the practice of research.

If such rules had been used in the past, we would be certainly deprived the bulk of anthropological or sociological production related to studies and field surveys. But it is also true that this production of knowledge was claimed to be universal and blind to the relations of domination, which conditioned such production of knowledge. The problem is therefore not to seek for the absence of rules, but rather to verify that the establishment of codes, charters, standards is done with active participation of those who are the first affected, researchers, and not managers and administrative staff of the universities.

Higher education, as other fields of social sciences, reproduces in its own way (which varies from one country to another) a professional pattern that focuses on the teaching and research methodological canons or theoretical boundaries within which knowledge can be produced. Suddenly, certain steps, certain questions are becoming difficult to consider, except to adopt a non-conformist attitude that may prove to be costly in professional and career terms. Researchers, on the other hand, internalize more diffuse moral and political standards, which proscribe certain questions, or make it impossible to use certain categories, as if they did not have their place in society considered.

May the quest continue.

Filipa M. Ribeiro
University of Porto, Portugal

Yurgos Politis
University College Dublin (UCD), Ireland

Bojana Culum
University of Rijeka, Croatia

316

Compilation of References

Aghion, P., Dewatripont, M., Hoxby, C., Mas-Colelle, M., & Sapir, A. (2008). *Higher aspirations: An agenda for reforming European universities.* Brussels: Bruegel.

Aksnes, D., Benner, M., Brorstad Borlaug, S., Hansen, H., Kallerud, E., Kristiansen, E., et al. (2012). Centres of excellence in the Nordic countries: A comparative study of research excellence policy and excellence centre schemes in Denmark, Finland, Norway and Sweden. *Working Paper 4/2012.*

Alarcão, I. (2001). Novas tendências nos paradigmas de investigação em educação. In I. Alarcão (Ed.), Escola reflexiva e nova racionalidade (pp. 135-144). São Paulo: Artmed editora.

Alarcão, I. (Ed.). (1996). Formação reflexiva de professores: Estratégias de supervisão. Porto: Porto Editora, Colecção CIDInE.

Alarcão, I., & Roldão, M.C. (2008). *Supervisão: Um contexto de desenvolvimento profissional dos professores.* Mangualde: Edições Pedago.

Alarcão, I., & Tavares, J. (2003). *Supervisão da prática pedagógica: Uma perspectiva de desenvolvimento e aprendizagem.* Coimbra: Edições Almedina.

Aldrich, H., & Ruef, M. (2006). *Organizations evolving.* London: Sage.

Altbach, P. G., & Salmi, J. (2011). *The road to academic excellence: The making of world-class research universities.* Washington, DC: World Bank Publications. doi:10.1596/978-0-8213-8805-1

Altrichter, H., Posch, P., & Somekh, B. (2000). *Teachers investigate their work: An introduction to action research across the professions.* New York: Routledge.

Amaral, A., Neave, G., Musselin, C., & Maassen, P. (2010). *European integration and the governance of higher education and research.* Dordrecht, The Netherlands: Springer.

Anderson, T. (2013). *Promise and/or peril: MOOCs and open and distance learning.* Retrieved from http://www.col.org/SiteCollectionDocuments/MOOCsPromise-Peril_Anderson.pdf

Angelova, M., & Riazantseva, A. (1999). If you don't tell me, how can I know: A case study of four international students learning to write the US way. *Written Communication, 16*(4), 491–525. doi:10.1177/0741088399016004004

APEC. (2004). *Indicators of knowledge based economy.* APEC Economic Committee.

Apple, M. (2000). *Official knowledge - Democratic education in a conservative age.* London: Routledge.

Apple, M. W., & Jungck, S. (1990). You don't have to be a teacher to teach this unit: Teaching, technology, and gender in the classroom. *American Educational Research Journal, 27*(2), 227–251. doi:10.3102/00028312027002227

Apple, M., & Beane, J. A. (Eds.). (1995). *Democratic schools.* Alexandria, VA: Association for Supervision & Curriculum.

Arendt, H. (1968). *Between past and future.* New York: Penguin.

Aresta, M. (2009). *As ferramentas web 2.0 e as comunidades de aprendizagem: Estudo de casos sobre as comunidades de aprendizagem no mestrado em multimédia em educação.* (Master thesis). Universidade de Aveiro, Aveiro, Portugal.

Argyris, C. (1999). *On organizational learning.* Blackwell Publishing.

Argyris, C., & Schon, D. A. (1996). *Organizational LEARNING II: Theory, method, and practice.* New York: Addison-Wesley.

Arnett, J. (1989). Caregivers in day-care centers: Does training matter? *Journal of Applied Developmental Psychology, 10*(4), 541–552. doi:10.1016/0193-3973(89)90026-9

Arora, A., & Gambardella, A. (1997). Public policy towards science: Picking stars or spreading the wealth? *Revue d'Economie Industrielle, 79*(79), 63–75. doi:10.3406/rei.1997.1653

Asheim, B., Coenen, L., Moodysson, J., & Vang, J. (2007). Constructing knowledge-based regional advantage: Implications for regional innovation policy. *International Journal of Entrepreneurship and Innovation Management, 7*(2), 140–155. doi:10.1504/IJEIM.2007.012879

Aspin, D. N., Chapman, J., Evans, K., & Bagnall, R. (Eds.). (2012). *Second international handbook of lifelong learning.* Dortrecht, The Netherlands: Springer; doi:10.1007/978-94-007-2360-3

Australia Bureau of Statistics (ABS). (2002). *Measuring a knowledge-based economy and society – An Australian framework* (Discussion Paper cat. No. 1375.0). Author.

Australian Qualifications Framework Advisory Board. (2007). Australia qualifications framework: Implementation handbook (4th ed.). Carlton South, Australia: Australian Qualifications Framework (AQF) Advisory Board.

Avison, D. E., Lau, F., Myers, M. D., & Nielson, P. A. (1999). Action research. *Communications of the ACM, 42*(1), 94–97. doi:10.1145/291469.291479

Ball, S. J., Reay, D., & David, M. (2002). Ethnic choosing: Minority ethnic students, social class and higher education choice. *Race, Ethnicity and Education, 5*(4), 333–357.

Bamber, V. (2013). Evidence, chimera and belief. *SEDA Special, 34.*

Bamber, V. (2013). A desideratum of evidencing value. *SEDA Special, 34.*

Bamber, V. (2008). Evaluating lecturer development programmes: Received wisdom or self-knowledge? *The International Journal for Academic Development, 13*(2), 107–116. doi:10.1080/13601440802076541

Bamber, V., & Anderson, S. (2012). Evaluating learning and teaching: Institutional needs and individual practices. *The International Journal for Academic Development, 17*(1), 5–18. doi:10.1080/1360144X.2011.586459

Bamber, V., & Trowler, P. (2005). Compulsory higher education teacher training: Joined-up policies, institutional architectures and enhancement cultures. *The International Journal for Academic Development, 10*(2), 79–93. doi:10.1080/13601440500281708

Bandura, A. (1994). Self-efficacy. In V. S. Ramachaudran (Ed.), *Encyclopedia of human behaviour* (pp. 71–81). New York: Academic Press.

Baptista, A. V., & Huet, I. (2012). Postgraduate research supervision quality: Rethinking the value of doctoral supervision to design an integrative framework. *International Journal of Learning, 18*(5), 175–194.

Baptista, A. V., Huet, I., & Jenkins, A. (2011). Quality of doctoral supervision: Supervisors' conceptions of learning, supervision and students' profiles. In N. Jackson, L. Frick, C. Nygaard, & N. Courtney (Eds.), *Postgraduate education: Form and function* (pp. 43–58). Faringdon, UK: Libri Publishing.

Barnett, S. W. (2003). *Better teachers, better preschools: Student achievement linked to teacher qualifications.* New Brunswick, NJ: National Institute for Early Education Research.

Barroso, J. M. (2006). *More Europe where it matters: Speech delivered to the European Parliament, Strasbourg, March 15.* Brussels: European Commission.

Bartelese, J., & Huisman, J. (2008). The Bologna process. In M. Nerad & M. Heggelund (Eds.), Toward a global PhD? Forces and forms in doctoral education worldwide (pp. 101-113). University of Washington Press.

Barton, D., & Lee, C. (2013). *Language online: Investigating digital texts and practices.* London: Routledge.

Basov, N., & Oleksandra, N. (2011). *Understanding knowledge creation - Intellectuals in academia, the public sphere and the arts.* Amsterdam: Editions Rodopi.

Batista, J. (2011). *O Uso das tecnologias da comunicação no ensino superior.* (PhD thesis). Universidade de Aveiro, Aveiro, Portugal.

Batista, J., Morais, N. S., & Ramos, F. (2011). Frequency and user satisfaction on using communication technologies to support learning: the case of Portuguese higher education. In A. Moreira, M.J. Loureiro, A. Balula, F. Nogueira, L. Pombo, L. Pedro, & P. Almeida (Eds.), *International council for educational media (ICEM) and the international symposium on computers in education (SIIE) joint conference (ICEM&SIIE'2011)* (pp. 372-380). Aveiro, Portugal: Universidade de Aveiro.

Batista, J., & Ramos, F. (2011). The institutional perspective on the use of communication technologies in Portuguese public higher education: A research proposal. In *Proceedings of 5th International Technology, Education and Development Conference*. Valencia, Spain: Academic Press.

Baume, D. (2008). A toolkit for evaluating educational development ventures. *SEDA, 9*(4).

Becher, T., & Trowler, P. (2001). *Academic tribes and territories: Intellectual enquiry and the cultures of discipline* (2nd ed.). London: Open University Press.

Beck, U., Giddens, A., & Lash, S. (1994). *Reflexive modernization: Politics, tradition and aesthetics in the modern social order*. Stanford, CA: Stanford University Press.

Beerkens, E. (2009). Centres of excellence and relevance: The contextualisation of global models. *Science, Technology & Society, 14*(1), 153–175. doi:10.1177/097172180801400106

Beerkens, E. (2010). Global models for the national research university: Adoption and adaptation in Indonesia and Malaysia. *Globalisation, Societies and Education, 8*(3), 369–381. doi:10.1080/14767724.2010.505099

Bennett, P., & Turner, G. (2012). *Postgraduate taught experience survey 2012 results: Report*. York, UK: Higher Education Academy.

Bennett, S., Bishop, A., Dalgarno, B., Waycott, J., & Kennedy, G. (2012). Implementing web 2.0 technologies in higher education: A collective case study. *Computers & Education, 59*(2), 524–534. doi:10.1016/j.compedu.2011.12.022

Benneworth, P., Coenen, L., Moodysson, J., & Asheim, B. (2009). Exploring the multiple roles of Lund University in strengthening Scania's regional innovation system: Towards institutional learning? *European Planning Studies, 17*(11), 1645–1664. doi:10.1080/09654310903230582

Bensimon, E. (2007). The underestimated significance of practitioner knowledge in the scholarship on student success. *The Review of Higher Education, 30*(4), 441–469. doi:10.1353/rhe.2007.0032

Bensimon, E., & Neumann, A. (1993). *Redesigning collegiate leadership*. Baltimore, MD: Johns Hopkins Press.

Bereiter, C. (2002). *Education and mind in the knowledge age*. Mahwah, NJ: Lawrence Erlbaum Associates.

Bergen. (2005). *The European higher education area: Achieving the goals*. Paper presented at the Conference of European Ministers Responsible for Higher Education. Bergen, Norway.

Berhmann, J., & Sams, A. (2012). *Flip your classroom: Reach every student in every class every day*. Alexandria, VA: Association for Supervision and Curriculum Development and International society for Technology in Education.

Bernstein, B. (2000). *Pedagogy, symbolic control and identity: Theory, research, critique* (rev. ed.). Lanham, MD: Rowman & Littlefield publishers.

Bielaczyc, K., & Blake, P. (2006). Shifting epistemologies: Examining student understanding of new models of knowledge and learning. In *Proceedings of the 7th International Conference on Learning Sciences (ICLS '06)* (pp. 50-56). International Society of the Learning Sciences.

Bielschowsky, C., Laaser, W., Mason, R., Sangra, A., & Hasan, A. (2009). *Reforming distance learning higher education in Portugal*. Lisbon: Ministry of Science, Technology and Higher Education.

Biggs, J. (2003). Aligning teaching and assessing to course objectives. *Teaching and Learning in Higher Education: New Trends and Innovations, 2*, 13–17.

Biglan, A. (1973). The characteristics of subject matter in different academic areas. *The Journal of Applied Psychology*, *57*(3), 195–203. doi:10.1037/h0034701

Bills, D. (2004). Supervisors' conceptions of research and the implications for supervisor development. *The International Journal for Academic Development*, *9*(1), 85–97. doi:10.1080/1360144042000296099

Bissett, A. (2009). Academics as entrepreneurs: The changing nature of academic professionalism. In iPED Research Network (Eds.), Academic futures: Inquiries into higher education and pedagogy (pp. 111-123). Newcastle upon Tyne, UK: iPED Research Network.

Blackwell, J., & Gamble, P. (2001). *Knowledge management – A state of the art guide*. London: Kogan Page Publishers.

Blair, E., Cline, T., & Wassis, J. (2010). When do adults entering higher education begin to identify themselves as students? The threshold-of-induction model. *Studies in Continuing Education*, *32*(2), 133–146. doi:10.1080/0158037X.2010.488355

Blau, P. M. (1964). *Exchange and power in social life*. New York: Wiley.

Bleiklie, I., & Mathisen, G. (2011). Organizing knowledge institutions – Standardizing diversity. Paper presented at the 24th Annual Conference of the Consortium of Higher Education Researchers. Reykjavic, Iceland.

Bleiklie, I. (2013). Comparing university organizations across boundaries. *Higher Education*, *67*(4), 381–391. doi:10.1007/s10734-013-9683-z

Bleiklie, I., & Byrkjeflot, H. (2002). Changing knowledge regimes: Universities in a new research environment. *Higher Education*, *44*(3/4), 519–532. doi:10.1023/A:1019898407492

Bleiklie, I., & Kogan, M. (2006). Comparison and theories. In M. Kogan & M. Bauer (Eds.), *Transforming higher education: A comparative study* (2nd ed., pp. 3–22). Dordrecht, The Netherlands: Springer.

Blin, F., & Munro, M. (2008). Why hasn't technology disrupted academics' teaching practices? Understanding resistance to change through the lens of activity theory. *Computers & Education*, *50*(2), 475–490. doi:10.1016/j.compedu.2007.09.017

Blumberga, S. (2012). Dimensions of epistemic authority of university professors. *Social and Natural Sciences Journal*, *5*(0), 1–5. doi:10.12955/snsj.v5i0.299

Bodycott, P., & Walker, A. (2000). Teaching abroad: Lessons learned about inter-cultural understanding for teachers in higher education. *Teaching in Higher Education*, *5*(1), 79–94. doi:10.1080/135625100114975

Bogdan, R. C., & Biklen, S. K. (2003). *Qualitative research for education: An introduction to theories and methods* (4th ed.). New York: Pearson.

Bonaccorsi, A., & Daraio, C. (Eds.). (2007). *Universities and strategic knowledge creation: Specialization and performance in Europe*. Cheltenham, UK: Edwar Elgar. doi:10.4337/9781847206848

Bond, G. C. (1981). Social economic status and educational achievement: A review article. *Anthropology & Education Quarterly*, *12*(4), 227–257. doi:10.1525/aeq.1981.12.4.05x1811q

Bostock, S. J. (1998). Constructivism in mass higher education: A case study. *British Journal of Educational Technology*, *29*(3), 225–240. doi:10.1111/1467-8535.00066

Boud, D., & Felleti, G. (Eds.). (1999). *The challenge of problem-based learning* (2nd ed.). London: Kogan Page. First published 1991, reprinted 1999. Retrieved February 15, 2014, from http://books.google.es/books?id=zvyBq6k6tWUC&pg=PA137&redir_esc=y#v=onepage&q&f=false

Bourdieu, P. (2004). *Science of science and reflexivity*. Chicago: University of Chicago Press.

Bowles, S., & Gintis, H. (2000). Schooling in capitalist America revisited. *Sociology of Education*, *75*(1), 1–18. doi:10.2307/3090251

Bowl, M. (2001). Experiencing the barriers: Non-traditional students entering higher education. *Research Papers in Education, 16*(2), 41–160. doi:10.1080/02671520110037410

Bowl, M. (2003). *Non-traditional entrants to higher education: They talk about people like me.* Stoke on Trent, UK: Trentham Books.

Braun, K., Moore, A., Herrmann, S. L., & Könninger, S. (2010). Science governance and the politics of proper talk: Governmental bioethics as a new technology of reflexive government. *Economy and Society, 39*(4), 510–533. doi:10.1080/03085147.2010.510682

Brebenel, A. (2013, April 22). Mariana campeanu: "Education is the only solution for integrating Roma people". *Adevarul.* Retrieved from http://adevarul.ro/news/societate/marianacampeanu-singura-solutie-integrarea-romilor-esteeducatia-1_517509d0053c7dd83f3464c4/index.pdf

Brew, A. (2001). Conceptions of research: A phenomenographic study. *Studies in Higher Education, 26*(3), 271–285. doi:10.1080/03075070120076255

Brew, A. (2007). Evaluating academic development in a time of perplexity. *The International Journal for Academic Development, 12*(2), 69–72. doi:10.1080/13601440701604823

Brew, A., & Peseta, T. (2004). Changing postgraduate supervision practice: A programme to encourage learning through reflection and feedback. *Innovations in Education and Teaching International, 41*(1), 5–22. doi:10.1080/1470329032000172685

Britton, C., & Baxter, A. (1999). Becoming a mature student: Gendered narratives of the self. *Gender and Education, 11*(2), 179–193. doi:10.1080/09540259920681

Brix, J., & Lauridsen, K. M. (2012). Learning styles and organisational development in practice: An exploratory study of how learning styles and individual learning strategies can facilitate organisational development. *International Journal of Innovation and Learning, 12*(2), 181–196. doi:10.1504/IJIL.2012.048353

Brix, J., & Lauridsen, O. (forthcoming). Improving learning competencies in the context of radical innovation: A team perspective. *International Journal of Innovation and Learning.*

Bron, A., & Thunborg, C. (2012). Higher education and lifelong learning in Sweden. In M. Slowey & H. G. Schuetze (Eds.), *Global perspectives on higher education and lifelong learners* (pp. 97–111). London: Routledge.

Brooks, J. G., & Brooks, M. G. (1999). *In search of understanding: The case for constructivist classrooms.* Alexandria, VA: Association for Supervision and Curriculum Development.

Brown, G., & Atkins, M. (1986). Academic staff training in British universities: Results of a national survey. *Studies in Higher Education, 11*(1), 29–42. doi:10.1080/03075078612331378441

Brown, T. (2008). Design thinking: Thinking like a designer can transform the way you develop products, services, processes—and even strategy. *Harvard Business Review, 2008*(June). Retrieved from http://www.lacountyarts.org/UserFiles/File/CivicArt/Harvard%20Business%20Review-on-Design-Thinking.pdf

Bruner, J. S. (2000). *Kultura obrazovanja [The culture of education].* Zagreb: Educa.

Brunsson, N., & Sahlin-Andersson, K. (2000). Constructing organizations: The example of public sector reform. *Organization Studies, 21*(4), 721–746. doi:10.1177/0170840600214003

Bryman, A., & Burgess, R. G. (Eds.). (1994). *Analyzing qualitative data.* London: Routledge. doi:10.4324/9780203413081

Burchinal, M., Hyson, M., & Zaslow, M. (2008). Competencies and credentials for early childhood educators: What do we know and what do we need to know? *NHSA Dialog Brief, 11*(1).

Burke-Johnson, R., & Onwuegbuzie, A. J. (2004). Mixed methods research: A research paradigm whose time has come. *Educational Researcher, 33*(14), 14–26. doi:10.3102/0013189X033007014

Burt, R. L. (2004). Structural holes and good ideas. *American Journal of Sociology, 110*(2), 349–399. doi:10.1086/421787

Bush, V. (1945). *Science: The Endless Frontier.* Washington, DC: US Government Printing Office.

Butler, M., & Gheorghiu, L. (2010). Exploring the failure to protect the rights of the Roma child in Romania. *Public Administration and Development, 30*(4), 235–246. doi:10.1002/pad.562

Caine, R. N., Caine, G., McClintic, C., & Klimek, K. (2009). *12 brain/mind learning principles in action.* Thousand Oaks, CA: Corwin Press.

Campbell, J., & Li, M. (2008). Asian students' voices: An empirical study of Asian students' learning experiences at a New Zealand university. *Journal of Studies in International Education, 12*(4), 375–396. doi:10.1177/1028315307299422

Capano, G., & Piattoni, S. (2011). From Bologna to Lisbon: The political uses of the Lisbon 'script' in European higher education policy. *Journal of European Public Policy, 18*(4), 584–606. doi:10.1080/13501763.2011.560490

Carroll, J. B. (1965). The contributions of psychological theory and educational research to the teaching of foreign languages. *The Modern Language Journal, 49*(5), 273–281. Retrieved February 15, 2014, from http://www.jstor.org/stable/322133

Carroll, D., & Patterson, V. (2011). *A profile of undergraduate mature new entrants.* Dublin: HEA.

Carr, W., & Kemmis, S. (1986). *Becoming critical: Education, knowledge and action research.* London: Falmer Press.

Carvalho, A. A. (2008). Os podcasts no ensino universitário: Implicações dos tipos e da duração na aceitação dos alunos. In A. A. Carvalho (Ed.), Actas do encontro sobre web 2.0 (pp. 179–190). Braga: Universidade do Minho. Retrieved from https://repositorium.sdum.uminho.pt/bitstream/1822/8566/1/Marques%26CarvalhoSIIE_08.pdf

Cassier, M. (1997). Compromis institutionnels et hybridations entre recherche publique et recherché privée. *Revue d'Economie Industrielle, 79*(1), 191–212. doi:10.3406/rei.1997.1661

Castaneda, L., & Camacho, M. (2012). Desvelando nuestra identidad digital. *El Profesional de la Información, 21*(4), 354–360. Retrieved February 15, 2014, from http://eprints.rclis.org/17350/1/2012EPI.pdf

Cavaliere, P. (2011). Catch me if you can: The OSCE report and the hunt for the elusive "human right to the internet". *Media Laws.* Retrieved February 15, 2014, from http://www.medialaws.eu/catch-me-if-you-can-the-osce-report-and-the-hunt-for-the-elusive-%E2%80%9Chuman-right-to-the-internet%E2%80%9D/

Čepić, R., & Krstović, J. (2008). Cjeloživotno učenje i organizacije koje uče za održivu budućnost: Izazovi i pitanja [Lifelong learning and learning organizations for a sustainable future: Challenges and Issues]. In L. Vujičić & V. Uzelac (Eds.), *Cjeloživotno učenje za održivi razvoj part I [Lifelong learning for sustainable development]* (pp. 139–144). Rijeka: Faculty of Teacher Education, University of Rijeka.

Chalmers, D., & Thompson, K. (2008). *Snapshot of teaching and learning practice in Australian universities.* Carrick Institute Report on Behalf of Australian Learning and Teaching Council.

Chalmers, D., & Volet, S. (1997). Common misconceptions about students from South-East Asia studying in Australia. *Higher Education Research & Development, 16*(1), 87–99. doi:10.1080/0729436970160107

Chipea, F., & Bottyan, Z. (2012). Issues regarding the integration of young Roma in higher education: Qualitative analysis at University of Oradea. In T. Kozma & K. Bernath (Eds.), *Higher education in the Romania-Hungary cross-border cooperation area* (pp. 73–85). Oradea, Romania: Partium Press.

Christensen, C. M. (2003). *The innovator's solution: Creating and sustaining successful growth.* Boston: Harvard Business Press.

Christensen, T. (2011). University governance reforms: Potential problems of more autonomy? *Higher Education, 62*(4), 503–517. doi:10.1007/s10734-010-9401-z

Clark, B. (2011). *Moving the technology into the classroom project blended delivery: A literature review.* College Sector Committee for Adult Upgrading. Retrieved from ProQuest

Clark, B. R. (1998). *Creating entrepreneurial universities: Organizational pathways of transformation.* New York: Pergamon.

Coaldrake, P., & Stedman, L. (1999). *Academic work in the twenty-first century: Changing roles and policies*. Australian Government, Department of Education Training and Youth Affaires: Higher Education Division.

Cohen, L., Manion, L., & Morrison, K. (2011). *Research methods in education* (7th ed.). London: Routledge Department for Education and Skills.

Cohen, M. D., & March, J. G. (1974). *Leadership and ambiguity: The American college president*. Hightstown, NJ: McGraw-Hill Book Company.

Cohen, S. (2004). *The nature of moral reasoning: The framework and activities of ethical deliberation, argument and decision-making*. Melbourne: Oxford University Press.

Colander, D., & Kupers, R. (2014). *Complexity and the art of public policy: Solving society's problems from the bottom up*. Princeton, NJ: Princeton University Press.

Collins, H. (1985). *Changing order: Replication and induction in scientific practice*. Chicago: Chicago University Press.

Conecta13. (2013). '#eduPLEmooc, un MOOC para el desarrollo profesional docente'. *EducaLab, spin-off de a Universidad de Granada*. Retrieved February 15, 2014, from http://conecta13.com/2013/12/eduplemooc-conecta13/

Connell, R. W. (1985). How to supervise a PhD. *Vestes*, 2, 38–41.

Connor, H., Dewson, S., Tyers, C., Eccles, J., Regan, J. & Aston, J. (2001). *Social class and higher education: Issues affecting decisions on participation by lower social class groups*. Sheffield, UK: DfES

Conole, G., & Alevizou, P. (2010). A literature review of the use of web 2.0 tools in higher education. Milton Keynes, UK: The Open University. Retrieved from http://www.heacademy.ac.uk/assets/EvidenceNet/Conole_Alevizou_2010.pdf

Conrad, L. (1999). Contextualising postgraduate supervision to promote quality. In G. Wisker & N. Sutcliffe (Eds.), *Good practice in postgraduate supervision* (pp. 13–24). Staff and Educational Development Association.

Cooke, P., Braczyk, H.-J., & Heidenreich, M. (2004). *Regional innovation systems: The role of governance in a globalized world*. London: Routledge.

Corbett, A. (2014). The globalisation challenge for European higher education: Convergence and diversity, centres and peripheries. *European Journal of Higher Education*. doi:10.1080/21568235.2014.903575

Corbett, A. (2005). *Universities and the Europe of knowledge: Ideas, institutions and policy entrepreneurship in European Union higher education policy, 1955-2005*. Basingstoke, UK: Palgrave Macmillan. doi:10.1057/9780230286467

Coromina, L., Capó, A., Coenders, G., & Guia, J. (2011). PhD students' research group networks: A qualitative approach. *Advances in Methodology & Statistics, 8*(2), 137-155.

Correia, J. A. (2010). Paradigmas e cognições no campo da administração educacional: Das políticas de avaliação à avaliação como política. *Revista Brasileira de Educação, 15*(45), 456–467. doi:10.1590/S1413-24782010000300005

Corson, D. (1997). The learning and use of academic English words. *Language Learning, 47*(4), 671–718. doi:10.1111/0023-8333.00025

Costes, N., Hopbach, A., Kekäläinen, H., van IJperen, R., & Walsh, P. (2010). *Quality assurance and transparency tools - Workshop report*. Helsinki: European Association for Quality Assurance in Higher Education.

Council of Europe. (1992). *The European charter for regional or minority languages (ECRML)*. Retrieved February 15, 2014, from http://conventions.coe.int/Treaty/en/Treaties/Html/148.htm

Council of Europe. (2001). *Common European framework of reference for languages: Learning, teaching, assessment (CEFR)*. Strasbourg, France: Language Policy Unit. Retrieved February 15, 2014, from http://www.coe.int/t/dg4/linguistic/Source/Framework_en.pdfOfficial

Council of Europe. (2003). *Guide for the development of language education policies in Europe: From linguistic diversity to plurilingual education*. Strasbourg, France: Language Policy Unit. Retrieved July 26, 2014, from http://www.coe.int/t/dg4/Linguistic/Source/FullGuide_En.pdf

Council of Europe. (2008). *White paper on cultural dialogue: Living together as equals in dignity.* Retrieved July 26, 2014, from http://www.coe.int/t/dg4/intercultural/source/white%20paper_final_revised_en.pdf

Council of Graduate Schools of the U.S. (1991). *The role and nature of the doctoral dissertation.* Washington, DC: Report from the Council of Graduate Schools of the U.S.

Coutinho, C., & Júnior, J. (2008). Web 2.0 in Portuguese academic community: An exploratory survey. In Proceedings of the 19th International Conference of the Society for Information Technology & Teacher Education (SITE 2008). Las Vegas, NV: SITE.

Coutinho, C., & Junior, J. (2007). Blog e wiki: Os futuros professores e as ferramentas da web 2.0. In M. Marcelino & M. Silva (Eds.), *Actas do SIIE'2007 – Simpósio internacional de informática educativa* (pp. 199–204). Porto: Escola Superior de Educação do Instituto Politécnico do Porto.

Coutinho, C., & Junior, J. (2008). Using social bookmarking to enhance cooperation/collaboration in a teacher education program. In *Proceedings of World Conference on Educational Multimedia, Hypermedia and Telecommunications.* Chesapeake, VA: AACE.

Cozma, T., Cucos, C., & Momanu, M. (2010). The education of Roma children in Romania: Description, difficulties, solutions. *Intercultural Education, 11*(3), 281–288. doi:10.1080/14675980020002439

Crane, D. (1972). *Invisible colleges: Diffusion of knowledge in scientific communities.* Chicago: Chicago University Press.

Creswell, J. W. (2013). *Research design: Qualitative, quantitative, and mixed methods approaches* (2nd ed.). Thousand Oaks, CA: Sage Publications.

Creswell, J. W., & Plano-Clark, V. L. (2011). *Designing and conducting mixed methods research.* Los Angeles, CA: Sage Publications.

Crossan, M. M., & Apaydin, M. (2010). A multidimensional framework of organizational innovation: A systematic review of the literature. *Journal of Management Studies, 47*(6), 1154–1191. doi:10.1111/j.1467-6486.2009.00880.x

Cross, R., Borgatti, S. P., & Parker, A. (2001). Beyond answers: Dimensions of the advice network. *Social Networks, 23*(3), 215–235. doi:10.1016/S0378-8733(01)00041-7

Cruz-Castro, L., & Sanz-Menéndez, L. (2005). Bringing science and technology human resources back in: The Spanish Ramón y Cajal programme. *Science & Public Policy, 32*(1), 39–53. doi:10.3152/147154305781779687

Cruz-Castro, L., & Sanz-Menéndez, L. (2005). The employment of PhDs in firms: Trajectories, mobility and innovation. *Research Evaluation, 14*(1), 57–69. doi:10.3152/147154405781776292

Cruz-Castro, L., Sanz-Menéndez, L., & Martínez, C. (2012). Research centres in transition: Patterns of convergence and diversity. *The Journal of Technology Transfer, 37*(1), 18–42. doi:10.1007/s10961-010-9168-5

Culkin, J. M. (1967). A Shoolman's Guide to Marshall McLuhan. *Saturday Review.* Retrieved February 15, 2014, from http://www.unz.org/Pub/SaturdayRev-1967mar18-00051

Cullen, D., Pearson, M., Saha, L., & Spear, R. (1994). *Establishing effective PhD supervision.* Australian Government Publishing Service, Department of Employment, Education and Training.

Cumming, J. (2010). Doctoral enterprise: A holistic conception of evolving practices and arrangements. *Studies in Higher Education, 35*(1), 25–39. doi:10.1080/03075070902825899

Daft, R. L. (2010). *Organization theory and design.* Mason, OH: South-Western Cengage Learning.

Dahlstrom, E., Boor, T., Grunwald, P., & Vockley, M. (2011). The ECAR national study of undergraduate students and information technology, 2011 (research report). Boulder, CO: EDUCAUSE Centre for Applied Research. Retrieved from http://www.educause.edu/ecar

Dasgupta, P., & David, P. A. (1994). Toward a new economics of science. *Research Policy, 23*(5), 487–521. doi:10.1016/0048-7333(94)01002-1

Datnow, A., Hubbard, L., & Mehan, H. (2002). *Extending educational reform: From one school to many.* London: RoutledgeFalmer.

Davies, P. (2001). *Widening participation in higher education in England: Report to Scottish executive.* Stirling, UK: Centre for Research in Lifelong Learning/Scottish Executive.

Dawson, J., & Bekkers, C. G. (2002). *Supporting international students' transition to university.* Paper presented at the 11th Annual Teaching and Learning Forum: Focusing on the Student, Perth, Australia.

de Freitas, S. (2013). *MOOCs: The final frontier for higher education?* Coventry, UK: Coventry University. Retrieved February 15, 2014, from http://benhur.teluq. uquebec.ca/ted/Ressources/mooc.pdf

De Grande, P. (2013). Aportes de Norbert Elias, Erving Goffman y Pierre Bourdieu al estudio de las redes personales. *Andamios, 10*(22), 237–258.

Deem, R., Mok, K., & Lucas, L. (2008). Transforming higher education in whose image? Exploring the concept of the 'world-class' university in Europe and Asia. *Higher Education Policy, 21*(1), 83–97. doi:10.1057/palgrave. hep.8300179

Demo, P. (2003). *Educação e Qualidade.* Campinas: Papirus Editora.

Department for Business Innovation and Skills. (2013). *The maturing of the MOOC: Literature review of massive open online courses and other forms of online distance learning.* London, UK: Department for Business, Innovation and Skills. Retrieved May 1, 2014, from https://www. gov.uk/government/uploads/system/uploads/attachment_ data/file/240193/13-1173-maturing-of-the-mooc.pdf

Dietrich, A. (2000). The cognitive neuroscience of creativity. *Psychonomic Bulletin & Review, 11*(6), 1011-1026. Retrieved February 15, 2014 from http://download.springer.com/static/pdf/163/ art%253A10.3758%252FBF03196731.pdf?auth66=1 392965651_1c41ea592320ab0865bef5c8dc28bef1&e xt=.pdf

Dietz, J. S., & Bozeman, B. (2005). Academic careers, patents, and productivity: Industry experience as scientific and technical human capital. *Research Policy, 34*(3), 349–367. doi:10.1016/j.respol.2005.01.008

DiMaggio, P., & Powell, W. (1983). The iron cage revisited: Institutional isomorphism and collective rationality in organizational fields. *American Sociological Review, 48*(2), 147–160. doi:10.2307/2095101

Dobrica, P., & Jderu, G. (2005). *The academic education of Roma children: Socio-cultural determinants.* UNICEF. Retrieved from http://www.unicef.org/romania/ro/ Educatie_romi.pdf

Douglass, J. A., Edelstein, R., & Hoareau, C. (2011). A global talent magnet: How a San Francisco/Bay Area higher education hub could advance California's comparative advantage. In *Attracting international talent and further build US economic competitiveness.* Berkeley, CA: CSHE Publications.

Downes, S. (2005). E-learning 2.0. *eLearn Magazine, 2005*(10). Retrieved from http://elearnmag.acm.org/ featured.cfm?aid=1104968

Downes, S. (2011). *The MOOC guide.* Retrieved July 26, 2014, from https://sites.google.com/site/themoocguide/3- cck08---the-distributed-course

Duarte, J., & Gomes, M. J. (2011). Práticas com a Moodle em Portugal. In P. Dias & A. J. Osório (Eds.), *Atas da VII conferência internacional de TIC na educação, challenges 2011* (pp. 871–882). Braga: Centro de Competência da Universidade do Minho.

Dunn, L. (1993). Proximal and distal features of day care quality and children's development. *Early Childhood Research Quarterly, 8*(2), 167–192. doi:10.1016/ S0885-2006(05)80089-4

Dybicz, P. (2011). Anything goes? Science and social constructions in competing discourses. *Journal of Sociology and Social Welfare, 38*(3), 101–122.

Edirisingha, P., Salmon, G., & Fothergill, J. (2007). *Profcasting – A pilot study and guidelines for integrating podcasts in a blended learning environment.* Retrieved from http://hdl.handle.net/2381/404

Education Statistics at Regional Level. (n.d.). Retrieved on July 15th 2012 from http://epp.eurostat.ec.europa. eu/statistics_explained/index.php/Education_statistics_at_regional_level

Edwards, R. (1993). *Mature women students: Separating or connecting family and education.* London: Taylor and Francis.

EHEA. (2012). *Transparency tools.* Flanders: Flemish Ministry for Education and Training. Retrieved from http://www.ehea.info/article-details.aspx?ArticleId=145

El Ansari, W. (2003). Satisfaction trends in undergraduate physiotherapy education. *Physiotherapy, 89*(3), 171–185. doi:10.1016/S0031-9406(05)61033-4

Elliot, J. (1991). *Action research for educational change.* Buckingham, UK: Open University Press.

Elliott, J. (1998). *The curriculum experiment, meeting the challenge of social change.* Buckingham, UK: Open University Press.

Enders, J. (2002). Serving many masters: The PhD on the labour market, the everlasting need of inequality, and the premature death of Humboldt. *Higher Education, 44*(3/4), 493–517. doi:10.1023/A:1019850524330

Enders, J. (2005). Border crossings: Research training, knowledge dissemination and the transformation of academic work. *Higher Education, 49*(1-2), 119–133. doi:10.1007/s10734-004-2917-3

Enders, J., De Boer, H., & Westerheijden, D. (Eds.). (2009). *Reform of higher education in europe.* Rotterdam, The Netherlands: Sense.

Enders, J., de Boer, H., & Weyer, E. (2013). Regulatory autonomy and performance: The reform of higher education re-visited. *Higher Education, 65*(1), 5–23. doi:10.1007/s10734-012-9578-4

Enders, J., & De Weert, E. (2004). Science, training and career: Changing modes of knowledge production and labour markets. *Higher Education Policy, 17*(2), 135–152. doi:10.1057/palgrave.hep.8300047

Engeström, Y., Reigjo, M., & Raija-Leena, P. (Eds.). (1999). *Perspectives on activity theory.* New York: Cambridge University Press. Retrieved July 26, 2014, from http://ebooks.cambridge.org/ebook.jsf?bid=CBO9780511812774

Engeström, Y. (1987). *Learning by expanding: An activity-theoretical approach to developmental research.* Helsinki: Orienta-Konsultit Oy.

ENQA. (2011). ENQA position paper on transparency tools. Helsinki: European Association for Quality Assurance in Higher Education (ENQA).

Entwistle, N. (2009). *Teaching for understanding at university.* London: Palgrave Macmillan.

Espinoza, Ó., & González, L. E. (2013). Accreditation in higher education in Chile: Results and consequences. *Quality Assurance in Education, 21*(1), 20–38. doi:10.1108/09684881311293043

Etzkowitz, H., & Leydesdorff, L. (2000). The dynamics of innovation: From national systems and "mode 2" to a triple helix of university-industry-government relations. *Research Policy, 29*(2), 109–123. doi:10.1016/S0048-7333(99)00055-4

Etzkowitz, H., Ranga, M., Benner, M., Guaranys, L., Maculan, A. M., & Kneller, R. (2008). Pathways to the entrepreneurial university: Towards a global convergence. *Science & Public Policy, 35*(9), 681–695. doi:10.3152/030234208X389701

EURASHE. (2012). EURASHE policy paper on quality assurance and transparency tools. Brussels: European Association of Institutions in Higher Education (EURASHE).

European Commision. (2006). *The new Lisbon strategy: An estimation of the economic impact of reaching five Lisbon targets.* Brussels: European Commission.

European Commission. (2003). *The role of the universities in the Europe of knowledge.* Brussels: European Commission.

European Commission. (2003). *Investing in research: An action plan for Europe.* Brussels: European Commission.

European Commission. (2005). *Common actions for growth and employment: The community Lisbon programme.* Brussels: European Commission.

European Commission. (2006). *Delivering on the modernisation agenda for universities: Education, research and innovation.* Brussels: European Commission.

European Commission. (2006). *Cluster "modernisation of higher education": Summary report of the peer learning activity on university-business partnerships (UBPs).* Brussels: Directorate-General for Education and Culture.

European Commission. (2008). *Guide to cost-benefit analysis of investment projects*. Brussels: Directorate General Regional Policy. Retrieved February 15, 2014 from http://ec.europa.eu/regional_policy/sources/docgener/guides/cost/guide2008_en.pdf

European Commission. (2012). *National Roma integration strategies: A first step in the implementation of the EU framework*. Belgium: European Commission. Retrieved from http://ec.europa.eu/justice/discrimination/files/roma_nat_integration_strat_en.pdf

European Commission. (2013). Startup Europe - Using MOOCs to foster web talent in Europe. *Open Education Europa: The Gateway to European Innovative Learning*. Retrieved February 15, 2014, from http://openeducationeuropa.eu/en/groups/startup-europe-using-MOOCs-foster-web-talent-europe

European Commission. (2013). Communication from the Commission to the European Parliament, the Council, the European Economic and social Committee and the Committee of the Regions. *Opening up Education: Innovative Teaching and Learning for all Through new Technologies and Open Educational Resources*. Retrieved February 15, 2014, from http://new.eur-lex.europa.eu/legal-content/EN/TXT/?qid=1389115469384&uri=CELEX:52013DC0654

European Commission. (2014). Annotated guidelines. *Erasmus Charter for Higher Education, 2014-2020*. Retrieved February 15, 2014, from http://eacea.ec.europa.eu/funding/2014/documents/annotated_guidelines_en.pdf

European Commission. (2014). EMOOCs 2014, the second MOOC European stakeholders summit, will be held on February 10-12, 2014 in Lausanne. *Open Education Europa: The Gateway to European Innovative Learning*. Retrieved February 15, 2014, from http://openeducationeuropa.eu/en/news/save-date-second-mooc-european-stakeholders-summit-be-held-february-2014

European Council. (2000). *Diverse systems shared goals: The contribution to the Lisbon strategy*. Brussels: Council of the European Union.

European Council. (2004). *The success of the Lisbon strategy hinges on urgent reforms*. Brussels: Council of the European Union.

European Higher Education Area. (2010). Welcome to the EHEA official website! *Bologna Process - European Higher Education Area*. Retrieved February 15, 2014, from http://www.ehea.info

European Institute for Comparative Cultural Research. (2008). *Sharing diversity: National approaches to intercultural dialogue in Europe*. Bonn, Germany: European Institute for Comparative Cultural Research. Retrieved July 26, 2014, from http://www.interculturaldialogue.eu/web/intercultural-dialogue.php

European Union. (1999). Joint declaration of the European Ministers of Education. *The Bologna Declaration of 19 June 1999*. Retrieved February 15, 2014, from http://www.ehea.info/Uploads/Declarations/BOLOGNA_DECLARATION1.pdf

European Union. (2013). Erasmus+ programme: Call for proposals 2013. *Official Journal of the European Union, C 362*, 62-65. Retrieved February 15, 2014, from http://new.eur-lex.europa.eu/legal-content/EN/TXT/PDF/?uri=OJ:JOC_2013_362_R_NS0004&from=EN

Facer, K., & Selwyn, N. (2013). Towards a sociology of education and technology. In R. Brooks, M. McCormack, & K. Bhopal (Eds.), *Contemporary debates in the sociology of education* (pp. 218–236). London: Palgrave Macmillan. doi:10.1057/9781137269881.0016

Faculty of Teacher Education, University of Rijeka. (2010). *Early childhood and preschool education – Course program*. Available from http://www.ufri.uniri.hr/data/RipO-eng.pdf

Feldman, M. S., & Pentland, B. T. (2003). Reconceptualizing organizational routines as a source of flexibility and change. *Administrative Science Quarterly, 48*(1), 94–118. doi:10.2307/3556620

Felton, S. (2008). *The student experience of supervision: Towards the student-supervisor agreement*. Retrieved January 2009, from http://www.lancs.ac.uk/celt/celtweb/files/SimonFelton.pdf

Felt, U., Igelsbo, J., Schikowitz, A., & Völker, T. (2013). Growing into what? The (un)disciplined socialisation of early stage researchers in transdisciplinary research. *Higher Education, 65*(4), 511–524. doi:10.1007/s10734-012-9560-1

Ferreira, M., & Vanhoudt, P. (2004). Catching the Celtic tiger by its tail. *European Journal of Education, 39*(2), 209–236. doi:10.1111/j.1465-3435.2004.00176.x

Figel, J. (2006). *International competitiveness in higher education: A European perspective.* Paper presented at the Association of Heads of University Administration Annual Conference. Oxford, UK.

Fink, L. D. (2013). The current status of faculty development internationally. *International Journal for the Scholarship of Teaching and Learning, 7*(2). Retrieved from http://w3.georgiasouthern.edu/ijsotl/v7n2.html

Fiocco, M. (2006). *An evaluation of a pathway program: The students' view.* Paper presented at the Australian International Education Conference, Perth, Australia. Retrieved from www.idp.com/aiec

Flecha, R., Gómez, J., & Puigvert, L. (2001). *Teoría sociologica contemporánea.* Barcelona: Paidós.

Flecha, R., & Soler, M. (2013). Turning difficulties into possibilities: Engaging Roma families and students in school through dialogic learning. *Cambridge Journal of Education, 43*(4), 451–465. doi:10.1080/030576 4X.2013.819068

Fleming, A. (2012). Developmental evaluation and the "double loop": Adding value to the evaluation of complex change. *SEDA Special, 33.*

Fleming, T., & Finnegan, F. (2011). *Non-traditional students in Irish higher education: A research report.* Retrieved from http://www.ranlhe.dsw.edu.pl/

Fleming, T., & Murphy, M. (1997). *College knowledge policy, power and the mature student experience at university. NUI Maynooth.* Centre for Adult and Community Education.

Flick, U. (2002). *An introduction to qualitative research* (2nd ed.). London: Sage.

Florida, R. (2006). The flight of the creative class: The new global competition for talent. *Liberal Education, 92*(3), 22–29.

Flynn, J. T. (2013). MOOCs: Disruptive innovation and the future of higher education. *Christian Education Journal., 10*(1), 149–162.

Foster, T. (2009). *Research paper no.4: Alternative routes into and pathways through higher education.* London: Department for Business Innovation and Skills (BIS). Accessed online at http://www.bis.gov.uk/assets/biscore/corporate/migratedD/publications/B/BIS-RP-004

Foszto, L., & Anastasoaie, M. V. (2001). Romania: Representations, public policies and political projects. In W. Guy (Ed.), Between past and future: The Roma of Central and Eastern Europe. University of Hertfordshire Press.

Franklin, T., & Harmelen, M. (2007). Web 2.0 for content for learning and teaching in higher education. Bristol: JISC - The Joint Information Systems Committee. Retrieved from http://www.jisc.ac.uk/media/documents/programmes/digitalrepositories/web2-content-learning-and-teaching.pdf

Freire, P. (2000). *Pedagogy of freedom: Ethics, democracy, and civic courage.* Lanham, MD: Rowman & Littlefield Publishers.

Freitag, M. (1995). *Le naufrage de l'université et autres essais d'epistémologie politique.* Paris: Ladécouverte.

Friedrich, P. (2013). University autonomy and professorial recruitment: A case study at the department of economic and social history. (Master Thesis). Oslo, Norway: Faculty of Educational Sciences, University of Oslo. Retrieved from http://www.sv.uio.no/arena/english/research/projects/flagship/publications/friedrich-ma-university-autonomy.html

Fullan, M. (2007). *The new meaning of educational change* (4th ed.). New York: Teachers College Columbia University.

Fullan, M. G. (1993). The complexity of the change process. In M. G. Fullan (Ed.), *Change forces: Probing the depth of educational reform* (pp. 19–41). London: Falmer Press.

Fullan, M. G. (1999). *Change forces: The sequel.* Philadelphia, PA: Falmer Press.

Fumasoli, T. (2011). *Strategy as evolutionary path: Five higher education institutions on the move.* Lugano: USI. Retrieved from http://doc.rero.ch/record/23135?ln=it

Fumasoli, T. (2013). *The role of organizational routines in academic recruitment: Strategic devices or institutional constraints?*. Paper presented at the EAIR 35th Annual Forum: The Impact of Higher Education. New York, NY.

Fumasoli, T., Gornitzka, Å., & Maassen, P. (2014). *University autonomy and organizational change dynamics* (ARENA Working Paper 08/2014). Retrieved from http://www.sv.uio.no/arena/english/research/publications/arena-publications/workingpapers/working-papers2014/wp8-14.xml

Fumasoli, T., & Goastellec, G. (2014). Global models, disciplinary and local patterns in academic recruitment processes. In T. Fumasoli, G. Goastellec, & B. Kehm (Eds.), *Academic careers in Europe - Trends, challenges, perspectives*. Dordrecht, The Netherlands: Springer.

Fumasoli, T., & Lepori, B. (2011). Patterns of strategies in Swiss higher education institutions. *Higher Education*, *61*(2), 157–178. doi:10.1007/s10734-010-9330-x

Fumasoli, T., & Stensaker, B. (2013). Organizational studies in higher education: A reflection on historical themes and prospective trends. *Higher Education Policy*, *26*(4), 479–496. doi:10.1057/hep.2013.25

Gallacher, J., Field, J., Merrill, B., & Crossan, B. (2002). Learning careers and the social space: Exploring fragile identities adult returners and the new further education. *International Journal of Lifelong Education*, *21*(6), 493–509. doi:10.1080/0260137022000016172

Gallimore, R., & Goldenberg, C. (2001). Analyzing cultural models and settings to connect minority achievement and school improvement research. *Educational Psychologist*, *36*(1), 45–56. doi:10.1207/S15326985EP3601_5

Gallon, R., & Lorenzo, N. (2013). Transcending space: Ubiquitous knowledge. *Crossing Boundaries: Implications for the Content Industries*. Retrieved from http://adobe.ly/15NgqPx

Gallon, R., & Lorenzo, N. (2013). *Crossing boundaries: Implications for the content industries*. Adobe Technical Communications White Paper. Retrieved February 15, 2014, from http://www.adobe.com/cfusion/entitlement/index.cfm?event=custom&sku=FS0003677&e=tcs_whitepaper

Gallon, R. (2013). Communication, culture, and technology: Learning strategies for the unteachable. In R. D. Lansiquot (Ed.), *Cases on interdisciplinary research trends in science, technology, engineering, and mathematics - Studies on urban classrooms*. Hershey, PA: IGI Global. doi:10.4018/978-1-4666-2214-2.ch005

Gardner, H. (2005). *Discipliniranium [Disciplined mind]*. Zagreb: Educa.

Garfield, E. (1979). Mapping the structure of science. In E. Garfield (Ed.), *Citation indexing: Its theory and application in science, technology, and humanities* (pp. 98–147). New York: John Wiley & Sons, Inc.

Garrison, D. R., & Anderson, T. (2003). *E-learning in the 21st century: A framework for research and practice*. London: Routledge. doi:10.4324/9780203166093

Gatfield, T. (2005). An investigation into PhD supervisory management styles: Development of a dynamic conceptual model and its managerial implications. *Journal of Higher Education Policy and Management*, *27*(3), 311–325. doi:10.1080/13600800500283585

Georgiadis, F., Nikolajevic, D., & van Driel, B. (2011). Evaluating a project on Roma education. *Intercultural Education*, *22*(1), 105–113. doi:10.1080/14675986.2011.549649

Geuna, A., & Muscio, A. (2009). The governance of university knowledge transfer: A critical review of the literature. *Minerva*, *47*(1), 93–114. doi:10.1007/s11024-009-9118-2

Giacalone, R. A., & Thompson, K. R. (2006). Business ethics and social responsibility education: Shifting the worldview. *Academy of Management Learning & Education*, *5*(3), 266–277. doi:10.5465/AMLE.2006.22697016

Gibbons, M., Nowotny, H., Schwartzman, S., Scott, P., & Trow, M. (1994). *The new production of knowledge: The dynamics of science and research in contemporary societies*. London: Sage.

Gibbs, G., & Coffey, M. (2004). The impact of training of university teachers on their teaching skills, their approach to teaching, and the approach to learning of their students. *Active Learning in Higher Education*, *5*(1), 87–100. doi:10.1177/1469787404040463

Giere, R. N. (1993). Science and technology studies: Prospects for an enlightened postmodern synthesis. *Science, Technology & Human Values, 18*(1), 102–112. doi:10.1177/016224399301800106

Gillani, N., & Eynon, R. (2014). Communication patterns in massively open online courses. *The Internet and Higher Education, 23*, 18–26. doi:10.1016/j.iheduc.2014.05.004

Gillett, A. J., & Wray, L. (2006). *Assessing the effectiveness of EAP programmes*. London: BALEAP.

Gitanjali, B. (2004). Academic dishonesty in Indian medical colleges. *Journal of Postgraduate Medicine, 50*(4), 281–284. PMID:15623972

Gladings, N. (2004, March 8). Blended learning in K-12 social studies instruction. *Literature Review*.

Gläser, J. (2007). The social orders of research evaluation systems. In R. Whitley & J. Glaser (Eds.), *The changing governance of the sciences: The advent of research evaluation systems* (pp. 245–266). Dordrecht, The Netherlands: Springer. doi:10.1007/978-1-4020-6746-4_12

Glater, J. (2006, May 18). Colleges chase as cheats shift to higher tech. *The New York Times*.

Godin, B. (2006). The linear model of innovation: The historical construction of an analytical framework. *Science, Technology & Human Values, 31*(6), 639–667. doi:10.1177/0162243906291865

Goldman, A. (1999). *Knowledge in a social world*. Oxford, UK: Clarendon Press. doi:10.1093/0198238207.001.0001

Gomes, M. J., Coutinho, C., Guimarães, F., Casa-Nova, M. J., & Caires, S. (2011). Distance learning and e-learning in Portugal: A study of the perceptions, concepts and teaching practices at the Institute of Education, University of Minho. In *Proceedings of EDULEARN11 Conference*. Retrieved from http://repositorium.sdum.uminho.pt/bitstream/1822/12852/1/edulearn11-1.pdf

Gonzalez, N., Moll, L. C., & Amanti, C. (Eds.). (2005). *Funds of knowledge: Theorizing practices in households, communities, and classrooms*. Mahwah, NJ: Lawrence Erlbaum.

Goodfellow, R. (2011). Literacy, literacies and the digital in higher education. *Teaching in Higher Education, 16*(1), 131–144. doi:10.1080/13562517.2011.544125

Gopnik, A., Meltzoff, A. N., & Kuhl, P. K. (2003). *Znanstvenik u kolijevci – što nama rano učenje kazuje o umu [A scientist in the crib - What early learning tells us about the mind]*. Zagreb: Educa.

Gornitzka, Å. (2007). The Lisbon process: A supranational policy perspective. In P. Maassen & J. P. Olsen (Eds.), *University dynamics and European integration* (pp. 155–178). Dordrecht, The Netherlands: Springer. doi:10.1007/978-1-4020-5971-1_8

Gornitzka, Å., Kogan, M., & Amaral, A. (2005). *Reform and change in higher education: Analysing policy implementation*. Dordrecht, The Netherlands: Springer. doi:10.1007/1-4020-3411-3

Gornitzka, Å., Maassen, P., Olsen, J. P., & Stensaker, B. (2007). Europe of knowledge: Search for a new pact. In P. Maassen & J. P. Olsen (Eds.), *University dynamics and European integration* (pp. 181–214). Dordrecht, The Netherlands: Springer. doi:10.1007/978-1-4020-5971-1_9

Gosling, D. (2009). Educational development in the UK: A complex and contradictory reality. *The International Journal for Academic Development, 14*(1), 5–18. doi:10.1080/13601440802659122

Grabinger, R. S., & Dunlap, J. C. (1995). Rich environments for active learning: A definition. *Association for Learning Technology, 3*(2), 5–34. doi:10.1080/0968776950030202

Grant, B. (1999). *Walking on a rackety bridge: Mapping supervision*. Retrieved November 2012, from http://www.herdsa.org.au/wp-content/uploads/conference/1999/pdf/grant.pdf

Grant, B. (2001). Dirty work: "A code for supervision" read against the grain. In A. Barlett & G. Mercer (Eds.), *Postgraduate research supervision: Transforming (r)elations* (pp. 13–24). New York: Peter Lang.

Grant, B. (2003). Mapping the pleasures and risks of supervision. *Discourse (Abingdon), 24*(2), 175–190. doi:10.1080/01596300303042

Grant, B. (2005). Fighting for space in supervision: Fantasies, fairytales, fictions and fallacies. *International Journal of Qualitative Studies in Education, 18*(3), 337–354. doi:10.1080/09518390500082483

Grant, B., & Graham, A. (1999). Naming the game: Reconstructing graduate supervision. *Teaching in Higher Education, 4*(1), 77–89. doi:10.1080/1356251990040105

Grant, R. M. (1996). Toward a knowledge-based theory of the firm. *Strategic Management Journal, 17*(S2), 109–122. doi:10.1002/smj.4250171110

Greenbaum, T. L. (2000). *Moderating focus groups: A practical guide for group facilitation.* Thousand Oaks, CA: SAGE. doi:10.4135/9781483328522

Greenwood, R., & Hinings, C. (1993). Understanding strategic change: The contribution of archetypes. *Academy of Management Journal, 36*(5), 1052–1081. doi:10.2307/256645

Griffin, G. (2009). *Governance of science in a complex world: Issues for the social sciences and humanities.* Paper presented at the International Conference 'Governance of Science in the 21st Century: Mechanisms and Perspectives'. Moscow, Russia. Retrieved from http://www.issras.ru/conference_2009/index.php

Grodecka, K., Wild, F., & Kieslinger, B. (Eds.). (2009). How to use social software in higher education: iCamp project. In *How to use social software in higher education: A handbook for the iCamp project.* Retrieved from http://www.icamp.eu/wp-content/uploads/2009/01/icamp-handbook-web.pdf

Guardian Professional – Higher Education Network. (2013). *Stick or twist: The postdoctoral dilemma.* Last accessed 15th March 2014 at http://www.theguardian.com/higher-education-network/blog/2013/jun/21/postfoc-dilemma-stick-or-twist

Gunasekara, C. (2006). The generative and developmental roles of universities in regional innovation systems. *Science & Public Policy, 33*(2), 137–150. doi:10.3152/147154306781779118

Gurr, G. M. (2001). Negotiating the "rackety bridge" – A dynamic model for aligning supervisory style with research student development. *Higher Education Research & Development, 20*(1), 81–92. doi:10.1080/07924360120043882

Habermas, J., & McCarthy, T. (1985). *The theory of communicative action: Reason and the rationalization of society* (Vol. 1). Boston: Beacon Press.

Haggard, S. (2011). *The coming MOOC copyright problem and its impact on students and universities.* Retrieved February 15, 2014, from http://moocnewsandreviews.com/category/commentary/

Hall, A. (2007). Vygotsky goes online: Learning design from a socio-cultural perspective. *Learning and Socio-Cultural Theory: Exploring Modern Vygotskian Perspectives, 1*(1), article 6. Retrieved from http://ro.uow.edu.au//llrg/vol1/iss1/6

Hall, A., & Beradino, L. (2006). Teaching professional behaviours: Differences in the perceptions of faculty, students, and employers. *Journal of Business Ethics, 63*(4), 407–415. doi:10.1007/s10551-005-2411-6

Hanbury, A., Prosser, M., & Rickinson, M. (2008). The differential impact of UK accredited teaching development programmes on academics' approaches to teaching. *Studies in Higher Education, 33*(4), 469–483. doi:10.1080/03075070802211844

Harloe, M., & Perry, B. (2004). Universities, localities and regional development: The emergence of the 'mode 2' university? *International Journal of Urban and Regional Research, 28*(1), 212–223. doi:10.1111/j.0309-1317.2004.00512.x

Harman, G. (2003). PhD student satisfaction with course experience and supervision in two Australian research-intensive universities. *Prometheus, 21*(3), 312–333. doi:10.1080/0810902032000113460

Harris, A., & Tienda, M. (2010). Minority higher education pipeline: Consequences of changes in college admissions policy in Texas. *The Annals of the American Academy of Political and Social Science, 627*(1), 60–81. doi:10.1177/0002716209348740 PMID:23077374

Harrison, R., & Hopkins, R. L. (1967). The design of cross-cultural training: An alternative to the university model. *The Journal of Applied Behavioral Science, 3*(4), 431–460. doi:10.1177/002188636700300401

Harvey, J., Donnelly, R., & McAvinia, C. (2013). *Engaging lecturers as students: Building sustainable professional development.* Paper presented at the 6th Annual Learning Innovation Conference: Sustainable Models of Student Engagement – Rhetoric or Achievable? Dublin, Ireland.

Harvey, L., Drew, S., & Smith, M. (2006). *The first year experience: A review of literature for the higher education academy.* York, UK: HEA.

Harvey, L., & Green, D. (1993). Defining quality. *Assessment & Evaluation in Higher Education, 18*(1), 26p. doi:10.1080/0260293930180102

Hawkins, B. (2008). Using sociocultural theory to examine the context(s) of language teaching and learning. *Working Papers in TESOL & Applied Linguistics, 8*(1).

Hayes, N., & Introna, L. D. (2005). Cultural values, plagiarism, and fairness: When plagiarism gets in the way of learning. *Ethics & Behavior, 15*(3), 213–231. doi:10.1207/s15327019eb1503_2

Hazelkorn, E. (2013). How rankings are reshaping higher education. In V. Climent, F. Michavila, & M. Ripolles (Eds.), *Los rankings universitarios: Mitos y realidades* (pp. 1–8). Tecnos.

Hazelkorn, H. (2009). Rankings and the battle for world-class excellence: Institutional strategies and policy choice. *Higher Education Management and Policy, 21*(1), 1–22. doi:10.1787/hemp-v21-art4-en

Hazelkorn, H. (2011). *Globalization and the reputation race in rankings and the reshaping of higher education: The battle for world class excellence.* London: Palgrave MacMillan. doi:10.1057/9780230306394

HEA. (2008). *National plan for equity of access to higher education 2008-2013.* Dublin: HEA.

HEA. (2010). *A study of progression in Irish higher education.* Dublin: HEA.

HEA. (2012). *Higher education: Key facts and figures 2011-12.* Dublin: HEA.

HEA. (2013). *Higher education: Key facts and figures 2012-13.* Dublin: HEA Higher Education Statistics Agency (HESA) Website. Accessed at https://www.hesa.ac.uk/pis/urg

Healy, T. (2000). *The appraisal of investments in educational facilities.* Paris: OECD Programme on Educational Building. Retrieved July 26, 2014, from http://files.eric.ed.gov/fulltext/ED439593.pdf

Hellsten, M. (2002). *Students in transition: Needs and experiences of international students in Australia.* Paper presented at the 16th Australian International Education Conference, Macquarie, Australia.

Henkel, M. (1998). Evaluation in higher education: Conceptual and epistemological foundations. *European Journal of Education, 33*(3), 285–297.

Hernard, F., & Leprince-Ringuet, S. (2008). *The path to quality teaching in higher education.* Unpublished.

Hicks, D. (1995). Published papers, tacit competencies and corporate management of the public/private character of knowledge. *Industrial and Corporate Change, 4*(2), 401–424. doi:10.1093/icc/4.2.401

Higher Education Authority (HEA). (1995). *Report of the steering committee on the future development of higher education.* Dublin: HEA.

Higher Education Authority (HEA). (2006). *An overview of applications and acceptances to higher education.* Dublin: HEA Website. Accessed at http://www.hea.ie/en/policy/national-access-office

Higher Education Authority (HEA). (2012). *A proposed reconfiguration of the Irish system of higher education.* Report of the International Expert Panel for the Higher Education Authority of Ireland. Retrieved from http://9thlevel.ie/wp-content/uploads/International_Panel_Report.pdf

Hill, P. (2013). Emerging student patterns in MOOCs: A (revised) graphical view. *E-Literate.* Retrieved from http://mfeldstein.com/emerging-student-patterns-in-moocs-a-revised-graphical-view/

Hodsdon, L., & Buckley, A. (2011). *Postgraduate research experience survey 2011 results: Report.* York, UK: Higher Education Academy.

Hodson, P., & Thomas, H. (2003). Quality assurance in higher education: Fit for the new millennium or simply year 2000 compliant? *Higher Education, 45*(3), 375–387. doi:10.1023/A:1022665818216

Hoffman, D. (2009). Changing academic mobility patterns and international migration—what will academic mobility mean in the 21st century? *Journal of Studies in International Education, 13*(3), 347–364. doi:10.1177/1028315308321374

Hoffman, D. M., Blasi, B., Culum, B., Dragsic, Z., Ewen, A., & Horta, H. et al. (2014). The methodological illumination of a blind spot: Information and communication technology and international research team dynamics in a higher education research program. *Higher Education, 67*(4), 473–495. doi:10.1007/s10734-013-9692-y

Holdaway, E. (1997). Quality issues in postgraduate education. In R. G. Burgess (Ed.), *Beyond the first degree: Graduate education, lifelong learning and careers* (pp. 60–78). Buckingham, UK: SRHE & Open University Press.

Honneth, A. (2007). *Disrespect: The normative foundations of critical theory.* Cambridge, MA: Polity.

Hood, C. (2011). Public management research on the road from consilience to experimentation. *Public Management Review, 13*(2), 321–326. doi:10.1080/14719037.2010.539098

Hopkins, D. (2001). *School improvement for real.* London: Falmer Press. doi:10.4324/9780203165799

Horta, H. V. F., & Grediaga, R. (2010). Navel gazing: Academic inbreeding and scientific productivity. *Management Science, 56*(3), 414–429. doi:10.1287/mnsc.1090.1109

Hountondji, P. J. (1973). *Libertés: Contribution à la révolution dahoméen.* Cotonou: Editions Renaissance.

Houston, D. (2008). Rethinking quality and improvement in higher education. *Quality Assurance in Education, 16*(1), 61–79. doi:10.1108/09684880810848413

Hsieh, J., & Huisman, J. (2012). Cross-national policy change in higher education and the Bologna process: a prelude to global convergence? In *Proceedings of the Policy Formation in Post-Secondary Education: Issues and Prospects in Turbulent Times.* Academic Press.

Huet, I., Baptista, A. V., & Figueiredo, C. (2012). Qualidade da investigação doutoral: Enfoque no processo de supervisão na perspectiva de estudantes e supervisores. In A. Noutel, E. Brutten, G. Pires, & I. Huet (Eds.), *Ensino superior: Saberes, experiências, desafios.* João Pessoa: Ideia.

Hughes, J. M. C., & McCabe, D. L. (2006). Understanding academic misconduct. *Canadian Journal of Higher Education, 36*(1), 49–63.

Huisman, J. (Ed.). (2009). *International perspectives on the governance of higher education: Alternative frameworks for coordination.* New York: Routledge Press.

Hung, W. (2006). *Researching the researcher: A social network analysis of the multidisciplinary knowledge creation process.* (Unpublished master dissertation). University of Waterloo.

IHEP. (2009). *Impact of college rankings on institutional decision making: Four country case studies.* Washington, DC: Institute for Higher Education Policy. Retrieved from http://www.ihep.org/assets/files/publications/g-l/impactofcollegerankings.pdf

Inglis, T., & Murphy, M. (1999). *No room for adults? The experience of mature students in University College Dublin.* Dublin: Social Science Research Centre & Adult Education Office, University College Dublin.

Institute of Medicine (IOM) & National Research Council. (NRC). (2012). The early childhood care and education workforce: Challenges and opportunities: A workshop report. Washington, DC: The National Academies Press.

International Organization for Standardization. (1998). *ISO 9241-11: Ergonomic requirements for office work with visual display terminals (VDTs) - Part 11: Guidance on usability.* Geneva: International Organization for Standardization.

Istance, D., Stoll, L., Jolonch, A., Martínez, M., & Badia, J. (2013). Liderar per aprendre: Del diàleg entre la recerca i la pràctica. *Informes Breus 46 EDUCACIÓ.* Retrieved February 20, 2014, from http://www.fbofill.cat/intra/fbofill/documents/publicacions/580.pdf

Ivankova, N. V., Creswell, J. W., & Stick, S. L. (2006). Using mixed-methods sequential explanatory design: From theory to practice. *Field Methods, 18*(1), 3–20. doi:10.1177/1525822X05282260

Jambes, J. P. (2011). Développement numérique des espaces ruraux: Peut-on transformer un problème en ressource Territoriale? *Networks and Communication Studies, 25*(3-4), 165-178. Retrieved February 15, 2014, from http://www.netcom-journal.com/volumes/articlesV253/Netcom165-178.pdf

Jarvis, P. (2004). *Adult education and lifelong learning: Theory and practice* (3rd ed.). London: Routledge.

JISC. (2012). *Researchers of tomorrow: The research behaviour of generation y doctoral students.* London: JISC/British Library. Retrieved from http://www.jisc.ac.uk/publications/reports/2012/researchers-of-tomorrow.aspx

Johnson, D. R. (2013). Technological change and professional control in the professoriate. *Science, Technology & Human Values, 38*(1), 126–149. doi:10.1177/0162243911430236

Johnson, L., Smith, R., Willis, H., Levine, A., & Haywood, K. (2011). *The 2011 horizon report.* Austin, TX: The New Media Consortium.

Joint Quality Initiative Informal Group. (2004). *Shared 'Dublin' descriptors for short cycle, first cycle, second cycle and third cycle awards.* Retrieved September 2012, from www.eua.be/.../pushFile.php?.../dublin_descriptors

Jordan, A., Carlile, O., & Stack, A. (2008). *Approaches to learning: A guide for teachers.* Maidenhead, UK: Open University Press.

Josefowicz, M. (2012). *Connecting to complexity & change: Connecting urban design to people.* The International Nemetics Institute. Retrieved February 15, 2014, from http://cochange.wordpress.com/2012/12/18/connecting-urban-design-to-people/

Jovchelovitch, S. (2007). *Knowledge in context, representations, communities and culture.* London: Routledge.

Junco, R., & Cole-Avent, G. A. (2008). An introduction to technologies commonly used by college students. *New Directions for Student Services, 124*(124), 3–17. doi:10.1002/ss.292

Kahn, P., Young, R., Grace, S., Pilkington, R., Rush, L., Tomkinson, B., & Willis, T. (2006). *The role and effectiveness of reflective practices in programmes for new academic staff: A grounded practitioner review of research literature.* York, UK: Higher Education Academy.

Kaipa, P. (1999). What is unlearning? *The Mithya Institute for Learning.* Retrieved February 15, 2014, from http://mithya.prasadkaipa.com/learning/whatunlearn.html

Kandlbinder, P., & Peseta, T. (2006). *In supervisors' words... An insider's view of postgraduate supervision.* Sydney, Australia: The Institute for Teaching and Learning.

Kandlbinder, P., & Peseta, T. (2009). Key concepts in postgraduate certificates in higher education teaching and learning in Australasia and the United Kingdom. *The International Journal for Academic Development, 14*(1), 19–31. doi:10.1080/13601440802659247

Katz, R. (Ed.). (2008). *The tower and the cloud: Higher education in the age of cloud computing.* EDUCAUSE.

Keane, E. (2009). Frictional relationships ... tension in the camp: Focusing on the relational in under-represented students' experiences in higher education. *Irish Educational Studies, 28*(1), 85–102. doi:10.1080/03323310802597358

Keeling, R. (2006). The Bologna process and the Lisbon research agenda: The European Commission's expanding role in higher education discourse. *European Journal of Education, 41*(2), 203–223. doi:10.1111/j.1465-3435.2006.00256.x

Kehm, B. M. (2007). Quo vadis doctoral education? New european approaches in the context of global changes. *European Journal of Education, 42*(3), 307–319. doi:10.1111/j.1465-3435.2007.00308.x

Kehm, B. M., Huisman, J., & Stensaker, B. (2009). *The European higher education area.* Rotterdam, The Netherlands: Sense Publishers.

Kehm, B. M., & Teichler, U. (2007). Research on internationalisation in higher education. *Journal of Studies in International Education, 11*(3-4), 260–273. doi:10.1177/1028315307303534

Kehm, B. M., & Teichler, U. (2013). *The academic profession in Europe: New tasks and new challenges.* Dordrecht, The Netherlands: Springer. doi:10.1007/978-94-007-4614-5

Kehm, B., & Lanzendorf, U. (Eds.), *(n.d.). Reforming university governance.* Bonn, Germany: Lemmens.

Kellner, D. (2002). Technological revolution, multiple literacies and the restructuring of education. In I. Snyder (Ed.), *Silicon literacies: Communication innovation and education in the electronic age* (pp. 154–169). London: Routledge.

Kelly, M. (2005). The effects of increasing numbers of mature students on the pedagogical practices of lecturers in the institutes of technology. *Irish Educational Studies,* 24(2-3), 207–221. doi:10.1080/03323310500435497

Kember, D. (2009). Promoting student-centred forms of learning across an entire university. *Higher Education,* 58(1), 1–13. doi:10.1007/s10734-008-9177-6

Kennedy, G., Dalgarno, B., Bennett, S., Judd, T., Gray, K., & Chang, R. (2008). *Immigrants and natives: Investigating differences between staff and students' use of technology.* Paper presented at the Hello! Where are You in the Landscape of Educational Technology? Melbourne, Australia. Retrieved March 3, 2011, from http://www.ascilite.org.au/conferences/melbourne08/procs/index.htm

Kephart, W. M. (1949). Minority group discrimination in higher education. *Journal of Educational Sociology,* 23(1), 52–57. doi:10.2307/2264358

Khan Academy. (2014). What's Khan Academy all about? *Khan Academy.* Retrieved February 15, 2014, from https://www.khanacademy.org/#mission-statement

Kilduff, M., & Krackhardt, D. (2008). *Interpersonal networks in organizations.* Cambridge, UK: Cambridge University Press. doi:10.1017/CBO9780511753749

King, R. (2011). Power and networks in worldwide knowledge coordination: The case of global science. *Higher Education Policy,* 24(3), 359–376. doi:10.1057/hep.2011.9

Kipper, H., & Mischke, W. (2008). *Uvod u opću didaktiku [Introduction to general didactics].* Zagreb: Educa.

Kivinen, O., & Rinne, R. (1991). How to steer student flows and higher education: The headache facing the Finnish Ministry of Education. In G. Neave & F. Van Vught (Eds.), *Prometheus bound: The changing relationship between government and higher education in Western Europe* (pp. 51–64). Pergamon Press.

Klein, J. T. (1990). *Interdisciplinarity: History, theory, and practice.* Detroit: Wayne State University Press.

Klein, J. T. (2010). A taxonomy of interdisciplinarity. In R. Frodeman, J. T. Klein, & C. Mitcham (Eds.), *The Oxford handbook of interdisciplinarity* (pp. 15–30). New York: Oxford University Press.

Klein, J. T. (2010). *Creating interdisciplinary campus cultures: A model for strength and sustainability.* Hoboken, NJ: Jossey-Bass.

Kleinman, D. L., & Vallas, S. P. (2001). Science, capitalism, and the rise of 'knowledge worker': The changing structure of knowledge production in the United States. *Theory and Society,* 30(4), 451–492. doi:10.1023/A:1011815518959

Knight, P., Tait, J., & Yorke, M. (2006). The professional learning of teachers in higher education. *Studies in Higher Education,* 31(3), 319–339. doi:10.1080/03075070600680786

Knoke, D., & Yang, S. (2008). *Social network analysis* (2nd ed.). Thousand Oaks, CA: Sage.

Knorr-Cetina, K. (1992). The couch, the cathedral and the laboratory: On the relationship between experiment and laboratory in science. In A. Pickering (Ed.), *Science as practice and culture.* Chicago: Chicago University Press.

Knowledge, N. N. G. c. (2011). *RS policy document 03/11.* London: Royal Society.

Kok, W. (2004). *Facing the challenge: The Lisbon strategy for growth and employment.* Luxembourg: European Communities.

Koshy, V. (2005). *Action research of improving practice: A practical guide.* London: Paul Chapman Publishing.

Kosmützky, A., & Krücken, G. (2014). Growth or steady state? A bibliometric focus on international comparative higher education research. *Higher Education,* 67(4), 457–472. doi:10.1007/s10734-013-9694-9

Kosmützky, A., & Nokkala, T. (2014). Challenges and trends in comparative higher education: An editorial. *Higher Education, 67*(4), 369–380. doi:10.1007/s10734-013-9693-x

Krackhardt, D. (1990). Assessing the political landscape: Structure, cognition, and power in organizations. *Administrative Science Quarterly, 35*(2), 342–369. doi:10.2307/2393394

Kretek, P., Dragšić, Ž., & Kehm, B. (2012). Transformation of university governance: On the role of university board members. *Higher Education, 65*(1), 39–58. doi:10.1007/s10734-012-9580-x

Kuhn, T. S. (1996). *The structure of scientific revolutions.* Chicago: University of Chicago Press. doi:10.7208/chicago/9780226458106.001.0001

Kyuchukov, H. (2007). Good practices in Roma education in Bulgaria during the years of transition. *Intercultural Education, 18*(1), 29–39. doi:10.1080/14675980601143645

Kyvik, S. (2009). *The dynamics of change in higher education: Expansion and contraction in an organisational field.* Dordrecht, The Netherlands: Springer.

Kyvik, S., & Lepori, B. (2010). *Research in the non-university higher education sector in Europe.* Dordrecht, The Netherlands: Springer.

Lai, K. W. (2011). Digital technology and the culture of teaching and learning in higher education. *Australasian Journal of Educational Technology, 27*(8), 1263–1275.

Lam, A. (2005). Work roles and careers of R&D scientists in network organizations. *Industrial Relations, 44*(2), 242–275. doi:10.1111/j.0019-8676.2005.00383.x

Lamont, M. (2009). *How professors think – Inside the curious world of academic judgement.* Harvard University Press.

Lane, L. M. (2012). Three kinds of MOOCs, Lisa's (online) teaching blog. Retrieved from http://lisahistory.net/wordpress/2012/08/three-kinds-of-moocs/

Lankshear, C., & Knobel, M. (2011). *New literacies: Everyday practices and social learning* (3rd ed.). Maidenhead, UK: Open University Press.

Latour, B. (1987). *Science in action: How to follow scientists and engineers through society.* Cambridge, MA: Harvard University Press.

Laurillard, D. (2001). *Rethinking university teaching: A conversational framework for the use of educational technology.* London: Routledge.

Law, J. (2004). *After method: Mess in social science research.* London: Routledge.

Lawton, M. (2005). *Working class heroes.* Paper presented at University of Wolverhamton, Wolverhamton, UK. Retrieved from http://asp.wlv.ac.uk/Level3.asp?UserType=11&Level3=1659

Lea, M. R., & Jones, S. (2011). Digital literacies in higher education: Exploring textual and technological practice. *Studies in Higher Education, 36*(4), 377–393. doi:10.1080/03075071003664021

Leask, B. (2006). Plagiarism, cultural diversity and metaphor: Implications for academic staff development. *Assessment & Evaluation in Higher Education, 31*(2), 183–199. doi:10.1080/02602930500262486

Leathwood, C., & O'Connell, P. (2003). It's a struggle: The construction of the 'new student' in higher education. *Journal of Education Policy, 18*(6), 597–615. doi:10.1080/0268093032000145863

Lee, A. (2008). How are doctoral students supervised? Concepts of doctoral research supervision. *Studies in Higher Education, 33*(3), 267–281. doi:10.1080/03075070802049202

Lee, A. (2010). New approaches to doctoral supervision: Implications for educational development. *Educational Developments, 11*(2), 18–23.

Lee, A. (2012). *Successful research supervision: Advising students doing research.* London: Routledge.

Lee, H. F., Miozzo, M., & Laredo, P. (2010). Career patterns and competences of PhDs in science and engineering in the knowledge economy: The case of graduates from a UK research-based university. *Research Policy, 39*(7), 869–881. doi:10.1016/j.respol.2010.05.001

Leese, M. (2009). Out of class - Out of mind? The use of virtual learning environment to encourage student engagement in out of class activities. *British Journal of Educational Technology*, 40(1), 70–77. doi:10.1111/j.1467-8535.2008.00822.x

Lepičnik-Vodopivec, J., & Vujičić, L. (2010). The development of professional competencies: The educator as a reflective practitioner in tertiary education. *Scientia Paedagogica Experimentalis: International Journal of Experimental Research*, 47(1), 111–131.

Leskovec, J. (2011). Tracking, modeling and predicting the flow of information through networks. in *KDD 2011 tutorial, social media analytics*. Stanford University. Retrieved February 15, 2014, from http://snap.stanford.edu/proj/socmedia-kdd/

Lester, R., & Sotarauta, M. (Eds.). (2007). *Innovation, universities and the competitiveness of regions*. Helsinki: Tekes.

Levy, R. (2005). Les doctorants CIFRE: Médiateurs entre laboratoires de recherche universitaires et entreprise. *Revue d'Economie Industrielle*, 111(1), 79–96. doi:10.3406/rei.2005.3083

Li, A., & Gasser, M. (2005). Predicting Asian international students' sociocultural adjustment: A test of two mediation models. *International Journal of Intercultural Relations*, 29(5), 561–576. doi:10.1016/j.ijintrel.2005.06.003

Light, G., Cox, R., & Calkins, S. C. (2009). *Learning and teaching in higher education: The reflective professional*. London: Sage Publications.

Li, L., & Pitts, J. (2009). Does it really matter? Using virtual office hours to enhance student-faculty interaction. *Journal of Systems Education*, 20(2), 175–185.

Livingstone, S. (2003). On the challenges of cross-national comparative media research. *European Journal of Communication*, 18(4), 477–500. doi:10.1177/0267323103184003

Liyoshi, T., & Kumar, M. (2008). *Opening up education: The collective advancement of education through open technology, open content, and open knowledge*. Boston: The MIT Press.

Lloyd-Smith, L. (2010). Exploring the advantages of blended instruction at community colleges and technical schools. *MERLOT Journal of Online Learning and Teaching*, 6(2), 508-515. Retrieved from http://jolt.merlot.org/vol6no2/lloyd-smith_0610.htm

Lomas, C. (2005). *7 things you should know about social bookmarking*. EDUCAUSE Learning Initiative. Retrieved from http://www.educause.edu/library/resources/7-things-you-should-know-about-social-bookmarking

Lord, G., & Lomicka, L. (2008). Blended learning in teacher education: An investigation of classroom community across media. *Contemporary Issues in Technology & Teacher Education*, 8(2), 158–174.

Lorenzo, N. (2013). Daily adventure with Neus Lorenzo. In *Daily Edventures: Anthony Salcito's 366-day Look at Global Heroes in Education*. Retrieved February 15, 2014 from http://dailyedventures.com/index.php/2013/10/23/neuslorenzo/

Lorenzo, N. (2014). Curso MOOC- Personal lerning environment: eduPLEmooc, del ministerio de educación, ciencia y deportes. In *NewsNeus blog de formación docente*. Retrieved February 15, 2014, from http://newsneus.wordpress.com/curso-mooc-pel/

Lorenzo, N., & Martínez, M. (2013). Col·legi sant pere claver (Barcelona). In *Lideratge per a l'aprenentatge: Estudis de cas a Catalunya*. Barcelona: Jaume Bofill Fundation.

Lubensky, R. (2006). The present and future of personal learning environments (PLE). In *Deliberations: Reflecting on learning and deliberating about democracy*. Retrieved February 15, 2014, from http://www.deliberations.com.au/2006/12/present-and-future-of-personal-learning.html

Lucas, L. (2006). *The research game in academic life*. London: Palgrave.

Lueddeke, G. R. (2003). Professionalising teaching practice in higher education: A study of disciplinary variation and 'teaching scholarship'. *Studies in Higher Education*, 28(2), 213–228. doi:10.1080/0307507032000058082

Lund, J. R. (2004). Plagiarism: A cultural perspective. *Journal of Religious & Theological Information*, 6(3/4), 93–101. doi:10.1300/J112v06n03_08

Maassen, P. (2009). The modernisation of European higher education: National policy dynamics. In A. Amaral, I. Bleiklie, & C. Musselin (Eds.), *From governance to identity* (pp. 95–112). Dordrecht, The Netherlands: Springer. doi:10.1007/978-1-4020-8994-7_8

Macdonald, C., & Stratta, E. (2001). From access to widening participation: Responses to the changing population in higher education in the UK. *Journal of Further and Higher Education, 25*(2), 249–258. doi:10.1080/03098770120050909

MacDonald, K., & Ritzer, G. (1988). The sociology of the professions: Dead or alive? *Work and Occupations, 15*(3), 251–272. doi:10.1177/0730888488015003001

MacFadgen, S. L. (2007). *Mature students in the persistence puzzle: An exploration of the factors that contribute to adult learners' qualify of life and retention in postsecondary education.* (Unpublished doctoral dissertation). Simon Fraser University, Burnaby, Canada.

Mackenzie, D. (2006). *An engine, not a camera: How financial models shape markets.* Cambridge, MA: MIT Press. doi:10.7551/mitpress/9780262134606.001.0001

Maclellan, E., & Soden, R. (2004). The importance of epistemic cognition in student-centred learning. *Instructional Science, 32*(3), 253–268. doi:10.1023/B:TRUC.0000024213.03972.ce

Mainhard, T., van der Rijst, R., van Tartwijk, J., & Wubbels, T. (2009). A model for supervisor-doctoral student relationship. *Higher Education, 58*(3), 359–373. doi:10.1007/s10734-009-9199-8

Major, E. M. (2005). Co-national support, cultural therapy, and the adjustment of Asian students to an English-speaking university culture. *International Education Journal, 6*(1), 84–95.

Manathunga, C., & Goozée, J. (2007). Challenging the dual assumption of the 'always/already' autonomous student and effective supervisor. *Teaching in Higher Education, 12*(3), 309–322. doi:10.1080/13562510701278658

Mangematin, V., & Nesta, L. (1999). What kind of knowledge can a firm absorb? *International Journal of Technology Management, 18*(3), 149–172. doi:10.1504/IJTM.1999.002771

Mangematin, V., & Robin, S. (2003). The double face of PhD students: The example of life sciences. *Science & Public Policy, 30*(6), 405–414. doi:10.3152/147154303781780209

Marav, D. (2013). *We can do anything in the cyberworld except conceive: Mongolian university students' everyday digital literacy practices.* (Unpublished doctoral dissertation). Monash University, Monash, Australia.

Marav, D., & Espinoza, M. (2014). Equity and access in higher education: A comparative perspective from Chile and Mongolia. In Z. Zhang, P. W. K. Chan, & C. Boyle (Eds.), *Equality in education: Fairness and inclusion* (pp. 169–182). Rotterdam, The Netherlands: Sense Publishers. doi:10.1007/978-94-6209-692-9_13

March, J. G., & Olsen, J. P. (1989). *Rediscovering institutions: The organizational basis of politics.* New York: Collier Macmillan.

March, J. G., & Olsen, J. P. (1995). *Democratic governance.* New York: The Free Press.

Marcus, G. E. (1998). *Ethnography through thick and thin.* Princeton, NJ: Princeton University Press.

Marginson, S. (2011). The new world order in higher education. In M. Rostan & M. Vaira (Eds.), *Questioning excellence in higher education: Policies, experiences and challenges in national and comparative perspective* (pp. 3–20). Rotterdam, The Netherlands: Sense Publishers. doi:10.1007/978-94-6091-642-7_1

Marginson, S., & Rhoades, G. (2002). Beyond national states, markets, and systems of higher education: A glonacal agency heuristic. *Higher Education, 43*(3), 281–309. doi:10.1023/A:1014699605875

Marin, L. (2012). *Contemporary challenges in accessing high quality education for Roma children.* Retrieved from http://romaeducationfund.ro/download/Policy%20Brief%205%20--%20Politici%20educationale%20pentru%20romi%20in%20context%20FSE-POSDRU.pdf

Marope, P., Wells, P., & Hazelkorn, E. (2013). *Rankings and accountability in higher education: Uses and misuses.* Paris: UNESCO.

Marques, C., & Carvalho, A. A. (2009). Contextualização e evolução do e-learning: Dos ambientes de apoio à aprendizagem às ferramentas da web 2.0. In *Challenges'09 - VI Conferência Internacional de TIC na Educação* (pp. 985-1001). Braga: Universidade do Minho. Retrieved from http://repositorium.sdum.uminho.pt/handle/1822/10028

Martínez i Muñoz, M., Badia i Pujol, J., & Jolonch i Anglada, A. (Eds.). (2013). *Lideratge per a l'aprenentatge: Estudis de cas a Catalunya*. Barcelona: Jaume Bofill Fundation. Retrieved February 20, 2014, from http://www.fbofill.cat/intra/fbofill/documents/publicacions/580.pdf

Mathers, J., & Parry, J. (2010). Older mature students' experiences of applying to study medicine in England: An interview study. *Medical Education*, *44*(11), 1084–1094. doi:10.1111/j.1365-2923.2010.03731.x PMID:20880007

Maxwell, T. W., & Smyth, R. (2011). Higher degree research supervision: From practice toward theory. *Higher Education Research & Development*, *30*(2), 219–231. doi:10.1080/07294360.2010.509762

Mayes, T., & de Freitas, S. (2007). Learning and Elearning: The role of theory. In H. Beetham & R. Sharpe (Eds.), *Rethinking pedagogy in the digital age*. London: Routledge.

McAdams, D. P. (1988). Personal needs and personal relationships. In S. W. Duck (Ed.), *Handbook of personal relationships* (pp. 467–484). New York: John Wiley & Son, lda.

McAlpine, L., & Norton, J. (2006). Reframing our approach to doctoral programs: An integrative framework for action and research. *Higher Education Research & Development*, *25*(1), 3–17. doi:10.1080/07294360500453012

McAvinia, C., Harvey, J., Donnelly, R., McDonnell, C., & Hanratty, O. (2014). *What has been the impact of accredited professional development for people teaching in higher education?* Paper presented at the UK Higher Education Academy 10th Annual Conference, Birmingham, UK.

McCabe, D. L. (2005). It takes a village: Academic dishonesty and educational opportunity. *Liberal Education*, *91*(3), 26–31.

McCabe, D. L., Butterfield, K. D., & Trevino, L. K. (2006). Academic dishonesty in graduate business programs: Prevalence, causes, and proposed action. *Academy of Management Learning & Education*, *5*(3), 294–305. doi:10.5465/AMLE.2006.22697018

McCabe, D. L., & Trevino, L. K. (1995). Cheating among business students: A challenge for business leaders and educators. *Journal of Management Education*, *19*(2), 205–218. doi:10.1177/105256299501900205

McCune, V., Hounsell, J., Christie, V., Cree, V., & Tett, L. (2010). Mature and younger students' reasons for making the transition from further education into higher education. *Teaching in Higher Education*, *15*(6), 691–702. doi:10.1080/13562517.2010.507303

McDonald, C. (2006). Roma in the Romanian educational system: Barriers and leaps of faith. European. *Journal of Intercultural Studies (Melbourne, Vic.)*, *10*(2), 183–200.

McFadyen, M. A., & Cannella, A. (2004). Social capital and knowledge creation: Diminishing returns of the number and strength of exchange relationships. *Academy of Management Journal*, *47*(5), 735–746. doi:10.2307/20159615

McFarland, D. A., Diehl, D., & Rawlings, C. (2011). Methodological transnationalism and the sociology of education. In M. Hallinan (Ed.), *Frontiers in sociology of education* (pp. 87–110). Springer. doi:10.1007/978-94-007-1576-9_5

McGill, S. (2008). Integrating academic integrity education with business law course: Why and how? *Journal of Legal Studies Education*, *25*(2), 241–282. doi:10.1111/j.1744-1722.2008.00053.x

McGivney, V. (2004). Understanding persistence in adult learning. *Open Learning*, *19*(1), 33–46. doi:10.1080/0268051042000177836

McGowan, U. (2005). Does educational integrity mean teaching students NOT to 'use their own words'? *International Journal for Educational Integrity*, *1*(1).

McGowan, U. (2005). Academic integrity: An awareness and development issue for students and staff. *Journal of University Teaching and Learning Practice, 2*(3), 6.

McGuire, D., Collins, M., & Garavan, T. (2003). Tackling social exclusion at third level: A profile of participants on access courses. *Irish Educational Studies, 22*(1), 41–68. doi:10.1080/0332331030220107

McLean, J. E. (1995). *Improving education through action research: A guide for administrators and teachers.* Corwin Press.

McLean, P., & Ransom, M. L. (2005). Building intercultural competencies: Implications of academic skills development. In J. Carroll & J. Ryan (Eds.), *Teaching international students: Improving learning for all* (pp. 45–63). New York: Routledge.

Means, B., Toyama, Y., Murphy, R. F., & Baki, M. (2013). The effectiveness of online and blended learning: A meta-analysis of the empirical literature. *Teachers College Record, 115*(3), 1–47. Retrieved from http://www.tcrecord.org/library

Means, B., Toyama, Y., Murphy, R., Bakia, M., & Jones, K. (2009). *Evaluation of evidence-based practices in online learning: A meta-analysis and review of online learning studies.* Washington, DC: U.S. Department of Education, Office of Planning, Evaluation, and Policy Development.

Mehaffy, G. L. (2012). Challenge and change. *EDUCAUSE Review.* Retrieved June 3, 2014, from http://net.educause.edu/ir/library/pdf/ERM1252.pdf

Meister, J. (2012). Job hopping is the 'new normal' for millennials: Three ways to prevent a human resource nightmare. *Forbes Magazine.* Retrieved June 3, 2014, from http://www.forbes.com/sites/jeannemeister/2012/08/14/job-hopping-is-the-new-normal-for-millennials-three-ways-to-prevent-a-human-resource-nightmare/

Merrill, B. (2001). Learning and teaching in universities: Perspectives from adult learners and lecturers. *Teaching in Higher Education, 6*(1), 5–17. doi:10.1080/13562510020029563

Merton, R. (1968). *Social theory and social structure.* London: Free Press.

Merton, R. K. (1973). *The sociology of science: Theoretical and empirical investigations.* Chicago: The University of Chicago Press.

Meyer, M., Grant, K., & Kuusisto, J. (2013). The second coming of the triple helix and the emergence of hybrid innovation environments. In R. Capello, A. Olechnicka, & G. Gorzelak (Eds.), Universities, cities and regions: Loci for knowledge and innovation creation (pp. 193-209). Milton Park, UK: Routledge.

Meyer, J. W., & Rowan, B. (1977). Institutionalized organizations: Formal structure as myth and ceremony. *American Journal of Sociology, 83*(2), 340–363. doi:10.1086/226550

Meyer-Krahmer, F., & Schmoch, U. (1998). Science-based technologies: University–industry interactions in four fields. *Research Policy, 27*(8), 835–851. doi:10.1016/S0048-7333(98)00094-8

Miles, M. B., & Huberman, A. M. (1994). *Qualitative data analysis: An expanded sourcebook.* London: Sage.

Ministry of Education and Science. (2014). *Statistics on the higher education sector.* Retrieved June 30, 2014, from http://www.meds.gov.mn

Ministry of Science, Education and Sports, Republic of Croatia. (1997). *Pravilnik o načinu i uvjetima napredovanja u struci i promicanju u položajna zvanja odgojitelja i stručnih suradnika u dječjim vrtićima [Ordinance on the conditions and opportunities for promotion in profession and promotion in position titles of preschool teachers and associates in Croatian kindergartens].* Zagreb, Croatia: Ministry of Science, Education and Sports.

Mintzberg, H. (1979). *The structuring of organizations.* London: Prentice-Hall.

Miranda, L., Morais, C., Alves, P., & Dias, P. (2011). Redes sociais na aprendizagem. In D. Barros, C. Neves, F. Seabra, J. Moreira, & S. Henriques (Eds.), Educação e tecnologia: Reflexão, inovação e práticas (pp. 211-230). Lisboa: Universidade Aberta.

Miskovic, M. (2009). Roma education in Europe: In support of the discourse of race. *Pedagogy, Culture & Society, 17*(2), 201–220. doi:10.1080/14681360902934442

Mohrman, K. (2008). The emerging global model with chinese characteristics. *Higher Education Policy, 21*(1), 29–48. doi:10.1057/palgrave.hep.8300174

Moise, I. (2013, September 19). UNICEF, the Cilibia school, and the fight against school dropout. *Sanatatea buzoiana.* Retrieved from http://www.sanatateabuzoiana.ro/

Moldoveanu, M., & Baum, J. (2008). *The epistemic structure and dynamics of social networks.* Science Research Network Paper No 88795. Available at SSRN: http://ssrn.com/abstract=1115311

Moolenaar, N. M., & Sleegers, P. J. C. (2010). Social networks, trust and innovation - The role of relationships in supporting an innovative climate in Dutch schools. In A. J. Daly (Ed.), *Social network theory and educational change* (pp. 235–160). Cambridge, MA: Harvard Education Press.

Moorman, J., & Bowker, A. (2011). The university Facebook experience: The role of social networking on the quality of interpersonal relationship. *The American Association of Behavioral and Social Sciences Journal (AABSS), 15*, 1-23. Retrieved February 15, 2014, from http://aabss.org/Journal2011/04MoormanFinal.pdf

Morais, N. (2012). *O género e o uso das tecnologias da comunicação no ensino superior público Português.* (PhD thesis). Universidade de Aveiro, Aveiro, Portugal.

Morais, N., Batista, J., & Ramos, F. (2011). Caracterização das actividades de aprendizagem promovidas através das tecnologia da comunicação no ensino superior público Português. *Indagatio Didactica, 3*(3), 6–18.

Muller, J. (2009). Forms of knowledge and curriculum coherence. *Journal of Education and Work, 22*(3), 205–226. doi:10.1080/13639080902957905

Murphy, N., Bain, J., & Conrad, L. (2007). Orientations to research higher degree supervision. *Higher Education, 53*(2), 209–234. doi:10.1007/s10734-005-5608-9

Murray, F. (2004). The role of academic inventors in entrepreneurial firms: Sharing the laboratory life. *Research Policy, 33*(4), 643–659. doi:10.1016/j.respol.2004.01.013

Musselin, C. (2005). European academic labour markets in transition. *Higher Education, 49*(1/2), 135–154. doi:10.1007/s10734-004-2918-2

Musselin, C. (2005). *Le marché des universitaires.* Paris: Science Po Les Presses.

Musselin, C. (2006). Are universities specific organizations? In G. Krücken, A. Kosmützky, & M. Torka (Eds.), *Towards a multiversity? Universities between global trends and national traditions* (pp. 63–84). Bielefeld, UK: Transcript.

Musselin, C. (2007). Are universities specific organisations? In G. Krücken, A. Kosmützky, & M. Torka (Eds.), *Towards a multiversity? Universities between global trends and national traditions* (pp. 63–84). Bielefeld, Germany: Transcript Verlag.

Musselin, C. (2007). *The transformation of academic work: Facts and analysis.* Center for Studies in Higher Education.

Musselin, C. (2009). The side effects of the bologna process on national institutional settings: The case of France. In A. Amaral, G. Neave, C. Musselin, & P. Maassen (Eds.), *European integration and the governance of higher education and research* (pp. 181–205). Dordrecht, The Netherlands: Springer. doi:10.1007/978-1-4020-9505-4_8

Nackerud, S., & Scaletta, K. (2008). Blogging in the academy. *New Directions for Student Services, 124*(124), 71–87. doi:10.1002/ss.296

Nahapiet, J., & Ghoshal, S. (1998). Social capital, intellectual capital, and the organizational advantage. *Academy of Management Review, 23*, 242–266.

National Committee of Inquiry into Higher Education (NCIHE). (1997). *Higher education in the learning society.* Norwich: Crown Copyright.

National Strategy for Higher Education to 2030. (2011). Dublin: Department of Education and Skills.

Nationalencyklopedin. (Ed.). (2010). *Världens 100 största språk 2010, the world's 100 largest languages in 2010.* Retrieved February 15, 2014, from http://www.ne.se/spr%C3%A5k/v%C3%A4rldens-100-st%C3%B6rsta-spr%C3%A5k-2010

Neave, G. (2009). Institutional autonomyu 2010-2020: A tale of Elan – Two steps back to make one very large leap forward. In B. Kehm, J. Huisman, & B. Stensaker (Eds.), *The European higher education area: Perspectives on a moving target* (pp. 3–22). Rotterdam, The Netherlands: Sense Publishers.

Neave, G., & Rhoades, G. (1987). The academic estate in Western Europe. In B. Clark (Ed.), *The academic profession: National, disciplinary, and institutional settings* (pp. 211–270). Los Angeles, CA: University of California Press.

Neave, G., & van Vught, F. (Eds.). (1991). *Prometheus bound: The changing relationship between government and higher education in Western Europe*. Oxford, UK: Pergamon.

Nelson, R. R. (1993). *National innovation systems: A comparative analysis*. Oxford, UK: Oxford University Press.

Nerad, M. (2004). The PhD in the US: Criticisms, facts, and remedies. *Higher Education Policy, 17*(2), 183–199. doi:10.1057/palgrave.hep.8300050

Nerad, M., & Heggelund, M. (2008). *Toward a global PhD? Forces and forms in doctoral education worldwide*. University of Washington Press.

Neuman, W. L. (2004). *Basics of social research: Qualitative and quantitative approaches*. Pearson Education Incorporated.

Newman, M. E. J. (2006). Modularity and community structure in networks. *Proceedings of the National Academy of Sciences of the United States of America, 103*(23), 8577–8582. doi:10.1073/pnas.0601602103 PMID:16723398

Niemi, H. (2007). The Bologna process and the teacher education curriculum. In *Proceedings of the European Union Conference: Teacher Professional Development for the Quality and Equity of Lifelong Learning* (pp. 50-65). Lisbon: Ministry of Education.

Nkuyubwatsi, B. (2014). Cultural translation in massive open online courses (MOOCs). *eLearning Papers, 37*, 23-32. Retrieved from http://www.openeducationeuropa.eu/en/paper/experiences-and-best-practices-and-around-moocs

Nonaka, I. (1994). A dynamic theory of organizational knowledge creation. *Organization Science, 5*(1), 14–37. doi:10.1287/orsc.5.1.14

Nonaka, I., & Nishiguchi, T. (1995). *The knowledge-creating company*. New York: Oxford University Press.

Noordegraaf, M. (2007). From "pure" to "hybrid" professionalism: Present-day professionalism in ambiguous public domains. *Administration & Society, 39*(6), 761–785. doi:10.1177/0095399707304434

Nowotny, H., Scott, P., & Gibbons, M. (2002). *Re-thinking science: Knowledge and the public in an age of uncertainty*. Cambridge, MA: Polity Press.

Nybom, T. (2007). A rule-governed community of scholars: The Humboldt vision in the history of the European university. In P. Maassen & J. P. Olsen (Eds.), *University dynamics and European integration* (pp. 55–80). Dordrecht, The Netherlands: Springer. doi:10.1007/978-1-4020-5971-1_3

O'Connell, T., & Dyment, J. (2006). Reflections on using journals in higher education: A focus group discussion with faculty. *Assessment & Evaluation in Higher Education, 31*(6), 671–691. doi:10.1080/02602930600760884

O'Higgins, N. (2009). *It's not that I'm racist, it's that they are Roma: Roma discrimination and returns to education in South Eastern Europe*. IZA discussion papers, No 4208. Retrieved from http://nbn-resolving.de/um:nbn:de:101:1-2009061932

O'Neill, G., Moore, S., & McMullen, B. (Eds.). (2005). *Emerging issues in the practice of university learning and teaching*. Dublin: AISHE.

O'Neill, R., & Colley, A. (2006). Gender and status effects in student e-mails to staff. *Journal of Computer Assisted Learning, 22*(5), 360–367. doi:10.1111/j.1365-2729.2006.00186.x

O'Nions, H. (2010). Divide and teach: Educational inequality and the Roma. *International Journal of Human Rights, 14*(3), 464–489. doi:10.1080/13642980802704304

OECD. (1996). *The knowledge-based economy: General distribution*. Paris: OECD. Retrieved February 15, 2014, from http://www.oecd.org/science/sci-tech/1913021.pdf

OECD. (2004). *Review of national policies for education: Review of higher education in Ireland.* Paris: Organisation for Economic Cooperation and Development.

OECD. (2005). *Building competitive regions: Strategies and governance.* Paris: Organisation for Economic Cooperation and Development.

OECD. (2013). *Innovative learning environments.* Paris: OCDE. Retrieved February 20, 2014, from http://www.oecd-ilibrary.org/deliver/fulltext?contentType=%2fns%2fOECDBook%2c%2fns%2fBook&itemId=%2fcontent%2fbook%2f9789264203488-en&mimeType=freepreview&containerItemId=%2fcontent%2fserial%2f20769679&accessItemIds=&redirecturl=http%3a%2f%2fwww.keepeek.com%2fDigital-Asset-Management%2foecd%2feducation%2finnovative-learning-environments_9789264203488-en&isPreview=true

OECD. (2013). *PISA 2015: Draft collaborative problem solving framework, March 2013.* Retrieved February 15, 2014, from http://www.oecd.org/pisa/pisaproducts/Draft%20PISA%202015%20Collaborative%20Problem%20Solving%20Framework%20.pdf

OECD/JRC. (2008). *Handbook on constructing composite indicators – Methodology and user guide.* Paris: OECD. Retrieved from http://www.oecd.org/dataoecd/37/42/42495745.pdf

Óhidy, A. (2008). *Lifelong learning interpretations of an education policy in Europe.* Wiesbaden: Verlag für Sozialwissenschaften.

Okazaki, S., & Mendez, F. (2013). Perceived ubiquity in mobile services. *Journal of Interactive Marketing, 27*(2), 98–111. doi:10.1016/j.intmar.2012.10.001

Olah, S. (2009). The school dropout in Bihor County: A qualitative approach. *Revista Universitara de Sociologie, 1*(11), 95–128.

Oliver, B., & Goerke, V. (2007). Australian undergraduates' use and ownership of emerging technologies: Implications and opportunities for creating engaging learning experiences for the net generation. *Australasian Journal of Educational Technology, 23*(2), 171–186.

Olivier, C. (1991). Strategic responses to institutional process. *Academy of Management Review, 16*(1), 145–179.

Olmos-Peñuela, J., Castro-Martíncz, E., & D'Este, P. (2014). Knowledge transfer activities in social sciences and humanities: Explaining the interactions of research groups with non-academic agents. *Research Policy, 43*(4), 696–706. doi:10.1016/j.respol.2013.12.004

Olsen, J. P. (2009). Change and continuity: An institutional approach to institutions of democratic government. *European Political Science Review, 1*(1), 3–32. doi:10.1017/S1755773909000022

Organisation for Economic Cooperation and Development (OECD). (2004). *Review of higher education in Ireland.* Paris: OECD.

Organisation for Economic Cooperation and Development (OECD). (2011). *Education at a glance.* Paris: OECD. Accessed online at http://www.oecdlibrary.org/docserver/download/fulltext/9611051ec008.pdf

Osbourne, M., Marks, A., & Turner, E. (2004). Becoming a mature student: How adult applicants weigh the advantages and disadvantages of becoming a mature student. *Higher Education, 48*(3), 219–315.

Owen-Smith, J. (2005). Trends and transitions in the institutional environment for public and private science. *Higher Education, 49*(1-2), 91–117. doi:10.1007/s10734-004-2916-4

Owen-Smith, J., & Powell, W. W. (2004). Knowledge networks as channels and conduits: The effects of spillovers in the Boston biotechnology community. *Organization Science, 15*(1), 5–21. doi:10.1287/orsc.1030.0054

Palfreyman, D., & Tapper, T. (2008). *Structuring mass higher education: The role of elite institutions.* New York: Routledge.

Pantazi, R. (2013, October 1). Mihnea Costoiu, the delegated minister for the higher education: The number of students in public universities has grown by approximately 10% from last year. *HotNews.* Retrieved from http://www.hotnews.ro/stiri-esential-15701687-mihnea-costoiu-ministrul-delegat-pentru-invatamant-superior-numarul-studentilor-universitatile-publice-crescut-aproximativ-10-fata-anul-trecut.htm

Pantea, M.-C. (2014). Affirmative action in Romania's higher education: Roma students' perceived meanings and dilemmas. *British Journal of Sociology of Education*. doi:10.1080/01425692.2013.869172

Paradeise, C., Reale, E., Bleiklie, I., & Ferlie, E. (2009). *University governance*. Springer. doi:10.1007/978-1-4020-9515-3

Paradise, C., Reale, E., Bleiklie, I., & Ferlie, E. (Eds.). (2009). *University governance: Western European comparative perspectives*. Dordrecht, The Netherlands: Springer.

Park, C. (2005). New variant PhD: The changing nature of the doctorate in the UK. *Journal of Higher Education Policy and Management*, *27*(2), 189–207. doi:10.1080/13600800500120068

Park, C. (2007). *Redefining the doctorate*. York, UK: The Higher Education Academy.

Park, C. (2008). *The taught postgraduate student experience: Overview of higher education academy survey*. York, UK: The Higher Education Academy.

Parsons, D., Hill, I., Holland, J., & Wills, D. (2012). *Impact of teaching development programmes in higher education*. York, UK: Higher Education Academy.

Patrício, M., & Gonçalves, V. (2010). Utilização educativa do Facebook no ensino superior. In *Proceedings of the l Conference Learning and Teaching in Higher Education* (pp. 1-15). Évora: Universidade de Évora, Gabinete para a Promoção do Sucesso Académico.

Pearson, M., & Brew, A. (2002). Research training and supervision development. *Studies in Higher Education*, *27*(2), 135–150. doi:10.1080/03075070220119986c

Pearson, M., & Kayrooz, C. (2004). Enabling critical reflection on research supervisory practice. *The International Journal for Academic Development*, *9*(1), 99–116. doi:10.1080/1360144042000296107

Pempek, T., Yermolayeva, Y., & Calvert, S. (2009). College students' social networking experiences on Facebook. *Journal of Applied Developmental Psychology*, *30*(3), 227–238. doi:10.1016/j.appdev.2008.12.010

Perkmann, M., Tartari, V., McKelvey, M., Autio, E., Broström, A., & D'Este, P. et al. (2013). Academic engagement and commercialisation: A review of the literature on university–industry relations. *Research Policy*, *42*(2), 423–442. doi:10.1016/j.respol.2012.09.007

Perry, B., & May, T. (2006). Excellence, relevance and the university: The "missing middle" in socio-economic engagement. *Journal of Higher Education in Africa*, *4*(3), 69–92.

Petersen, E. V. (2007). Negotiating academicity: Postgraduate research supervision as category boundary work. *Studies in Higher Education*, *32*(4), 475–487. doi:10.1080/03075070701476167

Petrović-Sočo, B., Slunjski, E., & Šagud, M. (2005). A new learning paradigm – A new roles of preschool teachers in the educational process. *Zbornik Učiteljske Akademije u Zagrebu*, *7*(2), 329-340.

Phelps, C., Heidl, R., & Wadhwa, A. (2012). Knowledge, networks, and knowledge networks. *Journal of Management*, *38*(4), 1115–1166. doi:10.1177/0149206311432640

Philips, S. U. (1976). Access to power and maintenance of ethnic identity as goals of multicultural education: Are they compatible? *Anthropology & Education Quarterly*, *7*(4), 30–32. doi:10.1525/aeq.1976.7.4.05x1657s

PIAAC. (2012). *Program for the international assessment of adult competencies*. Retrieved February 15, 2014, from http://nces.ed.gov/surveys/piaac

Picciano, A., Dziuban, C., & Graham, C. (2013). *Blended learning: Research perspectives* (Vol. 2). London: Routledge.

Pickering, A. (2006). Learning about university teaching: Reflections on a research study investigating influences for change. *Teaching in Higher Education*, *11*(3), 319–335. doi:10.1080/13562510600680756

Pinheiro, R., Normann, R., & Johnsen, H. C. (2012). *Knowledge structures and patterns of external engagement*. Paper presented at the 34th Annual EAIR (European Higher Education Society) Forum. Stavanger, Norway.

Pinheiro, R. (2012). Knowledge and the 'Europe of the regions': The case of the high north. In M. Kwiek & P. Maassen (Eds.), *National higher education reforms in a European context: Comparative reflections on Poland and Norway* (pp. 179–208). Frankfurt, Germany: Peter Lang Publishing Group.

Pinheiro, R. (2012). University ambiguity and institutionalization: A tale of three regions. In R. Pinheiro, P. Benneworth, & G. A. Jones (Eds.), *Universities and regional development: A critical assessment of tensions and contradictions* (pp. 35–55). Milton Park, UK: Routledge.

Pinheiro, R., Benneworth, P., & Jones, G. A. (Eds.). (2012). *Universities and regional development: A critical assessment of tensions and contradictions.* Milton Park, UK: Routledge.

Pinheiro, R., & Stensaker, B. (2013). Designing the entrepreneurial university: The interpretation of a global idea. *Public Organization Review, 13*(2), 1–20. doi:10.1007/s11115-013-0241-z

Pinto, M., Souza, F., Nogueira, F., Balula, A., Pedro, L., Pombo, L., et al. (2012). Tracing the use of communication technology in higher education: A literature review. In L. Chova, A. Martínez, & C. Torres (Eds.), *Proceedings of the 6th International Technology, Education and Development Conference* (pp. 850-859). Valencia: INTED2012.

Piquer, J. M. (2012). *Internet en Chile: 20 años después.* Retrieved February 19, 2014, from http://www.fayerwayer.com/2012/01/internet-en-chile-20-anos-despues/

Platts, J. (2003). Developing competence and trust: Maintaining the heart of a profession. *Professional Ethics (Gainesville, Fla.), 11*(1), 3–18. doi:10.5840/profethics20031116

Polkinghorne, D. E. (2004). *Practice and the human sciences: The case for a judgment based practice of care.* Albany, NY: State University of New York Press.

Pombo, L., Morais, N., Batista, J., Pinto, M., Coelho, M., & Moreira, A. (2013). Five years of communication technologies use in higher education in Portugal: An overview. In M. Marcelino, M. Gomes, & A. Mendes (Eds.), *XV International Symposium on Computers in Education* (pp. 99-103). Instituto Politécnico de Viseu.

Porritt, V. (2014). Evaluating the impact of professional learning. In S. Cowley (Ed.), *Challenging professional learning.* Abingdon, UK: Routledge.

Porter, M. E. (1998). *Competitive advantage: Creating and sustaining superior performance.* New York: Free Press.

Posavec, K., & Hrvatic, N. (2000). Intercultural education and Roma in Croatia. *Intercultural Education, 11*(1), 93–105. doi:10.1080/14675980050005424

Powell, J., & Dayson, K. (2013). Engagement and the idea of the civic university. In P. Benneworth (Ed.), *University engagement with socially excluded communities* (pp. 143–162). Dordrecht, The Netherlands: Springer. doi:10.1007/978-94-007-4875-0_8

Powell, W. W., & Owen-Smith, J. (2002). The new world of knowledge production in the life sciences. In S. B. Brint (Ed.), *The future of the city of intellect: the changing American university* (pp. 107–131). Stanford, CA: Stanford University Press.

Powell, W. W., & Snellman, K. (2004). The knowledge economy. *Annual Review of Sociology, 30*(1), 199–220. doi:10.1146/annurev.soc.29.010202.100037

Prescott, A., & Hellsten, M. (2005). Hanging together even with non-native speakers: The international student transition experience. In P. Ninnes & M. Hellsten (Eds.), *Internationalizing higher education: Critical explorations of pedagogy andf policy* (pp. 75–95). Springer Publications. doi:10.1007/1-4020-3784-8_5

Prinsloo, M., & Rowsell, J. (2012). Digital literacies as placed resources in the globalised periphery. *Language and Education, 26*(4), 271–277. doi:10.1080/09500782.2012.691511

Prosser, M., Rickinson, M., Bence, V., Hanbury, A., & Kulej, M. (2006). *Formative evaluation of accredited programmes.* York, UK: Higher Education Academy.

Provis, C. (2004). Guanxi, relationships and ethics. *Australian Journal of Professional and Applied Ethics, 6*(1), 47–57.

Puente, X. (2007). New method using wikis and forums to evaluate individual contributions in cooperative work while promoting experiential learning: results from preliminary experience. In *Proceedings of the WikiSym 2007 - International Symposium on Wikis - Wikis at Work in the World: Open, Organic, Participatory Media for the 21st Century* (pp. 87-92). Montréal, Canada: WikiSym 07. doi:10.1145/1296951.1296961

Quality Assurance Agency for Higher Education (QAA). (2012). *UK quality code for higher education: Part B: Assuring and enhancing academic quality: Chapter B11: Research degrees*. Retrieved August 2012, from http://www.qaa.ac.uk/publications/informationandguidance/pages/quality-code-B11.aspx

Quality Assurance Agency for Higher Education. (2008). The framework for higher education qualifications in England, Wales and Northern Ireland. Mansfield, UK: QAA's Publications.

Quivy, R., & Campenhoudt, L. (2005). *Manual de investigação em ciências sociais* (4th ed.). Lisboa: Gradiva.

Ramey, C. T., & Suarez, T. M. (1985). Early intervention and the early experience paradigm: Toward a better framework for social policy. *Journal of Children in Contemporary Society*, *17*(1), 1–13. doi:10.1300/J274v17n01_01

Raviv, A., Bar-Tal, D., Raviv, A., & Abin, R. (1993). Measuring epistemic authority: Studies of politicians and professors. *European Journal of Personality*, *7*(2), 119–138. doi:10.1002/per.2410070204

Rawlins, P., & Kehrwald, B. (2010). Education technology in teacher education: Overcoming challenges, realizing opportunities. In R. Luppicini & A. Haghi (Eds.), *Cases on digital technologies in higher education: Issues and challenges* (pp. 50–63). Hershey, PA: IGI Global. doi:10.4018/978-1-61520-869-2.ch004

Reale, E. (2014). Challenges in higher education research: The use of quantitative tools in comparative analyses. *Higher Education*, *67*(4), 409–422. doi:10.1007/s10734-013-9680-2

Reason, P., & Bradbury, H. (Eds.). (2001). *Handbook of action research: Participative inquiry and practice*. London: Sage.

Recotillet, I. (2007). PhD Graduates with post-doctoral qualification in the private sector: Does it pay off? *Labour*, *21*(3), 473–502. doi:10.1111/j.1467-9914.2007.00385.x

Redfield, R., Linton, R., & Herskovits, M. J. (1936). Memorandum for the study of acculturation. *American Anthropologist*, *38*(1), 149–152. doi:10.1525/aa.1936.38.1.02a00330

Reedy, G. B. (2008). PowerPoint, interactive whiteboards, and the visual culture of technology in schools. *Technology, Pedagogy and Education*, *17*(2), 143–162. doi:10.1080/14759390802098623

Regí, C., & Lorenzo, N. (2014). *Nuevas estrategias para la gestión de contenidos en educación: Análisis de la situación*. Retrieved February 15, 2014, from http://newsneus.wordpress.com/curso-mooc-pel/

Reid, A., & Marshall, S. (2009). Institutional development fot the enhancement of research and research training. *The International Journal for Academic Development*, *14*(2), 145–157. doi:10.1080/13601440902970031

Rhoads, R. A., Berdan, J., & Toven-Lindsey, B. (2013). The open courseware movement in higher education: Unmasking power and raising questions about the movement's democratic potential. *Educational Theory*, *63*(1), 87–110. doi:10.1111/edth.12011

Ribeiro, F. M., & Lubbers, M. (2013). *Social networks and knowledge creation in higher education: The role of similarity and tie strength*. Paper presented at the 10th Conference of Applications of Social Network Analysis. Zurich, Switzerland.

Ribeiro, F. M. (forthcoming). Interdisciplinarity in ferment: The role of knowledge networks and department affiliation. *Technological Forecasting and Social Change*.

Richardson, J. (1995). Mature students in higher education: An investigation of approaches to studying and academic performance. *Studies in Higher Education*, *20*(1), 5–17. doi:10.1080/03075079512331381760

Rinaldi, C. (2000). Utopia? Considerazioni tra passato e futuro sull' educare nelle istituzioni infantili. In G. Rabitti & P. Rametta (Eds.), Intorno a un percorso di formazione, il quaderno del now (pp. 55-61). Municipality of Reggio Emilia, Italy: Reggio Children.

Rinaldi, C. (2006). *In dialogue with Reggio Emilia: Listening, researching and learning*. New York: Routledge. doi:10.4324/9780203317730

Rios-Aguilar, C., Kiyama, J. M., Gravitt, M., & Moll, L. C. (2011). Funds of knowledge for the poor and forms of capital for the rich? A capital approach to examining funds of knowledge. *Theory and Research in Education*, 9(2), 163–184. doi:10.1177/1477878511409776

Robinson, K. (1999). *All our futures: Creativity, culture and education*. London: National Advisory Committee on Creative and Cultural Education.

Roldão, M. C. (2007). Research-based teacher education and reflective practice: Teacher professional development for the quality and equity of lifelong learning. In *Proceedings of the Council of the European Union Conference: Teacher Professional Development for the Quality and Equity of Lifelong Learning* (pp. 39-49). Lisbon: Ministry of Education.

Roma Education Fund Romania. (2014, August 7). *Mission*. Retrieved from http://romaeducationfund.ro/en/

Rooney, D., Hearn, G., & Ninan, A. (2008). *Handbook on the knowledge economy*. Cheltenham, UK: Edward Elgar.

Ros-Rodríguez, J., Encinas, T., Picazo, R., Labadía, A., Artalejo, A., Gutiérrez-Martín, Y., & Gilabert, J.A. (2011). Use of wikis as collaborative tools in a b-learning course of Pharmacology. In L. Chova, I. Torres, & A. Martínez (Eds.), *Proceedings of INTED2011 - International Conference on Technology, Education and Development* (pp. 586-590). Valencia: INTED2011.

Roth, M., & Moisa, F. (2011). The right to education of Roma children in Romania. *International Journal of Children's Rights*, 19(3), 501–522. doi:10.1163/157181811X584587

Rowland, S. (2002). Overcoming fragmentation in professional life: The challenge for academic development. *Higher Education Quarterly*, 56(1), 52–64. doi:10.1111/1468-2273.00202

Russell, D. R. (1991). *Writing in the academic disciplines, 1870-1990: A circular history*. Southern Illinois University Press.

Sá-Chaves, I. (2007). *Formação, conhecimento e supervisão: Contributos nas áreas da formação de professores e de outros profissionais*. Aveiro, Portugal: Universidade de Aveiro.

Sally, D. (1995). Conversation and cooperation in social dilemmas: A meta-analysis of experiments from 1958 to 1992. *Rationality and Society*, 7(1), 58–92. doi:10.1177/1043463195007001004

Santos, C., Pedro, L., Ramos, F., & Moreira, A. (2011). Sapo campus: What users really think about an institutionally supported PLE. In *Proceedings of PLE Conference 2011*. Southampton, UK: Academic Press.

Santos, B. S. (2004). *A universidade do século XXI: Para uma reforma democrática eda universidade* (pp. xix–lxii). São Paulo: Cortez Editora.

Santos, B. S., Nunes, J. A., & Meneses, M. P. (2007). Opening up the canon of knowledge and recognition of difference. In B. S. Santos (Ed.), *Another knowledge is possible*. London: Verso.

Sawir, E. (2005). Language difficulties of international students in Australia: The effects of prior learning experience. *International Education Journal*, 6(5), 567–580.

Scardamalia, M. (2002). Collective cognitive responsibility for the advancement of knowledge. In B. Smith (Ed.), *Liberal education in a knowledge society*. Chicago: Open Court. Retrieved February 15, 2014, from http://ikit.org/fulltext/2002CollectiveCog.pdf

Scardamalia, M. (2004). *Ask the experts: What's the next revolution in education going to be?* [Video series]. Toronto: Ontario Institute for Studies in Education, University of Toronto. Retrieved February 15, 2014, from https://tspace.library.utoronto.ca/handle/1807/2994

Scardamalia, M., & Bereiter, C. (2003). Knowledge building. In J.W. Guthrie (Ed.), *Encyclopedia of education* (2nd ed.). New York: Macmillan Reference. Retrieved February 15, 2014, from http://ikit.org/ulltext/2003_knowledge_building.pdf

Schaffer, S., Roberts, L., Raj, K., & Delbourgo, J. (2009). *The brokered world: Go-betweens and global intelligence, 1770-1820*. Sagamore Beach, MA: Science History Publications/Watson Publishers.

Schank, R. C. (2011). *Teaching minds: How cognitive science can save our schools.* New York: Teachers College Press.

Schlosser, L. A., & Simonson, M. (2009). *Distance education: Definitions and glossary of terms* (3rd ed.). Charlotte, NC: Information Age Publisher.

Schneckenberg, D. (2009). Understanding the real barriers to technology-enhanced innovation in higher education. *Educational Research, 51*(4), 411–424. doi:10.1080/00131880903354741

Schvey, A., Flaherty, M., & Higgins, T. (2005). The children left behind: Roma access to education in contemporary Romania. *Fordham International Law Journal, 29*(6), 1155–2006.

Scott, W. R. (1992). *Organizations: Rational, natural, and open systems.* Englewood Cliffs, NJ: Prentice Hall.

Seeber, M., Lepori, B., Montauti, M., Enders, J., de Boer, H., & Weyer, E. et al. (2014). European universities as complete organizations? Understanding identity, hierarchy and rationality in public organizations. *Public Management Review.*

Selwyn, N. (2010). Degrees of digital division: Reconsidering digital inequalities and contemporary higher education. *Redefining the Digital Divide in Higher Education, 7*(1), 33-41. Retrieved October 15, 2012, from http://rusc.uoc.edu/ojs/index.php/rusc/article/view/v7n1_selwyn/v7n1_selwyn

Selwyn, N. (2013). *Discourses of digital 'disruption' in education: A critical analysis.* Paper presented at the Fifth International Roundtable on Discourse Analysis, Hong Kong.

Selwyn, N. (2007). The use of computer technology in university teaching and learning: A critical perspective. *Journal of Computer Assisted Learning, 23*(2), 83–94. doi:10.1111/j.1365-2729.2006.00204.x

Selwyn, N. (2008). An investigation of differences in undergraduates' academic use of the internet. *Active Learning in Higher Education, 9*(1), 11–22. doi:10.1177/1469787407086744

Selwyn, N. (2008). From state of the art to state of the actual? Introduction to a special issue. *Technology, Pedagogy and Education, 17*(2), 83–87. doi:10.1080/14759390802098573

Selwyn, N. (2011). *Schools and schooling in the digital age: A critical analysis.* Hoboken, NJ: Taylor & Francis.

Senge, P., Kleiner, A., Roberts, C., Ross, R., Roth, G., & Smith, B. (2003). *Ples promjene – izazovi u razvoju učećih organizacija [The dance of the change – The challenges in development of learning organizations].* Zagreb: Mozaik knjiga.

Shinn, T. (1988). Hiérarchies des chercheurs et formes de recherche. *Actes de la Recherche en Sciences Sociales, 74*(1), 2–22. doi:10.3406/arss.1988.2430

Siemens, G. (2004). Connectivism: A learning theory for the digital age. *Elearnspace Everything Elearning.* Retrieved February 15, 2014, from http://www.elearnspace.org/Articles/connectivism.htm

Siemens, G. (2006). Knowing knowledge. *Elearnspace Everything Elearning.* Retrieved February 15, 2014, from http://www.elearnspace.org/KnowingKnowledge_LowRes.pdf

Siemens, G. (2009). *Connectivism and connective knowledge.* Retrieved February 15, 2014, from http://ltc.umanitoba.ca/connectivism/?p=189

Siemens, G. (2009). *Connectivism and the role of the teacher.* Retrieved February 15, 2014, from http://www.connectivism.ca/?p=220

Siemens, G., & Tittenberger, P. (2009). Handbook of emerging technologies for learning. Winnipeg, Canada: Learning Technologies Centre, University of Manitoba. Retrieved from http://umanitoba.ca/learning_technologies/cetl/HETL.pdf

Silva, F. (2012). *A utilização de recursos educativos digitais no ensino superior a distância: A perceção do estudante e o modo como utiliza os recursos digitais para fins educativos.* (Master thesis). Universidade Aberta, Lisbon, Portugal.

Slaughter, S., & Leslie, L. L. (1997). *Academic capitalism: Politics, policies, and the entrepreneurial university.* Baltimore, MD: The John Hopkins University Press.

Slowey, M. (2012). Lifelong learning and higher education in Ireland: Turbulent times. In M. Slowey & H. G. Schuetze (Eds.), *Global perspectives on higher education and lifelong learners* (pp. 60–81). London: Routledge.

Slowey, M., Kozina, E., & Tan, E. (2014). *The voices of Irish academics: Perspectives on professional development.* Dublin: All Ireland Society for Higher Education.

Slowey, M., & Schuetze, H. G. (2012). *Global perspectives on higher education and lifelong learners.* London: Routledge.

Slunjski, E. (2008). *Dječji vrtić: Zajednica koja uči: mjesto dijaloga, suradnje i zajedničkog učenja [A kindergarten: The learning community: The place for dialog, cooperation and mutual learning].* Zagreb: Spektar Media.

Slunjski, E. (2011). *Kurikulum ranog odgoja – Istraživanje i konstrukcija [Early childhood education curriculum – Research and construction].* Zagreb: Školska Knjiga.

Smyth, R. (2004). Exploring the usefulness of a conceptual framework as a research tool: A researcher's reflections. *Issues in Educational Research, 14*(2), 167–180.

Snyder, I., Marginson, S., & Lewis, T. (2007). An alignment of the planets: Mapping the intersections between pedagogy, technology and management in Australian universities. *Journal of Higher Education Policy and Management, 29*(2), 187–202. doi:10.1080/13600800701351769

Soothill, K. (2006). *Experience of supervision: Continuities and change.* Retrieved January 2009, from http://www.lancs.ac.uk/celt/celtweb/files/KeithSoothill.pdf

Sosa, M. (2007). *Faculty & research: Where do creative interactions come from? The role of tie content and social networks.* ISEAD.

Sousa, D. (2011). *How the brain learns* (4th ed.). Thousand Oaks, CA: Corwin.

Spack, R. (1998). Cultural backgrounds: What should we know about multilingual students? *TESOL Quarterly, 32*(4), 740–746. doi:10.2307/3588006

Staker, H., & Horn, M. B. (2012). *Classifying K-12 blended learning.* INNOSIGHT Institute. Retrieved from http://files.eric.ed.gov/fulltext/ED535180.pdf

Stake, R. E. (2004). *The art of case study research.* Thousand Oaks, CA: SAGE.

Stake, R. E. (Ed.). (2004). *Standards-based and responsive evaluation.* Thousand Oaks, CA: Sage Publications.

Steel, C., & Levy, M. (2009). *Creativity and constraint: Understanding teacher beliefs and the use of LMS technologies.* Paper presented at the Same Places, Different Spaces, Auckland, New Zealand. Retrieved December 14, 2013, from http://www.ascilite.org.au/conferences/auckland09/procs/steel.pdf

Steele, C. (2012). How the mobile phone is evolving in developing countries. *PC Magazine.* Retrieved February 15, 2014, from http://www.pcmag.com/slideshow/story/297822/how-the-mobile-phone-is-evolving-in-developing-countries

Stefani, L. (Ed.). (2011). *Evaluating the effectives of academic development: Principles and practice.* Abingdon, UK: Routledge.

Stephan, P. E. (1996). The economics of science. *Journal of Economic Literature, 34*(September), 1199–1235.

Stes, A., Clement, M., & Van Petegem, P. (2007). The effectiveness of a faculty training programme: Long-term and institutional impact. *The International Journal for Academic Development, 12*(2), 99–109. doi:10.1080/13601440701604898

Stokes, D. E. (1997). *Pasteur's quadrant: Basic science and technological innovation.* Washington, DC: Brookings Institution Press.

Stoll, L., & Fink, D. (2000). *Mijenjajmo naše škole: Kako unaprijediti djelotvornost i kvalitetu škola [We should change our schools: How to improve effectiveness and quality of schools].* Zagreb: Educa.

Sturdy, S., & Freeman, R. (2014). *Knowledge in policy: Embodied, inscribed, enacted.* Policy Press.

Styles, I., & Radloff, A. (2001). The synergistic thesis: Student and supervisor perspectives. *Journal of Further and Higher Education, 25*(1), 97-106.

Swanson, D. L. (2004). The buck stops here: Why universities must reclaim business ethics education. *Journal of Academic Ethics, 2*(1), 43–61. doi:10.1023/B:JAET.0000039007.06014.24

Tamas, J. (2001). A hidden minority becomes visible Romani refugee children in the schools. *Childhood Education, 77*(5), 295–302. doi:10.1080/00094056.2001.10521653

Tatalović Vorkapić, S., & Vujičić, L. (2012). Do we need positive psychology in Croatian kindergartens? The implementation possibilities evaluated by preschool teachers. *Early Years: An International Journal of Research and Development, 33*(1), 33–44. doi:10.1080/09575146.2012.662214

Tatalović-Vorkapić, S., Vujičić, L., & Čepić, R. (2014). Preschool teacher identity. In P. Breen (Ed.), *Cases on teacher identity, diversity, and cognition in higher education* (pp. 22–60). Hershey, PA: IGI-Global. doi:10.4018/978-1-4666-5990-2.ch002

Taylor, S. (2009). The post-Humboldtian doctorate: Implications for supervisory practice. In iPED Research Network (Eds.), Academic futures: Inquiries into higher education and pedagogy (pp. 61-74). Newcastle upon Tyne, UK: iPED Research Network.

Teichler, U. (1996). Comparative higher education: Potentials and limits. *Higher Education, 32*(4), 431–465. doi:10.1007/BF00133257

Teichler, U. (2009). *Higher education and the world of work: Conseptual frameworks, comparative perspectives, empirical findings.* Rotterdam, The Netherlands: Sense Publishers.

Teichler, U. (2014). Opportunities and problems of comparative higher education research: The daily life of research. *Higher Education, 67*(4), 393–408. doi:10.1007/s10734-013-9682-0

Teichler, U., Arimoto, A., & Cummings, W. K. (2013). *The changing academic profession: Major findings of a comparative survey.* Dordrecht, The Netherlands: Springer. doi:10.1007/978-94-007-6155-1

Teichler, U., & Höhle, E. A. (2013). The academic profession in 12 European countries – The approach of the comparative study. In U. Teichler & E. A. Höhle (Eds.), *The work situation of the academic profession in Europe: Findings of a survey in twelve countries* (pp. 1–11). Dordrecht, The Netherlands: Springer. doi:10.1007/978-94-007-5977-0_1

Tene, O. (2010). Privacy: The new generations. *International Data Privacy Law, 1*(1), 15-27. Retrieved July 26, 2014, from http://idpl.oxfordjournals.org/content/1/1/15.full#xref-fn-78-1

Tess, P. A. (2013). The role of social media in higher education classes (real and virtual) – A literature review. *Computers in Human Behavior, 29*(5), 60–68. doi:10.1016/j.chb.2012.12.032

Tett, L. (2000). I'm working-class and proud of it: Gendered experiences of non-traditional participants in higher education. *Gender and Education, 12*(2), 183–194. doi:10.1080/09540250050009993

THE. (2014). *World rankings 2014.* Accessed 15th March 2014 from http://www.timeshighereducation.co.uk/world-university-rankings/

Theodosiou, M., & Amir-Aslani, A. (2013). The polyvalent scientist: The added value of management training. *Journal of Commercial Biotechnology, 19*(3), 6–9. doi:10.5912/jcb602

Thibaut, J. W., & Kelley, H. H. (1959). *The social psychology of groups.* New York: Wiley.

Thomas, L. (2002). Student retention in higher education: The role of institutional habitus. *Journal of Education Policy, 17*(4), 423–442. doi:10.1080/02680930210140257

Thune, T. (2009). Doctoral students on the university-industry interface: A review of the literature. *Higher Education, 58*(5), 637–651. doi:10.1007/s10734-009-9214-0

Tibebu, D., Bandyopadhyay, T., & Negash, S. (2010). ICT integration efforts in higher education in developing economies: The case of Addis Ababa University, Ethiopia. In R. Luppicini & A. Haghi (Eds.), *Cases on digital technologies in higher education: Issues and challenges* (pp. 279–303). Hershey, PA: IGI Global. doi:10.4018/978-1-61520-869-2.ch019

Tinto, V. (2002). *Taking student retention seriously: Rethinking the first year of college.* Paper presented at the Annual Meeting of the American Association of Collegiate Registrars and Admission Officers, Minneapolis, MN. Retrieved from http://suedweb.syr.edu/Faculty/Vtinto/Files/AACRAOSpeech.pdf

Tinto, V. (1993). *Leaving college: Rethinking the causes and cures of student attrition* (2nd ed.). Chicago: University of Chicago Press.

Tobin, J., Karusawa, M., & Hsueh, Y. (2004). Komatsudani then and now: Continuity and change in a Japanese preschool. *Contemporary Issues in Early Childhood, 5*(2), 128–144. doi:10.2304/ciec.2004.5.2.2

Tomlinson, C. A., & Imbeau, M. B. (2013). *Leading and managing a differentiated classroom.* Alexandria, VA: Association for Supervision and Curriculum Development.

Trant, M. (2006). Creative and innovative teaching in the context of wider access to higher education in Ireland. Paper presented at the 4th Annual International Conference on Teaching and Learning, Galway, Ireland.

Trevino, L. K., Butterfield, K. D., & McCabe, D. L. (1998). The ethical context in organizations: Influences on employee attitudes and behaviors. *Business Ethics Quarterly, 8*(3), 447–476. doi:10.2307/3857431

Trigwell, K., Caballero-Rodrigues, K., & Han, F. (2012). Assessing the impact of a university teaching development programme. *Assessment & Evaluation in Higher Education, 37*(4), 499–511. doi:10.1080/02602938.2010.547929

Trowler, V. (2010). *Student engagement literature review.* Lancaster, UK: Lancaster University.

Tucker, B. (2012). The flipped classroom. *Education Next, 12*(1). Retrieved from http://educationnext.org/the-flipped-classroom

Turner, K., & Pointon, M. L. (2009). *Contextualising the learning of assessment practices: Meeting the academic skills of international students.* Paper presented at the ALTC First-year Experience Curriculum Design Symposium, Queensland, Australia.

UK Council for Graduate Education. (1996). *Quality and standards of postgraduate research degrees.* Retrieved January 2009, from http://www.ukcge.ac.uk/OneStopCMS/Core/CrawlerResourceServer.aspx?resource=6B22F9C5-DC02-4633-9964-579846D4B3A4& mode=link&guid=a57997aa5a9f4450bb141144a86634e6

UNESCO. (2002). *Final report: Forum on the impact of open courseware for higher education in developing countries.* Paris: UNESCO. Retrieved February 15, 2014, from http://unesdoc.unesco.org/images/0012/001285/128515e.pdf

UNESCO. (2009). *Guide to measuring information and communication technologies (ICT) in education.* Quebéc, Canada: UNESCO Institute for Statistics. Retrieved from http://unesdoc.unesco.org/images/0018/001865/186547e.pdf

UNESCO. (2013). *Rethinking education in a changing world: Meeting of the senior experts' group.* Paris: UNESCO. Retrieved February 15, 2014, from http://unesdoc.unesco.org/images/0022/002247/224743e.pdf

University of Adelaide. (2014). *Adelaide business school.* Retrieved 25 June 2014, from http://www.business.adelaide.edu.au/

University of South Australia. (2014). *Business school.* Retrieved 25 June 2014, from http://www.unisa.edu.au/Business/

Välimaa, J., & Hoffman, D. (2008). Knowledge society discourse and higher education. *Higher Education, 56*(3), 265–285. doi:10.1007/s10734-008-9123-7

Vallas, S. P., & Kleinman, D. L. (2008). Contradiction, convergence and the knowledge economy: The confluence of academic and commercial biotechnology. *Socio-Economic Review, 6*(2), 283–311. doi:10.1093/ser/mwl035

van Rooyen, P., Dixon, A., Dixon, G., & Wells, C. (2006). Entry criteria as predictor of performance in an undergraduate nursing degree programme. *Nurse Education Today, 26*(7), 593–600. doi:10.1016/j.nedt.2006.02.002 PMID:16624454 van Vught, F., & Ziegele, F. (2011). *Design and testing the feasibility of a multidimensional global university ranking*. Brussels: Consortium for Higher Education and Research Performance Assessment.

Vang, J., & Asheim, B. (2006). Regions, absorptive capacity and strategic coupling with high-tech TNCs lessons from India and China. *Science, Technology & Society*, *11*(1), 39–66. doi:10.1177/097172180501100103

Veà, A. (2013). *Cómo creamos internet: Grup editorial 62*. Barcelona: S.L.U. Edicions Península.

Velliaris, D. M., & Warner, R. (2009). *Embedding 'learning guides' in a flexible delivery mode: Improving academic acculturation for international students at an Australian university*. Paper presented at the 20th ISANA International Education Conference, Canberra, Australia.

Velliaris, D. M., & Willis, C. R. (2014). Getting personal: An autoethnographic study of the professional identit(ies) of lecturers in an Australian pathway institution. In P. Breen (Ed.), Cases on teacher identity, diversity, and cognition in higher education (pp. 87–110). Hershey, PA: IGI Global. doi:10.4018/978-1-4666-5990-2.ch004

Vercruysse, N., & Proteasa, V. (2012). Transparency tools across the European higher education area. Helsinki: European Association for Quality Assurance in Higher Education (ENQA).

Verhoest, K., Peters, B. G., Bouckaert, G., & Verschuere, B. (2004). The study of organisational autonomy: A conceptual review. *Public Administration and Development*, *24*(2), 101–118. doi:10.1002/pad.316

Vieira, F. (1993). *Supervisão: Uma prática reflexiva de formação de professores*. Rio Tinto: edições ASA.

Vieira, F., Moreira, M.A., Barbosa, I., Paiva, M. & Fernandes, I.S. (2006). *No caleidoscópio da supervisão: Imagens da formação e da pedagogia*. Mangualde: Edições Pedago.

Vilkinas, T. (2008). An exploratory study of the supervision of Ph.D./research students' theses. *Innovative Higher Education*, *32*(5), 297–311. doi:10.1007/s10755-007-9057-5

Vlase, I., & Voicu, M. (2013). Romanian Roma migration: The interplay between structures and agency. *Ethnic and Racial Studies*. doi:10.1080/01419870.2013.809133

Vujičić, L. (2011). *Istraživanje kulture odgojno-obrazovne ustanove [The research of the culture of the preschool institution]*. Zagreb: Mali professor d.o.o.

Vujičić, L. (2008). Research and improvement of one's own practice – Way to development of teachers'/preschool teachers' practical competence. In I. Žogla (Ed.), *Teacher of the 21st century: Quality education for quality teaching* (pp. 184–194). Riga, Latvia: University of Latvia Press.

Vujičić, L., Čepić, R., & Pejić Papak, P. (2010). Afirmation of the concept of new professionalism in the education of preschool teachers: Croatian experiences. In Ch ovaG.L.Belenguer,M.D.CandelT.I. (Eds.), *Proceedings of EDULEARN10 Conference* (pp. 242-250). Valencia, Spain: IATED.

Vukasovic, M., Maassen, P., Nerland, M., Pinheiro, R., Stensaker, B., & Vabø, A. (2012). *Effects of higher education reforms: Change dynamics*. Rotterdam, The Netherlands: Sense Publishers. doi:10.1007/978-94-6209-016-3

Vygotsky, L. (1978). *Mind and society: The development of higher mental processes*. Cambridge, MA: Harvard University Press.

Wainwright, E., & Marandet, E. (2010). Parents in higher education: Impacts of university learning on the self and the family. *Educational Review*, *64*(4), 449–465. doi:10.1080/00131911.2010.487643

Waller, R. (2006). I don't' feel like a 'student' I feel like 'me'! The oversimplification of mature learners' experiences. *Research in Post-Compulsory Education*, *11*(1), 115–130. doi:10.1080/13596740500508019

Wangenge-Ouma, G., & Langa, P. (2010). Universities and the mobilization of claims of excellence for competitive advantage. *Higher Education*, *59*(6), 749–764. doi:10.1007/s10734-009-9278-x

Warschauer, M. (2003). *Technology and social inclusion: Rethinking the digital divide*. Cambridge, MA: The MIT Press.

Washburn, J. (2005). *University Inc.: The corporate corruption of higher education.* New York: Basic Books.

Weinberger, D. (2012). *Too big to know: Rethinking knowledge now that the facts aren't the facts, experts are everywhere, and the smartest person in the room is the room.* London: Basic Books.

Weingart, P. (2000). Interdisciplinarity: The paradoxical discourse. In P. Weingart & N. Stehr (Eds.), *Practising interdisciplinarity* (pp. 25–41). Toronto, Canada: University of Toronto Press Incorporated.

Weingart, P. (2010). A short history of knowledge formations. In R. Frodeman, J. T. Klein, & C. Mitcham (Eds.), *The Oxford handbook of interdisciplinarity* (pp. 3–14). New York: Oxford University Press.

West, L. (1996). *Adults, motivation and higher education: A biographical analysis.* London: Taylor and Francis.

Whipp, J., & Lorentz, R. R. (2009). Cognitive and social help giving in online teaching: An exploratory study. *Educational Technology Research and Development, 57*(2), 169–192. doi:10.1007/s11423-008-9104-7

White, D. S., & Manton, M. (2011). *Open educational resources: The value of reuse in higher education.* Oxford, UK: University of Oxford. Retrieved February 15, 2014, from http://www.jisc.ac.uk/media/documents/programmes/elearning/oer/OERTheValueOfReuseInHigherEducation.pdf

Whitebook, M., Austin, L. J. E., Ryan, S., Kipnis, F., Almaraz, M., & Sakai, L. (2012). *By default or by design? Variations in higher education programs for early care and teachers and their implications for research methodology, policy, and practice.* Berkeley, CA: Center for the Study of Child Care Employment, University of California.

Whitebook, M., Howes, C., & Phillips, D. (1989). *Who cares? Child care teachers and the quality of care in America—Final Report of the National Child Care Staffing Study.* Oakland, CA: Child Care Employee Project.

Whitebook, M., & Ryan, S. (2011). *Degrees in context: Asking the right questions about preparing skilled and effective teachers of young children. NIEER Policy Brief (Issue 22).* New Brunswick, NJ: National Institute for Early Education Research.

White, D. S., & Le-Cornu, A. (2011). Visitors and residents: A new typology for online engagement. *First Monday, 16*(9). doi:10.5210/fm.v16i9.3171

Whitley, R. (2008). Universities as strategic actors: Limitations and variations. In L. Engwall & D. Weaire (Eds.), *The university in the market* (pp. 22–37). London: Portland Press.

Whittle, A., & Spicer, A. (2008). Is actor network theory critique? *Organization Studies, 21*(4), 611–629. doi:10.1177/0170840607082223

Wiley, D., & Hilton, J. III. (2009). Openness, dynamic specialization, and the disaggregated future of higher education. *International Review of Research in Open and Distance Learning, 10*(5), 1–16. Retrieved from http://www.irrodl.org/index.php/irrodl/article/view/768/1414

Witte, J. (2008). Aspired convergence, cherished diversity: Dealing with the contradictions of Bologna. *Tertiary Education and Management, 14*(2), 81–93. doi:10.1080/13583880802051840

World Bank. (2010). *Tertiary education in Mongolia: Meeting the challenges of the global economy* (Report No. 52925 – MN). Human Development Sector Unit, Mongolia Country Management Office, East Asia and Pacific Region.

Yang, D., Sinha, T., Adamson, D., & Rose, C. P. (2013). *Turn on, tune in, drop out: Anticipating student dropouts in massive open online courses.* Retrieved April 30, 2014, from http://lytics.stanford.edu/datadriveneducation/papers/yangetal.pdf

Yin, R. K. (2003). *Case study research, design and methods.* Thousand Oaks, CA: SAGE.

Yin, R. K. (2009). *Case study research: Design and methods* (4th ed.). Thousand Oaks, CA: Sage Publications.

Young, M. (2008). From constructivism to realism in the sociology of the curriculum. *Review of Research in Education, 32*(1), 1–28. doi:10.3102/0091732X07308969

Yuan, L., & Powell, S. (2013). MOOCs and open education: Implications for higher education – A white paper. Bolton, UK: The University of Bolton. Retrieved from http://publications.cetis.ac.uk/2013/667http://publications.cetis.ac.uk/wp-content/uploads/2013/03/MOOCs-and-Open-Education.pdf

Zagzebski, L. T. (2012). *Epistemic authority – A theory of trust, authority and autonomy in belief*. Oxford, UK: Oxford University Press. doi:10.1093/acprof:oso/9780199936472.001.0001

Zamfir, E. (2013). Roma people within the global process of change. *Revista de Cercetare si Interventie Sociala, 40*, 149–165.

Zamfir, E., & Burtea, V. (2012). *The present and future perspectives of Roma culture from the perspective of Roma intellectuals, leaders, and other successful individuals.* Bucharest: The Press, Typography, and Distribution PPB Group.

Zeichner, K., Grant, C., Gay, G., Gillette, M., Valli, L., & Villegas, A. (1998). A research informed vision of good practice in multicultural teacher education: Design principles. *Theory into Practice, 37*(2), 163–171. doi:10.1080/00405849809543800

Zhang, Y., & Mi, Y. (2010). Another look at the language difficulties of international students. *Journal of Studies in International Education, 14*(4), 371–388. doi:10.1177/1028315309336031

Zhao, F. (2003). Transforming quality in research supervision: A knowledge-management approach. *Quality in Higher Education, 9*(2), 187–197. doi:10.1080/13538320308149

Ziman, J. (2000). *Real science: what it is, and what it means.* Cambridge, UK: Cambridge University Press. doi:10.1017/CBO9780511541391

Zollman, K. (2007). *Network epistemology.* (Unpublished doctoral dissertation). University of California, Irvine, CA.

Zuccala, A. (2006). Modeling the invisible college. *Journal of the American Society for Information Science and Technology, 57*(2), 152–168. doi:10.1002/asi.20256

About the Contributors

Filipa M. Ribeiro is a PhD candidate at the Faculty of Psychology and Educational Sciences of the University of Porto. She graduated in Journalism and Communication (2003) and after some specialization courses in Genetics and Law (2006), she obtained a Master's in Sociology and Communication of Science at the University of Aveiro. She has worked in areas like digital media, innovation, and project management. Since 2009, she has been doing research on higher education. She was a member of the Portuguese team in the ESF-funded project Transforming Universities in Europe. Currently, she is the co-principal investigator of the project "Ethical Issues in Conducting Social Network Analysis Research in Health and Educational Settings." She is a member of the Early Career Higher Education Researchers' (ECHER) network. Her main topics of research are ubiquitous knowledge and education, sociology of science, social networks, ethics and research, diversity in higher education. Her academic publications can be found here: https://giesteira.academia.edu/FilipaRibeiro.

Yurgos Politis completed a four-year Physics degree at the University of Athens and qualified as a Physics teacher. He undertook a Master's in Education and a PhD in Physics Education in University College Dublin. He has taught at both second and third level and has been a teaching and research assistant and/or postdoctoral researcher in the Schools of Physics and Education in UCD, NUI Galway, UCC, and IT Tralee. He is currently a post-doctoral researcher on three EC-funded projects: 1) ESRALE (http://www.socio.uvt.ro/st-educ/wp-content/uploads/2014/03/Flyer_ESRALE_version01-1.pdf), 2) COMMIT (http://www.eucen.eu/COMMIT), 3) Inclusive Learning (http://www.inclusive-learning. eu/project). Previous significant research work he was involved in includes *The Academic Profession in Europe: Responses to Societal Change* (EUROAC) project and the European Commission MORE2 project. Dr. Politis secured funding from ESF to host a colloquium in Dublin (13-14 April 2013). He is a founding member of the Early Career Higher Education Researchers' (ECHER) network that was established in 2011.

Bojana Ćulum has a PhD and MSc in Higher Education from the University of Rijeka, where she works as Assistant Professor. Her main research interests cover higher education and civil society, university third and civic mission, university role in local community development, and changes in academic profession. She is engaged as a leading researcher in project *Academic Profession Competence Framework: between New Requirements and Possibilities* (APROFRAME), funded by the Croatian Science Foundation. Her teaching follows service-learning pedagogy and covers themes in education, didactics, civil society, evaluation research, and qualitative research methods. She has been a member of the National Committee for Volunteering Development, appointed by the Croatian Government. She has initiated the membership of the University of Rijeka in the Talloires Network and has been appointed as a university representative. She is a member of an executive committee of the Early Career Higher Education Researchers' (ECHER) network. Her academic publications can be found here: https://uniri. academia.edu/BojanaCulum/Papers.

* * *

Pedro Almeida got his graduation in New Communication Technologies by the University of Aveiro and his PhD in the same university in Communication Sciences and Technologies. Currently, he is a lecturer in the Communication and Art Department in undergraduate, master, and doctoral courses (PhDs in Information and Communication in Digital Platforms and Multimedia in Education). As a member of the research unit CETAC.MEDIA, he has special interests in multimedia communication systems and applications aiming to support social and collaborative practices in different contexts: Entertainment (interactive TV and content area) and Education (distance-learning support).

Ana Balula is a lecturer and researcher at Águeda School of Technology and Management, University of Aveiro, Portugal. She holds a PhD in Multimedia in Education and is an integrated member of the Research Centre "Didactics and Technology in Education of Trainers" and a team member of the research Project "The Use of Communication Technologies in the Portuguese Higher Education," granted by the Portuguese Foundation for Science and Technology. Her research interests are in the areas of e-learning, b-learning, e-assessment, evaluation of e-teaching, online interaction strategies, ICT use in Higher Education, and educational technology.

João Batista is an Assistant Professor at the Institute of Accounting and Administration, University of Aveiro, Portugal, where he teaches Informatics courses. He is a member of the Communication Sciences and Technologies Research Center (CETAC.MEDIA), where he works in the use of communication technologies in higher education and training contexts. He has previous experience in academic management and as a private consultant. He holds a PhD in Information and Communication in Digital Platforms (University of Aveiro and University of Porto), a Master's degree in Science and Information Technology (University of Coimbra), and a first degree in Geographic Engineering (University of Coimbra).

Birle Delia (PhD) is a licensed psychologist and a lecturer in experimental psychology, school counseling, and psychological statistics at the University of Oradea, Psychology Department. Her research interests that have been translated into books, numerous articles, and conference presentations include career counseling, school psychology, child development, and moral reasoning.

Laura Bochis is full-time Assistant Professor, PhD at University of Oradea, Department of Sciences of Education. She teaches the following courses: Psycho-Pedagogy of Intellectual Disabilities, Education and Methodology of Intellectual Disabilities, Didactics of Special Education, Theory of Education. She worked as a speech therapist and psycho-diagnostician (between 2004-2013) in special education at the Centre for Inclusive Education No. 1 of Oradea. In this capacity, Laura assessed children with special educational needs; she intervened in oral and written language disorders. She also designed and implemented personalized intervention plans for children with different types of disabilities in school. Focused on improving relations in primary classrooms in mainstream schools, she developed and defended in

2012 the PhD thesis entitled "Program of Rational Emotive and Behavioral Education: Applications in Primary School." This was a research conducted for promoting pro-social behavior in children and for developing an intervention program that includes recommendations and models for teachers' activity with children in school.

Elena Bonchis is a Full Professor at the University of Oradea, Romania, and the Head of Psychology Department. She is one of the founders of Educational Psychology School and Vocational Counseling Commission at Romanian College of Psychologists. In addition, she founded and is the president of Romanian Association of School Psychologists and the Chief Editor of *Romanian Journal of School Psychology*. She has authored more than 10 specialty books and is a coordinator and co-author for several works and scientific articles in the area of education, school psychology, and human development.

Željko Boneta (PhD) is assistant professor and currently teaches students at Faculty of Teacher Education, University of Rijeka, Croatia, in Sociology, Sociology of Childhood, Sociology of Family, Construction and Evaluation of Measuring Instrument, and Sociology of Education. His current research interests include social status of teaching profession, family social and cultural capital, and revitalization of religiosity in post-socialist society. He has published over 20 articles and participated in dozens of research projects.

Dalila Coelho holds a degree in Educational Sciences by the University of Coimbra (2004) and is doing her PhD studies in Education at the University of Aveiro (2012-). She has been working as research assistant in Portuguese public Higher Education for the last eight years, at the Polytechnic Institute of Beja (2005-2009) and more recently at the University of Aveiro (2011-2014) on the TRACER Project. She is member of the Research Centre Didactics and Technology in Education of Trainers (CIDTFF), of the Research Centre in Communication Technologies and Sciences (CETAC.MEDIA), and of the Global Open Educational Resources Graduate Network (GO-GN). Previously, she was also a teacher in undergraduate courses, teaching educational sciences and research methodology subjects. Her current research areas are Open Educational Resources—main PhD research topic—as well as open and distance education, ICT4D, development education, and cooperation.

Daniela Crisan is currently pursuing a Master's degree in Methodology and Statistics at Tilburg School of Social and Behavioral Sciences, Tilburg, the Netherlands. She was born and raised in Oradea, Romania, where she also obtained a BSc in Psychology from University of Oradea, Faculty of Social Humanistic Science (class of 2013). Her current interests are in Psychometrics and Educational Testing.

Roisin Donnelly works as an academic developer in the Learning, Teaching, and Technology Centre in DIT and is Programme Coordinator of the MSc Applied eLearning; she also teaches and has examining responsibilities on the Postgraduate Diploma in Third Level Learning and Teaching and both core and elective modules on the MA in Higher Education. She has supervised 25 MSc and MA students to completion and is currently co-supervising a PhD student in Computing. She is a fellow of the UK Higher Education Academy and was recently awarded a fellowship in SEDA. She is on the Steering Committee of the Irish Enquiry-Based Learning Network (Facilitate) and a member of Educational Developers in Ireland Network (EDIN). She is an invited peer reviewer on a number of international journals and co-editor of the *Irish Journal of Academic Practice* (IJAP).

Michelle Espinoza is a PhD candidate at the Faculty of Education, Monash University, Australia. She is researching the actual use of digital technologies at Chilean schools. Michelle has worked in teacher education for 12 years and has developed an interest in the challenges that educational institutions face today in relation to digital technology use in the 21st century.

Carlton J. Fitzgerald, for the past 40 years as a teacher and principal, has dedicated his professional life to helping people work to become successful in life through education. During his tenure, he has instituted alternative programs in elementary, middle schools, and a high school adult diploma program. Carlton has partnered with the U.S. and Romania embassies to work with teachers in Romania to teach the social skills associated with positive civic responsibilities. Carlton is a former Associate Dean of Education at New England College, where he is now an Associate Professor of Education. As such, he is working through a partnership agreement among New England College, the Association for Promoting Cooperation in Education, and the University of Oradea.

Tatiana Fumasoli is a post-doctoral fellow at ARENA, Centre for European Studies, and an Assistant Professor at the Faculty of Educational Sciences, University of Oslo. She presently works in the Flagship Project, which investigates institutional change dynamics in European universities and which is funded by the Research Council of Norway. Her interest lies on strategic agency of political and social actors and on its implications for the integration of the European and the national higher education systems. Her work has appeared in *Higher Education, Minerva, Higher Education Policy, International Journal of Public Administration, and with Springer Publishers.*

Ray Gallon is an international presenter and communications consultant, co-founder of The Transformation Society, a research and training organisation, and owner of Culturecom, a consultancy specializing in business process improvement through communication. He has taught at universities in North America and Europe, including New York University, The New School, Canadore College, Université de Toulouse Le Mirail, Université Paul Valéry (Montpellier 3), Université de Paris Diderot (Paris 7), and Universitat de Barcelona. He has over 20 years of experience in the technical content industries, having worked with major companies such as IBM, Alcatel, and General Electric Health Care. Previously, Ray was an award-winning radio producer and journalist. In the late 1980s, he was program manager of WNYC-FM, New York Public Radio, and has since moved on to innovate in the fields of electronic networking and content strategy.

Orla Hanratty is an academic developer in the Learning, Teaching, and Technology Centre in DIT and Coordinator of the Continuing Professional Development Programmes offered by the Centre. In addition, Orla contributes to the Postgraduate Diploma in Third Level Learning and Teaching, MSc Applied eLearning, and MA in Higher Education. She previously held educational development and lecturing positions in the School of Medicine and School of Education in Trinity College Dublin. She was programme director of the NUI Maynooth Postgraduate Diploma in Higher Education and involved in teaching on accredited programmes in other Irish institutes. She has also designed and developed programmes for postgraduate tutors and demonstrators. Research and development interests include reflective practice and workplace learning in Higher Education. She is currently pursuing a Doctorate in Education.

Jen Harvey is Head of the Learning, Teaching, and Technology Centre at DIT. Jen originally graduated from Aberdeen University with a BSc in Zoology and later completed an MPhil in Immunology while working in Edinburgh University. She then moved to Napier University where she obtained a Dip.Ed.Tech. from Abertay University and, in 1994, a PhD in Science Education in collaboration with Glasgow University. Jen became the DIT Head of Lifelong Learning in 2003; previously, she was the Head of Distance Education. Before moving to Dublin, she worked as an Implementation Consultant for the LTDI a SHEFC project based in ICBL, Heriot Watt University, Edinburgh. Current research interests relate to the use of technology to support learning, student assessment strategies, practitioner-based evaluations, and Communities of Practice.

Simona Laurian is a Lecturer at the University of Oradea's Sciences of Education Department. Her specialty is Romanian children's literature. She teaches classes in literature, drama in the classroom, practicum experiences, and the capstone research project for graduating students. Simona teaches and is a mentor in the university's weekend program for undergraduate students in the preschool and primary program. She is a founding member and current president of the Association for Promoting Cooperation in Education.

Kristin Lofthus-Hope was engaged as a post doctor to work for the TRUE (Transforming Universities in Europe) project, employed by the Department of Administration and Organization Theory, University of Bergen, Norway. Within the TRUE project, the topic of interest has especially been higher education implementation strategies. Currently, she works as a senior researcher at the Uni Research Rokkan Centre, Norway. She holds a PhD in Science and Technology Studies from the Department of Interdisciplinary Studies of Culture, Norwegian University of Science and Technology (NTNU), and holds a Master in Sociology from the same university.

Neus Lorenzo (PhD) is an international speaker on education leadership and organizational innovation, an author and co-author of educational material and textbooks, and expert in training methodology and assessment. She has worked at the Inspectorate General of Education in the Generalitat de Catalunya (Catalan Government) and she has headed the Foreign Language Service in the Departament d'Ensenyament, the local Ministry of Education in Catalonia (Spain). She has deep experience of educational change management, acquired in more than 30 years of teaching at university, secondary, and primary levels. Neus has coordinated the Lifelong Learning Project (LLP 2007-2014) of the European Union in Catalonia and has represented the Spanish autonomies before the education committee of the European Parliament. She has been a trainer, advisor, and researcher (Council of Europe, Anna Lindh Foundation, Jaume Bofill Foundation), and she continues her research as co-founder of the Transformation Society.

Miranda Lubbers is the Ramón y Cajal researcher and lecturer in the Department of Social and Cultural Anthropology of the Autonomous University of Barcelona (UAB), Spain. Her research is in the areas of social networks and methodology, among others. She has published in journals such as *Social Networks*, *Journal of School Psychology* and *Journal of Early Adolescence*.

Margarida Lucas is a postdoctoral research fellow at the Research Centre Didactics and Technology in Education of Trainers (CIDTFF) at the University of Aveiro. She received her PhD in Multimedia in Education, and her research interests focus on the use of Social Web tools in education and their potential for the process of shared knowledge construction, with specific emphasis on the analysis and visualization of interaction supported by such tools. She has published several peer-reviewed articles in international journals and participated and chaired international conferences dedicated to issues surrounding technology-enhanced learning.

Daariimaa Marav completed her doctoral study in the Faculty of Education, Monash University, Australia, in 2013. She is now a senior lecturer in the National University of Mongolia, with research interests in English language teaching, sociology of education, technology use in everyday and educational settings, and educational inequalities.

Claire McAvinia works as an academic developer in the Learning, Teaching, and Technology Centre in DIT and is Programme Coordinator of the Postgraduate Diploma in Third Level Learning and Teaching, contributing also to the MSc Applied eLearning and MA in Higher Education, as well as workshops and other programmes offered by the LTTC. She was previously a learning technologist at NUI Maynooth, and has worked in similar academic development/e-learning development roles for more than a decade. She is a Fellow of the UK Higher Education Academy and holds a PhD from Trinity College Dublin, with postgraduate qualifications in learning and teaching from University College London and the Open University. Her current research interests are in academic development generally, Activity Theory, and educational technology.

Nídia Morais holds a degree in New Technologies of Communication, a Master's in Education and Multimedia, and a PhD in Information and Communication in Digital Platforms, all obtained at the University of Aveiro, Portugal. She has taught at the Higher School of Education of Viseu since 1999. Her research interests have focused on the adoption of e-Learning solutions in higher education, and recently, she has developed research and published several papers about gender-related issues regarding the use of communication technologies in supporting learning activities in higher education contexts. She has also participated in National and European research projects and is a member of the CI&DETS Research Group.

António Moreira holds a PhD in Didactics of Languages and is currently the Director of the Department of Education at the University of Aveiro, where he also coordinates the Doctoral Programme on Multimedia in Education. He has supervised several MA, PhD, and Post-Doctoral students, both in Didactics and in ICT in Education. He also founded and was the chief editor of the online journal *Indagatio Didactica*. He has published various books and book chapters as well as articles and acts as a reviewer for several national and international journals.

Emma Murphy is a postdoctoral researcher at the Higher Education Research Centre (HERC) and the School of Computing at DCU. In 2014 she was awarded an Irish Research Council postdoctoral research fellowship investigating the potential of inclusive technology to support older adult learners. Emma has significant experience in the design and evaluation of user interaction techniques for older adults and people with disabilities and has published extensively in this area. Emma completed her PhD at the Sonic Arts Research Centre at Queen's University Belfast and is also a graduate of Trinity College Dublin.

Susana Pablo-Hernando obtained her PhD in Sociology at the Universidad Complutense de Madrid. She was awarded a four-year studentship by CSIC (the Spanish Research Council) to carry out her doctoral research in the group "Systems and Policies in Research and Innovation." She has received "the 2011-2012 Extraordinary PhD Award" for her doctoral research about the labour market for PhDs. At present, she works as a Research Assistant at the Sorbonne Business School in Paris, providing methodological support in qualitative and quantitative research methods to doctoral students and professors attached to the research laboratory GREGOR.

Luís Pedro is an Assistant Professor in the Department of Communication and Art, University of Aveiro, Portugal. He is engaged in teaching activities in the Communication Sciences and Technologies field, namely in the New Communication Technologies degree, in the Multimedia Communications MSc, and in the Multimedia in Education and the Information and Communication in Digital Platforms Doctoral programmes. His research interests are related with social media development and integration in educational and training contexts.

Janine M. Pierce is a Course Coordinator at the Eynesbury Institute of Business and Technology (EIBT) and the South Australian Institute of Business and Technology (SAIBT), as well as being both a lecturer and coordinator at the University of South Australia, where she has been involved in onshore/offshore teaching programs including the Master's program at Torrens University. She has been a finalist in the Australian University Lecturer of the Year for her work with Open Universities Australia. Janine's research has been both in Australia and overseas extending her PhD focus on sustainable communities, which she applies in developing strategies for working with international students and in the wider community in research projects with people with special needs.

Rómulo Pinheiro is Associate Professor in Public Policy and Management at the University of Agder, Norway. He is also a Senior Researcher at Agderforskning, Visiting Professor at the University of Tampere, Finland, and Affiliate Researcher with the HEIK Research Group at the University of Oslo, Norway. His research interests lie at the interception between organizational studies, public policy and management, and regional science and innovation.

Marta Pinto is a PhD student in Multimedia in Education of the University of Aveiro and developed her research within project TRACER. She has a degree in Art Education from Escola Superior de Educação de Coimbra and a Master's in Child studies and Visual Communication and Artistic Expressions from University of Minho. For eight years, she developed her work as an Art Teacher, and for the past three years she has been dedicated to research within national and international projects. Her research work relates to the use of information and Communication Technologies in Education.

Lúcia Pombo is an Auxiliary Professor at the Department of Education of the University of Aveiro and effective member of the CIDTFF-UA research centre, where she is a member of the Laboratory of Digital Contents. She holds a PhD in Education, a PhD in Biology, and a Master's degree in Science of Coastal Zones; she concluded a post-doc project on Evaluation the Quality of Teaching and Training of Science Teachers. Her research interests are related to Educational Technology, in particular in topics related to teacher professional development, online education, and ICT integration in education programs. She's been writing and publishing papers in the area, as well as participating in international and national projects. She lectures curricular units such as Natural Sciences and Distance Education, and she supervises/ed several MA and PhD students both in Didactics and in ICT in Education.

Carmen Popa is a reader at the University of Oradea's Sciences of Education Department. Her specialty is Education Sciences. She is organizing the courses and seminars: Theory and Methodology of Instruction, Pedagogy of Pre-School Teaching, Cooperative Learning, Theory and Methodology of Curriculum, coordinating the practicum classes for the entire department, guiding the research projects for graduating students. She acquired a research grant entitled A Cross-Cultural Study of Implementing the Cooperative Learning Model in Primary Schools in Finland and Romania from Finland, University of Helsinki, Department of Psychology, Centre for Research on Networked Learning and Knowledge Building (2004). Since 2010, she is the coordinator of the educational program for the blended weekend classes (IFR) of the Faculty of Social and Humanistic Sciences. She is also a member of the Senate of University of Oradea.

Fernando Ramos is a Full Professor of Communication Sciences and Technologies at the Department of Communication and Art of the University of Aveiro (UA), Portugal. He is the author/co-author of more than 200 papers published in peer-reviewed journals and proceedings of international conferences, director of a large number of research projects financed by several funding agencies and industry, director of the PhD programme in Information and Communication on Digital Platforms, vice-director of the PhD on Multimedia in Education, under the Technology Enhanced Learning-Societal Challenges PD-FCT programme, former Head of the Department of Electronics and Telecommunications and of the Department of Communication and Art, former Scientific Director of CETAC.MEDIA, former Director of the Multimedia and Distance Learning Centre, former Head of the Executive board of UNAVE, coordinator of several international projects in Digital Media and Distance Education in Angola, Cape Verde, and Mozambique, coordinator of the expert group for the reorganization of the National University of East Timor, consultant to several national and international boards: European Commission, EACEA-European Agency for Culture, Education and Audiovisual, Portuguese Ministries of Economy and Industry, Institute for Quality, Government of Macao, and INED-National Distance Educational Institute of Mozambique, and he acts as a reviewer for several national and international journals, and is the director of the TRACER project.

Rui Raposo is an Assistant Professor at the Department of Communication and Art of the University of Aveiro. He holds a PhD in Science and Technology in Communication and a degree in New Technologies in Communication both from the University of Aveiro, is a research fellow at CETAC.MEDIA, where he develops research focused on communication mediated through technology in contexts linked to information visualization, museology, and tourism.

Maria Slowey is Professor and Director of the Higher Education Research Centre (HERC), Dublin City University, Ireland, where she also served as Vice-President Learning Innovation. She was previously Professor and Director of Adult and Continuing Education in Glasgow University, Scotland

(1992-2004), and Head of the Centre for Continuing Education and Widening Access in Northumbria University, England (1984-1992). Maria's research and policy activities focus on lifelong learning, innovation, and equity of access to higher education. She has published widely on these matters and been advisor at national and international levels to a range of bodies, including OECD, UNESCO, EC, European Universities Association, Council of Europe, European Training Foundation, Scottish Parliament, Irish Universities Association, Economic and Social Research Council, and the Higher Education Funding Councils of England and Scotland. Educated in University College Dublin and Trinity College Dublin, in 2009 Maria was elected an Academician of the British Academy of Social Sciences. Recent publications include *Global Perspectives on Higher Education and Lifelong Learners* (with Schuetze; 2012, Routledge) and *Voices of Academics in Ireland: Perspectives on Professional Development* (with Kozina and Tan; 2014, All Ireland Society for Higher Education [AISHE]).

Francislê Souza has a Pos-doc in ICT Applied to Science Education (2008), PhD in Science Education (2006), MA in Computational Quantum Chemistry (1998), Undergraduate in Chemistry (1995). He currently works as an Invited Assistant Professor at the University of Aveiro, where he also supervises MA and PhD students in Science Education, ICT, and as a lecturer in these areas. He is co-author of some software, such as IARS®, WebQDA®, ArguQuest®, and uTRACER®. He is the author of papers, books, and book chapters in the fields of active learning, questioning, chemistry education, and educational technology, and editor of the *Internet Latent Corpus Journal*.

Sanja Tatalovic-Vorkapic (PhD) is an assistant professor and currently teaches students at the Faculty of Teacher Education, University of Rijeka, Croatia, in Developmental Psychology, Psychology of Early Learning and Teaching, General Psychology, Emotional Intelligence, Developmental Psychopathology, Methodology of Quantitative Research, Positive Psychology. Her contemporary research interests include biological basis of personality, personality of (pre)school teachers and child personality, contemporary issues from developmental psychopathology and methodology of quantitative research, positive psychology (well-being, optimism, life satisfaction, virtues), and (pre)school teachers' personal and professional development. She has published numerous psychology-related articles and has been actively involved within various interdisciplinary research projects.

Ana Vitoria-Baptista has a Master's degree from the University of Aveiro (Portugal) in Educational Sciences. Her dissertation was about non-traditional adult students entering Higher Education (HE). She finished her PhD with distinction and honors in Pedagogy and Training at the same Portuguese HE institution on the topic "Quality of Doctoral Research Supervision: Design of a Framework to Evaluate and Monitor the Process." At the moment, Ana is a Research Fellow at the University of Aveiro within the funded project entitled "Non-Traditional Students in Higher Education." Her research interests are particularly focused on HE pedagogy, namely postgraduate research supervision, non-traditional students, linking teaching and research, undergraduate research, innovative teaching and learning strategies and inclusive forms of assessment, teachers and postgraduate research supervisors' professional development.

Donna M. Velliaris is Academic Advisor at the Eynesbury Institute of Business and Technology (EIBT). EIBT is a specialist pre-university institution where international students work towards the goal of Australian tertiary entrance. Donna holds two Graduate Certificates in (1) Australian Studies and (2) Religious Education, two Graduate Diplomas in (1) Secondary Education and (2) Language and Literacy Education, as well as three Masters' degrees in (1) Educational Sociology, (2) Studies of Asia, and (3) Special Education. In 2010, she graduated with a PhD in Education focused on the social and educational ecological development of school-aged transnational students. Her research interests and expertise include academic literacies, human ecology, Third Culture Kids (TCKs), and schools as cultural systems. Donna is the first-author of more than 10 book chapters to be published in 2014-2015.

Lidija Vujičić (PhD) is Associate Professor and currently teaches at Faculty of Teacher Education, University of Rijeka, Croatia, in various pedagogy-related subjects at undergraduate and graduate level. Her current research interests include Early Child Care and Preschool Education, New Paradigms in Early Education (Child-Childhood), Culture of Educational Institutions, Co-Constructing Curriculum, Learning Communities, Professional Development (Pre-Service and In-Service Education), Action Research. She has written the book titled *Researching the Culture of Educational Institutions*, two manuals as a co-author, *Kindergarten as a Children's House* and *Kindergarten in Harmony with Children's Nature*, and numerous articles. She has been actively engaged in several research projects.

Craig R. Willis is Academic Coordinator at the Eynesbury Institute of Business and Technology (EIBT) as well as a Senior Lecturer in the School of Civil, Environmental, and Mining Engineering at The University of Adelaide. Teaching large classes of up to 550 students, Craig has developed innovative ways of providing continuous formative feedback using interactive teaching techniques, peer instruction, and professional engineering processes. In the space of two years, he was recognised with a total of seven awards for excellence in teaching and learning at faculty, university, and national levels. His research expertise extends to diverse themes, including the first-year experience, international students, active learning strategies, e-learning, engagement with large classes, peer feedback, multiple choice assessment, and quality management processes.

Index

CPSIA information can be obtained at www.ICGtesting.com
Printed in the USA
BVOW06*1435060415

394563BV00016B/91/P

9 781466 672444